D1165606

The Psychology of Good and Evil

Why Children, Adults, and Groups Help and Harm Others

This book gathers together the knowledge gained in a lifelong study of the causes of goodness and evil. Since the 1960s Ervin Staub has studied the roots of helpful, caring, generous, and altruistic behavior in adults and their development in children, as well as passivity in response to others' need. He has also studied bullying and victimization in schools, as well as youth violence and its prevention. He spent many years studying the origins (and prevention) of human destructiveness, genocide, and mass killing, and he has examined the Holocaust, the genocide of the Armenians, the disappearances in Argentina, the genocide in Rwanda, and other instances. He has applied his work in many real-world settings, in seminars, workshops, lectures, and in consultations with parents and teachers, police officers, and political leaders. He has appeared frequently in the media, since September 11 especially, to explain the causes and prevention of terrorism. Professor Staub has published, in addition to books, many articles and book chapters on these topics. A selection from these is gathered, with new writings added, in *The Psychology of Good and Evil*. The book presents a broad panorama of the roots of violence and caring and suggests how we can create societies and a world that are caring, peaceful, and harmonious. Two of the important themes of the book are how both evil and goodness evolve, step by step, and the great power of bystanders.

Ervin Staub is Professor of Psychology at the University of Massachusetts at Amherst. He was born in Hungary, and received his B.A. and his Ph.D. (Stanford University, 1965) in the United States. He has taught at Harvard University, Stanford University, the University of Hawaii, and the London School of Economics and Political Science. He is a Fellow of four divisions of the American Psychological Association and was President of the Society for the Study of Peace, Conflict, and Violence (as well as recipient of its Lifetime Contribution to Peace Psychology award), and of the International Society for Political Psychology. Professor Staub applies his work to the promotion of caring, helping, "active bystandership," and the prevention of violence through media appearances, work with organizations and schools, and working on healing and reconciliation in conflict settings such as Rwanda.

Other books by Ervin Staub:

Positive Social Behavior and Morality: Vol. 1. Personal and Social Influences

Positive Social Behavior and Morality: Vol. 2. Socialization and Development

Personality: Basic Aspects and Current Research (editor)

The Development and Maintenance of Prosocial Behavior: International Perspectives on Positive Morality (coeditor)

The Roots of Evil: The Origins of Genocide and Other Group Violence

Social and Moral Values: Individual and Societal Perspectives (coeditor)

Patriotism in the Lives of Individuals and Nations (coeditor)

The Psychology of Good and Evil

Why Children, Adults, and Groups Help and Harm Others

ERVIN STAUB
University of Massachusetts, Amherst

PUBLISHED BY THE PRESS SYNDICATE OF THE UNIVERSITY OF CAMBRIDGE
The Pitt Building, Trumpington Street, Cambridge, United Kingdom

CAMBRIDGE UNIVERSITY PRESS
The Edinburgh Building, Cambridge CB2 2RU, UK
40 West 20th Street, New York, NY 10011-4211, USA
477 Williamstown Road, Port Melbourne, VIC 3207, Australia
Ruiz de Alarcón 13, 28014 Madrid, Spain
Dock House, The Waterfront, Cape Town 8001, South Africa

http://www.cambridge.org

First published 2003

Printed in the United States of America

Typeface Palatino 10/12 pt. *System* LaTeX 2_ε [TB]

A catalog record for this book is available from the British Library.

Library of Congress Cataloging in Publication Data

Staub, Ervin.

The psychology of good and evil : why children, adults, and groups help and harm others / Ervin Staub.

p. cm.

Includes bibliographical references and index.

ISBN 0-521-82128-2 (hardback) – ISBN 0-521-52880-1 (pbk.)

1. Good and evil – Psychological aspects. I. Title.

BF789 .E94 S83 2003
155.2′32 – dc21 2002034797

ISBN 0 521 82128 2 hardback
ISBN 0 521 52880 1 paperback

To Macs and to all "active bystanders"

Contents

Preface

I received my Ph.D. in psychology at Stanford in 1965, started my work life as a professor at Harvard, and almost immediately began to focus on the topics of this book: goodness and evil. For many years, I have conducted research on, extensively written about, and more and more applied to the real world the understanding that is presented in this book on a variety of interrelated questions: What leads children and adults to be generous and helpful, and what leads them to respond to someone's urgent need in an emergency rather than remain passive bystanders? Why do children and adolescents bully, harass, and intimidate each other, and what can we do about it? What influences lead people, especially young people, to become aggressive and violent, and what socialization and experience in the home and school lead children and youth to become caring and helpful? What leads groups of people to engage in violent actions, especially in extreme forms of violence such as genocide and mass killing? How can groups (and individuals) heal from the trauma created by past victimization? How can members of perpetrator and victim groups, or members of groups that have mutually harmed each other, reconcile? What is the role of passive bystanders in allowing violence to unfold, and how can we use the great potential power of "active bystanders" for preventing violence or generating helping? And how can violence and other harm-doing by individuals and groups be prevented and caring, helping, and peace be promoted, and how can cultures that generate these be created? Since September 11, 2001, I have also applied my prior work to the understanding of the roots of terrorism and its prevention.

As I engaged with these issues over the years, I increasingly entered the "real world." I lectured and conducted workshops for parents and teachers on practices in the home and school that would help them raise caring and nonviolent children. In this book I write about positive (as well as negative) socialization in the home and about the practices of "caring schools." It is possible to provide all children, I believe, with experiences that foster in them caring about other people, while also helping them maximize their own personal and human potentials, that is, helping them to become optimally functioning persons. It seems profoundly important to me, and I hope it will seem so to readers of this book, to bring this about.

In another entry into the real world, after the famous incident that someone captured on film – in which a few police officers severely beat Rodney King while a group of officers stood by watching – I developed a training program for the agency responsible for police training in the state of California, aimed at preventing the use of unnecessary force by the police. Later, together with Dr. Laurie Anne Pearlman, I developed, trained people in, and carefully evaluated the effects of their use in the community of an intervention to help promote healing and reconciliation in Rwanda, in the wake of the terrible genocide there in 1994. We have also worked with some of that country's leaders to help them understand the roots of violence and develop policies and practices they might use to prevent renewed violence and to break the cycle of violence.

As I am writing this, in December 2002, we are about to leave for Rwanda to try to help channel the feelings that arise from the *gacaca*, so that instead of retraumatization and renewed rage and hostility, the country can move toward reconciliation. The *gacaca* is a community justice system, newly created and initiated in 2001–2002. It was inspired by a traditional practice in Rwanda for resolving conflict and reconciling wrongdoers with the community. The large majority of 115,000 people who have been in prison since 1994, accused of perpetrating the genocide, will be tried in *gacaca* courts by 250,000 members of the community who were elected to serve as judges and trained over a period of several months.

As I have mentioned, I have done extensive writing in books, articles, book chapters, and at times in newspaper columns, about the topics I have just described: the roots and prevention of evil and the roots and creation of goodness. This book is a selection from my writings, covering primarily the period from the publication of my book on evil, *The Roots of Evil*, in 1989, to 2003; it also includes a number of earlier publications that I regard as especially important – particularly about influences that lead people to help others in need – and substantial new writings.

The Roots of Evil provides a thorough, detailed examination of the roots of genocide and mass killing at many levels, from culture and society to individual characteristics and human relationships, with detailed analyses of a number of important instances. The current book is much broader in its focus. It focuses on goodness as much as evil, on what leads individuals to help others, and on how caring and helping develop in children. Although I do not provide here the same deep exploration of the roots of genocide and mass killing, I summarize the material from *The Roots of Evil* in an award-winning publication that I have recently updated. I include publications that focus on new examples, especially Rwanda. I describe influences I have identified since *The Roots of Evil* – for example, the role of past victimization and woundedness in making violence by groups more likely. In *The Roots of Evil* I also discuss how violence by groups might be prevented. In the writings in this book I add to that exploration, addressing profoundly important matters such as healing, reconciliation, and even forgiveness, specific actions "bystander nations" can and ought to take to prevent violence by groups, and democratization as an avenue to culture change.

I wrote opening and concluding chapters for this book and included some other new or recent, not previously published pieces. The volume contains whole articles or book chapters, and parts of others. In a few selections, material that reports the results of research has been rewritten to make it easier to read and thus accessible to a wider audience. In putting together these selections, my aim has been to describe and interweave all the important elements in the understanding I have gained about goodness and evil in the course of my life's work, to represent what I know at this time about goodness and evil.

My life experience, and my lifelong work on good and evil, altruism and aggression, and helping and harm-doing, have been deeply intertwined. As one of the selections describes, I am what is nowadays called a child survivor of the Holocaust. I was a 6-year-old boy in Budapest in the summer of 1944 when about 450,000 out of about 600,000 Hungarian Jews were transported to Auschwitz and killed. I and members of my nuclear family survived because of Raoul Wallenberg, a Swede who heroically saved many lives in Hungary, and Maria, a Hungarian woman who worked for my family and did all she could to help us. We called Maria "Macs," an abbreviation of the Hungarian word for cat. I don't know how that came about. But Macs was my second mother, and I feel that her courageous actions and loving nature taught me, in spite of my experiences during the Holocaust and afterward in Hungary under communism, to have faith in human beings and in the possibility of our caring about each other, about the "other," and about all "others."

I believe that my beginning to work on what leads people to help others and what stops them from helping those in need, including my focus on the passive and active "bystander," and my lifelong concern with preventing violence, passivity, and promoting goodness, owe a great deal to Macs. On one of my visits to her in Hungary, when she was in her late eighties, I told Macs that the work I have been doing all my life was inspired by her. With her head with its beautiful fine silver hair shaking, as it did constantly in those days, she smiled and said, naturally and without pride, "I know." This book is dedicated to her, and to all others who have not and will not remain passive bystanders in the face of others' suffering and need, who act on behalf of others and thereby make this a more caring world.

Acknowledgments

This book summarizes what I have learned about goodness and evil in the course of 35 years. During that time I have done research in academic settings and research in the world outside the university on caring, helping, altruism, and the reduction of aggression, and I have engaged in efforts to raise caring children, prevent violence by individuals and groups, and promote healing by victimized groups and reconciliation among groups. I want to express my gratitude to the many people who have directly contributed to this book, or have been influential in my thinking and work over the years, and/or provided support by their friendship, affection, or in other ways. I will mention a few of them by name.

Vachel Miller was an outstanding collaborator in helping to make selections for the book. A few of the selections include research findings, and he was also extremely helpful in summarizing these in accessible language. Phil Laughlin, my editor at Cambridge University Press, was helpful in every possible way, as were others at Cambridge, like Helen Wheeler, who supervised the production. I am deeply grateful to associates, colleagues, and former students who have allowed me to include or reproduce coauthored material: Laurie Anne Pearlman, Darren Spielman, and Robert Schatz, as well as Daniel Goleman, whose article about my work in the *New York Times* (written when he was the behavioral science writer for the *Times*) is the only article by another person included in the this volume. Jen Borden was helpful in organizing materials for the book.

The late Perry London, the first person to study heroic rescuers, inspired my early work on altruism. Walter Mischel, my advisor and friend over the years, Eleanor Maccoby and Al Bandura, as well as Perry London, were all my teachers during my graduate school years at Stanford. The late Stanley Milgram and Robert Rosenthal were colleagues and friends during my years as a young professor at Harvard. Seymour Epstein, who I met when he was a visiting professor at Harvard and who has been my colleague for many years at the University of Massachusetts at Amherst,

George Levinger, Icek Aizen, James Averill, Robert Feldman, Susan Fiske, Linda Isbell, Ronnie Janoff-Bulman, Paula Pietromonico, all colleagues at UMASS, have all been supportive of my work. Daniel Bar-Tal, Janusz Reykowski, and Nancy Eisenberg were coauthors on various projects and intellectual companions. Many other colleagues, many of them members of the Society for Peace, Conflict, and Violence, the Peace Psychology Division of the American Psychological Association, or the International Society for Political Psychology, Psychologists for Social Responsibility, or social or child psychology groups, have influenced or inspired me. I am grateful to close, supportive friends, especially Jack Rosenblum, Corinne Dugas, Michael and Nina Shandler, Alan Hurwitz, Ana Lisano, John Mack, Marc Skvirsky, Pál Réti, Agnes Gáti, and Lane and Sarah Conn.

I am grateful to my sons, Adrian and Daniel, and to their wives, Sheri Kurtz and Kristin Brennan, for their love and presence in my life, and I am deeply appreciative of the values by which they live their lives.

And the adage last but not least truly applies in my thanking Laurie Anne Pearlman, my life partner and also my work partner in Rwanda, who supports with love and generosity of spirit all I do in the world.

PART I

INTRODUCTION AND CORE CONCEPTS

1

Good and Evil

Themes and Overview

This book is about understanding the roots of children, adults, and groups of people helping and harming others. It is about ways to create more caring for others' welfare and less harmful, aggressive, violent behavior. It is about how children, adults, small groups, and nations can become "active bystanders" who respond to others' suffering and help those in need, rather than remaining passive observers, even closing their eyes and hearts to others' fate.

There is much goodness in the world. A mother paying loving attention to a child. A father taking time off work to take his child to the first day of kindergarten – an act that saved the life of the president of a major bond-trading firm at the time of the terrorist attack on the World Trade Center. A grown son taking care of a sick old father. A popular girl spending time with a new, somewhat awkward girl in class, saving her from unkind behavior by classmates. A young Canadian boy, Craig Kielberger, hearing about child labor and with the help of an older brother and parents creating an international organization, of children and led by children with the help of adults, to eliminate child labor, to protect children, to promote their welfare. Another child, seeing homeless people on the streets, organizing a movement to bring blankets to homeless people.[1] A Hutu man in Rwanda coming to the home of a Tutsi woman after her husband is killed, sent there by another Hutu who used to work for this woman. He stays there protecting her from killers who come to the door to take her away, asking for nothing in return.[2]

Many people respond to the need of others, whether the need is to relieve suffering or to help enhance well-being. Some men and women organize their lives to serve others' welfare – whether by establishing the innocence of people in jail for a crime they did not commit, or finding money to lend to people in poor countries to start small businesses,[3] or by working for positive social change. Most of these people are not making sacrifices. The desire to contribute to others' welfare has become part of them. Helping people provides them with satisfaction and fulfillment.

Countries send food to other countries wracked by famine; give refuge to people who are fleeing from political repression; take action against the persecution of a minority at home or in other countries; intervene to stop violence. These and a million other acts of kindness, ranging from small to extreme, requiring little effort and sacrifice or involving great sacrifice or extreme danger, are all examples of goodness. When I asked a group of students who had expressed pessimism about human kindness to keep a diary of kind acts they received or observed, they were surprised by how much of it they witnessed.

On the "evil" side, individuals and groups harm others in small and big ways. Even if we encounter little significant violence in our own lives, we are surrounded by images on television, reports in newspapers and stories people tell us describing violent acts by individuals such as physical and sexual abuse of children, adult rape and murder, or youth violence ranging from physical attack to drive-by shooting and murder. We also hear about violence by groups against members of other groups in the course of "ethnopolitical" warfare, persecution and torture of groups of people, terrorist attacks on civilians, mass killing and genocide. And just about all of us experience, if not great violence, still hurtful, painful acts against us – when as children we are attacked by peers who call us names, spread rumors about us, hit us or exclude us, or when we are blamed or in other ways treated badly by adults, or as adults experience aggression against us.

A third very important part of this picture is the bystander, the individual or collection of individuals, including nations, who witness what is happening. While bystanders can be heroic in their efforts to help, they often remain passive. This passivity encourages perpetrators. When children in school intimidate, harass, or bully other children, peers who witness this usually remain passive – and some even join the perpetrators. Adults also often remain passive. When one group turns against another group, nations often remain passive. They may try hard to avoid both the feeling and the appearance of an obligation to act. For example, in Rwanda about seven hundred thousand Tutsis were killed in 1994, in the course of an attempt to eliminate all Tutsis. This was a genocide, since it aimed to eliminate a whole group of people. But the governments of the United States and other countries avoided the use of the term genocide.[4] By acknowledging that the killings were genocide, given the UN genocide convention, they would have had a moral obligation to act.

Bystanders have great potential power to do good. When two people hear sounds of distress from another room, what one person says can greatly influence whether the other witness helps or not. As a number of selections will show, individuals and groups can limit, stop, and even prevent violence, and encourage helpful actions by their words, actions, and example.

WHAT IS GOODNESS, WHAT IS EVIL?

To me, evil means human destructiveness. This can come in an obvious form, as great violence against others, such as a genocide. Or it can come in smaller acts of persistent harm-doing, the effects of which accumulate, like parents being hostile and punitive, or peers picking on a child day by day for a long time. Such actions can destroy a child's spirit, his or her dignity, self-worth, and ability to trust people.

At times, intense violence, destructive as it is, is not evil, but justified self-defense in response to unjustified attack – on oneself, one's family, one's group. The Nazi attacks on Czechs, Poles, Jews, and many others gave rise to violent but justified and necessary response by the Allies in World War II. The terrorist attacks on the World Trade Center and the Pentagon on September 11, 2001, are further examples of destructiveness that requires self-defense.

However, determining when violent acts are justified self-defense is not a simple matter. Perpetrators of evil acts often claim that they are defending themselves. Or they claim moral reasons or higher values for their actions, such as total social equality, which the Cambodian communists, the Khmer Rouge, claimed was their goal, or the purity of the group, which is often the "higher" purpose of nationalists who turn against minorities. In addition, the form of self-defense that is justified is also an issue. The actions of a teenager who is bullied day by day by peers and then takes a gun and shoots people, as in the case of some of the school shootings in the United States, seems unjustified, evil. It may be understandable – and this book is about both understanding and preventing evil – especially if bystanders are passive and uncaring and the child feels he or she has no one to turn to, even though it is still wrong and evil.

The view of evil inherent in this discussion is different from colloquial or theological views of evil. After my book *The Roots of Evil* was published, I was invited to be on a TV talk show by Ron Reagan, our former president's son, on evil. Others on the show were the author of a *Time* magazine cover story on evil, a priest who was known for conducting exorcisms (to drive the evil spirit out of people), the daughter of the leader of a Satanic cult (a group that worships Satan), a psychiatrist, and a professor of religion. The selection of these participants says a great deal about popular views of evil.

My definition of and concern with evil has to do with human actions that harm others (see also Chapter 4, on Evil). The focus is on evil actions. But individuals, as well as groups or societies, can develop characteristics that make it likely that they will repeatedly engage in such actions. Whether we do or do not want to call such individuals or groups evil, we must recognize their inclination for harm-doing. We must come to understand its roots and develop the knowledge required and the will to use this knowledge to prevent destructive behavior.

Especially when faced with great evil, such as genocide or seemingly senseless acts of great individual violence, there is a tendency in public discussion to regard them as incomprehensible. Perhaps we do not want to understand them because we want to keep them outside the common human realm that we are part of. But destructive actions are the outcome of certain basic, ordinary psychological and social processes and their evolution into extreme forms. Understanding their roots enables us to prevent them, and to prevent individuals and groups from developing the characteristics that make these acts likely.

Understanding itself can be of great value. In working in Rwanda in the aftermath of the genocide, we found that healing by both survivors and members of the perpetrator group who were not themselves perpetrators was furthered by understanding the circumstances, societal processes, and psychology of individuals and groups that created the genocide. Seeing the violence against them as understandable human acts and seeing the perpetrators not as embodiments of pure evil but as human beings whose evolution led them to their horrible acts helped survivors feel more human themselves (see Chapters 36 and 37).

Goodness is the opposite of evil. It refers to actions that bring benefit to individuals or whole groups: the greater the benefit and the more effort and/or sacrifice it requires, the greater the goodness. Goodness, like evil, can come in an obvious form, like a single heroic act that saves someone's life. Or it can take the form of persistent efforts to save people, as in the case of people in the United States who through the Underground Railroad helped slaves escape, or Hutus in Rwanda who endangered themselves to save Tutsis. Heroic acts and such persistent acts of goodness require great effort, courage, and at times even the willingness to endanger one's life.

But goodness can also take the form of persistent engagement in helping people or creating positive social change that does not involve great danger. It can consist of small, repeated acts that bring benefit to others, like kindness by a neighbor or relative toward a child who is neglected or badly treated at home, kindness that can help the child develop normally and even flourish in spite of adversity.

Nations often act in selfish and destructive ways. But goodness by groups, small and large, does exist, as I have already noted. In the case of nations, it sometimes comes from mixed motives, as in the case of the Marshall Plan, which rebuilt Europe but also aimed at preventing the spread of communism. At other times, as in Somalia, seemingly altruistic motives come to bad ends. The United States tried to help people suffering from starvation, but due to circumstances and some seemingly unwise decisions,[5]

U.S. soldiers were attacked and killed. The work of the Quakers in the abolition of slavery and of the villagers in La Chambon, France, saving thousands of Jews during the Holocaust, may also be regarded as group efforts born of humane values and expressing unselfish caring or altruism.

Like evil, goodness too is comprehensible. Like evil, goodness also evolves, individuals and groups changing by their own actions, which shape them to become more caring and helpful.

The material in this book presents a great deal of existing knowledge about the influences that generate either goodness or evil in individuals, nations, the whole world. My study of the roots of evil and goodness and my active efforts to help prevent violence and promote caring that this book presents have been motivated by my belief that evil can be prevented, goodness can be created, generated, helped to evolve, that bystanders can become "active." This was true even in the early stages, when I chose these topics and issues for my academic work out of deeply set psychological forces in me (see the next selection), without necessarily a conscious, well-formed intention to make a difference in the world. Over time, and at times in spite of despair over events in the world, I have come to hold these beliefs more consciously, and act out of them with greater self-awareness. With already existing knowledge, and further knowledge we will gain over time, we can engage in creating a more benevolent world.

THE PROGRESSIVE INCREASE IN, OR EVOLUTION OF, GOODNESS AND EVIL, AND THE ROLE OF BYSTANDERS

People who harm others tend to devalue those they harm, which makes it easier to harm them again; those who help others tend to value more the welfare of people they have helped, or of people in general, which makes it more likely that they will help again. This kind of change or evolution is a central feature of both goodness and evil. This does not mean, however, that an aggressive act will inevitably lead to more aggression, or a helpful act to more helping. It depends in part on the already existing characteristics of an individual or group. One of my students described the experience of a "friend" stealing a significant amount of money from him. He was very angry, invited this friend over, was waiting for him with other friends, and beat him up after he arrived. He was later horrified by his own actions and became very nonaggressive. When a person already holds caring values, and circumstances and his feelings (of anger, unjust treatment, and so on) lead him or her to act aggressively, this act need not contribute to an evolution of increasing violence.

The behavior of bystanders has a crucial influence on evolution. Unfortunately, as I have noted, when they witness others' need, or aggression against people, bystanders often see but do not act. They may even protect themselves from distress created by empathy, or from guilt due to inaction, by turning away, by closing their eyes to others' suffering. In one of my studies (see Chapter 6, Section E) some passersby, after a single look at a person who collapsed on the street, looked away and continued on their way without ever looking again. But when the passivity is in the face of harmful acts, it encourages the perpetrators and facilitates the evolution of greater harm-doing. I will propose that in extreme cases – like relatives or neighbors who know that a child is severely neglected or is physically or sexually abused but do nothing, or nations that take no action while a genocide is perpetrated in front of their eyes – passivity by bystanders may be regarded as evil (see Chapter 26).

At times people turn away internally, psychologically, from those in need. At other times bystanders see, know, but choose not to act and even become complicit: they directly or indirectly encourage perpetrators of violence. A country sells arms to and continues commerce and other normal relations with a country that engages in large-scale murder of people within its own population. A spouse or other family member continues warm relations with a person who physically, sexually, or psychologically abuses a child.

Bystanders also evolve. Some passive or complicit witnesses change and join evildoers. For example, a group of psychoanalysts in Berlin in the 1930s passively stood by as their Jewish colleagues were persecuted, accepted a nephew of Hermann Göring, the second highest Nazi after Hitler, as the head of their institute, and rewrote psychoanalytic theory to fit Nazi ideology. Some of them then participated in the euthanasia movement, identifying mentally ill, physically handicapped and other "inferior" Germans to be killed, and some later participated in the extermination of the Jews.[6]

Caring values and empathy with other people give rise to motives to help. But opposing perpetrators requires courage. In its early stages it may require moral rather than physical courage. Moral courage is the ability and willingness to act according to one's important values even in the face of opposition, disapproval, and the danger of ostracism. I will discuss moral courage in this book, although it has been little studied either in children or adults. It is an essential characteristic, however, for active bystanders, whether a child associating with or helping an unpopular peer, or a person speaking out against some policy or practice in a group.

THE POWER OF CIRCUMSTANCE AND THE IMPORTANCE OF WHO WE ARE

This book identifies influences that lead to great or persistent acts of harm or benefit. It also identifies ways that aggression, violence, and harm-doing in general may be prevented and caring, helping, and altruism may be promoted. The book examines psychological processes, such as anger, hostility, the devaluation of groups of people, empathy or its absence, and a feeling of responsibility for others' welfare that lead a person to act in destructive or caring ways. It looks at characteristics of persons that give rise to helping or harming others, the characteristics of cultures and social/political systems, and the evolution of these characteristics.

It also looks at circumstances to which individuals or groups respond that make either destructive or benevolent behavior likely. Certain circumstances have great power, leading many people to behave the same way. But even in the most extreme circumstances, who people are, their personalities and values (and in the case of groups, their culture), affects their reactions. Many people would not go into a burning house to save a life, but some do. If someone points a gun at us in a dark alley and demands our money, most of us hand it over. But some resist, willing to die in the process.

A man named Mark Bingham once wrested a gun from a would-be mugger. The same man was on Flight 93 on September 11, 2001, which crashed near Pittsburgh; presumably he was one of the passengers who attacked the terrorists. He and the other passengers died, but saved the lives of the people who would have been killed in the intended terrorist attack. What happened on that flight seems a good example of the combination of the power of the situation and individual characteristics. Without a passenger learning on his cell phone about the terrorist attacks on other targets, the passengers would probably have assumed that this was a normal hijacking, which they might survive without anyone getting hurt. But once they understood the nature of their situation, it still required some individuals to initiate action. The power of individuals can powerfully show itself in such a situation. One or two determined people can have great influence in mobilizing others.

The power of circumstance, of a specific situation, was clear in the many studies of bystander behavior in emergencies initiated by two social psychologists, John Darley and Bibb Latané.[7] They found that the larger the number of people present when someone suddenly needs help, due to an accident, an attack of illness, or some other reason, the less the likelihood that any one person will initiate help. Research on emergency helping is well represented in this volume, including research in which I found that what one witness says to another, which is an aspect of the circumstances that can influence action, greatly affects whether the other person helps or not.

The power of circumstance was also shown in the studies of Stanley Milgram on obedience to authority. A large percentage of people, the actual percentage depending on exact circumstances, obeyed a person in charge who put them in the role of "teacher" and told them to give stronger and stronger electric shocks to a "learner" when this person made mistakes on a task. When all that the teacher saw were signs on the machine indicating that the shocks were increasing and in the end extremely dangerous – when the supposed recipient of the shocks was in another room and no distress sounds were heard by the teacher – 69% of participants obeyed the person in charge and proceeded to administer the strongest shocks.[8]

But circumstances affect people in different ways. In this situation, 31% of the participants refused to continue to administer shocks. One study found that those who refused had a stronger feeling of moral responsibility than those who continued.[9] As in harming, so in helping others, our values, feelings of competence, and other characteristics strongly influence how we respond.

When the teachers heard distress sounds and loud complaints from the other room by the supposed recipient of the shocks (who did not actually receive the shocks), a smaller percentage of them obeyed. When the learner sat next to the teacher, who had to put the learner's hand on the shock machine, even fewer people obeyed.

The circumstances of a whole group of people, social conditions like the state of the economy – inflation, depression, and unemployment – or political turmoil, or threat or attack from the outside, powerfully affect group processes and actions. However, the characteristics of cultures, like a history of devaluation of a subgroup of society or overly strong respect for authority, and the nature of social and political systems also greatly affect how groups respond. Culture not only affects group behavior, but shapes individual psychology. Up to early in the twentieth century the popular view of children in Western countries such as England, the United States, and Germany, as presented in books on parenting, was that they are inherently willful (see again Chapter 4, on Evil). These books suggested that to become good people children's will must be broken, and broken early, using as much punishment as necessary. But as we shall see in this book, research shows that harsh treatment and cruelty to children *enhance* the potential for both individual and group violence.

HUMAN NATURE, GOODNESS, AND EVIL

Psychologists, social thinkers, and philosophers have written extensively about goodness and evil in human nature.[10] Some have assumed that humans are selfish and aggressive by nature. The philosopher Thomas Hobbes had an extreme view. According to him, if allowed to do so people would use any and all means to fulfill their own interests, resulting in constant violence, war by each against all. To prevent this, strong external controls by authorities were needed. Others, like the psychoanalyst Sigmund Freud, had similar but milder beliefs and thought that people need to acquire internal controls, in the course of growing up, to prevent harmful behavior by them.

Many others, like the French author/philosopher Jean-Jacques Rousseau and the American psychologist Carl Rogers, have assumed that humans are good by nature, that they care about others' welfare. However, in reality their views confuse nature and nurture. Both believed that this inherent goodness would be apparent under the right circumstances – that is, given the right "nurture" or experience. Rousseau's noble savage lost his goodness due to the bad institutions society created, and Rogers's child could lose his or her goodness by not receiving unconditional love. In other words, the right experiences are required to bring the inherent goodness to the fore. Still others, like David Hume, thought that relationships among people in groups can give rise to positive actions as people pursued their enlightened self-interest.

Sociobiologists think about human nature in the more modern terms of shared genetic makeup. They believe that both altruism and aggression have become part of the human genetic makeup. When others are in great need, this activates altruism. Threat to life activates aggression. When there is constant threat to life – for example, not enough game in the forest to feed people in surrounding areas – a culture may develop that promotes aggression in the service of survival. E. O. Wilson[11] has used this explanation for the culture of the Mundurucu, Brazilian headhunters who train children from an early age in fighting and attacking.

However, there have been nontechnological societies living in great scarcity that have been peaceful. A contrasting explanation would be that cultures that promote aggression develop for various reasons, which include scarcity and threat by other groups. These cultures then re-create themselves and over time even tend to evolve toward greater aggressiveness. Scarcity may contribute to, but does not make the development of a culture of violence inevitable. In seeming opposition to the sociobiological view, a group of scientists have signed the Seville Statement, expressing their belief that human beings are not aggressive by nature.

The assumption about human nature is an assumption about the shared genetic makeup of all humans. This is what sociobiologists write about. Evolutionary psychology, a recent development, is also concerned with shared human genetic makeup. It focuses on psychological mechanisms that have developed in humans because they help with "inclusive fitness," that is, they help us to survive so that we can transmit our genes and lead us to protect our children so that they can further transmit our genes.

David Buss has proposed that anger is such a mechanism, its purpose to prevent "strategic interference." Many theorists of aggression have viewed the interference with or blocking of goal-directed behavior as creating frustration, which in turn leads to aggression. While frustration-aggression theory has assumed that frustration leads to aggression, Buss does not assume that strategic interference leads to aggression. He proposes that it "motivates action designed to eliminate the interference or to avoid subsequent interfering events,"[12] leaving open the possibility of varied types of actions that may accomplish this goal. This is realistic, in line with much research that shows that frustration may, but does not necessarily, lead to aggression. It can also lead to a different approach to accomplish one's goals.

In addition to the shared human genetic makeup, the heredity of particular individuals is another important genetic influence. Are some people more aggressive while others are less aggressive by nature? Are some more altruistic while others are less so?

All that I have learned in the course of my studies of children and adults, my work with teachers and parents, my study of genocide and mass killing, my engagement with real-life situations like Rwanda, trying to help prevent renewed violence after the genocide of 1994 by promoting healing and reconciliation, my work with police officers and others, and my study of others' work tells me that human beings have the potential for both goodness and evil. Perhaps extreme conditions, such as attack, or the intense need of a helpless person – for example a young child's need in front of our eyes – do give rise to a natural inclination respectively for aggressive self-defense or help. But a young child who is attacked may cry, run away, or hit back. The "natural" inclination is not clear, and if it is there, it is only an inclination, not a genetically determined action.

But the experiences that children, adults, and groups have do develop characteristics that may lead them to be caring and helpful, or untrusting, hostile, and aggressive. Given these characteristics, circumstances give rise to psychological states and processes, like anger or empathy, and feelings of effectiveness or helplessness, that in turn can lead to helping or harming others. Over time an evolution to great kindness or cruelty can take place.

Individuals, of course, differ in heredity. One approach to hereditary origins is the search for particular genes associated with some behavior or characteristic. Most human characteristics and behaviors have highly complex origins and do not seem to be accountable by the nature of a single gene. When such a gene is identified, as in the case of manic-depressive or bipolar illness, over time the discovery has repeatedly turned out to be in error.[13]

Another approach, used in behavior genetics, is to identify a heritability statistic that aims to show the extent to which particular behaviors are due to genetic inheritance versus environment and experience.[14] This is done by comparing the degree to which relatives with greater and lesser hereditary similarity (identical twins, fraternal twins, adopted children and their adoptive versus birth parents) are more or less alike in particular behaviors, like alcoholism or aggression. Using heritability statistics is an appropriate strategy, but difficult to do correctly, since alternatives to a genetic explanation often exist. An obvious one is that identical twins are not only more genetically similar but are also treated more alike than fraternal twins. One way to properly establish hereditary influence is to compare identical twins and fraternal twins who have been separated early in life by adoption.

The most relevant heredity-based characteristic for goodness and evil seems to be temperament. Children differ in how active they are, how intense are their emotions, how comfortable they are with new places and people, and how easily they can learn to regulate their feelings and control their impulses. Some children, given their intensity and impulsiveness (that is, speedy reactions to stimuli around them), need more guidance to learn to be gentle in relation to others.

Certain temperamental characteristics of children can elicit reactions from parents as well as other people that lead to problems in their development. Very intense, impulsive children may evoke impatient, harsh reactions that shape them to become more intense and aggressive, rather than temper their temperament. But this does not have to be so, and many parents and adult caregivers offer children with more "difficult" temperaments – a somewhat unfortunate term used by early temperament researchers[15] – the love and patient guidance they require for optimal development.

Our shared human genetic makeup provides every child with the potential for caring and hostility, helping and aggression. But do all children have these potentials to an equal degree? So far, while there is some research showing differences in the heritability of aggression,[16] and to a lesser extent of helpful behavior, there is no evidence, at least in my view, that either aggression or altruism is directly inherited, that something other than differences in temperament are the sources of heritability. The best explanations for differences in people's inclinations to help or harm others are their experiences in life, and this book will focus on them. Until future research shows otherwise, the best hypothesis is that to the extent heredity plays a role in inclinations toward either kindness or cruelty, it does so through temperament, an indirectly related characteristic, which exerts its influence to a large extent through the reactions it creates to the child.

A shared genetic influence in humans is human needs, or what I have called "basic human needs." Like other human needs theorists,[17] I assume that all human beings share fundamental psychological needs. There is substantial overlap in the needs different theorists focus on. I have assumed that basic needs include needs for security, a positive identity, a feeling of effectiveness and control, positive connection to other human beings, autonomy, and a "usable" comprehension of reality. Basic needs are not directly linked to altruism or aggression; they exert influence in combination with experience. Experiences that constructively fulfill these needs make caring about other people more likely. Experiences that persistently frustrate them create vulnerability and generate negative feelings and hostility toward people (see Chapter 5).

Repeatedly in this book I will suggest the usefulness of a basic needs perspective in understanding goodness and evil in individuals and groups. The influences that I will describe as contributing to harm-doing and violence, or to their prevention and to caring and helpfulness, are not dependent on a basic needs perspective. But understanding the reasons why these influences have the effects they do will be enriched by considering how they fulfill or frustrate basic needs.

Humans also have an inclination to differentiate between "us" and "them," people they identify with, who are part of their group, and those outside the group. Identification with groups is rooted in both thought (perceiving oneself as a member of the group) and in feelings of connection that are often intense. The group may be defined by ethnicity, religion, nationality, race, family, political affinity, or in other ways. The differentiation between us and them is central to kindness and cruelty. Seeing others as them has an important role in violence by groups against others and seeing people as us contributes to empathy and caring.[18]

The inclination to differentiate us and them is based, in part, on aspects of our nature. One aspect is the infant's attachment to caretakers, accompanied by fear of strangers, which is a rudimentary form of the differentiation between us and them. Another is that our mind works by categorization, with those inside the group and those outside put into different categories.

This differentiation probably also has to do with basic needs. Being part of a group helps people feel secure. If one likes and respects one's group, membership provides a positive identity and positive connection to others in the group. The worldview propagated by the group is absorbed by its members. It is a natural, even inevitable basis of individuals' comprehension of reality.

ARE GOOD AND EVIL CULTURALLY RELATIVE?

Are goodness and evil relative, a matter of the norms and standards of behavior in particular societies? Or are certain actions good or evil even if they are not regarded so in particular societies?

One of the most surprising discussions I ever had with students took place many years ago, very early in a semester, when I lectured on and we discussed how we might infer or interpret an action as aggressive or cruel. The students argued that the behavior of a mother who is standing on the sidewalk next to a busy street and is spanking her very young child is always aggressive and unjustified, even if she had been explaining to her child a number of times on different occasions not to step into the street, the child had just done so, and her intention was not to hurt her child but to make sure that the child "gets it" and won't get killed. They insisted that the mother must find other ways to influence her child. In contrast, they said, we cannot make any judgment about the actions of Nazi Germany deliberately and methodically killing many millions of people, including Germans in their so-called euthanasia program, because they have their own culture and have the right to follow their own standards. I believe that the students' views were strongly shaped by prevailing perspectives at the time, at least in their environment, asserting on the one hand that we have no right to judge other cultures, that judging others is a presumption on our part, and on the other hand that hitting children is wrong (which I strongly agree with, although absolutes rarely hold in raising children and there can be exceptions).

Philosophers like Immanuel Kant and others have proposed universal standards of morality because societies (including small ones like families) can develop cruel, immoral standards of what is acceptable conduct. Cultures vary greatly, of course, in many ways. Much of this variation has nothing to do with kindness and cruelty. But some conduct, by groups toward other groups, and within groups, may have become normal for a group, even though it deeply harms human beings, whether by killing, inflicting physical pain, degrading people or in other ways frustrating basic needs. Societies also vary in goodness, in the extent to which they show respect and consideration for the welfare of human beings.

Goodness and evil may be regarded as endpoints of a dimension. When a group, whether a society or a family, has developed practices that make people suffer physically or psychologically, or inhibit their growth and development as persons, I would regard that society as on the evil side of that dimension. This is true even, or perhaps especially, when such practices are deeply ingrained and integrated into the life of the society. It is important to respect and value cultural variation and not regard one's own society as the standard by which to see and judge others. But it is also important to recognize when certain cultural practices persistently diminish and harm people.

In studying the extent to which rape exists in nontechnological societies, one anthropologist described rape-prone versus rape-free societies. In the former rape may be performed ceremonially, women who are accused of adultery may be gang-raped by their husbands and the husbands' friends, young men may be initiated into sex by finding women to rape.[19] Perhaps in such societies, since the practice is so deeply ingrained, it is not harmful. Perhaps women in such societies enjoy being raped or at least are not harmed by it. Such a possibility is made less likely by the generally antagonistic relation between men and women this anthropologist found in rape-prone societies.

Societies that treat people well and promote the fulfillment of their individual and human potentials are on the good end of the dimension. For example, in some societies children are treated with warmth and affection. They are well nurtured. In some others they experience much harshness. Such cultural practices persist because children, when they become parents, tend to treat their children in the same way, especially in societies in which there is substantial uniformity in behavior and standards. In the United States, with great cultural variations, children who are physically punished or abused by their parents are more likely to do the same with their children. But many such children realize that the treatment they received was wrong and engage in valiant efforts not to treat their children the same way.

GOOD AND EVIL AS OPPOSITES

An essential reason for studying goodness and evil and aggression and altruism together is that they are opposites of each other, in a variety of ways. Influences that lead to goodness inhibit evil and those that lead to evil inhibit goodness. Good actions enhance, evil ones diminish, human well-being. They are also opposite aspects of morality, which refers to actions that relate to human welfare and principles and rules that guide such actions.

Morality is our conception of how humans ought to behave. Moral rules and principles prescribe good (beneficial) actions and prohibit evil (destructive) ones. However, good and evil acts are not only guided by principles, rules, or values, but also by feelings – of connection to, versus disconnection from, other people, of affection, caring, and empathy versus anger and hostility. These feelings give rise to motives to help or harm others. As personality develops with experience, some people will be more inclined to feel empathy, others to feel anger or hostility. Thus, good and evil actions are opposites not only in their effects, and in our conception of what is right and wrong, but also in the feelings, values, and psychological processes that lead to one or the other.

In an early study, researchers found that among very young children, being empathic, feeling what another feels, did not diminish aggressive behavior toward peers. Young empathic children were very active socially and perhaps as a result their behavior was indiscriminate. They may not yet have learned to control their expression of anger. However, as they got slightly older, more empathic children became less aggressive.[20] In addition, some research studies have shown that feeling empathy when witnessing someone's need – especially the kind of empathy researchers have called sympathy, in which there is a feeling of concern for the other – is associated with more helping by children, as well as adults.[21]

My students and I studied a personality characteristic that I have called *prosocial value orientation*. This consists of a positive view of human beings, caring about other people's welfare, and a feeling of personal responsibility for others' welfare. People who possess a prosocial orientation are likely to be empathic. But they go beyond empathy, feeling something because another person feels it, and even beyond sympathy, which includes the special element of concern for the other person. They also believe and feel that they themselves have a responsibility for others' welfare. (However, some researchers see sympathy as including a feeling of responsibility.)[22] As selections in the book will show, we found in a series of studies that people with a greater prosocial value orientation help more. This is true when someone is in physical distress, with stomach pains, or in psychological distress, such as a woman having been left by a boyfriend after a serious relationship. It is true with self-reports of many different kinds of helping. We have also developed a version of this test for adolescents and found that aggressive boys have less of a prosocial value orientation than boys who are not aggressive.[23] Other relevant characteristics, such as advanced moral reasoning, have also been found to decrease aggression and increase helping.

Since people respond to circumstances, and since all of us have many and varied values, beliefs, goals, and relationships, which join with circumstances in complex ways, a generally kind and helpful person may at times harm others. A normally cruel and aggressive person may at times be kind. But different and opposing psychological states and processes are likely to be active in leading to one or the other kind of action.

I have already mentioned another pair of opposites, us versus them. We are more likely to help people we regard as us, see as similar to us, part of our community or group. We more easily harm people we define as them, different and separate.

GOOD AND EVIL IN INDIVIDUALS AND GROUPS

The same motives can lead both individuals and members of groups to be aggressive, or helpful. But a member of a group may also be aggressive, or helpful, because of his or her relationship to others in the group or the group as a whole, rather than due to personal motives. A person who would tend not to be violent (or helpful) on his or her own may become so as a member of a group.

A young person may join a gang not because he or she wants to harm others, but because being a gang member may satisfy needs that do not get satisfied elsewhere, like the need for security, positive connection to others, a positive sense of self, or a feeling of effectiveness. These are basic needs for everyone but especially powerful needs for adolescents. Once a member, if the gang engages in violence, this person is likely to participate due to his or her connection to other members and commitment to the group.

The same is true with regard to ideological movements. In group violence, particularly genocide and terrorism, ideologies have a central role. People may join for varied reasons, only one of which is an already existing affinity to an ideology, a vision about ideal social arrangements. Others include the need for connection, support, and the hope that an ideological vision offers in difficult times. A readiness to obey authority and/or a need to relinquish responsibility for their own lives, to give up a burdensome individual identity for identity as a group member, can lead people to join closely knit groups with authoritarian leaders.

With regard to violence by groups, the focus of this book is on mass killing and genocide. However, understanding the roots of these forms of group violence also enlightens us about other kinds of violence and harm-doing by groups, ranging from discrimination, to persecution, to terrorism. The preceding paragraph, which describes why people join and follow ideological movements that lead to mass killing or genocide,[24] also accurately describes why people join terrorist groups.[25]

People may also be *selected* for membership in an extreme group, which in turn shapes them. For example, Greek torturers at the time of the dictatorship of the Colonels in the 1970s were selected from members of the military police based on their anticommunist ideological orientation and their obedience to authority.

Once they are members, the group socializes or resocializes people through the ideas it propagates, through their relationship to others in the group, and through the actions they engage in as members. They may change toward goodness or toward readiness to destroy an "enemy." Socialization into the group may occur as a natural outcome of group life, or may be deliberate, such as indoctrination against an enemy. The Greek torturers underwent elaborate training. They themselves were tortured, in part to further develop their obedience to authority.[26]

Members of the reserve police battalions that were sent behind the German front to kill Jews had at least three kinds of preparation. First, the characteristics that led them to choose a police career prepared them. The second preparation was the change and evolution that all Germans underwent in the course of the increasing persecution of Jews in Germany in the 1930s. The third one was the change and evolution that police officers may undergo in the course of police work, which at times involves the use of force.[27] A fourth kind of preparation, described by Richard Rhodes, was prior participation in violence and killing in the service of the Nazi system.[28]

In the report by Christopher Browning about one of the police battalions, the first time they were ordered to gather and shoot groups of Jews, the power of the group was evident. Even though they were told they could excuse themselves if they felt they could not fulfill this task, and even though many later reported inner struggle and some claimed they avoided shooting the first time, they did not ask to be excused. It would have distanced them from the group, might have diminished them in the eyes of their fellow members, and in spite of the "permission" to excuse themselves, might have led to later punishment. Over time, shooting people became quite normal for them.[29] (Note, however, that in another report, Daniel Goldhagen[30] claimed that the members of this police group were cold-blooded killers from the start.)

The power of the group has also been shown among terrorists and suicide bombers. Terrorists often act for both "cause and comrades" (see discussion of this in the Conclusion to the book). Palestinian suicide bombers are often very young. While they are volunteers, once they accept their mission, they are usually continually surrounded by other group members, to limit their exposure to anything that might change their minds.[31]

We don't know how frequent it is in the realm of helping and harmdoing that people act because they are entrapped in a group, disagreeing with the group's actions but facing a combination of practical and psychological circumstances that stop them from freeing themselves. In spite of the difficulty and even danger of doing so, many recruits do leave terrorist groups. Since groups are powerful socializers, this is more likely to happen early, before the group resocializes them. However, as circumstances change, differences in seemingly monolithic groups emerge. Chinese Red Army soldiers, fierce fighters in Korea, began to split into communists and anticommunists in POW camps and to fight each other.[32]

In what Sam and Pearl Oliner have called "normocentric" rescue behavior by some people during the Holocaust, helping was based not on individual motivation, but on group membership. In Poland some priests and leaders of partisan groups led their members to save Jewish lives. Others, however, led their members to help the Germans kill Jews.[33] In Belgium, leaders in exile and church leaders at home influenced the population to help Jews. In European countries in general, the more anti-Semitic the leadership the larger was the percentage of Jews killed. However, when there was more anti-Semitic leadership there had usually been a history of anti-Semitic institutions and practices,[34] which shaped the population and prepared them to follow anti-Semitic leadership at the time of the Holocaust.

It can happen, of course, that an individual joins a group that turns out to be, or becomes over time, greatly at odds with his or her beliefs, values, and inclinations. Since such groups are difficult to leave, a person may stay, perhaps remaining internally opposed, perhaps changing. Or the values of the individual lead him to oppose what the group does. However, as a number of the selections in this book will show, members of children's peer groups, ethnic groups, and nations are frequently passive. Some of the selections examine what is required for people to oppose their group when they realize that it is moving toward or engages in evil acts.

A group, even a temporary one like a mob, can exert powerful influence on people. Still, the psychological processes and motivations leading individuals and groups to help and harm others can be quite similar. Both in individuals and groups self-interest (for example, wanting to make a good impression, or to gain friends, or to bring about reciprocal helping), empathy, a feeling of responsibility for others' welfare and commitment to moral principles are important motives for helping. Both individuals and groups harm others because they feel hostility, or want to protect themselves from attack, whether real or imagined, or desire revenge, or because they hope to gain something through aggressive actions.

However, groups can activate, give direction to, enlarge as well as add motivation. Ideology, a central motivator, is essentially a group phenomenon. As members, people can participate in group action automatically, guided by their embeddedness in the group. They may become "deindividuated," momentarily losing their identity so that they are guided not by their own but by the group's values and beliefs. They may experience a "contagion" of emotions that spreads through the group, for example, in case of mob violence, whether it is a lynching mob, a riot in inner-city violence in the United States, or soccer "hooligans."[35] They may be inspired by leaders, by group ideals, or may obey authorities. They may be motivated by the desire for status in the group, or to enhance their careers – a motivation among communist functionaries as well as SS members.[36]

SPIRITUALITY, GOODNESS, AND EVIL

For many people goodness and evil have spiritual meanings. What might such meanings be from the perspective of this book? One spiritual meaning of goodness may have to do with people finding meaning and purpose in their lives and in life in general. Another important meaning is service to others. I will describe, as a high-level basic need, the need for transcendence. This means going beyond the self, beyond a focus on one's own material and psychological needs and desires. Usually this becomes possible when other basic needs have been constructively fulfilled in a person's life. Transcendence can take varied forms; an important one is altruistic action to benefit other people.

A spiritual relationship to evil may mean the acceptance of evil in the world. This does not mean passivity. Instead, it has to do with how we orient ourselves to evil deeds and to the people who harm others. Can we learn from witnessing them, can we make some kind of peace with their existence, can we grow from an awareness of them? While the emphasis in this book is on both understanding and acting to prevent harmful, violent behavior, a spiritual perspective has great value. Given the amount and intensity of violence and harm-doing in the world, it is easy to despair. A spiritual perspective can help us find some inner peace even as we engage in the difficult and slow process of promoting goodness in the world.

THEMES OF THIS BOOK: ORGANIZATION BY TOPICS

This book attempts to answer several central questions. They include:

What personal or group characteristics, what specific circumstances and what psychological processes and states that arise from them, lead individuals and groups to commit either acts of goodness or acts of evil?

What childhood experiences, especially what kind of socialization by parents and schools, give rise to the characteristics that make it likely that individuals engage in caring, helpful acts, or hostile, violent acts?

What combination of conditions in a society and characteristics of cultures, institutions, political systems, and psychological processes these generate, produce destructive or helpful actions by groups?

How can people heal from past victimization? How can groups that have harmed each other reconcile?

How can the evolution of violence in individuals and groups be prevented and caring and helping be promoted? How can goodness become an organic outgrowth of children's upbringing, the personality they develop, the nature of societies?

The content of this book is organized into a number of sections or parts. The first section introduces the book. Following this introduction, there is an article from the *New York Times* Science Section by Dan Goleman on my work on bystanders. This is followed by a book chapter in which I briefly review my work, as well as describe some of my life experiences, from surviving the Holocaust in Hungary as a young child, to escaping from Hungary and coming to the United States, and much later beginning to address the impact of my early experiences. The combination of these experiences and a seemingly natural progression in my work shaped my concerns over time. This is followed by a discussion of my conception of basic human needs and their role in altruism and aggression, a perspective that has increasingly provided a framework for my thinking. Also included in this section is a brief discussion of the meaning of the term "evil."

The second part of the book is about the roots of people helping others or remaining passive in the face of others' needs. This part explores the influence of both circumstances and personal characteristics in helping. Many forms of helping are addressed, with emergency helping, people responding to others' sudden and intense need, a form of helping on which I and others have done a great deal of research, receiving some added attention. Most of the research on helping behavior and altruism in adults, my own and others', was done from the end of the 1960s to the mid to late 1980s (although one of the selections is from 1990). As a result, the material in this part of the book is older than the rest (much of which describes my latest work and thinking), but it identifies what I consider very important influences in leading a person to help others – or remain passive.

The third part looks at how caring and helping, in contrast to aggression, develop in children and youth. I discuss child rearing by parents and in schools and to some extent the influence of social conditions and culture. I look at peer relations, especially negative behavior by peers such as bullying, its sources, consequences, and the role of bystanders in it. In research in collaboration with Darren Spielman we used a method to reduce aggression in boys that included instruction about basic needs, with participants role playing both destructive and constructive ways of fulfilling needs. I also describe practices to create "caring schools" that develop in children a caring, helpful, and nonaggressive orientation to others. Included in this section is also a brief selection on the origins of father–daughter incest.

The fourth part of the book describes the origins of genocide, mass killing and other collective violence like violence by mobs and the police. In this part I describe the many influences leading to such extreme violence, and how it evolves step by step, with actions leading to changes in individuals and groups that make increasing violence possible and probable. The examples that are described in most detail are the Holocaust – the genocide against the Jews – and the genocide of the Tutsis in Rwanda.

I also examine the role of the United States in relation to collective violence, as perpetrator, passive or complicit bystander, or active helper. I focus on the United States both because this is my home, my country, to which I am committed and would like to see playing a constructive role in the world, and because of the power and tremendous potential influence of the United States. The material in this section also informs us about the roots of lesser harm inflicted on groups, like discrimination, persecution, and torture, as well as the roots of intractable conflict that can turn into severe violence. One of the articles also provides a summary of some of the research on and my conception of the behavior of rescuers, people who in the midst of the horrors of genocide endangered their lives to save others.

The fifth part of the book concerns itself with the prevention of genocide and mass killing. I discuss what the international community – organizations and nations – can do and needs to do to halt violence once it begins and, ideally, to prevent it before it begins. I and Laurie Anne Pearlman also describe healing and reconciliation that are necessary after intense conflict and violence between groups has taken place, in "war-torn" or "post-conflict" societies, to prevent new violence, together with our work in Rwanda on healing, forgiving, and reconciliation. I also explore why mass violence did not happen, or was limited, in some places where the conditions for it existed. In this part I also examine the NATO intervention in Kosovo, the experience of children of Nazi perpetrators, the experience and needs of refugees, and the spirit in which the United States and the world ought to act and the kind of actions they ought to take in the aftermath of the terrorist attacks on September 11, 2001, to combat terrorism and create a nonviolent world. I also discuss the constructive potential of Holocaust education, which has become widespread in schools and education centers. It has a constructive potential for everyone, children and adults, and especially for people who have suffered themselves, whether from mass violence, persecution, or violence in the inner cities.

In the sixth, final part of the book I discuss some aspects of creating caring, morally inclusive societies. I further consider what makes bystanders passive and how might they be transformed and become active. I consider the seemingly universal principle of reciprocity in human relations and the creation of systems of positive reciprocity. I address the important question of the relationship of the individual to the group. In doing so, I focus on "constructive patriots" who, in contrast to "blind patriots," are capable of a critical consciousness, an exploration and questioning of their group's actions, and are led by their love of their country to question and oppose destructive policies and practices. I examine what the ideal university might be like and the kind of students it would shape. In the conclusion to the book, which like the introduction (and some other selections) I wrote specifically for this book, I briefly explore some further issues, like terrorism and moral courage. I then summarize and extend the exploration of what is required for the evolution of goodness in individuals, and cultures and societies. My aim is to summarize what is required for creating caring, nonviolent, peaceful societies that nourish the human spirit and promote the optimal functioning of individuals, their capacity to grow and fulfill their human and personal potentials.

Notes

1. Staub, E. (in press). *A brighter future: Raising caring, nonviolent, morally courageous children*. New York: Oxford University Press.
2. Staub, E., & Pearlman, L. (2001). Healing, reconciliation and forgiving after genocide and other collective violence. In S. J. Helmick, & R. L. Petersen (Eds.), *Forgiveness and reconciliation: Religion, public policy and conflict transformation*. Radnor, PA: Templeton Foundation Press.
3. Kurlantzick, J. (2001, August). Muhammed Yunus. Part of Real Heroes: 20 men and women who risked it all to make a difference. *U.S. News and World Report*, p. 51.
4. Des Forges, A. (1999). *Leave none to tell the story: Genocide in Rwanda*. New York: Human Rights Watch; Power, S. (2001, September) Bystanders to genocide. *The Atlantic Monthly Magazine*.
5. See Staub, E. (1999). The origins and prevention of genocide, mass killing and other collective violence. *Peace and Conflict: Journal of Peace Psychology*, *5*, 303–337.

6. Staub, E. (1989). Steps along the continuum of destruction: The evolution of bystanders, German psychoanalysts, and lessons for today. *Political Psychology, 10*, 39–53 (see also "The psychology of bystanders, perpetrators, and heroic helpers," Chap. 22, this book).
7. Latané, B., & Darley, J. (1970). *The unresponsive bystander: Why doesn't he help?* New York: Appleton-Crofts.
8. Milgram, S. (1965). Some conditions of obedience and disobedience to authority. *Human Relations, 18*, 57–76; Milgram, S. (1974). *Obedience to authority: An experimental view.* New York: Harper and Row.
9. Kohlberg, L., & Candee, L. (1984). The relationship of moral judgment to moral action. In W. M. Kurtines & J. L. Gewirtz (Eds.), *Morality, moral behavior, and moral development*, pp. 52–73. New York: Wiley.
10. This is reviewed in chapter 1 (Positive behavior, morality, and human nature) of Staub, E. (1978). *Positive social behavior and morality. Vol.1. Personal and social influences.* New York: Academic Press.
11. Wilson, E. O. (1978). *On human nature.* New York: Bantam Books.
12. Buss, D. M. (2000). The evolution of happiness. *American Psychologist, 55*, 15–23, 17.
13. Peele, S., & DeGrandpre, R. (1995). My genes made me do it. *Psychology Today, 28*(4) (July/August), 50–53, 62, 64, 66, 68.
14. Ibid.
15. Thomas, A., Chess, S., & Birch, H. (1970). The origin of personality. *Scientific American, 223* (2), 102–109.
16. Rutter, M., Giller, H., & Hagell, A. (1998). *Antisocial behavior by young people.* New York: Cambridge University Press.
17. Maslow, A. H. (1987). *Motivation and personality* (3rd ed.). New York: Harper and Row (original work published in 1954); Kelman, H. C. (1990). Applying a human needs perspective to the practice of conflict resolution: The Israeli-Palestinian case. From J. Burton (Ed.), *Conflict: Human needs theory*. New York: St. Martin's Press.
18. Staub, E. (1989). *The roots of evil: The origins of genocide and other group violence*. Cambridge University Press, New York; Staub, E., & Bar-Tal, D. (in press). Genocide, mass killing and intractable conflict: Roots, evolution, prevention, and reconciliation. In D. Sears, L. Huddy, & R. Jervis, (Eds.), *Handbook of political psychology*. New York: Oxford University Press.
19. Sanday, P. R. (1981). The socio-cultural context of rape: A cross-cultural study. *Journal of Social Issues, 37* (4), 5–27.
20. Feshbach, N. D., & Feshbach, S. (1969). The relationship between empathy and aggression in two age groups. *Developmental Psychology, 1*, 102–107.
21. Batson, C. D. (1990). How social an animal? The human capacity for caring. *American Psychologist, 45*, 336–347; Eisenberg, N., & Fabes, R. A. (1998). Prosocial development. In W. Damon (Ed.), *Handbook of child psychology, fifth edition*, Vol. 3: N. Eisenberg (Ed.). *Social, emotional, and personality development*. New York: Wiley.
22. For example, Nancy Eisenberg, Lecture in the Department of Psychology, University of Massachusetts at Amherst, April 27, 2002.

23. Spielman, D., & Staub, E. (2000). Reducing boys' aggression. Learning to fulfill basic needs constructively. *Journal of Applied Developmental Psychology, 21*, 2, 165–181 (see "Reducing boys' aggression," Chap. 19, this book).
24. Staub, *The roots of evil.*
25. McCauley, C. R., & Segal, M. E. (1989). Terrorist individuals and terrorist groups: The normal psychology of extreme behavior. In J. Groebel & J. F. Goldstein (Eds.), *Terrorism.* Sevilla: Publicaciones de la Universidad de Sevilla.
26. Haritous-Fataurous, M. (in press). *The psychological origins of institutionalized torture.* New York: Routledge.
27. Staub, E. (2001). Understanding and preventing police violence. In S. Epstein & M. Amir (Eds.), *Policing, security and democracy.* Huntsville, TX: Office of Criminal Justice Press. See article in Section 4, this book.
28. Rhodes, R. (2002). *Masters of death: The SS-Einsatzgruppen and the invention of the Holocaust.* New York: Knopf.
29. Browning, C. R. (1992). *Ordinary men: Reserve batallion 101 and the final solution in Poland.* New York: HarperCollins.
30. Goldhagen, D. (1996). *Hitler's willing executioners: Ordinary Germans and the Holocaust.* London: Little, Brown.
31. Post, G. (in press). The mind of the terrorist. *Peace and Conflict: The Journal of Peace Psychology.*
32. McCauley & Segal, ibid.; McCauley, C. (in press). Making sense to terrorism after 9/11. In Moser, R. (Ed.), *Shocking violence II: Violent disaster, war and terrorism affecting our youth.* Charles C. Thomas, publisher.
33. Oliner, S., & Oliner, P. (1988). *The altruistic personality.* New York: The Free Press.
34. Fein, H. (1990). *Genocide: A sociological perspective.* Special issue of *Current Sociology, 38*, 1–126.
35. Buford, B. (1992). *Among the thugs: The experience, and the seduction, of crowd violence.* New York: Norton.
36. Steiner, J. M. (1980). The SS yesterday and today: A socio-psychological view. In J. Dimsdale (Ed.), *Survivors, victims and perpetrators: Essays on the Nazi Holocaust.* New York: Hemisphere Publishing Company.

2

Studying the Pivotal Role of Bystanders

Daniel Goleman

It was the summer of 1944, and 6-year-old Ervin Staub and his family, like other Jews in Budapest, were being set apart from their neighbors by laws imposed by the Nazis. Food was strictly rationed, and Ervin's 13-year-old cousin Eva, desperate to get a loaf of bread for her family, was waiting in a long bakery line after the curfew for Jews and without the yellow Star of David she was supposed to wear.

"Someone pointed her out as a Jew, and three young thugs tried to take her away," said Dr. Staub, now a psychologist at the University of Massachusetts, who vividly recalls the incident. "But she ran into our house to hide, and my aunt yelled at the thugs with such defiance that she scared them away."

That summer, members of the Staub family were given protective identity papers by Raoul Wallenberg, the Swedish ambassador who used the documents to shelter tens of thousands of Jews from the Nazis. Ervin's father had already been imprisoned in a Nazi labor camp, but was emboldened to try an escape when a close family servant smuggled the Swedish papers to him in the camp. He succeeded and hid in the house undetected until the end of the war.

"What happened to me as a child in Hungary has left me with a lifelong mission to get people to respond to those who need help," said Dr. Staub, who still speaks with a Hungarian accent, with luxuriantly rolled R's and sibilant S's. At 18, Dr. Staub fled Hungary during the 1956 uprising against Communist rule, and lived for two years in Vienna. Coming to the United States in 1959, he entered the University of Minnesota and began his studies in psychology, completing his graduate work at Stanford in 1965.

Reprinted from D. Goleman, Scientist at work: Ervin Staub. Studying the pivotal role of bystanders. *The New York Times*, Science Times. June 22, 1993. C1, C6. Reprinted by permission of *The New York Times*.

Dr. Staub exemplifies a growing breed of activist research psychologists who are finding ways to apply the lessons of the laboratory in addressing social concerns. Most recently, in the wake of the beating of Rodney King by police officers in Los Angeles, the California agency that sets training standards for police officers throughout the state commissioned Dr. Staub to design a training program to encourage officers to intervene when their colleagues use too much force. Part of that program will be given to the police there next month in a statewide training course.

It is the pivotal role of bystanders in abetting or preventing acts of evil that now captures Dr. Staub's scientific interest, whether it be nations standing back from intervening in the Balkans or individual cases like that of Sidney Brookins, a man who died from a concussion suffered in a beating this month in Minneapolis. Mr. Brookins lay dying for two days near the door to an apartment house while people walked past, ignoring him.

Dr. Staub's research career began with experiments involving carefully orchestrated simulations of just that sort of situation, where people are given the choice to help or ignore someone in dire need. The time was the mid-1960s, just after the 1964 murder of Kitty Genovese, who was knifed to death outside her apartment house in Kew Gardens, Queens, as 38 neighbors heard her pleas for help but did nothing, not even call the police.

Psychologists, at a loss to explain the inaction of the neighbors, began a series of studies in which, for example, unwitting volunteers for experiments were put in situations where they passed by someone who was moaning and in clear need of help.

In one of those now most often cited, students at Princeton Theological Seminary were asked to go to a nearby chapel and give an extemporaneous sermon on the Biblical parable of the Good Samaritan. As they walked to the chapel, they passed a man slumped in a doorway, moaning for help. About two-thirds of those who thought they had plenty of time stopped to help, but only 10% of the students who thought they were late did so.

Dr. Staub, then at Harvard University, took these studies one step further. "How you could increase the willingness to help had been ignored in social psychological studies of bystanders," he said. "I set out to identify the factors that make people more likely to come to someone's aid."

In one of Dr. Staub's studies, for example, volunteers were taken into a room in pairs for what they believed was an experiment in assessing people's personalities from written accounts about them. Actually one of each pair was a confederate of Dr. Staub's. Midway through their task, the people heard a loud crash from the next room, followed by sobbing and groans.

When the confederate said, "That probably has nothing to do with us," only about 25% of the volunteers investigated the source of the groans in the next room (actually a tape recorder). But when the confederate said, "That sounds pretty bad – I'll go get the experimenter and maybe you should go check what's happening next door," every one of the volunteers went to see what was wrong.

"It showed me the power of bystanders to define the meaning of events in a way that leads people to take responsibility," said Dr. Staub.

That principle – in the form of the assumption that police brutality can best be prevented by the intervention of onlooking fellow officers – is at the core of the training program Dr. Staub has designed for the police in California.

It proposes, for example, that chiefs and supervisors need to counter a drift toward overuse of violence by officers in their departments by holding them to strict accountability. The failure of supervisors to do or say anything about excessive violence is taken as a tacit acceptance, which encourages it. "That seems to have been the situation in the L.A. police force before the Rodney King incident," said Dr. Staub.

STOPPING POLICE BRUTALITY

"You need to shift the mindset, so officers realize that if they remain passive as bystanders they are responsible for what their fellow officers do," said Dr. Staub. "You have to do it in a way that does not undermine their loyalty to each other, but changes what loyalty means – stopping excess violence rather than hiding it behind a code of silence."

The program aims to make the police better able to readily recognize when a fellow officer is about to run the risk of using too much force, and encourage officers to step in to avert it by, for example, quickly explaining to the person being subdued what he needs to do to avoid being the target of even greater violence, or taking command of the situation from the other officer.

"Given the nature of police culture, this kind of intervention is easier before there is actual violence than once violence has started," said Dr. Staub.

Beyond that, the training seeks to help officers understand the forces that make police brutality more likely, such as seeing certain ethnic or racial groups in terms of negative stereotypes. Those attitudes make it easier for the police to justify the use of excessive force with members of those groups, Dr. Staub said.

In recent years, Dr. Staub's research has shifted from the experimental laboratory to case studies of events like the Holocaust, the genocidal reign of the Khmer Rouge in Cambodia, and the wholesale slaughter of enemies of right-wing military governments in Argentina.

"I wanted to understand in totality the dynamics of genocide and other group violence," said Dr. Staub. [I want to use the principles that lab studies yield for such larger purpose. E.S.]

His analysis of how such atrocities come about, and what might be done to prevent them, is summed up in his 1989 book, *The Roots of Evil*, published by Cambridge University Press.

THE PATH TO ATROCITY

The path to grave horror begins with minor transgressions. "The Holocaust began with much milder persecution, like laws forbidding Jews to hold positions in commerce or government," said Dr. Staub.

These steps are crucial junctures. "If bystanders – people who are neither perpetrators nor victims – object firmly at this point, it can slow or even stop the whole process," said Dr. Staub. "But if no one objects, it emboldens the transgressors." For example, he says, in the early days of Serbian aggression against Bosnia, "if a UN fleet had appeared offshore and said, 'Stop, or we'll bomb your artillery,' it would have sent a clear signal the world disapproved."

But just as perpetrators become more violent unless stopped, those who help, even in small ways, are often drawn to greater acts of altruism, Dr. Staub finds. He cites the case of Oskar Schindler, a German bon vivant who was given control of a Jewish-owned factory after the Nazi invasion of Poland in 1939. Starting with small acts of kindness to protect the welfare of his Jewish workers, Mr. Schindler eventually took greater and greater risks to protect them, getting permission to set up a work camp next to the factory and then finally surreptitiously setting up another factory outside Poland, taking along his entire contingent of "skilled workers" and saving the lives of more than 1,300 Jews.

Standing by passively while witnessing an evil act has a subtle effect on bystanders themselves. "If you empathize with the victim, but do nothing, you feel guilty," said Dr. Staub. "So there is a tendency to diminish the seriousness of the harm in your own mind, or to distance yourself from the victim. One way this happens is through the assumption that people who are suffering must somehow deserve it. Without quite realizing it, you can join the perpetrator in devaluing the victim."

By the same token, the passivity of bystanders has a demoralizing effect on victims. "When the rest of the world did nothing to help the Jews in Germany, Jews felt abandoned," said Dr. Staub. "When you feel helpless and alone, you are less likely to resist. But in Belgium, where the population resisted Germany in its persecution of the Jews, Jews themselves did much more on their own behalf."

In short, "actions by bystanders – even simply protesting what's being done – empower the victims, while passivity adds to their suffering," said Dr. Staub.

While that may seem self-evident, Dr. Staub finds that all too often people whose voices could have helped protect victims remain passive. "People don't realize the power they have as bystanders to make a difference," he said.

3

Studying and Promoting Altruism and Studying and Working to Prevent Genocide

The Guiding Role of Early Survival

INTRODUCTION

The connection between much of my work and my Holocaust experience is quite obvious. My work was probably also affected by my post-Holocaust experience of living under a communist system in Hungary, escaping from Hungary without my family, living in Vienna, then coming to the United States alone.

I did some early work on fear, control and lack of control, and the use of information and control to reduce fear. At the time, in no way did I connect this work to my own life experiences. I have spent most of my career studying what leads people to help others, what leads them to remain passive in the face of others' need, what leads them to harm others. The latter included the study of the origins of genocide and other collective violence. Underlying all my work has been an interest in change: How can we develop caring in children? How can people become more helpful? How can we reduce youth violence? How can we eliminate violence by groups against innocent people? A thread through all my work has been the study of the passivity and the potential power of bystanders, of individuals and groups who witness suffering or harm inflicted on others.

While the connection of this work to my Holocaust experience is quite clear, for many years I ignored and disregarded this connection, almost denied it. I survived the Holocaust and I was involved with my work, and I emotionally separated these two domains.

The connection broke through at some points. I started this kind of research in the late 1960s. I remember reading Leon Uris's book *Mila Seventeen*

Reprinted from E. Staub (2001). *Studying and promoting altruism and studying and working to prevent genocide: The guiding role of early survival.* In P. Suedfeld (Ed.), *Light from the Ashes: Social science careers of young Holocaust refugees and survivors.* Ann Arbor: University of Michigan Press. pp. 135–152. Included here are pp. 136–152.

sometime in the early to mid-1970s, a book about a German doctor in the post–World War II world, a seeming humanitarian and altruist, who was a Nazi doctor at a concentration camp during the war. He conducted some of the horrible, cruel, Nazi "medical experiments." I cried at one point and felt a renewed determination to do my work on helping and altruism. I felt deeply that I wanted to do what I could to help create a world in which human beings won't do horrible things to others.

Why did I need to disconnect my early experience and my work? Did I want to think that I was doing science, studying what was "objectively valuable," rather than indulging in something related to myself? Did my training in psychology lead me to believe that studying something that arose out of my life experience would make my work less valuable? Did I think that it would make my work less credible? Did I feel it would make me into a victim, treated condescendingly? Or was I defending myself from more directly engaging with the Holocaust, with my experiences and their impact on me? Perhaps all of these were true, to varying degrees.

FROM SURVIVAL TO BECOMING A PSYCHOLOGIST

I was six years old, living in Budapest, when in the summer of 1944 bad times were replaced by the worst of times. That summer all the Jews in Hungary who lived outside Budapest were driven or taken from their homes, packed into cattle cars, and transported to Auschwitz. Most of them were immediately killed. After the summer more were taken from Budapest. Out of a total of about 600,000 Jews in Hungary, about 450,000 were killed.

The bad times started for us way before that. Hungary was a voluntary ally of Germany, and it tried to match Hitler's anti-Semitic policies. In some ways it preceded them. For example, in 1920 a law was passed, the so-called numerus clausus, that limited Jewish entry into universities.

Our family and my mother's sister's family lived together in a large apartment in Budapest. The two families owned a small business together. They made trousseaus for women about to marry – bed linen, nightgowns, tablecloths, and so on. My earliest clear memory is of lying in bed at night as my uncle said good-bye to me and next morning waking up to sounds of crying as my family gathered to tearfully say good-bye to him as he left for a forced labor camp. All Hungarian Jewish men were called up for forced labor. I do not remember when my father left.

There were many "memorable" events in the years 1944 and early 1945, until the Soviet army liberated Budapest. In the spring of 1944 the ruler of Hungary, Admiral Horthy, realized that the war would be lost. He approached the Allies for a separate peace. The Germans discovered this and occupied Hungary. I was on the main street of Budapest, a street that encircled the city, with our maid Maria (nicknamed Macs, who joined our family before I was born and remained until she was the last surviving member in Budapest) when the German tanks rolled down the street. It was after this that a small group of Germans, helped by Hungarians, transported all Jews from the countryside to Auschwitz.

Things were bad in the city as well. Some people behaved in an intensely anti-Semitic manner. A coal merchant from across the street used to come into our apartment house around dawn, stand in the courtyard, and scream threats and degrading epithets at the Jewish residents of the building. In the fall the Hungarian Nazi Party, the Arrow Cross, took over the government. They gathered many Jews, took them down to the Danube, and shot them. Sometimes they tied several people together, shot some but not all of them, and pushed them all into the river.

My mother and aunt were courageous women and, like many survivors, did all that was in their power to save us. There were a number of incidents in which they showed courage and determination. For example, once we were told that all young men of a certain age were to gather in the courtyard, to be taken to work. My aunt prohibited my fifteen-year-old cousin from going. When he insisted, too scared to stay away, she slapped him, an unusual occurrence in our household. He stayed. Those who went did not return.

In an incident that vividly stands out in my memory my aunt also saved her thirteen-year-old daughter. There was a bakery right next to the entrance of the apartment house where we lived. One late afternoon my cousin Eva went outside, a perilous enterprise, to stand in line for bread. She did not wear a yellow star, perhaps because of a curfew on Jews. Someone recognized her and proclaimed that she was Jewish. She ran into the house, with three young Nazis chasing her. They wanted to take her away. My aunt encountered them just inside the entrance to the house. She shouted at them. She was so forceful that she intimidated them. They said they would come back with the police, but they never did. I watched this scene from the top of the stairs leading up from the entrance of the house to the mezzanine.

At some point my mother and aunt managed to get us protective passes. These passes were the creation of Raoul Wallenberg, a Swedish diplomat. Wallenberg was a member of an extremely wealthy and distinguished family, but he came from an impoverished branch of that family. He was the partner of a Hungarian Jew living in Sweden, with whom he operated an export-import firm. In this connection he had visited Hungary and met his partner's relatives who were still living there. After the terrible summer of 1944, he was asked to go to Hungary to try to save the lives of some of the remaining Hungarian Jews.

Wallenberg agreed. He threw himself into his mission with great intensity, determination, and courage. On his arrival in Budapest he immediately created a document that said that the bearer would move to Sweden after the war and would be under the protection of Sweden for the duration of the war. He cajoled the Hungarian authorities into respecting a certain number of these, constantly negotiating, threatening, persuading government officials. He as well as the underground created many more of these documents. He repeatedly endangered his life. He helped people in many ways: for example, pulling Jews off trains, handing them protective passes, and then claiming that they were under Swedish protection.

He bought apartment houses in Budapest, and people with protective passes moved into them. We were among these people. I remember the night when we left our apartment, pushing a cart with some belongings on the way to the protected house. We were very scared that someone, whether police, Arrow Cross, or hostile civilians, would stop us. At that time and place Jews were fair game for anyone.

On our arrival we first slept on mattresses in the basement with many other people. Later we graduated to the one-room apartment of an old woman who was ill. The old woman was in bed most of the time. I don't remember how we did this, but I believe eight of us stayed there.

I think that my lifelong concern with those who don't remain passive but instead help others, my interest in "active bystanders," was to an important extent inspired by Macs, even more than by Raoul Wallenberg. I regard her as my second mother, a woman who loved me, my sister, and my cousins dearly. In these terrible times she did all she could to help us. Sometime before we received the protective passes she took me and my sister into hiding with a Christian family. I remember walking with her on the street, holding on to her hand; arriving at the house and then standing in front of the door of the apartment where the family lived; entering the apartment and seeing a woman sitting on a stool peeling potatoes. That is just about all I remember from the week or two we spent there. When some people in the house where this family lived seemed suspicious of the "child relatives visiting from the countryside," Macs moved us to another family. After we received the protective passes, she brought us back home.

During our stay at the protected house, she prepared bread, which she took in a baby carriage to be baked at a bakery. The bread and other food she acquired fed many people in the house. Once she was stopped by Arrow Cross men and accused of helping Jews. She had to stand for hours with her hands held up, facing a wall. She firmly denied helping Jews. They let her go, and she continued helping us.

She went to the separate labor camps where my father and uncle were doing forced labor and brought them copies of the protective passes. These were useless in their situation. But perhaps possession of a pass gave my father courage. Whatever enabled him to do it, when his group was taken to Germany, during an overnight stopover at some army barracks in Budapest he escaped. He was the only one of the group to survive. He came to our protected house and hid there until the Soviet army arrived.

During a number of raids on our house, miraculously, he was not found. The protected houses were constantly raided, and many people were taken away. Once during a raid my father was hiding under an armchair that was pushed into the corner, with a blanket casually thrown over it. The Arrow Cross raiders searched every closet, every drawer, but did not find him. I was the one who saw them march down the street toward the house, called out to inform the rest of my family, and ran to the apartment door to check that they were actually entering the house. I don't know whether hiding my father under the armchair was a plan my mother had designed earlier or a strategy that she thought up in that terribly dangerous moment.

Finally, in late January 1945 our part of the city was liberated by the Soviet army. A number of my relatives did not survive. My uncle froze to death in the forced labor camp. My father's sister and her two children were killed in Auschwitz. But we were "luckier" than most people. The fathers of most of the Jewish boys who survived died in forced labor camps or in German death camps.

FROM COMMUNIST HUNGARY TO THE UNITED STATES

Life after the Nazi period was complicated and difficult but not life threatening to us. We moved back to our apartment. My parents restarted their business but on a very small scale, selling men's, women's, and children's underclothing at their small store. They had to start from scratch, since most of the people to whom they gave goods from their business for safekeeping did not return them. They claimed that the merchandise was taken by the Germans or the Russians. My mother later repeatedly saw tablecloths in the apartment of the superintendent of our apartment house, one of our trusted keepers of goods, that were supposedly taken by the Russians or Germans.

In 1948 the communists took power. After a wave of nationalization, they finally reached the bottom of the barrel and in 1953 nationalized very small businesses. My parents' business was closed, the goods in it taken away with nominal compensation. My parents were religious; my father did not want to work on Saturdays, so he went to work in a newly created Jewish toy making cooperative. At age fifty-seven, after a lifetime of working with textiles in some way or another, he started to work on a machine, making toys. My mother took orders for sweaters from individuals and had the sweaters made for them. This was illegal, since one was only allowed to sell sweaters that one had made oneself. We had an old weaving machine at home, a machine that did not actually work, in case the police came.

Our family had disintegrated. In 1949 my cousins escaped from Hungary. They had to escape, since the communist government did not allow people to leave. They went to Israel. In 1953 their mother was allowed to follow them.

In 1956 I finished high school, a technical high school. Not being of worker or peasant origin, and therefore considered politically unreliable, I was afraid of not getting into a university and of having few options after high school. Even though the engineering studies in my school did not appeal to me, I followed the only university possibility that seemed available. I succeeded in enrolling at a technical university in Miskolc, another Hungarian city, to study engineering.

Soon after this, in October 1956, the Hungarian revolution began. I had a variety of adventures during this time, of which I will mention one that says something both about me and about the persistent anti-Semitism in Hungary that probably reinforced some of the psychological effects of the Holocaust. One day the police barracks in Miskolc were raided and the police in them arrested. I was in front of the police building when this happened. A revolutionary council, or something like that, took over the city. My somewhat adventurous nature landed me, the day after, inside City Hall. Outside people were milling around, demanding that the now jailed police be handed over to them. A number of people, communists, secret police, whatever, had already been tied to cars and pulled around the city in revenge. There were discussions inside the building that I participated in. It was decided that a few students who were in the building would put on armbands to indicate they were from the university, go outside, and try to calm people.

Outside, people converged in small groups. Jews were one of the central points of their heated discussions. They believed that the new prime minister, who turned out to be quite temporary, before Imre Nagy took over, was Jewish. He was not, and I tried to assure them of that, acting as an informed, neutral person. I could have been in serious trouble had they found out I was Jewish.

When Miskolc calmed down, students with guns on their shoulder began to direct traffic, and I decided it was time to go home. I made my way to Budapest by train, by hitching rides on trucks and other vehicles, and by walking. Life there was very exciting, with hope for a better future. Then the Russian troops returned and after intense fighting put the revolution down. Even before this, an exodus to the West began. Mines and barbed wire that used to protect the border had been removed in the course of the easing of communist repression that was a precursor to revolt. Once the revolt started, the border was relatively unguarded. While some people were caught and some were shot, almost two hundred thousand people got through the borders surrounding Hungary.

I was one of them, leaving with two friends. I immediately wanted to go to the United States, but I did not get a visa. I lived in Vienna for two and a half years. I first did nothing, then enrolled at the technical university, then changed to the University of Vienna. Because I went to a technical high school in Hungary, in order to transfer I was required to take the final high school exams again. After one year at the university, in July 1959 I came to the United States.

I went directly to Minnesota, arranged to study at the university, and supported myself with varied jobs while doing so. I received my B.A. in psychology in 1962 and went to graduate school at Stanford, where I received a Ph.D. in 1965. I specialized in personality psychology my first year, then also took clinical courses and did clinical practica. In the fall of 1965 I started my first job as assistant professor of clinical psychology in the Department of Social Relations at Harvard University.

There were a couple of important influences on me during the graduate school years. One of them was the rigorous research orientation at Stanford, as represented at that time by my adviser, Walter Mischel; Al Bandura; Eleanor Maccoby; and others. Another was the cognitive-behavioral orientation of Arnold Lazarus, who during a one-year visiting professorship had a strong influence on a number of students. A third was the friendship I developed with Perry London, who at that time was involved in the first study of rescuers of Jews in Nazi Europe, a study he and his associates could not complete because they could not receive funding. This says something about the mood of the times. In psychology an attempt to understand behavior that took place two decades earlier was not regarded as credible. The public's and academics' attitude toward the Holocaust at the time was primarily to ignore it.

RESEARCH

Control, Information, and Fear

At Harvard I began a series of studies of the effects of lack of control on fear and physiological responses and of the impact of control and information in reducing fear. Enabling people to exercise control, whether over a snake (Staub 1968) or in setting and administering shock levels to themselves (Staub, Tursky, & Schwartz 1971), reduced fear and physiological responding. Providing people with information about snakes or about the properties of shocks (Staub & Kellett 1972) also reduced fear and physiological responding.

One may surmise that my interest in fear and control had to do in part with the tremendous threat, powerlessness, and lack of control over our lives that existed during my childhood. But perhaps my interest in control also had to do with the fact that in spite of this, within the narrow limits of still existing possibilities, my family did all it could to exercise control. We managed to survive because of those efforts. My mother and aunt standing in line with many people and somehow managing to get those letters of protection, my father escaping, our hiding him, and many other acts of control saved our lives.

I also had a strong interest in need for control. I developed a questionnaire to study it, but subsequent work crowded it out, and I never actually did the research. I was aware, by that time, that an overly strong need to exercise control, that is, difficulty in letting go, is counterproductive, in myself as well as others. Accepting circumstances one cannot control is, I believe, difficult for most survivors.

I wonder whether even my interest in information had some roots in my experience. I only have a foggy memory of this, but at one time I was in the basement of some building – probably the protected house. There was a raid, with uniformed men milling around. I believe I was sick and very scared that my parents would be taken away. I remember crying. My mother brought one of the uniformed men over, and this "kind" man assured (informed) me that my parents would not be taken (or, if this was the protected house, perhaps it was only my mother, since my father was in hiding during such raids). Obviously, such a connection between my work and a specific event is highly conjectural, but this and other life threatening events at the time had to have a great impact.

I did not continue with this line of research, which preceded most of the later interest in control in the field (although not Julian Rotter's early work on internal-external locus of control, which appeared around the time I began this work). It was supplanted by my increasing involvement with research on helping; generosity; altruism and the corollary of it, bystander passivity in the face of other people's need.

Sharing and Helping

My research in this domain was clearly stimulated by my Holocaust experience, while also at first greatly removed from it. It was in the course of conversations with Perry London at Stanford about his study of rescuers of Jews in Europe that I began to think of studying sharing. As the researcher I was trained to be at Stanford, I wondered how one might measure generosity. I arrived at Harvard with the thought that weighing the amount of candy children shared would be a good measure. This certainly does not seem a revolutionary idea, but with this idea my lifelong career in studying helpful and violent behavior began.

Our first study was one of reciprocity in sharing, an undergraduate honors project I supervised (Staub & Sherk 1970). Then, stimulated by the research of Latané and Darley (1970) on bystander behavior in emergencies, I did an extensive series of studies on children and adults responding to a crash and sounds of distress coming from the adjoining room. Among the many findings, a few were quite striking. We found that helping behavior increased from kindergarten to first and then to second grade, remained at the same level in fourth grade, and then declined in sixth grade to about the same level in helping by kindergarten children. This was true both when children heard the distress sounds alone and when they heard the noises in pairs (Staub 1970).

In this study, contrary to the findings of Latané and Darley that the presence of other bystanders decreases helping, when another bystander was present, that is, when kindergarten and first grade children were in pairs, helping increased. This seemed to be because young children did not hide their reactions from each other. There was no pluralistic ignorance, everyone looking unconcerned and thereby leading others to interpret what was happening was not an emergency. When young children heard the distress sounds, they reacted openly, talked to each other about them, and moved together to help.

I hypothesized that the decrease in helping in sixth grade was the result of children overlearning social rules that prohibited them from interrupting work on their task or entering a strange room in a strange place. In exploring this I found that when children received permission to enter the adjoining room, for an irrelevant reason, they were much more likely to help in response to the sounds of distress than children in a no information (control) group, who helped as little as children who were prohibited from entering the adjoining room (Staub 1971).

Many other studies with children and adults followed. I want to mention two series of studies, in my mind the most important of my work in this area. Unfortunately, I was running out of steam; my interest was turning to the study of the Holocaust, other genocides, and violence by groups against other groups. As a result, while I described these studies in several of my books and in chapters of edited volumes, I never published them in journals. [However some are included in the selections in this book. E.S.]

The first series of studies demonstrated that a particular personal characteristic, which I called prosocial value orientation, was strongly associated with a variety of different kinds of helping. My students and I first measured this using already existing measures (Staub 1974, 1978; Feinberg 1978; Grodman 1979). These were factor analyzed and provided a strong factor, with scores on these factors representing individuals' prosocial value orientation. Males who scored high on this measure were more likely to enter another room in response to distress sounds. Whether they entered or not, confronted with a person in distress they were more likely to engage in varied efforts to provide help (Staub 1974). Females who scored high on this test were more likely to respond to another person's psychological distress, primarily by suspending work on a task and attending to the person in need (Feinberg 1978; Grodman 1979; Staub 1978).

At one point, I developed my own measure of prosocial value orientation. This measure was published as part of a larger questionnaire developed for *Psychology Today* (Staub 1989b). An analysis of over two thousand responses indicated strong relationship of prosocial value orientation to various forms of self-reported helping. It also showed, together with other information gathered in the questionnaire, that people have different helping styles and domains of helping. Prosocially oriented persons helped in many different ways. A politically liberal orientation led people to work on positive social changes. Religiously oriented helpers tended to be volunteers and made donations. Materialistically oriented people (interested in wealth and financial security) tended to be unhelpful (Staub 1992, 1995a).

The second series of studies demonstrated learning by doing. It showed that children learn to become helpful when they are guided to engage in helping others. While the studies had complex results, overall they showed that children who participated in making toys for poor, hospitalized children or taught something to younger children were later more likely to be helpful (for a review of these studies, see Staub 1979, chap. 6; 1995a; 1995b). Providing children with information about the beneficial consequences of their initial helping tended to enhance the effects of participation. So did more positive interaction between teacher and helper in the teaching studies.

While doing all this research I was also working on a book on helping behavior, which turned out to be two books (Staub 1978, 1979). I edited a third book around the same time (Staub 1980). With all this done I collapsed for a while, fortunately during a sabbatical.

The Holocaust and Other Group Violence

Around the end of this sabbatical, I began to read about the Holocaust, for the first time in a serious way. Most likely, the interest in doing so evolved jointly from my own life experience and my work. As I studied helping, again and again the implicit question for me (and others) had been why people so often remain passive bystanders in the face of others' need. This was an essential question with regard to the Holocaust. As I began reading about the Holocaust, I felt that the concepts I had been using provided me with tools to make the incomprehensible at least understandable, to explain how the motivation for genocide could evolve and the inhibitions against killing could diminish.

I began to develop a conception of the origins of the Holocaust, progressively extending this conception to other genocides as well as to lesser forms of group violence (Staub 1989a). It was clear to me from the outset that to understand such horrible behavior by groups of people an interdisciplinary approach is necessary. The conception I developed started with difficult social conditions, which are the usual starting point for the evolution toward genocide. These conditions frustrate and thereby intensify intense human needs for security, positive identity, effectiveness, positive connection to others, and some meaningful comprehension of the world and one's place in it.

Frequently, groups of people impacted by difficult life conditions attempt to fulfill these needs by scapegoating some group for life problems and creating ideologies, visions of a better life, while also identifying enemies who stand in the way of fulfilling these visions. As they turn against the scapegoats and ideological enemies, an evolution begins. As individuals and groups harm others they change. Learning by doing occurs. Discrimination and violence become easier and more likely. A society can move, with "steps along a continuum of destruction," toward genocide.

Certain characteristics of the culture make all this more likely. These include a history of devaluation of a group of people, very strong respect for authorities, lack of pluralism, a past history of the use of violence to resolve conflict, and some others. Recently I have come to realize the importance of unhealed wounds in a group, due to past violence against them, as a cultural characteristic that can make genocide more likely (Staub 1996b, 1997, 1998).

Bystanders, tragically, are often passive, which has crucial impact. Passivity by internal bystanders – members of a perpetrator group who themselves are not perpetrators – and by external bystanders – outside individuals, groups, and nations – encourages perpetrators. As perpetrators move along the continuum of destruction, they frequently develop intense commitment to their ideology and to the destruction of their victims. Only actions by bystanders can halt their further evolution toward genocide. Bystanders have great potential power. But frequently they are not only passive but, by continuing with business as usual in their relationship to perpetrators or by actively supporting the perpetrators, they encourage genocide.

I described this conception and applied it to four instances of group violence in *The Roots of Evil: The Origins of Genocide and Other Group Violence* (1989a; see also Staub 1993, 1996a). These instances were the Holocaust; the genocide against the Armenians; the "autogenocide" in Cambodia; and a much smaller scale violence, the disappearances in Argentina. There are starting points or instigators of the process leading to genocide, which I mentioned in *The Roots of Evil* and also described in other places, in addition to the difficult life conditions noted previously in this chapter. They include conflict between groups, especially when these conflicts involve vital interests, such as territory needed for living, and especially when there has been a history of mutual antagonism between the groups. They involve conflict within a society between a superordinate group and a subordinate group with limited rights and privileges. Occasionally, the evolution starts with the pursuit of material self-interest by perpetrators (Staub 1989a, 1996a, 1997, 1999).

In *The Roots of Evil* I also began to write about the prevention of group violence. This is now one of my two major professional (and personal) concerns (see Staub 1996b, 1997, 1998, 1999, 2000). Prevention has to involve bystanders, individuals, nongovernmental organizations, international organizations, and nations. It requires motivation to act. For nations to act requires that their citizens expect them to act.

My other current major professional concern, related to prevention but also independent, is raising caring and nonviolent children. In addition to my work on the origins of altruism, and rescuers of Jews in Nazi Europe as exemplars of altruism (Staub 1989a, 1993), I have also done work on the origins of youth violence (Staub 1996a). In general, I have done a great deal of research, writing, parent training, and teacher training with a focus on raising caring, effective, nonviolent children. A major avenue for raising such children is through the schools. "Caring schools" (Staub 1995b) can be so structured that they provide children with experiences that promote connection, concern about others' welfare, and helpful action.

THE IMPACT OF THE HOLOCAUST ON ME

Even while I was studying the origins of the Holocaust, I ignored, neglected, the emotional impact that the Holocaust had on me. I simply avoided looking at it. I did not understand that one can be a professionally highly functioning person and still be deeply emotionally affected by traumatic experience.

I was pushed and pulled by a friend, Paul Valent, an Australian psychiatrist who is also a child survivor of the Holocaust from Budapest, and my wife, Sylvia (from whom I am now divorced), to go to the first meeting in New York of children hidden during the Holocaust. It was a powerful experience. I saw people who were all different but in some significant way all like me. Talking to them about experiences during the Holocaust and their impact on me was easy and natural. I realized that, like many of them, I have often experienced a film between myself and other people, a small divider. I am glad to say that since then, this film has more or less dissolved.

I believe that engagement with my personal past has affected my work. For the first time, I seriously began to think about victims. I became concerned about the importance of healing from genocidal violence in order to make it less likely that victims, in their intense need to defend themselves in a dangerous world, become perpetrators. My work has more firmly focused on prevention and, as part of prevention, on the need for groups of people with historical antagonism to reconcile (Staub 1998, 1999, 2000).

Some "Real World" Efforts

Increasingly over the years, I have wanted to do things that actually make a difference. One of my efforts in this direction was developing a training program for the state of California, following the Rodney King incident, to reduce police violence by training police officers to be active, constructive bystanders to each other who step in when confrontations move toward violence. Another has been engagement with Facing History and Ourselves, a national and now international organization. Central to its many activities has been to train teachers to use a curriculum that the organization has developed. Using the history of the Holocaust as its primary avenue, this curriculum teaches about human cruelty and about the possibilities of caring, of people becoming conscious of decisions they make and becoming concerned, active bystanders. I have done workshops for Facing History, especially as part of their teacher training institutes.

Also independently of Facing History I have done teacher training and have worked on the creation of caring schools. My vision is that in such schools a milieu is created in which all children feel part of a community, where children are participants in ways that affirm them, where they are guided to act in others' behalf and learn by doing. These are schools that help children develop inclusive caring and the moral courage not to be passive bystanders. As part of my concern with the development of caring I have been writing a book with the tentative title *A Brighter Future: Raising Caring and Nonviolent Children*, that is both scholarly and hopefully accessible to parents, teachers, and everyone else who is concerned about children.

Another of my real world efforts was organizing and leading a conference on activating bystanders that took place in Stockholm in June 1997 (Beyond Lamentation: Options for Preventing Genocidal Violence). A number of active efforts have emerged from this conference. One of them is the creation of a human rights organization led by young people (Staub & Schultz 1998). I have also engaged over the years with the media, in the hope that they can influence public attitudes about caring and violence.

Another effort has been an intervention research project that I and Dr. Laurie Anne Pearlman have been conducting since 1998. The purpose of this project, on healing, forgiveness, and reconciliation (supported by the John Templeton Foundation), is to make renewed violence between Hutus and Tutsis less likely, and to improve the lives of people deeply affected by the horrors of the genocide in Rwanda in 1994. The project is an intervention, with both psychoeducational and experiential elements. We have worked with the staff of local nongovernmental organizations, talking to them and discussing with them how genocide originates, what the effects of such trauma are on survivors, and what might be avenues to healing. They have also talked to each other, in small groups, about what happened to them during the genocide, supporting each other as they talk about very difficult experiences and feelings (Staub 2000).

The people we trained then worked with groups in the community. We set up an elaborate and formal research project, with varied control groups, to evaluate the effects of our training as it was transmitted to people in the community. Early results indicate that our training reduced trauma symptoms over a period of time, made people aware of the complex origins of violence, and led them to be more open to work with members of the "other" group for positive goals, such as the welfare of children and a better future. It also resulted in agreement with statements that they would forgive the other group if the other group acknowledged what they did and apologized. While healing, forgiveness, and reconciliation seem daunting tasks after a horrible genocide, they are of crucial importance.

WHERE AM I, AT THIS TIME IN MY LIFE?

I have had a very strong need to make a difference in the world, to improve the world. But the world is not visibly improving. In the last few years I have been less intensely upset as I read about, hear about, or see on television violence in the world. I seem to have developed some emotional distance, while still continuing to work hard on these issues. Perhaps I have also experienced some vicarious traumatization (Pearlman & Saakvitne 1995), through so much exposure in the course of my work to violence, brutality, killings. And after a period of distress about being less distressed, I am beginning to think that perhaps there is some good in a degree of emotional numbing, in being less impacted when I read about horrible things being done to people.

I have always worked extremely hard, not quite understanding the source of my intense motivation. And the number of things I am involved with seems to grow. What is my motivation in all this? What needs drive me? How much of this hard work is a compulsion that somehow derives from my Holocaust experience? In what part may it be the desire to create a better world; in what part a need to feel worthwhile and important that is dependent on doing; on what part a difficulty with just being? While working hard is satisfying, I also feel it is too encompassing. I will certainly continue but very much hope that I can learn to balance doing with being. I have long thought and talked about this desire for balance. Perhaps, it will come, any day now.

References

Feinberg, H. K. 1978. Anatomy of a helping situation: Some personality and situational determinants of helping in a conflict situation involving another's psychological distress. Ph. D. diss., University of Massachusetts, Amherst.

Grodman, S. M. 1979. The role of personality and situational variables in responding to and helping an individual in psychological distress. Ph.D. diss., University of Massachusetts, Amherst.

Latané, B., & J. M. Darley. 1970. *The unresponsive bystander: Why doesn't he help?* New York: Appleton-Crofts.

Pearlman, L. A., & K. Saakvitne. 1995. *Trauma and the therapist*. New York: Norton.

Staub, E. 1968. The reduction of a specific fear by information combined with exposure to the feared stimulus. *Proceedings, seventy-sixth annual convention of the American Psychological Association*, 3:535–37.

1970. A child in distress: The influence of age and number of witnesses on children's attempts to help. *Journal of Personality and Social Psychology* 14:130–40.

1971. Helping a person in distress: The influence of implicit and explicit "rules" of conduct on children and adults. *Journal of Personality and Social Psychology* 17:137–45.

1974. Helping a distressed person: Social, personality, and stimulus determinants, In *Advances in experimental social psychology*, vol. 7, edited by L. Berkowitz, 203–342. New York: Academic Press.

1978. *Positive social behavior and morality*. Vol. 1, *Social and personal influence*. New York: Academic Press.

1979. *Positive social behavior and morality*. Vol. 2, *Socialization and development*. New York: Academic Press.

1980. Social and prosocial behavior: Personal and situational influences and their interactions. In *Personality: Basic aspects and current research*, edited by E. Staub. Englewood Cliffs, NJ: Prentice-Hall.

1989a. *The roots of evil: The origins of genocide and other group violence*. New York: Cambridge University Press.

1989b. What are your values and goals? *Psychology Today*, 46–49.

1992. Values and helping. Manuscript, Department of Psychology, University of Massachusetts, Amherst.

1993. The psychology of bystanders, perpetrators, and heroic helpers. *International Journal of Intercultural Relations* 17:315–41.

1995a. How people learn to care. In *Care and community in modern society: Passing on the tradition of service to future generations*, edited by P. G. Schervish, V. A. Hodgkinson, M. Gates, and associates. San Francisco: Jossey-Bass Publishers.

1995b. The caring schools project: A program to develop caring, helping, positive self-esteem and nonviolence. Manuscript, Department of Psychology, University of Massachusetts, Amherst.

1996a. Cultural-societal roots of violence: The examples of genocidal violence and of contemporary youth violence in the United States. *American Psychologist* 51:117–32.

1996b. Preventing genocide: Activating bystanders, helping victims, and the creation of caring. *Peace and Conflict: Journal of Peace Psychology* 2:189–201.

1997. Halting and preventing collective violence: The role of bystanders. Background paper presented at symposium, Beyond Lamentation: Options to Preventing Genocidal Violence, Stockholm, Sweden, 13–16 June 1997.

1998. Breaking the cycle of genocidal violence: Healing and reconciliation. In *Perspectives on loss*, ed. by J. Harvey. Washington, DC: Taylor and Francis.

1999. Genocide, mass killing, and other group violence: Origins and prevention. *Peace and Conflict: Journal of Peace Psychology* 5:303–36.

2000. Genocide and mass killing: Origins, prevention, healing and reconciliation. *Political Psychology* 21:367–83.

Staub, E., & D. S. Kellett. 1972. Increasing pain tolerance by information about aversive stimuli. *Journal of Personality and Social Psychology* 21:198–203.

Staub, E., & T. Schultz. 1998. Youth movement targets violence prevention. *Psychology International* 9, no. 3:1–2.
Staub, E., & L. Sherk. 1970. Need for approval, children's sharing behavior, and reciprocity in sharing. *Child Development* 41:243–53.
Staub, E., B. Tursky, & G. Schwartz. 1971. Self-control and predictability: Their effects on reactions to aversive stimulation. *Journal of Personality and Social Psychology* 18:157–63.

4

Is Evil a Useful Concept for Psychologists and Others?

One focus of my work for many years has been the exploration of the roots of violence, especially of genocide and mass killing, which I referred to as *evil* (Staub, 1989). How does a group, a culture, as well as a person evolve so that they come to engage in "evil" actions or even develop a tendency for them? In recent years, I have also been greatly concerned with the prevention of genocide (Staub, 1996, 1998). Genocide and mass killing may seem obviously evil to most of us. However, because the concept of evil is becoming increasingly used in the social–psychological literature (Baumeister, 1997; Darley, 1992; Staub, 1989), it is important to ask whether it has useful meaning for psychologists. How would the meaning of evil be differentiated from the meaning of "violence"? Is evil the end point in the evolution of violence? In genocide, a plan is formulated to destroy a group. Usually, a decision is made to do this. Reactions to events and psychological and social processes turn into a plan. However, a conscious intention of extreme destructiveness does not seem a necessary aspect of evil. The real motivation is often unconscious, and a group's or person's habitual, spontaneous reactions to certain kinds of events can become highly destructive.

Evil has been a religious concept. The word also has been used as a secular term to describe, explain, or express aversion to certain actions and the human beings or natural forces from which they originate. The notion of a nonhuman force and origin often has been associated with evil, such as the devil, Satan, or Mephistopheles. Some have seen the forces of nature, when manifested in the destruction they sometimes bring, as evil. From a psychological standpoint, the forces of nature are surely neutral: They do, at times, cause harm but without conscious or unconscious intention.

Reprinted from E. Staub (1999). The roots of evil: Social conditions, culture, personality, and basic human needs. *Personality and Social Psychology Review*, *3*, 179–192. Included here are pp. 179–181.

The word *evil* is emotionally expressive for people: It communicates horror over some deed. People often romanticize evil. They want to see the abhorrent acts or events to which the word refers as having mythic proportions. Designating something as evil is sometimes used to suggest that the actions are not comprehensible in an ordinary human framework: They are outside the bounds of morality or even of human agency. However, evil is the outcome of basic, ordinary psychological processes and their evolution. Arendt's (1963) concept of the "banality of evil" seems to recognize this. However, the notion of the banality of evil also makes it seem as if its ordinariness diminishes the significance of evil.

I originally used the term *evil* to denote extreme human destructiveness, as in cases of genocide and mass killing (Staub, 1989), but evil may be defined by a number of elements. One of these is *extreme harm*. The harm can be pain, suffering, loss of life, or the loss of personal or human potential. Violent actions tend to arise from difficult, threatening circumstances and the psychological reactions of people to them. They are elicited by varied instigators, such as attack, threat, or frustration. Not all people react to such conditions with violence, but some do. Some individuals or groups engage in extremely harmful acts that are *not* commensurate with any *instigation* or *provocation* (Darley, 1992), another defining element of evil. Finally, some individuals, groups, or societies evolve in a way that makes destructive acts by them likely. The repetition or *persistence of greatly harmful acts* may be another defining element of evil. It is most appropriate to talk of evil when all these defining elements are present: intensely harmful actions, which are not commensurate with instigating conditions, and the persistence or repetition of such actions. A series of actions also can be evil when any one act causes limited harm, but with repetition, these acts cause great harm.

An important question is what might be the nature of the actor, whether a society or a person, that makes such acts probable. By "nature of the actor," whether a person or society, I do not refer to psychopathology. The evil I focus on and explore arises out of ordinary psychological processes and characteristics, although usually extreme forms or degrees of them: seeing people as hostile, devaluing certain groups of people, having an overly strong respect for authority, and others.

When a person or group is attacked, they have a right to defend themselves. If someone begins to shoot at me and I pull out a gun and kill the person, my action is not evil. Whether self-defense is justified can get complicated very fast, however. What if someone has threatened me, and I then lie in wait for him and shoot him when he leaves his house? If this person in a moment of anger has threatened to kill me, most of us would not see this as sufficient provocation to justify killing him, unless perhaps we know that this person has threatened other people in similar ways and then actually killed them.

A particular person, at a particular time, for idiosyncratic reasons, may take a threat extremely seriously and respond by killing another. This extremely violent act may not be evil: It may be peculiar to the circumstances and emotional state of the person at that time. Not arising from this person's personality, or from a combination of personality and the ongoing structure of circumstances, it is unlikely to be repeated. Evil usually has a more enduring quality. Thus, it might be best not to regard as evil a single act of intense harm that is out of balance with provocation. However, violence evolves, and individuals and groups change as a result of their actions (see subsequent discussion). As a person or group commits an intensely harmful act, there is an increased likelihood that they will do so again.

As well as action, omission may be evil, especially when it causes extreme harm, there is no strong justification for it in circumstances (such as lack of clarity of events or very high cost of action), and when it persists. Consider an extreme example: A person standing at the edge of a lake, taking no action while witnessing a child drowning in shallow water. Passivity in such an extreme situation is likely to arise from this person's nature, predicting other evil acts (or from this person's relationship to that particular child).

Evil acts are mainly directed at other human beings, although the destruction of animals or nature may also be considered evil. These actions often cause material harm: death, injury, pain, or severe deprivation and injustice. Persistent neglect or belittling of a child that causes physical harm, psychological pain, or psychological injury that diminishes the capacity for growth and satisfaction are also appropriately regarded as evil.

It may be most appropriate to regard it evil when destructive actions are intentional. However, intention is highly complicated psychologically because a person's real motive is often unconscious; individuals and groups tend to justify their actions, even to themselves; and various belief systems develop that propagate harmful actions in the service of some presumed good. Persons or groups who act destructively tend to claim self-defense or to claim that their victims are morally bad and dangerous or stand in the way of human betterment and, therefore, deserve suffering or death. They may simply use this as justification or may genuinely believe it even when it is completely untrue.

An example of a belief system leading people to act cruelly in the service of what they see as a good cause is the way children were treated in many societies (Greven, 1991; Miller, 1983). In many places, including Germany, England, and the United States, children were seen as inherently willful. Obedience by them was seen as a high virtue and important goal, and it was believed that children's will had to be broken early if they were to become good people. Such thinking often had religious roots (Greven, 1991). Any and all means, such as threatening children with the devil and in other ways scaring them, as well as physically punishing them or depriving them, were seen appropriate to break their will and teach them obedience and respect (Miller, 1983).

In the case of genocide, it is usually clear to outside observers that it is not justified by provocations even if it is a response to real violence by the other group. However, frequently the victim group has done nothing to justify violence against them, except in the perpetrators' minds. The Jews engaged in no destructive actions against Germans. Many of the intellectuals and educated people in Cambodia who were killed or worked to death by the Khmer Rouge did no harm that would justify such actions in the minds of most people. According to the Khmer Rouge ideology, however, these intellectuals had participated in an unjust system that favored them at the expense of others and were incapable of participating in a system of total social equality. To fulfill a "higher" ideal, to create total social equality, was the motivation to kill them or to reduce them to slaves working in the "killing fields" (Staub, 1989).

There is the same absence of provocation in many cases of recurrent violence against a spouse, or severe neglect, harsh verbal and physical treatment, and persistent physical violence against children. Some parents blame their children all the time: for having been noisy, thereby causing the car accident in which the parents were involved; for needing things that cost money, thereby depriving the family of other things; for anything and everything (L. Huber, school psychologist, personal communication, June 1997). Peck (1983) gave this as a primary example of evil. Such parents may completely lack awareness of what in themselves leads to their blaming and scapegoating, seeing their actions as justifiable reactions to the child.

Frequently, there are two levels of motivation in harmful behavior, including evil acts. One is to "harm" a person or a group, and another is to fulfill some goal that the harmful act supposedly serves. Perpetrators may present and often actually see their actions as in the service of higher ideals and of beneficial outcomes, even to the victims themselves (raising a good child), to society (creating social equality), or to all of humanity (creating a better world).

My discussion of the concept of evil suggests that it could be a useful concept for psychologists. It could lead, for example, to more focused exploration of the characteristics of persons, cultures, and situations that lead to harm doing that represents an overreaction to circumstances (provocation), is extreme and/or recurrent. It also could lead to more focused work on how cultures that promote such responses and persons who respond in these ways develop. Time will tell whether evil will be a comfortable concept for psychologists and whether it will become used.

Although the starting point for evil is usually the frustration of basic human needs (see next selection), evil actions are made possible by some or all of the following: lack or loss of concern with the welfare of other people; a lack of empathy with people, both lack of empathic feelings and lack of understanding how others feel; lack of self-awareness, the ability to understand one's own motives; having a negative view of others; a sense of entitlement, a focus on one's own rights; and devaluation, fear of, and hostility toward some or all human beings. How do the psychological tendencies that contribute to evil actions come about? How do motivations to intensely harm others arise? How do inhibitions decline? The material in this book will address these questions.

References

Arendt, H. (1963). *Eichmann in Jerusalem: A report on the banality of evil*. New York: Viking.

Baumeister, R. F. (1997). *Evil: Inside human violence and cruelty*. New York: Freeman.

Darley, J. M. (1992). Social organization for the production of evil. *Psychological Inquiry, 3*, 199–217.

Greven, P. (1991). *Spare the child: The religious roots of punishment and the impact of physical abuse*. New York: Knopf.

Miller, A. (1983). *For your own good: Hidden cruelty in child-rearing and the roots of violence*. New York: Farrar, Straus & Giroux.

Peck, M. S. (1983). *People of the lie: The hope of healing human evil*. New York: Simon & Schuster.

Staub, E. (1989). *The roots of evil: The origins of genocide and other group violence*. New York: Cambridge University Press.

Staub, E. (1996). Cultural–societal roots of violence: The examples of genocidal violence and of contemporary youth violence in the United States. *American Psychologist, 51*, 117–132.

Staub, E. (1998). Breaking the cycle of genocidal violence: Healing and reconciliation. In J. Harvey (Ed.), *Perspectives on loss: A sourcebook*. Washington, DC: Taylor & Francis.

5

Basic Human Needs and Their Role in Altruism and Aggression

A number of psychological theories include assumptions about central human needs. A few theories have *focused* on universal human needs. However, even though the need theories of Maslow and Murray are part of most personality psychology textbooks, human needs theory has not gained much prominence in psychology. Perhaps the reason is that the role of human needs in psychological functioning has not been extensively examined.

If there are basic, universal psychological needs, they must have a substantial role in human life. The purpose of this chapter is to offer a conception of basic psychological needs. They are important for this book because, in my view, the frustration of basic needs is central in the development of hostility and aggression, while their fulfillment is central in the development of caring about other people's welfare and altruism. While the work presented in this book is in no way dependent on a conception of basic needs, I believe that such a conception provides a useful framework for understanding helping and harm-doing.

BASIC PSYCHOLOGICAL NEEDS

One of the deepest concerns of psychologists and some other social scientists has been the identification of the springs of human action. What moves us to action and/or determines the direction of our strivings? Our motives, described by concepts like needs, desires, aims, goals and aspirations, not only shape our actions, but their fulfillment or frustration also deeply affect our inner life, our experience of ourselves and the world. Basic needs are conceptualized here as the most fundamental motives. Their satisfaction is essential for the growth, development, and well-being of human beings (Deci & Ryan, 1985). Basic needs have an imperative quality: they press for satisfaction. If they cannot be fulfilled by constructive means, people will attempt to fulfill them by destructive means, that is, in ways that harm themselves and/or other people. When basic needs are constructively fulfilled in the course of a person's life, they become transformed and give rise to purposive motives, such as personal goals (Staub, 1978). Such goals represent positive ends, or incentives, such as achievement or helping, which may guide people's lives.

A number of personality theorists have embedded in their theories central needs, motives, and beliefs that function as basic needs. These include Freud and the pleasure principle (or sex and aggression); Adler and the needs for overcoming inferiority or maintaining self-esteem, maintaining one's conceptual system, and relating to others; Jung and the need for transcendence and spirituality; Bowlby and object relations theories and the need for relatedness; Rogers and the need to maintain and enhance the self-concept; Kohut and the need for self-esteem (Epstein, 1993). Epstein (1990; 1993) proposed that people develop self-theories that have the function of enhancing the pleasure-pain balance, increasing self-esteem, organizing the data of experience and promoting relations to others. Janoff-Bulman (1992) proposed that people strive to maintain fundamental assumptions: that the world is benevolent, that they themselves are good, worthwhile people, and that the world is an orderly and just place.

Some theorists have made human needs central to their theory. Maslow (1968, 1987) proposed a hierarchy of needs including physiological needs, safety needs, belongingness and love needs, esteem needs, and growth or being needs. Murray (1938) has offered a long list of needs. Pearlman and her associates (McCann & Pearlman, 1990; Pearlman & Saakvitne, 1995), based on their work with trauma victims, have proposed five need areas that are affected by trauma: safety, trust or dependency, intimacy, esteem, and control. Deci and Ryan's (1985) self-determination theory posited three central needs: autonomy, competence, and relatedness. Stevens and Fiske (1995) noted that a large number of theorists have suggested the existence of one or more of five basic motives: to belong, to understand, to be effective, to find the world benevolent, and to maintain self-esteem.

Psychologists and other social scientists, have also advanced the concept of human needs as a way of understanding conflict, especially seemingly intractable conflict (Burton, 1990; Lederer et al., 1980). For example, Kelman (1990) has suggested that the failure to fulfill needs for identity, security, recognition, participation, dignity, and justice, or threat to such needs, significantly contributes to the origins, escalation, and perpetuation of conflict between groups. Christie (1997) has suggested that the fulfillment of the needs for security, identity, material well-being, and self-determination is central to peace building.

Most of the needs I will identify as basic have been regarded as fundamental or universal needs by a variety of theorists. They seem of special usefulness in understanding altruism and aggression. No claim is made here, however, that this list is exhaustive.

IDENTIFYING NEEDS: AN ANALYSIS OF GROUP VIOLENCE

The existence of basic human needs cannot be directly established. As Lederer (1980, p. 3) wrote: "Needs are theoretical constructs. . . . At best, the existence of a need can be concluded indirectly either from the respective satisfiers that the person uses or strives for or symptoms of frustration caused by any kind of nonsatisfaction." One source of the conception of basic needs presented here is the use of basic needs as explanatory concepts in an analysis of the origins of genocidal and other collective violence (Staub, 1989). The conditions preceding violence and the psychological-societal responses to them, which in turn gave rise to violence, made basic needs useful explanatory concepts.

This analysis indicated that difficult life conditions in a society such as intense economic problems, or intense political disorganization or conflict, or great, rapid social change, or some combination of these are frequently the starting point for genocidal violence. These conditions create social chaos and disorganization. Conceptualizing these conditions as frustrating basic needs makes the reactions they almost always generate understandable, as attempts at need satisfaction. These reactions – identification with the group, elevating the group, scapegoating, and ideologies – do not solve life problems, but offer some satisfaction for the basic needs frustrated by them. At the same time, they are the starting points for turning against another group: for discrimination, persecution, and violence that may end in genocide.

This view is consistent with, but not identical to the frustration-aggression hypothesis (Berkowitz, 1993). Considering the role of basic needs enhances our understanding of the avenue from frustration to aggression. When life conditions frustrate basic needs, people will make renewed attempts to satisfy these needs. The frustration of these needs does not lead to aggression, but it gives rise to psychological and social processes that make aggression more likely.

The nature of the instigating conditions and the type of responses to them suggest a particular set of needs as useful in explanation. These include needs for security (physical and psychological), positive identity, efficacy and control over events in one's life, positive connection to other people, and a comprehension of reality (Staub, 1989, 1996).

A tendency for increased identification by people with their group in difficult times is evident in many ethnic conflicts and genocides. Focusing on one's membership in a group diminishes insecurity, strengthens identity, creates connection and may give people at least the illusion of effectiveness and control. Elevating the group through the devaluation of others, another common response, further fulfills these needs.

Scapegoating, which identifies some group as the cause of life problems, is nearly universal in such times. It serves the need for a positive identity by diminishing one's own and one's group's responsibility for life problems, including the inability at times to provide food and shelter for oneself and one's family. It serves the need for comprehension of reality by providing an understanding of the reasons for life problems. It serves the needs for security, comprehension, as well as effectiveness and control by pointing to a way for dealing with life problems (which is to "deal" with its cause, the scapegoat). It is a means of creating connection, as members of the group join in scapegoating and in taking action against the scapegoat.

Another avenue to need fulfillment is to adopt ideologies, visions of a better society (like nationalism), or a better world (like communism and aspects of Nazism). Ideologies and movements to fulfill them offer a new comprehension of the world, connection to other followers, positive identity, effectiveness, and hope. Unfortunately, such ideologies are usually destructive, in that they identify some group as an enemy who must be destroyed if the ideology is to be fulfilled.

These group psychological and social processes are functional; they serve to fulfill the basic needs frustrated and activated by difficult life conditions. Unfortunately, they also lead the group to turn against some other group. Discrimination and limited violence against the victims bring about changes in the group and its individual members that make greater violence possible and probable. Without countervailing forces that inhibit this evolution, especially opposition by witnesses or bystanders, the progression of increasingly violent actions is likely to end in mass killing or genocide.

Certain cultural characteristics make genocide more likely (Staub, 1989; see also Staub, 1996). They can also been seen in basic needs terms. For example, strong respect for authority means that people are accustomed to guidance by and support from leaders and the group. As a result, the loss of effective leadership, as evidenced by severe life problems and social chaos, intensifies feelings of insecurity, disconnection, threat to identity, and loss of comprehension of reality.

A basic needs perspective can also be useful in developing strategies to prevent genocide and other collective violence. For example, in place of a destructive ideology that focuses on enemies, an inclusive, connecting vision can fulfill needs while enabling members of all groups to join together in responding to life problems. This happened to a degree in the United States during the Depression. It was made possible by relatively moderate life problems, certain characteristics of the culture, and the leadership that Roosevelt offered.

The road to intense group violence I sketched here is a common one. Even when the starting point is different, or is a combination of difficult life conditions with a history of antagonism between groups, or conflict between dominant and subordinate groups, or self-interest (Fein, 1990; Staub, 1989), many elements are common and much of the analysis applies.

BASIC NEEDS: DEFINITIONS AND ASSUMPTIONS

In the next section I will describe specific needs, accompanied by a few empirical or theoretical considerations to support the claim that they are basic needs. I will then present some assumptions about how needs operate. In addition to group violence, as this chapter and the discussion in later sections of the book will show, basic needs also have an important role in the development of individual altruism and aggression. Child-rearing practices that promote aggression in children frustrate basic needs, while those that promote caring and helping fulfill basic needs. The fulfillment of basic needs also leads to continued growth and personal evolution.

Security

The need to know or believe that we are and will continue to be free of physical and psychological harm (of danger, attack, injury to our body or self-concept and dignity) and that we are and will be able to satisfy our essential biological needs (for food, etc.) and our need for shelter.

Humans and other organisms have a strong tendency to respond to signals of potential harm. Sights, sounds, people, or places that have been associated with harm create fear, stress, avoidance, or attack. Attack and threat of attack, which frustrate the need for security (but can also frustrate other needs), are the strongest, most reliable instigators of aggression (Baron, 1977). Moreover, when humans and animals cannot escape from places associated with previous pain and suffering, they become withdrawn and depressed and stop efforts to exercise control, like dogs that have been exposed to unavoidable shocks (Seligman, 1975). Fear and stress associated with danger also reduce cue utilization. In sum, insecurity leads to significant deterioration in the functioning of organisms.

Effectiveness and Control

The need to know or believe that we have the capacity to protect ourselves from harm (danger, attack, etc.), to engage with the world and accomplish things we set out to do, like fulfilling important goals, and to lead purposeful lives and have the potential to impact our society or the world. While most elements of this need (and of other needs) come into play very early in life, some become relevant later in a person's life.

Security, and effectiveness and control, are inherently linked. The belief that we have control, the illusion of control, is essential for humans and other organisms (Lefcourt, 1973). By effective action we can protect ourselves from harm, and pursue desirable outcomes. Having or not having control, or believing that one does or does not have control, for example, over noise or electric shocks one receives in an experiment, can have a profound impact on physiological, cognitive, and psychological functioning, on success, health, and survival (Glass & Singer, 1972; Lefcourt, 1973; Seligman, 1975; Staub et al., 1971).

Human beings also engage in action for the sake of informational interaction with the environment characterized by interest in stimulation, curiosity, and exploration. This motivation has been called intrinsic because it is not done in the service of material or extrinsic reinforcers. Humans and other organisms will even sacrifice material rewards and endure pain in order to engage in intrinsically motivated activities. Intrinsic motivation has also been referred to as "effectence" or competence motivation (White, 1959; Deci, 1975). Intrinsically motivated activities both gather information about the world and develop competence and effectiveness.

Effective action can protect people from harm and bring about the fulfillment of their goals. However, the nature of the environment affects the relationship between action and its effects. In a benevolent environment, less control is necessary. People don't need to protect themselves from harm, and there are fewer barriers to the fulfillment of goals. In a malevolent or highly autocratic environment, what individuals do may have little relationship to what happens to them. Still, even in extremely malevolent environments, like Nazi concentration camps, people will do what they can to exercise control within the narrow range of possibilities (Des Pres, 1976). This helps maintain an illusion of control, in addition to any *real* contribution to survival.

Positive Identity

The need to have a well-developed self and a positive conception of who we are and who we want to be (self-esteem), which requires self-awareness and acceptance of ourselves, including our limitations. With increasing age, higher-level fulfillment of this need requires integration of different parts of ourselves. Coherence and inner harmony enable us, in turn, to lead increasingly purposeful lives.[1] Esteem from others has been regarded

[1] This description is clearly of a family of needs, where "members" of the family may at times conflict. For example, who we are and who we want to be can conflict with each other. A positive view is not the same as an integrated view. However, as a mature positive identity evolves, integration may come to enhance a positive view of the self, and who we want to be may become a part of who we are. The description of positive identity also includes processes required for continued growth, such as self-awareness.

by Maslow and other theorists as a basic need. Here it is seen as essential to fulfill certain basic needs, especially positive identity and positive connection.

There is probably no human need that has been posited by as many theories as this one. As I have noted, this need has been regarded as a central contributor to intractable conflict between groups (Burton, 1990; Kelman, 1990). It seems embedded in most stages in Erikson's (1959) developmental schema. Specifically the crises involving autonomy versus shame, initiative versus guilt, industry versus inferiority, identity versus role confusion, and ego integrity versus despair all seem to have significant consequences for identity.

Research and theory in social (Baumeister, 1991) and personality (Epstein, 1980) psychology suggest that both enhancement of one's self-esteem and maintaining the stability of one's self-concept are strong human motives. From the present perspective, the latter probably also has an important role in maintaining one's comprehension of reality.

Positive Connection

The need to have relationships in which we feel positively connected to other individuals or groups, such as close family ties, intimate friendships, love relationships, and relationships to communities.

Erikson's (1959) stage theory also stresses positive connection as crucial for continued growth. Connection is implicit in both his first developmental stage, which involves the crisis of trust versus mistrust, and stage six, which involves intimacy versus isolation. Baumeister and Leary (1995) gathered extensive empirical support for the existence of a need to belong, "the need to form and maintain strong, stable, interpersonal relationships" (p. 497).

The findings of the extensive research on attachment, quality of attachment (Ainsworth, 1974; Ainsworth et al., 1979; Bowlby, 1969, 1980; Bretherton, 1992), the positive consequences of secure attachment (Troy & Sroufe, 1987; Waters et al., 1979) and the extreme consequences of lack of attachment (Thompson & Grusec, 1970; Shaffer, 1995) suggest the profound importance of positive connection. Research showing strong positive associations between social support, that is, connections that people have to other people and community, and health, well-being, and even survival (Parks & Pilisuk, 1986) provides additional support.

Comprehension of Reality

The need to have an understanding of people and the world (what they are like, how they operate) and of our own place in the world; to have views or conceptions that make sense of the world. Our comprehension of reality in turn shapes our relations to the world and can create meaning in our lives. Since this is a basic need, any comprehension is better than none. However, certain kind of comprehension of reality, for example, seeing the world and people as hostile and dangerous, due to an earlier history of need frustration, make the fulfillment of other basic needs more difficult.

Not having some minimally coherent view of reality is a form of psychosis. Understanding or having a conception of how the world operates is required to predict and control events. The need for meaning is central in some theorizing (Frankl, 1959; Pearlman & Saakvitne, 1995). Meaning may be seen as an integration of one's comprehension of reality and identity and perhaps of other needs as well.

The need for consistency and the motivational power of inconsistency have been strongly established in psychology. This can be subsumed under the need for comprehension of reality: the need for various elements of reality (and identity) to fit together. Piaget's principle of assimilation, absorbing new information into existing schemas, a powerful principle of learning, appears to serve to maintain one's existing comprehension of reality.

But human beings and other organisms also seek the unknown. The attraction to and exploration of novelty may be means for developing and exercising one's comprehension of reality and sense of efficacy (Deci, 1975; White, 1959). The way needs interrelate is also crucial. For example, under conditions of security, in a benevolent environment, greater novelty may be tolerated and preferred. When positive connection is established, greater autonomy may be risked.

Independence or Autonomy

To make choices and decisions, to be one's own person, the ability to be separate.

Young children already work hard to assert their will. The famous terrible twos are an expression of this need. So are the often intense and hostile efforts of an adolescent in trying to become more independent and autonomous. Erikson (1959) has recognized the importance of autonomy by specifying the second of his eight stages of development as autonomy versus shame and doubt. While in well-functioning cultures all basic needs must find at least moderate fulfillment, different cultures emphasize and fulfill needs to different extents. Western cultures are seen as emphasizing individualism and autonomy, Eastern cultures as emphasizing connection and community (Triandis, 1994).

Transcendence of the Self

The need to go beyond a focus on, and concern with, the self. Forms of transcendence include experiencing connection with nature, the universe, or spiritual entities, devoting oneself to the welfare of others or working for significant social change.

Increasingly as other basic needs are fulfilled, the need to move beyond a focus on oneself emerges. People will experience dissatisfaction and restlessness, and continuing personal growth will be truncated, without the fulfillment of this need (Coan, 1977). Religions, Eastern and mystical traditions recount experiences of connection with something universal, whether a universal self, God, other spiritual entities, the universe or nature. There are many descriptions of "oceanic feelings" in which the boundaries of the self are lost.

States and capacities for transcendence may serve the need for transcendence. For example, experiences of absorption or deep engagement, what Csikszentmihalyi (1990) has called "flow," may be regarded as states of transcendence. These are times of self-forgetfulness. The focus is away from the self. Altruistic acts, motivated by the desire to diminish another's need, are inherently transcendent. Intense engagement accompanied by self-forgetful joy seems to exist in infancy, and altruistic acts may occur at an early age (Zahn-Waxler et al., 1979). Temporary states of transcendence are likely to be growthful; paradoxically, going beyond the self seems to serve the self. The growth of the self in turn creates the possibility of more persistent forms of transcendence.

In the present view the *need* for transcendence becomes powerful only after other basic needs have been fulfilled. However, "pseudotranscendence" may result from unfulfilled basic needs that motivate people to relinquish a burdensome self, often by giving themselves over to causes, beliefs, and movements. In such cases transcendence and pseudotrancendence may look similar, but the underlying motivations differ. Depending on the nature of the movement a person joins and subsequent experiences in it, basic needs may get fulfilled and pseudotranscendence may grow into genuine transcendence.

Long-Term Satisfaction

The need to feel and believe that things are good in our lives and that our life is progressing in a desirable way, not necessarily at the moment, but overall, in the long run.

People want to be contented, satisfied, and happy. Chronic unhappiness affects all aspects of life. I use the term long-term satisfaction rather than happiness to indicate stability even in the midst of temporary distress, sorrow, or pain. Pain due to loss, illness, separation, or the inability to fulfill important goals is inevitable in human life. Even in the midst of temporary unhappiness, however, people can have a basic, overall sense that their lives are progressing in a positive, satisfying way.

The fulfillment of this need is primarily a by-product of the fulfillment of other needs. Consistent with this view, self-esteem and internal locus of control or a feeling of efficacy have been strong correlates of happiness or well-being (Myers, 1992). However, a sense of goodness in one's life is already evident in well-cared-for infants. Their increasing capacity to soothe themselves when hungry or distressed (Shaffer, 1995) connotes the trust, hope, and good feelings that characterize long-term satisfaction.

Some Central Assumptions

I regard basic needs as primarily coexistent, not hierarchical. However, the need for security may be more fundamental than other needs. While the need for transcendence may press for fulfillment, it will arise to a significant degree and in an authentic form only when other basic needs are fulfilled to a reasonable extent. The need for long-term satisfaction is fulfilled primarily through the satisfaction of other needs. In a sense, therefore, these two needs are less basic.

Some needs and even components of a particular need may temporarily stand in opposition to each other. The need for connection can conflict with the need for autonomy. The need to maintain the self can conflict with the need to expand, further develop, or enhance the self. When needs are fulfilled, over time the self will become increasingly integrated with needs in increasing harmony.

Overall, needs have coherence and unity. Conditions and experiences that satisfy or frustrate one basic need often satisfy or frustrate others as well. For example, the infant's need for security will be satisfied by caretakers who in response to the infant's signals provide food or relieve pain and discomfort. But the caretaker's responsiveness also satisfies the infant's need for effectiveness and control. The total experience, the valuing of the child inherent in good caretaking, contributes to a positive identity and builds positive connection.

Constructive need satisfaction leads to continued growth. This means, first, that a need is satisfied in a way that does not frustrate (and might even satisfy) other needs. In the long run this is even true when needs or elements of needs stand in seemingly inherent contradiction to each other. Second, the satisfaction of one person's needs does not frustrate others' basic needs or others' ability to satisfy their needs. When it does, the resulting actions of the other are likely to be destructive in turn.

While at a specific moment the fulfillment of autonomy may frustrate the need for connection, in a family that accepts or encourages autonomy in children, autonomous behavior will not disrupt relationships. And connection will not close off or inhibit independence and autonomy. In the long run it is possible to develop a "connected self," in which connection and autonomy are in overall harmony. In contrast, in an "embedded self," connection to others is rooted in dependence (Staub, 1993). A person with a connected self is more capable of standing apart and opposing harmful actions by other people.

Destructive need satisfaction interferes with growth. It refers to modes of satisfaction of a need that frustrate the fulfillment of another need, or the needs of another person, or both. It normally also provides incomplete satisfaction of the need it serves. It limits personal growth. It is usually an attempt, either under conditions that frustrate need satisfaction, or by persons with a past history of need frustration, to gain some satisfaction of basic needs.

For example, a parent might do everything for a child, insisting that the child accepts and welcomes all that the parent does. This is destructive need fulfillment. It might temporarily fulfill the parent's need for connection, control, and perhaps the need to feel that the child is secure (Pearlman & Saakvitne, 1995). It might also temporarily fulfill the child's need for connection. But it frustrates the child's need for autonomy, effectiveness, and control, and the development of the child's identity. The relationship that develops between parent and child is likely, in the long run, to frustrate the fulfillment of the parent's needs as well.

Internal psychological processes may also serve destructive need fulfillment. A child (or an adult) is badly treated. By assuming that the bad treatment was his or her fault (Janoff-Bulman, 1992; Lerner, 1980) the child gains some feeling of security. Behaving well, doing the right thing, might avoid bad treatment.

While for a young child with abusive parents this may be a way to limit feelings of insecurity that arise out of unpredictable cruelty, it frustrates the need for a positive identity. In turn a child who sees herself as bad is less likely to engage in actions that create positive connections to other people. Under certain adverse conditions, like being a member of a persecuted minority, perceiving oneself (and one's group) as bad may be an avenue even for adults to somewhat greater feelings of security.

The widespread human tendency to believe that the world is a just place (Lerner, 1980) also seems to serve the need for security. It suggests that by being good, people will avoid pain and suffering. But it is a potentially destructive mode of need satisfaction. It often leads people to devalue those who suffer, since in a just world, they must somehow have deserved their suffering, either due to their actions or to their character. This can lead to harmful actions toward these devalued others, or increased passivity in the face of their suffering.

The constructive satisfaction of basic needs brings personal growth. An infant can begin to use less primitive signals, expressive sounds and words in place of crying, to communicate needs and bring about desired reactions (Shaffer, 1995). The more social nature of the interaction builds the child's language skills, nonverbal expressive capacities, and general social competence. The more social, interactive nature of the child's exercise of effectiveness and control builds social relationships and contributes to the satisfaction of the need for positive connection.

Need satisfaction is always temporary, but the effects of a history of need satisfaction or frustration are enduring. Enduring psychological processes also evolve that facilitate (e.g., self-awareness) or frustrate (e.g., a negative worldview) further need satisfaction.

The fulfillment of basic needs provides the preconditions for, and goes a long way toward creating, caring and altruism. Positive connections lead to the valuing of people, which makes empathy and caring possible. A feeling of security and a positive identity diminish a focus on oneself and one's own needs and make openness to others' needs more likely. Feelings of effectiveness and control help people fulfill their own goals; this also makes openness to others more likely. Feeling effective makes it probable that people will act on their empathy and caring. A realistic understanding of the world, when it is at least moderately benevolent, also makes it more likely that people will express caring and empathy in action.

There are elements of socialization that contribute to the development of caring, empathy, and helpfulness, beyond those intrinsically required to fulfill basic needs. This is the case with aspects of guidance: pointing out to children the consequences of their behavior on other people, the modeling of helpful behavior, and leading children to engage in helpful actions. Such practices, which are also need-fulfilling rather than need-frustrating, specifically socialize children for caring, empathy, and helping.

The fulfillment of basic needs creates strong connections to socializers. This enables them to teach, through words and deeds, devaluation of and hostility toward certain others. Thus, the practices and experiences that develop caring also give power to the socializers to generate hostility and aggression. However, while this can and does happen, it is not the usual reality. Usually, it is neglect and mistreatment of children that are associated with both individual violence as well as internal violence in a group and warfare (Ross, 1993).

Caring and Helping Born of Suffering

Some people who have greatly suffered seem to become intensely committed to helping others. This is true of some survivors of the Holocaust (Valent, 1998), as well as victims of other forms of cruelty and violence (Herman, 1992). We know little about this phenomenon, as yet. How frequently does it happen? What has been the totality of the experience of such people? How does it compare to the experience of abused children who become aggressors (Coie & Dodge, 1997; Widom, 1989 a, b)?

Some victims and survivors who turn to helping others may have had their basic needs fulfilled before their victimization. Many survivors of the Holocaust have come from loving and caring families. We know from research on resilience that children growing up in a difficult or harsh environment are sometimes greatly helped by connection to at least one caring adult (Rutter, 1987) or to caring peers (Freud & Dunn, 1951). Perhaps when basic needs are generally frustrated, even their limited fulfillment through a loving connection makes children (or adults) aware of the possibility of a better life, for themselves and others. The experience of great suffering combined with some fulfillment of basic needs may motivate people to create a world in which others will not suffer the way they have suffered. It may generate empathy and a feeling of responsibility for others' welfare.

Helping others may sometimes be a form of pseudotranscendence, a way of relinquishing a burdensome self by going beyond oneself. However, helping in the service of the self rather than giving oneself over to a violent group is a positive choice. In the course of helping, connections can develop to the people one helps and to other helpers. Identity can be strengthened, a feeling of effectiveness and control can develop, worldviews can change. The self can become more integrated (Colby & Damon, 1992). As basic needs are fulfilled genuine caring can develop and pseudotranscendence can turn into real transcendence.

FURTHER CONSEQUENCES OF THE FULFILLMENT OF BASIC NEEDS

The fulfillment of basic needs is always relative, a matter of degree. Along the way, there is inevitable frustration and pain: as a child learns the limits of his or her effectiveness, struggles with inherent conflict between needs such as autonomy and connection, and experiences conflict with parents and friends as well as rejection and loss. However, for people whose needs have been fulfilled to a substantial degree there is continuous personal growth. Such people will be similar in a variety of ways: their sense of security, their capacity for connection, their positive identity, their sense of effectiveness, and so on. At the same time, one person whose needs have on the whole been fulfilled may be quite different from another such person.

When basic needs are fulfilled in constructive ways, they undergo transformation. The push for need fulfillment evolves into the desire to bring about valued outcomes, or personal goals. What outcomes become valued will depend on specific experience. This is even true of outcomes related to the same need area, for example, effectiveness. One child, whose effectiveness has been channeled into cognitive and intellectual activities, may develop intellectual engagement and achievement as important personal goals. Another may come to value interpersonal effectiveness.

Selectivity, and desire rather than necessity, may characterize the motivation of people whose basic needs have been fulfilled. Such selectivity may apply to realms in which effectiveness is important, to connections a person chooses to foster, to aspects of identity, and so on. The origins of this selectivity will lie in the child's culture, family, and experience, the child's temperament, inherent capacities, gender, race, and the way others relate to the child due to them, and so on. While groups and families vary in the extent they facilitate or frustrate the fulfillment of basic needs, they also vary in the avenues they provide for need fulfillment. The extent to which different environments provide avenues for the fulfillment of basic needs or constrain need fulfillment is a profoundly important question to explore.

References

Ainsworth, M. D. S. (1979). Infant-mother attachment. *American Psychologist, 34,* 932–937.

Ainsworth, M. D. S., Bell, S. M., & Stayton, D. J. (1974). Infant-mother attachment and social development: Socialization as a product of reciprocal responsiveness to signals. In M. P. M. Richards (Ed.), *The integration of the child into a social world.* London: Cambridge University Press.

Baron, R. A. (1977). *Human aggression.* New York: Plenum Press.

Baumeister, R.F. (1991). *Escaping the self.* New York: Basic Books.

Baumeister, R.F., & Leary, M.R. (1995). The need to belong: Desire for interpersonal attachments as a fundamental human motivation. *Psychological Bulletin, 117(3),* 497–529.

Berkowitz, L. (1993). *Aggression: Its causes, consequences, and control.* New York: McGraw-Hill.

Bowlby, J. B. (1980). *Attachment and loss. Vol. 3: Loss, sadness and depression.* New York: Basic Books.

Bowlby, J. (1969). *Attachment and loss.* Vol. 1. *Attachment.* New York: Basic Books.

Bretherton, I. (1992). The origins of attachment theory: John Bowlby and Mary Ainsworth. *Developmental Psychology, 28,* 759–775.

Burton, J. W. (1990). *Conflict: Human needs theory.* New York: St. Martin's Press.

Christie, D. J. (1997). Reducing direct and structural violence: The human needs theory. *Peace and Conflict: Journal of Peace Psychology, 3,* 315–332.

Coan, R. W. (1977). *Hero, artist, sage, or saint? A survey of views on what is variously called mental health, normality, maturity, self-actualization, and human fulfillment.* New York: Columbia University Press.

Coie, J. D. and Dodge, K. A. (1997). Aggression and antisocial behavior. *Handbook of Child Psychology,* fifth edition. William Damon, (Ed.) Vol. 3. *Social, emotional, and personality development.* Nancy Eisenberg, vol. ed. New York: John Wiley and Sons.

Colby, A., & Damon, W. (1992). *Some do care.* New York: The Free Press.

Csikszentmihalyi, M. (1990). *Flow: The psychology of optimal experience.* New York: Harper and Row.

Deci, E. L. (1975). *Intrinsic motivation.* New York: Plenum Press.

Deci, E. L., & Ryan, R. M. (1985). The dynamics of self-determination in personality and development. In R. Schwarzer (Ed.), *Self-related cognition in anxiety and motivation.* Hillsdale, NJ: Erlbaum.

Des Pres, T. (1976). *The Survivor. An anatomy of life in the death camps.* Oxford: Oxford University Press.

Epstein, S. (1980). The self-concept: A review and the proposal of an integrated theory of personality. In E. Staub (Ed.), *Personality: Basic aspects and current research*. Englewood Cliffs, NJ: Prentice-Hall.
Epstein, S. (1990). Cognitive-experiential self-theory. In L. A. Pervin (Ed.), *Handbook of personality: Theory and research*, pp. 165–192. New York: Guilford Press.
Epstein, S. (1993). Emotion and self-theory. In M. Lewis and J. M. Haviland (Eds.), *Handbook of emotions*. New York: The Guilford Press.
Erikson, E. H. (1959). Identity and the life cycle. Selected papers. *Psychological Issues, 1* (Monograph 1.) New York: International Universities Press.
Fein, H. (1990). *Genocide: A sociological perspective*. Special Issue of *Current Sociology*, 38, 1–126.
Frankl, V.E. (1976/1959). *Man's search for meaning*. New York: Rochet.
Freud, A., & Dann, S. (1951). An experiment in group upbringing. In R. Eissler et al. (Eds.), *The Psychoanalytic study of the child*, Vol. 6. New York: International University Press.
Glass, D. C., & Singer, J. E. (1972). *Urban stress: Experiments on noise and social stressors*. New York: Academic Press.
Herman, J. L. (1992). *Trauma and recovery*. New York: Basic Books.
Janoff-Bulman, R. (1992). *Shattered assumptions*. New York: The Free Press.
Kelman, H. C. (1990). Applying a human needs perspective to the practice of conflict resolution: The Israeli-Palestinian Case. From J. Burton (Ed.), *Conflict: Human needs theory*. New York: St. Martin's Press.
Lederer, K. (1980). Introduction. In Lederer, K., Galtung, J., & Antal, D. (Eds.), *Human needs: A contribution to the current debate*. Cambridge: Oelgeschlager, Gunn and Hain.
Lefcourt, H. M. (1973). The function of the illusions of control and freedom. *American Psychologist, 28*, 417–425.
Lerner, M. (1980). *The belief in a just world: A fundamental delusion*. New York: Plenum Press.
McCann, I. L., & Pearlman, L. A. (1990). *Psychological trauma and the adult survivor: Theory, therapy, and transformation*. New York: Brunner Mazel.
Maslow, A. H. (1968). *Toward a psychology of being* (2nd ed.) New York: Van Nostrand.
Maslow, A. H. (1987). *Motivation and personality* (3rd ed.). New York: Harper and Row. (Original work published in 1954.)
Murray, H. A. (1938). *Explorations in personality*. New York: Oxford University Press.
Myers, D. G. (1992). *The pursuit of happiness*. New York: William Morrow and Company, Inc.
Parks, S. H., & Pilisuk, M. (1986). *The healing web: Social networks and human survival*. Hanover and London: University Press of New England.
Pearlman, L. A., & Saakvitne, K. W. (1995). *Trauma and the therapist: Counter transference and vicarious traumatization in psychotherapy with incest survivors*. New York: W. W. Norton.
Ross, M. H. (1993). *The culture of conflict: Interpretations and interests in comparative perspective*. New Haven: Yale University Press.
Rutter, M. (1987). Psychosocial resilience and protective mechanisms. *American Journal of Orchopsychiatry, 57(3)*, 316–331.
Seligman, M. E. P. (1975). *Helplessness: On depression, development and death*. San Francisco: W. H. Freeman.

Shaffer, D. R. (1995). *Social and personality development*. Monterey, CA: Brooks-Cole.
Staub, E. (1971). A child in distress: The influence of modeling and nurturance on children's attempts to help. *Developmental Psychology, 5*, 124–133.
Staub, E. (1978). *Positive social behavior and morality: Social and personal influences* (Vol. 1). New York: Academic Press.
Staub, E. (1989). *The roots of evil: The origins of genocide and other group violence*. New York: Cambridge University Press.
Staub, E. (1993). Individual and group selves, motivation and morality. In Wren, T., & Moam, G. (eds.), *Morality and the self*. Cambridge: MIT Press.
Staub, E. (1996). The cultural-societal roots of violence: The examples of genocidal violence and of contemporary youth violence in the United States. *American Psychologist, 51*, 117–132.
Staub, E., Schwartz, G., & Tursky, B. Self-control and predictability: Their effects on reactions to aversive stimulation. *Journal of Personality and Social Psychology*, 1971, *18*, 157–163.
Stevens, L. E., & Fiske, S. T. (1995). Motivation and cognition in social life: A social survival perspective. *Social Cognition, 13*, 189–214.
Thompson, W. R., & Grusec, J. (1970). Studies of early experience. In P. H. Mussen (Ed.), *Carmichael's manual of child psychology* (Vol. 2) (3rd ed.). New York: Wiley.
Triandis, H. C. (1994). *Culture and social behavior*. New York: McGraw-Hill, Inc.
Troy, M., & Sroufe, L. A. (1987). Victimization among preschoolers: Role of attachment relationships. *Child and Adolescent Psychiatry, 26*, 166–172.
Valent, P. (1998). Child survivors: A review. In J. Kestenberg & C. Kahn (eds.), *Children surviving persecution: An international study of trauma and healing*. New York: Praeger.
Waters, E., Wippmann, J., & Sroufe, L. A. (1979). Attachment, positive affect, and competence in the peer group: Two studies in construct validation. *Child Development, 50*, 821–829.
White, R. W. (1959). Motivation reconsidered: The concept of competence. *Psychological Review, 66*, 297–333.
Widom, C. S. (1989a). Does violence beget violence? A critical examination of the literature. *Psychological Bulletin, 106*, (1), 3–28.
Widom, C. S. (1989b). The cycle of violence. *Science, 224*, 160–166.
Zahn-Waxler, C., Radke-Yarrow, M., & King, R. A. (1979). Child-rearing and children's prosocial initiations toward victims of distress. *Child Development, 50*, 319–330.

PART II

THE ROOTS OF HELPING OTHER PEOPLE IN NEED IN CONTRAST TO PASSIVITY

6

Helping a Distressed Person

Social, Personality, and Stimulus Determinants

I. INTRODUCTION

There is an ancient and continuing human ideal which prescribes that people should help and do good for others. This ideal is communicated to us in many ways; in churches and schools, in family and community life, the moral imperative to aid our less fortunate or suffering fellows is often held up as one of the basic human values. Unquestionably, people's willingness to help each other is of great importance both for individuals and for the harmonious functioning of the social group. The consequences of not helping a person in need can be fatal for him or her. But just as important is the effect on the welfare of a whole society, on its social climate. What would life be like, what kind of relationships would we have with other people, and what would be our feelings toward them, if we could not count on anyone when we are in trouble?

Philosophers have long been concerned with the bases and origin of the individual's goodness toward his fellow man. Socrates believed that man is

Reprinted from E. Staub (1974). Helping a distressed person: Social, personality, and stimulus determinants. In L. Berkowitz (Ed.), *Advances in experimental social psychology: Vol. 7*. Academic Press, 1974. Included here are pp. 293–303, 309–311, 316, 321–322, and 335–341.

Two of the experiments reported in this paper were collaborative efforts. In the first series of experiments (V) the first experiment was Robert Baer's honors thesis, conducted under this writer's supervision at Harvard University. The last, large scale experiment (VIII) was conducted in collaboration with Sumru Erkut, Dan Jaquette, and John Murray, at Harvard University. I am grateful for their permission to report the findings here.

The experiments reported in this paper were supported by a Faculty Science Research Grant and a Biomedical Science Support Grant from Harvard University, and by a grant from the Milton Fund. The analysis of some of the data was facilitated by a Faculty Research Grant from the University of Massachusetts, Amherst.

The preparation of this paper was facilitated by a Social Science Department Development Grant from the National Science Foundation (Grant GU 4041) to the Department of Psychology, University of Massachusetts, Amherst.

capable of goodness: he can become good through self-examination, which leads to knowledge of virtue, which in turn will lead to virtuous action. Hobbes, on the other hand, viewed the individual as self-seeking, and needing strong external controls that would compel him to inhibit harmful actions and force him to do things that would benefit others. Compromise positions also emerged, such as that of Hume, who believed that, while basically selfish, man is capable of enlightenment. The demands placed on man by the conditions of social living will lead to the pursuit of enlightened self-interest, requiring that people be mutually concerned for each other's welfare.

These philosophical views also find expression in psychological theories. Rogers, Maslow, and others believe in the person's capacity for growth and development, including the ability to grow in love for, and kindness toward, others. The primary assumption of psychoanalysis, by contrast, is that man is self-seeking and must be controlled, by external restraints as well as by the education given him by parents and other socializers, to develop the capacity for social living. Hume's position seems fairly well expressed in social exchange theory: People learn to act in a manner that will maximize their mutual benefits because this is a condition for the satisfaction of their own needs and desires.

Perhaps these varied views, as expressed by both philosophers and psychologists, are representations of our varied behavior toward others, different observers having been inspired by different parts of the total vista. Obviously, people sometimes appear selfish or, more than that, "evil" – unconcerned with others' welfare, motivated by gain alone, cruel, even wantonly aggressive. At other times people appear to do things for others because it leads to mutual gain or ultimately to the benefit of the helper. But human beings also seem capable of concern with others' welfare, even of heroic action and supreme self-sacrifice. Many cases of heroism are recorded in which a stranger saved someone's life, or lost his own life in attempting to save another. People have also risked their lives to save others from persecution and death (London, 1970).

Although psychologists have made varied assumptions about human nature, until recently they neglected to study the positive sides of man (Staub, 1972a). In the past few years, however, there has been a dramatic increase in research on prosocial behavior – behavior that benefits other people. The increased interest may be due partly to the decline in the influence of theories that focused attention on how man went about gratifying his own needs, such as drive theory and psycho-analysis. Recent investigations have also been stimulated by research on helping behavior initiated by a few investigators, some with striking results.

In this chapter a series of related experiments will be described which show the multiplicity of influences promoting and/or inhibiting the giving of aid to those in physical distress. Physical distress represents one of the most basic and important conditions requiring assistance; this was the reason for selecting helping behavior in response to physical distress as the focus of study.

To start with, a brief account will be given of some prior research in this area which provided ideas and techniques upon which we drew. This survey will be followed by a general theoretical discussion of what motivates or restrains helping behavior, what are some reasons for helping or not doing so. Several groups of experiments will then be presented, each introduced by a more detailed discussion of certain relevant determinants of helping.

II. SOME RECENT RESEARCH ON HELPING BEHAVIOR

In a series of experiments, Berkowitz and his associates explored the conditions under which a person is willing to expend effort to help another person gain prestige (i.e., a positive evaluation of his activities) and material reward (Berkowitz, 1972). They found that, the greater the dependence of one person on another, the more likely it is that the latter will work hard in order to help. Berkowitz and Daniels (1963) suggested that a norm of social responsibility, which prescribes that people should help others who are dependent on them, guides this helping behavior.

Surprisingly, little is known about the individual's belief that there is an obligation to help others. Much of our knowledge of this is indirect (although not all; e.g., Almond & Verba, 1963; Schwartz, 1970). We can sometimes see evidence of people's belief in this obligation from their reactions to a violation of this obligation. When the *New York Times* reported that a young woman, Kitty Genovese, was murdered in New York City while 38 people witnessed the murder but did not intervene or call the police until it was too late, enraged writers of letters to the editor of the *Times* demanded that the names and addresses of these people be published so that they could be exposed to the public wrath they richly deserved (Rosenthal, 1964).

In a dramatic series of experiments, Latané and Darley (1970) explored the influence of the presence of other bystanders on the likelihood that people will take action in emergencies. They varied the number of people who the person thought had also witnessed the emergency. Subjects were either with other witnesses or were made to believe that other people were in adjoining rooms. A variety of different emergencies were used, ranging from subjects seeing a theft, to smoke filling the room where the subject was waiting or working, to a person in distress in an adjoining room. They found that, across these different settings, with an increase in the number of bystanders, there was some decrease in the subject's tendency to take action, and usually the decrease was very substantial. To explain their findings, Latané and Darley proposed, first, that people try to hide their emotions in public, creating a condition of "pluralistic ignorance" – people look around to see how others evaluate the event, and, since others seem unconcerned, they define the event as a nonemergency. Second, responsibility for action gets diffused when other people are present; although there is responsibility to help a person in need, it is unclear whose responsibility it is. Latané and Darley and others (e.g., Schwartz, 1970) developed decision-making models of helping behavior in emergencies. They suggested that, if a person is to be helpful in an emergency, he must notice the incident, must interpret it as an emergency, must decide that he has a personal responsibility to act, and then must believe that he can carry out the behavior demanded by the situation.

A normative explanation of helping behavior – that people help others because of existing social norms that prescribe help – was rejected by Darley and Latané as useless, primarily on the basis of findings in field experiments in which the cost to the potential helper of helping or not helping substantially affected helping behavior. It seems, however, that the diffusion of responsibility notion is primarily a normative explanation. At least implicit in this notion is the assumption that there are social norms which prescribe that people take action under certain circumstances, when, for example, another person is in distress. When other potential bystanders are present, the responsibility is shared and thus diffused – and so is the blame for not helping.

While a norm (of responsibility) is invoked to explain the findings, its influence is not independently demonstrated. In fact, the norm could be invoked to explain the opposite finding. When other people are present, fear of disapproval for not acting according to the norm – according to expectations widely held by members of a social group that people help others in need – could be a reason for each person to want to help. There is some research evidence, in fact, that when others are present, or when others may find out about one's behavior, a person is more likely to act in accordance with social norms (Liebert & Poulos, 1971; Hartshorne & May, 1928). In addition, norms are only one of the probable determinations of behavior. Like most, if not all, modes of conduct, helping behavior is apt to be multidetermined.

III. MOTIVES FOR HELPING (AND NOT HELPING) OTHERS

A. The Social Rewards and Costs of Helping and Not Helping

1. Adherence to Norms that Prescribe Helping Behavior. It is usually assumed that young children are self-seeking. Very early, however, they may learn that they are expected to do things for other people, and may be rewarded when they benefit others and punished for not doing this. Over time, they learn that other people consider it to be their obligation or responsibility to do certain things for others, at least under certain conditions. Thus, they presumably learn norms that prescribe prosocial behavior.

People may thus adhere to norms because of the rewards they expect for compliance and the punishments they expect for deviation. The approval and respect of specific others who witness or find out about one's behavior, and of one's whole social group, may hinge on behaving according to social norms that are regarded as important. At the extreme, being singled out for general recognition and honors (such as rewards for heroism, appearing in the newspapers and on television) or ostracism for inaction may result from helping or not helping.

We may therefore speak of rewards for helping and costs of not helping as a result of adherence to or deviation from social norms. Rewards and costs may take extreme forms; in several European countries, including the Soviet Union (*Time*, December 27, 1971), the obligation to help others is expressed in laws which make it a punishable offense not to help when the circumstances delineated in the law call for it.

2. ***Conflicting Social Influences.*** One complication in evaluating the influence of norms that prescribe helping is that we do not know actually what it is that people believe others expect of them. Particularly in complex, heterogeneous societies like ours, a differentiated set of beliefs may exist about the circumstances under which there is a greater or lesser obligation to help others, including exceptions to, and modifications of, the applicability of norms to specific conditions (Staub, 1972b).

Another complication is that a variety of social influences may conflict with (or add support to) the influence of helping norms. In any one situation a variety of norms and/or rules of appropriate social behavior are applicable. We learn that we are not supposed to interfere with other people's private business. Thus, a fight between lovers or a husband and wife is outside the jurisdiction of strangers; we are unwilling to interfere when a parent disciplines his child, even if the discipline seems too harsh, and so on. Dependency is not a desirable condition; people may believe that it lowers a person's status in relation to others, and this may make them unwilling to offer help unless the need for help is entirely clear (and, of course, one's offer may be rejected, perhaps in an abusive manner). An imaginary example illustrates the way in which rules of appropriate behavior can interfere with helping. Let us assume that one evening a student goes to his professor's house to work with him. After his attractive wife goes to bed, the professor has to leave the house for a few minutes. Then the student hears what may be, what appear to be, sounds of distress from the bedroom. What is the poor student to do? He may attempt to explain the sounds away – as coming from a television set, for example – but they continue. Should he go into his professor's bedroom and see what's wrong with the wife? The negative consequences may be great, particularly if he has misinterpreted the sounds. Such conflicts exist in many real life situations, and are likely to affect helping behavior.

Social influence, what other people who are present say and do, may also be an important source of conflict with helping norms. Other people's comments – how they define the meaning of a situation – what they themselves do, and what they may tell a person to do may affect the degree to which helping norms and other motives for helping are activated or inhibited. Reasons for this and detailed consideration of the nature of social influence will be presented later.

*3. **The Material and Physical Costs of Helping Behavior.*** In order to help others, people may have to sacrifice material possessions or time and effort or incur the emotional costs of involvement, sometimes even risk their personal safety. People obviously consider their own welfare and the personal consequences of helping others; as these costs increase, the likelihood of help will decrease. Sometimes as costs get larger, people probably believe, and undoubtedly with justification, that they are not even expected by others (that is, by norms) to help, since the likelihood of danger to themselves is unreasonably great. Few would blame someone who can barely swim for not trying to pull out a drowning person from a raging river.

Actually, sometimes people may help because they expect material gain for themselves as a result. There is an apparently powerful norm that is active in our society (and may even be universal): the norm of reciprocity (Gouldner, 1960; Gergen, 1968) which prescribes, among other things, that we ought to aid those who have helped us. There is evidence that this norm affects a wide range of behavior (Staub, 1972b). Thus, helping behavior may be motivated by the expected return of benefits from others. It is questionable, however, to what extent the reciprocity norm affects helping behavior in emergencies, when people face the need to help someone in distress whom they have never seen before and may never see again.

In general, people have feelings of obligation to themselves and to others, and a conflict often exists between their egocentrism and their willingness to help others. Thus, anything that increases the cost of helping may decrease the likelihood of helping behavior. Already existing concerns about the self (for example, about losses already suffered, about one's interests not having been satisfied, about one's competence or adequacy) may also shift the balance and decrease helping behavior (Berkowitz, 1970). This may be why making people feel good increases the help they extend to others (Isen & Levin, 1972; Berkowitz, 1972), while making them feel bad decreases help (Isen, 1970).

B. Internalized Values and Norms: Internal Rewards and Costs

A person may internalize beliefs, values, and standards of conduct, and then behave in accordance with them because *he* expects himself to act this way. He may then reward himself for adherence to his internalized values and punish himself for deviation; the self-reward may be either verbal (self-approval and praise, probably resulting in corresponding emotions) or material (a good meal, a night out, etc.).

I think it is worth distinguishing between two types of values and norms that are relevant to helping behavior. One type involves *concern with doing the right thing*, while the other has to do with *concern with others' welfare* – aiding others who need help because it enhances their welfare. This distinction may not be merely academic; a particular value may lead to a particular type of action. Durkheim (1961) differentiated between people who are "good" and those who are "responsible," the former being more concerned with others' welfare and doing good for others, the latter more concerned with the maintenance of societal rules and adherence to them. Relevant to this distinction, Hoffman (1970) found two types of value orientation among children. "Humanistic–flexible" children tend to be concerned with the consequences of behavior for others and seem more inclined to deviate from conventional social norms, if necessary, to enhance others' welfare. "Conventional–rigid" children, on the other hand, were more concerned with adherence to conventional societal norms.

The influence of internalized values and norms on helping behavior may be shown by a relationship between independently measured cognitive–affective indices of internalization and norm-prescribed behavior. Presumably, internalization is a matter of degree. Most people are likely to know what the important societal norms are – children apparently know many of them (Hartshorne & May, 1928; Bryan, 1970). Bryan, for example, found that most children can verbalize the desirability of sharing behavior, to the experimenter or to another child, whether they actually share or not. Some people may express greater belief in prosocial values and norms than others. In part, they may want to appear to people as individuals who believe in such norms. Nonetheless, this still means that they assign importance to prosocial norms and probably means that they have internalized them to some degree. Some people may have a network of associated cognitions that promote prosocial values and norms so that their thinking, and presumably their feeliings, are affected by considerations of their duty to help others and/or concern for others' welfare.

C. Empathy, the Vicarious Experience of Others' Emotions

Another person's distress may be vicariously experienced and his positive emotions upon being helped may be anticipated and vicariously experienced. Thus, the desire both to lessen one's own vicarious distress and to enhance one's own vicarious satisfaction may motivate helping behavior. It should be pointed out that, even though the helper's own emotions are emphasized, these emotions are activated by another person's condition or feelings, and thus the helping behavior is motivated by concern for another person. There is some recent evidence that empathy may inhibit aggression (Feshbach & Feshbach, 1969; Singer, 1971; Staub, 1971) and that it may activate prosocial behavior (Krebs, 1970; Aronfreed, 1970; Aderman & Berkowitz, 1970). [See also endnote on p. 170. E.S.]

IV. THE SITUATION AND THE PERSON AS DETERMINANTS OF HELPING BEHAVIOR

Whether any of the motives for promoting or inhibiting helping behavior will be activated, and to what degree, is a function of the characteristics of the situation in which the person finds himself, as well as his personal characteristics. The series of experiments to be reported here sought to examine a variety of characteristics of situations that induce people to aid another person in distress or inhibit aid, looked at the influence of personality characteristics on helping behavior, and also explored the interaction between the situation and personality in affecting helping behavior.

So far, social psychological research has focused on only a few of the situational conditions that influence helpfulness, such as the presence of other people and the behavior of a model (Bryan & Test, 1967; Macaulay & Berkowitz, 1970). In our research, the range of environmental influences has been extended to include: (1) the characteristics of the stimulus for help: the degree to which a person needs help and thus the utility of the help given; (2) the conditions surrounding the need for help: the types of norms or rules of appropriate behavior that operate in a situation, and the ease or difficulty of "escaping" from the situation without helping; (3) interpersonal influences on helping behavior: what other people say and do about an apparent stimulus for help and how they define appropriate behavior.

Although the importance of individual characteristics has been long emphasized, relatively few experiments studied the effects of personality on helping. Most of these studies were not successful in demonstrating such an influence (Latané & Darley, 1970, Korte, 1969). However, this failure was not complete (Schwartz, 1968; Schwartz & Clausen, 1970). It may be necessary to develop a conceptual approach pointing to certain research strategies if we are to show how personality affects helping behavior. This will be discussed more fully in conjunction with our research (see Section VIII).

V. THE EFFECTS OF CHARACTERISTICS OF THE STIMULUS FOR HELP AND OF SURROUNDING CONDITIONS ON HELPING BEHAVIOR

A major determinant of helpfulness may be the characteristics of the stimulus for help. Ambiguous distress cues may result in fewer attempts to help, while distress cues that indicate greater rather than less need for assistance may lead to more help.

As Latané and Darley (1970) emphasized, ambiguity often surrounds an emergency. When a person faces a distressed other, the nature or source of the other's distress is often unknown or unclear. Ambiguity and uncertainty about the need for help and about the type of action one should take may increase the observer's tension and discomfort, reducing the probability that he will approach the stimulus producing the discomfort. Ambiguity may also allow a person to interpret the distress cues in alternative ways. A person lying on the street may be seen as a bum or a drunk, even if he has just suffered a sudden attack of physical illness.

Several experimenters have found a very high frequency of helping behavior, perhaps in part because the stimulus for help minimized the ambiguity of the emergency. Piliavin et al. (1970) observed a high frequency of helping behavior across a variety of experimental conditions in response to staged emergencies on New York subways. The distressed person's visibility may have lessened the bystanders' uncertainty about the need for help. Other experiments also obtained high frequency of helpfulness in response to sounds of distress from adjoining rooms (Staub & Clawson, unpublished research; Clark & Word, 1972). Part of the distress sounds in our experiment and all of them in the Clark and Word experiment were live rather than tape-recorded, which might have minimized ambiguity and enhanced the credibility of the need for help.[1]

Generally, information about the source of a person's distress may reduce ambiguity and thus increase the likelihood that aid will be given him, but this information also specifies the degree of his need for help – that is, the utility of help, how important it is for him to receive aid, and how much benefit the help may produce. The greater the need, the more motives to help may be activated. Social norms as well as personal values that prescribe help are presumably more imperative when someone's need is great, and both the social and personal costs of not helping would

[1] Tape-recorded distress sounds, particularly when played to subjects on relatively simple tape recorders, may have a different, less real quality than live distress sounds. Hearing such distress sounds may not lead to clear awareness that the sounds are not genuine, but may introduce an element of uncertainty as to their origin or meaning. In experiments that we conducted with tape-recorded distress sounds we had to use a variety of devices – good tape recorders, a rug under the tape recorder, muffling the sounds by putting something over the speakers – to make the sounds appear in an adjoining room, to us and to pilot subjects, as genuine.

be greater. This concept of degree of need is similar to the concept of dependency employed by Berkowitz (Berkowitz & Daniels, 1963; Berkowitz, 1972). Berkowitz's research demonstrated that people extend more effort to aid another who is more rather than less dependent on them in acquiring rewards. Our research explored the influence on helping behavior of the degree of a person's physical distress, and thus his degree of dependence on others in alleviating distress.

Experiment One: Degree of Need for Help. The purpose of this experiment was to explore helping behavior in a natural setting, a city street, exploring the influence of the degree of need for help.[2] The experiment was conducted in a residential area of Cambridge, Massachusetts. As a passerby approached a corner opposite from a side street where a 21-year-old male confederate was waiting, the confederate did one of the following: a) collapsed on the sidewalk about 40 feet from the corner (no information); or b) approaching approximately the same spot, grabbed his knee after the subject appeared and collapsed holding his knee (bad knee) or, c) collapsed after grabbing his chest over his heart (bad heart).

Only 15 out of 60 subjects approached the victim to help him. The frequency of approach to the distressed person was 45% in the bad knee condition and 30% in the no information condition. However, not a single person approached the distressed person in the bad heart condition. This finding was not only surprising, but upsetting, since a person with a bad heart would presumably need help more urgently than would a person with a bad knee. One possible explanation for the lack of help is that subjects perceived the cost of help – the amount of effort and involvement demanded of them – as very great. The subjects might have even feared that the person with the bad heart would get worse while they were trying to help him and that they would be held responsible for his misfortune.

Experiment Two: Ability to Escape from Distress Cues. When the need for help is great, the perceived cost of helping may also be great, as in the case of a person having a heart attack. When the perceived cost is great, people will be less likely to help. But perhaps they will help if it is difficult to escape from the distress cues. When circumstances make escape difficult, helping behavior may be more likely because of the greater social cost of not helping.

To test this reasoning, we varied the ease of escaping from distress cues – from the presence of the distressed person. A male confederate appeared from a side street and walked toward a passerby, either on the same side of the street (difficult escape), or crossed over and walked toward the passerby

[2] The description of the four experiments that follows is a summary. For a complete description, see original publication.

on the other side of the street (easy escape). When he was about 40 feet from the passerby, he grabbed his chest or his knee. After three attempts to get up, he remained on the ground.

When escape was more difficult, people helped more often. Many more people approached the victim when he was in their path (72%) than when he was on the other side of the street (27%). Thus, a distressed person in the path of a passerby appears to have a greater chance of being helped than one who is easier to bypass. Moreover, in both escape conditions people approached the victim more when he appeared to have heart problems. In the difficult escape condition the victim with the heart problem was almost always approached.

In the difficult escape condition being closer to the victim may have activated motives for helping, including internalized norms, empathy, and a feeling of personal responsibility to help. When circumstances make escape difficult, sustained exposure is likely to focus attention on the person in need, activating processes that contribute to helping.

In addition, when escape was difficult, getting away from the distressed person looked like obvious avoidance. People may have feared social disapproval, either by other bystanders or the distressed person himself, if they did this. Some people did it anyway; they simply walked by him without stopping, or left the sidewalk and made a circle around him. Some crossed over to the other side of the street.

Of the people who passed on the other side of the street, a number of them glanced at the victim once or twice, and then hurried on without looking at him again. Apparently, some people minimized their exposure to the distress cues in this manner. They noticed something, but then avoided further exposure.

The greater helpfulness in response to the heart problem was in contrast to what happened in the first experiment. A reason for the difference may have been that the first confederate looked strong and vigorous, while the second one was obviously overweight. People may have doubted the authenticity of the first confederate's heart problem, but may have found it credible that the second confederate would have heart trouble.

Experiment Three. To explore this possibility, in this study the confederate of the second experiment enacted both the knee problem and the heart problem, following the exact procedures of the first experiment. While the frequency of help in the bad knee condition was about the same as in the first experiment, the frequency of help in the bad heart condition was substantially greater. Thus, the characteristics of the person needing help may affect the credibility that he (or she) has a particular type of need.

Experiment Four. To increase our confidence in accounting for the different findings in Experiment One and Experiment Three, we asked participants in this study to rate their perceptions of the two confederates. A group of undergraduate students was asked to watch film clips of the performance of the bad heart condition by the two confederates and make judgments about the nature of their distress. The second (overweight) confederate was significantly more often judged to have a heart problem. A number of the judges explained the collapse of the first, more sporty looking confederate by saying that he was hit by a bullet.

A. General Discussion

It was suggested in the Introduction that helping behavior is multiply determined. Our findings from this series of experiments were complex, but they probably reflect the complexities governing helping behavior in everyday life.

A clear result was that when the victim was not in the path of a would-be helper he was helped less, perhaps because the social and personal costs of not helping were smaller. When the victim was not in their path a number of people looked away after a first glance. When faced with a sudden unexpected event, many people may prefer to avoid the difficulties of decision-making and the sacrifices involved in helping. Milgram (1970) has suggested that people in large urban areas are so frequently exposed to others' needs and suffering that they have to defend themselves if they are to maintain a private life. With some people this self-defense may include maneuvers that will minimize their involvement with others' needs. However, if involvement is forced on them by circumstances, psychological and social processes may be activated that will lead to helping behavior, possibly even to a true concern for another's welfare and a desire to help him.

When information about the source of distress suggested greater need for help, in one experiment more help resulted, in another less. Our subsequent attempts to uncover the reason for this difference suggested that the characteristics of the stimulus person were responsible. The subjects on the street, much like those who judged the films, presumably attributed the second confederate's difficulty to a heart problem, because he was overweight. In contrast, a healthy, vigorous young man is unlikely to have a heart attack, and so, when the first confederate acted as if he had a heart problem, there may have been confusion about what was wrong with him, even suspicion. A discrepancy between a person's general characteristics and his condition of need may create ambiguity, possibly suspicion, and as a consequence might reduce helping behavior.

Piliavin, Rodin, and Piliavin (1970) and Piliavin and Piliavin (1972) recently suggested that observation of an emergency is physiologically and emotionally arousing, that arousal is aversive, and that people will attempt to reduce this unpleasant state by helping directly or indirectly, or by leaving the scene. They proposed that holding arousal constant, as costs of helping increase the probability of direct intervention decreases, while as costs of not helping increase the probability of direct help increases. We also regard costs of assisting and not assisting someone as important influences on helping behavior. In addition, we regard the degree of need for help (and thus the utility or potential benefit to the helped person) as an additional influence. Furthermore, we regard the costs of not helping to be a function both of potential external negative consequences (social sanctions) and of internal negative consequences (self-punishment). Thus, personal values and standards affect the cost of not helping another person in need.

Finally, it should be pointed out that little experimental evidence exists in support of either the Piliavin et al. analysis or our model. The difficulty is that the two kinds of costs and the utility of help are often related, and to an unknown degree. Our procedure for varying the ease of escape may have produced variation only or primarily in one of these elements, the cost of not helping.

VI. INFLUENCES THAT CONFLICT WITH HELPING: IMPLICIT AND EXPLICIT RULES OF APPROPRIATE BEHAVIOR[3]

In an experiment with children (Staub, 1970a), we found an unexpected curvilinear relationship between age and children's attempts to help another child in response to sounds of distress from an adjoining room. Helpfulness increased from kindergarten to second grade, but then decreased from second to sixth grade. This decrease in assistance with increasing age was surprising. When we questioned the older children about the reasons for their behavior, their responses suggested that they feared disapproval by the experimenter for possibly improper behavior. Children seemed to feel that going into the adjoining room was not permissible, that it would have been a transgression of an implicit rule which prohibits this kind of exploratory behavior in a novel environment.

In the course of their socialization children learn rules that regulate appropriate, "proper" behavior in everyday life. In our society, examples of such standards of proper behavior include stipulations not to interfere with others' affairs, not to call undue attention to one's self, not to behave in idiosyncratic ways. Many, although not all, of these rules are inhibitory in nature, emphasizing what one should not do. Obedience to these rules is generally thought of as less obligatory than obedience to moral rules, which guide behavior that might affect others' welfare (Brown, 1965). Nevertheless, the former may have greater force in influencing children's (and perhaps adults') behavior because they are taught extensively and are enforced

3 The series of experiments in this section were originally reported, in a more extended form, in the *Journal of Personality and Social Psychology*, 1971, 17, 137–144.

across a variety of situations. Moreover, when the expected or appropriate behavior is not clear, fear of disapproval may reduce the willingness to initiate any kind of action, including giving aid to a person in distress.

Obedience to a specific person in authority may also affect helping behavior. Explicit statements of expectations by a person in authority may define the rules of appropriate behavior for a specific situation. It has been demonstrated that adults will conform to explicitly stated expectations or demands of an experimenter that they act counter to moral norms by administering extremely intense and potentially harmful electric shocks to another person (Milgram, 1963). In practice, those in authority seldom come right out trying to discourage people from helping others in distress, but, as with rules of appropriate social behavior, they may restrain helpfulness indirectly by encouraging incompatible behavior.

Several experiments were conducted to investigate the influence on helping behavior of unstated "rules" of appropriate behavior, and of explicit information about the permissibility of behavior that had to be performed in order to help a distressed other.

Experiment One: Permission to Enter. In this experiment, in one condition participants received permission to enter an adjoining room, in another condition they did not. Having permission to enter was expected to decrease the fear of disapproval for inappropriate behavior, and thus increase attempts to help a distressed child.

Forty seventh-grade students participated in this experiment. Each of them, while sitting alone in a room drawing a picture, heard sounds of distress from a girl in an adjoining room. The (tape-recorded) sounds of a crash were followed by crying and sobbing, interspersed with calls for help. Some of the seventh-grade participants had been told beforehand that they may go into the adjoining room if they needed more drawing pencils (permission group). Others only received instruction to make a drawing and were told nothing about entering the adjoining room (no information group).

Some of the children entered the room after hearing the distress sounds; a few reported the distress sounds when the experimenter returned to the room; and some did nothing. The children in the permission group attempted to help significantly more often than those in the no information group. No difference in behavior was observed between boys and girls.

Permission to enter the other room presumably decreased the subjects' concern that their behavior would result in disapproval or criticism. The behavior of one girl in the permission group dramatically demonstrated concern with acting appropriately. This girl listened for a while to the distress sounds, then broke the points of both of her drawing pencils in quick, deliberate movements, apparently to justify her going into the other room to get more pencils, and then she ran into the adjoining room. This suggested that some children who received permission might still have felt inhibited, believing that they were only justified in going into the other room if they needed more pencils.

Experiment Two: Permission and Prohibition. Based on the first experiment, it seemed that the frequency of help following permission might increase if permission is perceived as unconditional, so that all children feel that it is all right to go into the other room. In addition to using a different instruction for permission than in the first experiment, this experiment sought to explore the effects of prohibition about entering the adjoining room.

This experiment involved 33 seventh-grade girls. The subjects heard sounds of distress, including calls for help, from another seventh-grade girl in the adjoining room. Before hearing the sounds, some of the girls received permission to enter the adjoining room if they finished their task or wanted to take a break from their task (permission group). Other girls received no information about the permissibility of entering the adjoining room (no information group). A third group was told not to go into the other room because a girl in that room was working on the same task as the subject and the experimenter did not want the two of them talking to each other (prohibition group).

Participants in the permission group helped significantly more often than those either in the no information group or in the prohibition group. The frequency of help was similar in the latter two groups. Almost all subjects (10 of 11) in the permission group went into the other room to help. Only three in the prohibition group and four in the no information group did so. Active help in the permission group was significantly greater than active help in the permission group of the first experiment, leading to the conclusion that the nature of permission made a difference in helping.

The findings suggest that rules about proper social behavior can affect children's helping behavior. Children apparently feel it is inappropriate to stop their work on a task and/or to enter a room in a strange environment, and fear disapproval for doing so. Having no information about the permissibility of entering the adjoining room seemed to be functionally equivalent to a prohibition against entering.

Experiment Three: Extension to Adults. This experiment attempted to explore the impact on adults of unstated "rules" of appropriate behavior as well as statements by an experimenter specifying what is the desirable or permissible behavior in a specific situation. Although adults are sensitive to an experimenter's instructions about appropriate behavior, motives for helping others may become stronger with age and there may be an increase in the ability to discriminate between situations in which conventional rules apply and those in which moral norms or values of caring supersede them.

This experiment involved 56 female subjects. Some were given permission by the experimenter to enter the adjoining room to get coffee if they wished (permission group). In the prohibition group, the experimenters explained that the person in the adjoining room should not be interrupted. In a third group participants received information only about their task. As in the earlier experiments, the subject heard taped distress sounds coming from an adjoining room of a woman who had apparently fallen off a ladder. The results showed that prohibition substantially reduced active helping, while no information and permission resulted in almost identical, high-frequency helping behavior. Having no information apparently did not function for adults as an implicit rule prohibiting entry into the other room, as it had for children.

The inhibition by children in the no information condition suggests that socialization in our society may overemphasize the teaching of prohibitions against improper behavior, without sufficient emphasis on norms that prescribe caring and helping. Behavior that manifests concern about others' welfare appears to be fragile and yields to contrary influences. Even for adults, the prohibition against entering the other room inhibited helping behavior. It seems that adults are sensitive to the explicitly stated expectations of others and respond to these expectations even if, as a consequence, they deviate from presumably socially highly valued norms, and presumably in the case of some of them from personal values as well, which prescribe or make it desirable to help those who need help. The findings suggest that neither children nor adults learn that under conditions of someone's urgent and possibly intense need, helping should supersede norms of appropriate behavior or the instructions of a person in charge who had no reason to anticipate such need for help.

VII. INTERPERSONAL INFLUENCES ON HELPING: THE EFFECT OF ANOTHER ONLOOKER "DEFINING" THE STIMULUS AND THE "APPROPRIATE" BEHAVIOR

Previous research by Latané and Darley showed that the presence of inactive others may greatly reduce helpfulness. In addition, what other observers say and do may have an influence. One strong demonstration of this was provided by the previous set of experiments in which the experimenter's statements apparently defined appropriate behavior in that setting and strongly affected helping behavior. Furthermore, bystanders may communicate to others their perception of the meaning of a stimulus and their belief about what should be done, and thus imply or even explicitly state their expectations as to what others should do.

We know that people strongly influence each other's behavior through verbal communication, by acting as models, or in other ways. Research on conformity shows the amazing degree to which this can happen (Asch,

1955; Kiesler & Kiesler, 1970; Hollander & Willis, 1967; Milgram, 1963). In order to be able to predict and control what happens to us and thus assure our safety and effective functioning in the world, we must perceive reality as accurately as possible. However, our definition of reality is greatly dependent on the consensus of those around us. One reason why people exert such a strong influence on each other may be that they learn both to check their reactions by comparing them to others' behavior (Festinger, 1954) and to align their perception of events with those of others. Even a sense of sanity seems dependent on our perceiving and interpreting events as other people do (Valins & Nisbett, 1971). Another obvious reason may be that people are sensitive to and concerned about what others will think of them. Other persons may reward by approval and praise behavior that is in line with their own beliefs about the meaning of an event and with their expectations of how a person should behave, and they may punish contrary behavior by disapproval, making the actor feel foolish and incompetent, or in other ways.

In the following experiment we explored the effect on helping behavior of the actions of a confederate in response to distress sounds. The apparent distress sounds were verbally defined by the confederate either as distress sounds or as something else, the confederate either did or did not help indirectly, and the subject was told by the confederate either to help directly or not to help because she was not supposed to enter the adjoining room. This last variation attempted to extend the findings of the previous series of experiments by investigating the influence of a prohibition against entering the adjoining room espoused by a person of same status as the subject.

This experiment also explored the relationship between personality characteristics of the subjects and helping behavior, and subjects' reactions to the female confederate as a function of her behavior.

A Study of Bystander Influence

The study involved 103 adult female participants. While completing a task, participants heard distress sounds from an adjoining room. There were two control groups and five experimental groups. In one control group subjects were alone, in another they were together with another subject (pairs). In the five experimental conditions subjects heard distress sounds together with a confederate acting as a subject. The confederate was always sitting with her back toward the door of the adjoining room while the subject faced the confederate and thus the door. Five seconds after the distress sounds started the confederate always interpreted or "defined" the meaning of the sounds.

In the positive verbal definition condition, the confederate said: "That sounds bad. Maybe we should do something." In the negative verbal definition group, the confederate said: "That sounds like a tape recording.

Maybe they are trying to test us. Or I guess it could be part of another experiment. But it does sound like a tape." In both conditions she then remained seated and did nothing herself. Whatever the subject did, the confederate followed her initiative, always staying behind her. In other conditions the confederate defined the distress sounds positively, and then did one of several additional things. In one condition she jumped up, hurried to a door leading out of the room (but not to the adjoining room) and said, "I'd better go and get the experimenter." In another condition she did the same and said, "I'd better go get the experimenter. You'd better not do anything; I don't think we are supposed to go into that room." Or she said, "I'd better go and get the experimenter. You go into the other room and see what happened." In each of these cases the confederate then hurried out of the room.

The words and actions of the confederate greatly affected the frequency of active help, i.e., subjects going into the room from which the distress sounds were heard. Subjects helped significantly more in the positive definition (66%) than in the negative definition condition (25%). When the stimulus was defined as an emergency and the appropriate behavior for the subject was defined as going into the other room, all subjects (100%) helped. The frequency of help was statistically significantly greater than in the positive definition condition (66%), in which the confederate defined the sounds as distress sounds but did not start any action and did not tell the subject what to do. The way the stimulus and the appropriate reaction to it were defined by one person affected the behavior of the other person.

The experiment demonstrates the strong effect of interpersonal influence, the influence of other witnesses or bystanders, on helping behavior. Verbal definition of the meaning of the sounds by one person affected the actions of another person. Subjects exposed to "maximum influence," in which the confederate interpreted the sounds as requiring a response, instructed the subject how to respond (defining also the appropriate behavior) and engaged in action herself helped more than those who only heard the other person give a "positive definition." These findings suggest that what people say, what they do, and the combination of what they say and do all powerfully affect people's behavior in response to an apparent emergency. Why and how does this happen?

Verbal communications by one person about the meaning of distress sounds may affect the second person's interpretation of both the distress sounds and the appropriate response, which in turn affects her behavior. Or it may communicate the first person's belief about what ought to be done, and her expectations of what the second person will do. Both of these effects may be present at the same time. We are not only strongly affected by, but probably often rely on or use other people's reactions as at least one important source of information in defining the meaning of events for us. We look at other people, we see what they think about an event, and we make up our minds about its meaning – partly on the basis of others' reactions. Another reason for the powerful effect of other people is our concern about their reaction to us – whether they will evaluate us positively, negatively, as good or bad, competent or incompetent. To avoid negative evaluation people try to behave in a manner that is consistent with other people's expectations of them.

A finding contrary to expectations was that the verbal prohibition to enter the adjoining room did not inhibit helping behavior. In fact, 75% of those people in the prohibition group helped, in contrast to 25% in the negative definition group and 66% in the positive definition group. A probable reason for this is that the prohibition conflicted with the confederate's definition of the sounds as distress sounds and with her example of indirect help. Moreover, no reason was provided about why it was not permissible to go into the adjoining room. It is also possible, of course, that prohibition from a fellow subject, with no more authority than oneself, might not be perceived as a real prohibition. But given the generally strong impact of this fellow subject's words and actions, this seems a less plausible explanation.

Control subjects who were alone helped almost as much as subjects exposed to "maximum influence." All except one person helped. The high frequency of help by single witnesses to an emergency that has been found in most research suggests that when a person is alone he feels that responsibility is focused on him. Other circumstances, for example, a person being told that he is in charge in case something happens (which we found in another study to increase first-grade children's helping), may also focus responsibility on an individual, increasing feelings of obligation toward a person in need and leading to helpful action.

VIII. PERSONALITY, COMMUNICATIONS ABOUT PERMISSIBLE BEHAVIOR, AND HELPING UNDER "LIFELIKE" CONDITIONS

The division of the determinants of social behavior into two classes, the situation and the personality of the actor, has a long tradition in psychology. Unfortunately, the attempts that have been made to demonstrate the relationship between personal dispositions and social behavior have often focused on only one personality variable at a time (Singer & Singer, 1972), and/or studied the influence of a personality characteristic on a single behavior, in a single setting. On the whole, the attempts to demonstrate how personal dispositions affect social behavior have not proved very satisfactory. Perhaps it is no wonder, then, that some theorists suggest (Jones & Nisbett, 1971; Mischel, 1968) that consistency in behavior is partly a function of situational similarity and partly in the eye of the beholder rather than real – that we have overestimated the effects of personality on behavior.

We felt, however, that a certain conceptual and related experimental approach would enable us to show that personality does affect helping behavior, and the manner in which this influence comes about. First, several types of personality characteristics may contribute to helping, and their combination may be necessary for certain types of helping behavior to occur. Therefore, we measured (1) the degree of "prosocial orientation" of subjects, which includes a concern about the welfare of others, a feeling of responsibility for others' welfare, and a belief in moral and prosocial values; (2) the tendency to take action rather than remain passive in the face of events; and (3) speed in making judgment about events. People who tend to suspend judgment may be slower to initiate action and may thus lose the opportunity to do so.

Second, personality and the nature of surrounding conditions are likely to interact in determining helping behavior. To demonstrate this, we again varied the experimenter's communications to subjects about the permissibility of entering an adjoining room from which they would later hear distress sounds. In doing this we also explored the influence on adult male subjects of behavioral rules communicated by an experimenter.

Third, we asked whether certain personality characteristics would be related to certain types of helping behaviors but not to others, depending on the kind of demands that providing help places on the person. To explore this we not only had subjects hear distress sounds from an adjoining room, but, whether they helped or not, subjects were also confronted by the confederate who produced the distress sounds and were provided with several further opportunities for help. All three types of personality characteristics described above seem important in affecting reactions to distress sounds, but only prosocial orientation seems important when a person faces a direct request for a certain type of help, because then the definition of the stimulus and of what needs to be done is already provided.

In laboratory experiments of our own and of other researchers tape-recorded distress sounds are usually used. If the subject helps by going to the "distressed person," he discovers the tape recorder. The present procedure enabled us to study the subjects' reactions to a real, live person "in distress," and the degree of sacrifice they are willing to make when several avenues of help are available, varying in effort but also in the utility of the help provided.

Finally, the sounds of distress that subjects heard were relatively mild in intensity. Very powerful situational influences, including extremely intense sounds, may have a relatively uniform effect on people, reducing the likelihood that personality characteristics will affect behavior.

Description of Study

This experiment involved 130 male undergraduate students. Groups of subjects completed paper and pencil personality tests. A number of these measures were used together to evaluate a prosocial value orientation.

Several weeks later, subjects were tested individually on speed of judgment and reaction time. Subjects were exposed to one of three experimental treatments. One group had no information about the adjoining room. In the permission group, the same instructions were used as in previous experiments, i.e., that there was coffee brewing in the adjoining room which would soon be ready and the subject could go in to get some. In the prohibition group, subjects were told that they were working on a timed task and were asked not to interrupt their work. These instructions aimed at extending the prohibition beyond the immediate response to the distress sounds to subsequent opportunities for helping.

Shortly after the experimenter left the room, the subjects heard distress sounds from an adjoining room, groaning by a person that was intended to sound as the result of stomach cramps. Several males acted as confederates, all trained to act similarly. If the subject entered the room, the confederate said that his stomach was "killing" him, asked whether he could lie down in the room where the subject had come from (a larger room with a couch), then went ahead and lay down. If the subject did not enter the room, after about two minutes the confederate entered the subject's room, asked about lying down on the couch and proceeded to do so. During the subsequent interaction each participant's reactions to the confederate's behavior and statements were carefully noted.

While lying on the couch, the confederate always added that he had a stomach problem and had run out of pills. Then he provided further opportunities for the subject to respond in a helpful manner. First he said, after a short time had elapsed, "I don't want to bother you. There is a lounge on the fifteenth floor where I can lie down for a longer time." The confederate slowly began to get up and started to take a few steps toward the door. The purpose of this was to test the subject's willingness to get rid of the burden of responsibility placed on him by the confederate's presence.

After a few steps, however, the confederate sat down on the arm of the couch and said, calmly but still in distress, "Maybe there is something you can do for me. I have a prescription for my pills with me, but I forgot to have it filled. If you could call my roommate for me, he would come over and take the prescription down to Harvard Square to have it filled. Or if you have the time maybe you could take it down to the square. That would be much quicker." The participants' helping behavior varied greatly. A couple of them had to be chased down the steps, as they ran down from the fourteenth floor of the building where all this took place, not wanting to wait for the elevator so that they could get to the pharmacy faster. One person reached the pharmacy in Harvard Square before the experimenter caught up with him. Following this sequence of interaction, participants were told the nature of the study.

The subjects' responses were categorized in several ways, according to the form of help offered. Of the 130 subjects, 41 actively responded to the distress sounds by entering the adjoining room while 89 did not. Correlations among measures of help showed that subjects who responded more to the original distress sounds continued to help more at each opportunity offered to them. There was a marginally significant difference among the different groups in active attempts to help. The frequency of active help was about equal in the prohibition group and the no information group but greater in the permission group.

The subjects in this experiment did not respond as the female subjects did in the earlier experiment using similar treatments, but more like the seventh graders with whom no information and prohibition both resulted in low frequencies of active help, while permission enhanced helping. The distress cues were milder in this experiment, not strong enough perhaps to overcome, in the no information condition, inhibitors of helping present in this situation. Also, the victim was male, and male subjects may have been concerned about intruding on another male.

Personality was strongly related to helping behavior in this experiment. Subjects who were more prosocial, as indicated by their scores on *specific* tests relevant to helping, helped more, but the relationships were affected by the treatment conditions, the exact nature of the personality characteristics, and the nature of help needed. But our analysis suggests that beyond the specific aspects of personality measured by each test, there is a more *general* personal characteristic, which I named *"prosocial value orientation."*

We created a measure of this using a statistical procedure called factor analysis. This technique helps to find common aspect of, and helps to combine, different tests. The varied tests we used (see the original publication for details; but note that in subsequent selections I describe a single test I created to measure prosocial value orientation) together appeared to assess three primary dimensions: a positive in contrast to negative evaluation of human nature and human beings; a feeling of concern about other people's welfare or its absence; and a feeling of personal responsibility for people's welfare or its absence. The values of equality and leading a helpful life were also part of prosocial orientation. Individuals who had high scores on this measure helped more, in every way, in all treatment conditions.

Our attempt to show a direct relationship between perceptual and action tendencies and helping behavior was not successful. A possible reason for this was inadequate measurement of those tendencies. However, we did find that participants who scored high on a measure of impulsiveness responded faster to the distress sounds from another room. Participants were more impulsive if they made faster (although because of the speed often incorrect) judgments in matching the picture of an object with its exact replica out of a number of very similar objects, in contrast to reflective participants who made slower (and thus more accurate) judgments. Impulsive persons stopped working on their task earlier and looked at the door of the adjoining room; some got up and walked around. But they did not help more unless they had a stronger prosocial value orientation. An "action tendency" still seems important for a person to actively initiate help, at least under certain conditions. It may consist of impulsiveness, feelings of effectiveness, and other perceptual or instrumental characteristics. However, it may have to combine with relevant values and the motives that arise from them, to lead to purposeful action.

When combined personality-situational influences are explored, it seems important to consider the kind of motives that may be activated by a situation and the degree to which conflicts between motives may arise. In our experiment subjects were exposed to the need for helping a distressed person while working on a task. Subjects who ranked the value "ambition" highly were less helpful when asked for help in getting a prescription filled, presumably because this meant interrupting work on their task for a longer period of time. More "ambitious" subjects may have experienced more conflict between helping and working on their task.

In studies that will be reported in subsequent selections, we found prosocial orientation related to quite varied forms of helping.

IX. GENERAL DISCUSSION AND CONCLUSIONS

The source of people's motivation for helping others may vary greatly, from expected external rewards (or the avoidance of punishment), to self-reward, to emphatic "reinforcement" – satisfaction gained from another person's increased well-being. In order to predict helping behavior, we have to consider the possibilities for rewards and punishments inherent in the situation, as well as characteristics of individuals which affect their internal reactions.

We found that several types of influences affect the willingness to help a person in distress. The nature of distress cues may indicate the degree of need to help, and also the type of behavior that is required – whether it demands initiative or not, and whether it demands more or less sacrifice. The circumstances surrounding the need for help may make it easy to avoid helping or exceedingly difficult in terms of embarrassment, social punishment, and later shame or guilt. The circumstances may also make helping behavior seem perfectly appropriate, or in conflict with other norms relevant to the situation. The influence of others on helping behavior has been particularly strongly demonstrated: this influence is varied, and many-faceted.

Personality characteristics also affect helping behavior, and they may modify the influence of the determinants that were just enumerated. The "prosocial orientation" that exerted its influence in our last experiment probably represents, primarily, a way of looking at, of thinking about, other people's welfare, and one's own responsibility toward other people. Depending on how one thinks about such matters, one's interpretation of the meaning of a specific instance of another person's distress and one's judgment of the appropriate resolution of it (reaction to it) are likely to be affected. Depending on how one interprets such arousal-producing events as a person's distress, one's emotional reactions are also likely to be affected. A network of cognitions (that is, beliefs and values) concerning other people's welfare may lead not only to self-reward or self-punishment, depending on how one behaves toward others, but also to empathy with the sufferer. This is strongly suggested by current theories of emotion which maintain that physiological reactions to an event and the interpretation of these reactions are codeterminants of emotion. The assessment of an event may determine both the degree of physiological reactions to it and their interpretation.

We have emphasized that circumstances and personality characteristics interact in affecting helping behavior. Individuals who are prosocially oriented appear to be sensitive to social influences just like other people. At least when subjects scoring high on specific measures of prosocial orientation were considered, their helping behavior was greater than that of low-scoring subjects when the circumstances were favorable (permission) to being helpful, but not when they were less favorable. However, persons with a strong general prosocial orientation were more helpful under all conditions. Still, moral and caring values, including the value of helping others in need, may be regarded as ideals. While some individuals hold such ideals more than others and strive to achieve them more, many people seem to need social support to behave according to them. Even feelings like empathy and sympathy are affected by particular conditions.

Nevertheless, people with a prosocial orientation seem willing to endure greater sacrifices and to give up more of their self-interest for the sake of others. But perhaps this is not the best way of thinking about it. For people with a prosocial orientation, helping others may be a satisfying activity, so that it is not simply a question of self-interest versus others' interest. After all, when they help, they act according to their ideals, and therefore are maintaining a positive self-image. Unfortunately, sometimes the satisfaction inherent in helping behavior and in its end results may not be salient, because of the interference of conditions that lead to self-concern. When such interfering conditions do not exist (or are eliminated), satisfaction may be anticipated and experienced. It would be desirable to explore the extent to which helping behavior or its beneficial outcome for others produces satisfaction.

A. Ethical and Methodological Issues. There are several ethical and methodological issues with regard to our own research and to this type of research generally. In the first set of experiments, we conducted research "in the field." To do so seems important because suspicion and demand characteristics may affect the behavior of subjects in the laboratory, and thus lifelike conditions and experiences are difficult to create there. However, a variety of problems exist in field research as well. First, the people who are involved are not only being deceived but have not even agreed to partake in interaction with the experimenter, as do laboratory subjects. Subjects in our research did not seem to be upset by this. However, we do not know how people who did not stop, and others who made the requested phone call and did not return, felt about the experience.

A question of some importance is the effect of participation in our research on future behavior. Will participants be less helpful because they were deceived, and because their help was in vain? Or will they be more helpful because through our experiments and in the course of extensive discussion with the experimenter (particularly in laboratory experiments) they become more aware of the need to help? Unfortunately, we have no ready answer. It is of interest, however, that in one of our experiments with a high frequency of helping behavior, in 70% of the experimental units (one-, two-, or three-person groups) at least one subject gave as a reason for his behavior that he had heard about people often not helping when they ought to, and did not want to "be like that" (Staub & Clawson). If such knowledge was a genuine influence on behavior, perhaps psychological research can have an educative influence.

B. Implications for Developmental Psychology. Our research findings about the social and personality determinants of helping behavior also have implications for developmental psychology. If one is concerned with how a tendency for acting prosocially develops among children it may be helpful to consider what determines prosocial behavior, and what personal characteristics, including orientation toward situations, would children have to acquire in order to act prosocially. For example, our findings with seventh-grade subjects (as well as adults) and our general reasoning suggested that often there is a conflict between the desire to help and the desire to act "appropriately." To increase helping behavior, we may reduce the conflict by letting a child know that under certain circumstances it is permissible to engage in certain behaviors which may otherwise be proscribed. More specifically, we may teach him that the need to help others often supersedes other obligations.

We conducted an experiment designed in part to do this (Staub & Buswell, unpublished data). It provided the hoped-for result but in an unexpected fashion. In one experimental group, one child (the subject) was working on a task, while another child (a confederate) played with games in the same room. Sometimes the confederate needed help: to reach something high up on a shelf, or because she had fallen off a chair, or for some other reason. Using a buzzer as a signal, we tried to teach our subjects that under some circumstances, when another person needs help, they should interrupt whatever they are doing in order to provide help.

The confederates were children from the same population as the subjects. The experimenter took them to the experimental room before the subject had arrived, and trained them to perform the different behaviors in response to cue cards. They performed these activities after the subject joined them in the room. Either a day or a week after training, we evaluated both children's helping and sharing behavior, testing the confederates also for the sake of completeness. The confederates helped more than subjects in the experimental group (and more than subjects in three other experimental groups). A number of them spontaneously verbalized a principle that they learned in the experiment – that one ought to help others, or something similar.

Our hypothesis about why the confederates learned but not the subjects may be briefly stated. Being directly instructed in prosocial behavior may arouse tension (as a result of being the object or target of instruction), and because social norms make helping behavior obligatory it is also likely to arouse psychological reactance (Brehm, 1966), a desire to maintain one's freedom of action; both may reduce learning. On the other hand, acting as a collaborator of an experimenter in teaching others, the child is in a position of responsibility, which probably enhances his self-esteem. For this reason (and perhaps others – the child has responsibilities just as he does when he helps someone), it may enhance the acceptance by the child of the material taught (see Staub, 1973).

As we suggested earlier, a belief that people in need ought to be helped, whether an internalized belief or simply knowledge of a social norm, if it exists at all, probably exists in the form of a differentiated set of beliefs about the conditions under which one is or is not obliged to help others. In Rokeach's (1969) terms, there may be attitudes toward the object (a person in need, in this case), as well as toward situations in which the object is found. It seems important to shape attitudes toward situations also, not only toward persons in need, to teach the relative importance of norms referring to different situations, if one is to foster a generalized tendency toward helping others.

Another important factor in the development of a tendency to act prosocially may be learning to assume responsibility for the welfare of others. In our earlier discussion we suggested that responsibility for help may be diffused in nature, and that certain conditions may focus responsibility on a specific individual. Feelings of personal responsibility may also be a characteristic of a person (Schwartz & Clausen, 1970) and affect his behavior in many situations.

One way to develop or increase such feelings of personal responsibility might be to focus responsibility on children to engage in behavior that will enhance another's welfare. Over a period of time this may lead to learning that others expect that one will help a person in need, that others regard it as one's obligation, and it may even become an internalized standard. In one of our experiments (Staub, 1970b), children were left "in charge" by the experimenter, were told to "take care of things," and subsequently heard distress sounds. This increased first graders' attempts to help. Kindergarten children, who may not have felt competent to help, tended to deny that they heard distress sounds more than control subjects who did not have responsibility for helping focused on them, presumably because they feared disapproval for not helping. By frequently or regularly assigning children responsibility to help others and having them actually exercise their responsibility, they may develop a feeling of personal responsibility for others' welfare (Staub, 1973).

References

Aderman, D., & Berkowitz, L. Observational set, empathy, and helping. *Journal of Personality and Social Psychology*, 1970, *14*, 141–168.

Almond, G. A., & Verba, S. *The civic culture*. Princeton: Princeton University Press, 1963.

Aronfreed, J. The socialization of altruistic and sympathetic behavior: Some theoretical and experimental analyses. In J. Macaulay & L. Berkowitz (Eds.), *Altruism and helping behavior*. New York: Academic Press, 1970.

Asch, S. E. Opinions and social pressure. *Scientific American*, November 1955.

Berkowitz, L. The self, selfishness and altruism. In J. Macaulay and L. Berkowitz (Eds.), *Altruism and helping behavior*. New York: Academic Press, 1970.

Berkowitz, L. Social norms, feelings, and other factors affecting helping behavior and altruism. *Advances in Experimental Social Psychology*, 1972, *6*, 63–108.

Berkowitz, L., & Daniels, L. Responsibility and dependency. *Journal of Abnormal and Social Psychology*, 1963, *66*, 429–436.

Brehm, J. W. *A theory of psychological reactance*. New York: Academic Press, 1966.

Brown, R. *Social psychology*. New York: Free Press, 1965.

Bryan, J. H. Children's reactions to helpers: their money isn't where their mouths are. In J. Macaulay & L. Berkowitz (Eds.), *Altruism and helping behavior*. New York: Academic Press, 1970.

Bryan, J. H., & Test, M. A. Models and helping: Naturalistic studies in aiding behavior. *Journal of Personality and Social Psychology*, 1967, *6*, 400–407.

Clark, R. D., & Word, L. E. Why don't bystanders help? Because of ambiguity? *Journal of Personality and Social Psychology*, 1972, *24*, 392–401.

Durkheim, E. *Moral education*. New York: Free Press, 1961.

Feshbach, N. D., & Feshbach, S. The relationship between empathy and aggression in two age groups. *Developmental Psychology*, 1969, *1*, 102–107.

Festinger, L. A theory of social comparison processes. *Human Relations*, 1954, *7*, 117–140.

Gergen, K. J. *The psychology of behavior exchange*. Reading, MA.: Addison-Wesley, 1968.

Gouldner, A. The norm of reciprocity: A preliminary statement. *American Sociological Review*, 1960, *25*, 161–178.

Hartshorne, H., & May, M. A. *Studies in the nature of character*. Vol. 1. *Studies in deceit*. New York: Macmillan, 1928.

Hoffman, M. Moral development. In P. Mussen (Ed.), *Carmichael's manual of child development*. New York: Wiley, 1970.
Hollander, E., & Willis, R. Some issues in the psychology of conformity and nonconformity. *Psychological Bulletin*, 1967, *74*, 62–76.
Isen, A. M. Success, failure, and reaction to others: The warm glow of success. *Journal of Personality and Social Psychology*, 1970, *15*, 249–301.
Isen, A. M., & Levin, P. F. Effect of feeling good on helping: Cookies and kindness. *Journal of Personality and Social Psychology*, 1972, *21*, 384–388.
Jones, E. E., & Nisbett, R. E. *The actor and the observer: Divergent perceptions of the causes of behavior*. New York: General Learning Press, 1971.
Kiesler, C., & Kiesler, S. *Conformity*. Reading, MA: Addison-Wesley, 1970.
Korte, C. Group effects on help-giving in an emergency. *Proceedings of the 77th Annual Convention of the American Psychological Association*, 1969, *4*, 383–384.
Krebs, D. L. Empathically-experienced affect and altruism. Unpublished doctoral dissertation, Harvard University, 1970.
Latané, B., & Darley, J. M. *The unresponsive bystander: Why doesn't he help*? New York: Appleton, 1970.
Liebert, R. M., & Poulos. R. W. Eliciting the "norm of giving": Effects of modeling and presence of witness on children's sharing behavior. *Proceedings of the 79th Annual Convention of the American Psychological Association*, 1971.
London, D. The rescuers: Motivational hypothesis about Christians who saved Jews from the Nazis. In J. Macaulay and L. Berkowitz (Eds.), *Altruism and helping behavior*. New York: Academic Press, 1970.
Macaulay, J. R., and Berkowitz, L. *Altruism and helping behavior: Social psychological studies of some antecedents and consequences*. New York: Academic Press, 1970.
Milgram, S. A behavioral study of obedience. *Journal of Abnormal and Social Psychology*, 1963, *67*, 371–378.
Milgram, S. The experience of living in cities. *Science*, 1970, *167*, 1461–1468.
Mischel, W. *Personality and assessment*. New York: Wiley, 1968.
Piliavin, J. A., & Piliavin, I. M. Effect of blood on reactions to a victim. *Journal of Personality and Social Psychology*, 1972, *23*, 353–362.
Piliavin, I. M., Rodin, J., & Piliavin, J. A. Good Samaritanism: An underground phenomenon. *Journal of Personality and Social Psychology*, 1970, *13*, 289–299.
Rokeach, M. *Beliefs, attitudes and values*. San Francisco: Jossey-Bass, 1969.
Rosenthal, A. M. *Thirty-eight witnesses*. McGraw-Hill, 1964.
Schwartz, S. H. Words, deeds, and the perception of consequences and responsibility in action situations. *Journal of Personality and Social Psychology*, 1968, *10*, 232–242.
Schwartz, S. H. Moral decision making and behavior. In J. Macaulay & L. Berkowitz (Eds.), *Altruism and helping behavior*. New York: Academic Press, 1970.
Schwartz, S. H., & Clausen, G. T. Responsibility, norms and helping in an emergency. *Journal of Personality and Social Psychology*, 1970, *16*, 299–310.
Singer, J. L. (Ed.), *The control of aggression and violence*. New York: Academic Press, 1971.
Singer, J. L., & Singer, D. Personality. In P. H. Mussen & M. K. Rosenzweig (Eds.). *Annual review of psychology*. Annual Reviews, Inc.: Palo Alto, 1972.

Staub, E. A child in distress: The influence of age and number of witnesses on children's attempts to help. *Journal of Personality and Social Psychology*, 1970, *14*, 130–140 (a).
Staub, E. A child in distress: The effects of focusing responsibility on children on their attempts to help. *Developmental Psychology*, 1970, *2*, 152–154. (b)
Staub, E. The learning and unlearning of aggression: The role of anxiety, empathy, efficacy and prosocial values. In J. Singer (Ed.), *The control of aggression and violence: Cognitive and physiological factors*. New York: Academic Press, 1971.
Staub, E. Self-sacrifice for the sake of others. Review of Macaulay, J. R., & Berkowitz, L. (Eds.), Altruism and Helping Behavior: Social Psychological Studies of Some Antecedents and Consequences. *Contemporary Psychology*, 1972, *17*, 20–22. (a)
Staub, E. Instigation to goodness: The role of social norms and interpersonal influence. *Journal of Social Issues*, 1972, *28*, No. 3. (b)
Staub, E. The development of prosocial behavior in children. Andover: Warner Modular Publications, Inc. 1973.
Valins, S., & Nisbett, R. E. *Attribution processes in the development and treatment of emotional disorders*. New York: General Learning Press, 1971.

7

Spontaneous (or Impulsive) Helping

The Piliavins and their associates have proposed that "there will be (a) special circumstances that give rise to and (b) specific personality types who engage in rapid, impulsive, noncalculative irrational helping or escape behavior following observation of an emergency." (Piliavin et al., 1975, p. 430). Piliavin (1976) presented a variety of studies in which impulsive helping was supposed to take place, as defined by either average latencies of help in at least one condition of 15 seconds or less or 85% or greater frequency of help. What conditions lead to impulsive helping? Piliavin specifies four conditions that appear at least somewhat related to impulsive helping; in combination they are significantly associated with impulsive helping: (a) The victim must be visible, or there must be clear cries for help; (b) the victim must not be perceived as part of an experiment; (c) the subject must be moving or at least standing; and (d) there must have been a prior meeting between the bystander and the victim. Other conditions that lead to impulsive helping behavior are rapid onset of need and perceived time pressure for help.

Impulsive helping in Piliavin's view is high-probability and/or high-speed helping when rational calculation of costs does not take place. An example par excellence of impulsive helping is provided by Markowitz (1973, p. 75): A passerby sees a boy who is falling out of a sixth-story window, runs over, and catches him. The phenomenon of impulsive helping appears to exist. Some environmental conditions may induce impulsive helping in many people. Under other conditions, perhaps when some of the situational influences are not active and/or when costs associated with helping seem high, fewer people may engage in impulsive helping. What may the cognitive decision-making processes in impulsive helping be? Are

Reprinted from E. Staub (1978). *Positive social behavior and morality: Vol. 1. Personal and social influences*. Academic Press, from Ch. 3, pp. 114–116.

there any? There probably are, but perhaps decision making does not have to deal with the resolution of conflict. The costs involved in helping may not be considered by the actor, and self-concern may not be activated. The circumstances may arouse only prosocial motivation, and strategies of action that promote help.

Are most people impulsive helpers under the conditions specified? Are people who have a generalized tendency to be impulsive, to react fast to any kind of sudden or attention-getting stimulus, more likely to be impulsive helpers? General impulsivity may be insufficient. In one study (Staub, Erkut, & Jaquette, as described in Staub, 1974) we found that male subjects who heard sounds of discomfort and distress from an adjoining room reacted faster to the sounds if the subjects appeared impulsive on a measure administered to them earlier, but they did not necessarily help more. Subjects were earlier administered Kagan's Matching Familiar Figures Test, a measure on which they were supposed to match one figure with the only identical one of six other figures that varied only in small details. The individuals who made fast (and thus more frequently erroneous) responses on this test responded faster to the distress sounds – by interrupting their work, standing up, and so on – but they did not help more. Perhaps they would have helped more if the distress sounds had been more intense or if the victim had been visible. I would expect, however, a combination of prosocial motives and impulsiveness to be necessary for impulsive helping to occur.

In closing this brief discussion of impulsive helping, I would like to suggest that an important determinant of such helping is the lack of certain types of decision-making processes. We are likely to be dealing with a continuum, ranging from conditions (external and internal) that clearly focus responsibility on a potential helper and demand fast response of a specific kind, which lead to a short-circuiting of decisional processes, to those that evoke uncertainty, conflict, and complex affective reactions and/or decision making. Lack of an elaborate decisional process does not mean, however, that the behavior is "irrational." In fact, in addition to prosocial motivation that enables people under certain external conditions to make a rapid or instantaneous decision to help, prior experience that led to the availability to people of plans or strategies for action or enables them to speedily construct such plans probably increases the likelihood of this type of help. Consequently, *spontaneous* helping may be a better label than impulsive helping, since the latter has the connotation that the behavior is not controlled by reason.

References

Markowitz, J. A. *Walk on the crust of hell*. Brattleboro, VT: The Stephen Greene Press, 1973.

Piliavin, I. M., Piliavin, J. A., & Rodin, J. Costs, diffusion and the stigmatized victim. *Journal of Personality & Social Psychology*, 1975, *3*, 429–438.

Piliavan, J. A. Impulsive helping, arousal and diffusion of responsibility. Paper presented at the XXI International Congress of Psychology, Paris, 1976.

Staub, E. Helping a distressed person: Social, personality and stimulus determinants. In L. Berkowitz (Ed.), *Advances in experimental social psychology*, Vol. 7. New York: Academic Press, 1974.

8

Social and Prosocial Behavior

Personal and Situational Influences and Their Interactions

As I crossed Harvard Square one day, I noticed a young woman waving her arms and shouting in the middle of the street. She was standing in front of a car, demanding that the driver run her over. Just before I reached her, a policeman appeared and escorted her to the sidewalk. She sobbed, said that she did not want to live, that life is miserable. A local professor-type tried to take her into the restaurant that we happened to be standing in front of, offering her a cup of coffee, presumably wanting to give her a chance to calm down. I was trying to talk to the policeman – who began to disentangle himself from this scene, busily giving information to a driver who stopped near us – telling him that we need to take some action, that the woman needs psychiatric attention. The woman suddenly turned, walked away and disappeared around the bend of the street. An older man and I started to walk after her. Not wanting to seem to chase her, we did not run; and by the time we turned the bend, she was nowhere to be seen. I looked into a couple of stores and a restaurant further down the street, but could not see her.

What happened to this young woman that led to her actions? How would other people, with different personal characteristics, have reacted to the same experiences? What influences guided her behavior and the behavior of those of us who responded to her, however ineffectively?

A major goal of psychology has always been to study and come to understand human behavior. In this chapter, I am concerned with two large questions. First, what determines the way people behave toward each

The dissertations described in this chapter, and my own research since 1973, as well as the preparation of this chapter, were facilitated by Grant MH 23886 from the National Institutes of Mental Health. Reprinted from E. Staub (1980). *Social and prosocial behavior: Personal and situational influences and their interactions*. In E. Staub (Ed.), *Personality: Basic aspects and current research*. Prentice-Hall, from Ch. 6, pp. 237–294. Reprinted by permission of Pearson Education, Inc., Upper Saddle River, N.J.

other; what influences guide their social behavior? Second, what influences guide *positive* interactions among human beings? Can we understand why people do or do not behave toward each other in a positive fashion – why they do or do not help each other, share with each other, show sensitivity and kindness to each other? Can we predict the occurrence of such behavior?

These two questions are related. In order to understand positive social behavior, we have to consider how social behavior in general is determined. Frequently, people face conflicts between benefiting others and engaging in behavior that promotes their own interests. They may want to reach a high level of achievement in some activity, gain social approval, enjoy others' company, or enrich themselves. What determines how they resolve their conflict and how they act? In this chapter I will attempt to develop a conception of how social behavior is determined, while focusing on the more specific question, examining influences on positive social behavior. Some of the same principles are likely to account for how varied social behaviors are determined, although specific types of behaviors will also have special or unique influences on them.

By positive social behavior I refer to actions that benefit other people. Usually, such behavior demands some form of self-sacrifice. Helping, sharing, cooperation, sensitivity, and responsiveness to other people can all be considered positive acts. In order for an act to be positive behavior, it has to be voluntary and intended to benefit another person. However, the reasons or motives for intending to benefit others can vary. Concern with others' welfare and the desire to enhance their welfare may be one reason. Personal values and norms may be the source of such concern, or the source may be an affective involvement with others and the experience of empathy. The reason for positive acts may also be the desire for social approval or the avoidance of social disapproval, or the desire for other forms of self-gain, including the hope of material rewards that a person can gain by inducing other people to reciprocate their kindness or generosity. In cooperative activities, a person can benefit himself or herself while benefiting others.

A person's tendency to behave positively is important even if the positive behavior intends to gain benefit for the actor. After all, attempting to further the interest of the self through positive acts, in contrast to aggressive, harmful acts, promotes everyone's welfare. The philosopher Hume suggested that human beings are capable of learning through their experience in social living to promote their self-interest in an enlightened fashion, by considering the interrelationship between their own and others' interests. Some current theories and research seem in agreement with this conception. For example, exchange theories assume that social systems and personal relations are guided by exchange relationships, in which people exchange goods and services, and engage in a give-and-take that is mutually beneficial (Chadwick-Jones, 1976; Homans, 1961; Staub, 1972, 1978; Thibaut & Kelley, 1959).

A number of years ago I talked to a Carnegie Hero, someone who received a medal from the Carnegie Hero Foundation for having endangered his life in the course of saving someone else's life. This happened ten days after his combined gallbladder and appendectomy operations, on his first day out of the house. He went to the beach with his girlfriend. Hearing the cries of a drowning woman, he jumped into the water, swam to her, and pulled her toward the shore, keeping her afloat until a rescue boat arrived. When pulled from the water, he himself was in a state of collapse.

Many questions can be asked that highlight our inquiry. What motivated him to act? Why was it he, a man still recovering from surgery, rather than others on the crowded beach? Would he help people in other ways too? Would he give money to a needy person, or try to console someone who is sad or upset? Is he usually kind and generous with his friends and acquaintances? Is it reasonable for us to expect that he would be helpful in any of these ways? What do we have to know about him to predict whether he will behave positively in these ways and/or whether he will show consistency in positive behavior?

To state these issues in a general way, to what extent are people consistent in their behavior? Can people be characterized by tendencies to behave one way or another? Is it possible to gather information about people that enables us to predict how they will behave on specific occasions? Can we develop a theoretical model to make such predictions? What do we have to know about people, about their environment, and about the relationship between individual characteristics and environments to understand (and predict) social behavior?

The purpose of this chapter is to examine these and related questions and to describe a conceptualization, or theoretical model, for understanding and predicting (positive) social behavior. Research findings about influences on positive social behavior are too extensive to review here in detail. Instead, generalizations derived from the research findings will be presented, based on this author's recent elaborate reviews of this literature (Staub, 1978, 1979). Some examples of the research on which these generalizations are based will be presented. Research that is specifically relevant to the theoretical model will be reviewed.

SITUATIONAL AND PERSONAL INFLUENCES

When will the external environment or situation exert primary influence on behavior? While situations exert influence, they do so as a function of their meaning to people, of the thoughts and feelings they give rise to, and of the motives they arouse. It is people, not situations, who act. Under certain circumstances most people may act similarly because the situation activates very basic common goals or needs. Sometimes, such goals or needs may be common to most of humanity, such as the desire for survival, perhaps aroused by a wild animal, or by a fire, or by someone with a gun. When someone pulls a gun on us and demands our money, most of us will hand it over. Other times, communality among people in basic goals or needs, and the manner in which they try to satisfy goals, will be a function of similarity in socialization and of norms and rules that guide social behavior in particular cultures. For example, the desire for respect by one's peers may be strongly inculcated in one culture and less so in another. The ways to gain respect may also vary. Usually, circumstances do not exert such a powerful influence that most people who face them would behave in a similar way. Particularly in a culture like ours, in which great variability in values and motives exists across subcultures and individual families, there will be variations among people in how they interpret and react to most situations.

People not only respond to events, but seek them out and create opportunities for varied kinds of conduct. Here, personal – in contrast to environmental – influences are even more important. Obviously, some people like to go to the movies, and frequently do so, while others who like football may spend endless hours in the stadium or in front of the television set. People also shape their environment, and the circumstances they create will in turn influence their own behavior. For example, Kelley and Stahleski (1970) found that some subjects believed that people in general are competitive rather than cooperative, and these subjects behaved competitively from the start in a prisoner's dilemma game. This resulted in competitive reactions by their partners. By their own behavior, they apparently brought about the competitive behavior they expected, which then confirmed their original belief and further affected their behavior. Cross-cultural research with children showed cultural differences in degree of competitiveness, and showed that patterns of interaction develop within particular pairs that affect the continued interaction of the pair even more than cultural origin or other conditions. Some children act so competitively that they provoke competition in even potentially cooperative partners (Toda, Shinotsuka, McClintock, & Stech, 1978). A substantial body of research shows reciprocity in human interactions: by what we do, we shape others' reactions to us (Staub, 1978). Our relationship to the world is usually transactional. We continuously shape our environment. The influence of the environment, whether we ourselves shaped it or not, in turn interacts with our characteristics in affecting our further conduct.

THE MEANING AND NATURE OF INTERACTION

The controversy about the relative influence of persons and situations on behavior led to renewed interest in their interaction. The concept of interaction has a long history (Ekehammar, 1974). Magnusson and Endler (1977) presented a recent view of interactionist approaches. In this view, "persons and situations are regarded as indispensibly linked to one another.... Neither the person factors nor the situation factors per se determine behavior in isolation; it is determined by inseparable person by situation interactions" (Magnusson & Endler, 1977, p. 4). This view is consistent with my own, implying that a major concern we must have is not the relative influence of persons versus situations – to what *degree* it is the characteristics of the person and to what *degree* it is the situation that determines behavior. Instead, we must be concerned with how personal characteristics and situations *join*. What will result from particular personality environment combinations, and why?

In spite of the long history of the interaction concept, most personality research employed a single measure of some personal characteristic and correlated it with behavior in a specific instance. Interactions were usually not tested. When situation-personality interactions were tested, researchers usually explored the influence of a single personality characteristic in conjunction with limited situational variation. For example, one study explored how persons who vary in their feeling of responsibility for others' welfare are affected by the number of people who are present when someone needs help – a variation in one personal characteristic and one aspect of the environment each. Generally, the presence of a greater number of people allows the diffusion of responsibility for others' welfare, and results in less help. People with a stronger sense of personal responsibility were less affected by such variation in the number of bystanders (Schwartz & Clausen, 1970).

Perhaps the limited influence of interactionist approaches on empirical research may partly be explained by the theoretical nature of "classical" interactionism (Ekehammar, 1974). However, theoretical notions have been proposed that may be useful in understanding the manner in which personal characteristics and environments relate to each other in guiding perception, thought, affect, and behavior. Murray (1938) described personal needs and environmental presses that are relevant to these needs and would activate them. Lewin (1938, 1948), who was perhaps the most powerful advocate of behavior being a joint function of persons and their environments, suggested the importance of goals, and of valences or forces within persons that move them toward relevant environmental "regions" where the goals may be satisfied.

If the current, more research-oriented interactionist approaches are to be fruitful and ultimately successful, several conditions must be fulfilled. It is certainly not a single characteristic of a person that guides his or her actions on any one occasion, that determines how he or she reacts to circumstances. We need to specify the classes of personality characteristics and situations that we regard important in determining particular types of behavior. We need to consider interrelationships among personal characteristics, and their joint influence. Situations not only activate relevant characteristics, but must affect their relationships. That is, the organization of personality characteristics is not static; it is dynamic, changing, active (Carlson, 1971, chap. 1). Further, we have to specify the psychological processes that are aroused by varied situations, as a function of personal characteristics. Situations give rise to meanings; they activate personal values, norms and beliefs, empathic reactions toward other persons, and other thoughts and affects. We have to provide a theoretical model that will specify the interrelationships among personal characteristics, situations, the psychological processes that result, and behavior. Finally, we have to develop elaborate measures of both persons and situations. Without their proper measurement, no theoretical model can be tested.

A THEORETICAL MODEL FOR PREDICTING PROSOCIAL BEHAVIOR

A Brief Outline of the Theory

In this section I will discuss each component of the theory in some detail. To provide a coherent picture, I will start with a brief outline. The theory presumes that people are purposeful organisms who develop varied motivations, which will be called *personal goals*, in the course of their growth and development. Personal goals can be activated by characteristics of the environment, either the external environment or a person's internal environment, his thoughts or imagination. The environment can be described in terms of its activating potential for particular personal goals. Depending on the activating potential of the environment and on the extent that a person possesses various personal goals, an environment may activate no goal, or one, two, or more goals. When two or more goals are activated, they may conflict with each other, when their satisfaction cannot be pursued by the same course of action. Alternatively, one of the goals may be dominant; or the goals may join with each other, when a particular course of action can lead to the satisfaction of all of them. Sometimes, helping another person can satisfy a prosocial goal, an approval goal – since helping others is a socially valued activity that often leads to approval and praise by other people – and even an achievement goal, since, in the course of helping, a person can show skill, competence, or excellence. When two or more goals conflict with each other, action may be inhibited, or the conflict may be resolved. Whether a goal is activated or not, and whether an activated goal will be pursued in action, depends also on personal characteristics other than goals. Perceptual tendencies – which include the speed of defining events and role taking, the capacity of viewing events from others' points of view – can affect the interpretations of events.

Varied types of competencies may affect the likelihood that a person will take action. Lack of competence may also interfere with the activation of goals.

Personal Goals

There has been a long history in psychology of concern with and emphasis on motivational constructs in attempting both to understand why people behave as they do and to predict how they will behave. The names of constructs have varied: *drive, need, reinforcement, reward value,* and other terms have been used. The purported properties of these constructs have also varied.

Long ago, McDougall (1908) suggested that people's behavior can be best understood by the goals they pursue – in contrast, for example, to the means by which they pursue their goals. Other writers echoed this belief (Murray, 1938; Lewin, 1938, 1948). Why have many writers stressed needs, or goals, as primary influences on human behavior? In addition to those cited, motivational constructs are included in many writers' theories of human behavior. For example, both Rotter (1954) and Mischel (1966) stressed the subjective value of outcomes as important determinants of behavior: people are inclined to move toward outcomes that are valued by them. Others have stressed the importance of specific motives such as need for approval, need for achievement, or need for affiliation.

A primary characteristic of human beings seems to be their purposefulness. We do not go about the world in a random fashion; nor do we simply follow rules all the time. Our adherence to rules itself probably, to a large extent, depends on our motives. While the nature of motivation that characterizes the social behavior of specific human beings varies across cultures, varies as a function of socialization in specific families and personal experiences in life, and perhaps varies due to heredity, the existence of motivation seems universal. Anthropologists and psychologists have found, for example, that cultures differ in the extent to which they lead members to be cooperative, competitive, or individualistic in their interactions with each other (Mead, 1937). In some cultures, people come to prefer to bring about mutual gain, to interact with others in a cooperative fashion. In other cultures, members come to prefer competition, to enhance their own gain in comparison to the gains of others, to increase their relative advantage over others. In either case, motivation exists, but its nature is different.

I assume that personal goals, the construct I will use to denote motivation, exert strong influence in directing our behavior, and that many other personality characteristics that need to be considered are primarily important in determining whether personal goals are activated and/or whether their satisfaction is pursued or not. The word *goal* implies a preference for certain outcomes or end states, or an aversion for certain outcomes and the desire to avoid them. It also implies a striving toward or away from these outcomes. The word *personal* refers to the fact that different people have different goals, and that the organization of goals within persons – their relative importance – varies. The same goal may be high in one person's hierarchy of goals and low in another's. Further, each person's goals have a special individual character, partly because of differences in cognitive elaboration and ranges of applicability (see below). Nonetheless, there is likely to be enough similarity among goals of different individuals that people can be grouped on the basis of communality in goals.

While people appear idiosyncratic in the outcomes they value (Mischel, 1973; Mischel & Mischel, 1976), for each individual there is probably a range of similar-valued outcomes. Certainly, all past conceptions of motives imply classes of outcomes that can reduce or satisfy a motivated state, or outcomes at which motivated behavior aims. Research findings on need approval (Crowne & Marlowe, 1964), and on other motives, provides some support. People with a strong need for approval desire and/or seek varied forms of approval, and are concerned about and want to avoid disapproval by people in general. With regard to outcomes related to a prosocial goal, minimally, a person who values diminishing others' physical pain is likely to hold this value with varied sources of pain. Certain classes of outcomes are likely to be valued by many people who grow up and live in a particular culture. Most people in our culture probably value, to varied degrees, positive evaluation and approval (and want to avoid negative evaluation and disapproval – the latter might be regarded as a negative goal), physical safety, and material welfare, among other goals.

Internalized values, norms, beliefs, and the tendency to react empathically to others' needs can all increase the value or desirability of benefiting other people, and thus contribute to a prosocial goal. Depending on the nature of the values, the extent to which empathy is involved, and so on, the specific character of the goal may differ. For some people, the desired outcome might be to improve others' welfare; for others, acting in a helpful manner might itself be the desired outcome. However, neither the component values and norms nor the exact nature of the desired outcomes which enter into defining goals have a piecemeal character. In order to qualify as a motivational orientation that is represented by the term *personal goal*, they have to combine into some kind of organized whole. In the case of prosocial goals, this organized whole may have the form of broad value orientations.

Variation in the nature of personal goals is likely to be found in most domains, not only the prosocial one. Some individuals who are characterized by a strong achievement goal may want to do well in comparison to some standard of excellence when their goal is activated; others may want to experience success; and so on. Regardless of their exact quality, when such achievement goals are activated, they may all gain expression in hard work and attempts to do well in varied activities.

I am implying that a family of personal goals of a particular kind may exist. However, the primary members of the family may be few. In the case of prosocial goals, two types of value orientations may give rise to two primary prosocial goals; and even those two can frequently be related to each other, or occur together. One value orientation I will call *prosocial orientation*; it emphasizes concern about the welfare of other human beings. I will discuss this in greater detail below. Another value orientation focuses on *duty and obligation* toward other human beings, on societal rules and/or abstract moral principles that prescribe positive behavior, rather than on the persons themselves who are to be helped. As I noted elsewhere (Staub, 1978, 1979), persons who are characterized by a prosocial orientation are likely to perceive, interpret, and think about events in a manner that gives rise to feelings of empathy. Thus, in the case of most people, the capacity for empathy, for vicariously experiencing others' feelings, is coded in the form of a value orientation. The arousal of empathy can, in turn, motivate prosocial acts.

Defining Characteristics of Goals. Personal goals are likely to have a number of defining characteristics. One I already noted is the desirability of certain outcomes. Another is a network of cognitions that is usually associated with a goal. It does happen, of course, that the inclination to reach some goal – or the desire to avoid an outcome, a negative goal – is primarily emotional, that a person has few conscious thoughts, beliefs, or values that are associated with the goal. Phobic reactions are not regarded as based on reason, as the result of thinking and evaluation.[1] The tendency to react with empathy or sympathy to another's fate can also be primarily a "gut reaction." Usually, however, we have varied thoughts, beliefs, and values associated with outcomes that are desirable (or aversive) to us. These cognitions function, in part, to tune us perceptually to the kind of circumstances that make it possible to satisfy our goal. They are also applied to the interpretation of situations. The manner in which events, situations, or outcomes are interpreted is likely, in turn, to determine our

[1] This is a debatable issue, however. While phobic individuals frequently say "I know that this (the object the person is afraid of) is not dangerous," they sometimes hold beliefs that can understandably give rise to strong fear. It is possible to argue that at some level they must evaluate the object of their fear as dangerous or terrifying, or, depending on one's theory, they use the object as a symbol for something that is terrifying to them. Providing people with information can, in fact, reduce fear and even the experience of pain produced by electric shocks (Staub & Kellett, 1972).

emotional reactions to them. This view is consistent with current cognitive theories of emotion (Arnold, 1960; Lazarus, 1966; Leventhal, 1974; Stotland, 1969). Thus, the cognitive network presumably leads to interpretations that give rise to emotions, which make the goal desirable and motivate attempts to reach the goal. Over time, many circumstances may acquire well-developed meanings and give rise to strong emotions without much cognitive elaboration. Seeing a child standing in the path of an onrushing car will give rise to strong emotion, in most people, with little or no thinking about or processing of the meaning of the event.

Personal goals can lead to experiences that help people learn to perceive the relevance of events to their goals. If our Carnegie Hero possessed a prosocial goal, the range of applicability of which extended to people in physical distress or at risk, he may have had past experience in responding to cries for help. In the course of his experience, he may have come to take such cries of distress seriously. He may have come to believe that when people call for help they are in trouble. One reason for his responding before others did may have been that he did not need to think about the meaning of those calls for help to decide whether or not they were serious. If so, he did not need to engage in cognitive work to determine the meaning of the event, and thus could respond faster.

A third related characteristic of personal goals is the arousal of tension upon the activation of the goal, which continues to exist until either the goal has been reached or it has been deactivated in some manner. The notion that tension is aroused and maintained by the activation of a goal has been proposed by Lewin (1948; see also Deutsch, 1968) and currently extended to the realm of prosocial behavior by Hornstein (1976). The limited evidence that is available about tension systems and their properties supports the concept. An example is the well-known Zeigarnik (1927) effect. Consistent with Lewinian assumptions, Zeigarnik found that interrupted tasks are remembered better than completed ones. Tasks that are interrupted nearer their completion – nearer to reaching the outcome – are remembered better than tasks interrupted further from completion (Deutsch, 1968). The latter finding provides support for another Lewinian concept, that of a goal gradient.

The concept of personal goal implies some generality of the motivation, a class of outcomes that are valued, rather than a single outcome.[2] Still,

[2] Although personal goals usually point to classes of outcomes, seemingly it can happen that a single end satisfies a personal goal. Consider, for example, that a major personal goal for someone may be finding and experiencing love. This person may focus his or her energies on satisfying this goal. Let's assume that he or she encounters someone who perfectly satisfies the goal, for a lengthy period of time. What happens to a goal once so fulfilled (whether by a single outcome, or by repeated experiences or cumulatively, e.g., when someone whose goal is wealth feels sufficiently wealthy)? Presumably, it will be replaced by others in a

among people with similar personal goals – such as the goal of benefiting other people – the *range of applicability* of goals can vary. Some people might have learned to apply their concern about others' welfare at times when another person was in physical need but not in psychological distress; others might have learned to apply such concern only to people of certain kinds, perhaps people whom they think of as similar to themselves or as coming from the same ethnic or racial background. Thus, the personal goal that motivates prosocial action might have different specific ranges of applicability. The range can be relatively narrow, or it can be broad, applicable to varied circumstances, varied needs. We have to develop devices to measure not only the existence of various personal goals and their intensity, but also the specific ranges in which they are applicable, and their breadth or narrowness.

Further specification of the range of applicability of goals is also possible. We can specify domains to which each goal is *likely* to be applied. The desire for excellence, as it is embodied in achievement goals, may be applied to intellectual activities, to a person's work and/or profession, to interpersonal interactions, to sports, or to several of these domains. In Feinberg's (1977) study, for example, which will be described later in detail, high-achievement women applied themselves to consoling, advising, and generally extensively talking to another (distressed) female. With regard to prosocial goals, domains of applications may be divided into physical distress and psychological distress, or into family and friends versus others – the latter further subdivided into potential ingroups and outgroups (people with the same or different religion, race, etc.).

The range of applicability of a prosocial goal can also be affected by specific values and norms that people ascribe to, which qualify or further define the general goal. A prosocial orientation implies concern about other people's welfare; still, people with a strong prosocial orientation may differ in the importance of the value of equity (people should receive benefits as a function of their inputs or accomplishments) and equality (people should receive benefits equally) to them. Those who value equity more may apply their prosocial orientation less to people who they feel are less deserving – on the basis of their characteristics, or due to lack of effort, or to some prior wrongdoing. People who value equality, in contrast to equity, may discriminate less in the application of their prosocial goals as a function of deserving. People who believe that the world is a just place where people get what they deserve (Lerner & Simmons, 1966) may sometimes not react to others' suffering, believing (or rationalizing) that, since the world is just, the suffering must be deserved (Rubin & Peplau, 1973; Staub, 1978).

person's hierarchy of goals. The goal would not be an activated state, and would not be pursued in action.

Would any outcome that a person tries to reach be an expression of a personal goal? Presumably not. Some outcomes or end states may reflect a temporary desire evoked by particular conditions, neither recurrent nor of a class of outcomes valued by the person, nor an expression of the person's cognitive network. Such desires would best not be considered examples of personal goals.

The Activating Potential of Situations and Goal Conflict

Every person has varied goals, which can be arranged in a hierarchy according to their importance to the person. These goals, as described so far, represent potentials. At any one time, the desire for a certain outcome or end state, which is the primary defining component of the goal, may be dormant. Alternatively, goals may be in an activated state. Sometimes, thoughts, images, or internal stimuli can activate a goal; at other times, aspects of the environment can activate it.

In a particular situation, varied motives or personal goals may be aroused in a person. Sometimes when a person is faced with another's need for help, that is the only force acting on him or her: given some degree of motivation to be helpful, the person will act. At other times, a person might be faced with a situation which potentially activates a variety of motives: to be helpful, to achieve well on some task, to affiliate with other people, to pursue adventure, or to behave in proper social ways. Whether such goals are activated will depend on the nature of the situation and on its activating potential, as well as on the characteristics of the person and the degree to which the person possesses the personal goals that might be activated by the situation. For example, someone might be working on a task, or might be simply sitting in a room waiting. Somebody in another room seems to be in distress. If it is important for this person to both do well on tasks and to help other people, he will experience conflict when he is working on the task. His two goals conflict with each other. This will not happen when he is simply waiting, because then his goal of achievement will not be activated. Neither will this happen if doing well on tasks is unimportant to him.

What is the utility of the conception of personal goals and activating potentials? Their utility lies in the recognition that, frequently, circumstances activate varied personal goals. If we are to understand how prosocial behavior in particular and social behavior in general are determined, we have to consider the joint influence of varied motives. Different goals may sometimes conflict, and may sometimes join and support each other. The goal to achieve may lead a person to work hard on a task and diminish helping; or it may be applied to helping someone in need, adding to the influence of a prosocial goal. Using motivational constructs that apply to varied motives and classes of outcomes can improve our ability to understand and predict social behavior. For this to happen, we will have to be able to measure personal goals, ranges of applicability, and the activating potentials of situations.

A retrospective analysis of an extreme form of helpful behavior can provide an example of how personal goals affect helping, and of the match that is required between personality and the situation for help to occur (Staub & Feinberg, 1980). This example draws on a report by London (1970). He concluded, on the basis of extensive interviews with "rescuers" – people who were involved in an underground system of saving Jews and other persecuted individuals in Nazi Germany – that they had three characteristics in common. These were: a strong conscious identification with moral parents; adventurousness; and a sense of marginality in relation to the community. Presumably, strong moral identification led to personal values promoting helpful behavior, thus to the motivation to help. The costs of helping in this situation were potentially extremely high – with the loss of life likely and the loss of liberty certain – if discovered. A sense of adventurousness, gaining satisfaction from dangerous activities and perceiving them as exciting, which apparently led these individuals to also participate in other dangerous activities in the course of their lives, seems important. This characteristic might have not only have enhanced the likelihood that they would carry out their prosocial goal, but might be thought of as an additional goal that could be satisfied by helping. Marginality might have helped rescuers in not accepting the definition of their environment of the persecution of Jews and others, a definition which would have minimized the perception of the need or the justification for involvement.

The study of conflicts among goals that are activated in specific situations has been surprisingly neglected. While psychoanalytically oriented writers, and Dollard and Miller (1950), in translating psychoanalytic concepts into a behavioral framework, clearly recognized the importance of goal conflict, even they stressed the role of conflict between approach and avoidance tendencies toward a single goal. Frequently, multiple goals are activated by circumstances; and the manner in which one or another comes to predominate, or the extent to which they mutually inhibit (or sometimes promote) each other, needs to be considered.

What determines which personal goal in a particular situation will exert dominant influence on behavior? The strength of intensity of an activated personal goal must be a joint function of the strength or importance of the personal goal to the individual and the strength of the activation potential of the environment for that goal. As an initial assumption, I will suggest that the intensity of the activated goal will be a function of the multiplicative relationship between intensity of the personal goal and the activating potential. The greatest sum that results from this multiplication will determine which activated goal will be dominant and will influence behavior. When the intensity of two or more activated goals is nearly identical, action required to pursue any of them may be inhibited, and/or various processes may be involved in conflict resolution. One of these, justification processes, will be discussed below.

The Nature of Prosocial Goals and the Measurement of Goals

How can personal goals be measured? One possibility is to ask people to rank order their goals, similar to Rokeach's (1973) method for rank ordering values. Values and goals are quite similar concepts, in fact, in that values also imply the desirability of certain outcomes. Rokeach presents people with two lists of 18 values. They are asked to rank order each in their order of importance for them. The rank ordering has reasonable stability over time intervals of a year and a half. In measuring personal goals in a similar manner, we must recognize that the hierarchy of personal goals may not only change over time, but may vary over the circumstances of a person's life. For example, such a hierarchy may be different for students during the academic year and during their vacation.

A second index of personal goals can be the cognitive network associated with them. With regard to prosocial goals, varied research findings suggest to me that the important aspects of the cognitive network of a prosocial goal of some generality and breadth are: a) positive orientation toward other people – positive evaluation of human beings; b) concern about – value placed on – others' welfare; and c) a feeling of personal responsibility for others' welfare. These three dimensions are interrelated. Clearly, these are dimensions of both thought and affect: they will be regarded here as cognitive dimensions, which represent a cognitive network, since even when we collect information about affects, we tap a person's perceptions and cognitive representations of his or her emotions. The information that we receive consists of people's cognitive representations of their beliefs, values, feelings, and desires, and of relevant portions of the world around them.

The importance of the second and third cognitive components listed above is suggested both by findings of research that explored situational influences on helping (which show that the degree of another's need or dependence affect helping, and that circumstances that focus responsibility on a person enhance helping; Bar-Tal, 1976; Rosenhan et al., 1976; Staub, 1978) and by findings of research that explored personality correlates of positive behavior (which show that people who have a sense of personal responsibility for others' welfare, or hold values or personal norms that favor helping, tend to help more; Huston and Korte, 1976; Schwartz, 1977; Staub, 1974, 1978). The first component is likely to be a basic, important, but generally neglected influence (Staub, 1976, 1978). In one study, Wrightsman (1966) found that subjects' evaluations of human nature were related to their trust and trustworthiness in a laboratory game. Christie's test of Machiavellian orientation has many items testing beliefs about human nature and human beings: scores on this test were found to be associated with helpful conduct (Staub, Erkut & Jaquette, as described in Staub, 1974; Feinberg, 1977; Grodman, 1979). A test Midlarz (1973) developed to measure trust also explored this basic orientation toward others (e.g., people's evaluation of human beings, the extent of their positive regard for them). Scores on this test were significantly related to the acceptance of another's need as real, when there were reasons to question it, and to the resulting helping behavior. Positive orientation to people is likely to be a basic element, a precondition for the other two cognitive components of the prosocial goal.

The above three central dimensions of the cognitive network are characteristic of a value orientation that I called prosocial orientation, which gives rise to one kind of prosocial goal (Staub, 1978, 1979). Earlier, I suggested that a second primary prosocial goal centers on feelings of duty and obligation – imposed by society, by principles that one has adopted or developed, or by the commandments of God. Duty or obligation is clearly related to a feeling of responsibility for others' welfare – the third cognitive component discussed above. To what extent are the two goals different, and what reason is there to believe that there are two such separable goals? Prosocial orientation is more person centered; duty orientation is based more on norms and principles. The first and second cognitive components may be less important for orientation toward duty or obligation, or may be different in quality. Consider, as an extreme, that a person feels obligation or duty to help people even if he or she assumes that people are basically selfish and untrustworthy. A person may believe on religious grounds that human beings are sinful and bad, but that it is nonetheless one's obligation to do good to others. Or a person may feel that, while people are basically unworthy, and though he has little liking for them and even fears them, the social contract demands that one helps others. The two types of prosocial goals may be regarded as distinct: people may be characterized by one or the other to varied extents, but also by some mixture of the two.

A relevant differentiation between value orientations was suggested by Hoffman (1970b). He found that children's thinking, as measured primarily by story completions, can be characterized by either an external orientation (judgments of right and wrong based on what might be punished or rewarded by people in authority) or by two different "internal" orientations. Children who have internalized certain values – who accepted them as their own, and tended to evaluate conduct not in terms of positive or negative reactions by other people but in terms of these internalized values – were regarded as having an internal orientation. One of the two internal orientations Hoffman called humanistic, the other conventional. Humanistic children seemed concerned with others' welfare and were willing to deviate from conventional rules and standards if this would benefit another person. Conventional children tended to give legal and religious bases for moral judgments and tended to ignore extenuating circumstances for wrongdoing. Moreover, they would indicate that story characters experienced guilt not so much because of harm that they actually caused to other people, but as a result of awareness of an unacceptable impulse in themselves. Hoffman's stories concerned themselves with moral judgment – the resolution of some type of moral conflict – and with reactions to having harmed someone or not having helped someone, and with transgressions of rules. They provide little direct information about thoughts and feelings about positive actions. Nonetheless, the findings are relevant to the distinction between the two types of prosocial goals. They indicate, however, that conventional children are concerned not only with acting according to societal rules (a duty or obligation type of orientation), but also with the inhibition of their impulses.

Other relevant discussion comes from Durkheim (1961), who believed that some people are concerned with promoting the "good" and are inclined to respond to others' need even if that demands a break with conventions, while other people are concerned with the maintenance of the social order.

In discussing prosocial or other goals, one cannot assume universality across cultures in any of the aspects of goals that I specified. Cultures vary in how much certain outcomes of behavior are valued. In some cultures, benefiting other people is apparently not valued – as indicated by the absence of such behavior and by the contrary behavior seemingly promoted by the culture (Benedict, 1934; Turnbull, 1972). Even if similar types of outcomes are valued in different cultures, the nature of the goal, as represented by the cognitive network associated with it, may differ. The form or circumstances of relevant conduct may, therefore, also vary. Cohen (1972) states that the idea of unselfish helpfulness (which is embodied in prosocial orientation and is an ideal in Western cultures) is alien to most social groups. It is assumed that when you do things for other people, you do it for self-gain. In hunting-and-gathering societies, for example, where cooperation and mutual help was essential and food sharing was obligatory, the person who contributed the most gained thereby the greatest power and prestige.

In different societies – and in different families, which may be regarded as small societies – the extent of cognitive elaboration of goals can vary. In some groups, the affective components – perhaps of great intensity – of goals may be directly socialized, and the network of relevant beliefs and thoughts restricted. This makes it important to include intensity measures of the desire for outcomes or end states.

A third way of establishing individual differences in personal goals, which may be done after people rank order their personal goals and provide information about their cognitive networks, is experimental. We can examine the extent to which the importance of goals, and the presence of relevant thoughts and feelings, can be affected by varying conditions of activation. That is, if a prosocial goal moves up in a person's hierarchy of goals, and/or a person's thinking shows greater evidence of the cognitions characteristic of a prosocial goal when circumstances are expected to activate the prosocial goal, that would provide further evidence for the importance of the goal for that person. We can expose people to activating conditions and then, rather than examining their behavior, provide them with opportunities to describe what they think (and how they feel).

OTHER PERSONALITY INFLUENCES

A variety of personal characteristics, in addition to personal goals, can affect social behavior, primarily by affecting the likelihood that motivation for action will be aroused, or that it will be expressed in behavior.

Perceptual Tendencies

Several perceptual tendencies can contribute to the activation of prosocial goals. The capacity for *role-taking*, which was mentioned earlier, may be an important one. Sometimes, another person's need is so obvious that no special skill or sensitivity is needed to perceive it. This is usually the case in emergencies, when suddenly the need emerges to respond to someone's physical distress or to danger to a person's life. At other times, the need is subtly expressed, and well-developed role-taking capacity is needed for perceiving it, particularly for perceiving it accurately. Role taking affects not only perception but also the manner in which what is perceived is then processed. Role taking varies in kind (perceptual, communicative, affective), and, of course, not all kinds are equally involved in the activation of prosocial goals (Staub, 1979).

The capacity to accurately perceive how another feels can certainly exist without concern about others' welfare. However, the likelihood that a person takes another's role will itself be increased by a prosocial orientation or values which increase the sensitivity to others' welfare. Providing people with different perceptual orientations – instructing them to impersonally observe another person, or to imagine what an experience might be like for him or her, or to imagine what it would be like for the observer to have that experience (imagine the self in the other's place), or to simply watch the other person – results in different degrees of physiological reactions, and in different emotional experiences and/or behavior (Stotland, 1969; Aderman & Berkowitz, 1970; Aderman et al., 1974). Prosocial values and empathic capacity may, in everyday life, lead to such differences in perceptual orientation toward others' experiences. That is, values, empathy, and role taking are likely to be related to some degree. There are, in fact, research findings which show that a positive relationship exists between certain types of role-taking capacities and level of moral reasoning (see Staub, 1978).

Another relevant perceptual-cognitive tendency is the speed of making judgments about the meaning of events in one's environment. People seem to vary in this (Denner, 1968). By suspending judgment, the opportunity for taking action may frequently pass. Role-taking is a perceptual tendency primarily relevant to prosocial goals. Other perceptual tendencies may exist that are relevant to other specific goals. The speed of making judgment can be relevant to varied goals. The opportunity to gain approval or avoid disapproval, or the possibility of taking initiative in beginning a relationship with other people, can depend on the speed of assessing circumstances and events. The speed of judging events itself appears to be related to, or be a function of, other characteristics. Denner suggests, on the basis of his discussion with subjects, that people who are slow in judging events distrust their own judgment, and perhaps also the world, in that they do not want to be taken in by the appearance of things. Self-esteem and belief in one's competence may be involved.

Competencies and the Execution of Goals

A person's competence is probably a crucial determinant of whether he or she will take action in executing personal goals. Lack of the subjective experience of competency may also inhibit the activation of personal goals.

Assume that you are walking across a deserted bridge. You see a person ahead of you who appears to begin to climb up the railing. As he notices you, he stops and remains standing there, looking at the water. You assume that he intended to jump – to commit suicide – and that he is waiting for you to pass by and disappear from sight. You believe that you ought to intervene in some fashion. Depending on how you feel about your capacity to intervene, the chances that you will take action, and the kind of action you will take, would be greatly affected. If you trust your ability to initiate a conversation, to talk to another person, and to exert an influence on another person's thoughts, feelings, and behavior, you may start a conversation, and continue until you establish some kind of contact with this person. It may then become possible for this person to talk about his problems and his reasons for being on the bridge, or for you to introduce the question. Alternatively, you may feel that you cannot start a conversation with a stranger, who probably does not want to have anything to do with you anyway. If you feel sufficiently strongly this way, the feeling may even interfere with the activation of your prosocial goal, your awareness of the need, and your desire to help.

Competence refers to a person's subjective evaluation of his capacities as well as to his possession of skills and capacities in an objective sense. Here, competence is a summary term that refers to a class of variables.

The most general one is the person's belief in his or her ability to influence events, to bring about desired outcomes – described by the concept of locus of control. Belief in their ability to influence events and to bring about desired outcomes makes it worthwhile for people to initiate action and actively pursue their goals.

Existing plans or strategies for action in various situations, and the capacity to generate plans, seem another important aspect of competence (Miller, Galanter, & Pribram, 1960; Mischel, 1973). When the behavior that is required is clearly specified by someone's need or by the existing circumstances, such competence is not needed. However, the kind of action that would be helpful is frequently unclear, and the need to generate plans is great. One may even move further back along the chain of events and consider that cognitive competencies are involved in deciding whether values and beliefs that one holds are applicable to a current situation. Values and beliefs tend to be relatively general: when one cannot rely on past experience with similar situations, one needs to derive standards and norms of conduct ("In this situation, I ought to help") which are applicable to the specific situation that one faces.

Schwartz (1970, 1977) suggested that a person's awareness of the possible consequences of his behavior on other people is an important determinant, in combination with other characteristics, of helping behavior. Awareness of potential consequences of one's action may be the result of joint variation in role-taking, in a person's sense of his ability to exert influence over events, and in the capacity to generate plans of action. It is the combination of these characteristics that would lead a person to consider what consequences his behavior may have, and to realize and appreciate its potential beneficial consequences. Schwartz found that persons who scored high on a paper-and-pencil measure of awareness of consequences were more helpful under some circumstances than those who scored low on this measure. Under other circumstances – for example, in an emergency, where the potential consequences of action may have been clear to everybody – scores on this measure did not affect helping. I would expect that a strong personal goal combined with awareness of consequences – or more generally, with awareness of and belief in one's capacity to affect others' welfare – would lead to most help for a person in need.

A further aspect of competence is the possession of behavioral skills and/or a person's belief in possessing the skills that are necessary for prosocial action on a particular occasion. One has to swim in order to pull someone out of the raging river. One has to have certain interpersonal skills or believe that one possesses them, in order to attempt to help a person distressed about some aspect of his life and, certainly, to actually be helpful to him.

Varied aspects of competence contribute to the expectations of success in reaching a desired outcome (Rotter, 1954; Mischel, 1966), which in turn affect the likelihood of taking action to reach that outcome. All of these competencies may contribute to a feeling of control on a particular occasion. The feeling of control over aversive events increases tolerance for them and diminishes both the physiological arousal they produce and their negative effects on task performance (Glass & Singer, 1972; Staub et al., 1971; Staub & Kellett, 1972). Lack of control produces a sense of helplessness (and/or lack of hope), which reduces the likelihood of subsequent attempts at taking action and exerting influence (Lefcourt, 1973; Seligman, 1975). Lack of competence, subjective or objective, may not only diminish attempts to reach the outcomes implied by personal goals, but may also diminish the likelihood that goals are activated, since a goal activated but not pursued is likely to create distress and discomfort. Lack of competence may exert its influence by minimizing attention to activating stimuli, or by creating a desire to avoid the activating stimuli. That is, subjective incompetence may be a source of motivation itself, a negative goal that gives rise to the desire to avoid situations where competence is called for.

Related to competence, to some extent an outcome of variation in competence, is a person's capacity to take initiative, to engage in action under ambiguous or difficult conditions – his or her "action tendency." Variation in subjective or objective competence is certainly not the only determinant, however, of action tendency; independence, impulsiveness, courage, adventurousness, and anti-conformity may all contribute to a person's tendency to initiate action consistent with his goals. Depending on circumstances, some of these characteristics may be more important than others. In one study, for example, we found a significant positive correlation between subjects' ranking of *courageous* on Rokeach's test of values (a term that was defined as standing up for one's beliefs) and their entering an adjoining room in response to mild sounds of distress coming from there (Staub, Erkut, & Jaquette, in Staub, 1974).

Our Carnegie Hero had served as a parachutist during World War II. To do his job as a parachutist, he had to deal with physical danger and must have possessed physical coordination and skill. I do not know how parachutists were selected during World War II; if he volunteered, that would suggest that he liked to face physical challenge. All these characteristics could be important in leading him to take action and to be successful in saving the drowning woman. A liking of danger and of the exercise of his physical capacities may have also contributed (in spite of his weakened condition) to his motivation to help.

Disposition Toward "Justifications"

Frequently, people engage in cognitive activities to minimize the activating potential of certain conditions on themselves. To different degrees, people will hold beliefs and values that can be applied to inhibit the arousal of a personal goal, as well as to deactivate an already activated goal. Certain cognitions, when used in this manner, will be called *justifications*. Many conditions make the inhibition of a personal goal, or its deactivation, desirable. They include foreseeing or experiencing conflict among goals. A high cost of helping – when, in order to benefit someone, a person has to sacrifice a great deal of time or valued material resources, to expend substantial energy, or to risk his or her safety – frequently results in conflict between a prosocial goal and the goal of promoting the interests of the self. Both high cost and lack of competence in pursuing a goal may lead to justifications. Conflict can also be inherent in the quality of a person's goal itself. When a person experiences goal conflict, it can be disturbing to simply proceed with the pursuit of the strongest, activated goal. Justifications can minimize the activating potential of certain conditions, or can deactivate goals, and thereby decrease the experience of conflict and distress about not pursuing some goal.

Not all thoughts that lead to not helping or to not acting according to some goal are properly called justifications. The analysis of how personal goals affect behavior suggests that a person can decide that he or she wants to pursue one goal rather than another, for good reasons. A person may weigh the degree of another person's need, or the legitimacy of another person's request, and decide that his or her own needs or goals are more important to pursue. However, a person may use reasons for not helping (or not acting according to some other goal) that rationalize, that justify the decision or the fact that one has not helped. Often we have no objective criteria to differentiate between good reasons and justifications; the distinction can be a matter of judgment or point of view, and can be argued. A potential helper may think that a person in need does not deserve help – because of the kind of person he is (and a little suffering may even be good for him), or because his own actions brought about the need for help – and thus may think that his suffering is deserved. If a man is lying on the street, someone may think he is a bum, probably drunk, and that he either needs or deserves no help (Staub & Baer, 1974). While the passerby who thinks this way is likely to not check out his judgment, which is then used as justification, he or she can approach this person and see if he is drunk, or sick and in need of help. If a person believes that there is no need for civil-rights action, and does nothing to promote such action or legislation, claiming that blacks are poor and "disadvantaged" not because of the way society treated them but because they are not interested in education and do not work as hard as whites, direct "checking out" of the correctness of such beliefs is more difficult. This can make it relatively easy to use such thinking for justifications. A person with a strong prosocial goal, who frequently uses justifications to eliminate the need for help, either has strong conflicting motives or has conflict inherent in his or her prosocial goal.

Justifications can also be applied to goals other than prosocial ones. When they are applied to a goal that conflicts with a prosocial goal, they can contribute to helping. For example, a person may justify not trying to do well on a task, by judging it a poor task or by devaluing the people who gave the task, thereby decreasing conflict about helping someone.

There seem to be certain beliefs and values that make justifications of not helping easier. Lerner (Lerner & Simmons, 1966; Lerner, 1971) proposed that people believe that the world is just. When they see an innocent person suffer (innocent in the sense that this person has not *done* anything to bring about or deserve suffering), in order to maintain their belief in a just world, people will devalue the suffering victim. They will assume that, due to his character or personality, this person deserves to suffer. Rubin and Peplau (1973) found that people greatly vary in their belief that the world is just. Individuals who more strongly hold the just-world view are more inclined to devalue people who suffer, members of minority groups who are discriminated against, or others whom the world apparently does not treat in a just fashion.

Reactance and Sensitivity to Pressure

Another person's need for help can arouse resentment about the imposition that it represents (Berkowitz, 1973; Staub, 1978). Brehm (1966) proposed that people are sensitive to demands placed on them that either limit their freedom of action or imply or threaten a limitation on their freedom. Frequently, people respond against such pressures by acting contrary to them. People may be particularly sensitive to such pressure in the realm of prosocial behavior. Others' need for help invokes societal norms that make it an obligation to help. The obligatory nature of these norms may often create psychological reactance. The feeling of reactance can also be used as a justification: "I will not let my freedom be limited; I am not going to oblige with demands placed on me."

There is evidence that children, particularly boys, respond to some conditions that aim at increasing their helping behavior with opposition, presumably arising out of reactance. Boys respond with opposition to verbal communications about the desirability or usefulness of help or about its beneficial consequences for the recipients (Staub, 1971c, 1975a, 1975b, 1979). Since, in our culture, boys are trained to be independent, it is understandable that they would respond more negatively than girls when such demands are placed on them. Boys, and males in general, evidence less concern about others' welfare on various paper-and-pencil tests than do girls and women, at least in our culture (Hoffman, 1977; Staub, 1978); this would also increase the likelihood of oppositional reactions to requests for help.

Sensitivity to pressure, and an oppositional tendency, may be dominant characteristics of some individuals. Under many circumstances, people may respond differently to conditions that potentially activate a prosocial goal, or other goals, as a function of variation in this characteristic. The desire to not be unduly influenced by other people, to not be controlled by them – independence or self-determination – may be an important personal goal for many people.

DIMENSIONS OF SITUATIONS RELEVANT TO HELPING

A staggering amount of research, considering that almost all was conducted within the last decade, shows that varied aspects of situations affect positive behavior. The findings of this research can help us specify dimensions of situations that vary in activating potential for prosocial goals. Variations along some of the dimensions can also determine whether personality characteristics other than goals – for example, the feeling of competence in reaching an outcome – will be important. Still other variations can affect the activation of goals that conflict with a prosocial goal. The summary of situational dimensions below was derived from Staub (1978). These dimensions are conceptual: many different actual characteristics of stimuli can specify their location on one of these conceptual dimensions, or on several of them at the same time.

1. The extent to which the nature of stimulus for help (someone's physical or psychological need, its degree, nature, and manner of presentation), the surrounding conditions, or social influence that is exerted by other people provide an unambiguous definition of someone's need for help. The less ambiguity, the more help will follow. Ambiguity diminishes the likelihood that the stimulus is interpreted as representing someone's need, and thereby diminishes activating potential. Ambiguity can also give rise to concern that a helpful act would be inappropriate or appear foolish, and thus may activate an approval goal.

Yakimovich and Saltz (1971) had a workman fall off a ladder in front of the subject's window – an event enacted to provide a stimulus for help. The frequency of help substantially increased when, in addition to other indications of distress, the workman eliminated ambiguity by calling for help. Other studies also found that clearly defining a situation as one in which someone needs help increases helpful responses by people (Bickman, 1971; Staub, 1974).

2. The degree of need for help. Usually, the greater the need for help, the more help will follow (Staub & Baer, 1974). However, exceptions may exist, partly because when someone's distress, discomfort, or the danger to a person are great, which make the need for help great, the costs associated with helping – the sacrifices demanded from, or the potential danger for a helper – are frequently also great.

3. The extent to which responsibility for help is focused on a particular person rather than diffused among a number of people. The more clearly the circumstances focus the responsibility on a particular person, the greater the likelihood that this person will provide help. Responsibility is focused on a person if he or she is the only witness to another's need; if he or she is the only person who is in a position to help, although not necessarily the only witness; if he or she has special skills that are required for helping; if he or she has a special relationship to the person in need; if a leadership position makes this person the natural one to take charge; and in other ways.

In the well-known studies by Latané and Darley (1970), the number of people who witnessed emergencies varied. As the number of witnesses who were present, or whom participants believed were present, increased, the likelihood that a participant would respond to sounds of distress coming from another room decreased. Presumably, diffusion of responsibility was one reason for this. People who were alone when they heard the sounds were most likely to attempt to help. In a study by Korte (1969), the subject, who witnessed through an intercom an ostensible asthma attack by the experimenter, was led to believe either that another person who also witnessed the emergency was in a position to help, or that the other person was tied to electrodes and thus could not leave. In the latter condition, which appears to focus responsibility on the subject to a greater degree, participants helped more.

Conditions that strongly focus responsibility to help on a person can lead to helping, even if that person has little personal motivation to help. Societal norms strongly prescribe that we help people with certain kinds of needs. When responsibility is focused on a person, compliance with these norms is more likely. When a need exists, but responsibility is not directly focused on particular individuals, people with personal motivation to help should be more likely to do so. In one study, female subjects who (in responding to questionnaire items) ascribed more responsibility to themselves for others' welfare helped more and were less affected by variation in the number of bystanders in an emergency (Schwartz & Clausen, 1970). The findings of another study also showed that personal characteristics modify the influence of other witnesses (Wilson, 1976). Esteem-oriented individuals who (on the basis of sentence-completion tests) appeared to have feelings of strong personal adequacy, the belief that "they can master situations in realistic and functional ways" (Wilson, 1976, p. 1079), and a need for efficacy in interpersonal relationships, responded more in an emergency, and were unaffected by variation in the number of bystanders – in comparison to "safety-oriented" subjects or a mixed group. Safety-oriented subjects appeared dependent and mistrustful, characterized by feelings of personal incompetence and a view of the world as uncontrollable. The difference in helping was particularly great when subjects witnessed the emergency with two passive bystanders. In addition to being more action-oriented and more resistant to external influence, more concern about the distressed person's welfare may have been aroused in esteem-oriented individuals. The presence of others – and particularly that of bystanders who, by their passivity, defined the situation as one in which no action was necessary – may have created fear of disapproval and self-concern in safety-oriented persons. Self-concern, however, appears to strongly interfere with the capacity to respond to others' needs (Staub, 1978).

4. The degree of impact of the instigating stimuli. Closeness in space and the length of exposure to a distressed person, and the ease or difficulty of getting away from his or her presence (affecting length of exposure) seem to be conditions that affect the impact of the stimulus for help on a potential helper. In studies where people were exposed to an emergency on the subway, somebody usually helped, regardless of the number of people who were present (Piliavin et al., 1969, 1975). In some cases, the emergency occurred on the express train that did not stop for several minutes. Although several influences may be at work, the impact of continued exposure to a person in physical need was probably important in leading people to initiate help.[3] In another study (Staub & Baer, 1974) bystanders helped a distressed person on the street, who fell down in their path, substantially more than they helped a person who fell down on the other side of the street. In the latter instance, the impact of the stimulus was smaller, and the opportunity for bystanders to escape from its presence greater. Greater impact presumably embodies a greater activating potential for prosocial goals. However, the social cost of not helping and the attendant desire to avoid social punishment can also increase with greater impact.

5. The extent to which circumstances specify the response to someone's need for help or leave the required response undefined. Sometimes, the stimulus for help and/or surrounding conditions clearly indicate not only

[3] In one study, Piliavin et al. (1975) attempted to test the effects of length of exposure by having the emergency occur either four stops or one stop before the end of the line. While they found no effect of length of exposure, in both conditions the emergency occurred right after the subway train left a station. Thus, length of exposure till the next station, where bystanders *could* leave the train, was equal. "Escape" from the situation was possible in both conditions, although inconvenient in one treatment condition for passengers who intended to travel beyond the next station.

that help is needed, but also the kind of action that is required; a potential helper may even receive a specific request for a specific act. At other times, a person may have to decide both that help is needed and what needs to be done. In such cases, more decision making and greater initiative are required, and varied competencies are involved in helping. For example, Schwartz and Clausen (1970) found that when a person in need asked for a pill that he had in his coat pocket, he received help much more frequently than in another condition, where the need was presented, but ways of helping were not specified.

6. The "direct" costs of helping. How much effort, time, energy, material goods, or risk to oneself is demanded? The greater such costs, the less help can usually be expected. Greater costs create conflict between a goal that is powerful for most people, to protect and promote one's interests, and other goals that may promote helping.

7. Indirect costs. In everyday life, it is a common occurrence that in order to help others, one has to sacrifice the pursuit of goals that one is actively pursuing. There has been little research about how attention to others' needs is affected, what kinds of conflicts are created, and how they are resolved when a person is engaged in the pursuit of some activity or personal goal and has to sacrifice that pursuit in order to help another person. It is one thing to talk to a seemingly upset neighbor who stops by, when one has free time; it is a somewhat different thing when one is about to go to play tennis, or to meet one's lover, or has only a couple of hours to finish some important work for a deadline. In a study that is relevant to this kind of conflict, Darley and Batson (1973) found that seminary students who were to deliver a lecture were less helpful to a person lying on the ground, whom they passed by on their way to the lecture, if they were told that they were late and had to hurry to get to their lecture on time. Being engaged in the pursuit of goals must frequently diminish people's willingness to help others.

8. The social appropriateness of the behavior required for help. Circumstances can suggest that the type of action that is required for help is socially acceptable or that it may be undesirable, inappropriate, or socially unacceptable. For example, implicit or explicit rules – that a child is to continue working on a task, or that going into a strange room in a strange environment is inappropriate (Staub, 1970, 1971b, 1974) – may inhibit responses to another person's apparent distress. When circumstances activate an approval goal, it may promote helping by inducing people to act according to social norms or specific situational rules that prescribe help for others, or it may inhibit helping, depending on the nature of the circumstances.

9. Temporary psychological states of a person that result from positive or negative experiences concurrent with or just prior to the opportunity to benefit others. Such experiences can result in positive or negative moods, different levels of temporary self-esteem, or differences in other internal states. Positive states usually enhance, negative states frequently (although not always) diminish, help for others. Presumably, a person's own psychological state affects his or her capacity to perceive or seriously consider others' needs and affects the feeling of connection between the self and others: both would affect the activation of prosocial goals. Notice that the conceptual-stimulus dimension here is a person's own internal state.

I proposed a theory of "hedonic balancing" which specifies how people balance their own and other people's states of well-being at any particular time (Staub, 1978). In the course of this "balancing," people consider how they themselves feel at the moment, how much better or worse they feel than their usual state of well being. They compare this to how the other person feels, how much better or worse than the other might usually feel. The outcome or hedonic balance can affect both the activation of prosocial goals and whether activated goals will be acted upon. Many hedonic balance conditions are possible. A person who had a success experience and feels good would be more likely to show positive behavior, according to this conception, if his usual state of well-being is neutral rather than highly positive, so that his current feelings represent a positive hedonic discrepancy. He may show even more positive behavior if the person who needs help appears to experience a negative hedonic discrepancy, a state worse than his usual state – if he is usually healthy but now sick, rather than if he is usually sick and is now sick as well.

Researchers found that even seemingly minimal experiences, such as finding a dime in a telephone booth or receiving a cookie from someone, can increase people's subsequent willingness soon afterwards to help a person who appears to need help (Isen & Levin, 1972). Providing information to people about their competence on a task (whether or not this competence is relevant to the kind of action that needs to be taken to help another person); their success and failure on tasks; children thinking about past positive or negative experiences; communications to people that they will be evaluated on some task (this perhaps arousing self-concern) – all have been found to affect prosocial behavior (for reviews, see Rosenhan et al., 1976; Bar-Tal, 1976; Staub, 1973, 1978). However, the extent to which persistent individual differences in self-esteem and/or characteristic moods of individuals modify the influence of the momentary experiences has remained largely unexplored (although not completely – see Staub, 1978). Such persistent characteristics may directly influence the activation of prosocial goals or the feeling of competence in executing positive action. They may also affect what internal states are created by everyday experiences.

10. Past experience with the potential recipients of positive behavior. A person's sense of relatedness to or connectedness or identification with another person seems to be an extremely important determinant of whether this person will take action to benefit another (Hornstein, 1976; Reykowski, 1975; Rosenhan et al., 1976; Staub, 1978). This connection between others and the self may be a function of a person's orientation toward other people in general, an aspect of a prosocial goal, or an aspect of past experience with or knowledge about particular others.

The existence of a relationship to a person in need, its degree and kind, will affect the extent to which the interests of the self and others are regarded as identical or unrelated or opposing, and will affect the kind of special rules or principles that guide the relationship. Our relationships to other people frequently place special obligations on us to respond to their needs, to promote their welfare. The existence of a close relationship, as well as certain other conditions (knowledge of shared group membership, or of similarities of opinions, beliefs, and personality) can lead to identification with another person; and this makes the arousal of a prosocial goal, or specifically of empathy and of other motives that promote help, more likely. Other conditions, those which give rise to antagonism, may make help less likely. An ongoing relationship also provides others' needs with greater impact, since it makes it difficult to physically remove oneself, to escape from the presence of another's distress or need.

Principles that guide positive social behavior among people in close relationships probably differ somewhat from those that guide positive behavior among strangers or acquaintances. In responding to a stranger's need for help, the prior behavior of that person toward us is not an issue; we may anticipate future reciprocity, but we do not respond to the past behaviors of this person. However, reciprocity does guide our behavior toward people with whom we had past interactions: we return favors, and frequently retaliate harm. Interpersonal relations and positive interactions are certainly transactional. Past actions by one person affect subsequent responses by another, which in turn influence the next behavior of the first actor, and so on. Reciprocity applies less in relationships among friends than among acquaintances and strangers who are participating in a "minimal interaction," a limited exchange of behaviors (Floyd, 1964; Staub & Sherk, 1970; Staub, 1978). Presumably, in close relationships, benefits that people provide for each other and sacrifices that they make can be balanced over a longer time interval.

In sum, the existence of a positive relationship with another person may not only increase the likelihood of the activation of prosocial goals, but can invoke varied obligations and special principles that guide positive (and negative) interactions. Finally, people in continuing relationships can develop norms, rules, standards, and values that are applicable to that relationship, which guide their behavior toward each other. Unfortunately, our knowledge of principles of prosocial, helpful behavior in close relationships is quite limited, as yet.

SUPPORTING RESEARCH

What research findings exist that provide support for the theoretical conceptions described above? Some of our own research attempted to explore both the influence of a prosocial goal as a function of its activation by stimulus conditions, and/or the joint influence of several goals, on positive behavior. Some previously existing research is also relevant.

Research Conducted to Test the Theoretical Model

The findings of one of our studies provided one impetus to the conception advanced above; it also provides support for it (Staub, Erkut, & Jaquette, as reported in Staub, 1974). In this study, responses to sounds of distress, and help for the distressed person in the course of subsequent interaction with him, were affected by a combination of the characteristics of the situation and personality characteristics of subjects. Male participants worked on a number of personality tests, some of which measured values and beliefs relevant to a prosocial goal. In a second session, while working on a personality measure, the subject heard sounds of distress from an adjoining room. Previously he either received permission to enter the adjoining room, or was told not to interrupt work on the task (prohibition), or received no information about rules that might affect freedom of action. If the subject did not enter the adjoining room in response to the sounds, the "distressed" confederate entered the subject's room. An interaction followed in the course of which the confederate presented the subject with several sequences of behavior, each providing a separate opportunity for a helping act. The final sequence presented the subject with a choice between going to a pharmacy to fill a prescription, and thereby help the confederate's stomach problem, or calling the confederate's roommate – which demanded less effort but would result in much slower help – or refusing to help.

Subjects with a more advanced level of moral reasoning (Kohlberg, 1969), or those who tended to ascribe responsibility to themselves for others' welfare, (Schwartz, 1970) helped more, but only when the experimenter previously indicated that it was permissible to interrupt work on their task and to enter the adjoining room for an irrelevant reason – to get a cup of coffee (permission condition). As in other experiments (Staub, 1971b), permission presumably reduced concern about disapproval. People who held prosocial values such as helpfulness or equality – as indicated by their ranking of these values on Rokeach's (1973) measure – tended to help more in the permission condition. In the prohibition condition, where subjects were told that their task was timed and were asked to work on it without interruptions, and in the no information condition where the experimenter said nothing, only slight relationships existed between scores on these varied value-related measures and subjects' behavior. Values that conflicted with helping, such as ambition, reduced helping. The negative relationship between valuing ambition and helping was particularly strong in the prohibition condition, which would be expected to activate ambition or the desire for achievement by subjects on their tasks.

A factor analysis of measures that expressed positive values about people or about helping produced a strong factor with a high loading of most of the measures on this factor. These included the measures mentioned above, as well as scores on a measure indicating negative evaluation of human beings and manipulativeness (Christie & Geis, 1968), which had negative loading. Scores on this "prosocial-orientation" factor were related to most of the helpful actions that the subjects had opportunities to perform, and the relationship was relatively unaffected by situational variation.

The findings of this study showed that situations and prosocial values and beliefs interact in affecting behavior, but people characterized by a combination of these beliefs and values were less affected by situational variation. Since in all treatments a need existed, a prosocial goal could be activated in all conditions. The findings also suggested that a number of existing measures can be used together as a preliminary index of a prosocial goal.

In two dissertations, Feinberg (1977) and Grodman (1979) further tested the theoretical model. In both of these studies, a little explored but extremely important type of helping was studied: people's reactions to someone's psychological distress. We all have the frequent experience that someone we know or interact with is upset, frustrated, sad, or disappointed. What determines our willingness to attempt to console, advise, or in other ways help?

In both studies, female participants were administered most of the value-related personality measures that in the above study had a high loading on the prosocial-orientation factor, and a couple of additional ones. In addition, in Feinberg's study the subjects also filled out a group of measures to test values and beliefs related to an achievement goal. A factor analysis of scores on the measures of prosocial values and beliefs provided a strong factor in both studies: factor scores were used to divide subjects into high and low prosocial groups. In Feinberg's study the factor analysis of achievement-related measures also provided a strong factor, and subjects divided by factor scores were assigned to high and low achievement groups.

In Feinberg's study these divisions resulted in groups of subjects who were either low in both achievement and prosocial goals, high in both, or low in one and high in the other. In a second session, each subject was working together with another person – a confederate – on a personality test. In response to a story that was part of this test, the confederate began to tell the subject about a very upsetting experience that occurred the night before (*high need*). She described how her boyfriend of two years' standing, with whom she had talked about marriage, suddenly broke up with her. Not only did he not explain why, but he refused to discuss the matter. The confederate presented several pieces of information, if the subject allowed, and additional information if the subject elicited it by what she said, all in a carefully prepared and structured manner. In a *low need* condition the confederate provided the same information, but reported that the event occurred a year ago, and did not act upset. She seemed to reminisce rather than need help.

Varied behaviors of the subjects were recorded, either by observers or on a tape recorder, and were later categorized. These included verbal behaviors such as the total amount that subjects talked, their expression of sympathy, giving advice, and others; nonverbal behaviors such as working on or looking at the task, or looking at and smiling at the confederate; ratings by the confederate and the observer following the interaction of the subjects' helpfulness and orientation toward the confederate; and an index of the subjects' willingness to continue the conversation after the experimental participation was over. Subjects also provided information on a post-experimental questionnaire about their feelings about the confederate, and about other aspects of their experience.

As expected, people helped more in high need than in low need, both verbally and nonverbally. Contrary to expectations, persons who valued achievement more helped more than those who valued achievement less, particularly in verbally responding to the confederate. It was originally expected that achievement orientation would be expressed in task-related activity, not recognizing that an achievement goal can also be satisfied by doing well in helping a distressed person. This points to the importance of carefully evaluating the activating potential of situations for varied goals. High-prosocial subjects helped less in low need than did low-prosocial subjects, but more in high need. This difference was particularly strong in nonverbal responses, attention to the confederate rather than the task. Responses on the post-experimental questionnaire indicated that in low need, the high-prosocial subjects felt an obligation to help the experimenter by completing the task. High need apparently activated their desire to help the confederate, which was expressed by a moderate degree of verbal help and by substantial nonverbal interest and responsiveness, and a willingness to later continue the interaction.

Contrary to expectations, persons with high achievement and low prosocial goals talked substantially more to the confederate than did any other group of subjects. This happened both under high need and low need, suggesting that these people were not simply responding to a strong need, but to any claim on their attention. People high on the prosocial goal and low on the achievement goal tended to behave as high prosocial subjects in general, but showed the same trends toward helping somewhat more strongly. Under high need, high-prosocial low-achievement subjects paid more attention to the confederate than did subjects in any other condition. Finally, answers on the post-experimental questionnaire indicated that when faced with strong need, high-prosocial subjects, particularly high-prosocial, low-achievement ones, tended to like the confederate more and perceive her distress as more genuine than did low-prosocial subjects, particularly low-prosocial, high-achievement ones. The latter group of subjects, in addition to talking a substantial amount and paying moderate attention to the confederate, also worked a substantial amount on their task. Seemingly, they wanted to do a great deal, but they indicated – although generally not to a significant degree – that they gained less gratification from helping behavior than did any other group of subjects. The findings of this study provide some support for the theory. However, they also point to certain issues – for example, that *assumptions* by researchers about the meaning (activating potential) of stimuli for people can be incorrect. Moreover, they show that people are highly discriminative in their behavior, which is a complex function of their personality and the existing conditions.

In another study, Grodman (1979) used the high-need condition described above. In addition to dividing subjects by their prosocial goal into low and high groups, on the basis of their performance on personality measures (see Feinberg's procedure described earlier), she varied the costs associated with helping the distressed confederate. By attending to the confederate and helping her, and thereby neglecting their task, people provided less information about themselves to the experimenter – who, in the high-cost condition, promised to give the subjects information about their personality on the basis of test results. No such promise was made in the low-cost condition. Thus in high cost, by helping, people diminished the value of the feedback that they would receive about themselves.

In this study, subjects with a strong prosocial goal helped more than those with a weak prosocial goal. The difference was not only significant on varied measures of help, verbal and nonverbal, but was also quite substantial. On several measures, this was true regardless of costs. On other measures, prosocial goal and cost each affected helping; and on still others, only the interaction between the two affected behavior. In the latter case, usually the high-prosocial subjects helped significantly more than the low-prosocial ones, verbally or by showing interest, in the low-cost condition. Frequently, they also helped numerically more in the high-cost condition, but the difference was insubstantial.

The differences in helping that are associated with a prosocial goal are consistent with, but stronger than, the findings of Feinberg, whose high-prosocial subjects were more helpful than low-prosocial ones in the high-need condition, but mainly in nonverbal ways. Conflict between helping and the possibility of acquiring knowledge about themselves reduced helping by high-prosocial subjects. Grodman noted, on the basis of responses by subjects on a post-experimental questionnaire, that acquiring knowledge about themselves seemed very important for high-prosocial subjects, more important than for low-prosocial ones. This is consistent with research findings showing that among young adolescents those who are more sensitive and responsive to others are more concerned about their interaction with others and about their effects on other people (Reese, 1961). To such individuals, information about themselves and about how they appear to other people would be important. Consequently, Grodman's high-cost condition may have created greater conflict for high-prosocial subjects than some other kinds of costs would have.

Other Relevant Research

A few existing research studies seem relevant to the theoretical model described in this chapter. In one study, Schwartz and his associates (1969) provided subjects with an opportunity to cheat on a task on one occasion, and with an opportunity to be helpful on another occasion. Subjects could cheat in solving multiple-choice vocabulary problems; and while working on a puzzle they could help someone who had trouble putting the puzzle together and had made requests for help. Before either activity, three personality characteristics were measured: the participants' need for achievement, their need for affiliation, and their level of moral reasoning. The authors made differential predictions about the relationship between personality characteristics and behavior in the two situations. Stronger need to achieve was expected to be positively related to not cheating, because the desire for excellence cannot be satisfied by getting the right answers through cheating; but it was expected to be negatively related to helping, because helping would interfere with solving the puzzle. Need for affiliation was expected to be unrelated to cheating, which is an impersonal activity, but positively related to helping, which involved a positive interpersonal interaction. More advanced moral reasoning was expected to be positively related to both honesty and helping, since both can be regarded as moral behaviors. Essentially, the hypotheses were confirmed by the data. At the same time, the two behaviors, cheating and helping, were unrelated to each other.

From the perspective of our theory, these researchers considered the activating potential of each of two situations with regard to three values or motives, and measured individual differences in these values or motives.

By doing so they could correctly predict the relationship between these personal motives and behavior.

In another study, Liebhart (1972) measured some form of a prosocial motive or goal of eleventh- to thirteenth-grade German male high-school subjects, by administering a projective test of "sympathetic orientation." The subjects' disposition to take instrumental action to relieve their own distress was measured by a Lickert-type scale that the author devised. Subjects with a sympathetic orientation helped more quickly in response to sounds of distress from the adjoining room – a bang followed by cries and moans – if they were also disposed toward instrumental action. This finding supports the notion that when personality characteristics which make it a desirable goal to assist another are activated, a person is likely to help if he is characterized by an orientation toward taking action.

Also relevant are findings of a study by Gergen and associates (1972), and their discussion of their findings. Members of an undergraduate class could indicate their willingness to aid the psychology department with five ongoing projects – counseling male students from a nearby high school; counseling female students; helping with a faculty research project on deductive thinking; with a research project on unusual states of consciousness; or collating and assembling materials for further use by the class. In the preceding class session the students completed a battery of personality tests, measuring a variety of characteristics or "traits."

Gergen and associates found that different personality characteristics were significantly related to volunteering help with different tasks. Also, the pattern of correlations differed for males and females. The findings are consistent with the present model: people selected tasks to help with that seemed to satisfy some personal goal or lead to some outcome desirable for them. For example, need for nurturance in males was significantly related to their willingness to help with counseling other males ($r = .41$), but not to volunteering with other forms of help. Presumably, students with a strong need for nurturance expected to experience satisfaction in the course of a nurturant relationship that they anticipated in counseling. Sensation seeking as a personality characteristic was positively related to helping with research on unusual states, but negatively related to volunteering for research on deductive thinking. The correlations between personality and volunteering showed a similar kind of specificity among female subjects. The authors stressed that helping behavior is determined by specific situational payoffs. People have different payoff preferences, and depending on them, they will move toward one or another social context. They discourage the notion that certain trait dispositions or individual differences will be found to account for variability in prosocial behavior.

Helping behavior was not measured in this study: rather, the subjects' stated intentions to help were evaluated, in a group situation. The relationship between measures of the intention to help and actual helping is poor (Staub, 1978). However, for the purposes of considering the theoretical meaning of the data, this is not a prohibitive problem. Since subjects were not confronted with someone's immediate need for help, and since the class consisted of 72 people, the students probably did not feel an obligation to provide substantial help with most of the five tasks. Our theoretical model suggests that they would choose the kind of help that, either in terms of the activities inherent in them or the outcomes they lead to, would be satisfying and meaningful from the standpoint of their personal goals.

A further important consideration is that no attempt has been made in this study to evaluate personality characteristics that are relevant to helping per se, that make helping a desirable activity; that is, the kinds of characteristics that enter into or might be components of a prosocial goal. Only a high degree of motivation for prosocial behavior can be reasonably expected to lead to any generality in helping behavior or generality in the expressed intention to be helpful, and only under certain conditions. An "irrelevant" characteristic, such as sensation seeking, would be expected to sometimes add to, other times detract from, the influence of a prosocial goal. When considered by itself, it can be expected to lead to helping only when it so happens that the helping behavior satisfies sensation seeking; that is, for accidental reasons. However, given the existence of a strong prosocial motivation, a positive relationship between such motivation and several helping acts can be expected, at least when other personality characteristics are supportive and no conflicting goals are active.

In conclusion, both our own initial research efforts and research conducted by others, based on varied theoretical conceptions, provide findings that can be viewed as encouraging initial support for the theoretical model (see also Schwartz & Clausen, 1970; Wilson, 1976; both reviewed above). In most of this research, the joint, interactive influence of some personality variables and environmental variation led to behavior in a specific setting that can be meaningfully explained in terms of the theoretical model. In addition to further research of this kind, future studies can also explore the extent to which people with certain personal goals and/or related competencies will seek out situations in which they can pursue their goals, and the extent to which they behave consistently across varied circumstances in pursuing their goals. The conditions under which such consistency can be expected have been specified at earlier points in the chapter.

Self-Regulation in the Pursuit of Goals

How do personal goals, stimulus conditions and associated activation potentials, competencies, and other relevant personal characteristics jointly affect behavior? As noted earlier, a precise formulation of the interrelationship among these determinants of behavior may be premature. The intensity of a personal goal and of the activating potential of the situation may join to determine the intensity of an activated goal in a multiplicative fashion. Competencies may affect the expectancies that one can or cannot successfully pursue an outcome that would satisfy a goal. As a function of the specific nature of their competencies, people may carry with themselves such expectancies toward certain outcomes, this affecting goal activation. Such expectancies may also arise (may be constructed) on specific occasions as a function of circumstances following the activation of a goal, and may inhibit or promote the pursuit of goal satisfaction. In the initial stages of testing the theory, it is sufficient to assume that strong competencies for pursuing some outcomes may be promotive, weak ones may be prohibitive of goal-directed behavior. Either an analysis-of-variance model or a regression model can be used to test the joint influence of goals and competencies.

How does self-regulation of behavior take place? Several authors, writing about determinants of helping behavior, propose that people progress through a series of decisions; their nature determines whether they will help others or not (Latané & Darley, 1970; Schwartz, 1970, 1977; Pomazal & Jaccard, 1976). Latané and Darley proposed a decisional sequence in emergencies. In their view, people first have to notice an event, then they have to decide that it means that someone needs help, then they have to assume that they are responsible for providing help. Given all these positive decisions, they still have to execute some action.

Such a specification of decision steps is useful. By varying the nature of the environment – for example, providing people only with the stimulus for help, or providing them with that as well as with a definition of its meaning, or also focusing responsibility on them, and so on – we can affect where people will be along the decisional sequence. By also considering personality characteristics, and by measuring the joint effects of situational variations and personality on thought and feeling – before behavior could have taken place – as well as on behavior, we can progressively elaborate on what takes place internally, on how varied influences affect thinking and feeling.

At the same time, this conception of decisional steps is likely to be an oversimplification. Our actual flow of consciousness is probably more formless, with less definite junctures, without definite decision points. This flow is likely to include interpretations of events and the considerations of what actions one might take. If there is no conflict due to great demands on the helper, or to conflicting goals, or to other thoughts and feelings that block the flow of consciousness, a person's "will" may gain uninhibited expression in action (William James, 1890).

The flow of consciousness can include thoughts about the ease or difficulty of interpreting an event and dealing with it, verbal self-reinforcements or self-punishments that accompany action (a person thinking about how well or poorly he is doing, how good, clever, and skillful, or how bad, stupid, and incompetent he is) with corresponding feelings. There is substantial evidence that the way people "speak to themselves," their internal dialogue, affects their behavior (Meichenbaum 1980). Mischel, Ebbesen, and Zeiss (1972, 1973) showed that, with young children at least, whether or not children have in front of them valued material objects that function as rewards, and instructions that lead them to engage in varying cognitive processing of such stimuli, affects their delay of gratification, their capacity to wait for delayed, larger rewards, in contrast to accepting immediate but smaller rewards. Masters and Santrock (1976) demonstrated that asking children to think varied positive or negative thoughts while they were working on tasks affected their persistence, whether these thoughts were relevant to the task itself or not.

I have suggested all along that personal goals are the primary organizers of a person's thinking about, feelings toward, and actions related to the pursuit of varied classes of outcomes. Personal goals provide general orientations. I suggested that ranges of applicability of goals can be different for different people. Schwartz (1977) elaborated a decisional model that is based on the assumption that specific moral norms that people hold will determine whether they behave prosocially on specific occasions (e.g., "It is my obligation to donate blood"). I believe that specific norms are likely to be one determinant of the range of applicability of more general personal goals. While personal goals are more basic and general in their applicability, both would enter into guiding the flow of consciousness. By setting standards of conduct for specific occasions, they will affect self-reinforcement, self-punishment, and other elements of the flow of consciousness which guide people's behavior. The specification of the nature of self-regulation, of the flow of thoughts and feelings and their relationship to conduct, is an important task.

References

Aderman, D., & Berkowitz, L. Observational set, empathy and helping. *Journal of Personality and Social Psychology*, 1970, *14*, 141–148.

Brehm, S. S., & Katz, L. B. Empathic observation of an innocent victim: The just world revisited. *Journal of Personality and Social Psychology*, 1974, *29*, 342.

Arnold, M. *Emotion and personality*. New York: Columbia University Press, 1960.

Bar-Tal, D. *Prosocial behavior: Theory and research*. Washington, D.C.: Hemisphere Publishing Company, 1976.

Benedict, R. Anthropology and the abnormal. *Journal of General Psychology*, 1934, 59–82.

Berkowitz, L. Reactance and the unwillingness to help others. *Psychological Bulletin*, 1973, *79*, 310–317.

Bickman, L. The effect of another bystander's ability to help on bystander intervention in an emergency. *Journal of Experimental Social Psychology*, 1971, *7*, 367–380.

Brehm, J. W. *A theory of psychological reactance*. New York: Academic Press, 1966.

Carlson, R. Where is the person in personality research? *Psychological Bulletin*, 1971, *75*, 203–219.

Chadwick-Jones, J. K. *Social exchange theory: Its structure and influence in social psychology*. New York: Academic Press, 1976.

Christie, R., & Geis, F. (Eds.) *Studies in Machiavellianism*. New York: Academic Press, 1968.

Cohen, R. Altruism: human, cultural or what? *Journal of Social Issues*, 1972, *28*, 39–57.

Crowne, D. P., & Marlowe, D. *The approval motive: Studies in evaluative dependence*. New York: Wiley, 1964.

Darley, J., & Batson, C. "From Jerusalem to Jericho": A study of situational and dispositional variables in helping behavior. *Journal of Personality and Social Psychology*, 1973, *27*, 100–108.

Deutsch, M. Field theory in social psychology. In G. Lindsey & E. Aronson (Eds.), *Handbook of social psychology*, Vol. I. Addison Wesley Publishing Company, 1968.

Denner, B. Did a crime occur? Should I inform anyone? A study of deception. *Journal for Personality*, 1968, *36*, 454–466.

Dollard, J., & Miller, N. E. *Personality and psychotherapy*. New York: McGraw-Hill, 1950.

Durkheim, E. *Moral education*. New York: The Free Press, 1961.

Ekehammar, B. Interactionism in personality from a historical perspective. *Psychological Bulletin*, 1974, *81*, 1026–1048.

Feinberg, H. K. Anatomy of a helping situation: Some personality and situational determinants of helping in a conflict situation involving another's psychological distress. Unpublished doctoral dissertation, University of Massachusetts, Amherst, 1977.

Floyd, J. Effects of amount of reward and friendship status of the other on the frequency of sharing in children. Unpublished doctoral dissertation, University of Minnesota, 1964.

Gergen, K. J., Gergen, M. M., & Meter, K. Individual orientations to prosocial behavior. *Journal of Social Issues*, 1972, *8*, 105–130.

Glass, D. C., & Singer, J. E. *Urban stress. Experiments on noise and social stressors*. New York: Academic Press, 1972.

Grodman, S. M. The role of personality and situational variables in responding to and helping an individual in psychological distress. Unpublished dissertation, University of Massachusetts, 1979.

Hoffman, M. L. Conscience, personality, and socialization technique. *Human Development*, 1970, *13*, 90–126. (b)

Sex differences in empathy and related behaviors. *Psychological Bulletin*, 1977, *84*, 712–720.

Homans, G. C. *Social behavior: Its elementary forms*. New York: Harcourt, Brace & World, 1961.

Hornstein, H. A. *Cruelty and kindness. A new look at aggression and altruism*. Englewood Cliffs, N.J.: Prentice-Hall, Inc., 1976.

Huston, T. L., & Korte, C. The responsive bystander: Why he helps. In T. Lickona (Ed.), *Moral development and behavior*. New York: Holt, Rinehart, & Winston, 1976.

Isen, A. M., & Levin, F. Effect of feeling good on helping: Cookies and kindness. *Journal of Personality and Social Psychology*, 1972, *21*, 384–388.
James, W. *The principles of psychology*. Vols. I and II. New York: Henry Holt, 1890.
Kelley, H. H., & Stahleski, A. J. Social interaction basis of cooperators' and competitors' beliefs about others. *Journal of Personality and Social Psychology*, 1970, *16*, 66–91.
Kohlberg, L. Stage and sequence: The cognitive-developmental approach to socialization. In D. Goslin (Ed.), *Handbook of socialization theory and research*. Chicago: Rand McNally, 1969.
Korte, C. Group effects on help-giving in an emergency. *Proceedings of the 77th Annual Convention of the American Psychological Association*, 1969, *4*, 383–384.
Latané, B., & Darley, J. M. *The unresponsive bystander: Why doesn't he help?* New York: Appleton-Century-Crofts, 1970.
Lazarus, R. S. *Psychological stress and the coping process*. New York: McGraw-Hill, 1966.
Lefcourt, H. The function of the illusions of freedom and control. *American Psychologist*, 1973, *28*, 117–125.
Lerner, M. J. Observer's evaluation of a victim: Justice, guilt, and veridical perception. *Journal of Personality and Social Psychology*, 1971, *20*.
& Simmons, C. H. Observer's reactions to the "innocent victim": Compassion or rejection? *Journal of Personality and Social Psychology*, 1966, *4*, 203–210.
Leventhal, H. Emotions: A basic problem for social psychology. In C. Nemeth (Ed.), *Social psychology: Classic and contemporary integrations*. Chicago: Rand McNally, 1974.
Lewin, K. The conceptual representation and measurement of psychological forces. *Contributions to psychological theory*, 1938, *1*.
Resolving social conflicts. New York: Harper, 1948.
Liebhart, E. Empathy and emergency helping: The effects of personality, self-concern, and acquaintance. *Journal of Experimental Social Psychology*, 1972, *8*, 404–411.
London, P. The rescuers: Motivational hypothesis about Christians who saved Jews from the Nazis. In J. Macauley & L. Berkowitz (Ed.), *Altruism and helping behavior*. New York: Academic Press, 1970.
Magnusson, D., & Endler, N. S. *Personality at the crossroads: current issues in interactional psychology*. Hillsdale, N.J.: Lawrence Erlbaum Associates, 1977.
Masters, J. C., & Santrock, J. W. Studies in the self-regulation of behavior: Effects of verbal and cognitive self-reinforcement. *Developmental Psychology*, 1976, *12*, 334–348.
McDougall, W. *Social psychology*. London: Methuen, 1908.
Mead, M. *Cooperation and competition among primitive peoples*. New York: McGraw-Hill, 1937.
Meichenbaum, D. Stability of personality change and psychotherapy. In Staub, E., *Personality: Basic aspects and current research*. Englewood Cliffs, N.J.: Prentice-Hall, 1980.
Midlarz, S. The role of trust in helping behavior. Unpublished masters thesis, University of Massachusetts, Amherst, 1973.
Miller, G. A., Galanter, E., & Pribram, K. H. *Plans and the structure of behavior*. New York: Holt, Rinehart & Winston, 1960.

Mischel, W. Theory and research on the antecedents of self-imposed delay of reward. In B. A. Maher (Ed.), *Progress in experimental personality research*, Vol. III. New York: Academic Press, 1966.

Towards a cognitive social learning reconceptualization of personality. *Psychological Review*, 1973, *80*, 252–283.

Ebbesen, E. B., & Zeiss, A. R. Cognitive and attentional mechanisms in delay of gratification. *Journal of Personality and Social Psychology*, 1972, *21*, 204–218.

Selective attention to the self: Situational and dispositional determinants. *Journal of Personality and Social Psychology*, 1973, *27*, 129–142.

& Mischel, H. N. A cognitive social-learning approach to morality and self-regulation. In T. Lickona (Ed.), *Moral development and behavior*. New York: Holt, Rinehart & Winston, 1976.

Murray, H. A. *Explorations in personality*. New York: Oxford University Press, 1938.

Piliavin, I. M., Rodin, J., and Piliavin, J. A. Good Samaritanism: An underground phenomenon. *Journal of Personality and Social Psychology*, 1969, *13*, 289–299.

Piliavin, J. A., & Rodin, J. Costs, diffusion and the stigmatized victim. *Journal of Personality and Social Psychology*, 1975, *3*, 429–438.

Pomazal, R. J., & Jaccard, J. J. An informational approach to altruistic behavior. *Journal of Personality and Social Psychology*, 1976, *33*, 317–327.

Reese, H. Relationships between self-acceptance and sociometric choices. *Journal of Abnormal and Social Psychology*, 1961, *62*, 472–474.

Reykowski, J. Introduction. In J. Reykowski (Ed.), *Studies in the mechanisms of prosocial behavior*. Wydaevnictiva Universytetu, Warszawskiego, 1975.

Rokeach, M. *The nature of human values*. New York: Macmillan Publishing Co., 1973.

Rosenhan, D. L., Moore, B. S., & Underwood, B. The social psychology of moral behavior. In T. Lickona (Ed.), *Moral development and behavior*. New York: Holt, Rinehart & Winston, 1976.

Rotter, J. B. *Social learning and clinical psychology*. Englewood Cliffs, N.J.: Prentice-Hall, 1954.

Rubin, Z., & Peplau, L. A. Belief in a just world and reactions to another's lot: A study of participants in the national draft lottery. *Journal of Social Issues*, 1973, *29*, 73–93.

Schwartz, S. H. Moral decision making and behavior. In J. Macauley & L. Berkowitz (Eds.), *Altruism and helping behavior*. New York: Academic Press, 1970.

Normative influences on altruism. In L. Berkowitz (Ed.), *Advances in experimental social psychology*, Vol. 10. New York: Academic Press, 1977.

& Clausen, G. T. Responsibility, norms and helping in an emergency. *Journal of Personality and Social Psychology*, 1970, *16*, 299–310.

Feldman, K. A., Brown, M. E. & Heingarter, A. Some personality correlates of conduct in two situations of moral conflict. *Journal of Personality*, 1969, *37*, 41–57.

Seligman, M. E. P. *Helplessness: On depression, development, and death*. San Francisco, Calif.: W. H. Freeman and Company, 1975.

Staub, E. A child in distress: The influence of age and number of witnesses on children's attempts to help. *Journal of Personality and Social Psychology*, 1970, *14*, 130–140.

Helping a person in distress: The influence on implicit and explicit "rules" of conduct on children and adults. *Journal of Personality and Social Psychology*, 1971, *17*, 137–145. (b)

The use of role playing and induction in children's learning of helping and sharing behavior. *Child Development*, 1971, *42*, 805–811. (c)

Instigation to goodness: The role of social norms and interpersonal influence. *Journal of Social Issues*, 1972, *28*, 131–151.

Children's sharing behavior: Success and failure, the "norm of deserving," and reciprocity in sharing. Paper presented at the Symposium: Helping and Sharing: Concepts of Altruism and Cooperation, at the meeting of the Society of Research in Child Development, Philadelphia, Pennsylvania, March, 1973.

Helping a distressed person: Social, personality, and stimulus determinants. In L. Berkowitz (Ed.), *Advances in experimental social psychology*, Vol. 7, Academic Press, 1974.)

The development of prosocial behavior in children. Morristown, N.J.: General Learning Press, 1975.(a)

To rear a prosocial child: Reasoning, learning by doing, and learning by teaching others. In D. DePalma & J. Folley (Eds.), *Moral development: Current theory and research*. Hillsdale, N.J.: Lawrence Erlbaum Associates, 1975.(b)

The development of prosocial behavior: Directions for future research and applications to education. Paper presented at Moral Citizenship/Education Conference, Philadelphia, Pennsylvania, June 1976.

Positive social behavior and morality: Volume 1, Personal and social influences. New York: Academic Press, 1978.

Positive social behavior and morality: Volume 2, Socialization and development. New York: Academic Press, 1979.

& Baer, R. S., Jr. Stimulus characteristics of a sufferer and difficulty of escape as determinants of helping. *Journal of Personality and Social Psychology*, 1974, *30*, 279–285.

& Feinberg, H. Personality, socialization, and the development of prosocial behavior in children. In D. H. Smith & J. Macauley (Eds.), *Informal social Participation: The determinants of socio-political action, leisure activity, and altruistic behavior*. San Francisco: Jossey-Bass, Inc., 1980.

& Kellett, D. S. Increasing pain tolerance by information about aversive stimuli. *Journal of Personality and Social Psychology*, 1972, *21*, 203.

& Sherk, L. Need approval, children's sharing behavior, and recriprocity in sharing. *Child Development*, 1970, *41*, 243–253.

Tursky, B., & Schwartz, G. Self-control and predictability: Their effects on reactions to aversive stimulation. *Journal of Personality and Social Psychology*, 1971, *18*, 157–163.

Stotland, E. Exploratory studies of empathy. In L. Berkowitz (Ed.), *Advances in experimental social psychology*, Vol. 4. New York: Academic Press, 1969.

Thibaut, J. W., & Kelley, H. H. *The social psychology of groups*. New York: Wiley, 1959.

Toda, M., Shinotsuka, H., McClintock, C. G., & Stech, F. J. Development of competitive behavior as a function of culture, age, and social comparison. *Journal of Personality and Social Psychology*, 1978, *36*, 825–839.

Turnbull, C. M. *The mountain people*. New York: Simon & Schuster, 1972.

Wilson, J. P. Motivation, modeling and altruism: A person X situation analysis. *Journal of Personality and Social Psychology*, 1976, *34*, 1078–1086.

Wrightsman, L. S. Personality and attitudinal correlates of trusting and trustworthy behaviors in a two-person game. *Journal of Personality and Social Psychology*, 1966, *4*, 328–332.

Yakimovich, D., & Saltz, E. Helping behavior: The cry for help. *Psychonomic Science*, 1971, *23*, 427–428.

Zeigarnik, B. Uber das Behalten von erledigten und unerledigten Handlungen. *Psychol. forsch.*, 1927, *9*, 1–85.

9

The Power to Help Others

Report on a Psychology Today *Survey on Values, Helping, and Well-Being*

A distressing feature of the decade just past is the selfishness that was one of its most salient characteristics. Not since the Gilded Age have so few reveled publicly in having so much, while the gap between rich and poor Americans widened and the middle class shrank. There is growing agreement that one key task of the '90s is to build a society that values helping as much as getting. The quality of individual life, the social good and even the welfare of humanity – protection of the environment and peace – depend on it.

But how do we move from a me-generation mentality to a more caring America? One way is to understand more about the people who *do* consistently reach out to others – what they are like, what leads them to help, what makes them different from the people who don't help.

Past studies other researchers and I have done show that altruism (caring about and helping others) is as basic a part of human nature as caring about ourselves. But how each of us develops – into caring, loving adults or people who ignore the needs of others – depends largely on how we are treated, what we see and what guidance we receive as we go along.

So it's vital to us as a society to know as much as we can about what leads to caring and helping. And it's important to us as individuals, too. There is strong evidence that helping makes us feel better and makes our lives more satisfying.

This is an issue whose importance extends well beyond our shores. Altruism research makes it clear that the willingness of people to help the persecuted is one of the few forces that can counter tyranny and genocide – two

This manuscript was to appear in *Psychology Today* in the month that the magazine suspended publication in 1990 for about two years. The questionnaire referred to in this article is included in the Appendix.

The questionnaires were coded by a group of students led by Sheri Rosenblum (who also did the computer analysis) and Adrian Staub. The group also included Emma Dickinson, Jill Robbins, Peter Gibowitz, Lawrence Elliot, and Laura Cohen.

of the scourges that shattered the hope of progress with which we entered the 20th century. The recent reports of Azerbaijani citizens who hid their Armenian neighbors from the racial riots that shook the Soviet Union is but the newest example of the kind of heroism that saved some people from the Holocaust half a century ago.

As the evidence reviewed in my recent book, *The Roots of Evil*, makes clear, either genocide or resistance to it gains support from the acts of individuals. Harmful actions dehumanize the victims; helpful actions place value on their lives and challenge those who persecute them.

Psychology Today readers seem very aware of the enormous importance of gaining new insight into what builds altruism. More than 7,000 of you took time to respond to *PT*'s in-depth survey on values and goals last May, many including provocative and thoughtful letters. From these responses I randomly selected 2,000 questionnaires to analyze for this report.

Psychologists and philosophers have debated the meaning and roots of altruism for years. The responses to *PT*'s survey offer a fresh perspective on much of what we already knew about helping, and supply new information that corrects other beliefs.

WHAT VALUES ARE MOST IMPORTANT TO PEOPLE WHO CONSISTENTLY HELP OTHERS?

As you'd expect, their values are "other-oriented." We measured a constellation of other-oriented values – beliefs that directly or indirectly express regard for human beings and identify their welfare as desirable and good. Our survey shows that combining two of these beliefs – holding a positive view of human beings and believing that you are personally responsible for their welfare, a combination I call "prosocial orientation" – is especially important in altruism.

We also measured people's belief in their ability to help others. This feeling of competence is, by itself, associated with helping. But when we combine prosocial orientation (which expresses caring) with competence (which is the belief that one can translate caring into helping), the result is very substantial altruism. I named this combination "active caring" (see "How World Views Influence Helping").

In the past psychologists have considered prosocial orientation, empathy and a commitment to moral rules as potential motivators of unselfish helping. Our survey found each of them connected to helping, but prosocial orientation played a much bigger part in determining who helped and how much.

One reason, I suspect, is that rules themselves and adhering to them can become so important to people that the underlying spirit of concern for human welfare becomes secondary. And feeling distressed because someone is in trouble may not be translated into action unless you feel personally responsible for the sufferer's welfare and competent to do something about it.

Common courtesies we asked about, such as giving directions to strangers, holding elevator doors open or giving up one's seat on a bus or train, affect the quality of public life. Still, it is reassuring to me that these easy-to-do actions aren't the primary expressions we found of other-oriented values (see "How We Help"). These values – specifically prosocial orientation and active caring, as we have seen – are more strongly linked to the other forms of helping, including volunteering, that require more time and effort.

DO OTHER-ORIENTED VALUES PRODUCE HELPING?

The survey's results tell us that prosocial orientation and helping go together, but which causes which? I suspect it works both ways. The values and feelings that comprise prosocial orientation motivate helping, and the experience of being helpful leads people to value others' welfare more. The helpers also come to see themselves as more caring individuals.

Helpfulness that demands considerable sacrifice usually evolves gradually, starting with small acts that prepare the way. This evolution happened with many who risked their lives to save Jews and others threatened by genocide in Nazi Europe. Some who at first agreed to hide a family briefly ended up hiding them for years. Others started by helping a friend and eventually saved the lives of many strangers.

Some of the comments readers made to supplement their answers to our survey show how different values and experiences work to induce or reduce helping. A 38-year-old director of a crisis hotline wrote, "We are not our brother's keeper, we are his brother." She is highly other-oriented and helpful. In contrast, a 30-year-old software engineer refuses "to fritter away time on community organizations" and just says no to "charitable organizations attempting to impose burdens on me." He helps very little.

Others are less self-aware, prey to the natural tendency to believe in one's good intentions. A 23-year-old public relations executive writes that she is in a "state of apathy" because the help anyone can provide is so "insufficient that it isn't worth doing." She helps little, but not just because she feels powerless. Her answers show that other-oriented goals are simply less important to her than self-oriented ones.

WHAT ARE TRULY OTHER-ORIENTED GOALS?

In addition to asking readers about their values – what it is they consider good and desirable – we also asked about their goals – the desirable ends they personally strive for. I looked separately at how two kinds of other-oriented goals relate to helping. Not surprisingly, people who strive to help individuals, improve society, increase equality, lessen the threat of war and achieve other broad goals are especially helpful.

But I was surprised that the goals of friendship, cooperation and connection to others were not similarly related to helping. Perhaps people who value *only* these goals are not truly other-oriented but interested in fulfilling their own needs through friendship.

DO SELF-ORIENTED GOALS AUTOMATICALLY MEAN LESS HELPING?

This question hasn't really been addressed in previous research. We found that the answer depends on the specific goals. Men and women help much less if they consider as most important what I call "materialistic-competitive" goals such as wealth, career success and power. But caring strongly about other kinds of self-oriented goals – such as emotional support and security, approval from others, pleasure and fun, privacy, personal growth, adventure, competence and control – doesn't reduce helping.

To check further on this, I looked at the answers given by the people who were most helpful and found that most of them considered both other-oriented goals and the second sort of self-oriented ones important in their lives. Many helpful people, it seems, aren't simply self-sacrificing, they consider and balance their own and others' needs.

HOW HELPING MAKES YOU FEEL GOOD

We found something else among the caring: the joy of helping. There hasn't been much research on how people feel after they help, but what exists agrees that it's usually good. When we asked people to think of specific times they helped and tell us how they felt afterward, 81% of the descriptions they selected were positive – such as good, joyful, needed – rather than negative – bad, let down, taken advantage of.

What we didn't know before the survey is that it's clearly a case of the rich (in caring) getting richer. Most people feel better after they help. But those who are *generally* more helpful, or more other-oriented, felt even better than people for whom helping is less in character. The altruists' comments back this up. A typical answer to the question. "Why do you help people?" ran something like, "It gives back more than anything else I know."

Another woman answered simply, "I help because I'm good at it. I listen carefully, I find people's strengths and mobilize them." And from a third woman, a social worker. "The day a new adopting father walked out of my office with year-old twins, one in each arm, followed by his formerly childless wife, I knew it was all worthwhile."

HOW HEALTH AND WELL-BEING RELATE TO HELPING

We expected to find that helpful people were healthier – see "Helper's High," *PT*, October 1988 – but that didn't happen. How people rated their health and how often they had seen the doctor during the previous year had nothing to do with how much they helped or how much volunteer work they did. But we did find a strong link between helping and a general feeling of well-being, which involves a combination of satisfaction with life and self-liking.

Again, I think this is a two-way street. It seems that those whose lives are more satisfying feel they have more to give others. And people feel better about themselves, feel their life is enriched, when they see the benefits of their help. As a man who manages an adolescent substance-abuse program explained, "I help people because it gives meaning to my life."

This speaks to one of the most hotly argued points in altruism research: the feeling on the part of some theorists that helping isn't really altruism if the helper gets something out of the deal. It's certainly true that people can help others for selfish reasons – to gain recognition, for example, or even material rewards. I don't consider this altruism. Or people can help because they are guided by enlightened self-interest, believing that we are all better off if we help one another – a worthwhile motive, if not quite altruism.

But true altruists, people who really care about others' welfare, get the most meaning and satisfaction out of helping. Such people don't act to make themselves feel good. The satisfaction they experience is due to the improved welfare of the "other" they helped. It's certainly better for us as individuals and for the world in general if we learn to gain satisfaction by helping others rather than ignoring or hurting them. Acts of helping, whatever their genesis, can lead to greater caring, as we have seen.

WHICH IS THE MORE HELPFUL SEX?

Psychologist Carol Gilligan's research suggests that, in general, men and women listen to two different voices when they face moral questions. Women's "caring voice" is concerned mainly with how a decision or action will help or hurt the people involved. In similar situations men's "justice voice" worries about the abstract rightness or wrongness of what happens. So it would seem – and common wisdom agrees – that women are generally more helpful than men.

We found, however, that men and women helped equally and often similarly. Among the 12 different ways of helping we asked about (see "How We Help"), we uncovered only three significant gender differences: Women console more, and men are more likely to donate blood and to pick up hitchhikers.

Another difference: While the most helpful men and women in our survey are equally other-oriented, women as a group are more likely to exhibit this orientation. Why this doesn't translate into more helping by women is suggested by something else we found: a closer relationship between other-oriented values and helping in men than in women. To put it another way, men seem to translate more of their caring into action.

So while as a group men describe themselves less as other-oriented, they actually help about as much as women. This is not due to any greater feeling of competence: women actually report somewhat greater belief in their ability to help. Being caring is, of course, regarded as part of the traditional female role. Perhaps some women express these "feminine" values without a real commitment to act on them. Or they may act more in ways we didn't ask about in detail – such as in everyday interactions with family and friends.

Because caring is associated more with the female role and women have more other-oriented values than men, it may be that our questionnaire especially appealed to them. More than 70% of the respondents were women, compared to the approximately 60% female readership of *PT*.

THOSE HELPFUL THIRTYSOMETHINGS

Research shows that in most ways helping increases throughout childhood and adolescence. But we haven't known much about age differences in helping beyond the school years.

Many think of youth as the time people are hot to change and improve the world. But the kind of real-life helping our survey assessed increases as people get older, though it is not a completely gradual process. There is a sudden surge, stronger in volunteering than other forms of helping, in the early 30s. I suspect that most of us are preoccupied with our personal lives – education, career, marriage, children – before our attention turns outward and we are willing to devote considerable time to others.

People who have children also help more than those who don't. Perhaps what they learn and feel as they care for their children makes parents more sensitive to the needs of others. Children also bring more involvement with schools, with religious institutions, with the community in general – which automatically creates more opportunities for helping.

THE ROOTS OF HELPING: WHAT HAVE WE LEARNED?

What people reveal in their answers, and show even more clearly in their letters, confirms and expands previous research on altruism. Some mention growing up in a loving family: "In choosing a career in social work," one man wrote, "I felt I was fortunate to have had a wonderful family. I wanted to help others achieve the same goal." Receiving love gives children self-confidence and produces adults who value others.

Some people say they had models of helping, usually parents but sometimes others. One woman who helped others often mentioned her Aunt Carol, "who would always help in any situation." She mentioned one specific case in which the aunt stopped to aid an elderly black couple whose car had broken down. They had been stranded in the desert for three hours because no one else had stopped to help them.

Such models play an important role in developing altruism. Children learn by doing. My own research has shown that when children are encouraged to help others, they become more helpful, especially if they see the beneficial results. But what children see others do also strongly affects their actions.

So a good example can start a cycle. It leads to helping, which leads to caring, which in turn leads to more helping. Children increasingly learn to value others' welfare and start to see themselves as the kind of people who help others.

The process can work in reverse, too, if the models are of violence or apathy. Acts that cause only a little harm prepare the way for less caring and more harmful acts in the future.

I saw an unusual example of positive modeling – in this case, the parent followed a son's example – in a *New York Times* article this January. A donation to the *Times* Neediest Cases Fund was accompanied by a letter explaining: "I had a son named John who passed away from cancer this past July. He was 21. He was one who always championed the cause of the underprivileged. I would like to make the enclosed donation in his name in the hope that it will help to provide some food or shelter to a homeless person."

Some people wrote to *PT* at length about how they'd been helped at a crucial time, while others expressed deep pain about getting no assistance when they needed it. Whether this led them to mistrust and nonhelping or to caring and helping seemed to depend largely on their beliefs and world view (see "How World Views Influence Helping"). As one woman put it, "I have chosen work in a helping profession. I needed help as a teenager and couldn't find it."

Another, after telling how she and some other teachers had been accused of abusing the children in her school, wrote, "It's a terrible thing not to get help and support and understanding when you need it most. It reinforces my most basic belief that if you need help, you'd better be willing and able to help yourself."

We also found that there may be a substantial commitment to making changes in America that represent more caring, even if such changes are costly. For example, two-thirds agree or strongly agree that relief to needy people "requires, first and foremost, changes in social and economic

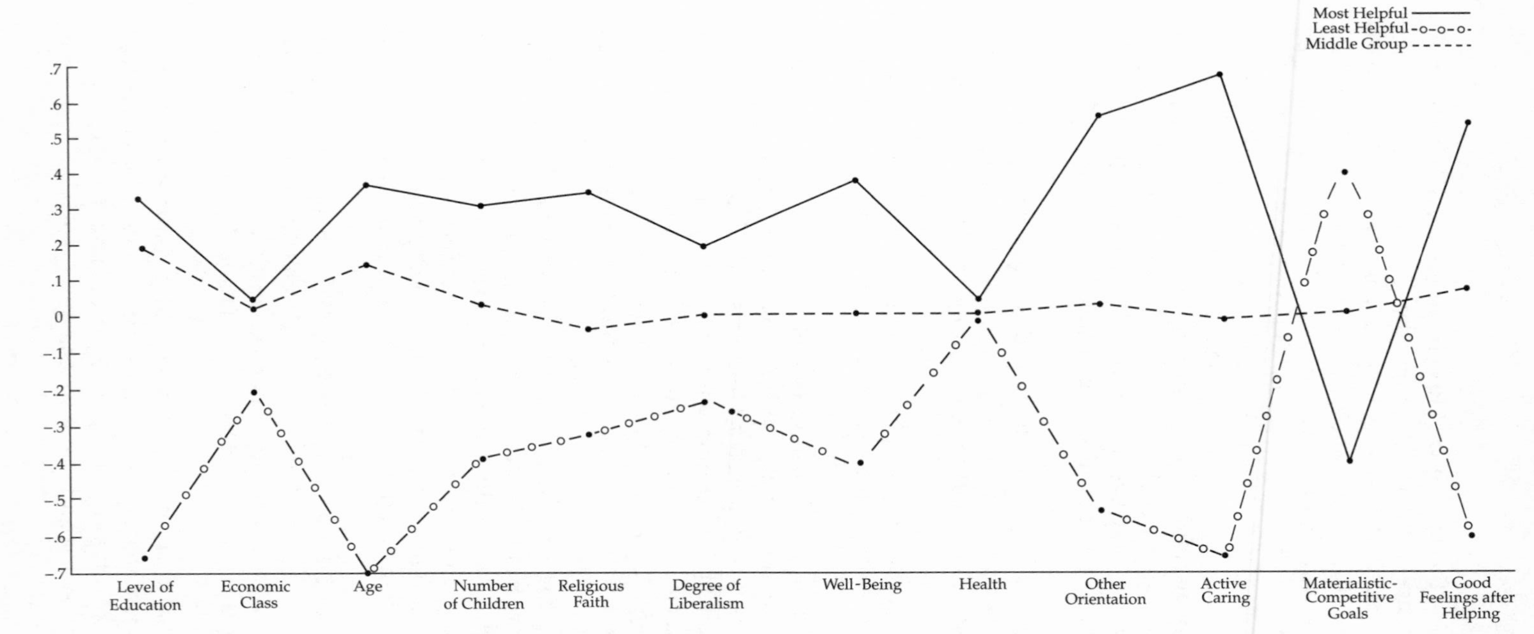

FIGURE 9.1. Differences in altruists and non-altruists. To show in what other ways people who are more or less helpful differ, we translated the answers that measured some important characteristics of our respondents into identical units (standard scores). The chart above compares altruists (the men and women who helped the most, the top 15%), non-altruists (the men and women who helped the least, the bottom 15%), and a middle group (the 25% whose helping was nearest to the average). The chart shows the extent to which each group is above or below the average on a number of characteristics that we measured, such as values (active caring), well-being, health, good feelings after helping, and others. Zero on the chart is the average of the whole group. Of the many differences between altruists and non-altruists, the greatest is in the value I have called here *active caring*, a brief measure of a prosocial value orientation. All the differences, except in health, are statistically significant.

TABLE 9.1. *More Information about Helping and Helpers*

1. How We Help[a]

The table below shows how frequently readers say they helped in 12 specific ways. Helping that doesn't call for much effort was frequent, but there was a great deal of more-demanding helping and volunteering as well.

	Percentage Who Help Each Way				
	Very often	Quite often	A few times	Once	Never
1. I have tried to console someone who was upset.	44	33	20	1	2
2. I have given money to a charity.	32	35	28	3	2
3. I have given directions to a stranger.	25	44	31	0	1
4. I have delayed an elevator for a stranger.	24	38	33	2	4
5. I have done volunteer work for a charity.	15	22	34	10	25
6. I have spent some time working for causes (like peace, social justice, or the environment).	15	13	30	10	12
7. I have helped a friend to move.	10	20	48	11	11
8. I have donated blood.	8	11	24	12	45
9. I have helped a stranger in an emergency (sudden illness, accident).	6	11	44	15	24
10. I have offered my seat on a bus or train to a stranger.	4	13	50	12	21
11. I have picked up a hitchhiker.	2	4	27	16	52
12. I have served food in a soup kitchen.	1	2	6	5	86

[a] Because figures are rounded off, some rows don't add up to 100%.

(continued)

TABLE 9.1. (*continued*)

2. How World Views Influence Helping[b]

Most of the survey questions address distinct values (such as responsibility to others and belief in moral rules), goals (improving society, privacy, financial security) and feelings (political, religious, spiritual). These factors can be arranged into four constellations. I call world views: religious, liberal, active caring and materialistic-competitive. The chart below shows how each of these views relates to people's goals, their other-orientation and their preferred types of helping.

For example, active caring is deeply rooted in other-oriented beliefs. People with this world view help most and in a broad range of ways. Those with a liberal view tend not to believe the world is just – a belief that leads people to see sufferers as somehow deserving to suffer. They feel concern for a broad range of human beings and have strong other-oriented goals.

People with a religious world view believe strongly in rules. They are more likely than liberals to work for charities and donate money, while liberals tend to work for social causes. As you'd expect, a materialistic-competitive world view is associated with less caring and helping.

	Religious	**Liberal**	**Active Caring**	**Materialistic-Competitive**
GOALS:				
Other oriented	+	++	+++	NM
Materialistic-competitive	–	–	– –	NM
SOME COMPONENTS OF OTHER ORIENTATION:				
Personal responsibility	++	o	++++	– –
Social responsibility	+	++	++++	– – –
World is not just	o	++	++	– –
Rule orientation	++++	o	+++	– –
Positive view of people	o	+	+++	–
Inclusiveness	+	++	++++	– –
SOME TYPES OF HELPING				
Dorating to charity	++	o	++	–
Volunteering for charity	++	o	+++	– –
Helping strangers in emergencies	+	o	++	o
Consoling people in distress	+	+	++	–
Working for social causes	o	++	+++	– –

[b] The symbols + and – indicate positive and negative connections and the degree, from slight (+ or –) to very strong (+ + + + or – – – –). o means that no connection exists. NM means that due to the method of assessment reporting a connection is not meaningful.

TABLE 9.1. (*continued*)

3. Who Answered the Survey[c]

Age: From 11 to 81.
Average age: 38
Sex: Women 72%
Men 28%

HIGHEST LEVEL OF EDUCATION	
High school or less	13%
Some college/ Associate's degree	25
Bachelor's degree	24
Some graduate school	6
Master's degree/ Addtl. grad. school	24
Doctorate/Professional degree	8

SOCIOECONOMIC CLASS	
Working class/blue collar	7%
Lower middle	12
Middle	50
Upper middle	30
Upper	2

POLITICAL ORIENTATION	
Liberal	43%
Moderate	39
Conservative	18
Libertarian	1

RELIGIOUS AFFILIATION	
None	15%
Atheist/agnostic	3
Protestant/Christian/Unitarian	48
Catholic	27
Jewish	6
Other	1

MARITAL STATUS	
Single	36%
Married	43
Divorced/separated	19
Widowed	2

NUMBER OF CHILDREN	
None	50%
One	11
Two	20
Three or more	20

RACE	
White	82%
African-American	2
Asian	2
Hispanic	2
Other	2
No answer	11

[c] Because figures are rounded off, some columns don't add up to 100%.

Note: Many readers who answered the questionnaire noted a discrepancy between the instructions for Part I, which said that the scale ran from 1 (strongly disagree) to 5 (strongly agree), and how we labeled the scale below the instructions. After discovering the mistake too late to fix it, we did two things to see if it seriously compromised the survey:

1. We administered the questionnaire to 297 people and found that 97% of them followed the correct designation. [The measure in the Appendix has the correct instructions. E.S.]
2. In scoring the answers, we adjusted the scoring for the 57 respondents who specifically mentioned that they had followed the incorrect instructions and for 24 others whose answers to Part I were so discrepant with their other answers on the questionnaire that we assumed they had also followed the incorrect instructions.

policies," while less than 6% strongly disagreed with the statement. And a plurality of more than 41% would be willing to "pay more taxes to expand social welfare programs."

The survey shows that whatever their mode or motivation, helping seems to improve the helpers' lives as well as those of the people they help. But it also suggests that deciding to help others simply to better one's own life doesn't quite do the trick. While there is nothing wrong with fulfilling one's own needs while helping others, deep satisfaction from helping requires genuine, unselfish caring.

The good news is that this can be learned. Even if you're preoccupied largely with yourself when you start, your motivations can change as you go along. One woman told us how "after I divorced and my children left home, I found myself in a self-centered existence . . . I realized I needed to focus on others sometime. So I found a 'cause' I felt compassion for and have been working with children through the Council on Child Abuse ever since. I can honestly say that I feel better after my sessions with these children . . . We all want to be wanted, loved and needed. So what better way than to go to those in need?"

PART III

HOW CHILDREN BECOME CARING AND HELPFUL RATHER THAN HOSTILE AND AGGRESSIVE

10

The Origins of Caring, Helping, and Nonaggression

Parental Socialization, the Family System, and Cultural Influence

What kind of socialization is required to raise caring, cooperative, helpful persons? What kinds of experiences are necessary for the development of characteristics that help people deal with crises by turning toward rather than against others, by inclusion rather than exclusion? What will help them resist movements, ideologies, and group influences that lead to confrontation and violence? How can they become self-assertive, able to stand up for their own rights and pursue their own goals, but also consider the rights, needs, and goals of others? What kind of socialization is required to develop people who are willing to make sacrifices to help others?

The way children are socialized is a basic manifestation of the culture and its institutions. Through socialization the culture recreates itself or creates itself anew. In order to socialize children in ways that lead to caring and nonaggression, a society (and its individual members) must value these characteristics. Currently, this is the case to a limited degree only in most countries; as compared with wealth, personal success, or patriotism, *the relative value* of caring about and helping others tends to be low. Therefore, changes in the socialization of children and in the values and institutions of society must progress simultaneously, supporting and reinforcing each other.

Sociobiologists (Trivers 1971; Wilson 1975) have proposed that altruism, the willingness to sacrifice in order to benefit others, is part of the human genetic makeup. However, our observations of each other clearly tell us that human beings vary greatly in their caring and help giving. While it is reasonable to believe that we possess a genetic potential for altruism (as

Reprinted from E. Staub (1992). The origins of caring, helping, and nonaggression: Parental socialization, the family system, schools, and cultural influence. In P. M. Oliner, S. B. Oliner, L. Baron, L. A. Blum, D. L. Krebs, and M. Z. Smolenska. *Embracing the other: Philosophical, psychological, and historical perspectives on altruism*. New York: New York University Press, pp. 390–412, with brief sections deleted. Copyright 1994, New York University Press. Reprinted with permission of the publisher.

well as aggression), the evolution of this potential depends on experience. Experience greatly affects even animals' response to the needs of other animals (see Staub 1978). Beyond a genetic potential, we possess "genetic building blocks" out of which altruism as well as aggression can evolve (Staub 1989). The fate of these potentials depends, however, on experience.

Socialization, the process whereby a culture transmits its values, rules, and roles to the child, is one type of important experience. What the culture teaches – by reward and punishment, through stories, and by example – is one source of the values and personal characteristics of individuals.

While the purpose of cultural transmission is to socialize children into prevailing values, norms, conceptions, and modes of behaving, none of these are static. Cultures evolve, as individuals do. For a group of people to survive, for group life to be possible, the culture must evolve values and rules that limit aggression and promote consideration for others' welfare and interest. However, the exact nature of standards and values that societies evolve will greatly differ as a result of different environmental conditions that groups have faced, different solutions they have created to resolve problems, their different routes of evolution. The rules and values they transmit represent their accumulated wisdom. Religions often elevate the accumulated wisdom of a culture to universalistic strivings.

In some cultures, the child is also exposed to human ideals that go beyond the existing culture. Philosophers as well as other thinkers have often gone beyond the peculiarities of the evolution of their own group and offered universal values and rules that would maximize human welfare. These ideals usually derive from conceptions of enlightened self-interest, the view that we can maximize our own welfare by considering the welfare of others, so that they will consider ours. Principles such as Kant's categorical imperative, according to which we are to act only in ways that we are willing to have others act, expand moral consideration beyond the group to all humanity. A less absolute principle is offered by utilitarianism, which regards the best conduct as the one that maximizes the ratio of benefit to harm (the greatest good for the greatest number). The combination of an absolute principle like the categorical imperative and the principle of utility may offer the best guide to moral conduct (Frankena 1973).

Yet another source of caring and nonaggression is the experience of a child in his or her relationships with both other human beings and the social system. How others behave towards the child, how as a result of the influences affecting him the child behaves towards others, as well as the limitations and opportunities within the social system itself determine whether the child feels valued or disregarded, comes to value rather than devalue other human beings, and sees others as benevolent or malevolent, as trustworthy or untrustworthy. Valuing people is essential for wanting to reach out to them and to respond to their needs. When socializing experiences are positive, the developing persons will come to value both themselves and others, and evolve generative capacities so that they can create values and ways of being that go beyond what is learned from transmission and direct experience.

Another likely source of values of mutual caring, connectedness, and love is the experience of connectedness. Having experienced such states (as a result of conditions that I will describe below) we transform them into values. Such experiences can be highly gratifying, which is reason for optimism; they make it possible to develop and/or adopt connectedness to others and caring for them as central values.

A constellation of characteristics, rather than a single one, is optimal both for individual positive functioning and positive human relationships. They include a *prosocial value orientation* – a positive view of others, concern for their welfare, and a feeling of personal responsibility for others' welfare (Staub 1974, 1978, 1980, 1989) – as well as *moral rule orientations*, which can be as general as holding a basic moral principle like justice, or specific such as adopting norms that prescribe helping. *Empathy* is a third important characteristic; it probably arises from a positive view of human beings, feelings of connection to them, and in case of sympathy concern about their welfare. (See endnote on empathy, sympathy, and personal distress on p. 170).

A prosocial value orientation was related to people helping others in either physical (Staub 1974, 1978) or psychological (Feinberg 1978; Grodman 1979; Staub 1978) distress. It was found to be more strongly related to self-reports of helping than either moral rule orientation or empathy (Staub 1990b). Nonetheless, a combination of these characteristics, especially an integration in which rule orientation is not predominant, provides a strong basis for helpfulness while making it unlikely that the welfare of individuals will be sacrificed for abstract ideals.

Personal goal theory suggests that in order to be frequently activated, to be dominant over other motives and thus lead to helping, these value orientations should be high in people's hierarchy of values and goals (Staub 1978, 1980, 1989). This is to be one of the central outcomes of the positive socialization in the home and in schools that I will describe in this chapter. Supporting characteristics such as competencies and the capacity to infer or perceive others' internal states and take their roles are also essential for caring, empathy, and their expression in behavior (Staub 1978, 1980, 1989).

CHILD REARING THAT PROMOTES CARING, HELPING, AND NONAGGRESSION

The education of the child in values and rules is less basic than the child's direct experience. Interpersonal relations and experiences with caretakers, with people in authority, and with peers are the sources of feelings, values, and beliefs about self, about other people, and about connections to others.

Attachment and Differentiation

An important *genetic building block* is the capacity for attachment. Except under the most extreme conditions of deprivation in caretaking and stimulation, found in some institutions (Thompson & Grusec 1970), and probably also present in some of the fractured and disorganized families increasingly common in our society, the child will develop an attachment – an affectional tie – to a caretaker. The quality of attachment will vary. Researchers have identified three primary kinds: secure, anxious, and conflictual or avoidant. Secure attachment is the result of the caretaker touching and holding the infant, mutual gazing, the responsiveness of the caretaker to the infant's needs. The latter is an essential component. Infants who develop secure attachment to caretakers are less upset when this person leaves them with a stranger, more loving and responsive when he or she returns. They show less anxiety in strange situations and appear secure and loving with the person who is the object of their attachment.

Recent research findings confirm the long-held belief that the earliest relationships influence later ones. When they later interact with peers, securely attached infants are able to initiate interaction effectively, and are the recipients of positive behavior from peers (Sroufe 1979). Secure attachment is probably a rudiment of trust both in others and in the self, of positive valuing of other people and a positive identity.

The connection to some people that is inherent in attachment is also a starting point for fear of other humans. As attachment manifests itself, evolving gradually but becoming evident after infants develop object constancy, stranger anxiety also appears. This is a powerful rudimentary manifestation of the fear and distress by which both humans and animals respond to the strange, the unfamiliar, what is discrepant from the known. Experience, however, shapes the degree and extensiveness of fear of strangers. For example, infants who develop a secure attachment or are exposed to more people show less stranger anxiety (Shaffer 1979). Attachment and stranger anxiety are manifestations, both as metaphors and in reality, of the separation of us and them, the known and liked from the unknown that is feared. Continuing experience shapes the evolution of positive ties to some people and the inclination to separate from others.

Children learn to differentiate between their primary group, the family, and the rest of the world, and are frequently taught not to trust those outside the family. Moreover, there is often specific indoctrination against outgroups, be they religious, ethnic, national, or political. At a very early age children evaluate their nation, for example, in a positive way, while expressing stereotypic and negative views of other nations (Piaget & Weil 1951).

Having learned to make differentiations between in-groups and outgroups, people will naturally create them under novel circumstances. Even if they develop prosocial and moral rule orientations and empathy, unless they become inclusive, that is, come to include a broad range of people in the human and moral domain, their helping and caring may remain restricted to a narrow in-group (Oliner & Oliner 1988; Staub 1989, 1990a).

Positive Socialization and the Child's Experience

Research findings from the last two or three decades, obtained both from examination of parental socialization practices and from laboratory settings, indicate that a *pattern of parental practices* contributes to prosocial behavior and values (for reviews, see Grusec 1981; Eisenberg 1986; Radke-Yarrow, Zahn-Waxler, & Chapman 1983; Staub, 1979, 1981, 1986; Zahn-Waxler et al. 1986). These include parental warmth, affection, or nurturance; the tendency to reason with the child, to explain why the parents expect certain behaviors while they disapprove of others, and especially "induction," pointing out to children the consequences of their behavior on others, both negative and positive; firm but not forceful control, the parents leading the child to actually act according to values they regard as important, to follow important rules; and natural socialization, the parents guiding the child to engage in behavior that benefits others, to cooperate with others, so that learning by doing can follow (Staub 1975, 1979). Modeling by parents, the example of the parents' own behavior, is also an important source of what children learn.

Parental warmth and affection, especially when combined with sensitivity in perceiving and responding to the child's needs, have important consequences. The child experiences the parents as loving and kind, as trustworthy and benevolent. Since interaction with parents is usually the young child's primary experience of people, these feelings will generalize to others. The parents' caring and kindness lead the child to experience himself or herself positively, to the evolution of positive self-esteem. Warmth and nurturance make the child feel safe, so that he or she can initiate new behaviors and experiment in the world without fear of punishment. Even a limited ten-minute-long interaction with a nurturant rather than an indifferent adult leads kindergarten-age children to initiate more action upon hearing sounds of another child's distress from another room (Staub 1970a). Finally, warmth and nurturance by parents lead to identification, to the child wanting to be like the parents. This increases cooperation with parents, and makes the relationship of parents and children more mutually satisfying and the socialization of the child easier.

The quality of interaction with adults results in selective attention to the world, a striking finding. Nursery school children who were cared for, over a two-week period, by either a warm or an indifferent adult remembered the same number of actions of small dolls that were manipulated by the adult. However, *what* they remembered differed; the former children remembered more positive, helpful acts, the latter more negative, aggressive acts (Yarrow & Scott 1972). In general, children's orientation to other people probably affects how they experience events and what they learn from experience.

Reasoning with children is a mild form of influencing and controlling them. As a mode of relating to them, it is consistent with affection and nurturance. Induction, the parents (or anyone else) pointing out to the child the consequences of his or her behavior for other people, communicates to the child his or her power to affect others' well-being, as well as his or her responsibility toward others. In addition, induction focuses attention on others' internal states, on how they feel and what they think, on their inner world. This is crucial for learning to consider others' needs, hopes, and desires.

Children have their own desires, intentions, their own agenda. If parents are to guide the child to a consideration of other people, or if they are to lead the child to respect values and rules, they must at times exert additional influence. Firm enforcement of at least a limited set of rules that the parents regard as highly important is necessary. It is essential, however, that this does not take forceful and violent forms (see below). Firm enforcement of rules that express important values can coexist with allowing the child substantial autonomy, choice, and self-guidance, to an increasing degree as the child's capacity for responsible choice and competence develops.

Parents can also guide children to act in helpful, generous, cooperative ways, an example of what I have called *natural socialization* (Staub 1975, 1979). Natural socialization is a pervasive but hidden aspect of socialization. In order to develop interest in and motivation to engage with activities, objects, and people, the child has to experience them. He or she has to engage with mathematical games and problems to evolve an interest in math, a desire to work with math, and to experience such activity as satisfying. Engagement can result in learning by participation: under supporting conditions, participation will enhance motivation. Such learning is of great importance for helping and harm-doing.

In a series of studies my associates and I found that children who teach younger children, or make toys for poor hospitalized children, or write letters to hospitalized children are later more likely to be helpful or generous (Staub 1975, 1979). These findings were stronger for girls, in that participation in a broader range of prosocial acts enhanced their later prosocial behaviors. With girls the combination of participation and pointing out the beneficial consequences of their behaviors to them had the strongest effect in increasing subsequent helpfulness or generosity.

Boys were more likely to later act to benefit others if they participated in helpful acts that responded to lesser and/or less personal need. Direct helping of needy others seemed to evoke their resistance. For example, when boys participated by making toys for poor hospitalized children, their helping behavior immediately afterwards declined. Still, this experience had a positive impact with the passage of time, in that these boys' helping was somewhat elevated on a "delayed posttest" several weeks later. In contrast, helping behavior that was not directed to alleviate distress or personal need, making toys to help an art teacher develop materials for teaching art, enhanced boys' subsequent helping of poor, hospitalized children. For girls, the initial experience of making toys for poor hospitalized children enhanced later helping most.

In our society, boys may see some acts of kindness as "goody goody," especially when adults induce them or guide them to engage in those acts. The caring these acts express may be inconsistent with the masculine image boys try to adopt. Being put in a situation where they were to engage in such acts may have resulted in resistance and evoked an oppositional tendency.

Finally, the parents' example, their kindness not only toward their own children but in interaction with people in general, is essential. Values, rules, and modes of behaving will not be acquired by children if they are verbally propagated by adult socializers but not manifested in their conduct.

The consequences of these experiences on children's personality appear manifold. First, they lead to a positive evaluation of other people, a respect for and concern about other people's welfare, and a feeling of responsibility to help others – that is, a prosocial value orientation. Second, out of their connection to other people and their capacity to understand others' internal states, feelings of empathy can arise. The experiences that I described, especially if they are combined with parents setting relatively high standards for their children that they can successfully fulfill at least some of the time, will also lead to the evolution of a positive self-esteem (Coopersmith 1967).

A pattern of child-rearing practices that is in essence the opposite of the one I just discussed will lead to the opposite consequences: to hostility and aggression. They include indifference and rejection by parents; hostility, especially between boys and their fathers; and the use of control over the child that relies on the parents' power, or power-assertive control, such as depriving the child of privileges and especially the frequent use of physical punishment. Such practices are related to aggressive behaviors in boys (Aronfreed 1968; Bandura & Walters 1959; Eron 1982; Huesmann et al. 1984; Huesmann, Lagerspetz, & Eron 1984; Staub 1986, 1989). One likely effect of their use is that children come to view people as hostile and aggressive; another is that they learn that aggression is normal, acceptable, even inevitable in human relations. Their own mistreatment may generate anger and hostility in them toward other people. In extreme cases, they may develop an *antisocial orientation*, a negative evaluation of people and the desire to harm them.

Experiences that are afforded by the culture and life in a society both affect parental socialization and combine with it to shape individual characteristics. For example, children who habitually watch aggressive television are more aggressive. But these tend to be children who are rejected, criticized, or are in other ways the objects of parental hostility (Eron 1982; Huesmann et al. 1984; Huesmann, Lagerspetz, & Eron 1984). Personal experiences affect the elements of culture to which children voluntarily expose themselves. But even children who experience positive socialization will usually be exposed to elements of culture that stress competition and focus on self-interest. And they often lack guidance as to how to integrate conflicting values and goals.

Self-Awareness and Positive Identity

An essential aspect of *positive socialization* is to develop self-awareness and self-acceptance in children. Too much anxiety and threat make it necessary for children to defend themselves from feelings, to deny them and repress them. Even when socialization practices and the family environment are optimal, however, children require help to correctly read and code their own feelings and those of others. They require support to experience and be aware of their own sadness, disappointment, hurt, and anger. Parents can help children learn to perceive, accept, and deal with the whole range of feelings. Alternatively, they can guide children not to attend to and thereby not to perceive, or to negatively evaluate, deny, and repress some feelings.

The consequences can be profound. One of them is the projection of unacceptable feelings onto others, which generates moral indignation, anger, and hostile behavior. Another is diminished well-being and happiness and diminished capacity for informed choice which affect all relationships.

Life can never be painless. Even feelings of love often result in pain: the person we love returns less caring and love, or turns to another for love, or dies. It is essential for people to be able to experience feelings of sadness, grief, sorrow, anxiety, anger, and other painful and conflictful emotions. Only by experiencing them can people move through them, be done with them. The inability to perceive, accept, or experience such feelings in ourselves makes it unlikely that we will perceive them in others or, if we do, that we will respond with empathy, support, and help. It diminishes our capacity to accurately see and experience others; combined with our diminished well-being, it makes us less open to others' needs, pain, or suffering; and it decreases our willingness to subordinate our own needs and goals to helping others in distress.

Another essential consequence of positive child rearing is self-reliance, emotional independence, and the capacity for independent judgment. Such qualities will result from providing children with love and nurturance, from helping them become aware of their feelings, from allowing them increasing degrees of autonomy, from involving them in family decision making, and from exposing and guiding them to a wide range of activities. Such child rearing enables children to differentiate themselves from members of their family, to evolve separate identities. It provides the emotional strength to endure the vicissitudes and turmoils of life. All this reduces the likelihood that people will seek guidance from leaders and solace from ideologies that tell them how to live, or that they will accept definitions of reality by experts and those in authority that would lead them to harm other people (Staub 1989).

Being part of and committed to a valued group, like a nation, or to a faith or an ideology, gives people great courage, physical and moral. Frequently such courage serves destruction, as evidenced by kamikaze pilots, Shiite terrorists, or men in battle. However, great courage is evident as well in service to others that is nonviolent and at times requires deviation from a larger social group. When lives are in danger, due to accidents or persecution, some people respond in heroic ways, endangering and at times losing their own lives in saving others. The challenge of raising children is to help them evolve strong, well-developed but at the same time connected identities that embody caring about others' welfare and the experience of deep feelings of satisfaction from connection to other people. The term *connected identities* implies both such connection and the capacity to stand apart and, at times, in opposition.[1]

The preceding discussion shows the importance for children's development of feeling safe, secure, and protected, especially when young. A great problem today, at least in the U.S., is the large numbers of children who grow up without either a family or an alternative child-care arrangement that provides this.

THE INFLUENCE OF THE FAMILY AS A SYSTEM

It is increasingly recognized that the family is a system with explicit and implicit, hidden rules. For children, these rules tend to become blueprints of the world and of how to function in it. In coercive family environments, members rely on aggression to exert control over each other and to defend themselves from attack (Patterson 1982). Children come to learn that human beings are aggressive, and that only by aggression can they defend themselves or exert influence.

In many families parents set rules in an authoritarian fashion. They often prohibit not only aggression by children within the family but also the expressions of anger or other feelings they regard as antisocial or contrary

[1] I have proposed a classification of types of selves according to degree and nature of connection to others: disconnected; autonomous or independent; selves-in-relation (Surrey 1985); and embedded (Staub, 1993). The connection of embedded selves to others includes dependency and need, which make deviation and independent action difficult. The term "connected selves" or "identities" has a similar meaning to, but for my purposes is preferable to "self-in-relation."

to their ideals. The consequences can include denial and repression of hostile feelings, lack of self-awareness and self-acceptance, and a liking of or preference for hierarchical relationships. Children who grow up in a democratic family, where values and rules are negotiated and children participate in making decisions, will obviously learn greater independence.

Family systems also have other characteristics. One parent may be passive, with decisions made by the other. Once the system evolves around this division of power, change will be resisted. The greater power of one parent may arise from, or may be maintained by, a coalition with children. The child's personality will manifest both his or her own position or role in the system and what the system teaches about the roles, responsibilities, and relative power of males and females, adults and children.

Recent work by Boszormenyi-Nagy and Spark has focused on justice as a profoundly important aspect of family life (Boszormenyi-Nagy & Spark 1984). Injustice that the child suffers in the family will remain a legacy that the person will have to work out in his or her own life. The abuse of children, in this view, can be the balancing out of injustice that a person suffered as a child at the hands of parents.

One difficulty in raising children in ways that promote caring and nonaggression lies in the parents' own personalities. Even if parents value these characteristics in their children, they are limited by their own personalities in promoting them. Their ease or difficulty in allowing their growing children participation in family decisions, the extent to which they are aware of their own feelings and perceive those of their children, and the family rules they unknowingly establish are the result of their own past history and who they have become. People need mirrors to see themselves and to grow. To become capable of raising caring and nonaggressive children, many people need experiences that would bring to their awareness both their modes of relating to their children and the family systems they have unconsciously shaped.

To overcome the limitations imposed by the negative impact of certain parental characteristics, we ought to expand the range of adults with whom the child has significant contact. More cooperative child rearing would facilitate intimate contact with more people. My observations suggest to me that children whose early experience was potentially highly damaging, as a result of abandonment or bad treatment at the hands of adults, were sometimes "saved" by people who had reached out to them and become significant positive figures in their lives.

Methods of disciplining children and modes of relating to them are also affected by the parents' own life conditions. For loving, affectionate relationships with children, the use of reasoning, and the use of nonforceful modes of control, it is necessary that parents have relatively ordered and secure life circumstances. If their basic needs for food, shelter, health care, and emotional support are unfulfilled, and if they lack a feeling of reasonable control over their lives, positive socialization becomes less likely.

When unemployment increases, reports of child abuse increase, and economic problems are associated with increased societal violence (Hovland & Sears 1940; Landau 1982). [See also Staub 1989; however, a reanalysis found that Hovland and Sears' findings did not support the latter. E.S.]

If we are to raise children who feel connected to other human beings, who are willing to help others, and who can resist pressures towards individual or group aggression, society will have to provide parents with at least a modicum of security and the fulfillment of basic needs. Thus, for the evolution of a pattern of personal characteristics that significantly increase the potential for kindness versus cruelty, in a large enough group of children to represent a noticeable cultural change, at least minimally supportive societal conditions are required.

We can instruct parents – train them in specific skills of child rearing. This is not enough, however. Methods of raising children partly derive from parents' values. Up to the twentieth century, parents in many places – in Germany, but also in England and elsewhere (DeMauss 1974; Stone 1977) – regarded children as innately willful. Forceful means were required if the child was to be capable of goodness and obedience. Obedience to parents was regarded as perhaps the highest of all values. Belief in the use of physical punishment with children (Straus, Gelles, & Steinmetz 1980) and other destructive beliefs, values, and practices still abound.

How do such societal views change? Partly through the education of parents. They must be convinced that beneficial consequences follow from children acquiring characteristics that promote positive behavior and diminish harm-doing: on the life of the family, on the future success and happiness of the child, and on the harmony and well-being of society. Some of these characteristics, like positive self-esteem and a feeling of efficacy, are also important for people pursuing self-related goals. A positive orientation to other people contributes to harmonious, satisfying interpersonal relationships and, thereby, to personal satisfaction and happiness. Reciprocity is perhaps the most basic law of human relationships (Gouldner 1960): people return kindness and are unlikely to harm someone who has benefited them. However, reciprocity depends not only on actions but also on the motives attributed to actors. We will best gain others' kindness, cooperation, trust, and affection if we impress them with our caring and unselfish actions *and* intentions. The best way to accomplish this is to be caring and unselfish. Self-assertion is also important, standing up for one's rights, so that those who might exploit a person's kindness will not be able to do so.

Creating Change

Information, advocacy, and the availability of services with specifiable benefits may lead parents to accept and even seek education in parenting. Training parents in specific skills of child rearing can be highly effective.

The state of Missouri, for example, initiated a demonstration project, starting with prospective parents and continuing until the children reached age three. Participants were taught simple skills such as setting clear limits for their children beginning in the first year of life, and creating stimulating environments and experiences (Meyerhoff & White 1986). Formal evidence showed that children whose parents received this training functioned at a more intellectually advanced level than children whose parents had not. Less formal evidence suggested that they also functioned better socially.

If such programs were widely available, and their benefits known, many prospective parents might turn to them to reduce the uncertainties of parenting and acquire the skills of "positive parenting." In the context of training in parenting skills, parents could examine and discuss their beliefs about the nature of children and evolve an attitude of benevolence, care, and consideration. As parents realize that positive modes of relating to children are effective in gaining their cooperation, they will acquire both a sense of power and an increased feeling of benevolence. They are likely then to be receptive to new views and positive practices. Social scientists and psychologists have an essential role in communicating information to the public that has accumulated in research, which provides the bases for new assumptions about and techniques for raising children.

It would also be of great value to create and make available *family systems diagnoses* to the general public. The purpose of this would be to make family members aware of – by the use of vivid procedures like viewing and discussing videos of family interaction – the rules and procedures by which the family operates. The discussion of what is happening in the family could entail education in alternative ways of functioning, and their possible results. Such services may someday be practical tools to increase happiness and well-being in families, decrease the frequency of divorce, and contribute to the positive socialization of children.

Note: Empathy, Sympathy, Personal Distress, and Prosocial Orientation

Some researchers, such as Eisenberg, have described a type of empathy, "sympathy," in terms somewhat similar to my description of prosocial value orientaion, empthy with another's distress that includes concern for the other (although without explicit focus on a feeling of responsibility). Eisenberg and Batson both have differentiated empathy, sympathy, and personal distress. Sympathy seems associated with helping. Personal distress looks similar to empathy, but it is not "feeling with the other." Instead, a person is impacted by someone's distress and experiences distress. In personal distress the motivation is to reduce one's own distress, sometimes by reducing another's distress, sometimes by simply getting away. Eisenberg and her associates have shown, in an extensive series of studies, that parents who help children regulate their emotions foster sympathy, while difficulty in the self-regulation of emotions is associated with personal distress (see, e.g., Nancy Eisenberg, Empathy-related emotional responses, altruisms, and their socialization. In R. J. Davidson & A. Harrington (Eds.), *Versions of compassion*. New York: Oxford University Press, 2002).

References

Aronfreed, J. (1968). *Conduct and conscience.* New York: Academic Press.
Bandura, A., & Walters, R. H. (1959). *Adolescent aggression: A study of the influence of child training practices and family inter-relationship.* New York: Ronald.
Boszormenyi-Nagy, I., & Spark, G. M. (1984). *Invisible loyalties: Reciprocity in intergenerational family therapy.* New York: Bruner-Mazel.
Coopersmith, S. (1967). *Antecedents of self-esteem.* San Francisco: Fremont.
DeMauss, L. (Ed). (1974). *History of childhood.* New York: Psycho-history Press.
Eisenberg, N. (1986). *Altruistic emotion, cognition, and behavior.* Hillsdale, NJ: Erlbaum.
Eron, L. D. (1982). Parent-child interaction, television violence, and aggression of children. *American Psychologist, 37,* 197–211.
Feinberg, H. K. (1978). Anatomy of a helping situation: Some personality and situational determinants of helping in a conflict situation involving another's psychological distress. Doctoral dissertation, University of Massachusetts, Amherst.
Frankena, W. (1973). *Ethics* (2nd ed.). London: Prentice-Hall.
Gouldner, A. W. (1960). The norm of reciprocity: A preliminary statement. *American Sociological Review, 25,* 161–79.
Grodman, S. M. (1979). The role of personality and situational variables in responding to and helping an individual in psychological distress. Unpublished doctoral dissertation, University of Massachusetts, Amherst.
Grusec, J. (1981). Socialization processes and the development of altruism. In J. P. Rushton & R. M. Sorrentino (Eds.), *Altruism and helping behavior*. Hillsdale, NJ: Erlbaum.
Hovland, C. I., & Sears, R. R. (1940). Minor studies of aggression: Correlation of lynchings with economic indices. *Journal of Psychology, 9,* 301–10.
Huesmann, L. R., Eron, L. D., Lefkowitz, M. M., & Walder, L. O. (1984). Stability of aggression over time and generations. *Developmental Psychology, 20,* 6, 1120–34.
Huesmann, L. R., Lagerspetz, K., & Eron, L. D. (1984). Intervening variables in the television, violence-aggression relation: Evidence from two countries. *Developmental Psychology, 20,* 746–75.
Landau, S. F. (1982). Trends in violence and aggression: A cross-cultural analysis. Paper presented at the Tenth International Congress of Sociology, Mexico City.
Meyerhoff, M. K., & White, B. L. (1986). Making the grade as parents, *Psychology Today, 20,* September, 38–45.
Oliner, S. B., & Oliner, P. M. (1988). *The altruistic personality: Rescuers of Jews in Nazi Europe*. New York: Free Press.
Patterson, G. R. (1982). *Coercive family processes*. Eugene, OR: Castilia.
Piaget, J., & Weil, A. (1951). The development in children of the idea of the homeland and of relations with other countries. *International Social Science Bulletin, 3,* 570.
Radke-Yarrow, M. R., Zahn-Waxler, C., & Chapman, M. (1983). Children's prosocial dispositions and behavior. In P. H. Mussen (Ed.), *Carmichael's manual of child psychology*, Vol. 4 (4th ed.). New York: Wiley.
Shaffer, D. R. (1979). *Social and personality development*. Monterey, CA: Brooks-Cole.
Sroufe, L. A. (1979). The coherence of individual development: Early care, attachment, and subsequent developmental issues. *American Psychologist, 34,* 834–42.

Staub, E. (1970a). A child in distress: The influence of modeling and nurturance on children's attempts to help. *Developmental Psychology, 5*, 124–33.

(1974). Helping a distressed person: Social, personality, and stimulus determinants. In L. Berkowitz (Ed.), *Advances in experimental social psychology*, Vol. 7. New York: Academic Press.

(1975). To rear a prosocial child: Reasoning, learning by doing, and learning by teaching others. In D. DePalma & J. Folley (Eds.), *Moral development: Current theory and research*. Hillsdale, NJ: Erlbaum.

(1978). *Positive social behavior and morality: Social and personal influences*, Vol. 1. New York: Academic Press.

(1979). *Positive social behavior and morality: Socialization and development*, Vol. 2. New York: Academic Press.

(1980). Social and prosocial behavior: Personal and situational influences and their interactions. In E. Staub (Ed.), *Personality: Basic aspects and current research*. Englewood Cliffs, NJ: Prentice-Hall.

(1981). Promoting positive behavior in schools, in other educational settings, and in the home. In J. P. Rushton & R. M. Sorrentino (Eds.), *Altruism and helping behavior*. Hillsdale, NJ: Erlbaum.

(1986). A conception of the determinants and development of altruism and aggression: Motives, the self, the environment. In C. Zahn-Waxler, E. M. Cummings, & R. Iannotti (Eds.), *Altruism and aggression: Biological and social origins*. New York: Cambridge University Press.

(1989). *The roots of evil: The origins of genocide and other group violence*. New York: Cambridge University Press.

(1990a). Moral exclusion, personal goal theory, and extreme destructiveness. In S. Opawa (Ed.), Moral exclusion and injustice. *Journal of Social Issues, 46*, 47–65.

(1990b). The power to help others. Unpublished manuscript, University of Massachusetts, Amherst.

(1993). Individual and group selves, motivation and morality. In W. Edelstein & T. Wren (Eds.), *Morality and the self*. Cambridge: MIT Press.

Stone, L. (1977). *The family, sex and marriage in England, 1500–1800*. New York: Harper & Row.

Straus, M. A., Gelles, R. J., & Steinmetz, S. (1980). *Behind closed doors: Violence in the American family*. Garden City, NY: Anchor/Doubleday.

Surrey, J. (1985). *Self-in-relation: A theory of women's development*. Wellesley, MA: Stone Center, Wellesley College.

Thompson, W. R., & Grusec, J. (1970). Studies of early experience. In P. H. Mussen (Ed.), *Carmichael's manual of child psychology*, Vol. 2 (3rd ed.). New York: Wiley.

Trivers, R. L. (1971). The evolution of reciprocal altruism. *Quarterly Review of Biology, 46*, 35–37.

Wilson, E. O. (1975). *Sociobiology: The new synthesis*. Cambridge, MA: Belknap Press of Harvard University Press.

Yarrow, M. R., & Scott, P. M. (1972). Imitation of nurturant and nonnurturant models. *Journal of Personality and Social Psychology, 23*, 259–70.

Zahn-Waxler, C., Cummings, E. M., & Iannotti (Eds.). (1986). *Altruism and aggression: Biological and social origins*. New York: Cambridge University Press.

11

Natural Socialization

The Role of Experience or Learning by Doing

FOCUSING RESPONSIBILITY ON CHILDREN AND LEARNING BY PARTICIPATION

Enacting or rehearsing prosocial behavior is important if children are to learn to behave prosocially. Certain types of influences on children, such as verbal communications, will acquire meaning and gain acceptance when they are experienced in conjunction with ongoing prosocial action.

I have previously suggested (Staub, 1975a, 1975b, 1978c; Staub & Feinberg, 1978) that an important influence on children learning to behave prosocially is the focusing of responsibility on them by parents and other socializing agents to engage in behavior that enhances others' welfare. Focusing responsibility refers to the demand by the parent that the child engage in prosocial behavior. It does not refer to a method of discipline, such as love withdrawal or power assertion, which does not specify what values and behavior the parents wish to promote. Like induction, focusing responsibility on children to behave prosocially refers to a particular content area, to a particular type of behavior the parents wish to promote. Although responsibility assignment is likely to lead to knowledge of desirable behavior, knowledge of "family norms" or social norms, it can only be expected to lead to internalization and self-guidance if socializers employ effective controls so that the child will actually behave prosocially. Thus, effective focusing of responsibility on children might result from a combination of parental values and parental actions that induce behavior consistent with these values in the child. However, focusing responsibility on children for activities that are in some sense prosocial might also be motivated by other values and by self-interest. At the extreme parents may insist that the child work around the house to the point of exploitation and

Reprinted from E. Staub (1979). *Positive social behavior and morality: Vol. 2. Socialization and development*. New York: Academic Press. From Ch. 6, pp. 189–219.

an inequitable distribution of labor. Obviously the motives for responsibility assignment, equity, and many other conditions may determine its effect on the child.

A distinction may be made between two types of responsibility assignment, according to the degree to which they are structured. The need to act prosocially may emerge in the course of ongoing events; and may result in sharing toys with others, helping someone who had an accident or hurt himself in other ways, or consoling someone who is upset. Rewarding children for doing these things, punishing them for not doing them, and generally communicating to them that they are expected to behave prosocially under conditions like these would be one form of responsibility assignment. Such *less-structured* responsibilities may lead to the development of initiative on the part of children, since they often have to use their own judgment to determine what prosocial action is appropriate. Responsibility assignment may also be *more structured*; a child may be expected to take care of a younger sibling whenever the mother is not home or when she is otherwise occupied, or may have obligations for the maintenance and welfare of the family or some of its members. The more clearly specified the task – what it is, how it is done, and when it is done – the more structured the responsibility assignment.

An early study found that children who had pets acted more sympathetically toward their peers (Bathurst, 1933). Although the responsibility of taking care of pets might have increased these children's sensitivity to others, it is also possible that more sensitive children are more interested in having pets. Baumrind (1971, 1975) reported that part of the pattern of child rearing by parents of friendly and sociable children was the assignment of household duties to children. Mussen et al. (1970) reported that encouragement of responsibility by mothers was associated with peers' perceptions of a child's helpfulness, particularly in boys. Other relevant data came from several sources.

Evidence that provides tentative support for the influence of "structured" responsibility assignment on prosocial behavior comes from the cross-cultural research of John and Beatrice Whiting (1969, 1975). These investigators examined the behavior of children in six cultures and the relationship between the characteristics of the culture, child rearing, and children's behavior. They found that in some cultures children were more altruistic (they made more responsible suggestions to others, were more helpful, and so on), whereas in other cultures children were more egoistic (they sought help and attention for themselves). These cultures differed in a number of characteristics, including social organization and level of technological development. However, what was most strongly related to and in the researchers' view responsible for the differences among cultures in children's altruistic-egoistic tendencies was the degree to which children were assigned responsibilities that contributed to the maintenance of the family. The more the children had to tend animals, take care of younger siblings, and assume other "responsible" duties, the more altruistic their behavior. The children were found to be most egoistic in the "Yankee" town in the United States, in "Orchardtown." There, children's obligations in the family consisted primarily of keeping order in their own rooms, which was unlikely to give them much of a sense of importance for contributing to the welfare of the family.

Whiting and Whiting noted that parents did not use induction or gentle persuasion in the cultures that assigned extensive responsibility to children; rather, they exerted influence in a straightforward manner, to make sure that children actually did their (prosocial) tasks. What children learn from actually engaging in prosocial behavior will depend on a variety of surrounding conditions: the manner in which they are induced to do it, whether they are reinforced for it, the degree of satisfaction that they experience from the activity itself, the degree to which they learn to gain satisfaction from the positive consequences of their action, how demands on them compare to demands placed on other children in their culture, and so on.

If strong force is exerted on children to behave prosocially, a variety of negative consequences might follow. First, psychological reactance might be created, resulting in resistance or in children trying to outsmart the authority exerting force. They may either not behave prosocially, or, if they do, they will make external rather than internal attributions about reasons for their prosocial behavior. However, several conditions might alter such consequences. First, in some cultures responsibility for others' welfare and efforts to contribute to the welfare of the group might be basic, universally enforced elements of the culture, so that the need to behave that way and the value underlying it will not be questioned. Moreover, a child's contribution to the welfare of his family or group can be so necessary, and important, that participation in prosocial behavior confers importance on the child.

When children's participation in prosocial activity is enforced over a period of time – even if this is done in a manner that on a single occasion might lead to resentment, reactance, and external attribution for acting prosocially – they might accept the values and norms inherent in such conduct and come to guide their behavior according to them. A person who consistently behaves in a particular way would find it difficult to maintain that he does so for purely external reasons.

One culture that seems to use responsibility assignment extensively, according to Bronfenbrenner (1970), is the Soviet Union. The whole social milieu of children is shaped to make them learn that their conduct affects other children and others' conduct affects them, and that they are responsible to follow the rules of the collective and to make others follow the rules. A variety of methods are set up to make children assume responsibility for their collectives – which are defined at various levels: a small group the child is a member of, the child's whole class, his school, and his society. These methods include shaming, depriving a group of privileges when any one member's behavior is objectionable, and making children responsible for supervising and monitoring one another's activities. Thus children are both objects of others' supervision and agents in monitoring and guiding others' behavior. One specific example is that elementary-school children are assigned younger classmates, for whom they are responsible. They walk the child to school and are expected to help the child with any problems, particularly schoolwork. Their responsibility for the younger child is part of the curriculum; they receive a grade. Another example is that classwork is done in groups of about five peers, with each member responsible for all others. Still another example: When a child has been late in coming to school, one or two other children get the task (from their teacher, or from their small collective) to stop by his house and escort him to school in the morning. Bronfenbrenner (1970) reported relatively low occurrence of disruptive and inconsiderate behavior among children in the Soviet schools.

In addition to such practices in schools, parents are educated in practices that will maximize rule obedience and cooperative behavior. Manuals in child rearing, which include specific examples of how to deal with particular problems, are prepared for both teachers and parents. Structured assignment of responsibility, and the opportunity to participate in prosocial behavior, often in a manner that might be intrinsically satisfying because it puts the child into a position of importance, seem fundamental aspects of these child-rearing practices, together with group supervision and enforcement of responsible activity.

What might be the effect of children's experiences in Russian schools on their prosocial behavior toward individuals in everyday settings – for example, on their willingness to respond to someone in an emergency? Although Bronfenbrenner describes instances in which teachers encouraged prosocial behavior in interaction among individual children and discouraged negative behavior, it seems that the primary aim of the social education children receive is to instill a sense of responsibility toward the group and the collective society (Tschudnowski, 1974). An important aspect of this is rule-following behavior and a subjugation of one's interest to the group. It would be important to know to what extent this sense of responsibility is evoked when there is no accountability to an authority and when individual initiative is required. Would intensive socialization in following rules interfere with individual initiative?

In many societies, including our own, the older children in a family, particularly if the family is large, are especially likely to have responsibility focused on them to care for their younger siblings and protect them from mishaps, and to assume various responsibilities in maintaining the family. Bossard and Boll (1956) provided detailed descriptions of the characteristics of large families, on the basis of an interview-questionnaire study of

100 such families. In these families responsibility was frequently focused on older children to care for the younger ones, to administer discipline while doing so, and often to run the house. These authors noted that several personality types developed among the children. One was the "responsible" type, which was seen most often in children, particularly older girls or the oldest one, who had responsibilities in the rearing of the younger children. Since the family circumstances often made it necessary for older children to assume responsibility, such a child could consider her role an important and meaningful one. Such responsibilities might therefore be accepted as legitimate and a sense of responsibility for others might become internalized. However, because such responsibilities are not a way of life for children in our culture, so that in comparison to others the child may feel heavily burdened, sometimes rebellion ensues. This might be particularly likely if the child or adolescent feels exploited because the parents and other children do not sufficiently share in the care of the family. Both issues are exemplified in the report of a girl, the oldest of eight children:

> By the time I was in the third grade, I was always helping mother while the others played with the neighboring children. This made me old beyond my years, serious, and quite responsible for all that went on in the household.... Each Saturday, my mother went into the city six miles away for the groceries and stayed for the day. In the evening she and dad visited friends and came home about midnight. From age fifteen to nineteen, I found myself responsible for seeing that the housework was finished, cooking lunch and dinner for the children, and caring for the newest baby. At night, I bathed six children, washed their heads, and tucked them into bed. Saturday nights continued like this until I rebelled. I wanted to have time for dates like other girls had. (Bossard & Boll, 1956, pp. 159–160)

I am proposing that involvement with responsible activities will lead to a sense of personal responsibility toward others, which is an important influence on prosocial behavior. However, the nature, magnitude, and other aspects of such responsible activities would modify what is learned from them. Actually, the girl in the foregoing example, even though she ultimately rebelled against her exploitation, might still have acquired a prosocial tendency that she expressed in her interaction with others.

The proposed relationship between birth order and prosocial behavior has been found in experimental studies of children's reactions to sounds of distress from another child in an adjoining room. Oldest siblings tend to be most helpful (Staub, 1970b, 1971a,c), whereas youngest ones tend to be least helpful (Staub, 1970b). In pairs of children who together heard sounds of distress and did not actively help by going into the adjoining room, upon the return of the experimenter about a minute and a half after the distress sounds were over, the children in the pairs who were oldest siblings were more likely to report that something happened, or to be the first to respond to the experimenter's questions, than children in other birth positions (Staub, 1970b). These findings are somewhat surprising, because oldest siblings appear less certain of themselves in social situations and are less popular with their peers (Hartup, 1970). That they initiate more helping acts may be the result of greater demands placed on them to be responsible for others' welfare. An alternative hypothesis should also be considered, however: Oldest siblings have a more intense relationship with their parents and, to the degree that the parents hold prosocial values, they are more likely to adopt them.

Like older siblings, older children who are part of a social group may have responsibility focused on them to respond to the needs of younger children, or awareness of their greater competence may lead them to assume responsibility and to respond helpfully to the needs of younger children.

Children who spend substantial amounts of time in a social group in which the ages of peers vary may learn to be helpful by observing helpful acts done by older children, by experiencing such acts when they are directed at them, and by acting in a "responsible" prosocial manner when they themselves are older. Bizman, Yinon, Mitzvari, and Shavit (1978) found, in fact, that children 5 years of age and older in age-heterogeneous kindergartens in Israeli cities and kibbutzim were more helpful than same-age children who came from age-homogeneous kindergartens. The former children were more likely to choose helpful alternatives in deciding what was the best response to two situations that were described to them, and they shared more pretzels that they won in a game with children who would not have a chance to play. The authors note that the 5-year-olds in the heterogeneous kindergarten "already learned with older children when [they] were only four years old" (Bizman et al., 1978, p. 156). Since apparently they did so in the same kindergarten, whereas children attended the homogeneous kindergarten for a shorter time, the findings may have been affected by the greater familiarity of children in the heterogeneous kindergarten both with the setting and with the other children, the recipients of their generosity. There were no differences between city and kibbutz children in this study.

In several foregoing examples, responsibility was focused on children with some degree of pressure, although in some cases, as with older siblings, responsibility may be "naturally theirs." Because of their greater competence, older siblings may naturally assume the roles of protector of younger siblings from harm and of caretaker for them. Sometimes these and other responsibilities will be regarded by children, or can be presented to them, as a privilege rather than a duty. The role they are cast into, the demands placed on them, indicate trust in their competence or ability, have prestige attached to them, and might have varied intrinsically rewarding aspects. Given these surrounding conditions participation in prosocial activity would not produce reactance or resistance. On the contrary, it would be a rewarding experience to the actor. In earlier writings (Staub, 1975a,b; Staub & Feinberg, 1978) I distinguished between children being the targets of instruction, instruction being aimed at them, and children learning through participation in activities that are meaningful and rewarding to them (indirect instruction).

What experiences might be regarded as indirect instruction? At an early age a child might be asked to "help Mommy." The implication that the child's help is needed makes the child a valued collaborator. In the cultures that Whiting and Whiting studied, the children's responsible duties were important for the maintenance of the family. The children may have gained a sense of importance from being collaborators in an important enterprise.

An incidental finding of one of our experiments (Staub & Buswell, unpublished research) also suggested the positive results of children acting as collaborators of adults, and of indirect instruction. We used several procedures in this study in our attempt to enhance prosocial behavior. In one treatment group one child, the subject, was working on a task, while another child, a confederate, was doing other things in the same room. Sometimes these were play activities, but in the course of other "activities" the confederate needed help (for example, once she fell off a chair, and another time she could not reach an object high up on a shelf). Using a buzzer as a signal, we tried to teach our subjects that under some circumstances, when another person needs help, it is "appropriate" (Staub, 1971b) to interrupt whatever they are doing in order to provide help. The confederates, children from the same population as the subjects, were taken to the experimental room by the experimenter before the subjects entered and trained to engage in a variety of activities in response to cue cards. They performed these activities after the subject joined them in the room. Either 1 day or 1 week after the training, both the subjects' and the confederates' helping and sharing behavior was evaluated. The confederates attempted to help significantly more in response to sounds of distress by another child than subjects in any of four experimental groups. A number of these children spontaneously verbalized the principle that we tried to teach the subjects in the experimental session, that one ought to help others when they need help.

Children who are provided with the opportunity to teach other children benefit the child they teach, but being given the responsibility to teach can be viewed by them as a privilege, and might be intrinsically rewarding. There has been, since the 1960s, an apparently nationwide movement in the schools to use older children as tutors for younger ones (Allen, 1976; P. Lippitt, 1969; R. Lippitt, 1968; Thelen, 1969). This has been called *cross-age tutoring*.

In such programs, both well-functionig children and children with behavioral problems are used as tutors. Informal reports provided by the writers cited suggest that participation may improve the academic performance of both the child being taught and the tutor (who is usually the focus of interest). It may reduce the behavioral problems of both participants and may result in greater self-confidence as well as other positive personality changes in the tutor. Based on her observations, Lippitt (1968) wrote that "dramatic" changes result from participation as tutors and explained this as a result of the students' being in a collaborative effort with the teachers. In a few primarily unpublished studies, when low achieving or poorly motivated children tutored younger children for an extended period, the tutors showed positive gains in self-attitudes or self-concepts (see Feldman, Devin-Sheehan, & Allen, 1976).

What kind of learning results from doing? Focusing responsibility on children will, minimally, make them aware of parental and/or societal values. When they are successfully induced to engage in prosocial behavior, in a consistent fashion, they might learn, at the least, that people are expected to do things for others; that other people regard such behavior as an obligation, and that one can expect rewards for doing so and punishment for not doing so. Under certain conditions children are likely to internalize values and norms of prosocial conduct. First, they might come to believe that people ought to assume responsibility in relation to other people. Second, they may come to regard it as their own obligation to assume responsibility for others. If they evaluate their own behavior as internally guided, they might come to regard themselves as people who do and will assume responsibility when others' welfare is involved. Their concern about others' welfare and their empathic capacity may also increase. Some of the conditions that may make these consequences more or less probable have already been mentioned. They include (probably in our culture, where values of individuality and self-interest often conflict with prosocial values, and where children's contributions, in many segments of society, are not essential for survival) not overly coercive ways of inducing children to behave responsibly or prosocially and an association between prosocial behavior and cognitions that amplifies reasons for and positive consequences of behaving prosocially. Participation in responsible prosocial action can be induced so it will be perceived as an important, privileged activity, or as a collaborative activity with an adult socializer, or as an activity that is intrinsically satisfying. The association of the rewarding nature of such responsibilities with others' welfare and with the sense of power or competence that results from being able to enhance others' welfare might lead the child to view his own interests as identical with those of others – or at least as associated rather than conflicting. Helping others might then be experienced not as a sacrifice, but as a contribution to the self, the increase in others' welfare resulting in empathic reinforcement – in a parallel change in the actors' own emotions. (Such a change in personal orientation will not, of course, always gain expression in behavior, which is determined in a complex fashion.)

Learning by doing and by participating may be regarded as examples of experiential learning. Teaching others, or participating in helping other people, can also provide opportunities for role-taking experiences in interaction with others, which, according to cognitive developmental theory, is crucial for the moral development of children. The notion of interactive experience as a source of learning and development and the exploration of experiential learning is extremely important not only from the cognitive developmental perspective, but from any perspective that seriously concerns itself with the child's growth and development. The dimensions of experiences that contribute to the development of prosocial behavior and morality in general will have to be progressively elaborated and defined, and the processes by which they induce learning and the kind of learning or change that results from them will have to be specified. Moreover, children's personalities – what they have learned from parents, the kinds of persons they have already become – will determine the effect of particular experiences on them. Depending on prior learning and experience they will perceive objectively identical experiences differently and they will learn different things from them.

EXPERIMENTAL RESEARCH ON LEARNING BY PARTICIPATION AND INTERACTIVE EXPERIENCE

Direct Instruction for and Participation in Prosocial Action

A variety of experiments suggest that telling children what to do will affect their behavior, at least in the short run, as much as or more than exposure to a model. This has been found in studies in which verbalizations to children clearly specified that they were expected to donate (Grusec, 1972; Grusec & Skubicki, 1970; Rice & Grusec, 1975). Experiments in setting standards for self-reinforcement showed that verbally imposing standards on children resulted in greater adherence to the standards than did exposure to models (Masters & Mokros, 1974: chapter 4). Other studies also show that focusing responsibility on people for others' welfare, in a specific manner, affects their behavior. In one study (Staub, 1970a), first-graders' attempts to help a child apparently in distress in an adjoining room were greater when they were left "in charge" by the experimenter, to "take care of things," and subsequently heard the distress sounds. Moreover, kindergarten children, whose helping behavior did not increase as a result of responsibility being focused on them, perhaps because they were too young to know what to do upon the experimenter's return, tended to deny that they heard distress sounds more often than those who did not have responsibility focused on them, presumably because they feared disapproval for not helping. In another study Tilker (1970) found that subjects who were asked to observe another person administering shocks to a learner, in a Milgram-type situation, were more likely to interfere with the further administration of shocks when they were made responsible for the learner's welfare, and when there was more feedback about the consequences of the shocks, that is, more signs of distress of the person receiving the shocks.

These studies show the immediate consequences of imposing standards of conduct on people or making them responsible for others' welfare. By frequently or regularly assigning responsibility to children (and adults?) in this manner, the consequences described earlier may occur. However, one cannot assume from the immediate consequences of responsibility assignment on behavior in the same setting that more extensive responsibility assignment will produce generalized and enduring consequences. Other experimental studies, however, have provided further information about delayed or generalized effects of responsibility assignment and participation in prosocial action.

Groups of experiments that were reviewed elsewhere (Staub, 1978) showed that the experience of positive behavior affects subsequent performance of similar behavior and/or related feelings. Being part of a group of co-operating individuals enhanced liking for both others in the group and persons outside the group (for example, class members) by children. When people were induced to engage in a single positive act of some sort they were more likely to engage in a second positive act, in comparison to persons in control groups.

Rosenhan and White (1967) found that children who donated more of the rewards that they earned when they privately played a bowling game were those who donated in the model's presence during a training period, when the model and the child took turns playing the bowling game. These researchers proposed that the rehearsal of modeled behavior was an important contributor to later prosocial behavior. Possibly, however, the individual characteristics of certain children led them to donate both in the model's presence and in her absence.

Participation, Teaching Others, and Induction

My students and I conducted a series of experiments to explore the influence of participation in various types of prosocial activities – sometimes by itself, sometimes in combination with induction – on various types of subsequent prosocial behavior.

In one of these experiments (Staub, 1975b; Staub & Fotta, 1978) the combination of repeated participation in a prosocial activity (making puzzles for hospitalized children) and induction increased girls' but not boys' subsequent prosocial behavior and expressed prosocial intentions; boys were somewhat affected by the separate procedures.

In another study (Staub, Leavy, & Shortsleeves, 1975) we explored the effects of teaching others on children's later prosocial behavior. Some fifth- and sixth-grade girls learned a prosocial activity, first-aid techniques; others learned a neutral activity, making puzzles. In one condition the girls were individually trained in these activities and then practiced them for a period of time (no teaching). In another condition the girls were told, before the training period, that they would teach these activities to younger children; following the training each subject did indeed teach a younger child. Teaching another child resulted in participants writing significantly more letters to hospitalized children, about a week after the training session, clearly a generalized and delayed effect of the training. Interestingly, there was an interaction in the effects of teaching and its content: The experience of teaching had a greater effect on children who taught a younger child to make a puzzle. At least two interpretations of this seem reasonable. First, the children who taught first-aid skills did not directly benefit the learner, but potentially benefited other people whom the learner could in turn help. In contrast, the children who taught puzzle making were told that the purpose of this was to enable children to make their own toys, which might be satisfying to them. These children might have felt that they were directly benefiting the child they taught, which may have resulted in a stronger association between the satisfaction experienced in teaching and the awareness of benefiting another person. Second, learning and teaching first-aid skills was more complicated, and perhaps the participants experienced less mastery and consequently less satisfaction from their role.

A potentially important finding of this study was that ratings by the experimenter (who observed the children through a one-way mirror) of the teacher's responsiveness to the child she taught – the teacher considering the younger child's ability in setting the pace, listening and responding to the learner, and so on – were significantly positively related to the number of letters that the teacher wrote. Responsiveness by the teacher was also significantly related to the learner's responsiveness to the teacher. First, existing characteristics of some children might have enabled them to be more responsive as teachers, perhaps experiencing more satisfaction as a result, and being more affected by the experience. Second, the characteristics of the learner may have affected the teacher's and the learner's responsiveness to each other, with a similarly positive effect on the teacher. Both could be true. However, responsiveness by teachers was also a function of the children's experience in training. Children who participated in the training with one of the experimenters later wrote more letters than those who participated with the other experimenter, regardless of treatment conditions. Similar differences were found in the influence of the two experimenters on the children's responsiveness to each other. It should not be surprising at this point that the characteristics of a "socializer," no matter how temporary a socializer that person is, modify her influence.

As in our earlier study (Staub & Fotta, 1978), the experimental treatments did not affect the number of gift certificates that children donated for needy children immediately after the training, probably for similar reasons. They received these gift certificates for their participation, and could put their donations into a box outside the room on their way back to the classroom. Having just earned them, and believing that they deserved them, they might have been unwilling to part with them, in all treatment conditions.

In a further experiment we attempted to explore the effects of three experimental procedures – participating in a prosocial activity, teaching others, and induction – on subsequent prosocial behavior (Staub & Jancaterino as presented in Staub, 1975b). I will communicate some of the complex findings and experiences with this project that highlight important issues about the methodology of such research.

In exploring the effects of teaching, we intended to make several improvements. In the previous experiment, the content of instruction varied in different experimental groups. In this experiment the content was the same, puzzle making, but the reason for making the puzzles was varied. In one of the direct instruction (no teaching) groups children learned to make puzzles so they could make some for hospitalized children, then continued to work on the puzzles for a while (prosocial group). In another group children learned to make puzzles for hospitalized children but were also given a list of induction statements to read and rehearse that pointed out the benefits that making puzzles for hospitalized children were likely to produce (prosocial–induction group). They were told that knowing the consequences of their behavior was likely to make helping others enjoyable. Then they spent some time working on the puzzles.[1] In a third group (not prosocial) children learned to make puzzles and then spent time working on them; they were asked to do this because it might be enjoyable for them to learn to make their own toys. In three parallel conditions children taught another child puzzle making. In the prosocial teaching group children learned to make puzzles so they could teach younger children to make puzzles for hospitalized children. Then they taught a younger child how to make the puzzle. In a second teaching group children also received and rehearsed the list of induction statements, to be used while teaching the younger child. They were told that the younger children would find helping more enjoyable if they knew the consequences of their behavior, and that they would be more likely to help. In a third group the children taught the younger child how to make puzzles because "it might be enjoyable for children to learn how to make their own toys." With subjects

[1] This group served primarily as a control for the teaching–prosocial–induction group described later. In that group, teachers read and rehearsed induction statements so that they could use them in teaching other children. Although reading and rehearsing induction statements to make the task more enjoyable might have appeared contrived to the children in the no-teaching condition, we wanted both to expose children who did not teach to induction and to equate their degree of familiarity with the induction statements, because that might be an important determinant of whether children are affected by them.

varying in sex, we had a 2 × 3 × 2 design (teaching–not teaching; prosocial activity–prosocial activity with induction–no prosocial activity; and sex).

Following the treatment sessions, subjects' willingness to donate gift certificates was tested. They received the gift certificates either 1 or 2 days after the treatment or several days, mostly 5–6, afterward, and then they were asked to donate some of the gift certificates to a group of needy children.

Eleven days after the gift-certificate test, the next posttest, the envelopes test, was administered. Each subject received two large manila envelopes and was told that he or she might want to fill the envelopes with pictures, stories, or poems, cut out of magazines or copied from magazines and books, and other items. The children were told that these envelopes would be given to children who did not have families and had few attractive objects or toys of their own. Finally, 2 weeks after the envelopes test, the subjects were administered the puzzles test. They received three large envelopes containing unmade puzzles of the same kind that they had previously worked on. When they received the puzzles, they were asked how many of these puzzles they thought they would make for hospitalized children (intentions measure). The puzzles that they actually made were collected in 3 days.

Scores for both the envelopes test and the puzzles test were derived by two independent raters on the basis of how much work the material that the children handed in represented and, in the case of the envelopes test, how much material sacrifice it involved. Agreement between the raters was over 90% in both cases.

Analysis of variance showed a significant effect of teaching on donating gift certificates. Children who taught other children donated more gift certificates. There was a highly significant sex effect; girls donated more. The timing of the test of donation was varied, to explore the possibility that children who receive gift certificates later, when the feeling of deserving might be less acute, would share more. Correlations computed within each treatment group between the number of days that the donation test followed the treatment and the number of gift certificates that children donated showed that in the three nonteaching groups and in one of the teaching groups (prosocial–no induction) the relationship was negligible. However, in the other two teaching groups, the longer the delay after the treatment session, the more gift certificates children donated. This might be interpreted as support for the hypothesis that teaching would enhance children's donations when their feeling that the gift certificates were earned and deserved was less acute.

Other measures of helping were affected by treatments in interaction with gender. Boys in the treatment groups tended to make more puzzles for other children. In contrast to earlier experiments that involved only female experimenters, in this study male experimenters conducted the treatment sessions with boys and female experimenters conducted the treatment sessions with girls. The findings suggest that sex differences might, in part, be caused by the gender of the experimenter. Additional analysis showed that helping behavior varied not only according to gender (of the experimenters and subjects) but, to some extent, according to the specific person who conducted the session. These findings suggest that more must be learned about the different effects of male and female experimenters on boys and girls as well as the influence of different modes of interaction with subjects.

There were also differences found in classroom membership. These differences suggest that the atmosphere established in a classroom can have important effect on children's behaviors independent of other background variables. The importance of the overall environment was further shown in a project aimed at reducing boys' aggression (reported later in the book). We found that differences in school climates influenced the effectiveness of our procedures. The attitude teachers communicated about the experiment might also have affected the results. Classroom differences became significant over time, as the cooperation of one of the teachers declined.

How participants perceive an experiment or intervention and what attitudes develop toward it is important. The shared view of a project that inevitably develops may be a powerful influence on children's behavior. It is important to learn about such shared views, but is not usually done. Asking participants to describe their thoughts and feelings about the experiment, and evaluating how these relate to the behavior of later participants, might be one approach to this.

We conducted another elaborate experiment, with fourth-, fifth-, and sixth-grade children, to explore further the effects of induction, of participating in a prosocial activity, and of teaching on children's varied prosocial behaviors (Staub & Feinberg, 1977). We again made several changes, what we regard as improvements, in our procedures. A deficiency in the last study was the lack of a control group in which children would have a truly neutral experience. As my conception of the influence of participation in prosocial activity evolved, it led to the belief that both kinds of participation, making puzzles for hospitalized children, and teaching others, would increase later prosocial behavior. Thus, all the treatment conditions in the previous experiment might be expected to increase, to some extent, later prosocial behavior. Therefore, in this experiment, we included a control group in which children were simply asked to make toys during the training. They were not given a specific reason for doing so. We also thought that induction might be more effective if children could participate in thinking up the benefits that would result from their activity. Therefore, in the treatment group where children experienced induction they were asked to suggest what benefits might follow from making toys for hospitalized children. The experimenter wrote down their ideas, suggesting others so that the same basic set of positive consequences was always included. It is important to note that we sacrificed somewhat the ability to draw theoretical conclusions, for meaningfulness. In all relevant experimental groups children were briefly told about some beneficial consequences of making toys for poor hospitalized children, since to ask children to do that without some explanation seemed artificial and unreasonable. Thus we contrasted minimal with elaborate induction. We also thought that puzzle making might be too restrictive an activity, that some children might not like it. Therefore, we had materials prepared for a variety of different toys that children could make (puzzles; pogo horses; fish with a magnet and a fishing line with a magnet; beanbags) about equal in difficulty, and the children could select which toy they wanted to make.

Treatments varied the reason for the children's being asked to make toys. In one group they were asked (participating individually, one child at a time) to make them for poor hospitalized children whose parents could not provide them with toys. In another group the reason was the same but children also experienced induction. In a third group the subjects were asked to make toys to help art teachers find out what kinds of toys children like to make and are good at making, thereby helping the art teachers to prepare the best materials for art classes. In all these conditions the children participated in some prosocial activity (participation conditions). In a fourth condition, the children were simply asked to make the toys, without a particular reason. In all groups, after the treatments were administered and the children were trained to make a toy, they proceeded for 15 minutes to make toys, and then continued to make toys (a different one, if they so desired) in another session 2 days later.

In another set of three experimental conditions (teaching) the children experienced the same training as in the three participation conditions, but in preparation for teaching a younger child to make toys, for the reasons described (for example, so that the younger child could make toys for hospitalized children). After the training experience, each child proceeded to teach a younger child for 15 minutes. Two days later they taught again; the learner was another younger child of the same sex.

Half of the subjects from each group received and had the opportunity to share gift certificates 1–2 days after the second experimental session (already a delayed posttest), and were administered the toy-making posttest about 2 weeks after that. The other half were administered these tests in the reverse order. In the toy-making posttest, after children selected the kind of toy they wanted to make they received materials for four toys, and were told to make as many toys as they wished. About 2 weeks following the second, delayed posttest, children were asked to write letters for hospitalized children, in a manner similar to that described earlier.

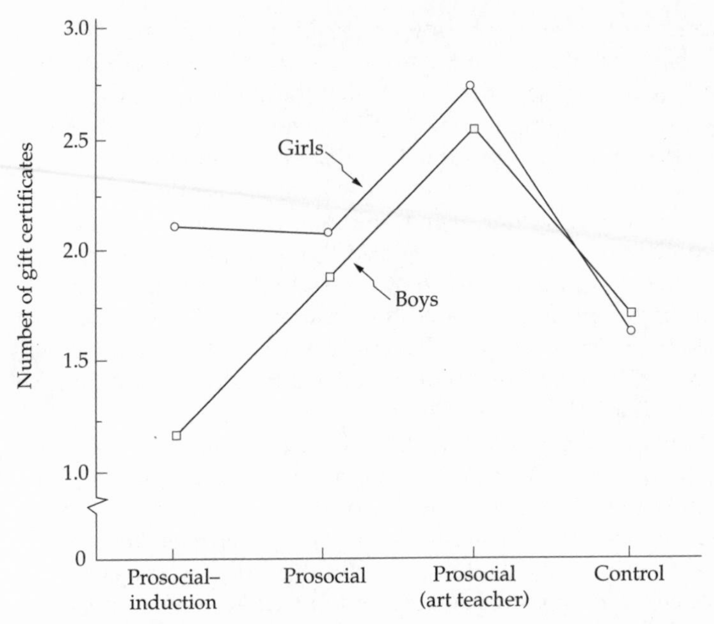

FIGURE 11.1. The average number of gift certificates that children donated in each experimental group.

The teaching and participation conditions had comparable effects on all dependent measures; therefore, the parallel teaching and no-teaching (participation) conditions were combined for further analyses. The effects of various forms of participation were compared to one another and to the effects of the control treatment.

The number of gift certificates that children shared was significantly affected by treatments ($p < .04$). The children in the prosocial–art teacher condition shared significantly more than those in the control group or those in the prosocial–induction group. As Figure 11.1 indicates, the latter difference is due to the low level of sharing by boys in the prosocial–induction group. The analysis of toy scores showed a significant treatment by sex interaction ($p < .03$). As with gift certificates, boys in the prosocial–art teacher condition had substantially and significantly higher scores than those in the other treatment groups. Girls, on the other hand, made more toys in the prosocial–induction group than in the other groups (Figure 11.2). Analyses of the number of letters that children wrote to hospitalized children, and the amount of effort expended in letter writing, showed only a significant sex difference; girls did more than boys. The findings clearly show that in comparison to a control group, participation in a prosocial activity of a certain kind, helping an art teacher (and thereby, indirectly, the art teacher's pupils) enhanced boys' later prosocial behavior. The same

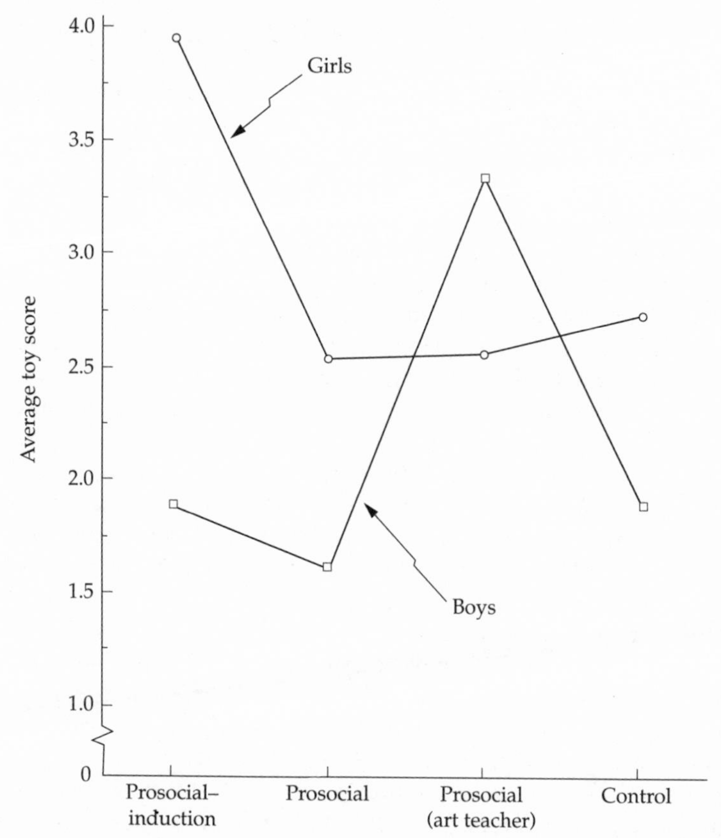

FIGURE 11.2. Average toy scores in each experimental group.

activity also enhanced girls' prosocial behavior on one measure, sharing gift certificates; helping hospitalized children and experiencing induction enhanced girls' prosocial behavior of another kind.

It is important to emphasize that the nature of the activities of children in the prosocial and prosocial–art teacher conditions was identical; only the stated reasons for their activities were different. The substantial effect of the prosocial–art teacher treatment on boys' and on girls' sharing of gift certificates may be due to one or more of several factors: that helping in this condition was not a behavior that would be regarded as "good" (or even goody-goody), thus creating reactance; that their involvement in or help with the selection of materials or activities for art classes made the children feel important; and that this was a kind of goal they could understand and empathize with. The helping behavior of boys in this condition was as great as that of girls in any treatment group. Thus, although in these studies there was a tendency for girls to behave more prosocially, some conditions appear to induce boys to prosocial behavior.

It seems clear from these findings, and earlier ones, that elaborate verbal communications that point out the consequences of positive behavior on other children, combined with actual participation in such prosocial behavior, frequently enhance girls' later prosocial behavior but either have no effect on boys or decrease boys' later prosocial behavior. Bernstein (1975) also found that a verbal communication of an inductive nature decreased the number of puzzles that seventh-grade boys later made for hospitalized children; it slightly (not significantly) increased the number of puzzles that girls made. When this verbal communication was accompanied by another kind that provided personal information about the would-be recipients of the puzzle, the decrease in boys' helping behavior did not occur.

What may be the explanation of the sex difference in reactions to verbal communications? A variety of other experiments also showed that girls are more responsive to verbal communications than boys (Grusec & Skubicki, 1970; Hovland & Janis, 1959; Staub, 1972) in that their attitudes or behaviors are more likely to be affected by them. For one thing, in everyday life there may be less control exercised over boys than girls, in that verbal communications that give guidance or direction to them are less frequently enforced and translated into behavior. If so, then boys may learn to disregard verbal influence attempts to a greater degree. Second, if boys are taught to be independent and self-directing to a greater degree than girls, they may resent verbal communications or other influence procedures that would diminish their freedom more than girls; these would be more likely to evoke reactance and opposition. This may be particularly true of communications that promote other people's welfare, because such communications invoke social norms that have an obligatory character. If greater reactance is created, the boys' prosocial behavior would be reduced more.

One finding may be viewed as providing support for the latter proposition. Analyses were performed in which the effects of the order of administering the tests of sharing gift certificates and making toys were evaluated. Order had no effect on sharing gift certificates. However, with toy scores as the dependent variable, a highly significant treatment by sex by order interaction was found ($p < .01$). This appeared mainly due to boys making significantly and substantially fewer toys in the prosocial–induction group than in other groups when toy making was their first posttest ($\overline{X} = .29$). However, they made more toys in this than in other conditions when toy making was their second posttest ($\overline{X} = 2.91$), even though the tendency in the other experimental groups was for children to make fewer toys on the delayed than on the immediate posttest. If induction statements evoked reactance and this diminished toy making by boys on the immediate posttest, it is reasonable to assume that in a period of over 2 weeks this reactance would have declined.

How Does Experiential Learning Occur?

Teaching others and participating in prosocial behavior can be regarded as examples of what may be called *natural socialization*. Socialization mostly refers to the influence of socializers on children through the child-rearing techniques they employ and through direct tuition. Natural socialization refers to participation in activities and interpersonal experiences that result in some kind of learning. Socialization is involved here in an indirect manner, in that socializing agents can lead the child to participate in these activities and can create surrounding conditions that will maximize learning from such participation, but they do not directly teach the child to behave prosocially. Learning is primarily the result of the experience of, or participation in, an activity. Parents, teachers, and socializers in general are heavily involved in such indirect socialization in the child's everyday life. The circumstances that exist in the child's life are also important in determining whether the child will get involved in such activities. The various examples of natural socialization that have been explored seem to lend themselves to application, to being used in schools and other settings to promote children's prosocial behavior, and, more generally, to promote the development of positive characteristics such as self-esteem and positive orientation toward others.

A related type of learning occurs through role playing, which may be regarded as "as if" participation (Staub, 1976). Although in the course of role playing children do not aim to reach the same goals at which the real behavior (like helping someone) would aim, they do perform the behavior and may have some of the experiences that are usually associated with it. Role playing is at least partly an enactive form of learning, as are other types of participation. Moreover, since in role playing the behavior has an "as if" quality, variations in and experimentation with behavior are possible, and learning may take place that would not occur in the course of the real performance of the behavior. The shifting or exchange of roles can contribute to the development of awareness of others' perspectives, to role taking.

What are the significant elements of such experiences, which determine whether children's later prosocial behavior is affected or not? To briefly summarize earlier discussion, several (interrelated) conditions seem important:

1. A sense of benefiting others, of doing something that increases others' welfare.
2. A sense of responsibility for others' welfare. Certain conditions may focus responsibility on children to a greater degree, make them feel

that they are personally responsible for another person's welfare; other conditions may do so to a lesser extent or not at all. However, too much responsibility or too great a need by another person or lack of identification with beneficiaries of one's behavior may not activate or may interfere with processes that would lead to learning through participation.

3. A sense of the significance of one's activities, a belief that they are important and worthwhile.
4. A sense of agency or personal effectiveness. I would not expect participation in positive behavior that creates a sense of incompetence in the actor to enhance later positive behavior.
5. Other conditions that make the experience a satisfying one, in contrast to an unpleasant one: for example, the nature of the activity, whether it is liked or disliked.
6. Verbal communications to children can affect the degree to which self-attribution takes place and can contribute to the development of a cognitive network about the self, the welfare of others, and the behaviors for benefiting others that would enhance later positive behavior.
7. The opportunity for role taking, which may enable a child to appreciate others' needs and their related feelings.

Presumably, not all of these conditions have to be present at the same time.

To summarize again, in addition to those mentioned, several kinds of changes may result from experiences that include the just mentioned components. The association between benefiting others and the experience of self-enhancement or self-gratification may contribute to the expectations of gratification from benefiting others. It may also contribute to experiencing empathy with others. Over time a person may come to respond with an experience of empathic reinforcement to others' increased welfare that results from his actions. Having responsibility focused on the self may contribute to a sense of responsibility or obligation toward others. Having engaged in positive behavior may lead to setting higher standards for future positive conduct. Having benefited others, awareness of one's capacity to benefit others may increase. Clearly, some of these changes are interrelated.

An important task of future research in this and in other domains is to explore the cognitive and affective consequences of learning opportunities and the relationship between these consequences and behavioral ones. Do the presumed consequences really follow? Are they the mediators of the increased positive behavior that follows participatory learning? As I have repeatedly suggested, how existing personal characteristics modify experiential learning is also important. There is some indication that personality modifies how having engaged in some behavior affects people (Staub, 1978, chapter 5).

INTERACTIVE EXPERIENCE, ROLE TAKING, AND EXPERIENTIAL LEARNING

What is the relationship between role taking in interaction with peers as a form of experiential learning, which was assigned the central role, in both Piaget's (1932) and Kohlberg's (1969, 1976) theories, as a source of development, and the kind of experiential learning that I have emphasized? The two types of learning are related, complement each other, but are also different from each other. Piaget regarded the adjustments required in interaction with others, the demand for coordination between individuals to resolve conflict and engage in cooperation, as sources of cognitive and moral growth. Thus, the more opportunity for peer interaction (and the more varied roles available to children in the course of interaction), the greater the expected rate of change in role taking and in moral reasoning. Although the research on the influence of exposure of children to reasoning more advanced than their own and on the influence of guiding children's moral discussions suggests that socializers have an important role, the theory stresses that children learn from their own experience.

My reasoning about experiential learning is similar on the last point: Socializers exert influence, but their effect is indirect. The actual learning or change results from the child's own experience. Extensive opportunities for interaction may lead to the development of role taking and sensitivity to others. They may also promote children's tendencies to consciously process their experiences, to make attributions (to the self, or to external agents), and to evaluate aspects of their environment. Thus, the opportunity for varied interactive experiences may make it more likely that children learn from participation. However, for children to engage in positive (in contrast to negative) behavior, adults and the rules or structure of an environment have to provide guidance. Progressively, such behavior can become self-maintaining. Thus, more directive influence is required by adults than that posed by Piaget and Kohlberg, for experiential learning of a behavior tendency and of related values and norms to occur.

Does the opportunity for interactive experience contribute to the development of role taking and moral reasoning? Based on Piagetian theory, several investigators assumed that environments that allow or lead to more early peer interaction would lead to the development of greater role-taking skills. None of the studies explored affective role taking: They focused on perceptual, communicative, or cognitive role taking. Hollos and Cowan (1973) found no differences in the role-taking capacity of children in farming communities in Norway and those in nonfarming communities (which provided presumably greater opportunities for social interaction).

West (1974) found no differences between children from Israeli kibbutzim, moshavs (which are cooperative agricultural settlements, but not as communal as kibbutzim), and cities. Hollos and Cowan suggested that, beyond minimal threshold level, the sheer amount of social interaction does not affect the development of role-taking skills. In West's view, a basic level of varied social experience is necessary for the development of decentered thought, and other factors must be looked to as sources of individual differences in role-taking skills.

Beyond the amount and even the variety of social experience it allows, the rules and structure of a social environment can be expected to affect the nature of peer interaction. For example, how restrictive environments are would affect the extent to which children consider the consequences of their behavior on others and why others behave toward them as they do, in contrast to children primarily following existing rules and interpreting behavior as normative.

In contrast to the preceding studies, Nahir and Yussen (1977) found that first- and fifth-grade kibbutz children were better able to modify their descriptions of objects as a function of the age of the children who were the recipients of their communications than were city children. First-grade kibbutz children were also significantly better than city children at describing pictures to other children, without including information that was available to them but not represented in the pictures. These tasks seem to involve communicative skills that experience with peer interaction should contribute to: The findings have face validity. The differences in the findings of the varied studies may be partly due to different role-taking tasks that were employed.

Differences in opportunities for interactive experience, in socialization practices, and in rules laid down for children in groups must combine and jointly affect development. With regard to city and kibbutz, socialization practices appear to differ, at least as judged by reports of children about their experiences with their mothers, fathers, peers, and teachers (Avgar, Bronfenbrenner, & Henderson, 1977). Children in the kibbutz received more support and less discipline at home than did children in the city. Kibbutz parents were more concerned with encouraging autonomous behavior than were city parents. In reporting about their experiences outside the family, kibbutz children received more support than city children but also experienced more discipline from teachers and peers. Moshav children fell in between city and kibbutz children on all these dimensions but were closer to kibbutz than to city children.

It seems that older kibbutz children (the subjects were fifth, sixth, and seventh graders) receive a substantial amount of support and encouragement for autonomy by their parents, but discipline and responsibility in interacting with others is promoted by teachers and peers. The combination of emphasis on autonomy – which presumably included stressing the child's own responsibility – and the emphasis by teachers and by the peer group on responsibility in social interaction, as well as joint possession of play material with peers from an early age, can enhance cooperation and diminish competition among kibbutz children (in games, this has been found in comparison to children in the United States, in West Germany, and in Israeli cities; Madsen & Shapira, 1977) and probably contribute to other types of positive social behavior.

One of the profound issues facing research and theory on personality and social development and on the development of positive behavioral orientations is exploration and specification of the manner in which varied parental practices or socializing influences directed at specific children by parents and others, natural socialization and learning by participation, and the nature of the environment and the peer interaction it promotes jointly affect what children learn, how they develop, and even the principles by which their learning and development occur. Not only are these influences intertwined in shaping children, but the personal characteristics that children develop also enter into the transactions between them and their environments and affect further development.

References

Allen, V. L. *Children as teachers: Theory and research on tutoring*. New York: Academic Press, 1976.

Avgar, A., Bronfenbrenner, U., & Henderson, C. R. Jr. Socialization practices of parents, teachers, and peers in Israel: Kibbutz, moshav and city. *Child Development*, 1977, *48*, 1219–1227.

Bathurst, J. E. A study of sympathy and resistance among children. *Psychological Bulletin*, 1933, *30*, 625.

Baumrind, D. Child care practices anteceding three patterns of preschool behavior. *Genetic Psychological Monographs*, 1976, *75*, 43–88.

Baumrind, D. Current patterns of parental authority. *Developmental Psychology*, 1971, *4*, 1–101.

Baumrind, D. *Early socialization and the discipline controversy*. Morristown, New Jersey: General Learning Press, 1975.

Bernstein, M. R. Helping in children: The effects of recipient-centered verbalizations, the role of empathy. Unpublished masters thesis, University of Massachusetts, 1975.

Bizman, A., Yinon, Y., Mitzvari, E., & Shavit, R. Effects of the age structure of the kindergarten on altruistic behavior. *Journal of School Psychology*, 1978, *16*, 154–160.

Bossard, J. H. S., & Boll, E. S. *The large family system*. Philadelphia: University of Pennsylvania Press, 1956.

Bronfenbrenner, U. *Two worlds of childhood*. New York: Russell Sage Foundation, 1970.

Feldman, R. S., Devin-Sheehan, L., & Allen, V. L. Children tutoring children: A critical review of research. In V. L. Allen (Ed.), *Children as teachers*. New York: Academic Press, 1976.

Grusec, J. E. Demand characteristics of the modeling experiment: Altruism as a function of age and aggression. *Journal of Personality & Social Psychology*, 1972, *22*, 139–148.

Grusec, J. E., & Skubicki, L. Model nurturance demand characteristics of the modeling experiment and altruism. *Journal of Personality & Social Psychology*, 1970, *14*, 352–359.

Hartup, W. W. Peer interaction and social organization. In P. H. Mussen (Ed.), *Carmichael's manual of child psychology*. New York: Wiley, 1970.

Hollos, M., and Cowan, P. A. Social isolation and cognitive development: Logical operations and role-taking abilities in three Norwegian social settings. *Child Development*, 1973, *44*, 630–641.

Hovland, C. I., & Janis, I. J. *Personality and persuasibility*. New Haven: Yale University Press, 1959.

Kohlberg, L. Stage and sequence: The cognitive-developmental approach to socialization. In D. Goslin (Ed.), *Handbook of socialization theory and research*. Chicago: Rand McNally, 1969.

Kohlberg, L. Moral stages and moralization: The cognitive-developmental approach. In T. Lickona (Ed.), *Moral development and behavior*. New York: Holt, 1976.

Lippitt, P. Children teach other children. *Instructor*, 1969, *78*, 41–42.

Lippitt, R. Popularity among preschool children. *Child Development*, 1941, *12*, 305–322.

Lippitt, R. Improving the socialization process. In Clausen (Ed.), *Socialization and society*. Boston: Little, Brown, 1968.

Madsen, M. C., & Shapira, A. Cooperation and challenge in four cultures. *Journal of Social Psychology*, 1977, *102*, 189–196.

Masters, J. C., & Mokros, J. R. Self-reinforcement processes in children. In *Advances in child development and behavior*, Vol. 9. New York: Academic Press, 1974.

Mussen, P. H., Rutherford, E., Harris, S., & Keasey, C. B. Honesty and altruism among pre-adolescents. *Developmental Psychology*, 1970, *3*, 169–194.

Nahir, H. T., & Yussen, S. R. The performance of kibbutz and city reared Israeli children on two role-taking tests. *Developmental Psychology*, 1977, *13*, 450–455.

Piaget, J. *The moral judgment of the child*. London: Kegan Paul, 1932.

Rice, M. E., & Grusec, J. E. Saying and doing: Effects on observer performance. *Journal of Personality & Social Psychology*, 1975, *32*, 584–593.

Rosenhan, D., & White, G. Observation and rehearsal as determinants of prosocial behavior. *Journal of Personality & Social Psychology*, 1967, *5*, 424–431.

Staub, E. A child in distress: The effects of focusing responsibility on children on their attempts to help. *Developmental Psychology*, 1970, *2*, 152–154. (a)

Staub, E. A child in distress: The influence of age and number of witnesses on children's attempts to help. *Journal of Personality & Social Psychology*, 1970, *14*, 130–140. (b)

Staub, E. A child in distress: The influence of modeling and nurturance on children's attempts to help. *Developmental Psychology*, 1971, *5*, 124–133. (a)
Staub, E. Helping a person in distress: The influence of implicit and explicit "rules" of conduct on children and adults. *Journal of Personality & Social Psychology*, 1971, *17*, 137–145. (b)
Staub, E. The use of role playing and induction in children's learning of helping and sharing behavior. *Child Development*, 1971, *42*, 805–817. (c)
Staub, E. The effects of persuasion and modeling on delay of gratification. *Developmental Psychology*, 1972, *6*, 168–177.
Staub, E. *The development of prosocial behavior in children*. Morristown, New Jersey: General Learning Press, 1975. (a)
Staub, E. To rear a prosocial child: Reasoning, learning by doing, and learning by teaching others. In D. DePalma & J. Folley (Eds.), *Moral development: Current theory and research*. Hillsdale, New Jersey: Lawrence Erlbaum, 1975. (b)
Staub, E. The development of prosocial behavior: Directions for future research and applications to education. Paper presented at Moral Citizenship/Education Conference, Philadelphia, June, 1976.
Staub, E. *Positive social behavior and morality, Vol. 1: Social and Personal influences*. New York: Academic Press, 1978. (a)
Staub, E. Socialization by parents and peers and the experiential learning of prosocial behavior. In J. H. Stevens & M. Mathews (Eds.), *Mother/child, father/child relationships*. National Association for the Education of Young Children, 1978. (c)
Staub, E., & Buswell, S. Incidental effects of helping an adult teach other children prosocial behaviors. Unpublished research, University of Massachusetts.
Staub, E., & Feinberg, H. Experiential learning and induction as means of developing prosocial conduct. Unpublished research, University of Massachusetts, Amherst, 1977.
Staub, E., & Feinberg, H. Personality, socialization, and the development of prosocial behavior in children. In D. H. Smith & J. Macauley (Eds.), *Informal social participation: The determinants of socio-political action, leisure activity, and altruistic behavior*. Jossey-Bass, 1978.
Staub, E., & Fotta, M. Participation in prosocial behavior and positive induction as means of children learning to be helpful. Unpublished manuscript, University of Massachusetts, Amherst, 1978.
Staub, E., & Jancaterino, W. Learning to be helpful by participation in a positive behavior: The effects of teaching others. Unpublished research, University of Massachusetts.
Staub, E., Leavy, R., & Shortsleeves, J. Teaching others as a means of learning to be helpful. Unpublished research, University of Massachusetts, Amherst, 1975.
Tschudnowski, P. Paper delivered at the Conference on Mechanisms of Prosocial Behavior. Sponsored by the Committee of Psychological Sciences of the Polish Academy of Sciences, Poland, October 1974.
Thelen, H. A. Tutoring by students. *School Review*, 1969, *77*, 229–244.
Tilker, H. A. Socially responsive behavior as a function of observer responsibility and victim feedback. *Journal of Personality & Social Psychology*, 1970, *14*, 95–100.

West, H. Early peer-group interaction and role-taking skills: An investigation of Israeli children. *Child Development*, 1974, *45*, 1118–1122.
Whiting, B., & Whiting, J. W. M. *Children of six cultures*. Cambridge, Massachusetts: Harvard University Press, 1975.
Whiting, J. W. M., & Whiting, B. The behavior of children in six cultures. Unpublished manuscript, Department of Social Relations, Harvard University.

12

The Origins of Hostility and Aggression

When affection and nurturance are absent and especially when there is hostility and violence against the child, the likelihood of aggression increases and the child's capacity to function effectively in the world – in terms of interpersonal relations, school performance, and adjustment to school – decreases. The research literature has begun to delineate the influences, and at times their combinations, that lead to aggressiveness, to its frequent correlate ineffectiveness in socially (conventionally) valued realms, and to the psychological processes, the feelings and modes of thinking, that mediate these outcomes.

THE ORIGINS OF AGGRESSION IN NEGLECT, HARSH TREATMENT, VIOLENCE, AND LACK OF GUIDANCE

Parental negativity, hostility, and punitiveness stand out as core elements in the pattern of childrearing that creates aggression and ineffectiveness in socially valued realms. The degree of punitiveness and whether punishment expresses hostility or occurs in an otherwise affectionate or caring context appear to determine their impact.

What is the meaning of the terms *child neglect, maltreatment,* and *abuse* (Kinard, 1979; Youngblade & Belsky, 1990)? Parental neglect and punitiveness are often treated as a single dimension. At one endpoint is lack of care so that the child's physical needs are not satisfied, progressing to lack of nurturance, affirmation, and support so that the child's emotional and identity needs remain unfulfilled. This side of the dimension points to omissions and corresponds to what is usually identified as neglect. It moves

Reprinted from E. Staub (1996). *Altruism and aggression: Origins and cures.* In R. Feldman (Ed.), *The psychology of adversity.* Amherst, MA: University of Massachusetts Press, pp. 120–144. Included here are pp. 120–130.

on to increasing degrees of commission or harmful behavior: punitive discipline or the use of parental power to withhold privileges and restrict the child's freedom and rights, rejection of the child in the form of criticism and negative evaluation, verbal abuse, the use of physical punishment of varying intensity and frequency, and finally physical abuse (violence that leads to physical injury) and sexual abuse. In reality, there may be two separate dimensions, one involving neglect, the other punitiveness. A child can receive good physical caretaking and affection from parents who regularly use physical punishment (see below).

Harsh discipline consisting of physical punishment or abuse is associated with aggression in children, youth, and adults (Dodge, Bates, & Pettit, 1990; Gelles & Conte, 1990; Weiss, Dodge, Bates, & Pettit, 1992; Widom, 1989b; Youngblade & Belsky, 1990). Weiss et al. (1992) found that harsh (severe, strict, often physical) discipline early in life was associated with aggression by children. In most research, however, physical punishment and abuse on the one hand and neglect on the other hand are not treated independently. Moreover, different points on the neglect-abuse dimension are often not identified. The influence of the context is usually not separated, for example, whether physical punishment is used in a generally hostile or affectionate context, or in an orderly functioning or disorganized family.

Maltreated (both neglected and abused) toddlers are more aggressive, less prosocial, and respond to others' distress with aggression rather than empathy. Maltreated children exhibit more anger, have more conflict in their families, and are more aggressive with peers (see Youngblade & Belsky, 1990). Vissing, Straus, Gelles, and Harrop (1991) found that the physical punishment of young children was associated with aggression, delinquency, and interpersonal problems at age 18; the more intense the physical aggression against the child, the stronger the relationship. The frequency of verbal aggression by parents, such as swearing at and insulting the child, was independently related to aggression, delinquency, and interpersonal problems (Vissing et al., 1991).

Researchers who study aggressive boys find that they have experienced more rejection, hostility, physical punishment or abuse by parents (Bandura & Walters, 1959; Huesmann, Eron, Lefkowitz, & Walder, 1984; Olweus, 1979). Moreover, a high percentage of violent adult criminals have been abused as children (Lewis, Mallouh, & Webb, 1989). Widom (1989b) found, comparing validated cases of abuse and neglect 20 years earlier with a control group of nonabused cases, that children who were abused and neglected were later more frequently arrested for delinquency, adult criminality, and violent criminal behavior.

Aggressive behavior shows at least moderate stability with age, with greater stability in males than females (Huesmann et al., 1984; Olweus, 1979). Peer-rated aggression when a child is 8 years old is related to later aggression against spouse, physical punishment of one's children, and criminality at age 30. There is, moreover, intergenerational stability of aggression in families. First, parents' aggression (physical punitiveness) when their children are 8 years old relates to the children's aggression at age 8 and to these children's use of aggression when they are 30 against their own children, whose modal age is 8. Second, the strongest relationship has been found between a person's aggression at age 8 and the aggressive fantasy of this person's child when the child is about age 8 (Huesmann et al., 1984).

A variety of studies have shown that people who were abused as children tend to abuse their own children (Kaufman & Zigler, 1987), and young unmarried adults who were abused show a heightened potential to abuse (Milner, Robertson, & Rogers, 1990). The majority of physically abused children do not become abusive parents, however (Widom, 1989a). According to one estimate, the rate of intergenerational transmission is 30% (Kaufman & Zigler, 1987), in comparison to the 2%–4% abuse rate found in the general population (Gelles & Conte, 1990). This should not be surprising, for several reasons. Aggression can have varied objects. Some abused children may be partly or wholly healed through contact with caring adults (Garmezy & Rutter, 1983), peers, or later in life. Others may become fearful and avoidant rather than aggressive; this would also affect their parenting.

Punitiveness is not the only source of the development of aggression. Permissiveness, a lack of standards, or lax discipline was associated with high aggressiveness as measured by the recorded offenses of a group of delinquent youths (DiLalla, Mitchell, Arthur, & Pagliococca, 1988). In a permissive setting, aggression may be reinforced by its consequences (Patterson, 1986; Patterson, Littman, & Bricker, 1967), teaching children that aggression pays (Buss, 1971). This may occur especially in environments that instigate but do not control aggression. Permissiveness also means a lack of guidance, contributing to ineffectiveness and poor self-control. However, the motivations for aggression would differ as a function of its origins in permissiveness or punitiveness, and of the reason for permissiveness.

Permissiveness can be a form of neglect associated with lack of love or disinterest in the child. However, it can also have other origins: an at least theoretically benevolent desire not to stifle the child, based on an ideology of children's inherent potential for growth; family disorganization and chaos; or parents' incapacity to exercise control.

Sexual abuse is a significant form of aggression against children and adolescents. So far primarily female victims have received attention, but boys are also abused sexually, with the extent, nature, and consequences less well known. When the abuser is an older male with power who is part of the family, that is, the father or stepfather, the traumatic impact is especially great (Finkelhor, 1979; Herman & Hirschman, 1981). The use of force adds to the traumatic impact (Browne & Finkelhor, 1986). Females have historically been less likely to respond to abuse and trauma by becoming aggressive, but with an increase in the United States in antisocial aggression by females (Summary Report of the APA's Commission on Violence and Youth, 1993), this may be changing. One reason that sexual abuse by fathers or stepfathers is especially traumatic may be that the child has no "safe haven" to escape to and therefore lives in constant insecurity and danger. The same is true of children in physically abusive families.

Aggression against the child not only impacts the child, but also teaches by modeling. So does violence by one parent against the other. In abusive couples, frequently males and females are both violent (Morgan, 1993), but male violence against females has more destructive effects. The many forms of modeling of aggression – others' aggression toward oneself, toward others, on TV and in films, in neighborhoods – lead to a strongly established view in which aggression is normal, acceptable, even the right form of behavior, at least in dealing with conflict (Huesmann & Eron, 1984).

In some families a coercive pattern of interaction leads to the use of aggression both to defend oneself and to get what one wants (Patterson, 1982, 1986). Both the reinforcement of aggression (Buss, 1971) and principles of reciprocity (Rausch, 1965; Staub & Feinberg, 1980) create and maintain aggressive behavior in the children.

Parents abusing each other, or spouse battering, contributes to aggressive behavior by children. In some studies its influence is even greater than that of physical punishment of children (Widom, 1989a). In one study, parental conflict and general aggressiveness (yelling, throwing things, attempting to injure someone when frustrated) was associated with a greater degree of criminality in children than parental punitiveness (McCord, 1988).

External influences, like TV watching, interact with parental negativity toward the child and negativity in the family. The amount of violent television 8-year-old boys watch is associated with more fantasy aggression at a later age and with aggressively delinquent behavior at age 19 (Eron, Walder, & Lefkowitz, 1971). However, rather than TV watching itself, the interaction of a large amount of TV viewing and the experience of abuse by either mother or father has been found to be related to violent crime (Health, Krutt Schnitt, & Ward, 1986). As the findings of Yarrow and Scott (1972) reported earlier suggest, whether an environment is affectionate or indifferent (or hostile) is likely to affect what children remember of their experience. It is also likely to affect how they process the television aggression they are exposed to.

How does heredity affect the development of individual aggressiveness? To the extent it does, it is likely to be through temperamental characteristics, as they evoke or simply interact with certain parental behaviors or environmental influence. For example, temperamentally difficult children raised in unsupportive environments by disorganized, distressed caretakers are more likely to develop delinquency than those with nurturant caretakers in a supportive environment (Werner, 1987). Both premature and temperamentally difficult children are more likely to be abused (Widom, 1989a), presumably because the attachment ties that parents develop to them are weaker and the parents' frustration in their caretaking efforts are greater.

Physical Punishment in an Affectionate Context

Like caring and altruism, aggression is a function of a pattern of childrearing and environmental influences. While frequent and severe physical punishment often occurs in the context of neglect and lack of love, physical punishment can also occur in the context of affection, care, and guidance, which moderate its effects. A limited amount of physical punishment, in the context of love and responsiveness, was associated with "humanistic" values in children (Hoffman, 1970). The combination of an affectionate, loving relationship with mother, consistent standards, physical punishment for violating standards, and church attendance by mother and child (which suggests the presence of guiding values) characterized nonaggressive African-American boys, in contrast to institutionalized aggressive and noninstitutionalized aggressive boys (Boone, 1991). The physical punishment of the nonaggressive boys may have also been of lesser magnitude, since parents were likely to be less provoked. The investigator suggests that in the context of caring and guidance, adolescents seem to experience the physical punishment as an indication of parental love (Boone, 1991).

In the first phase of their longitudinal study, Eron and his associates (1971) found that the less nurturant and accepting parents were and the more they punished the child for aggression at home, the more aggressive were the children in school. But boys who were punished for aggression and strongly identified with their fathers tended not to be aggressive either at home or in school. The presumably more benevolent pattern of childrearing that led to boys' identification with their fathers also influenced the meaning and effect of punishment. However, when punitiveness is intense and chronic, it is likely to be the primary determining influence of the child's experience in the family, and to shape his or her relationship to the adults.

THE EFFECTS OF PARENTAL NEGATIVITY AND PERMISSIVENESS: MEDIATORS OF AGGRESSION IN CHILDREN AND YOUTH

Beliefs, Norms, and Cognitive Structures

Current views of the acquisition of aggression stress the reinforcement of aggression (Patterson, 1982, 1986), the imitation of aggressive models (learning aggressive behavior and the expectation that it leads to rewards) (Bandura, 1986), learning norms and developing cognitive structures that make aggressive behavior acceptable and appropriate (or even right) (Huesmann & Eron, 1984), and the acquisition of sociocognitive processes such as schemas, scripts, perceptions, and attributions of hostility to people (Dodge, 1993). Neglect, hostility, or physical aggression by parents, or psychological, physical, or sexual abuse can define for the child the nature of the world and the way life is lived. Aggressive children and adolescents (Dodge, 1993, Dodge et al., 1990), as well as adults (Toch, 1969), see people as hostile. Aggressive children see hostility especially toward themselves, but also see and describe others' behavior not directed toward them in terms of aggression (Steinberg & Dodge, 1987; Stromquist & Strauman, 1992). The child develops "memory structures of the world as a hostile place that requires coercive behavior to achieve desired outcomes" (Dodge, 1993, p. 579. These theoretical views, while extremely useful and supported by research findings, place insufficient emphasis on the emotional consequences of the child's experiences and on the resulting emotional orientations and motives as the sources of aggression.

Motives for Aggression

Persistent motives may result from parental negativity. Cognitive schemas and attributional styles, which guide the perception and interpretation of current events and of one's relationship to them, are both rooted in and activate feelings and motives. A view of other people or of the world as hostile toward the self (Dodge, 1993), or as malevolent in general, and low self-esteem and an insecure self (Staub, 1993) can jointly activate strong needs to protect and elevate the self. Aggression can provide feelings of strength, power, and control.

Intense parental negativity, especially abuse, is likely to lead to hostility toward people. An antisocial value orientation may develop, the opposite of a prosocial value orientation, a personal disposition embodying a negative evaluation of people and a desire and intention to harm them. That childhood victimization leads to hostility is suggested by a strong association between physical abuse in childhood and expressive but not instrumental crimes of violence in adulthood (Widom, 1989a), or angry reactive violence but not proactive aggression or nonviolent criminal behavior (Dodge, 1993).

For young children, parental negativity intensifies the need for security, which they can only gain through connection to the hostile or abusive parent(s). An early psychological strategy to increase a feeling of security may be to see oneself as bad and deserving of punishment. This offers the hope of avoiding punishment by learning how to be good. While this places the focus of responsibility within the self and creates a negative self-concept, it does not stop children from also learning that the world is a hostile place, at least for them. In adolescence, perhaps because parental punitiveness paradoxically intensifies the need for connection to the abusive parents, the normal process of separation from parents and developing psychological independence becomes more difficult.

Types of Attachment

Parental negativity is related to insecure infant attachment to caretakers. Neglect is associated with resistant attachment, abuse with avoidant attachment, and their combination with a composite of resistant and avoidant attachments (Youngblade & Belsky, 1990). After World War II there were reports of the absence of attachment in children reared in extremely neglectful institutions (Thompson & Grusec, 1970). Some writers now again mention "unattached" children (Keogh, 1993), whose affective connections to caretakers and by generalization to other people have not developed or have been disrupted. They are usually children who have been passed around in child care agencies and foster homes and may well have been abused.

Resistant and avoidant attachment in infants is associated in the preschool years with aggressive behavior (Youngblade & Belsky, 1990). Boys who had been classified as avoidant, when paired with another insecurely attached child, are either aggressors or victims in the interaction or alternate between the two. This is not the case when they are paired with securely attached children, who manage to create friendly interactions regardless of the other child's attachment classification (Troy & Sroufe, 1987). Avoidant attachment creates a disconnection from people in general, perhaps of a lesser degree and without the disorganized emotionality that is found in unattached children.

As noted above, recent research and theory has focused on schemas, scripts, or the social-cognitive consequences of child maltreatment as moderators of aggressive behavior in children (Dodge, 1993; Huesmann & Eron, 1984). However, attachment is primarily an affective relationship. Different types of attachments, as they generalize to other people (possibly cognitively encoded in mental models or assumptions about and evaluations of people), represent a continuum of emotional connection to, ambivalence toward, disconnection from, or hostile turning against people.

The Self-Concept

Experiences of hostility and abuse are likely to lead to problems with self-esteem. In a recent study, aggressive boys did not differ from others in their perceived self-competence (see Dodge, 1993). However, incarcerated violent criminals (Newman, 1974; Toch, 1969), first-time violent offenders

(Gillooly & Bond, 1976), and violent gang members (Copeland, 1974) all had lower self-esteem than either control groups or nonviolent delinquents who themselves differed from control subjects (Offer, Marohn, & Ostrov, 1975). Moreover, college students who had low self-esteem found aggressive reactions more acceptable in their responses to vignettes that described frustrating, threatening, or aggressive behavior directed at them than students with high self-esteem did (Theiss, 1985).

Subcultural beliefs and norms may teach strength and power as the ideal male characteristic and strong response to provocation as the required behavior (Nisbett, 1993). A need to look strong in one's own and others' eyes can lead to the tendency to perceive and react aggressively to slight or even imagined provocation (Staub, 1971; Toch, 1969). The combination of personal experience, subcultural norms, cultural influence through TV and film, and violent neighborhoods with rules of reciprocity explain why retaliation-revenge for past insult or harm is the most frequent reason adolescents give for their violent acts (Agnew, 1990).

Socialization Void and Self-Socialization

Some hostile and abusive parents set firm rules in an authoritarian fashion, but others are permissive or neglectful, so that guidance and structure are lacking. This makes it unlikely that children learn impulse control and effective self-guidance. The combination of abuse with neglect and lack of guidance combine the child's victimization with the absence of socialization. One conceptualization of this is as a "socialization void" (Friedrich & Stein, 1973). The environment does not provide learning opportunities for prosocial behavior and skills in effective interaction. Children do not learn how to satisfy their goals by prosocial means. They are not guided to participation in activities that develop socially and academically useful skills and interests. They lack, as a result, the cognitive capacities, motivation, and self-regulatory skills required for effective participation in school. Young children who experience physically punitive discipline are less likely to attend to relevant social cues and to use competent responses (Dodge, 1993; Dodge et al., 1990).

Aggressive behavior toward peers leads to unpopularity in school (Hartup, 1970). Unpopularity and poor school performance both express and perpetuate lack of stable connections to people and social institutions. Engagement in school makes delinquency less likely (Zigler et al., 1992).

Aggressive boys' perception of hostility toward themselves is correct; in a new group more aggression is directed toward them (Dodge & Frame, 1982). This is a form of self-socialization. Aggressive boys' behaviors create reactions toward them that presumably further develop their already existing perceptions, feelings, and behavioral tendencies. Given strong reciprocity in aggressive behavior (Rausch, 1965; Staub & Feinberg, 1980), children's own aggression may elicit reciprocal aggression, or their poor social skills and inappropriateness in joining with others (Dodge, 1993) may lead to aggression against them. In contrast, securely attached children create peaceful interactions with normally aggressive, avoidantly attached children (Troy & Sroufe, 1987). Empathic children (especially girls) are the recipients of more positive behavior from their classmates (Staub & Feinberg, 1980).

One form of self-socialization occurs when already existing characteristics lead to behavior that elicits reactions that strengthen and further evolve these characteristics. Another form is the selection of associates, contexts, or environments that further develop these existing characteristics. Delinquent, antisocial friends or gangs may serve important and developmentally appropriate needs for belonging, identity, and security. Aggressive adolescents may select antisocial friends or antisocial groups partly because of a match in inclinations, partly because they are the only ones available to them.

A new form of grouping that has received attention, as a result of "wildings" (Gibbs, 1989), has been named a pack (Scheidlinger, 1992; Staub & Rosenthal, 1995). The pack is a relatively temporary joining together by a group of teenagers in antisocial acts, without the rules and stability of traditional gangs. As yet we know little about packs' frequency and nature. It might be that a reason for their appearance is that adolescents are not developing the capacities required for sustained friendship or social organization.

Bystander Behavior and Perceptions of Abandonment or Benevolence

The impact of bad treatment by parents may be modified if the child or adolescent realizes that his or her experience is not universal. The child may come to feel betrayed at home and abandoned by "bystanders," other family members, or people outside the family who are in a position to know but do nothing. In families with father-daughter incest, mothers who know frequently remain passive (Scott & Flowers, 1988). Their reactions to daughters who approach them for help is often punitive, which intensifies the trauma (Browne & Finkelhor, 1986; Herman & Hirschman 1981). Similar abandonment by the other parent or other bystanders may be experienced by sons and daughters who are neglected, badly treated, or physically abused. While an awareness of one's own bad fate relative to others can intensify hostility, realizing the existence of benevolence and especially experiencing benevolence can build connections and create hope for the future. The experience of benevolence, or of an affectionate connection with people outside the immediate family, has been identified as an important source of resilience in children who grow up in difficult home environments (Garmezy & Rutter, 1983). We know little as yet about the consequences for children of different roles that nonabusive parents and relatives assume: supporter of the perpetrator (as sometimes happens in father-daughter incest, see Staub 1991), passive bystander, silent ally, active defender, or source of love and affection.

Spouse abuse not only provides aggressive models, but also interferes with the child's relationship to both parents. Depending on the child's experience with each parent, it may create hostility to, identification with, or ambivalence toward the perpetrator. Empathy with the victim gives rise to empathic distress. Given the child's incapacity to help, as in the case of other passive observers of victimization (Staub, 1989), over time the child is likely to distance himself or herself by devaluing the abused parent.

References

Agnew, R. (1990). The origins of delinquent events: An examination of offender accounts. *Journal of Research in Crime and Delinquency, 27*, 267–294.

Bandura, A. (1986). *Social foundations of thought and action: A social cognitive theory*. Englewood Cliffs, NJ: Prentice-Hall.

Bandura, A., & Walters, R. H. (1959). *Adolescent aggression: A study of the influence of child training practices and family interrelationships*. New York: Ronald Press.

Boone, S. L. (1991). Aggression in African-American boys: A discriminant analysis. *Genetic, Social, and General Psychology Monographs, 117*(2), 203–228.

Browne, A., & Finkelhor, D. (1986). Impact of child sexual abuse: A review of the research. *Psychological Bulletin, 99*(1), 66–77.

Buss, A. H. (1971). Aggression pays. In J. L. Singer (Ed.), *The control of aggression and violence*. New York: Academic Press.

Copeland, A. (1974). Violent black gangs: Psycho- and sociodynamics. *Adolescent Psychiatry, 3*, 340–353.

DiLalla, L. F., Mitchell, C. M., Arthur, M. W., & Pagliococca, P. M. (1988). Aggression and delinquency: Family and environmental factors. *Journal of Youth and Adolescence, 73*, 233–246.

Dodge, K. A. (1993). Social cognitive mechanisms in the development of conduct disorder and depression. *Annual Review of Psychology, 44*, 559–584.

Dodge, K. A., Bates, J. E., & Pettit, G. S. (1990). Mechanisms in the cycle of violence. *Science, 250*, 1678–1683.

Dodge, K. A., & Frame, C. L. (1982). Social cognitive biases and deficits in aggressive boys. *Child Development, 53*, 620–635.

Eron, L. D., Walder, L. O., & Lefkowitz, M. M. (1971). *Learning of aggression in children*. Boston: Little, Brown.

Finkelhor, D. (1979). *Sexually victimized children*. New York: The Free Press.

Friedrich, L. K., & Stein, A. H. (1973). Aggressive and prosocial television programs and the natural behavior of preschool children. *Monographs of the Society for Research in Child Development, 38* (4), (Serial No. 151).

Garmezy, N., & Rutter, M. (1983). *Stress, coping, and development in children*. New York: McGraw-Hill.

Gelles, R. J., & Conte, J. R. (1990). Domestic violence and sexual abuse of children: A review of research in the eighties. *Journal of Marriage and the Family, 52*, 1045–1058.

Gibbs, N. C. (1989). Wilding in the night. *Time*, May 8, pp. 20–21.
Gillooly, D., & Bond, T. (1976). Assaults with explosive devices on superiors. *Military Medicine, 141* (10), 700–702.
Hartup, W. W. (1970). Peer interaction and social organization. In P. H. Mussen (Ed.), *Carmichael's manual of child psychology*. New York: Wiley.
Health, L., Krutt Schnitt, C., & Ward, D. (1986). Television and violent criminal behavior: Beyond the Bobo doll. *Violence & Victims, 1*, 177–190.
Herman, J. L., & Hirschman, L. (1981). *Father-daughter incest*. Cambridge, MA: Harvard University Press.
Hoffman, M. L. (1970). Moral development. In P. H. Mussen (Ed.), *Carmichael's manual of child development*. New York: Wiley.
Huesmann, L. R., & Eron, L. D. (1984). Cognitive processes and the persistence of aggressive behavior. *Aggressive Behavior, 10*, 243–251.
Huesmann, L. R., Eron, L. D., Lefkowitz, M. M., & Walder, L. O. (1984). Stability of aggression over time and generations. *Developmental Psychology, 20*(6), 1120–1134.
Kaufman, J., & Zigler, E. (1987). Do abused children become abusive parents? *American Journal of Orthopsychiatry, 57*, 186–192.
Keogh, T. (1993, January/February). Children without a conscience. *New York Age Journal*.
Kinard, E. M. (1979). The psychological consequences of abuse for the child. *Journal of Social Issues, 35*(2), 82–100.
Lewis, D. O., Mallouh, C., & Webb, V. (1989). Child abuse, delinquency, and violent criminality. In D. Cicchetti & V. Carlson (Eds.), *Child maltreatment: Theory and research on the causes and consequences of child abuse and neglect*. New York: Cambridge University Press.
McCord, J. (1988). Parental behavior in the cycle of aggression. *Psychiatry, 51*, 14–23.
Milner, J. S., Robertson, K. R., & Rogers, D. L. (1990). Childhood history of abuse and adult child abuse potential. *Journal of Family Violence, 5*, 15–34.
Morgan, H. (1993). *Spouse abuse*. Unpublished doctoral dissertation, University of Massachusetts, Amherst.
Newman, D. E. (1974). The personality of violence: Conversations with protagonists. *Mental Health and Society, 1*, (5–6), 328–344.
Nisbett, R. E. (1993). Violence and U.S. regional culture. *American Psychologist, 48*, 441–450.
Offer, D., Marohn, R. C., & Ostrov, E. (1975). Violence among hospitalized delinquents. *Archives of General Psychiatry, 32*(9), 1180–1186.
Olweus, D. (1979). Stability and aggressive reaction patterns in males: A review. *Psychological Bulletin, 86*, 852–875.
Patterson, G. R. (1982). *Coercive family processes*. Eugene, OR: Castilia Press.
Patterson, G. R. (1986). Performance models for antisocial boys. *American Psychologist, 41*, 432–444.
Patterson, G. R., Littman, R. A., & Bricker, W. (1967). Assertive behavior in children: A step toward a theory of aggression. *Monographs of the Society for Research in Child Development, 32* (Serial No. 113).
Rausch, H. (1965). Interaction sequences. *Journal of Personality and Social Psychology, 2*, 487–499.

Scheidlinger, S. (1992). *On adolescent violence: Some preliminary group process observations.* Unpublished manuscript on file with the author, Albert Einstein College of Medicine, Bronx, NY.

Scott, R. L., & Flowers, J. V. (1988). Betrayal by the mother as a factor contributing to psychological disturbance in victims of father-daughter incest: An MMPI analysis. *Journal of Social and Clinical Psychology, 6*(1), 147–154.

Staub, E. (1971). The learning and unlearning of aggression: The role of anxiety, empathy, efficacy and prosocial values. In J. Singer (Ed.), *The control of aggression and violence: Cognitive and physiological factors*. New York: Academic Press.

Staub, E. (1989). *The roots of evil: The origins of genocide and other group violence.* New York: Cambridge University Press.

Staub, E. (1991). Psychological and cultural origins of extreme destructiveness and extreme altruism. In W. Kurtines & J. Gewirtz (Eds.), *The handbook of moral behavior and development*. Hillsdale, NJ: Lawrence Erlbaum Associates.

Staub, E. (1993). Individual and group selves, motivation and morality. In T. Wren & G. Noam (Eds.), *Morality and the self.* Cambridge: MIT Press.

Staub, E., & Feinberg, H. (1980). Regularities in peer interaction, empathy, and sensitivity to others. Presented at the symposium: Development of Prosocial Behavior and Cognitions. American Psychological Association meeting, Montreal.

Staub, E., & Rosenthal, L. (1995). Mob violence: Social-cultural influences, group processes and participants. In *Summary report of the American psychological association's commission on violence and youth*, Vol. 2. Washington, DC: American Psychological Association.

Steinberg, M. D., & Dodge, K. A. (1987). Attributional bias in aggressive adolescent boys and girls. *Journal of Social Clinical Psychology, 1*, 312–321.

Stromquist, V. J., & Strauman, T. J. (1992). Children's social constructs: Nature, assessment, and association with adaptive and maladaptive behavior. *Social Cognition, 9*, 330–358.

Summary Report of the American Psychological Association's Commission on Violence and Youth. (1993). *Violence and youth: Vol. 1, Psychology's response.* Washington, DC: American Psychological Association.

Theiss, A. (1985). Self-esteem and attitudes towards violence: A theory about violent individuals. Unpublished dissertation, University of Massachusetts at Amherst.

Thompson, W. R., & Grusec, J. (1970). Studies of early experience. In P. H. Mussen (Ed.), *Carmichael's manual of child psychology*, 3rd ed. (Vol. 2). New York: Wiley.

Toch, H. (1969). *Violent men.* Chicago, IL: Aldine.

Troy, M., & Sroufe, L. A. (1987). Victimization among preschoolers: Role of attachment relationships. *Child and Adolescent Psychiatry, 26*, 166–172.

Vissing, Y. M., Straus, M. A., Gelles, R. J., & Harrop, J. W. (1991). Verbal aggression by parents and psychosocial problems of children. *Child Abuse and Neglect, 15*, 223–235.

Weiss, B., Dodge, K. A., Bates, S. E., & Pettit, G. S. (1992). Some consequences of early harsh discipline: Child aggression and a maladaptive social information processing style. *Child Development, 63*, 1328–1333.

Werner, E. E. (1987). Vulnerability and resiliency in children at risk for delinquency: A longitudinal study from birth to young adulthood. In J. D. Burchard &

S. N. Burchard (Eds.), *Primary prevention of psychopathology, 10, Prevention of delinquent behavior* (pp. 16–43). Newbury Park, CA: Sage.

Widom, C. S. (1989a). Does violence beget violence? A critical examination of the literature. *Psychological Bulletin, 106*(1), 3–28.

Widom, C. S. (1989b). The cycle of violence. *Science, 224,* 160–166.

Yarrow, M. R., & Scott, P. M. (1972). Limitation of nurturant and non-nurturant models. *Journal of Personality and Social Psychology, 8,* 240–261.

Youngblade, L. M., & Belsky, J. (1990). Social and emotional consequences of child maltreatment. In R. T. Ammerman & M. Hersen (Eds.), *Children at risk: An evaluation of factors contributing to child abuse and neglect.* New York: Plenum Press.

Zigler, E., Taussig, C., & Block, K. (1992). Early childhood intervention: A promising preventive for juvenile delinquency, *American Psychologist,* 47 997–1006.

13

Cultural–Societal Roots of Violence

Youth Violence

CULTURAL–SOCIETAL SOURCES OF THE SOCIALIZATION AND EXPERIENCES THAT LEAD TO AGGRESSION

Difficult Life Conditions

To understand the increase in aggression by youth, we must specify not only cultural–societal influences, but also changes in those influences. In my view, there have been moderately difficult life conditions in the United States in the past quarter of a century, created primarily by tremendous cultural–societal change. Great, rapid social change, even of a positive kind, creates psychological dislocation and frustrates basic needs in people, which affects their treatment of children.

The following have been some of the elements of difficult life conditions in the United States. Starting in the 1960s, a number of important leaders were assassinated. The United States fought a major war that created a great schism within the country. The United States lost economic power and prestige. The civil rights movement and feminism brought major changes to social arrangements and individual lives. There have been changes in gender relations and sexual mores, an increase of women in the workforce, and great increases in divorce rates and in single parenting. The drug culture (both taking and selling drugs) has affected many people's lives. Some of these changes, and the loss of clear guiding values associated with them, have had direct effects on family life, parenting, and the experiences of children, effects that are the proximal causes of youth violence. There have also been economic changes, like the flight of manufacturing from the inner cities, that have especially affected minority groups living in the inner cities.

Reprinted from E. Staub (1996). The cultural–societal roots of violence: The examples of genocidal violence and of contemporary youth violence in the United States. *American Psychologist, 51,* 117–132. Included here are pp. 123–127.

Given the presence of difficult life conditions in the United States, why has there not been genocidal violence, or developments seemingly leading to it? Democracies in general tend not to engage in genocidal violence, to an important extent because of the cultural characteristics that evolve within democracies. Life conditions have not been as difficult in the United States as in many countries where mass killings or genocides have occurred. Moreover, various cultural conditions for genocide are currently absent in the United States.

Although there has been a long and continuing history of devaluation of minorities, and although substantial structural inequities remain, improvement in civil rights and procedural protections have decreased crude, obvious forms of prejudice and discrimination. The United States has long been a pluralistic society. Pluralism has been strengthened in the last few decades by the greater inclusion in the public domain of previously excluded groups, like African Americans, with greater access to representation in government and the media. Finally, whereas in most societies there is some tendency to respect and obey authorities, in the United States this is moderated by both pluralism and individualism.

However, great social changes in society and in family life, combined with certain cultural characteristics, have created conditions that foster youth violence.

EFFECTS OF DIFFICULT LIFE CONDITIONS AND CULTURE ON CHILDREN'S SOCIALIZATION AND EXPERIENCES

Social conditions such as difficult life conditions and cultural characteristics will have both independent and interactive effects. Sometimes the two are strongly connected, for example, the cultural devaluation of minorities and discrimination or structural inequities. In the case of genocide, difficult life conditions intensify cultural characteristics such as devaluation and authority orientation. In the case of youth violence, difficult life conditions either directly, or by both affecting and combining with relevant cultural characteristics and social processes, intensify aggression-generating socialization practices in the home and in society in general.

Harsh Treatment and Limited Guidance

Difficult life conditions, especially when combined with cultural devaluation, can lead to harsh treatment of minorities, a starting point for the evolution of genocide. Difficult life conditions in a society can also lead to harsh treatment and less guidance of children.

Single parents – whose number has greatly increased – abuse their children more, especially if they are young or poor, or both (Gelles, 1981; Gelles & Conte, 1990). In the long run, the social changes may create equalitarian homes that provide better parenting. But in the short run, because of newly changed and still changing gender roles, conflict within families has probably increased, resulting in less structure and more violence. The focus of child rearing has shifted away from obedience (Edwards, 1986) – a potentially positive development. But there has also been a weakening of guiding values and standards, which has diminished structure and guidance. An increased focus on the self, perhaps due to societal changes frustrating the fulfillment of basic needs, has been accompanied by less feeling of responsibility to children and family (Baumeister, 1992; Bellah, Madsen, Sullivan, Swindler, & Lipton, 1985).

Negative Views of Children

The devaluation of subgroups of society makes it more likely that under difficult life conditions they become scapegoats and ideological enemies. Negative views of children are persistent cultural sources of negative socialization, which difficult life conditions intensify.

Views of children as willful and disobedient have historically contributed to their harsh treatment by parents in a number of Western societies such as Germany (Miller, 1983), England (Stone, 1977), and the United States (Greven, 1991). It was traditionally believed that for children to become good people, their will had to be broken and their obedience ensured. Any means were acceptable to accomplish this.

Many parents still believe that physical punishment is necessary in raising children (Greven, 1991; Straus, Gelles, & Steinmetz, 1980). At the beginning of the 1990s, over 90% of parents reported using physical punishment with their young children (Straus, 1992). As societal changes and life problems impact people, threaten their identity, lead to a loss of their traditional comprehension of reality, and make positive connections across gender lines more difficult, self-focus and frustration are created. They are likely to reduce patience with children and bring to the fore negative views that are still part of the culture.

The conditions of parents' lives affect parenting. Improvement in the conditions of mothers' lives leads to more secure attachment by infants to them, obviously by affecting the mothers' interactions with their infants (Sroufe, 1979). Economic problems and unemployment create less consistent, harsher parenting by some fathers (Elder & Caspi, 1985).

Conceptions of Maleness

Parenting is affected by the prevalent conception of maleness in a society, and changes in them in response to difficult life conditions and societal change. Historically, in the United States (Miedzian, 1991) and many other societies, men have been expected to be strong, tough, and powerful. In the

United States, part of the cultural revolution of the past quarter century has been to soften maleness, in some subcultures. But in others, especially when men have difficulty fulfilling their roles effectively, a focus on masculinity intensifies.

Sanday (1981) compared rape-prone and rape-free societies. The former is characterized by male dominance and hostile relations between the sexes. These seem to have evolved in response to scarcity and the experience of weakness and powerlessness it has created in men. Elder and Caspi (1985) found that men who lost their jobs during the Great Depression were more punitive and unpredictable with their children. This was true primarily of fathers who were less stable and more irritable before they lost their jobs, and especially when mothers were aloof. Affectionate mothers buffer fathers' behavior. Other stressors, like changes in sex roles and gender relations and the feelings of helplessness engendered by difficult life conditions, may similarly impact male identity and parenting.

Although I did not emphasize conceptions of maleness in genocidal violence, they are likely to have a role there as well. In response to persistent difficulties of life, both individuals – especially those with histories of harsh treatment and exposure to violence – and groups or collections of individuals and their culture seem to move towards greater toughness in self-image and harshness in interaction with others.

Poverty, Prejudice, and Discrimination

Poverty is the strongest predictor of violence, including homicide (Hill, Soriano, Chen, & LaFromboise, 1994). The conditions that surround poverty and shape its meaning are important. For example, high rates of mobility in poor areas are significantly associated with crime rates (Sampson, 1993). Instability in the community limits mutual support and adds to social disorganization. Poverty and high rates of mobility in a particular segment of society or within a minority group are social conditions that can be the result of internal culture, or of the culture of the larger group and its resulting social and institutional arrangements, especially discrimination.

As McLoyd (1990) suggested, poverty is likely to impact children primarily by reducing parents' capacity for consistent, supportive parenting and by leading to harsher behavior towards children. This is even more likely when poverty is combined with other difficult life conditions and the local community and general societal disorganization such conditions create. Poverty – especially when combined with prejudice, discrimination, and structural inequities that impede social mobility (Hill et al., 1994) – creates frustration and feelings of relative deprivation, injustice, and anger, as well as self-devaluation and hopelessness. All this can give rise to compensatory processes such as a culture of toughness in which honor becomes highly valued and an image of strength essential to maintain (Hammond & Yung, 1993).

Strong guiding values, community cohesion, and hope can counteract the violence-producing potential of poverty (Staub, 1996; Tajfel, 1982), even in the face of prejudice and discrimination. Perhaps this explains the reason that, when San Francisco's Chinatown was one of the poorest areas of the city, the murder rate remained extremely low (J. Q. Wilson & Herrnstein, 1985). This, however, is a best case scenario. Usually poverty, disadvantage, and discrimination give rise to violence within homes and whole communities (Belsky & Vondra, 1992; Garbarino et al., 1992).

Prejudice, discrimination, exclusion from participation in societal processes, and the poverty that is frequently associated with all this can lead to demands for change and, when such demands are ineffective, to mob violence or revolution (Staub & Rosenthal, 1994). On rare occasions, victorious rebellion leads to genocide, as it did in Cambodia. At other times, when the cultural conditions I described exist, those in power respond to demands for change, rebellion, and attendant social disorganization with mass killing, as they did in Argentina (Staub, 1989), or with genocide (Fein, 1990). Prejudice and discrimination can also lead to internal reactions in victim groups, such as ingroup devaluation (Tajfel, 1982), and can weaken community ties and support, effects magnified by poverty and by difficult life conditions in the larger society. Their joint impact on parenting can be great, with continuing impact on youths.

The culture of the group that is suffering from poverty – to the extent that it does not promote social, vocational, or educational skills and capacities and does not have a strong internal organization that provides community and support – accentuates the impact of poverty. The culture and social structure and institutions of the larger society – to the extent they convey prejudice, create discrimination, and limit support – are important contributors to the relationship between poverty and youth violence.

Black Culture and the Larger Society

Homicide was the leading cause of death for African American youth, both male and female, between 1978 and 1988, primarily perpetrated by other African American youths (Hammond & Yung, 1993, 1994). In Prothrow-Stith's (1991) view, changes in social conditions that had direct impact on Black families and communities were the reason for this.

W. J. Wilson (1987) has suggested that a Black underclass was essentially created by two societal trends. The first was millions of manufacturing jobs disappearing from the cities between 1960 and 1980 in the face of foreign competition, and the resulting changes in the U.S. economy. As a consequence, many Black people lost their jobs, without new job possibilities for them or their children. Second, the Black middle class moved to the suburbs, changing the composition of the previously "vertically integrated" Black neighborhoods. Now these had come to consist of primarily poor people, with a drastic increase – rooted in male unemployment – of poor Black families headed by women.

Prothrow-Stith (1991) wrote,

> Regardless of the race or class of individuals, when large numbers of men are out of work and large numbers of families are headed by women the rate of crime and violence in that community rises sharply. This fact is as true for whites as for blacks. (p. 72)

She noted that White communities with chronic male unemployment and high rates of female-headed households are as troubled by violence and crime as underclass Black neighborhoods, but that there are fewer such neighborhoods. Unemployment hit Black communities much harder than it had White ones.

Although Prothrow-Stith (1991) and others have stressed that violence is associated with class and social conditions and not race, it may be worthwhile to introduce a cultural perspective as well. The external culture and social conditions – that is, slavery followed by continued intense discrimination and violence against Black people – may have created internal cultural elements in the Black community that affect family life. The impact of past discrimination and violence may have intensified the destructive consequences of both the conditions described by W. J. Wilson (1987) and the difficult life conditions in society.

Cohesion within families and even within communities had to be affected by the practice of selling off individual members. One effect may be the greater value placed on communal ties by African Americans (Hill et al., 1994); another may be the fragility of such ties and the increased vulnerability to life problems and social disorganization.

The violence perpetrated on African Americans – at the time of slavery and later in the form of lynchings and other ways (Staub & Rosenthal, 1994) – must have had traumatic effects. Such traumas are often handed down through the generations. At the time of slavery, Black people were severely punished for learning to read or write. Later, hard work and success continued to be dangerous, resulting in raids by the Ku Klux Klan or accusations of wrongdoing by White business competitors that led to lynchings (Brown, 1965). These historical influences, combined with continued discrimination and limited opportunity, would diminish expectations of success and create fear in those who would try to achieve it. Although discrimination has eased, lack of quality education and of inner city jobs along with welfare policies that weaken families and continued racism limit the process of internal cultural change. In turn this limits the capacity to seize existing opportunities.[1]

The unfulfilled possibility of participation in the materialistic American culture increases relative deprivation. African Americans as a group are "aware of, and aggrieved about, their disadvantaged status in American life" (Major, 1994, p. 297). The possibilities for economic and social improvement, without the capacity to make use of them, increase powerlessness and anger. This would be the case especially among Black men, because the inability to live up to expectations, including one's own, and to have respected roles intensify masculine values. Black males' ineffectiveness in schools and other institutions valued by mainstream society would further hopelessness, alienation, and anger. Hispanics and other immigrant groups in which men lose their traditional roles as a result of their move to the United States might be similarly affected.

All this would affect the fathering of children as well as directly affect youth. Frustrated expectations and the unresponsiveness of authorities and the social system to grievances appear to be primary causes of riots, in which adolescent and young adult men are the primary participants (Staub & Rosenthal, 1994).

Gangs and the Fulfillment of Basic and Developmental Needs

Gangs are a major source of violence, although contrary to popular belief, nongang-related violence, including homicide, is substantially more common than gang-related violence (Hammond & Yung, 1994).

Gang membership is at least partly the outcome of a course of development. Neglectful, hostile, and permissive parenting – combined with the observation of violence in the home, in surrounding communities, and on television – lead to a negative orientation toward people, to the belief that aggression is normal, acceptable, and unavoidable or even good, and to poor social skills. These lead to aggressiveness toward peers that creates unpopularity among them. The resulting combination leads to poor school performance and lack of connection to school (Pepler & Slaby, 1994). Connection to other social institutions is also absent. Just like bonds to people, bonds to social institutions like school or church diminish

[1] There is a danger that some readers may interpret this analysis as blaming the victims for their plight; my intention is just the opposite. It is inevitable that a long history of slavery and subsequent discrimination and persecution would affect Black culture. Ignorance or denial of this makes it unlikely that the larger society will engage in appropriate efforts to help with positive cultural change such as early education efforts. Denying or ignoring the impact of the past is, however, likely to lead to blaming the victims, as less intelligent, less motivated, or less deserving.

aggressiveness (Huesmann & Eron, 1984; Hill et al., 1994; Pepler & Slaby, 1994).

Youths with such a developmental course turn to and associate with other less socially and educationally successful youths. The attraction of gangs for such youths is strong. Gangs can satisfy unfulfilled basic needs, including those developmentally central to adolescence (e.g., needs for a positive identity, connection to peers, and feelings of effectiveness and control). However, some of the avenues of need fulfillment gangs promote are destructive. Gangs promote self-concepts as well as self-presentations of strength and power, norms of violence toward outgroups, and violent action. The differentiation between "us" and "them" is intensified; violence against outsiders is often accompanied by intense support for a limited social network of friends and family (Gillis & Hogan, 1990). This is extremely similar to what happens in, and is in part intentionally created by, perpetrator groups like the SS or torturers in Greece (Staub, 1989) and in police units (Staub, 1992).

Like other kinds of violence, gang violence has greatly increased in the last decade. Old and new sources of violence include the protection of territory, honor, and drugs (A. P. Goldstein & Soriano, 1994). Drugs disinhibit violence; involvement in the sale of drugs provides resources not otherwise available to youths who predominantly come from disorganized, low income, and minority environments (A. P. Goldstein & Soriano, 1994); and the drug trade provides purpose and direction for gang activities. When gangs become normative in a community, youths will also join for the sake of their own safety. As in the case of ideological movements, membership in gangs can also become a source of prestige.

Given their personal history and societal role, the youths who join gangs are likely to have strong though unacknowledged feelings of humiliation and shame. This makes it understandable that gangs would create cultures in which respect and honor become central issues. The reasons that certain youths join and give themselves over to a gang and its culture and ideology have a similarity to members of groups who have suffered from difficult life conditions giving themselves over to ideological movements that elevate them.

A further manifestation of societal and individual disorganization may be "wildings" by loosely connected groups of youths. Wildings are violent actions generated among youths who happen to congregate at some place. In contrast to traditional, more organized gang violence, wildings are a form of mob violence (Staub & Rosenthal, 1994).

If many adolescents who join gangs feel mistrust and hostility to people, can they develop real connections to their peers? Does emotional resocialization take place in gangs, increasing the capacity for connection to people in general? Psychological research on gangs has been limited

(A. P. Goldstein & Soriano, 1994), and we do not have answers to such questions. But even if such resocialization does take place, it is likely to be strongly connected to both the values of strength and power and the differentiation between ingroup and outgroups that gangs promote.

Minority Cultures

Minority cultures can have either a protective or a facilitating effect on youth violence (Hill et al., 1994; see Eron et al., 1994). For example, family connection, collectivism, and respect for authority are among central values in Hispanic culture. These can protect youths from influences leading to violence. However, given family instability and dysfunction and the harsh parenting and lack of guidance that accompany them, gangs may come to substitute for family (Hill et al., 1994; A. P. Goldstein & Soriano, 1994). Further contributors to youth violence are the frustrations, stresses, confusions of identity, limits on effectiveness, and difficulties in developing a coherent understanding of the world that minority children and adolescents may experience as they negotiate their lives in two cultures, their minority culture and the larger culture and institutions of the United States. Helping children develop "bicultural competence" (Hill et al., 1994) can reduce violence.

Lack of knowledge by parents of the larger culture, and by teachers of the culture of minority students, can have significant effects. For example, unaware of the communalism of African Americans (Hill et al., 1994) or of the interdependent orientation (Markus & Kitayama, 1991) of many ethnic cultures in the United States, teachers may demand independent work without proper help in readjustment. Or, unaware that Mexican culture teaches children to show respect by not looking at a reproving adult's face, many teachers interpret such behavior in children they admonish as hostile (Staub, 1996).

Evolution of an Increasingly Violent Culture in the United States

Violence has been increasing in the U.S. in the realms of child abuse, sexual abuse, and spouse battering, although the extent to which such violence versus the reporting of it has increased is unclear (Gelles & Conte, 1990). Violence in television and the movies, youth violence, school violence, neighborhood violence like drive by shootings – which a decade ago were unheard of – and the use of guns in violence by youths, which substantially contributes to homicide rates (Prothrow-Stith, 1991), have all increased. In the case of genocide, difficult life conditions initiate an evolution of increasing violence against a victim group. In the U.S., there has been an evolution toward increase in these varied forms of symbolic and real violence among individuals.

As a result of this culture change, forms and levels of violence that 30 years ago would have been unacceptable have become ordinary. As in the case of the evolution of genocidal violence, in this case also, individuals and the whole group have progressively changed. A higher level of violence has become a societal characteristic.

As in the case of genocide, such evolution unfolds when there are no countervailing forces (Staub, 1989). Until recently, "bystanders" – for example, government, legislators, and the public – have remained largely passive. There are several likely reasons for this. First, there was gradual, progressive change, which allowed people to habituate to each new form or level of violence. Second, great societal changes and social disorganization made people preoccupied with their own lives and with many societal issues. Third, people could explain one form of violence that has received much attention – by African Americans and predominantly against other African Americans – by referring to the still existing cultural devaluation of Black people. As the devaluation of victims contributes to bystander passivity when a society moves toward genocide, so it contributed to passivity in the face of youth violence to the extent that a devalued group was identified as the main victim.

Fourth, some of the constituting elements of societal violence, like television violence and the availability of guns, are supported by central ideological and cultural elements of U.S. society. These include a focus on constitutional rights – including freedom of expression and the right of citizens to defend themselves – and free enterprise, which justifies both any television programming that sells, and the sale of guns. Fifth, violence in a family, although it may be known to a few people, is private – its extent has until recently been unknown. Sixth, as people first became aware of the degree of physical and sexual violence within the long-idealized institution of the family, denial and other defensive processes slowed down and diminished response. In addition, longstanding historical roots of both individualism and violence in the U.S. have provided a cultural basis for the evolution of greater violence and have reduced bystander response.

References

Baron, R. A. (1977). *Human aggression*. New York: Plenum Press.

Baumeister, R. F. (1992). *Meanings of life*. New York: Guilford.

Baumrind, D. (1975). *Early socialization and the discipline controversy*. Morristown, NJ: General Learning Press.

Bellah, P. N., Madsen, R., Sullivan, W. M., Swindler, A., & Lipton, S. M. (1985). *Habits of the heart: Individualism and commitment in American life*. New York: Harper & Row.

Belsky, L., & Vondra, L. (1992). Lessons from child abuse: The determinants of parenting. In D. Cichetti & V. Carlson (Eds.), *Child maltreatment* (pp. 153–203). New York: Cambridge University Press.

Brown, R. W. (1965). *Social psychology*. New York: Free Press.
Edwards, C. D. (1986). *Promoting social and moral development in young children*. New York: Columbia University Teachers College Press.
Elder, G. H., Jr., & Caspi, A. (1985). Economic stresses in lives: Developmental perspectives. *Journal of Social Issues*, *44*, 25–45.
Eron, L. D., Gentry, J. H., & Schlegel, P. (Eds.). (1994). *Reason to hope: A psychosocial perspective on violence & youth*. Washington, DC: American Psychological Association.
Fein, H. (1990). *Genocide: A sociological perspective* [Special issue]. *Current Sociology*, *38*, 1–126.
Garbarino, J., Dubrow, N., Kostelny, K., & Pardo, C. (1992). *Children in danger*. San Francisco: Jossey-Bass.
Gelles, R. J. (1981). Child abuse and violence in single parent families: Parent absence and economic deprivation. *American Journal of Orthopsychiatry*, *59*, 492–502.
Gelles, R. J., & Conte, J. R. (1990). Domestic violence and sexual abuse of children: A review of research in the eighties. *Journal of Marriage and the Family*, *52*, 1045–1058.
Gillis, A. R., & Hogan, J. (1990). Delinquent samaritans: Networks, structures, social conflict and the willingness to intervene. *Journal of Research in Crime and Delinquency*, *27*, 30–51.
Goldstein, A. P., & Soriano, F. I. (1994). Juvenile gangs. In L. D. Eron, J. H. Gentry, & P. Schlegel (Eds.), *Reason to hope: A psychosocial perspective on violence & youth* (pp. 315–333). Washington, DC: American Psychological Association.
Greven, P. (1991). *Spare the child: The religious roots of punishment and the impact of physical abuse*. New York: Alfred A. Knopf.
Hammond, W. R., & Yung, B. (1993). Psychology's role in the public health response to assaultive violence among young African American men. *American Psychologist*, *48*, 142–154.
Hammond, W. R., & Yung, B. (1994). African Americans. In L. D. Eron, J. H. Gentry, & P. Schlegel (Eds.), *Reason to hope: A psychosocial perspective on violence & youth* (pp. 105–118). Washington, DC: American Psychological Association.
Hill, H., Soriano, F. I., Chen, A., & LaFromboise, T. D. (1994). Sociocultural factors in the etiology and prevention of violence among ethnic minority youth. In L. D. Eron, J. H. Gentry, & P. Schlegel (Eds.), *Reason to hope: A psychosocial perspective on violence & youth* (pp. 59–97). Washington, DC: American Psychological Association.
Huesmann, L. R., & Eron, L. D. (1984). Cognitive processes and the persistence of aggressive behavior. *Aggressive Behavior*, *10*, 243–251.
Major, B. (1994). From social inequality to personal entitlement: The role of social comparisons, legitimacy appraisals, and group membership. In M. Zanna (Ed.), *Advances in experimental psychology* (Vol. 26, pp. 293–355). New York: Academic Press.
Markus, H. R., & Kitayama, S. (1991). Culture and the self: Implications for cognition, emotion, and motivation. *Psychological Review*, *98*, 224–253.
McLoyd, V. C. (1990). The impact of economic hardship on Black families and children: Psychological distress, parenting, and socioemotional development. *Child Development*, *61*, 311–346.

Miedzian, M. (1991). *Boys will be boys. Breaking the link between masculinity and violence*. New York: Doubleday.

Miller, A. (1983). *For your own good: Hidden cruelty in child-rearing and the roots of violence*. New York: Farrar, Straus, and Giroux.

Pepler, D. J., & Slaby, R. G. (1994). Theoretical and developmental perspectives on youth and violence. In L. D. Eron, J. H. Gentry, & P. Schlegel (Eds.), *Reason to hope: A psychosocial perspective on youth & violence* (pp. 27–58). Washington, DC: American Psychological Association.

Prothrow-Stith, D. (1991). *Deadly consequences: How violence is destroying our teenage population and a plan to begin solving the problem*. New York: Harper-Collins.

Sampson, R. J. (1993). The community context of violent crime. In W. J. Wilson (Ed.), *Sociology and the public agency* (pp. 259–286). Newbury Park, CA: Sage.

Sanday, P. R. (1981). The socio-cultural context of rape: A cross-cultural study. *Journal of Social Issues, 37*, 5–27.

Sroufe, L. A. (1979). The coherence of individual development: Early care, attachment, and subsequent developmental issues. *American Psychologist, 34*, 834–842.

Staub, E. (1989). *The roots of evil: The origins of genocide and other group violence*. New York: Cambridge University Press.

Staub, E. (1992). Understanding and preventing police violence. *Center Review, 6*, 1–7.

Staub, E. (1996). Altruism and aggression in children and youth: Origins and cures. In R. Feldman (Ed.), *The psychology of adversity*. Amherst: University of Massachusetts Press.

Staub, E., & Rosenthal, L. (1994). Mob violence: Social-cultural influences, group processes and participants. In L. Eron, J. H. Gentry, & P. Schlegel (Eds.), *Reason to hope: A psychological perspective on violence & youth* (pp. 281–315). Washington, DC: American Psychological Association.

Stone, L. (1977). *The family, sex and marriage in England, 1500–1800*. New York: Harper & Row.

Straus, M. A. (1992). *Corporal punishment of children and depression and suicide in adulthood*. Paper presented at the Society for Life History Research, Philadelphia, PA.

Straus, M. A., Gelles, R. J., & Steinmetz, S. K. (1980). *Behind closed doors: Violence in the American family*. Garden City, NY: Anchor Press/Doubleday.

Tajfel, H. (1982). Social psychology of intergroup relations. *Annual Review of Psychology, 33*, 1–39.

Wilson, J. Q., & Herrnstein, R. J. (1985). *Crime and human nature*. New York: Simon and Schuster.

Wilson, W. J. (1987). *The truly disadvantaged: The inner city, the underclass and public policy*. Chicago: University of Chicago Press.

14

Bystanders and Bullying

Following the recent school shooting in Santee, California, students, parents, and school personnel agonized over what might have happened had those who heard the perpetrator talk about his intention to take a gun to school and shoot people intervened. In a number of earlier school shootings peers reported such conversations and violence was averted. But students, and adults, have other important responsibilities as witnesses or bystanders as well. The perpetrators of many school shootings have been described as victims of bullies, with others passively witnessing their suffering.

Many students who are victims are themselves not aggressive. Many suffer quietly. Others are both victims and bullies themselves. A very few – perhaps those who have had hurtful, painful experiences outside the school as well or at least have no support and loving connection to parents, relatives or peers – strike out with the level of violence manifested in the school shootings we have seen in the past few years.

Until recently, much of the world, both students and adults, has seen kids in school picking on each other as simply the way things are. The teen arrested for the Santee, California shootings was picked on, but not more than other kids, according to his peers. They saw his experience as "normal."

My collaborators and I at UMass have conducted, at the invitation of the Belchertown schools, a very detailed study of students' experience of their lives in school, including aggression and bullying. We studied students from second grade through high school. We have found that, even in good schools, which the schools in Belchertown appear to be, with

Reprinted from E. Staub (2001). Bystanders and bullying. *Daily Hampshire Gazette*, April 26, 2001, p. A10. Reprinted with permission of the *Daily Hampshire Gazette*.

a lot of positive behavior among the students, a minority of students are victims of harassment, intimidation, or are "picked on" by other students. Other students are not victims of aggression, but simply are excluded from the mainstream of student life. Not surprisingly, both groups of students report less positive and more negative feelings about their lives in school than their peers.

Whether students described incidents of bullying as victims, as perpetrators, or simply as witnesses, they said that while some of the time other kids join in with bullies, most of the time peers who are witnesses/bystanders remain passive, and only occasionally does a peer try to help. They report that adults also often remain passive. Students who report occasional intervention by others when they are picked on are less unhappy in school. At all ages except late in high school, being someone who intervenes is also associated with positive feelings about life at school.

Although kids-treating-other-kids-badly has long been accepted as simply part of growing up, some legislators have started talking seriously about writing laws that would outlaw bullying in schools, as a result of these horrific acts of violence. Many pundits have suggested we offer character education in schools. But what kind of character do we shape when we foster an environment that produces victims, perpetrators, or passive observers, over years and years of elementary and secondary education? It should not be surprising that a group of eighth-grade students in our study agreed that bullying would never stop.

We as parents, educators, and citizens must make it stop. This requires that we create communities in classrooms and schools which includes everyone – students who are strong academically or not, jocks or unskilled at sports, those alike or those different from most of the others. Taking care of animals at a young age, which everyone can do, putting on plays in which everyone has a role – whether as actor, responsible for make up or costumes – a class acting together to help in the community or help with an important cause in the world, are some of the many ways community can be created. Students participating in deciding about and maintaining values and rules the group should live by is another important way to give everyone a sense of importance and belonging. Teachers and students together can agree, as they build this community, that harassment will not be tolerated.

While teachers obviously have to lead, a classroom and school can become a community in which students and teachers share the responsibility for speaking out when one student harasses another. The potential power of bystanders is great. Bystanders in a classroom can speak not only to perpetrators, but also to victims. Imagine what would happen if one kid called another a hurtful name, and other children turned to the victim and said, "We are sorry; he is wrong to say that. We are your friends." Imagine the effect such support and empathy would have on the victim, the perpetrator, and the bystanders themselves.

Such a supportive community would help develop positive values and the moral courage to act on them. It would improve the possibility of teaching and learning. And it would do away with kids shooting others at school.

15

Students' Experience of Bullying and Other Aspects of Their Lives in Middle School in Belchertown

Report Summary

Ervin Staub and Darren A. Spielman

INTRODUCTION

In recent years an awareness has developed of the frequency and destructive consequences of harassment, intimidation, students picking on each other – what may all be called bullying – in the schools. These are forms of aggression that make the lives of students painful. They affect classroom climate and make teaching and learning more difficult. The personality, interpersonal relations, and happiness of students who are persistent targets of bullying may be seriously affected. While past research and observation suggest that many students who are bullied suffer quietly, the frustration and anger bullying can generate seem to have had a role in motivating some of the students who have become killers of their fellow students and teachers in school shootings in the United States.

Motivated by the desire to create safe, caring schools, and supported by a grant from the Department of Justice, questionnaires were developed to assess bullying, as well as the broader aspects of students' experience of their lives in the Belchertown schools.[1] Three questionnaires were developed with questions worded to be appropriate for students in grades two and three, four to six, and seven to twelve. Here we summarize our report on middle school students' responses to the questionnaire.

Part one of the questionnaire asked students about behavior directed at them, behavior they performed, and behavior they observed in the course of the past week in school. Negative behaviors directed at them included name calling, threats, being hit, exclusion from groups, rumors and lies about the student; positive behaviors directed at students included others being friendly to them, asking them to join fun activities and making them feel important.

This part of the questionnaire also asked students about their own negative and positive behavior toward others. It asked them about positive and negative behavior by adults toward themselves (praise, affirmation, versus being embarrassed and having their feelings hurt by adults) and toward others. The students were also asked to report passive bystandership (witnessing a student being picked on and doing nothing) and active bystandership (witnessing and taking positive action) by peers, by themselves, and by adults when peers badly treated the student or other students. We believe that passivity and, even more, complicity (joining others in negative behavior) by bystanders greatly contributes to bullying. Students were also asked to describe their feelings in school in the past week: feeling left out, angry, lonely, scared, happy, accepted, part of the group, listened to by peers, listened to by adults.

Part two of the questionnaire asked students to describe an incident when a student bullied them, an incident when they witnessed bullying and an incident when they bullied others. They were asked about the recency of these events (more recent bullying suggesting that it happens more often) and about how frequently such things happen. They were asked about motives for negative behavior and about where negative behavior takes place in the school.

Part three asked students how they feel about treatment from peers. It asked how often they worry about bullying, how safe they feel from bad treatment, how respectfully they feel that peers treat them and how comfortable they feel in school. It asked these same questions about treatment from adults. Part three also asked students about where and why they feel unsafe and uncomfortable in school.

OVERVIEW OF FINDINGS

Students report a great deal of positive behavior directed at them by peers, by adults and performed by themselves. Students also report a great deal of positive feelings about their lives in school. Students report much less, but still a substantial amount, of negative behavior directed at them, both by peers and to a lesser extent by adults, and negative feelings about their lives in school.

Positive behaviors by peers tend to be associated with each other: students who receive more of one kind of positive behavior from peers also tend to receive more of other kinds. The same is true of positive behavior directed at students by adults. In addition, positive behaviors from peers and adults are associated with each other. Students who receive more positive behavior from peers also tend to receive more positive behavior from adults.

These associations are also true of negative behavior, some students receiving more of different kinds of negative behavior from peers, others less, and some students receiving more of different kinds of negative behavior from adults, others less. As with positive behavior, students who receive more negative behavior from peers also tend to receive more from adults; those who receive less from peers tend to receive less from adults.

Receiving positive behaviors is associated with having positive feelings about one's life in school. Receiving negative behaviors tends to be associated with having negative feelings about one's life in school. Some students report they are bullied a lot and report worrying about bullying a great deal.

There are students who receive no negative behavior, while others receive quite a bit, with corresponding difference in feelings about school experience. There are students who receive a lot of positive behavior, and others who receive none or very little. The latter group of students also receives relatively little negative behavior. These students seem excluded, not part of the flow of life in their peer group. They have even fewer positive feelings about school than students who receive many negative behaviors.

Some students who receive a lot of negative behavior report that they direct little negative behavior at others. This is consistent with past research. Others who receive negative behavior from peers and adults also direct negative behavior at others. Such students may be part of negative cycles of interaction, with the actions of each party resulting in harmful and hurtful reactions by the other party.

While some negative behavior and bullying takes place everywhere in the school, the hallways and the school bus are reported as especially likely places for them.

DETAILED SUMMARY

Students' Reports of Positive and Negative Behavior Directed at Them

Students report fairly high frequency of being bullied, witnessing bullying, and worrying about bullying. One third of the students reported they were bullied the past week, 10% that they were bullied the day they filled out the questionnaire. Thirteen percent of the students report that they are bullied at least once a day. Eight percent of the students report that they worry about bullying all the time. Another 7% checked the next highest number on a 5 point scale indicating worry about bullying.

Students report fairly high frequencies of negative behavior directed at them by peers (being called names, 62%, someone kicking, hitting or pushing them, 42%, being excluded, others spreading lies or gossip about them, and so on), with many students reporting that such behaviors occurred multiple times in the course of the week.

Negative behaviors tend to be associated. They tend to go together, at least to a moderate extent. A student who is the object of one kind of negative behavior tends also to be the object of other kinds. This means that while some students receive very few negative behaviors, others receive a great deal.

There is substantial positive behavior in the interaction of students, but many students also report receiving no or very little positive behavior in the course of the past week. Thus, 27% report that no one asked them to join a fun activity, 24% that no one made them feel important. Positive behaviors also tend to go together, some students receiving more of different kinds of positive behavior, others less.

Students report a great deal of positive behavior by adults. But many of them report receiving no positive behavior or little of it. While most of them report no negative behavior by adults toward them, a significant minority do report actions that embarrassed them, adults treating them unfairly or hurting their feelings or someone else's feelings. Reports of negative behaviors by adults also tend to go together, some students receiving less, others more. Students who are the targets of more negative behavior by peers also report receiving more negative behavior from adults.

STUDENTS' FEELINGS ABOUT THEIR LIVES IN SCHOOL

Students report a great deal of positive feelings. A substantial majority feel happy almost always or a lot of the time, and say that other students treat them with respect. Not quite as many report that they feel part of the group – nearly 10% say this is almost never the case. Most students also report that adults and other students treat them well and that they feel safe from students or adults treating them badly at school. But just as with positive behavior, there is a significant minority of students who do not report these positive feelings or experiences. About 18% of students feel unsafe or very unsafe from students, 15% from adults, treating them badly in school. Positive feelings tend to be associated. Those who report feeling happy also tend to report feeling comfortable, accepted, safe and part of the group.

The predominant response of students was that they almost never or only once in a while have negative feelings, like anger, loneliness, feeling left out or scared in school. But a substantial number of students do report having such negative feelings and experiences. Sixteen percent report that they feel angry, 13% feel left out of the group, a lot of the time or almost always. Negative feelings also tend to go together, some students experiencing more of the varied negative feelings, others less.

Associations among Behaviors and Feelings

Students who report receiving negative behavior from peers tend to have more negative feelings about their lives in school (they report feeling angry, scared, lonely, excluded and so on) and less positive feelings (less happy, accepted, listened to). The same is true of students who receive more negative behavior from adults. Students who report receiving more positive behaviors from peers report more good feelings about their lives in school. The same is true, although somewhat less strongly, of students who report more positive behavior from teachers.

Students also report directing negative behavior at others, although less than the amount of negative behavior they report receiving. These negative behaviors also go together. Students who perform more of them also report more negative and fewer positive feelings about their lives in the school.

There is an association between negative behavior directed at students by peers, as well as by adults, and students own negative acts. Students who receive more negative acts by others also perform more negative acts. They also report more negative and fewer positive feelings.

Students report that they perform many positive acts toward peers. These also tend to go together: students who report more positive acts of one kind tend to report that they also engage in more positive acts of other kinds. Performing such behaviors is associated with receiving such behaviors from others and with more positive feelings and fewer negative feelings.

Girls report less negative behavior directed at them by peers and by teachers, and more positive behavior directed at them than boys. It is not surprising, in light of this, that the experience by girls of their lives in school is more positive, that they report more positive feelings than boys.

There are only a few grade differences. An important one among them is that in comparison to sixth and seventh graders, eighth graders report receiving more negative behavior and less active bystanding from other students.

The Profiles of Extreme Groups: Recipients of Negative and Positive Behavior

The 15% of the students who received the least negative behavior from peers in the past week (who may be called "low negatives" – these students actually report that they received no negative behavior) differ in important ways from the 15% who report receiving the most negative behavior ("high negatives"). The latter report more negative behavior from adults as well, more negative behavior of their own, more negative feelings and less positive feelings (see Figure 15.1).

As a group students who receive the most negative behavior report that they engage in more negative behavior than those who receive the least negative behavior. But there is great variation in the former group. Some students in that group report that they themselves engage in little or no

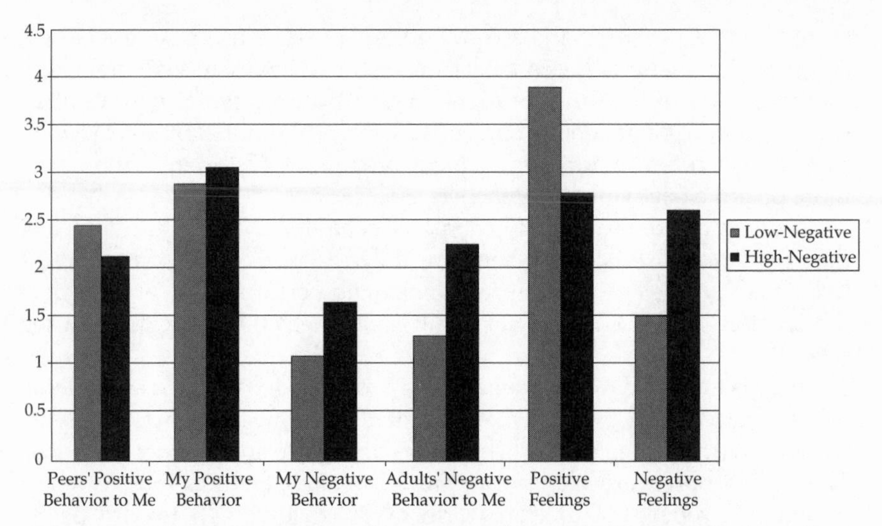

FIGURE 15.1. Some comparisons between students who receive the least (low-negative) and the most (high-negative) negative behaviors from peers.

negative behavior. These students report receiving more negative behavior from peers than students who report that they themselves engage in negative behavior, but report receiving less negative behavior from teachers.

The 15% of the students who receive the most positive behavior from their peers (they check the highest number in reporting each of the positive behaviors on the questionnaire, which means that they received each of those behaviors at least three times in the past week) differ in important ways from the 15% who receive the least positive behavior (who report receiving such behavior not at all or once in the prior week). The latter students report less positive behavior of their own, less positive feelings and slightly more negative feelings. These students report even less positive feelings than the 15% of the students who are the most frequent recipients of negative acts (see Figure 15.2).

Bystanders

Students report about equal amounts of passive bystanding by other students (a witness who saw that they were picked on and did not try to stop it – 24%) and active bystanding by fellow students (a witness who did try to stop it – 26%. Boys report that they are bullied more often than girls and that others witness them being bullied more often than girls. But girls report receiving more active bystanding than boys.

Many students report that they witnessed bullying of others (79%). They report that they frequently remained passive, as well as frequently intervened. Boys and girls report equal witnessing, with boys reporting

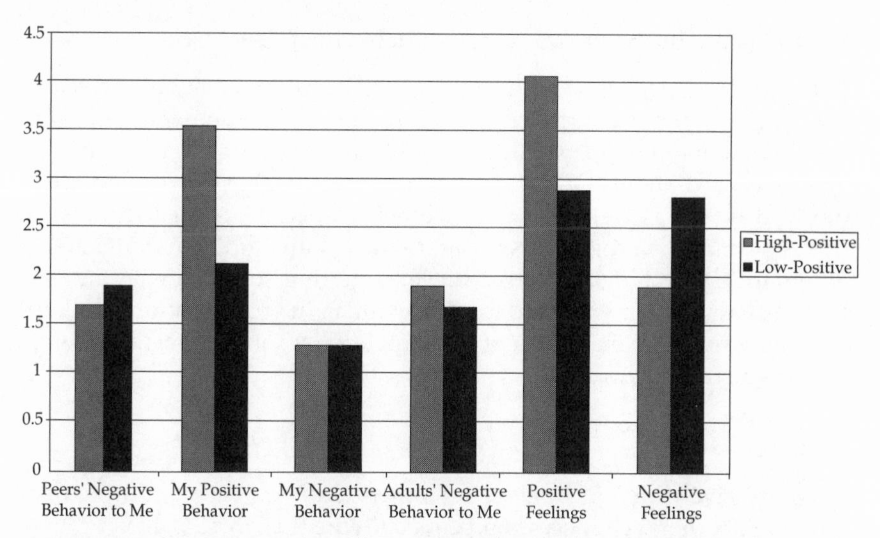

FIGURE 15.2. Some comparisons between students who receive the most (high-positive) and the least (low-positive) positive behaviors from peers.

more passivity. Older students, eighth graders, report they witness more bullying, and also that they more often remain passive bystanders.

Students report frequent witnessing by adults of students picking on other students. They report that adults often intervened (64%), but also fairly often remained passive (28%). Fewer students reported that adults witnessed someone picking on them. This may be due to the wording of the question – students were asked whether an adult saw a student picking on someone, but when the question related to themselves they were asked whether "an adult saw another student trying to hurt me." Of those who said yes, 16% said an adult intervened on their behalf, 8% saying an adult did not help them. Eighth graders report more witnessing by adults, which may be because they are more often bullied. They also report more passivity by adults in the face of this.

Children who receive more negative behavior from peers and adults, and who themselves perform more negative behavior, report more active bystanding and substantially more passive bystanding by peers and adults than do other students. These reports suggest that with students who are often picked on, others sometimes intervene to help, but more often do not.

There are many associations between bystander behavior and students' feelings. The strongest associations are that the more either peers or adults are passive bystanders when students are picked on, the more negative feelings and the less positive feelings students report. There is a slight association between active bystandership by students and their own positive feelings.

Places Where Bullying and Negative Behavior Takes Place

Students are especially concerned about hallways, next about the school bus and next about the locker room. But about 16% also express concern about what might happen to them in the classroom, with the same percentage concerned about the cafeteria. In some places there is concern about physical as well as verbal harm from others (especially in the hallways), in others primarily verbal attacks (classroom). Many younger students fear older students. Many students fear encountering students who they believe dislike them or who tend to pick on them. In some locations students describe adults as part of the problem (cafeteria, school bus), acting in ways that are distressing to students.

Motives

Students give different motives for others bullying them, and for their bullying of others. They see their peers bullying them first of all in order to look good, then because the peer does not like them, then in order to feel good. Boys report as the fourth most frequent reason for being bullied that they did something to their peer, but for girls this is the reason given least often. The predominant reason students give for bullying another is that the other did something to them, the next most frequent is that they do not like the student. Other reasons are reported very infrequently.

Conclusions

What this report shows is likely to be the picture of a normal middle school. The experience of many students in the school is mainly positive. But the experience of some students seems quite negative. There are two groups of students whose life at school should concern us.

One group reports a lot of negative behavior toward themselves, by peers and adults. These students have much more negative feelings and less positive feelings about school than students who receive little negative behavior.

Some students may be part of a cycle of negative behavior. Children's own negative behavior toward peers and their peers' negative behavior toward them were associated with each other. Knowing that there is such association does not tell us which one causes the other, or whether both are caused by something else. We do not know from the information we gathered to what extent the cycle starts with negative behavior by a child, to which others react with negative behavior, or with negative behavior by peers, or even adults, to which the child reacts with negative actions.

The starting point for such a negative cycle may vary. But, once the negative cycle exists, a negative act by one participant in the system may elicit negative responses from other participants. It is important for teachers to manage their relationship to even difficult students without contributing to such an ongoing negative cycle, and to help break such cycles among students. Breaking such cycles is important for the functioning of a class and especially for the long-term welfare of the students who are the primary objects of negative actions by peers and adults.

We also know from past research and observation that many kids who are picked on don't engage in evidently negative behavior of the kind we asked about, which might "reasonably" elicit negative reactions from others. The same seems true of students in Belchertown. About half of the students who receive the most negative behavior report little negative behavior of their own. Some students may simply be picked on, badly treated, especially by peers: they receive even more negative behavior by peers, but less negative behavior from teachers, than those who report that they themselves engage in negative acts. Perhaps unwilling or unable to defend themselves their peers pick on them more.

Another group of students receives a moderate amount of negative behavior (only a little more than those who receive a lot of positive behavior from peers), but no positive acts or very few positive acts are directed at them. They report even less positive feelings about their lives in school than the students who are the recipients of many negative acts by others. Perhaps they feel invisible, excluded, even ostracized.

It may also be that negative behavior toward some students is elicited, or positive behavior toward them is made less likely, by their negative mood or general unhappiness that is the result of difficult experiences at home or in the outside world in general. Researchers have noted that children with low self-esteem and with seeming inability to defend themselves are more likely to be the target of bullying. But perhaps even more profound a reason for negative behavior and lack of positive behavior by peers (and adults) is children's overall mood state. In other words, it is possible that the origin or initial cause of the negative moods or lack of positive moods these children report is not their school experience. Even then, however, their problems are likely to become worse due to difficulties in their relationship to peers and adults in school. Positive relationships to peers and adults would almost certainly help, in contrast, to ameliorate past hurt and the difficulties that arise from that. Caring relationships with one or more people is an important source of resilience by children – of functioning well despite difficult backgrounds and difficult circumstances.

Students' descriptions of their lives in school indicate that certain changes in the school environment would be important to improve the well-being of some of the students, seemingly a minority but a substantial minority. Negative behavior, students picking on some students and in general acting in aggressive and hurtful ways toward each other, ought to diminish. The way adults interact with students, at least with some students, should change. Positive behavior should increase toward students who do not receive positive behavior from their peers. Joining those who pick on students and passive bystandership needs to diminish.

Some students, because they feel badly about their lives in school, or have bad experiences outside school and feel badly about their lives in general, may have a biased perception. This may explain why they perceive adults' actions, not only toward themselves but also toward others, as negative. But certain things increase the credibility of students' reporting. For example, high-negative and low-negative students are quite similar in reporting others' positive behavior toward themselves and their own positive behavior toward others. High- and low-positives are quite similar in reporting their peers' negative behavior toward themselves, and high-positives report that they perform much more positive behavior than low-positives. Since human interactions are often reciprocal, this makes sense.

The relationships described by "high-negative" and "low-positive" students with their peers and teachers also shape the rest of the student body. When students witness negative behavior toward others, when they join or remain passive, they themselves are negatively affected. In contrast, students who are active bystanders have somewhat more positive feelings. Students must also be affected when they interact with peers who worry a lot about being bullied or are unhappy in school. The development of students, their personality and character, is shaped by all this.

Students report more bullying and negative behavior and more worry about such behavior in certain places than others. But while the hallways and the school bus are the most problematic places, students are concerned about such behavior everywhere. This, together with all the rest of the information indicates that, in spite of the predominantly positive experience of a clear majority of students, an overall change in school climate and in people's way of relating in the school would be highly desirable.

Recommendations for Action

It seems reasonable to conclude that the experience of life in the school can be and ought to be improved for some students. This is likely to improve school life for everyone and enhance the beneficial effects of school on children's personality, character, and later happiness in life. Ideally, for this to happen, apart from any specific "interventions," changes should be in the school climate. It should be in the life of the school, and of each classroom, as a community. A few preliminary suggestions follow, for further discussion by the school community. To institute them requires teacher training, or the "training" of students, or both. However, most of the suggestions don't require the teaching of new or additional material in the classroom. They have to do with a way of life, rather than special activities.

1. *Discuss with students the issue of negative behavior and bullying, as well as the exclusion of some peers, and develop with the participation of students desirable rules of peer interaction.* Participation by students creates community and gives students a sense of responsibility for maintaining rules. It is important also to discuss what is required for students to actually live by these rules and to participate in maintaining them. Some of the items that follow can contribute to make living by these rules a reality.

The "discussion" should include emotionally involving descriptions of what it is like to be a victim. It should indicate that such behavior is not acceptable and lead to an agreement that it will not be tolerated by the community. At the same time it should include an empathic exploration of why students may act in ways that are harmful and/or hurtful to others. The reasons may be psychological (wanting to look good, to feel good, be included – the discrepancies between how students perceive their own and others' motives shown in the report may be used). Negative actions may also be instigated by others' actions and the way students interpret them. Aggressive children tend to see others as hostile to themselves, and then respond to the hostility they perceive. Lack of skills to effectively and non-aggressively deal with what students see as challenging or negative behavior by others also contributes.

2. *Bystandership training.* Students should be trained in effective ways of intervening when they see peers bully or act in hurtful ways towards others. While effective bystandership can require force and confrontation, good bystandership usually involves early action, knowing how to exert influence in positive ways and the ability to recruit others as active bystanders. Teachers may also benefit from some aspects of such training.

Responses on the questionnaire indicate that victims of negative behavior benefit from intervention that attempts to protect them. Active bystandership by others is associated with less negative feelings about school life. We also know from research that students who have friends who speak up for them are not likely to be bullied. Such protection can be extended to all students.

3. *Creating community in each classroom and in the school as a whole.* It is important to create a community that includes everyone, both students who are marginal because they are aggressive, antisocial, because they present problems in their behavior and relationships to others (who, when not included, tend to associate with each other and develop greater problems), and students who are marginal for other reasons.

There are many possible ways to do this. Putting on plays, finding worthwhile causes that groups of students can work for (to benefit the school, the community, the outside world), putting on cultural events with the involvement of families, are some examples of community building. It is important to include everyone in these activities, for every student to be part of the community. It is important to provide all students with opportunities to use whatever skills they possess and to have these skills and their contributions be appreciated by others. The connections that develop among students in the course of activities in the pursuit of shared goals are likely to lead to more positive attitudes toward individual students who may otherwise be devalued.

4. *Conflict resolution training.* Such training, which is now widely used, can help students deal better with potentially aggression-generating situations.

5. *Learning to fulfill needs and goals in constructive ways.* Some students, who tend to be aggressive, might get training in how to respond to what they see as provocative acts in effective, nonaggressive ways that fulfill their needs and goals. These needs include "basic needs" that human beings share – to feel secure, to feel effective, to feel good about oneself, to have positive connections to other people. The training includes role play, as well as learning about one's own motives, the habitual (aggressive) ways one fulfills them and alternative (constructive) ways of fulfilling them. In the course of this training students also learn social skills and come to understand others' needs and motives better (see Chapter 19).

6. *Healing from psychological injuries.* Many students are likely to have had painful and difficult experiences in their lives. The injuries these create affect students' feelings about themselves and other people and the way they act towards others. Engagement with such experiences, for example, by writing about them, or through reading assignments that can give rise to discussions which may have a healing effect, can bring benefits in students' emotional life and interpersonal relationships.

While this recommendation is less "mainstream" than some of the others, and while it requires some special training and the use of class time, it can be instituted in schools in a natural manner. It may bring substantial benefits to students, in their emotional life, in increased self-awareness and even in writing and other skills. (The training provided to teachers may also help teachers engage with some of their own difficult experiences from the past, which may affect their relationship to students).

7. *Helping teachers develop positive methods of guidance and discipline.* The findings of the survey, together with much research and common sense, suggest that providing guidance to students and using discipline techniques that do not embarrass and hurt students is important. Given teachers' extensive experience, developing positive guidance and discipline practices may best be accomplished by teachers working together in brainstorming, constructing and developing the use of such methods.

8. *Adult supervision in certain settings.* We interpret the findings of the survey as requiring changes in the school and classroom climates. But the findings do suggest the value of more adult supervision in certain settings,

especially the hallways, and helping adults develop effective but positive methods of dealing with problem situations in certain settings, like the school bus.

9. *Focus groups*. The use of focus groups for gathering additional information. To the extent focus groups are used, they can be vehicles for change. In addition to gathering information, students could engage with the question of what is required for reducing negative behavior and enhancing positive behavior and how they can contribute to accomplishing these goals.

10. *Community forums, for students, teachers, and parents*. Presenting the information we collected about school life may itself contribute to change. It can provide a context for discussion among students, teachers, parents and between these groups. Training for parents that enables them help their children interact effectively with peers, in order to minimize negative behavior by them or directed at them, would also be worthwhile. Such training might contribute to the use of positive socialization techniques by parents.

In order to get many parents involved, the school may need to create special incentives. The participation of their children in events may motivate parents to come to the school.

Finally, creating the changes that are suggested and implied here would, we believe, also contribute to more effective learning in school. The recommendations include elements that might themselves further cognitive growth in children. The changes in relationships and emotional experiences that can be expected should make both learning and teaching easier and more effective.

Note

1. We were invited by the Belchertown schools to conduct this research, under a grant from the Department of Justice to the Belchertown police and schools. This report summary was prepared for distribution by the school system to its staff and not as a formal description of research. However, both in this selection and in the selection that follows, references to "association" (for example, among positive behaviors) mean statistically significant and often very substantial correlations, and statements of "differences" between groups refer to statistically significant differences based on appropriate statistical analyses.

16

Passive and Active Bystandership across Grades in Response To Students Bullying Other Students

Ervin Staub, D. Fellner, Jr., J. Berry, and K. Morange

The previous selection is about student life in middle school. However, we actually did the study described in that selection in the whole school system, from grades two to twelve. Here, we will briefly describe some striking findings about students and teachers witnessing and responding to bullying, and changes in this over the years. We regard positive bystandership to be of great importance in reducing bullying – which may be defined as negative behavior such as harassment, intimidation, and verbal or physical aggression, especially when this is repeatedly directed at the same persons.

In general, the findings of the study across all grades were similar to the findings in middle school. For example, positive behaviors directed at students were associated with each other, and negative behavior directed at students were associated with each other, at every grade level. However, there were also differences. For example, fewer students reported that they were bullied in the previous week in the lower grades, before the fifth grade, than in subsequent grades (see Figure 16.1).

When someone is badly treated, the response of a witness can have an enormous impact on the severity and frequency of such negative behavior. A witness who does not act when he or she sees one student bullying another we consider a "passive bystander." Active bystanders react in a positive or helpful manner, such as trying to stop the bullying, speaking on the behalf of the victim, or alerting an authority figure. A bystander's reaction may, of course, also be negative, such as joining in the bullying. For the purposes of this report, however, we will consider "active bystanding" as a *positive* action.

This chapter is a section from E. Staub, D. Fellner, Jr., J. Berry, & K. Morange. Students' experience of bullying and other aspects of their lives in the Belchertown school system – Overview report. Unpublished manuscript, Department of Psychology, University of Massachusetts at Amherst.

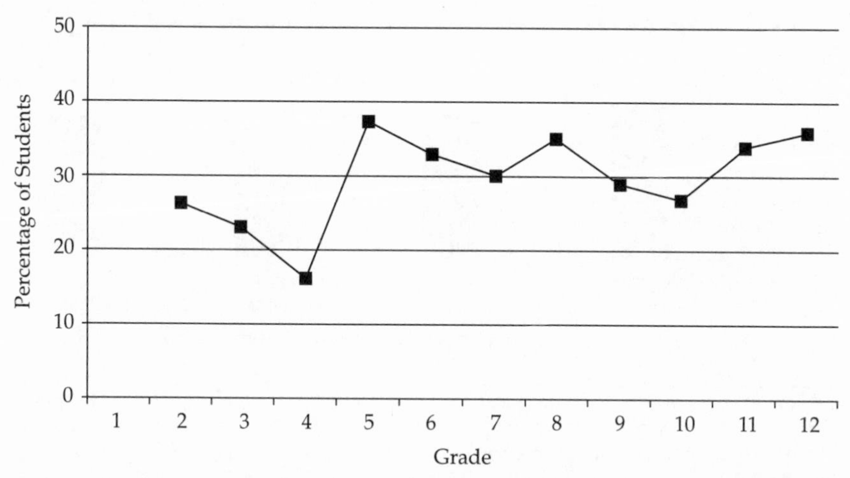

FIGURE 16.1. Percentage of students who reported that they were bullied in the past week, by grade.

Students witness peers' negative behavior with great frequency. With the exception of the fourth grade, where there is a drop in frequency, as grade level increased larger percentages of students reported that they had recently witnessed bullying. Forty-seven percent of primary school children, 50% of fifth graders, 51% of middle school children, and 71% of high school students reported witnessing bullying in the previous two weeks.

There is a strong association between other students being passive (in contrast to active) bystanders and the negative feelings and behaviors of bullied students. Active bystandership is often reciprocal. Receiving active bystandership from other students or from teachers is associated with being an active bystander to others. Passive bystandership is also reciprocal. While active bystanders reported more positive behaviors toward their peers in school, passive bystanders reported that they performed more negative behaviors. Passive bystanders also reported receiving more negative behaviors from the teacher and having more negative feelings (see Figure 16.2).

Overall, students reported more active bystandership by adults than by other students, both in their own conflicts and in conflicts they witnessed. When asked about the last time they were bullied, 45% of all students bullied in the presence of an adult reported that the adult came to their aid. Only 32% reported that other students were active bystanders for them.

Active bystandership decreases across grades – older students receive less help when bullied – either from teachers or other students, with greater declines in help by teachers. Complicity (joining in the bullying) remains relatively stable across grades, with a dip in the ninth grade, but then return to higher levels. Passive bystandership, however, *increases* with grade.

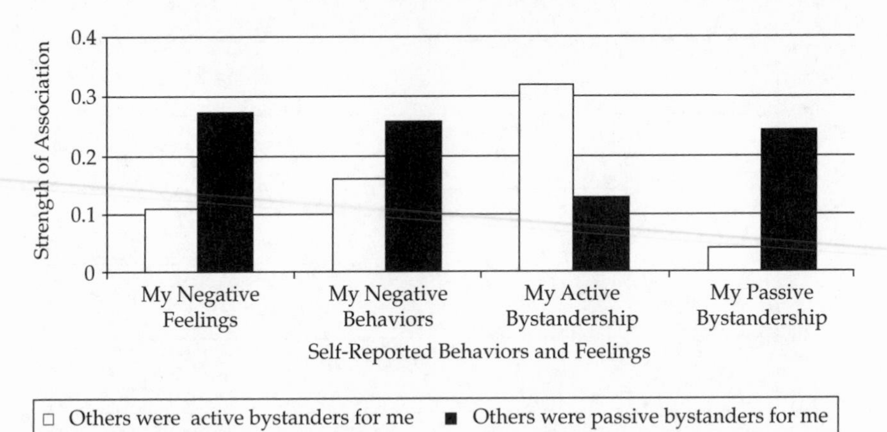

FIGURE 16.2. Strength of association between others' bystander behaviors and self-reported behaviors and feelings.

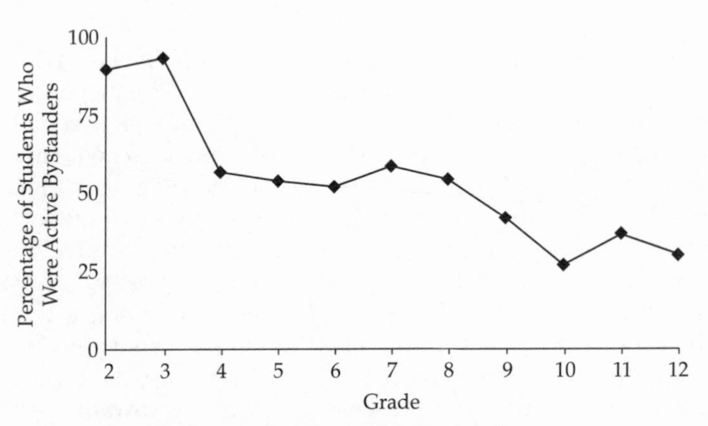

FIGURE 16.3. Students' reports of active bystanding.

Possibly as children get older they are expected (by both their teachers and peers, and by themselves) to handle their own conflicts. The result of the decrease in active bystandership, however, may be that adolescents feel more endangered and abandoned, their need for security and positive connection less fulfilled. Girls are more likely to report that other students intervened the last time they were bullied, while boys are more likely to report that other students joined in the last time they were bullied. Boys and girls are similar in their self-reported bystandership behaviors.

Students' reports of their own bystander behaviors are similar to what they report of others' behaviors. As grade level increases, the percentage of students who report being active bystanders drops substantially (see Figure 16.3). While over 80% of students in the second grade reported coming to the aid of a bullied peer at least once in the past week, less than 30% of twelfth graders reported this. There is an especially large drop in active bystandership between the third and fourth grades.

When students were asked about their own bullying, and consistent with the preceding findings, those who answered the questions (many left this part of the survey blank, or wrote, "I never bully" on the top of the page) reported that passive bystandership in response to their negative behaviors *increases* and active bystandership *decreases* with increasing grade level. However, they reported less active bystandership overall than did students describing their own bystandership behaviors, or the behaviors of others when they themselves were the victims of bullying.

The older they were, the larger the percentage of students who reported that bystanders joined in the bullying, with a sharp drop in eleventh grade and a return to its previous level in the twelfth grade. It is possible that bullies interpret others' passive behaviors as "joining in." For example, while bullying another child, a group of students witness the incident, do nothing to stop the bully, and are laughing. The bully could interpret this as "joining" in, while the bystanders may report doing nothing. Another possibility is that students do not truthfully report the frequency with which they join in the bullying when they are witnesses.

As suggested in the previous selection, training in constructive, positive bystandership and classroom and school climates that encourage students to be active bystanders will likely improve the lives of all students: those who are victimized, those who are inclined to bully but would change in positive ways as a result, and also those who come to feel better about themselves as they become more caring people through their actions as active bystanders.

17

Self-Esteem and Aggression

Earlier in the book, I mentioned that aggressive behavior and low self-esteem have been found, in a variety of studies, to go together. In recent works, however, this relationship has been challenged. Here I will discuss some important characteristics of aggressive boys and men, including self-esteem.

Aggressive boys see other people as hostile, especially to themselves. They see others as intending to harm. For example, when they see pictures showing boys playing soccer and one boy kicking another while trying to get the ball away from him, they interpret this as intentional harmdoing (Coie & Dodge, 1997). Aggressive adults, both college students and prison inmates, also see other people as hostile (Galvin & Spielman, 1999). However, intentional rather than accidental harm caused by others is especially likely to provoke retaliatory aggression (Mallick & McCandless, 1966). Boys who are not aggressive assume that such acts are accidental. Some children who are badly treated, given their specific circumstances, may come to feel hostility and even hatred toward people. However, the need for connection to other people is profound, and even such children and the adults they grow into will desire and seek connection to some others.

Negative beliefs and hostility, as they come to be expressed in behavior, create a self-fulfilling prophecy. Reacting to others as if they had aggressed against us makes them respond aggressively. A group of unfamiliar boys, after spending a period of time with an aggressive boy, becomes aggressive toward him (Dodge, 1980). Our early experiences shape us, but we, in turn, tend to create circumstances that further develop our personalities in the same direction, a form of "self-socialization." Thus, both in youth and later

Reprinted from E. Staub (1999). The roots of evil: Personality, social conditions, culture and basic human needs. *Personality and Social Psychology Review*, 3, 179–192. Included here are pages 188–189.

in life, the characteristics such boys develop lead to expressively violent behavior, apart from any tendency for instrumental violence they may develop. Later in life, they also aggress against their children (Huesmann, Eron, Lefkowitz, & Walder, 1984). It is estimated that about 30% of children who have received harsh physical punishment treat their children the same way, in contrast to 2% to 3% of physical abuse in the general population (Ziegler, Taussig, & Black, 1992).

Harsh treatment also leads to difficulty in liking and accepting oneself. As Freud has proposed, rather than seeing, examining, and accepting conflicting, problematic aspects of oneself, one projects them into other people. Alternatively, it becomes extremely important to affirm one's own value, relative to other people. Because in many parts of our society and in the world men are supposed to be strong and powerful, affirming one's value becomes showing that one is strong and powerful. Many men who have been imprisoned for violent crimes report that they used to pick fights either to feel good about themselves or to look good in others' eyes (Toch, 1969).

Olweus (1979, 1993) found that bullies, who tend to pick on and repeatedly victimize other children, do not have low self-esteem. Coie and Dodge (1997), in reviewing research on aggression in children, reported that aggressive boys do not have low self-concepts and that they tend to blame others rather than themselves for "negative outcomes." Baumeister (1997) proposed that it is high self-esteem and injured narcissism that are associated with aggression.

However, the background and experience of aggressive boys that I have described earlier make it unlikely that they have "genuinely" high self-esteem, as does further information I describe later. How might we understand the evidence, then? First, such boys, and later the men they become, may compensate for their sense of vulnerability and social and academic difficulties by proclaiming their own worth, thereby affirming themselves to others and even themselves. Related to such a compensatory self-esteem may be projection, seeing weakness, vulnerability, and various bad qualities in others, rather than themselves, and blaming others for negative outcomes.

Second, there may be important, alternative avenues in the development of aggression. One of these is permissiveness and lack of punishment for aggression. Another is an environment that may or may not be harsh and punitive but encourages aggression, so that children, youth, and the adults they grow into feel when they aggress that they are doing the right thing. In fact, although many aggressive children are ineffective, and although their aggressive behavior is disorganized, with limited self-control and easy flare-up of anger (Rausch, 1965), others are effective aggressors. Although the former are unpopular among their peers, among the latter, aggression is unrelated to popularity (Coie & Dodge, 1997).

A group of peers, for example, antisocial friends or members of a gang, may also help to maintain self-esteem. Often a seeming focus in such groups, and probably the most important function of the group for its members, is to help create and maintain positive identity and connection to like-minded others. Thus, members of such groups would have a heightened sense of self, at least while they are members.

Perhaps another important issue is not simply the level of self-esteem but what it is based on and how stable and reliable rather than how fragile it is. Many boys who become aggressive do not have the socially valued means to gain a positive image through competence and good performance in school and good relationships with peers. Therefore, they organize their self-esteem around strength, power, and physical superiority over others. Their early experiences as victims, the models of aggression around them, and the culture's focus on male strength and superiority all facilitate this. It is how self-esteem is constituted, what self-esteem is based on, that may matter. However, the self-esteem of aggressive boys and of aggressive men (Baumeister, 1997) appears to be very vulnerable and fragile. Its maintenance may require the continued feeling of and perhaps use of strength and power over others.

Thus, the level of self-esteem, how it is constituted, and its fragility and sources may all matter. As I have written elsewhere

> In groups and in individuals very high self-evaluation often masks self-doubt. Persistent life difficulties may contradict the high self-evaluation and bring self-doubt to the surface. Even when there is no underlying self-doubt, a very high self-evaluation may be associated with limited concern for others. Among individuals, a *moderately* positive self concept is most strongly associated with sensitivity and responsiveness to other people. (Staub, 1989, p. 55; see also Jarymowitz, 1977; Reese, 1961)

People have to value themselves to value other people, but not value themselves so strongly that others do not matter.

"High self-esteem" for some people (but not for many others) may include a sense of superiority that must be defended. When it is frustrated, it is likely to lead to aggression. Low self-esteem may lead some people to affirm themselves in their own and others' eyes by aggression or to have a greater sense of insecurity in the world and feel that they must defend themselves. I have suggested that both "group self-concepts" of superiority and of weakness and vulnerability (and sometimes their combination) are cultural elements that may make genocide more likely (Staub, 1989).

However, in many instances of violence or with many actors, self-esteem may not have a primary role. Instead, orientations to people and the world – perceptions of hostility, valuing or devaluing people, and feelings of hostility – may have strong influence, even though the experiences that have affected these orientations also have had an impact on self-esteem.

References

Baumeister, R. F. (1997). *Evil: Inside human violence and cruelty*. New York: Freeman.

Coie, J. D., & Dodge, K. A. (1997). Aggression and antisocial behavior. In W. Damon (Series Ed.) & N. Eisenberg (Vol. Ed.), *Handbook of child psychology: Vol. 3. Social, emotional, and personality development* (5th ed.). New York: Wiley.

Dodge, K. A. (1980). Social cognition and children's aggressive behavior. *Child Development, 51*, 162–170.

Galvin, D., & Spielman, D. (1999). *Poor social perspective taking and hostile attribution bias in aggressive men*. Unpublished manuscript, Department of Psychology, University of Massachusetts at Amherst.

Huesmann, L. R., Eron, L. D., Lefkowitz, M. M., & Walder, L. O. (1984). Stability of aggression over time and generations. *Developmental Psychology, 20*, 1120–1134.

Jarymowitz, M. (1977). Modification of self-worth and increment of prosocial sensitivity. *Polish Psychological Bulletin, 8*, 45–53.

Mallick, S. K., & McCandless, B. R. (1966). A study of catharsis of aggression. *Journal of Personality and Social Psychology, 4*, 591–596.

Olweus, D. (1979). Stability of aggressive reaction patterns in males: A review. *Psychological Bulletin, 86*, 852–875.

Olweus, D. (1993). *Bullying at school: What we know and what we can do*. Oxford, England: Blackwell.

Rausch, H. (1965). Interaction sequences. *Journal of Personality and Social Psychology, 2*, 487–499.

Reese, H. (1961). Relationships between self-acceptance and sociometric choices. *Journal of Abnormal and Social Psychology, 62*, 472–474.

Staub, E. (1989). *The roots of evil: The origins of genocide and other group violence*. New York: Cambridge University Press.

Toch, H. (1969). *Violent men*. Chicago: Aldine.

Ziegler, E., Taussig, C., & Black, K. (1992). Early childhood intervention: A promising preventive for juvenile delinquency. *American Psychologist, 47*, 997–1006.

18

Father–Daughter Incest

A parent or parent substitute sexually engaging his or her child may be seen as violent or as evil – even if there is no physical force or overt intimidation. A child cannot freely give or withdraw consent. Engaging sexually with a child breaks a moral barrier and, in a large percentage of cases, creates significant long-term harm (McCann & Pearlman, 1990).

I will analyze the influences that lead to such behavior with one type of perpetrator I will call *needy-dependent*. He is insecure, and has strong needs for being cared for. Given who he is, it is difficult for him to exercise control in shaping his life, and he easily feels powerless. His important motives have been satisfied by his wife at the beginning of their marriage. According to Gelinas (1983), the wife tends to be a "parentified" child, who had been led to assume adult responsibilities of caretaking in her family of origin. She naturally continued in her caretaking role in relation to her husband.

However, at some point, the additional demands of children result in her withdrawal, sometimes precipitated by illness. Her emotional and sexual withdrawal powerfully activate the husband's needs for being cared for and nurtured, and probably for the feelings of strength and power he gained from this. His insecurity and poor social skills prevent him from seeking satisfaction of his emotional and sexual needs outside the family. Sometimes additional inhibitions exist, for example, religiousness that inhibits him from extramarital sexual relations. An added motive for incest, according to Groth (1982), for both kinds of offenders (see below), is revenge or retaliation against the wife for failing or opposing him.

Reprinted from E. Staub (1991). Psychological and cultural origins of extreme destructiveness and extreme altruism. In W. Kurtines & J. Gewirtz (Eds.), *The handbook of moral behavior and development*. Hillsdale, NJ: Lawrence Erlbaum Associates, pp. 425–446. Included here are pp. 437–440.

According to Groth, the wife's withdrawal may have to do with lack of fulfillment of her own needs by a husband who relates to her more like a dependent child than a competent adult. She may seek to satisfy her needs outside the family. In any case some form of family dysfunction precipitates incest. The man feels abandoned. With his limited capacity to cope, the avenues available to satisfy his needs seem limited. The child who becomes the incest victim is known to him, is under his control, and her inexperience and lack of power make her an attractive sexual partner for him.

The evolution toward incest often begins with the parentification of one of the daughters, usually the oldest. She gradually replaces the withdrawn mother, first in physical caretaking (preparing food, etc.), then in providing emotional closeness. Since the woman has withdrawn from both the husband and the children, this emotional closeness may also fulfill the daughter's emotional needs. Ultimately, the father violates the parent-child boundary. This provides him with the satisfaction of his emotional needs, sexual needs, and need for feelings of control and power. Although the child's needs and the appropriate parental role are disregarded, in such cases a specific devaluation of the victim need not (but can) exist.

Another type of perpetrator plays a dominant role in his family. He assumes an authoritarian position, acting as if members of his family were his property, to do with as he pleases. His behavior is reminiscent of some perpetrators of genocide (for example, the Nazi concentration camp commandant, Amos Goeth; see Staub, 1989). Some such men physically abuse members of their family, and specifically the child who is their incest victim. The motives that lead such a man to incest appear to include power needs, anger and the desire to hurt, and sexual gratification. He may experience sexual access to his child as part of his "narcissistic entitlement as head of the family" (Groth, 1982, p. 223). Finally, in a small group of incestuous fathers the primary motivation appears to be inappropriate sexual responsiveness to children. Groth (1982) calls these men "fixated" offenders.

How do inhibitions decline? Many perpetrators may start with deficient moral values. Usually there is an evolution toward incest. There is gradual increase in the physicalness of contact, which can be accompanied by a progression of psychological changes including "moral equilibration" (Staub, 1989). Both published literature and my discussions with therapists indicate that some perpetrators use fantastic justifications, treating them as if they provided moral reasons for their actions. For example, perpetrators have claimed that the incest educates the child in sexuality; that it is better for the child to have sex in the home than unsupervised sex in the rough, dangerous world outside; that it gives the child love. Some have claimed that the child was too young to be affected.

Stepfathers are relatively frequent perpetrators. In their case the emotional connection to the child may not be as strong, the child may be seen more as a "them." The taboos against sex with children still operate, but the strong taboos against incest may not.

Perpetrators seem deficient in role taking capacity and empathy. This deficiency enables them to objectify victims, which further lessens empathy. Victims are viewed as objects, without considering their inner world, their needs or feelings of pain. This enables perpetrators to deny the harm, and believe that their victims enjoy the experience.

As brutality in the treatment of victims of torture and genocide serve to distance perpetrators from victims (Staub, 1989), so physical abuse by perpetrators of incest can be a means of self-distancing. It can stimulate their use of just world thinking and their further devaluation of victims.

Bystanders play an important role, as they do in most forms of ongoing victimization. The mother is frequently a passive bystander. At times she may (unconsciously) defend herself from awareness, especially when not being burdened by her family is one of her important needs. Or she may avoid becoming informed through active inattention (Staub & Baer, 1974). When the perpetrator is the second type, the mother's general submissiveness, as well as her fear and habitual submission to the wishes and commands of the husband, must contribute to her passivity. Occasionally, mothers join fathers or stepfathers as accomplices or coperpetrators.

To understand better the role of bystanders, it would be important to explore how often passive mothers and other family members are aware of the incestuous relationship, and "choose" (whether consciously or through psychological processes that are automatic) not to react. It should also be explored how accessible was information about the incest to other family members, in the form of unusual and inappropriate interactions between father and daughter, signs of distress in the child, and so on.

Incest usually has severe long-term effects on a victim (Gelinas, 1983). This is not surprising: In her own home, where she should be most secure, she is victimized by one parent, and abandoned (not helped) by the rest of her family. The abandonment at the time of their victimization of Holocaust survivors by their countrymen and the rest of the world (Staub, 1989) may be one contributor to the extremely severe and lasting effects of their victimization (Danieli, 1988).

The conception that I presented can be helpful in guiding the treatment of perpetrators. One aim of therapists must be to make perpetrators aware of their responsibility; another to humanize victims, to create awareness of their suffering and empathy with them. Perpetrators also need to become aware of their own needs. Therapy must aim at reducing the inhibitions that stop them from fulfilling their motives in acceptable ways and helping them develop skills to do so. Therapists must also work with bystanders and the family system. Ultimately society will have to attend to the predisposing elements in the culture.

References

Danieli, Y. (1988). Treating survivors and children of survivors of the Nazi Holocaust. In F. M. Ochberg (Ed.), *Post-traumatic therapy and victims of violence* (pp. 278–294). New York: Brunner/Mazel.

Gelinas, D. (1983). The persisting negative effects of incest. *Psychiatry, 46,* 312–331.

Groth, N. A. (1982). The incest offender. In S. M. Sgrio (Ed.), *Handbook of clinical intervention in child sexual abuse* (pp. 215–239). Lexington, MA: D.C. Heath.

McCann, L. I., Pearlman, L. A. (1990). *Psychological trauma and the adult survivor: Theory, therapy and transformation.* New York: Brunner/Mazel.

Staub, E. (1989). *The roots of evil. The origins of genocide and other group violence.* New York: Cambridge University Press.

Staub, E., & Baer, R. S., Jr. (1974). Stimulus characteristics of a sufferer and difficulty of escape as determinants of helping. *Journal of Personality and Social Psychology, 30,* 279–285.

Part 2. Interventions to Reduce Aggression and Promote Caring and Helping

19

Reducing Boys' Aggression

Learning to Fulfill Basic Needs Constructively

Darren A. Spielman and Ervin Staub

In the past decade, youth violence has increased dramatically in the United States (Blumstein, 1995). This has led to a proliferation of interventions aimed at reducing aggression (Eron, Gentry, & Schlegel, 1994). Both basic research and interventions have focused on boys, who are more physically aggressive. The aim of the present study was to design, implement, and evaluate an intervention that focused on aggressive boys' basic needs, their interpersonal goals, and their ability to fulfill these in a constructive, nonaggressive manner.

Extensive research has shown that reactively aggressive boys lack the cognitive tendencies (see Crick & Dodge, 1994) and social skills (see McFall, 1982) to fulfill their goals in prosocial ways. They tend to interpret the intentions that underlie other's behavior toward them as hostile. This leads them to retaliate against people whose actions are ambiguous and who may mean them no harm (Dodge & Crick, 1990). Aggressive boys tend to have a limited ability to take the perspective of others and to understand what others think and feel (e.g., Pepler, Byrd, & King, 1991). They also see aggression as normal, acceptable behavior (Huesmann & Eron, 1984). It is not surprising, therefore, that in many situations, especially those involving conflict, they become aggressive.

In one promising approach to reducing aggression, children and adolescents receive training in the cognitive and social skills that underlie social

Reprinted from D. Spielman & E. Staub (2000). Reducing boys' aggression: Learning to fulfill basic needs constructively. *Journal of Applied Developmental Psychology, 21, 2,* 165–181. Some sections are summaries of the material in the original article.

A Grant from the National Institute of Mental Health (MH-18827) supported Darren Spielman while he conducted this intervention. Faculty Research Grant 1-03245 to Ervin Staub from the University of Massachusetts provided funds for the project. The authors express gratitude to Brett Amundsen, Chris Duff, Jahmal Mosley, James McDonough, and Seth Cohn for their roles as research assistants, intervention facilitators, or both.

behavior (Kazdin, 1994). Specific interventions have attempted to reduce participants' hostile perceptions of others (e.g., Pepler et al., 1991), improve their ability to take the perspective of others (e.g., Chandler, 1973), and increase the production of alternative solutions to potential conflict situations and provide specific behavioral tools for social interaction (e.g., Shure, 1992). Although these treatments often have positive effects, the magnitude of their impact on behavior is relatively limited.

Traditional cognitive interventions have not addressed the motivational and emotional bases of aggressive behavior. Researchers are now moving to address the affective along with the cognitive sources of aggression (e.g., Goldstein & Glick, 1994). The current intervention addresses motivation and emotion through the theoretical background of basic human needs (e.g., Staub, 1989, 1996). The theory suggests that: (a) all human beings share certain basic psychological needs, (b) basic needs give rise to powerful motives, (c) aggressive children's needs have been frustrated, and (d) aggressive children have learned to meet their needs in destructive ways.

An extensive literature suggests that harsh treatment in the family (for a review see Coie & Dodge, 1998) and coercive interactions with family members (Patterson, Reid, & Dishion, 1992) contribute to the development of boys' aggression. Such experiences frustrate children's basic needs and are instrumental in developing destructive modes of need fulfillment (Staub, 1996).

The basic human needs considered here are: *security*, the need to feel one is and will continue to be free from physical and psychological harm and will be able to meet physical needs; *positive identity*, the need for a well-developed and positive conception of who one is; *positive connection*, the need to have relations in which one feels connected to and valued by people; *effectiveness/control*, the need to feel one can accomplish things, can stop bad things from happening, and can make good things happen; and *comprehension of reality*, the need to have an understanding of how people and the world operate (Staub, 1989, 1996).

Need fulfillment is considered destructive if it fulfills one or more needs while interfering with the fulfillment of other needs. For example, aggressive boys may fulfill their needs for effectiveness and control, positive identity (e.g., feeling important, being taken seriously), and safety (e.g., protecting themselves from harm, real or imagined) through aggression. However, as a result their peers dislike them (Coie & Dodge. 1997), which interferes with their fulfillment of the need for positive connection. Hostile responses from others also frustrate their need for security. Need fulfillment is also considered destructive if it harms others.

In light of this theoretical ground and the empirical evidence on the cognitive characteristics of aggressive youth, an intervention was developed to reduce the aggressive behavior of seventh-grade boys. One aim of the intervention was to provide aggressive boys with a basic needs perspective and, with this perspective as a guide, to help them become aware of their motives and their customary ways of fulfilling these motives. Progressively, in the course of the intervention, the various basic needs were described and their connection to specific goals that boys may have in everyday situations was explored. A second aim was to help boys understand the concepts of constructive and destructive need fulfillment and how these concepts related to themselves: to their actions, to the goals they satisfy by their actions, and to the basic needs connected to these goals. A third aim was to develop behavioral strategies and skills to fulfill basic needs constructively – in ways that serve the actor and do not harm others. It was expected that, in the course of accomplishing these goals, aggressive participants' perceptions of others' motives would change. They would come to understand that others, like themselves, possess and act to fulfill basic needs. The treatments were expected to decrease the aggressive behavior of aggressive boys, decrease their attributions of hostile intentions to others, and increase their social role-taking ability.

Over the course of the intervention, participants developed, role played, and discussed different strategies for responding to potential conflicts. They explored the different motives that can underlie people's behavior. The purpose of the intervention was to help aggressive children acquire the knowledge, skills, and preferences necessary for constructive need fulfillment.

In this study, we also explored the role of a potentially important, but so far unexplored, personal characteristic in aggression. In a variety of studies a *prosocial value orientation* (PVO) has been associated with helping other people: in physical distress (Staub, 1974), in psychological distress (Feinberg, 1978; Grodman, 1979), and in self-reports of a variety of different kinds of helping (Staub, 1986, 1992, 1995). Prosocial orientation measures individuals' evaluation of human beings, concern about others' welfare, and a feeling of personal responsibility for others' welfare. Given the nature of this personality dimension and prior findings related to helping, it seemed a likely inhibitor of aggressive behavior. We expected differences in PVO between aggressive and nonaggressive boys. We were also interested in exploring the possibility that higher PVO scores may predict greater effectiveness of our treatments on boys' aggression. Boys with a higher score may be more open to the information and experience provided by our treatments.

HYPOTHESES

Premeasures

Relative to nonaggressive participants, aggressive participants were expected: to make more hostile attributions in response to hypothetical situations, to produce more aggressive responses to the hypothetical situations, and to demonstrate poorer social role-taking ability and weaker PVO.

Postmeasures

Relative to aggressive participants in the control group, aggressive participants in the treatment group were expected: to make less hostile attributions, to produce less aggressive responses, to demonstrate improved social role-taking ability, and to behave less aggressively, as measured by disciplinary records and teacher evaluations. Prosocial value orientation was expected to moderate the effects of treatment on aggressive behavior. We also considered the possibility that prosocial value orientation may itself change as a result of the intervention.

METHOD

Participants

The 47 participants ranged in age from 11 to 14. All were seventh-grade boys divided evenly between two urban middle schools (school A and school B). Both schools have a population which ranges from lower-middle to lower class, although school B lies closer to the upper end of this range. The student body in both schools includes African American, Puerto Rican, white, and Asian students.

School A provided 15 aggressive and 8 nonaggressive participants. School B provided 10 aggressive and 14 nonaggressive participants. One treatment "crew" of 6 boys was formed at each school, for a total of two treatment crews and 12 treatment boys. The remaining aggressive boys formed a no-contact control group.[1] Boys in the control group completed the same premeasures and postmeasures as the boys in the treatment group, but had no other contact with the intervention team.

Procedure

Letters and consent forms were sent to the homes of all boys in the seventh-grade class at the beginning of the school year. At the same time, sixth-grade teachers evaluated each of their homeroom students from the previous year (current seventh graders).

[1] Original plans included a placebo-control group. Because of the low number of aggressive participants, it was impossible to form one. However, boys' aggressive behavior is resistant to change and is unlikely to be affected by a neutral social experience. See Discussion for further treatment of this issue.

The evaluation form asked teachers to agree or disagree, on a 5-point scale (from 1 = strongly disagree to 5 = strongly agree), with statements about each student's aggressive behavior and negative relations with peers. Students who received an average score of 3 or more were placed in the aggressive group while students who received only 1s, 2s, or both were placed in the nonaggressive group. Other students who returned permission slips were informed that they would not be part of the study.

Aggressive participants were put into matched pairs on the basis of teacher ratings and randomly placed into the control group or treatment group. Boys from different schools were not placed in the same treatment crew.

Premeasures

Teacher Evaluation Form. As noted above, sixth-grade homeroom teachers completed the form for all of their students from the previous year. Current seventh-grade homeroom teachers completed evaluation forms one month after termination of the intervention.

In-House Suspensions. In-house suspensions records were selected for analysis because they are maintained comparably across schools and provide higher frequencies than out-of-school suspension records. Students receive in-house suspensions for behaviors such as fighting or serious verbal confrontations. School B provided records for the second half of the sixth-grade school year; both schools supplied records for the first half of the seventh-grade year.

Interview Measures. Before the intervention began, research assistants who were blind to the participants' status administered measures in interviews with participants. Those measures included:

HOSTILE ATTRIBUTION BIAS. Participants listened to a series of short vignettes, and were asked to imagine that they were in the event described. Each vignette described an event in which the actions of a character produced a negative outcome for the participant, such as being hit with a ball thrown by another student. After hearing the vignette, participants were asked about the character's intentions and how they would respond. Answers to these questions were scored for nonhostile or hostile attribution and level of aggressive response.

PROSOCIAL VALUE ORIENTATION. An adolescent version of Staub's prosocial value orientation measure (Staub 1989, 1992) was prepared for this study. Participants indicated how much they agreed or disagreed with statements regarding their positive versus negative evaluation of people, concern for others' welfare, and sense of their own responsibility for others' welfare. (See the Appendix in this book for the adult version.)

Postmeasures

In addition to teacher evaluation and in-house suspension data, post-measures were administered after the completion of the intervention. The same prosocial value orientation measure was administered a second time. An improved, updated version of the hostile attribution bias was used. As with the earlier version, students responded to events described in a series of vignettes. After each vignette, participants were asked five questions: 1) What do you think was going on in the mind of_____when this happened? (responses were coded as hostile, ambiguous, or nonhostile); 2) Do you think that_____did_____because she/he/they were being mean to you? 3) Do you think that_____did_____for some other reason? (respondents answered on a scale from not possible to very likely). The last two questions asked were, 4) What would you do or say if this happened to you? and 5) What could you do in this situation to meet your goal? These questions were open-ended and received scores for both content and level of effectiveness. (We are grateful to Kenneth Dodge who provided this measure.)

INTERVENTION

Treatment participants met after school, 1 day per week for 1 hour, for 14 weeks. The first 7 sessions were run by a graduate student and a trained undergraduate assistant. The last 7 sessions were run by the graduate student alone.

The elements of the training were developed, rehearsed, and role played by the senior investigator and the graduate student who conducted the training. Together, they explained the training to the undergraduate research assistants and extensively role played and rehearsed the procedures. This provided further training for the graduate student facilitator. A six-session pilot intervention was conducted with aggressive boys at an alternative middle school for students with aggressive/antisocial behavioral problems. This pilot intervention further tested and developed the procedures and provided experience for the graduate facilitator.

At the opening of the first session it was explained that

> We're going to think up short scripts about different social situations. The kind of situations that could turn into a conflict, where a problem might develop, or it might not. Then, you guys are going to act them out and film them. Then, we'll watch the tapes and talk about them and see what we think. The idea is to learn about different ways to interact with people, destructive, negative ways and more positive ways. Helpful ways and harmful ways. But that's not all we'll be doing. We're also learning about acting and making good films. Hopefully, you'll really improve and the movies will get better and better with practice.

In the first session, the participants acted out the following scene that the facilitators planned ahead of time.

A boy gets to the lunch room early. He sits at a table where some of his friends usually sit and puts his stuff down. Then, he realizes he left his jacket in a classroom. He leaves to get the jacket. Meanwhile, a group of kids comes and sits at the table. One of the newcomers sits in his seat. When the boy returns, his stuff has been shoved to the side and he has no place to sit.

The graduate facilitator explained the scene to the participants. The participants then thought of a way to act out the scene that would "create a problem." They were encouraged to make the scene as lifelike as possible (dialogue was not written down, but was generated spontaneously within the parameters of the scene). They then named the characters, chose roles (e.g., camera man, protagonists, bystanders), and acted out the scene. They enacted it several times, switching roles each time. The participants and the facilitators then watched the video. The graduate facilitator led the group through a discussion of the scenario. The discussion challenged the participants to understand why the characters behaved as they did, what the characters were feeling, and what purposes their behaviors served. Two basic human needs were introduced (positive connection and positive identity) and suggested as motivators of some of the action in the scene.

Participants then figured out a way to satisfy these needs that may not cause a problem or result in a fight. Again, they were encouraged to make the scene as lifelike as possible, "to do it in a way that could really happen." They spent time, with the facilitators' help if necessary, generating alternative solutions to the situation. They then acted out and filmed the scene, rotating through different roles. The participants and facilitators watched the new film and went through another discussion. The second discussion addressed the same questions as the first one. It was noted that the same needs that motivated behavior in the first scene motivated totally different behavior in the second scene. For example, to earn the respect of his friends and regain his seat, in the first scene the protagonist may insult and threaten the "offending" boy. In the second scene, the protagonist may explain the situation to the boy, and another friend at the table may suggest grabbing another chair and squeezing in.

Each session followed the general format of the first week: produce a conflict, film "negative" scene, discuss, film "positive" scene, discuss. However, given the session length, a full cycle was not completed every week. Yet, sessions did not end after acting the negative scene without some discussion of and thought about positive possibilities. Also, as the project evolved the facilitators and participants decided that it was not always necessary to act and film the negative versions of the scenarios.

After the first session, a new need was introduced each week until all needs had been introduced. Participants invented their own scenes (but the facilitators always came with backup scenes prepared). As the sessions progressed, the scenes became more complex. The facilitator suggested taking more factors into account (e.g., the history between individuals involved in the interaction, gradually developing conflicts). In addition to focus on basic needs and goals in specific situations, sessions focused on understanding the position of others in a situation, as well as on specific strategies and behaviors useful for positive interaction.

An example of a scene created by the participants goes as follows. Students are sitting in class. The teacher is handing back a test. The teacher says. "I'm quite pleased with how most people did" (hands back an A test to student 1). Then the teacher says, "With other people, I'm not so pleased." The teacher gives student 2 a direct look and hands him his test, which earned an F. Student 2 is upset (and publicly embarrassed). The teacher dismisses class (school is dismissed). Student 1 and student 2 go separate ways. On his walk home, student 2 steps into a muddy puddle with his new sneakers. He is upset. He exclaims angrily. As he continues walking, he sees student 1 heading toward him on the sidewalk. As they approach each other, student 1 says something and student 2 thinks it is an insult. He yells harshly at student 1, and so forth. In the positive version of the scene, everything is the same except (a) student 2 says something different to himself when he steps in the mud. He notes how mad he is getting because of the bad day he is having, (b). When he passes Student 1, he starts to get mad in the same way as before. Then, he checks himself. He apologizes to student 1, explaining that he is mad because of the test and stepping in the mud.

RESULTS

Premeasures

It was predicted that aggressive participants would score lower on a measure of prosocial value orientation than nonaggressive participants. Results confirmed this prediction. Aggressive participants had significantly lower PVO scores than nonaggressive participants. No significant differences were found between aggressive control and treatment groups.

The analysis showed no significant differences between groups on the measure of hostile attribution bias. However, hostile attributions were followed by more aggressive responses than nonhostile attributions. Nineteen percent of responses following hostile attributions fell in the most aggressive category, compared with 8% of responses following nonhostile attributions.

Sixth-grade disciplinary records from school B were consistent with teacher ratings. Eighty percent of aggressive participants, as selected through teacher evaluations, received in-house suspensions in the second half of their sixth-grade year. Only 21% of nonaggressive participants received such suspensions. School A never provided sixth-grade disciplinary records.

Postmeasures

We expected that aggressive boys with higher prosocial value orientations scores might have benefited more from treatment. Although there was a negative correlation between PVO scores and change in suspensions experienced by boys in the treatment group, it was not significant. The PVO scores of treatment participants did not increase relative to the scores of aggressive control participants.

The treatment reduced hostile attribution. On question one both aggressive control and nonaggressive participants attributed more hostile intentions to ambiguously acting characters than treatment participants. Nonaggressive participants made fewer, but not significantly fewer, hostile attributions than aggressive control participants.

Treatment and nonaggressive participants responded similarly to question three and were more likely than control participants to believe that the characters in the stories acted with nonhostile intentions. Question two, in contrast, revealed no significant differences among groups. No differences were found in content or effectiveness of group members' responses to questions four and five.

Analysis of responses to questions one and four indicated a significant relationship between attribution and behavior. All responses following ambiguous and nonhostile attributions were coded as competent, while nearly 12% of responses following hostile attributions were coded as aggressive.

We conducted an analysis of in-house suspensions for the schools separately; only school B provided sixth-grade information and the climate in the schools was quite different. For school B, treatment participants' suspension counts declined and then remained low. However, control participants' suspension counts declined and then spiked in the three months after the intervention. There were no significant differences in suspensions between the groups in the semester before or in the two months before the intervention. But the treatment group received substantially fewer suspensions in the three months after the intervention than the control group.

For school A, analysis indicated no significant effects for the treatment. No differences were found between control or treatment groups before or after the intervention.

Grouping the two schools together, further analysis indicated that treatment participants improved over time relative to control participants. Over time, the number of suspensions in school B increased relative to school A.

The control group in school B deteriorated substantially over time, while the other groups remained stable.

Comparison of disciplinary records from the two months before the intervention revealed no significant differences between school A and B aggressive participants, nor between school A and B treatment participants, nor school A and B control participants.

Changes in behavior were assessed, in part, by teachers' evaluations of students. It was predicted that the teacher scores of treatment participants would decrease relative to the scores of aggressive control participants. Analysis revealed no such effect. Over time, both groups showed a reduction in scores. Scores declined significantly across groups between the first evaluation, conducted by the prior year's sixth-grade teachers, and the second evaluation, conducted by seventh-grade teachers one month after the intervention.

DISCUSSION

The intervention produced several positive results. It reduced the boys' tendency to attribute hostile intentions to others. In one school, it reduced their aggressive behavior, as measured by counts of in-house suspensions. It also provides the first evidence that prosocial value orientation – previously positively associated with helping behavior – is negatively associated with aggressive behavior. The latter findings also provide the first test of an adolescent measure of PVO.

Postmeasure assessment of hostile attribution bias points to the positive effect of the intervention. Comparisons revealed that boys in the treatment group were less likely than boys in the control group to attribute hostile intentions to others. The treatment group was also less likely than the nonaggressive group to attribute hostile intent. This effect was consistent across schools.

The lower hostile attribution by aggressive treatment participants, relative to nonaggressive participants, may raise concern that treatment participants were attempting to provide "good" or "right" answers. However, the participants had not previously met the research assistants who collected the postmeasures, and these measures were collected a substantial length of time after the intervention.

The intervention focused on exploring motives behind actions. It focused on pausing and thinking before reacting. It emphasized basic needs as the source of specific motives that affect both one's own and others' actions. It emphasized the many motives that guide behavior and suggested that even aggressive action often stems from the need for a positive identity, feeling of effectiveness, and other nonhostile sources. Awareness of the variability and complexity of motives should make one less likely to assume that others act with hostile intent. Treatment participants discussed motives in the context of role playing real-life situations. The real-life quality of role playing often helps people integrate concepts into their experience. For example, in prior research, kindergarten-age children who role played helping scenes were later more helpful (Staub, 1971). The reduction in aggressive boys' hostile attributions is likely to be genuine, rather than the result of social desirability. Because the postmeasures were administered 4 to 6 weeks after treatment, there is also some evidence of stability.

The finding that hostile attributions tend to precede aggressive acts directly whereas nonhostile attributions tend to precede nonaggressive acts, replicates past results (Crick & Dodge, 1994). However, we do not know to what extent the changed attributions of aggressive boys have come to guide their real-life actions and whether they are responsible for the effect of treatment on detentions.

Further evidence for the positive effect of the intervention comes from the analysis of disciplinary records. The records of the boys in the treatment group improved relative to the records of the boys in the control group. However, an increase in the suspensions of the school B control group accounts for this result. Over the same period, the suspensions of the school B treatment group and the school A control and treatment groups remained relatively stable.

DIFFERENCES IN SCHOOL ENVIRONMENTS

Our observations of the climate in the two schools throughout the project suggest that school B was a more difficult environment for students. The first author, who was the primary facilitator in the project, recorded events he observed at the schools in a weekly log. The differences in school climate indicated by these observations may account for the worsening behavior of school B aggressive boys in the control group. The intervention may have prevented the behavior of the treatment boys from declining in the same manner. School A seemed to provide a more constructive environment, where students' aggressive behavior may tend to improve, or at least not spiral downward as often happens with aggressive adolescents (Kupersmidt, Coie, & Dodge, 1990; Coie & Dodge, 1997). The moderate disparity in school demographics does not appear to explain these differences. If anything, the slightly higher socioeconomic status of the school B population should predict better outcomes for that school.

According to our observations, school B provided a harsher and more variable environment than school A. It was more common to hear teachers or administrators from school B insulting, threatening, and shouting at students. The teachers were often sarcastic and disrespectful. The research assistants who collected premeasure data noted the tendency of school B teachers to communicate bad things about individual students in the students' presence. Also, the school B principal generally remained in his office with the door closed.

School A teachers and administrators were strict, but rarely seemed arbitrary or belligerent. The principal was part of the life of the students and teachers, frequently seen interacting with them. Harsh, variable, and arbitrary authority, such as that observed at school B, is likely to contribute to aggressive behavior and other behavior problems in schools (Dodge & Frame, 1982; Kupersmidt et al., 1990; Pratt, 1973). It is unlikely to ameliorate already existing aggressive tendencies.

The students' impressions of the teachers support the facilitator's observations. The issue of student–teacher interactions consumed two intervention sessions. As part of the exercise, the boys described teacher behaviors that they did not like or thought were unfair. School B boys responded quickly with a list of complaints. A few excerpts follow:

"They feel that all kids are bad and they yell at them for no reason."
"They don't like their jobs, but they have nothing better to do. They're sick of us."
"We get mad because they yell at us and embarrass us in front of our friends."
"Last year I got in trouble a lot. I was really bad. So this year, if I do one little thing bad, they get on my case. They expect me to be bad."
"They threaten you. That doesn't help you. It makes you worried."
"If I break a rule, they have every right to yell at me. But, if it's just some little thing, like not sitting down the second they say, that's wrong."

In contrast, an excerpt from the facilitator's school A log (11/14/96) appears below:

"We acted out the teacher problem scene. Not as smooth as school B. They had some trouble coming up with a good scene, with specific situation and behaviors of the teacher.... They said 'none of the teachers are that mean, they're not so bad.' (Big difference from school B)."

The next week, one of the school A students did say the following:

"They puttin' you down so we think, 'why can't we put them down?' That's how it starts. They say, 'treat others how you would want to be treated.' Then they treat you bad and you figure... (note: he trails off)."

The findings on behavior change are complex and based on a small number of participants. However, the qualitative observations do support our explanation of the differences in the aggressive boys' posttreatment behavior in the two schools. Suggestive as they are, the findings point to the potentially crucial issue of the larger context in generating aggression and presumably also facilitating its reduction.

Teacher evaluations provide another measure of change in the boys' behavior. Collapsing across groups and schools, teachers rated the boys as less aggressive on the postmeasure than on the premeasure. At face value, the behavior of control and treatment boys improved in the eyes of homeroom teachers. The aggressive boys were selected for their high scores on the premeasure. On average, postmeasure scores declined. Regression to the mean may explain the result.

The final measure assessed participants' PVO. Measures of PVO have been highly predictive of helping behavior both in laboratory settings (e.g., Feinberg, 1978; Staub 1974) and large-scale self-report studies (Staub, 1992, 1995). We reasoned that aggressive and harmful behavior should be negatively associated with PVO. Following prediction, aggressive participants produced significantly lower PVO scores than nonaggressive participants. There was a moderate, negative correlation between PVO scores in the treatment group and change in suspensions, but it did not approach significance.

It should be noted that the small number of aggressive participants made it impossible to form a placebo-control group. Without such a group, one cannot determine if results stem from the specific features of the intervention, or the effect of participation in a creative activity, in a small group, with positive and productive peer interaction, and positive personal attention from an adult. However, aggressive behavior and related cognitive tendencies are hard to change. Even elaborate interventions frequently produce only limited effects. This makes it unlikely that mere contact would substantially reduce either the cognitive or the behavioral aspects of aggression (Eron et al., 1994; Goldstein, 1999; Kazdin, Seigel, & Bass, 1992).

Considering the limited number of participants and the typical tenacity of aggressive behavior, the results, although complex, are highly encouraging. Not only did the intervention reduce hostile attributions, it did so 4 to 6 weeks after treatment. It also improved the behavior of aggressive boys. The literature suggests that aggressive boys' behavior tends to deteriorate over time. This was true of aggressive boys in school B who were in the control group, but not of boys who were in the treatment group. The improvement of the behavior of aggressive boys in school A is interesting, suggesting that school environment can ameliorate already manifest antisocial tendencies.

This study is the first test of an intervention approach that focuses on motives and their expression through aggressive behavior. The approach combines a number of elements. First, it attempts to promote awareness of basic needs and a conceptualization of one's own and others' actions in terms of constructive and destructive modes of need fulfillment. It provides opportunities to learn constructive strategies for need fulfillment, both by developing plans and enacting them. It thus offers both conceptual and active modes of learning. Learning takes place in a setting that simulates real life: role play in interaction with peers. Thus although this is not a multilevel intervention (Reid & Eddy, 1997) involving parents and teachers, it is an intervention that provides opportunities for change in the course of interactions with peers, rather than in isolation. It has the promise of ecological validity.

This study attempted to show change in behavior as well as change in hostile attribution tendency – which research suggests is an important mediator of aggressive behavior. Future research may attempt to evaluate changes specific to this intervention. It may assess awareness of one's own and others' motives as well as awareness of and ability to generate constructive strategies for need fulfillment. Peer interaction in school may be observed to assess the extent to which the treatment engenders the use of constructive approaches to need fulfillment.

References

Blumstein, A. (August, 1995). Violence by young people: Why the deadly nexus? *National Institute of Justice Journal, 229*, 2–9.

Chandler, M. J. (1973). Egocentrism and antisocial behavior: The assessment and training of social perspective-taking skills. *Developmental Psychology, 9*(3), 326–332.

Coie, J. D., & Dodge, K. A. (1998). Aggression and antisocial behavior. In W. Damon (Series Ed.) & N. Eisenberg (Vol. Ed.), *Handbook of child psychology: Vol. 3. Social, emotional and personality development* (5th ed., pp. 779–862). New York: Wiley.

Crick, N. R., & Dodge, K. A. (1994). A review and reformulation of social information-processing mechanisms in children's social adjustment. *Psychological Bulletin, 115*(1), 74–101.

Dodge, K. A., & Crick, N. R. (1990). Social information-processing bases of aggressive behavior in children. *Personality and Social Psychology Bulletin, 16*(1), 8–22.

Dodge, K. A., & Frame, C. L. (1982). Social cognitive biases and deficits in aggressive boys. *Child Development, 53*, 620–635.

Eron, L. E., Gentry, J. H., & Schlegel, P. (Eds.), (1994). *Reason to hope: A psychosocial perspective on violence and youth.* Washington, D.C.: American Psychological Association.

Feinberg, H. K. (1978). *Anatomy of a helping situation: Some personality and situational determinants of helping in a conflict situation involving another's psychological distress.* Unpublished doctoral dissertation, University of Massachusetts, Amherst.

Goldstein, A. P. (1999). Aggression reduction strategies: Effective and ineffective. *School Psychology Quarterly, 14*(1), 40–58.

Goldstein, A. P., & Glick, B. (1994). Aggression replacement training: Curriculum and evaluation. *Simulation & Gaming, 25*(1), 9–26.

Grodman, S. M. (1979). *The role of personality and situational variables in responding to and helping an individual in psychological distress.* Unpublished doctoral dissertation, University of Massachusetts. Amherst.

Huesmann, L. R., & Eron, L. D. (1984). Cognitive processes and the persistence of aggressive behavior. *Aggressive Behavior, 10*, 243–251.

Kazdin, A. E. (1994). Interventions for aggressive and antisocial children. In L. D. Eron, J. H. Gentry, & P. Schlegel (Eds.), *Reason to hope: A psychosocial perspective on youth and violence* (pp. 341–382). Washington. D.C.: American Psychological Association.

Kazdin, A. E., Seigel. T., & Bass, D. (1992). Cognitive problem-solving skills training and relationship therapy in the treatment of antisocial child behavior. *Journal of Consulting and Clinical Psychology, 60*, 733–747.

Kupersmidt, J. B., Coie, J. D., & Dodge, K. A. (1990). The role of poor peer relationships in the development of disorder. In S. R. Asher & J. D. Coie (Eds.), *Peer rejection in childhood* (pp. 247–308). Cambridge, England: Cambridge University Press.

McFall, R. M. (1982). A review of and reformation of the concept of social skills. *Behavioral Assessment, 4*, 1–33.

Patterson, G. R., Reid, J. B. & Dishion, T. J. (1992). *A social learning approach, Vol. 4: Antisocial boys*. Eugene, OR: Castalia.

Pepler, D. J., Byrd, W., & King, G. (1991). A social-cognitively based social skills training program for aggressive children. In D. J. Pepler & K. H. Rubin (Eds.), *The development and treatment of childhood aggression* (pp. 361–379). Hillsdale, NJ: Erlbaum.

Pratt, T. M. (1973). Positive approaches to disruptive behavior. *Today's Education, 62*, 18–19.

Reid, J. B., & Eddy, J. M. (1997). The prevention of antisocial behavior: Some considerations in the search for effective interventions. In D. M. Stoff (Ed.), *Handbook of antisocial behavior* (pp. 343–356). New York: Wiley.

Shure, M. B. (1992). *I can problem solve: An interpersonal cognitive problem-solving program*. Champaign, IL: Research Press.

Staub, E. (1971). The use of role-playing and induction in children's learning of helping behavior and sharing behavior. *Child Development, 42*, 805–816.

Staub, E. (1974). Helping a distressed person: Social, personality, and stimulus characteristics. In L. Berkowitz (Ed.), *Advances in experimental social psychology* (Vol. 7, pp. 294–339). San Diego, CA: Academic Press.

Staub, E. (1986). A conception of the determinants and development of altruism and aggression: Motives, the self, the environment. In C. Zahn-Waxler (Ed.), *Altruism and aggression: Social and biological origins* (pp. 135–164). New York: Cambridge University Press.

Staub, E. (1989). *The roots of evil: The origins of genocide and other group violence*. New York: Cambridge University Press.

Staub, E. (1992). *Values, helping, and well being*. Unpublished manuscript. Department of Psychology, University of Massachusetts at Amherst.

Staub, E. (1995). How people learn to care. In P. G. Schervish, V. A. Hodgkinson, M. Gates, & Associates (Eds.), *Care and community in modern society: Passing on the tradition of service to future generations* (pp. 51–67). San Francisco: Jossey-Bass.

Staub, E. (1996). The cultural-societal roots of violence: The examples of genocidal violence and of contemporary youth violence in the United States. *American Psychologist, 51*, 117–132.

20

Creating Caring Schools

Design and Content of a Program to Develop Caring, Helping, Positive Self-Esteem, and Nonviolence

BACKGROUND AND OBJECTIVES

In this chapter I will describe a program to create schools in which students' experiences in their classrooms promote caring about the welfare of others and the inclination to help others. The influences that give rise to caring and helping are in many respects the opposite of those that develop hostility and aggression in children and youth (Staub, 1986, 1996a, in preparation), and an additional central aim of this program is to lessen hostility and aggressiveness. The latter is best accomplished, however, by creating conditions and experiences that promote caring, cooperation, and helpfulness. Part of the focus of this program is to develop caring about members of racial, religious, or ethnic groups other than one's own, what I will refer to as inclusive caring. The program also aims to foster positive self-esteem, since children and adolescents have to value themselves to a reasonable degree if they are to value and help others. Beyond caring about individuals, the program also promotes feelings of responsibility for the social good. As a by-product of the classroom milieu created and the students' experiences in the classroom, positive effects on learning are also expected.

The program consists of workshops with teachers and other school personnel, and follow-up training with them to translate the ideas, perspectives, and skills they had acquired in the workshops into classroom practice. It also includes workshops with parents, so that their ways of relating to and guiding children at home may become supportive of the school effort. Most of the elements of the program are directly relevant to educating parents for practicing "positive socialization." The program is based on past research and my past experience with presenting the ideas and practices described in this proposal to teachers and parents in lectures and workshops. Since this program has not been fully implemented, the description I present is essentially a proposal. Hence, while many of its elements are based on research findings, the program as a whole has not been evaluated. I prepared an earlier version of this manuscript in 1995, and updated it for this volume.

While my work with children has been primarily in the United States, this description is also informed by my travel and work outside the U.S. Certainly the issues and questions I address, and the general methodology – although not necessarily all its details – are relevant to many places in the world. This is true even with regard to the background conditions that make socialization in schools especially important, "difficult life conditions" that can have many elements. In the U.S. these have included social upheavals related to the Vietnam War, the assassination of leaders, race relations, the civil rights movement, feminism and in recent times the terrorist attacks of 9/11/2001 and the war against terrorism. They include tremendous social changes that have deeply affected family life and parenting. In many places in the world in addition to social changes poverty, political conflict, and war have had deeply disrupting effects on parenting, making the role of schools as socializers extremely important. In the United States as well, shifts from a booming economy to recession have had significant effects on people's psychological states.

Schools, where so much of the life of children and adolescents is lived, inevitably shape children and youth as social beings. They shape their values, their personality, their character and social behavior, their orientations to themselves and other people. In the U.S. the question of whether schools should "teach values" is frequently debated. But the *core* influence of schools in the realm of values is not through teaching but through experiential learning. Schools inevitably affect students' *valuing* of other people and of themselves, and their beliefs and values, through the students' experiences of interaction with teachers and other students, the guidance they receive, the actions they themselves engage in, their roles and experiences in the classroom. While this is one reason for focusing on schools in this project, another is the condition of families in the U.S. at this time. Tremendous changes have been taking place in American society in the last several decades (Staub, 1989, 1996a, 1996b), creating some degree of social disorganization and frustrating basic needs.

The substantial social changes have greatly affected the life of families and the behavior of parents toward their children. Currently there are many one-parent families, with the parent who is the main presence in the child's life preoccupied with work, economic and personal problems.[1] Single parents are more likely to abuse their children than parents in two

[1] Parents' personal characteristics, such as having themselves been harhsly treated as children, often interact with current circumstances in affecting their behavior toward their children. For example, during the Depression in the 1930s in the U.S. fathers who had been irritable before they lost their jobs were likely to become especially irritable with their

parent families, especially if they are young and poor (Gelles, 1981; Gelles & Conte, 1990). Physical harshness and emotional abuse both tend to increase, in turn, hostility and aggression in childhood (Dodge, 1993; Weiss et al., 1992) and later in life (Widom, 1989a, 1989b). There are also many dysfunctional two-parent families in which children experience lack of structure, neglect, or abuse, whether the dysfunction is due to poverty and the experience of relative deprivation, alcohol or drugs, a breakdown of community life, or other circumstances. These conditions, together with lack of community support, create disorganization in the home and ways of treating children and youth that contribute to the development of hostility and aggression rather than caring and helpfulness.

The conditions in society and the home also impact the schools. They shape students' characteristics and lead to less cooperative and more aggressive behavior toward teachers and peers. They contribute to racial and other types of conflict. They reduce the capacity of many children and adolescents for self-regulation and effective participation in learning.

The practices of school can be shaped to provide positive socialization. The earlier schools begin to provide positive socializing experiences, the greater their potential impact. Therefore this proposal will focus on elementary schools, but it can be adapted to higher grade levels. Ideally entire schools will participate in the project, thereby creating continuity in children's classroom experiences and maximizing the impact of the program.

A great deal of research has been conducted in the last two and a half decades to identify the influences that contribute to the development in children of prosocial behavior – behavior that aims to benefit others – including the development of underlying characteristics that lead them to value and want to help other people. These characteristics include empathy, feelings of responsibility for others' welfare, belief in moral rules that prescribe helping people, an "inclusive" definition of human beings that lessens the differentiation between "us" and "them," and feelings of competence to help. (For reviews of relevant research see Eisenberg, 1986, 1992; Eisenberg & Fabes, 1998; Grusec, 1981; Hoffman, 1970, 1975, 2000; Radke-Yarrow et al., 1983; Staub, 1979, 1981, 1986, 1992, 1996a, 1996b, in preparation.)

The research findings indicate that the groundwork for valuing others and their welfare, as well as for valuing oneself, is laid by *experiences* in interaction with people. It requires, therefore, experiential learning. The same is true for devaluing others and for the development of hostility and aggression. The essence of the program is the way of life in the classroom. The primary purpose of the workshops and of the follow-up training is to

children (Elder and Caspi, 1985). However, this was made less likely given certain maternal characteristics. In countries where war has traumatized parents, this trauma is likely to be continually reactivated by enduring life problems.

introduce and develop ideas, perspectives, and skills that will help teachers create classrooms that provide experiential learning. A secondary purpose is to communicate concepts and perspectives that prepare teachers to introduce a limited amount of classroom instruction, which supports and expands the experiential learning.

Creating classrooms that promote a positive orientation in children to the self and others will also improve, I believe, conditions for academic instruction and enhance children's learning and performance. The security, benevolence, and feelings of personal significance combined with guidance that children experience in such classrooms can free them from self-concern and increase their attention to and motivation for learning. Their experience can promote a feeling of enablement, a belief by children in their capacity to learn (in addition to the belief that by their actions they can benefit other people or the classroom community). The positive spirit in the classroom would also improve the teachers' capacity to teach. Better learning is likely to be an important secondary benefit.

Parents would also be invited to participate in workshops, although less extensive ones than those for teachers. It seems of great value to involve parents, so that they both come to understand the school effort and learn about positive socialization themselves. All too often, schools call on parents to address their children's misconduct or poor performance. In this program, parents will be called upon as allies, to join the school in a shared purpose. Many parents would also benefit from the experience of community with other parents, and a sense of community imparted by their alliance with the schools. Special techniques will be used to involve parents, such as connecting the initial information meeting and invitation to the workshop with showing work by or presenting a performance by their children. The influence on parents of their workshop experience can lead to the creation of home environments that support the experiential learning in the classroom.

Over time the schools can become self-sufficient in perpetuating the practices of positive socialization. Whenever possible the resources that exist within the schools, especially the expertise of the teachers, will be drawn upon. It is part of the program plan to create a committee of school staff that, following the workshops, will both further develop and disseminate within each school practices that serve the program's goals, and introduce new teachers and parents to the program. The joining of teachers and parents can be instrumental in creating a community of shared purpose. It can be a vehicle for "cross-cutting relations" (Staub, 1988, 1989), or deep contact among the members of different subgroups that constitute the school district.

The program draws on and develops the resources that exist within schools, and at a relatively low cost could be adopted in many school districts.

METHODS AND SPECIFIC CONTENT

Program Components

The program begins with a one-week (5 days) workshop for teachers, consisting of presentations, extensive discussion, and small group meetings that include experiential learning activities. Each morning and each afternoon there is to be a presentation with discussion, followed by small group meetings, followed by reassembly in the large group and reports and discussion of the experiences, ideas and skills developed in the small groups. On the fifth day there is to be a summary in the morning, and discussion of the activities that are to follow the workshop in the afternoon.

The small groups will deal with specific topics introduced in the presentations and where appropriate include role-playing exercises and other forms of experiential training. Among the aims of the small group activities is to demonstrate, further develop, and learn to use positive discipline practices with children, and rules for positive peer interaction; to examine the assumptions that teachers and parents have about children and how these guide their actions; and to discuss and develop strategies for participation by students in classroom life as well as in activities that benefit others (to create "learning by doing"), and community building in the classroom.

Following the workshops members of the project staff (and ideally also at least one member of the school staff) are to attend classes and work with teachers to further develop the use of specific practices within the classroom. A committee of teachers and other school staff is to be created to further develop and disseminate information about classroom practice.

Separate workshops are to be conducted with parents, possibly to consist of one all-day and two evening sessions, but their length and timing will be determined by what would maximize, in each setting, parents' willingness to participate. Opportunities are to be created for contact and interaction between school staff and parents, to be organized by or at least with the involvement of the committee established in each school. Meetings might focus on particular content areas of the program, and how they might be dealt with at home and in the schools.

AN OVERVIEW OF PROGRAM ELEMENTS AND WORKSHOP CONTENT

The following overview describes the primary substantive content areas for the workshop, developed on the basis of research findings. Each component will be presented and ways of implementing it discussed and rehearsed. Except for #1, which will be introduced in the course of discussions of #2 and #3 and further discussed after #3, the sequence of presentation here corresponds to the sequence in the workshop.

1. Assumptions by Teachers and Parents About the Nature of Children

Different assumptions that teachers and parents hold, for example, that children are by nature willful and disobedient, or that they are basically cooperative, affect their behavior toward children and can become self-fulfilling prophecies. In many Western nations, for example Germany (Miller, 1983), England (Stone, 1977), and also the U.S. (Greven, 1991), there have been deeply ingrained beliefs that children are willful, that it is essential to make them obedient early, and that highly forceful means are acceptable and even necessary to accomplish this. The belief in the importance of using physical punishment with children is still widespread in the U.S. (Straus, Gelles & Steinmetz, 1980), and physical punishment is still widely used, even with young children (Straus, 1992). However, the research findings show that harsh, physically punitive and verbally hostile behaviors by parents create negative orientation to people and aggressiveness (Weiss et al., 1992; Gelles, 1981; Eron et al., 1971; Dodge, 1993; Staub, 1996a).

In contrast, warmth, nurturance, and responsiveness to children's needs by caretakers create a secure rather than anxious or avoidant attachment in infants to their caretakers (Ainsworth, 1979). Such experiences contribute to cooperation with parents in even very young children (Ainsworth, Bell, & Stayton, 1974). Rather than spoiling children, fast response to infants's needs, when they cry, is associated with less crying by them at age one (Stayton et al., 1973). Children who were securely attached to their caretakers as infants are less aggressive and manage to maintain positive interactions with normally aggressive children in nursery school (Troy & Sroufe, 1987) and have positive peer relations in elementary school (Sroufe, 1979).

But parental warmth, nurturance, and responsiveness are also essential beyond infancy. They are likely to lead children to trust and value other people, as well as themselves. It is not surprising that these ways of relating to children are associated with both helpful, prosocial behaviors by them and positive self-esteem (Coopersmith, 1967; Eisenberg, 1992; Hoffman, 1970, 1975; Staub, 1979, 1986, 1996a).

The workshop will concern itself with the impact that our assumptions have on our behavior. It will draw on research findings to show that the modes of child rearing and the experiences that children have, as well as the influences that currently operate on them, greatly affect their personality and behavior, and that nurturance and responsiveness to children's needs contribute to cooperation and positive behavior by them. In the small groups teachers will have an opportunity to examine their own assumptions about the nature of children in general, as well as differences in their assumptions about boys and girls, and about children who come from different racial, ethnic, religious, socioeconomic, and cultural backgrounds.

2. Modes of Relating to Children: Warmth and Sensitivity

Warmth, nurturance, and sensitivity to children are the central elements in developing caring and helpful tendencies in children. It is a pattern of child-rearing practices that is required (Staub, 1979), and no one element is sufficient, but warmth and sensitivity are central to this pattern. Concern about children's welfare and responsiveness to their needs create in them the experience of benevolence. They create feelings of trust, of valuing people, and a perception of positive intentions underlying other people's behavior. In contrast, children who are harshly treated attribute hostility and negative intentions to others (Weiss et. al, 1992; Dodge, 1980). Appropriate forms of warmth and nurturance vary at different ages, and can take different forms depending on adult characteristics. Parents of high self-esteem boys, for example, are genuinely concerned about their sons' welfare, but are not necessarily physically affectionate (Coopersmith, 1967).

Sensitivity is also important. For example, while responding to a child's needs is important, subtlety is required in providing comfort to a child who has in some way been humiliated. Very overt expressions of support and affection may be counterproductive. It may not be experienced as empathic and supportive (Staub, in preparation). At the same time, it can be extremely valuable to create a classroom culture in which feelings, needs, the culture that children brought with themselves, and other important issues can be discussed. For this to work, teachers have to create a framework that encourages openness but is protective of children at the same time.

The consequences of warmth and benevolence versus indifference or hostility are very far-reaching. In one study Yarrow and Scott (1972) had preschool children in playgroups be supervised, on repeated occasions, by either a warm or an indifferent adult. The children were later shown scenes enacted by small diorama figures. Subsequently they remembered the same amount of what they were shown, but the children supervised by the warm adult remembered more of the positive actions of the diorama figures; those supervised by the indifferent adult remembered more of the negative actions.

3. Guidance and Discipline

Children need structure in their lives. Over time, external structure can become internal structure, and external guidance can be replaced by inner guidance. Warmth or affection combined with permissiveness, lack of rules, and guidance does not lead to the development of prosocial behavior tendencies (Eisenberg, 1992; Eisenberg & Fabes, 1998). Permissiveness in the home is associated with aggressiveness as measured by the recorded offenses of a group of delinquent youth (Di Lalla et al., 1988).

a. *Setting rules and standards of conduct.* Rules can function as guides to what is expected, reasonable, and right. Ideally, especially as children become older, rules will be flexible. Ideally, rules will not be primarily proscriptive, prohibiting undesirable behavior, but prescriptive, promoting desirable actions. Children whose parents use more prescriptive rules have been found more generous (see Staub, 1979). The balance of rules versus autonomy is important, and should increasingly shift to the latter as children become older (Staub, in preparation).

Both in schools and in the family, the participation of children in rule setting has important benefits. One benefit is cognitive growth, as children examine the consequences of particular rules for themselves, for others (including the teacher), and for the life of the classroom. Another benefit is greater commitment by children and youth to rules that they have participated in creating. A highly significant benefit is that participation in rule making contributes to children developing critical consciousness and "critical loyalty" (Staub, 1989) or moral courage. In the course of discussing and negotiating about rules, they can learn to use their own judgment rather than simply accept the word of authorities and to express views that may be in opposition to the majority. In the course of this they can develop moral courage, which may enable them to oppose practices by their group, whether it is their peer group, or later on their country, that are contrary to basic human values such as respect for the welfare of individuals and subgroups of the society.

It is the unwillingness or inability to question and oppose that leads people to remain passive bystanders and frequently contributes to the evolution of increasing violence by groups against other groups, including minorities within a country (Staub, 1989). The unwillingness to speak out also makes bullying and other antisocial behavior by children and youth more likely.

b. *Strategies to shape the standards and rules of peer interaction* will be discussed and developed in the workshops. It is essential to develop and maintain, as noted above, as much as possible jointly with children, adherence to standards that express the basic value of respect for others' welfare. Peer interaction is a powerful arena for children to learn about themselves and other people, and to develop positive habits of relating to others (Hartup, 1983; Staub, 1979; Staub & Feinberg, 1980). It is also an important domain for learning by doing. A number of related topics and issues will be discussed in the workshops: Reasons for children's aggression, and of their mistreating or bullying other children; the importance of teachers not being passive bystanders to hostile and aggressive interactions among children; modes of intervention that can create a classroom spirit that makes such behaviors unlikely (both direct and "indirect" interventions like seating arrangements); and the balance of "control" by teachers in important domains while allowing autonomy in other domains.

There will be some attention to *conflict resolution* techniques, so that teachers can guide children to work out their conflicts peaceably. Such techniques have been used in many contexts. They include teaching children to describe how they themselves feel and what they want (rather than commenting on the others' actions), and to listen to each other. This avoids insult, attack, and the escalation of conflict, and offers the possibility of compromise and agreement. The effectiveness of mediation and conflict resolution is likely to increase in the context of caring classroom practices.

c. *Reasoning and explanations.* Reasoning with children and adolescents, explaining to them and discussing with them the reasons for specific rules, is an important form of guidance (Hoffman, 1970; Baumrind, 1975). Ideally reasoning will refer to values, such as the protection of everyone's needs, or making it possible for the teacher to teach and students to learn.

"Induction" or pointing out to children the consequences of their behavior on others – how certain of their acts harm others, while others benefit there – is an important aspect of reasoning (Hoffman, 1970; 1975; Staub, 1971; 1979). Induction makes children aware both of the inner world of others, thereby promoting the capacity for empathy, and of the child's impact on others, thus promoting feelings of responsibility.

In schools (and in the home) children and adults can discuss the consequences (benefits and disadvantages) of various rules for individuals and the group. Adults can guide children to talk about issues and problems, including interpersonal conflicts and internal conflicts. In the process they can help children develop awareness as well as self-awareness. As I have noted, it is extremely important that teachers create a framework for such discussion in which the children's feeling of safety is protected.

d. *Modeling.* The example of others is important in developing caring and helping. Obviously, teachers model by their own actions. Progressively, the behavior of students can serve to model for each other caring, helping, and cooperation.

e. *Positive discipline.* Children have their own needs and desires, and they bring with themselves orientations to other people and behavioral tendencies that can lead them to act in harmful rather than helpful ways. It is important for teachers to practice firm but non-forceful discipline (Baumrind, 1975), especially in domains they consider important. For example, when children are not guided to actually act in helpful rather than uncooperative, selfish, and aggressive ways, they can develop a positive way of talking about helping without becoming genuinely caring and helpful (see Staub, 1979).

The extensive use of power and force by adults, even nonphysical force, is not productive for the development of caring and helping. But the development of techniques for and the practice of positive discipline is one of the more difficult things to learn for many parents and teachers. It will receive special focus in the workshops.

4. Learning by Doing

A profoundly important avenue to becoming a helpful person is engagement in helpful action. My own research with children shows that leading or guiding children to engage in behavior that benefits others, like making toys for poor hospitalized children, or older children teaching younger children, later results in more helpful and generous behavior by them (Staub, 1975, 1979). My review and examination of both psychological research and life events show that when people help others under reasonably supportive conditions they become more helpful; when they harm others without negative consequences to themselves they become more capable of doing harm to others (Staub, 1979, 1989) (see Chapter 11 in this volume).

Many opportunities exist and can be created within schools for children to benefit other children or the group. The schools can also be instrumental in guiding students to engage in helpful, socially responsible behavior outside the school. I have called the role of adults in this process "natural socialization" (Staub, 1979). Instead of rewarding, punishing, or even instructing children, adults can guide them to engage in behavior that benefits others. It is their *experience* in the course of performing prosocial behavior, both their awareness of its beneficial consequences and their experience of their own effectiveness and power to benefit others, that leads children to become more helpful, as well as more caring. As they help others, children (and adults) tend to become more concerned about the welfare of those they help, and progressively about the welfare of people in general, and come to see themselves as more willing (and able) to help others. Specific activities will be suggested for learning by doing and will also be designed by participants.

5. Learning About Us–Them Differentiation, and the Acceptance of "Them"

Even children who learn to be caring and helpful often learn to draw sharp distinctions between "us" and "them," and apply their helpful orientation only to members of their "in group."

a. In the workshop, *psychological processes or ways of thinking* that lead children and adults to turn against members of other groups will be discussed. One of them is the tendency to differentiate between "us," our group, and "them," people who don't belong to our group. It is helpful to understand the origins of this tendency in individuals, and in the culture or society (Allport, 1954; Staub, 1989, 1996a; Tajfel, 1982). A second tendency is to devalue those who are regarded as "them," and to think about them in terms of stereotypes – that is, exaggerated beliefs and images (Allport, 1954; Piaget and Weil, 1951). In many societies the devaluation of certain groups has become part of the culture and is transmitted to children. A third tendency is "just world" thinking (Lerner, 1981), the widely held belief that the world is a just place. Therefore, people who suffer, who are poor or the victims of discrimination or mistreatment, are seen as deserving their fate – due either to their actions or to their character. As a result, they are devalued. These and other ways of thinking that lead people to diminish others will be discussed both to inform teachers and to prepare them to introduce these concepts into the classroom.

b. *Differences and similarities.* Learning about differences in customs, habits, and ways of life of different groups of people, together with considering basic similarities among human beings in needs, strivings, hopes, and aspirations, can lead to a greater acceptance of "them." Part of this learning about similarities and differences may take place in special exercises for children, like making lists of "What do I want?" and comparing and discussing lists. Part of the learning may take place in the course of classroom instruction, for example, by teaching children about cultures from a "functional" perspective. This means the exploration of how characteristics of cultures evolve as they face and develop modes of solving life problems, like scarcity, threat, enmity, and war. By considering how different cultures evolved in part because of life circumstances, children can come to understand how this has happened in their own culture. This makes it possible to see the way of life in their society as just one way of life, not the only right way of life.

c. How *us–them differentiation in the peer group manifests itself* is to be discussed in the workshops. This involves discussing reasons for children devaluing, bullying, and "scapegoating" others who are different. One reason is fear of becoming like these children, especially since children's own identity is not yet well formed. Another is fear of ostracism by peers if one does not sharply differentiate oneself from children who are different, devalued, the victims of bullying. A third reason is the feeling of superiority and power that children can gain by acting against others. A further reason is learned prejudice toward certain others based on race, class, religion, or other criteria.

The value of acknowledging, discussing, and affirming differences among children in the classroom (in clothing, orientation to time, etc.) and methods for doing this will be discussed. The origins of some of these differences in cultural backgrounds will also be discussed, including their origins in families as cultures. How the satisfaction children may derive from connection with those who scapegoat or bully can be replaced by connections that are more "inclusive" needs to be discussed.

6. Participation and Community Building

Participation in the life of the classroom in significant ways can contribute to the development of a positive sense of self, feelings of responsibility for others' welfare, and social responsibility – responsibility for the social good and human welfare. It can also build connections among children and create a feeling of community. The satisfactions inherent in being a member of a community can reduce antisocial behavior in the classroom, and can draw in children who otherwise might remain marginal. Aggressive children usually feel little connection to school or community. The experience of such connection is negatively related to aggressiveness (see Eron, Gentry & Schlegel, 1994; Kaufman & Zigler, 1987; Staub, 1996b).

The types of participation discussed earlier can also serve community building, like participation in rule making, the class and teacher creating a student-teacher bill of rights, and so on. Students can also take care of animals, participate in theater projects, and engage together in community projects designed "for learning by doing," for benefiting people outside the school and thereby developing their own caring and helpful tendencies.

7. Cross-Cutting Relations, with Equal Status

For members of different groups to work, learn, and play together is of great value in creating positive connections across group lines (Deutsch, 1973; Staub, 1988, 1989). Deep involvement in shared activities, significant contact between members of different groups, can serve as well as create shared goals and overcome negative attitudes. For positive attitudes to develop it is important for members of different groups who work together on joint projects to have equal power (Allport, 1954), especially if they traditionally differ in status. It is important for the adults in the school to approve of and support their engagement in joint activities.

Cooperative learning is one form of cross-cutting relations. In one kind of cooperative learning, called the "jigsaw" technique (Aronson et al., 1978), each of six children learn part of the material they need to know for a project, and teach it to each other. Each child teaches others and is taught by others. Cooperative instruction enhances academic learning by minority students, and prosocial peer interaction among all students (Johnson et al., 1984). These and other examples of cross-cutting relations can be discussed.

8. Increasing Children's Capacity to Understand Others

Greater understanding of others' internal states, feelings, and motives (or increased "role-taking" capacity) increases the tendency for helpful behavior (Eisenberg, 1986; Eisenberg & Fabes, 1998; Hoffman, 1970, 2000; Staub, 1979). In the workshop, sensitivity to children's feelings, affirming them by recognizing their feelings and needs, guiding them to affirm each other in this way, and guiding children to share their feelings will be discussed. The use of "induction" in the classroom as a means to increase role taking will be discussed and role played. The use of videos will be demonstrated in increasing children's understanding of others' internal states. This involves asking children to describe what the different characters in a video film want, feel, or think.

9. Working with Aggressive/Antisocial Children and Youths

The last explicit component of the workshop will be about teaching children who tend to be antisocial/aggressive or disruptive in the classroom alternative modes of expressing feelings and fulfilling needs and desires. Some children experience hostility, physical violence, or other conditions at home that give rise to mistrust, perception of hostility by others, and both defensive and hostile aggression. Such children often lack the skills and habits of fulfilling their needs through positive behavior due to a "socialization void." That is, without examples or guidance at home, and with the habit of watching primarily aggressive television programs (Eron et al., 1971; Friedrich & Stein, 1973; Heussman et al, 1984a, 1984b), they have not developed the skills and habits of expressing feelings and fulfilling desires in positive ways. What they bring to the peer group, like aggressive or hostile behaviors, often results in aggressive and hostile responses from others (Dodge, 1980, 1986; Dodge & Frame, 1982; Rausch, 1965; Staub & Feinberg, 1980) and leads to a cycle of hostility.

There will be some exploration in the workshops of how teachers can help such children both to become aware of their needs, motives, and desires and to learn to fulfill them in positive ways. Apart from time limitations, the circumstances of teachers do not allow them to "retrain" antisocial children. Nonetheless, the training within the workshop should influence the teachers' views of such children and guide them to deal with their behavior in ways that can help them change.

Whenever possible, a *special program* is to be set up for such children, to be conducted by the project staff. As a starting point, children can be helped to identify their important needs and goals, especially those served by aggressive or disruptive behavior. These are likely to include self-defense, instrumental gain, and connection and recognition. They can then be helped to think of and experiment with other, more positive behaviors by which they can fulfill these goals. Role playing (Staub, 1971, 1981; Chandler, 1973), videotaping children's behaviors, and video feedback and modeling can be used to help children experiment with and learn constructive modes of need fulfillment (see Chapter 19 in this book on reducing boys' aggression).

10. Promoting Self-Awareness and Change in Teachers

In addition to providing information and developing new skills, the workshop experience may bring about some transformation in teachers. Assumptions about children may be connected to assumptions about human beings that teachers have developed on the basis of their own life experience, including childhood experience. Change in deeply set views, orientations, and motives best occurs through experiential relearning. The workshop may offer, nonetheless, some opportunity for change in relevant beliefs and orientations through discussion and exploration in a community of peers. To promote this, in addition to exploring their assumptions about children and human beings in general, teachers will discuss what they need and want from their students, what they believe is right or wrong in children's way of behaving that they took from their families and hold "automatically" rather than in a considered manner, and what are their own central values, especially as they express themselves in their interaction with children.

11. Trauma and Healing

Trauma has become in the last couple of decades a central concept in understanding the needs and characteristics of people who have experienced intensely stressful, painful, humiliating, or violent events (Herman, 1992; Pearlman & Saakvitne, 1995). Working in schools in areas where many children or their parents have been trauma victims, it will be important to provide teachers with information about the effects of trauma. Understanding how children's inner world and behavior are affected by trauma can enhance teachers' empathy, patience, and success in creating caring classrooms. Physical and sexual abuse, violent neighborhoods, victimization as the member of some group, and the emotional states and actions of parents who are survivors of genocide (in Europe, Cambodia, Turkey, or anywhere else) can all have traumatic effects on children.

Helping children heal from trauma can significantly contribute to their becoming caring and helpful people. Engagement with the traumatic experiences and the feelings they have generated, under supportive conditions, so that these experiences and feelings can lose their traumatizing power, and positive connections to other people are both avenues to healing. The former can be facilitated by reading and talking about stories in which children or adults have painful experiences. Training can be especially helpful here, to enable teachers to guide the discussion in a constructive, supportive manner, and to make appropriate decisions about engaging children about their own experience or limiting the discussion to the story characters. The latter, positive connection to others, will be facilitated by the creation of the kind of classroom community and peer relations that I discussed earlier.

THE CLASSROOM AND THE OUTSIDE WORLD

It is important for teachers to let students know that the rules in the classroom may be different from what they are accustomed to in the outside world. This will maximize the effectiveness of the program. For some children, the difference between their experience in the outside world and in a caring classroom will be great. It should be easier to get their cooperation if this difference is clearly acknowledged and explained, if the rules of the classroom "world" are clearly specified and their difference from the outside world is noted and even highlighted. The positive socialization practices and positive standards of peer interaction can bring about experiential relearning in children who have come to devalue and fear people, or have learned to devalue and mistreat peers who are members of ethnic, religious, or social groups other than their own.

A further reason for teachers to discuss the difference between the classroom and the outside world is the issue of transition. Some children live in environments where cooperative and helpful behaviors may lead to exploitation or abuse, unless they are cautiously and selectively employed. Discussing effective transition, transition rules, and skills not only protects children but also makes the helpful tendencies they develop in the school more resistant to the pressures of the outside world.

PARENT WORKSHOPS

The workshops for parents should include many of the same components, with some differences. For example, in discussing modes of relating to children and discipline practices, examples relevant to the home should be used. Participation and community building are to be discussed primarily in relation to the home. It is useful to also discuss, however, these practices in relation to the school, so that parents can support the practices of a caring school.

FOLLOW-UP WORK IN SCHOOLS

For several months after the workshop, staff associated with the program, and when possible a member of the school staff who works with the program, should observe participating classrooms on a regular basis. Observers and teachers can discuss events in the classroom, jointly evaluate what aspects of the program have or have not yet been successfully introduced into the classroom, discuss problems that teachers encounter, and plan specific ways to introduce and improve the implementation of the program in the classroom.

Members of the program staff are to be trained before the workshop and then participate in the workshop. They are to meet afterward to discuss and elaborate on the workshop experience. Subsequently, they are to meet regularly to discuss the ongoing work with teachers, to resolve specific problems that arise in specific classrooms, and to work on the ongoing implementation of the program.

The tasks of the teachers' committees include developing specific ideas to implement program components and creating participation in the continuing evolution of the program by all the school personnel. Specific ideas may include projects or activities for community building in the classroom beyond those presented and developed in the workshop, or ways to make practices more accessible to and usable by teachers.

One of the goals of such committees ought to be the involvement of parents in the program. The committees can bring parents and teachers together to work on various aspects of the program, for example, on creating "learning by doing" opportunities outside the classroom. The involvement of parents can have many beneficial effects: mutual support by parents and teachers, a feeling of significance by parents, and an alliance between parents and the school.

In summary, in the training workshop, positive socialization practices will be discussed, developed, and tried out through role play and other ways. One goal of the workshop is to provide ideas, develop skills, and create confidence in teachers that they can use positive means to bring about classroom discipline. Requirements for and components of positive discipline include an atmosphere of warmth and caring; sensitivity to cultural, subcultural, and individual differences among children; the capacity to disapprove of and inhibit behavior without putting down and rejecting children; helping children fulfill their needs by constructive, positive actions; the explanation of rules that allows discussion and questioning; and the participation by children in creating rules.

The program will benefit children as they develop positive identities and greater capacity for helpful, positive, and satisfying relationships with other people. It will benefit teachers and parents as they develop more positive means of guiding children and more satisfying relationships with children. And it will benefit society as a whole, since the project will help develop caring and responsible rather than hostile and aggressive citizens, individuals who contribute to others' welfare and the social good, and to positive relations among subgroups of society. As noted, it is also expected that students will benefit through improved academic learning, that teachers will benefit through greater ease of instruction and increased effectiveness, and society will benefit through better educated citizens.

(Ideas for program evaluation and for research possibilities associated with this program are available from the author.)

References

Ainsworth, M. D. S. (1979). Infant-mother attachment. *American Psychologist, 34,* 932–937.

Ainsworth, M. D. S., Bell, S. M., & Stayton, D. J. (1974). Infant-mother attachment and social development: Socialization as a product of reciprocal responsiveness to signals. In M. P. M. Richards (Ed.), *The integration of the child into a social world.* London: Cambridge University Press.

Allport, G. W. (1954). *The nature of prejudice.* Reading, MA: Addison-Wesley.

Aronson, E., Stephan, C., Sikes, J., Blaney, N., & Snapp, M. (1978). *The jigsaw classroom.* Beverly Hills, CA: Sage Publications, Inc.

Baumrind, D. (1975). *Early socialization and the discipline controversy.* Morristown, NJ: General Learning Press.

Chandler, M. J. (1973). Egocentrism and antisocial behavior: The assessment and training of social-perspective taking skills. *Developmental Psychology, 9,* 326–332.

Coopersmith, S. (1967). *Antecedents of self-esteem.* San Francisco: Fremont & Company.

Deutsch, M. (1973). *The resolution of conflict: Constructive and destructive process.* New Haven, CT: Yale University Press.

DiLalla, L. F., Mitchell, C. M., Arthur, M. W., & Pagliococca, P. M. (1988). Aggression and delinquency: Family and environmental factors. *Journal of Youth and Adolescence, 73,* 233–246.

Dodge, K. A. (1980). Social cognition and children's aggressive behavior. *Child Development, 51,* 162–170.

Dodge, K. A. (1986). Social information processing variables in the development of aggression and altruism in children. In C. Zahn-Waxler, M. Cummings, & M. Radke-Yarrow (Eds.), *The development of altruism and aggression: Social and biological origins.* New York: Cambridge University Press.

Dodge, K. A. (1993). Social cognitive mechanisms in the development of conduct disorder and depression. *Annual Review of Psychology, 44,* 559–584.

Dodge, K. A., & Frame, C. L. (1982). Social cognitive biases and deficits in aggressive boys. *Child Development, 53,* 620–635.

Eisenberg, N. (1986). *Altruistic emotion, cognition and behavior.* Hillsdale, NJ: Lawrence Erlbaum Associates.

Eisenberg, N. (1992). *The caring child.* Cambridge: Harvard University Press.

Eisenberg, N., and Fabes, R. A. (1998). Prosocial development. In W. Damon (Ed.), *Handbook of child psychology* (Vol. 3) (5th ed.) N. Eisenberg (Ed.). Social, Emotional, and Personality Development.

Elder, G. H., Jr., & Caspi, A. (1985). Economic stress in lives: Developmental perspectives. *Journal of Social Issues, 44* (4), 25–45.

Eron, L. D., Gentry, J. H., & Schlegel, P. (Eds.) (1994). *Reason to hope: A psychosocial perspective on violence and youth.* Washington, DC: American Psychological Association.

Eron, L. D., Walder, L. O., & Lefkowitz, M. N. (1971). *Learning of aggression in children.* Boston: Little, Brown.

Friedrich, L. K., & Stein, A. H. (1973). Aggressive and prosocial television programs and the natural behavior of preschool children. *Monographs of the Society for Research in Child Development, 38* (4, Serial No. 151).

Gelles, R. J. (1981). Child abuse and violence in single parent families: Parent absence and economic deprivation. *American Journal of Orthopsychiatry, 59,* 492–502.

Gelles, R. J., & Conte, J. R. (1990). Domestic violence and sexual abuse of children: A review of research in the eighties. *Journal of Marriage and the Family, 52,* 1045–1058.

Greven, P. (1991). *Spare the child: The religious roots of punishment and the impact of physical abuse.* New York: Alfred A. Knopf.

Grusec, J. E. (1981). Socialization processes and the development of altruism. In J. P. Rushton & R. M. Sorrentino (Eds.), *Altruism and helping behavior.* Hillsdale, NJ: Lawrence Erlbaum Associates.

Hartup, H. (1983). Peer relations. In P. H. Mussen (Ed.), *Carmichael's manual of child psychology* (Vol. 4) (4th ed.). New York: Wiley.

Herman, J. (1992). *Trauma and recovery.* New York: Basic Books.

Hoffman, M. L. (1970). Conscience, personality, and socialization technique. *Human Development, 13,* 90–126.

Hoffman, M. L. (1975). Altruistic behavior and the parent-child relationship. *Journal of Personality and Social Psychology, 31,* 937–943.

Hoffman, M. L. (2000). *Empathy and moral development.* New York: Cambridge University Press.

Huesmann, L. R., Eron, L. D., Lefkowitz, M. M., & Walder, L. O. (1984). Stability of aggression over time and generations. *Developmental Psychology, 20,* 6, 1120–1134.

Huesmann, L. R., Lagerspetz, K., & Eron, L. D. (1984). Intervening variables in the television violence-aggression relation: Evidence from two countries. *Developmental Psychology, 20,* 746–775.

Johnson, D. W., Maruyama, G., Johnson, R., Nelson, D., & Skon, L. (1981). The effects of cooperative, competitive and individualistic goal structures on achievement: A meta analysis. *Psychological Bulletin, 89,* 47–62.

Kaufman, J., & Zigler, E. (1987). "Do abused children become abusive parents?" *American Journal of Orthopsychiatry, 57,* 186–192.

Lerner, M. (1981). *The belief in a just world: A fundamental delusion.* New York: Plenum Press.

Miller, A. (1983). *For your own good: Hidden cruelty in child-rearing and the roots of violence.* New York: Farrar, Straus and Giroux.

Pearlman, L. A., & Saakvitne, K. (1995). *Trauma and the therapist.* New York: Norton.

Piaget, J., & Weil, A. (1951). The development in children of the idea of the homeland and of relations with other countries. *International Social Science Bulletin, 3,* 570.

Radke-Yarrow, M. R., Zahn-Waxler, C., & Chapman, M. (1983). Children's prosocial dispositions and behavior. In P. H. Mussen (Ed.), *Carmichael's manual of child psychology* (Vol. 4) (4th ed.). New York: Wiley & Sons.

Rausch, H. (1965). Interaction sequences. *Journal of Personality and Social Psychology, 2,* 487–499.

Sroufe, L. A. (1979). The coherence of individual development: Early care, attachment, and subsequent developmental issues. *American Psychologist, 34,* 834–842.

Staub, E. (1971). The use of role playing and induction in children's learning of helping and sharing behavior. *Child Development, 42,* 805–817.

Staub, E. (1974). Helping a distressed person: Social, personality and stimulus determinants. In L. Berkowitz (Ed.), *Advances in experimental social psychology* (Vol. 7). New York: Academic Press.
Staub, E. (1975). To rear a prosocial child: Reasoning, learning by doing, and learning by teaching others. In D. DePalma & J. Folley (Eds.), *Moral development: Current theory and research.* Hillsdale, NJ: Erlbaum.
Staub, E. (1979). *Positive social behavior and morality: Socialization and development* (Vol. 2). New York: Academic Press.
Staub, E. (1980). Social and prosocial behavior: Personal and situational influences and their interactions. In E. Staub (Ed.), *Personality: Basic aspects and current research.* Englewood Cliffs, NJ: Prentice-Hall.
Staub, E. (1981). Promoting positive behavior in schools, in other educational settings, and in the home. In J. P. Rushton & R. M. Sorrentino (Eds.), *Altruism and helping behavior*. Hillsdale, NJ: Erlbaum.
Staub, E. (1986). A conception of the determinants and development of altruism and aggression: Motives, the self, the environment. In C. Zahn-Waxler (Ed.), *Altruism and aggression: Social and biological origins.* Cambridge: Cambridge University Press.
Staub, E. (1988). The evolution of caring and nonaggressive persons and societies. In R. Wagner, J. DeRivera, & M. Watkins (Eds.), Positive approaches to peace. Special issue of the *Journal of Social Issues*, *44*, 81–100.
Staub, E. (1989). *The roots of evil: The origins of genocide and other group violence.* New York: Cambridge University Press.
Staub, E. (1990). The psychology and culture of torture and torturers. In P. Suedfeld (Ed.), *Psychology and torture*. New York: Hemisphere Publishing Group.
Staub, E. (1991). Psychological and cultural origins of extreme destructiveness and extreme altruism. In W. Kurtines & J. Gewirtz (Eds.), *The handbook of moral behavior and development*. Hillsdale, NJ: Lawrence Erlbaum Associates.
Staub, E. (1992). The origins of caring, helping and nonaggression: Parental socialization, the family system, schools, and cultural influence. In S. Oliner & P. Oliner et al. (Eds.), *Embracing the other: Philosophical, psychological and historical perspectives on altruism*. New York: New York University Press.
Staub, E. (1993). The psychology of bystanders, perpetrators and heroic helpers. *International Journal of Intercultural Relations*, *17*, 315–341.
Staub, E. (1996a). Altruism and aggression in children and youth: Origins and cures. In R. Feldman, *The psychology of adversity*. Amherst: University of Massachusetts Press.
Staub, E. (1996b). The cultural-societal roots of violence: The examples of genocidal violence and contemporary youth violence in the United States. *American Psychologist*, *51*, 117–132.
Staub, E. (in preparation). *A brighter future: Raising caring and nonviolent children.* New York: Oxford University Press.
Staub, E., & Feinberg, H. (1980). Regularities in peer interaction, empathy, and sensitivity to others. Presented at the symposium: Development of prosocial behavior and cognitions. American Psychological Association Meetings, Montreal.
Staub, E., & Rosenthal, (1994). Mob violence: Social-cultural influences, group processes and participants. In *Summary report of the American Psychological*

Association's Commission on Violence and Youth (Vol. 2). Washington, DC: American Psychological Association.
Stayton, D. J., Ainsworth, M. D. S., & Main, M. B. (1973). Development of separation behavior in the first year of life: Protest, following, and greeting. *Developmental Psychology, 9*, 213–225.
Stone, L. (1977). *The family, sex and marriage in England, 1500–1800*. New York: Harper & Row.
Straus, M. A. (1992). Corporal punishment of children and depression and suicide in adulthood. Paper presented at the Society for Life History Research, Philadelphia, PA.
Straus, M. A., Gelles, R. J., & Steinmetz, S. K. (1980). *Behind closed doors: Violence in the American family*. Garden City, NY: Anchor Press/Doubleday.
Tajfel, H. (1982). Social psychology of intergroup relations. *Annual Review of Psychology, 33*, 1–39.
Troy, M., & Sroufe, L. A. (1987). Victimization among preschoolers: Role of attachment relationships. *Child and Adolescent Psychiatry, 26*, 166–172.
Weiss, B., Dodge, K. A., Bates, S. E., & Pettit, G. S. (1992). Some consequences of early harsh discipline: Child aggression and a maladaptive social information processing style. *Child Development, 63*, 1321–1335.
Widom, C. S. (1989a). Does violence beget violence? A critical examination of the literature. *Psychological Bulletin, 106* (1), 3–28.
Widom, C. S. (1989b). The cycle of violence. *Science, 224*, 160–166.
Yarrow, M. R., & Scott, P. M. (1972). Limitation of nurturant and nonnurturant models. *Journal of Personality and Social Psychology, 8*, 240–261.

PART IV

THE ORIGINS OF GENOCIDE, MASS KILLING, AND OTHER COLLECTIVE VIOLENCE

21

A Note on the Cultural–Societal Roots of Violence

When there is large-scale or widespread violence in a society, either cultural characteristics, societal conditions or, most likely, a combination of the two are exerting influence.

Genocidal violence is a societal process. To understand its origins and evolution, we must consider beyond individual psychology group psychological processes and their roots in culture, social conditions, and societal institutions (Fein, 1990; Staub, 1989). For the sake of simplicity in language, I will use the term *genocidal violence* to include both genocide – the attempt to eliminate a whole group of people, whether defined by race, religion, ethnicity, or political beliefs – and mass killing, in which there is no intention to eliminate a whole group. Genocides and mass killings often have fuzzy boundaries and shared determinants (Staub, 1989).

By considering only individual psychology, without the role of culture, social conditions, and group process, we will be unable to understand these phenomena and hampered in taking action to deal with them. My intention is to show the role of cultural characteristics and societal conditions in genocide or mass killing, including the way they generate and shape psychological processes and actions that contribute to violence.

Culture refers to the perspectives and meanings shared by members of a group: their views of the world and of themselves; their beliefs, values, and norms of conduct; their myths and conceptions of God and the spiritual; and so on. Social institutions, like schools, the legal system, religion, police, and the family, embody culture. They express and maintain culture, helping it shape and express the characteristics and psychology of individuals.

Reprinted from E. Staub (1996). Cultural–societal roots of violence: The examples of genocidal violence and of contemporary youth violence in the United States. *American Psychologist, 51*, 117–132. Included here are parts of pp. 117–118.

Social conditions are the economic, political, technological, and other important states of the group at a particular time. Stable social conditions (e.g., level of technological development, poverty or wealth of different groups, etc.) arise from culture and social organization. Even temporary variations in social conditions can be culture based, like the cycles of economic growth and recession in the United States. But temporary social conditions, like the difficult life conditions in a society that will be discussed below, are the result of a combination of influences that may include culture, the way social institutions operate, international events and conditions, and other influences. Their origins are not well understood. The best method to establish the role of culture and social conditions in violence may be to demonstrate the existence of patterns of cultural-societal characteristics that precede and accompany particular forms of violence in different societies and historical periods.

References

Fein, H. (1990). *Genocide: A sociological perspective* [Special issue]. *Current Sociology, 38*, 1–126.

Staub, E. (1989). *The roots of evil: The origins of genocide and other group violence.* New York: Cambridge University Press.

22

The Psychology of Bystanders, Perpetrators, and Heroic Helpers

What leads groups of people or governments to perpetrate genocide or mass killing? What are the characteristics and psychological processes of individuals and societies that contribute to such group violence? What is the nature of the evolution that leads to it: What are the motives, how do they arise and intensify, how do inhibitions decline?

A primary example in this article will be the Holocaust, the killing of between 5 and 6 million European Jews by Nazi Germany during World War II. Other examples will be the genocide of the Armenians in Turkey in 1915–1916, the "autogenocide" in Cambodia between 1975 and 1979, the genocide in Rwanda in 1994, and the disappearances and mass killing in Argentina, mainly between 1976 and 1979. Many of the same influences are also present both in the widespread uses of torture and in terrorist violence.

In the United Nations charter on genocide the term denotes the extermination of a racial, religious, or ethnic group. Although not included in the charter, and although some scholars call it politicide (Harff & Gurr, 1990), the destruction of a whole political group is also widely regarded as

Reprinted from a chapter of the same title by E. Staub in L. S. Newman & R. Erber (Eds.). (2002). *What social psychology can tell us about the Holocaust: Understanding perpetrator behavior*. New York: Oxford University Press, with permission from Oxford University Press. An earlier version of this chapter was published as an article by E. Staub (1993). The psychology of bystanders, perpetrators, and heroic helpers. *The International Journal of Intercultural Relations, 17*, 315–341. Copyright 1993, with permission from Elsevier Science. This was an updated version of a paper with the same title that won the Otto Klineberg International and Intercultural Prize of the Society for the Psychological Study of Social Issues (also a division of the American Psychological Association).

For the current chapter a figure was added from E. Staub (2001). The role of the individual and group identity in genocide and mass killing. In R. D. Ashmore, L. Jussim, and D. Wilder (Eds.), *Social identity, intergroup conflict, and conflict reduction*. New York: Oxford University Press. Copyright 2001 by Oxford University Press. Used with permission of Oxford University Press, Inc.

genocide (Kuper, 1981). In mass killing, the boundaries of the victim group are less well defined, and the elimination of a whole racial, religious, or ethnic group is not intended. For example, in Argentina the victims included Communists, people seen as left leaning, and liberals who wanted to help the poor or supported social change. Usually, although not always, mass killings have fewer victims. The Holocaust, the killings of the Armenians, and the killings in Rwanda were genocides; the killings in Cambodia were genocidal but with less well defined group boundaries, in that Khmer as well as members of minority groups were killed; the disappearances in Argentina were a mass killing. Genocides and mass killings have similar psychological and cultural origins.

This chapter will focus on the psychology and role of both perpetrators and bystanders. Bystanders to the ongoing, usually progressively increasing mistreatment of a group of people have great potential power to influence events. However, whether individuals, groups, or nations, they frequently remain passive. This allows perpetrators to see their destructive actions as acceptable and even right. As a result of their passivity in the face of others' suffering, bystanders change: They come to accept the persecution and suffering of victims, and some even join the perpetrators (Staub, 1989a, 1989b, 1999a, 2000a,b).

All of us are bystanders to many events – neither actors nor victims but witnesses. We witness discrimination and the fate of the homeless. We have known about torture in many countries, the death squads in Guatemala and El Salvador, the use of chemical weapons by Iraq to kill its own Kurdish citizens while our government and many others supported Iraq, the imprisonment of dissidents in mental hospitals in the Soviet Union (Bloch & Reddaway, 1977, 1984), and the nuclear policies of the United States and the USSR. Examination of the role of bystanders in genocides and mass killings may enlighten us about our own role as bystanders to others' suffering, and to policies and practices that potentially lead to the destruction of human beings.

Another focus of this chapter is the psychology of those who attempt to save intended victims, endangering their own lives to do so. Bystanders, perpetrators, and heroic helpers face similar conditions and may be part of the same culture: What are the differences in their characteristics, psychological processes, and evolution?

BRIEF REVIEW

A conception is presented in this chapter of the origins of genocide and mass killing, with a focus on how a group of people turns against another group, how the motivation for killing evolves and inhibitions against it decline. The conception identifies characteristics of a group's culture that create an enhanced potential for a group turning against others. It focuses on difficult life conditions as the primary activator of basic needs, which demand fulfillment. Conflict between groups is another activator. The pattern of predisposing cultural characteristics intensifies the basic needs and inclines the group toward fulfilling them in ways that turn the group against others. As they begin to harm the victim group, the perpetrators learn by and change as a result of their own actions, in ways that make the increasing mistreatment of the victims possible and probable. The perpetrators come to see their actions as necessary and even right. Bystanders have potential influence to inhibit the evolution of increasing destructiveness. However, they usually remain passive and themselves change as a result of their passivity, becoming less concerned about the fate of the victims, some of them joining the perpetrators.

THE PSYCHOLOGY OF PERPETRATORS

Violence against a subgroup of society is the outcome of a societal process. It requires analysis at the level of both individuals and society. Analysis of the group processes of perpetrators, an intermediate level, is also important.

Instigators of Group Violence

Difficult Life Conditions and Basic Human Needs. Why does a government or a dominant group turn against a subgroup of society? Usually difficult life conditions, persistent life problems in a society, are an important starting point. They include economic problems such as extreme inflation, or depression and unemployment, political conflict and violence, war, a decline in the power, prestige, and importance of a nation, usually with attendant economic and political problems, and the chaos and social disorganization these often entail.

Severe, persistent difficulties of life frustrate powerful needs, basic human needs that demand fulfillment. Certain "predisposing" characteristics of the culture and social organization tend to further intensify these needs (Staub, 1989a, 1996, 1999b). These include needs for security, for a positive identity, for effectiveness and control over important events in one's life, for positive connections to other people, and for a meaningful understanding of the world or comprehension of reality. Psychological processes in individuals and social processes in groups can arise that turn the group against others as they offer destructive fulfillment of these needs.

Germany was faced with serious life problems after World War I. The war and defeat were followed by a revolution, a change in the political system, hyperinflation, the occupation of the Ruhr by the French, who were dissatisfied with the rate of reparation payments, severe economic depression, conflict between political extremes, political violence, social chaos, and disorganization. The intense conflict between political extremes and the collapse of traditional social mores were both manifestations and further causes of life problems (Craig, 1982; A. DeJong, 1978). Intense life problems also existed in Turkey, Cambodia, Rwanda, and Argentina (Staub, 1989a, 1999a). For example, in Argentina, severe inflation, political instability, and repression, followed by wide-scale political violence, preceded the policy of disappearances: the kidnapping and torture of tens of thousands of people and the killing of at least 9,000 but perhaps as many as 30,000 people (Nunca Mas, 1986).

The inability to protect oneself and one's family and the inability to control the circumstances of one's life greatly threaten security. They also deeply threaten identity or the psychological self – self-concept, values, beliefs, and ways of life – as well as the need for effectiveness and control. The need for comprehension of reality (Epstein, 1980; Janoff-Bulman, 1985, 1992; Staub, 1989a), and a conception of the world, one's place in it, and how to live is frustrated as the social chaos and disorganization render the existing views of reality inadequate. The need for connection to other people and the group is frustrated at a time when people need it most, by the competition for resources and self-focus that difficult life conditions foster. Finally, people need hope in a better future. These psychological needs join material ones, such as the need for food and physical safety, and rival them in intensity and importance. Since the capacity to control or address life problems and to satisfy material needs is limited, the psychological needs become predominant in guiding action (Staub, 1989a, 1996, 1999b).

The motivations just described can be satisfied by joining others in a shared effort to solve life problems. But constructive solutions to a breakdown in the functioning of society are difficult to find and take time to implement. Certain cultural-societal characteristics, present in most societies but to greatly varying extents, add to the likelihood that these needs will be fulfilled in ways that turn the group against another group. They create a predisposition for group violence.

In Germany a two-step process led to the genocide. The difficult life conditions gave rise to psychological and social processes, such as scapegoating and destructive ideologies, which are described later. Such processes do not directly lead to genocide. However, they turn one group against another. In Germany, they brought an ideological movement to power and led to the beginning of an evolution, or steps along the continuum of destruction, also described later. Life conditions improved, but guided by ideology, the social processes and acts of harm-doing they gave rise to continued to intensify. In the midst of another great social upheaval, created by Germany, namely, World War II, they led to genocide.

Group Conflict. Another instigator that frustrates basic needs and gives rise to psychological conditions in individuals and social processes in groups that may lead to genocide is conflict between groups. The conflict may revolve around essential interests, such as territory needed for living space. Even in this case, however, psychological elements tend to make the conflict intractable, such as attachment by groups to a particular territory, unhealed wounds in the group, or prior devaluation and mistrust of the other.

Or the conflict may be between superordinate or dominant groups and subordinate groups with limited rights and limited access to resources. Such conflicts deeply affect the needs for security and positive identity, as well as other basic needs. They have often been the originators of mass killing or genocide since World War II (Fein, 1993). When group conflict turns into war and the other predisposing conditions are present, mass killing or genocide becomes especially likely (Harff, Gurr, & Unger, 1999). In Rwanda, preceding the genocide by Hutus of Tutsis in 1994, there were both difficult life conditions and conflict between groups, a combination that is an especially intense instigator. Starting in 1990, there was also the beginning of a civil war (des Forges, 1999; Staub, 1999a).

Cultural-Societal Characteristics

Cultural Devaluation. The differentiation between in-group and out-group, us and them, tends by itself to give rise to a favoring of the in-group and relative devaluation of the out-group and discrimination against its members (Brewer, 1978; Tajfel, 1982; Tajfel, Flamant, Billig, & Bundy, 1971). Devaluation of individuals and groups, whatever its source, makes it easier to harm them (Bandura, Underwood, & Fromson, 1975; Duster, 1971).

A history of devaluation of a group, negative stereotypes, and negative images in the products of the culture, its literature, art, and media, "preselect" this group as a potential scapegoat and enemy (Staub, 1989a). In Germany, there had been a long history of anti-Semitism, with periods of intense mistreatment of Jews (Dimont, 1962; Girard, 1980). In addition to early Christian theological anti-Semitism (Girard, 1980), the intense anti-Semitism of Luther (Hilberg, 1961; Luther, 1955–1975), who described Jews in language similar to that later used by Hitler, was an important influence. Centuries of discrimination and persecution further enhanced anti-Semitism and made it an aspect of German culture. Even though at the end of World War I German Jews were relatively assimilated, anti-Semitism in the *deep structure* of German culture provided a cultural blueprint, a constant potential, for renewed antagonism against them. In Turkey, deep-seated cultural devaluation of and discrimination against Armenians had existed for centuries. In Rwanda, there was intense hostility by Hutus toward Tutsis, as a result of prior dominance by Tutsis.

At times devaluation of the potential victims is the result of a newly emerging ideology that designates a group as the enemy. The ideology usually draws on existing differentiations and divisions in society. For example, in Cambodia, there had been a long-standing rift between the city, inhabited by those who ruled, the officialdom, the aristocracy, and the educated, and the country, with its peasant population (Chandler, 1983; Etcheson, 1984). The Khmer Rouge ideology drew on this division, defining all city dwellers as actual or potential enemies (Staub, 1989a).

This is a probabilistic conception, with different elements enhancing or diminishing the likelihood of one group turning against another. Not all probabilities become actualities. For example, intense anti-Semitism had existed at least in parts of Russia before the revolution of 1917. While it was perhaps not as embedded in the deep structure of the culture as in Germany, it did create the potential for Jews to become scapegoats or ideological enemies. Deep divisions had also existed between rulers and privileged members of society, on the one hand, and the peasants and workers, on the other. The ideology that guided the leaders of the revolution led them to focus on this latter division.

Respect for Authority. Overly strong respect for authority, with a predominant tendency to obey authority, is another important cultural characteristic. It leads people to turn to authorities, old or new, for guidance in difficult times (Fromm, 1965). It leads them to accept the authorities' definition of reality, their views of problems and solutions, and stops them from resisting authorities when they lead them to harm others. There is substantial evidence that Germans had strong respect for authority that was deeply rooted in their culture, as well as a tendency to obey those with even limited authority (Craig, 1982; Girard, 1980). German families and schools were authoritarian, with restrictive and punitive child-rearing practices (Miller, 1983; Devereux, 1972). Strong respect for authority has also characterized the other societies that engaged in genocide or mass killing, such as Turkey, Cambodia, and Rwanda, although in some cases it was especially strong in the subgroup of the society that became the perpetrator, as in Argentina, where the military was both the architect and the executor of the disappearances (Nunca Mas, 1986).

A Monolithic Culture. A monolithic in contrast to pluralistic society, with a small range of predominant values and/or limitations on the free flow of ideas, adds to the predisposition for group violence. The negative representation of a victim group and the definition of reality by authorities that justifies or even necessitates the victims' mistreatment will be more broadly accepted. Democratic societies, which tend to be more pluralistic, are unlikely to engage in genocide (Rummel, 1994), especially if they are "mature" democracies, with well-developed civic institutions (Staub, 1999a).

German culture was monolithic: It stressed obedience, order, efficiency, and loyalty to the group (Craig, 1982; Staub, 1989a). As I noted earlier, the evolution of the Holocaust can be divided into two phases. The first one brought Hitler to power. During the second phase, Nazi rule, the totalitarian system further reduced the range of acceptable ideas and the freedom of their expression. In the other cases, the societies, and at times particularly the perpetrator groups in them, such as the military and paramilitary groups in Argentina, were also monolithic. In the frequent cases of genocide or mass killing when the political-ideological system was highly authoritarian and even totalitarian, monolithic tendencies were further intensified.

Cultural Self-Concepts. A belief in cultural superiority (that goes beyond the usual ethnocentrism), as well as a shaky group self-concept that requires self-defense, can also contribute to the tendency to turn against others. Frequently the two combine, a belief in the superiority of one's group with an underlying sense of vulnerability and weakness. Thus the cultural self-concept that predisposes to group violence can be complex but demonstrable through the products of the culture, its literature, its intellectual and artistic products, its media.

The Germans saw themselves as superior in character, competence, honor, loyalty, devotion to family, civic organization, and cultural achievements. Superiority had expressed itself in many ways, including proclamations by German intellectuals of German superiority and of their belief in Germany's right to rule other nations (Craig, 1982; Nathan & Norden, 1960; Staub, 1989a). Partly as a result of tremendous devastation in past wars (Craig, 1982; Mayer, 1955) and lack of unity and statehood until 1871, there was also a deep feeling of vulnerability and shaky self-esteem. Following unification and a brief period of strength, the loss of World War I and the intense life problems afterward were a great blow to cultural and societal self-concept.

The combination of a sense of superiority with weakness and vulnerability seems to have been present in Turkey, Cambodia, and Argentina as well. In Argentina, progressively deteriorating economic conditions and political violence deeply threatened a belief in the specialness and superiority of the nation, especially strongly held by the military, and an elevated view by the military of itself as protector of the nation (Crawley, 1984). In both Cambodia and Turkey, a past history of empire and national glory were deeply embedded in group consciousness (Staub, 1989a). The existing conditions sharply contrasted with the glory of the past. Difficult life conditions threaten the belief in superiority and activate the underlying feelings of weakness and vulnerability. They intensify the need to defend and/or elevate the self-concept, both individual and cultural.[1]

To a large extent, people define themselves by belonging to groups (Mack, 1983), which makes their social identity important (Tajfel, 1982; Turner, 1987). Group self-concepts become especially important in difficult times as the inability to deal with life problems threatens personal identity. Over time, the group's inability to help fulfill basic needs and societal disorganization also threaten group self-concept, people's vision and evaluation of their group.

Unhealed Wounds Due to Past Victimization. Another important cultural characteristic that contributes to a sense of vulnerability is a past history of victimization. Just like victimized individuals (Herman, 1992; McCann & Pearlman, 1990), groups of people who have been victimized in the past are intensely affected. Their sense of self is diminished. They come to see the world and people in it, especially outsiders, individuals as well as whole groups, as dangerous. They feel vulnerable, needing to defend themselves, which can lead them to strike out violently. Healing by victimized groups is essential to reduce the likelihood that they become perpetrators (Staub, 1998, 1999a).

The limited evidence, as yet, indicates that the effects of group victimization are transmitted through the generations. This is suggested both by the study of individual survivors and their offspring, and group culture. For example, Craig (1982) has suggested that long-ago wars in which large percentages of the German population were killed led to the strongly authoritarian tendencies in Prussian and then German society. People in authority became especially important in providing protection against danger.

A History of Aggressiveness. A history of aggression as a way of dealing with conflict also contributes to the predisposition for group violence. It makes renewed aggression more acceptable, more normal. Such a tradition, which existed in Germany before World War I, was greatly strengthened by the war and the widespread political violence that followed it (Kren & Rappoport, 1980). It was intense in Turkey; it existed in Cambodia as well (Chandler, 1983), intensified by tremendous violence during the civil war between 1970 and 1975; it expressed itself in repeated mass killing of Tutsis in Rwanda (des Forges, 1999); and it existed in Argentina, intensified by

[1] In Cambodia, especially, the focus on past national glory may have been not so much an expression of a feeling of superiority as a defense against feelings of inferiority. The glory of the Angkor empire faded hundreds of years earlier, and in the intervening centuries Cambodia was frequently invaded by others and ruled for very long periods by Vietnam and France.

the mutual violence between guerrilla groups, right-wing groups and the government preceding the disappearances (Staub, 1989a).

In Germany, an additional predisposing factor was the presence of war veterans. We now know about the existence and prolonged nature of post-traumatic stress disorder in Vietnam War veterans. The disorder was probably widespread among German veterans who had similar experiences – direct combat, a lost war, and lack of appreciation by society. Decline in self-esteem, loss of faith in the benevolence of the world and in legitimate authority, and a search for alternative authority are among the characteristics of this disorder in Vietnam veterans (Card, 1983; Egendorf, Kadushin, Laufer, Rothbart, & Sloan, 1981; Wilson, 1980; see also Herman, 1992). In Germany, they would have intensified needs created by the difficult life conditions and added to the guiding force of cultural predispositions. For example, they would have given special appeal to alternate authority, given the weakness and collapse of traditional authority.

Turning Against Others: Scapegoating and Ideology

Scapegoating and ideologies that arise in the face of difficult life conditions or group conflict are means for satisfying basic needs. However, they offer destructive satisfaction of basic needs in that they are likely to lead to harmful actions against others.

In the face of persistently difficult life conditions, already devalued outgroups are further devalued and scapegoated. Diminishing others is a way to elevate the self. Scapegoating protects a positive identity by reducing the feeling of responsibility for problems. By providing an explanation for problems, it offers the possibility of effective action or control – unfortunately, mainly in the form of taking action against the scapegoat. It can unite people against the scapegoated other, thereby fulfilling the need for positive connection and support in difficult times.

Adopting nationalistic and/or "better-world" ideologies offers a new comprehension of reality and, by promising a better future, hope as well. But usually some group is identified as the enemy that stands in the way of the ideology's fulfillment. By joining an ideological movement, people can relinquish a burdensome self to leaders or the group. They gain connection to others and a sense of significance in working for the ideology's fulfillment. Along the way, members of the "enemy" group, usually the group that is also scapegoated for life problems, are further devaluated and, in the end, often excluded from the moral realm. The moral values that protect people from violence become inoperative in relation to them (Staub, 1989a).

The ideology that the Nazis and Hitler offered the German people fit German culture. Its racial principle identified Aryans, and their supposedly best representatives, the Germans, as the superior race. The material

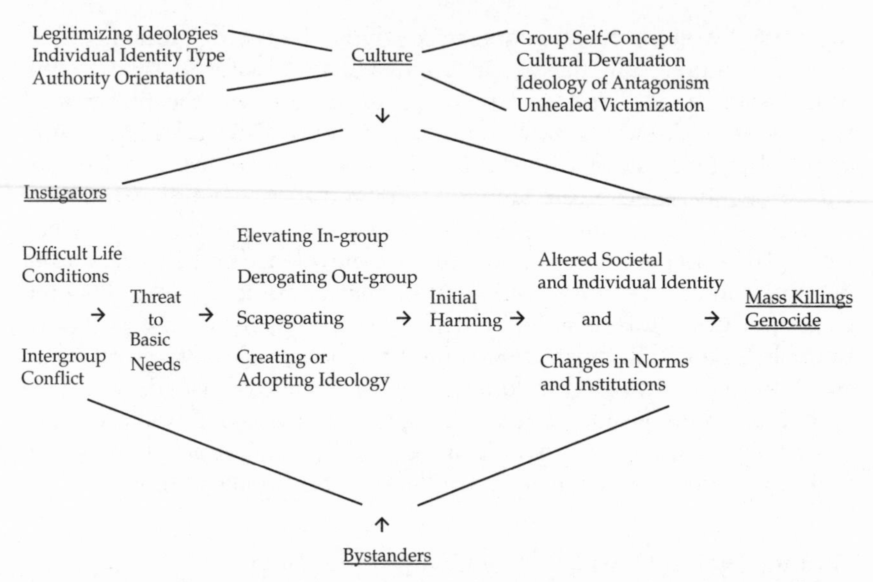

FIGURE 22.1. Influences and processes contributing to genocide and mass killing.

needs of the German people were to be fulfilled (and their superiority affirmed) through the conquest of additional territories, or living space. The ideology identified Jews as responsible for life problems and as a primary barrier to the creation of a pure, superior race. Later Jews were also identified as the internal enemy that joined the external enemy, the Soviet Union, to destroy Germany (Dawidowicz, 1975; Hilberg, 1961; Kren & Rappoport, 1980). In the *Fuhrerprinzip*, the leadership principle, the ideology prescribed obedience and offered the guidance of an absolute authority.

Ideology has been important in all the other instances of genocide as well. We may differentiate between "better-world" ideologies, which offer a vision of a better future for all human beings, and nationalistic ideologies, which promise a better life for a nation (Staub, 1989a). Although the German ideology was nationalistic, it had better-world components, in that racial purity was supposed to improve all humanity – except, of course, the impure, who were to be destroyed or subjugated.

In Turkey, the genocide of the Armenians was guided by a nationalistic ideology: pan-Turkism. Part of this was a vision of a new Turkish empire. In Cambodia, the genocide was guided by a Communist better-world ideology but with intense nationalistic components. To create a world of total social equality, all those privileged by their position, wealth, or education had to be eliminated or totally subjugated. In Rwanda, "Hutu power," the total elevation of Hutus over Tutsis, was a form of ideology (des Forges, 1999; Staub, 1999a). In Argentina, the mass killings partly evolved out of a conflict of interest between more and less privileged groups. However, the perpetrators of the mass killing were also protecting their worldview and subscribed to an intense anti-Communist ideology and visions of a Christian society (Staub, 1989a).

SELF-SELECTION AND THE SELECTION OF PERPETRATORS

Those who supported Hitler at the start, by voting for him, were quite heterogeneous with regard to class and occupation (Abraham, 1987; Platt, 1980). Initially, those who were perpetrators of violence were SA and SS members, and over time, increasingly SS members. They were joined by others as the evolution of violence progressed. A by now well-known example of this is the German auxiliary police, who were sent to kill Jews before the machinery of killing in the concentration and extermination camps was established (see Browning, 1992; Goldhagen, 1996). Some people in areas occupied by the Germans, like the Ukraine, Lithuania, and Latvia, also joined in the killing (Goldhagen, 1996), probably motivated by a combination of factors, including hostility toward the Soviet Union, of which they were part, which led them to join its enemy, the Germans; deep-seated anti-Semitism; and subservience to the occupiers and conquerors and the desire to gain their favor.

Members of the SS, who were central in the killing process, had strong authority orientation, along with a preference, and perhaps need, for a hierarchical system (Dicks, 1972; Steiner, 1980) that was even stronger than the general German orientation to authority. This may have been partly the result of self-selection (Staub, 1989a), partly of special training in obedience (Kren & Rappoport, 1980), partly of learning by doing (see later discussion). Other characteristics of SS members were belief in Nazi ideology and a preference for military-type activities (Steiner, 1980). The early SS joined Hitler to serve as his bodyguards at political meetings. Fighting political opponents was their first major task. Those who joined had to accept, if not welcome, violence.

The importance of ideology was also evident in the selection of ideologically devoted Nazi doctors for the euthanasia program, where they were the direct perpetrators of murder, and for the extermination camps, where they directed the killing process (Lifton, 1986). Given a cultural devaluation, the people who are attracted to an ideology that elevates them over others and promises them a better world need not be *personally* prejudiced against a devalued group that is designated as the enemy. They might have greater needs aroused in them by life problems or might carry more of the cultural predispositions that shape motivation and guide modes of dealing with them. However, in research concluded in 1933 on SS members, although not all respondents reported personal anti-Semitism, most of them were openly and viciously anti-Semitic (Merkl, 1980). The SS members who expressed the most intense anti-Semitism tended to be in leadership positions (Merkl, 1980).

The Role of Obedience

Since the dramatic experiments of Stanley Milgram (1965, 1974), obedience to authority has been viewed as a crucial determinant of the behavior of perpetrators. The importance of obedience is also suggested by the training that direct perpetrators receive in fostering submission to authority, whether the SS (Kren & Rappoport, 1980) or torturers in Greece (Gibson & Haritos-Fatouros, 1986; Haritos-Fatouros, 1988). It is suggested by the self-selection for the SS of individuals oriented to obedience (Dicks, 1972; Steiner, 1980) and the greater obedience in the Milgram experiments (Elms & Milgram, 1966) of high scorers on the F Scale, a measure of the "authoritarian personality." In Greece, the authorities selected especially obedient – as well as ideologically sympathetic – military police recruits for training as torturers (Gibson & Haritos-Fatouros, 1986; Haritos-Fatouros, 1988).

However, many of the direct perpetrators are usually not simply forced or pressured by authorities to obey. Instead, they *join* leaders and decision makers, or a movement that shapes and guides them to become perpetrators. Decision makers and direct perpetrators share a *cultural-societal tilt*. They are part of the same culture and experience the same life problems; they probably respond with similar needs and share the inclination for the same potentially destructive modes of their fulfillment. Many who become direct perpetrators voluntarily join the movement and enter roles that in the end lead them to perpetrate mass killing.

The Role of Leaders

Leaders who propagate scapegoating and destructive ideologies are often seen as acting to gain followers or consolidate their following. Even Gordon Allport (1954) suggested that this was the case with Hitler. However, leaders are members of their group, affected by the instigators that affect the rest of the group and by cultural characteristics that predispose the group to violence. For example, in previously victimized groups the leaders, like the rest of the population, tend to carry unhealed wounds. It is this joining of the needs and inclination of populations and leaders that creates great danger of mass killing or genocide.

While in difficult times groups often turn to leaders with the potential to generate violence, and while leading the group toward constructive resolution of life problems and group conflicts can be difficult and dangerous, except under the most extreme conditions leaders still have the potential to try to do so. Instead, unfortunately, leaders and elites often propagate scapegoating and destructive ideologies, use propaganda against devalued groups and "enemies," and create paramilitary groups or other institutions that become instruments of violence (Staub, 1999b).

LEARNING BY DOING, EVOLUTION, AND STEPS ALONG THE CONTINUUM OF DESTRUCTION

Mass killing or genocide is usually the outcome of an evolution that starts with discrimination and limited acts of harm-doing. Harming people changes the perpetrators (and the whole society) and prepares them for more harmful acts.

In a number of studies with children, my associates and I found that involving children in efforts to help other children – for example, having them spend time making toys for poor, hospitalized children or teaching younger children – increased their later helping behavior (Staub, 1975, 1979, 1986). Prior helping (Harris, 1972) and even the expressed intention to help (W. DeJong, 1979; Freedman & Fraser, 1966) also increase adults' later helping. Similarly, harming others increases the degree of harm people subsequently inflict on others. When "teachers" shock "learners" who make mistakes on a task, teachers who set their own shock levels increase the intensity of shock over trials (Buss, 1966; Goldstein, Davis, & Herman, 1975). This is the case even with control for the learner's error rate (Goldstein et al., 1975).

People learn and change as a result of their own actions (Staub, 1979, 1989a). When they harm other people, a number of consequences are likely to follow. First, they come to devalue the victims more (Berkowitz, 1962; Goldstein et al., 1975; Sykes & Matza, 1957; Staub, 1978). While in the real world devaluation normally precedes harm-doing, additional devaluation makes greater mistreatment and violence possible. Just-world thinking (Lerner, 1980; Lerner & Simmons, 1966) may be an important mechanism in this. Assuming that the world is just, and that people who suffer must have brought their fate on themselves by their actions or character, ironically, perpetrators are likely to devalue people they themselves have harmed. The self-perception of perpetrators is also likely to change (Bem, 1972; Grusec, Kuczynski, Rushton, & Simutis, 1978; Staub, 1979). They come to see themselves as able and willing to engage in harmful, violent acts – against certain people, and for good reasons, including higher ideals embodied in an ideology.

Personal goal theory (Staub, 1980) suggests moral equilibration (Staub, 1989a) as another mechanism of change. When a conflict exists between moral value(s) and other motives, people can reduce the conflict by replacing the moral value with another value that either is less stringent or is not a moral value but is treated like one. Eisenberg (1986) reported research findings that support such a process: Cost and other conditions led both children and adults to shift to less evolved moral reasoning. The Nazis replaced respect for the lives of certain people with the values of racial purity, and obedience and loyalty to leaders.

Consistent with this model, in Nazi Germany there was a progression of "steps along a continuum of destruction." First, Jews were thrown out of government jobs and the military, then from other important positions. They were pressured into selling their businesses and later were forced to sell. Marriage and sexual relations between Jews and Aryan Germans were prohibited. Having lost all their property, earning their livelihood with menial jobs, and identified by yellow stars, the Jews were moved into ghettos. In addition to sporadic violence against them, there was organized violence (e.g., the Kristallnacht, in 1938). Many Jews were taken to concentration camps (Dawidowicz, 1975; Hilberg, 1961) before mass extermination.

Steps along a continuum of destruction often start long before those who lead a society to genocide come to power. In Turkey, the legal rights of Armenians and other minorities were limited for centuries. Armenians were the frequent victims of violence. From 1894 to 1896, over 200,000 Armenians were killed by special troops created mainly for this purpose (Greene, 1895; Toynbee, 1915). In Rwanda, about 50,000 Tutsis were killed in 1959, with massacres of large numbers of Tutsis in the early 1960s and 1970s and sporadic killings of smaller numbers after that (des Forges, 1999; Prunier, 1995).

Harm doing and violence normally expand. Even when torture was part of the legal process in Europe, in the Middle Ages, over time the circle of its victims enlarged. First it was used only with lower-class defendants, later also with upper-class defendants, and then even with *witnesses*, in order to obtain information from them (Peters, 1985). In Germany, in addition to the increasing mistreatment of Jews, other forms of violence, such as the euthanasia program and the killing of mentally retarded, mentally ill, and physically deformed Germans (Dawidowicz, 1975; Lifton, 1986) – who in the Nazis' view diminished the genetic quality of the German race – contributed to psychological and institutional change and the possibility of greater violence. In Rwanda, in addition to Tutsis, Hutus who were seen as politically moderate or as not supportive of the leadership were also targeted (des Forges, 1999). In the course of the genocide, some Hutus were killed for personal reasons, and in addition to Tutsi women, some Hutu women were also raped.

In both Argentina and Cambodia, the form of the evolution was not simply increasing violence against the victim group but a cycle of increasing violence between opposing parties. In Cambodia, the Khmer Rouge and government forces fought each other with increasing brutality from 1970 to 1975. In Argentina, left-wing guerrilla groups abducted and killed people, blew up buildings, and created chaos, while right-wing death squads were killing people identified as left-wing enemies. In both cases one of these parties became the perpetrator of extreme violence. The circle of victims was tremendously enlarged beyond those who participated in the initial cycle of violence.

In the course of this evolution, the perpetrators exclude the victims from the moral universe. Moral principles become inapplicable to them (Staub, 1989a). The prohibitions that normally inhibit violence lose force. The killing of the victims can become a goal in its own right. Fanatic commitment develops to the ideology and to the specific goal of eliminating the victims. Even goals basic to persons and groups, like self-protection, come to be subordinated to this "higher" goal (Staub, 1989b; von Maltitz, 1973), which becomes the dominant guide to action. There is a reverse of morality, so that killing becomes the right thing to do. The example of terrorist groups shows that even life itself can be subordinated when overriding fanatic commitment has developed to a murderous cause.

Group processes come to dominate the psychology of perpetrators. Embedded in a group, trained in submission to authority, and further indoctrinated in ideology, people give up individual decision making to the group and its leaders (Milgram, 1974; Zimbardo, 1969). The "We" acquires substantial power, in place of the "I." With the boundaries of the self weakened, there will be emotional contagion, the spread of feelings among group members (Milgram & Toch, 1969; Staub, 1987; Staub & Rosenthal, 1994), and shared reactions to events. The members' perception of reality will be shaped by their shared belief system and by the support they receive from each other in interpreting events. Deviation from the group becomes increasingly unlikely (Staub, 1989a; Toch, 1965).

As a whole society moves along the continuum of destruction, there is a *resocialization* in beliefs, values, and standards of conduct. New institutions emerge that serve repression, discrimination, and the mistreatment of identified victims. They represent new realities, a new status quo. Paramilitary groups develop into institutions of murder (des Forges, 1999). For example, in Guatemala a civilian group was created, "who killed and abducted on the orders of G-2," the intelligence division of the Guatemalan army. This group acquired a life of its own and also began to initiate killings (Nairn & Simon, 1986).

THE PSYCHOLOGY OF BYSTANDERS

In the face of the increasing suffering of a subgroup of society, bystanders frequently remain silent, passive – both *internal* bystanders and *external* ones, other nations and outside groups (Staub, 1989a, 1999a). Bystanders also learn and change as a result of their own action – or inaction. Passivity in the face of others' suffering makes it difficult to remain in internal opposition to the perpetrators and to feel empathy for the victims. To reduce their own feelings of empathic distress and guilt, passive bystanders will distance themselves from victims (Staub, 1978). Just-world thinking will lead them to see victims as deserving their fate, and to devalue them. While in Cambodia the population was completely brutalized, in Turkey and Germany, and initially in Argentina, the majority accepted, if not supported, the perpetrators' actions. In Rwanda, a small but significant percentage of the population participated in killings.

Most Germans participated in the system, in small ways such as using the Hitler salute (Bettelheim, 1979) and through organizations and group activities. Moreover, as bystanders, most Germans were not just passive: They were *semiactive participants*. They boycotted Jewish stores and broke intimate relationships and friendships with Jews. Many benefited in some way from the Jews' fate, by assuming their jobs and buying their businesses. Repeatedly the population initiated anti-Jewish actions before government orders, such as businesses' firing Jewish employees or not giving them paid vacations (Hilberg, 1961).

The German population shared a societal tilt with perpetrators – the cultural background and difficult life conditions, and the resulting needs and the inclination to satisfy them in certain ways. This might have made the Nazi movement acceptable to many who did not actually join. Moreover, after Hitler came to power, the lives of most Germans substantially improved (Craig, 1982): They had jobs and they were part of a community in which there was a spirit of togetherness and shared destiny.[2]

Their passivity, semiactive participation, and connections to the system had to change the German people, in ways similar to the changes in perpetrators. Consistency theories, and specifically balance theory (Heider, 1958), suggest that given Hitler's hatred for the Jews, the Germans' gratitude to and admiration of Hitler (Craig, 1982) would have intensified their anti-Jewish attitudes. The majority apparently came to accept and even support the persecution of Jews (Staub, 1989a). Others became perpetrators themselves.

The Berlin Psychoanalytic Institute

Some members of the Berlin Psychoanalytic Institute provide an example of bystanders who became perpetrators (Staub, 1989b). Many members left Germany. Those who remained presumably had at least tolerance for

[2] In June 1987, I gave a lecture at the University of Trier, in Germany, on the psychology of genocide. I asked my hosts beforehand, and they kindly arranged for me a meeting with a group of older Germans who lived under Hitler – 20 individuals aged 60 to 75. In our 4-hour-long discussion, these people repeatedly and spontaneously returned to the satisfactions they experienced under Hitler. They could not keep away from it. They talked about far more than just the material security or the existence of jobs and a livelihood. The camaraderie and feelings of community sitting around campfires, singing songs, and sharing other experiences of connection and group spirit stood out in their memories.

the Nazi system from the start. Over time, they changed. They accepted a new name, the Goering Institute, and a new head, the cousin of the second-ranking Nazi, Hermann Goering. They were silent when Jewish colleagues were removed (and used ideologically based euphemisms to refer to them – e.g., not pure Germans). Some of the members advanced ideas or reinterpreted psychoanalytic concepts to support the Nazi ideology (Friedrich, 1989). Ideas, such as the theory of sluggish schizophrenia used in the Soviet Union to place dissidents in mental hospitals (Bloch & Reddaway, 1977), can be important steps along the psychological continuum of destruction. In Germany, the evolution of ideas about eugenics before Hitler came to power formed a basis of the euthanasia program (Lifton, 1986) and probably contributed to the Nazi ideology itself. In the end some institute members participated in the euthanasia program, and some became perpetrators in the extermination of Jews (Lifton, 1986; Staub, 1989a).

In the other instances as well, bystanders were either passive or supportive of perpetrators. In Argentina, the violence by guerrilla groups created fear in the population. When the military took over the government, a recurrent event in Argentina during the post–World War II years, the population initially supported the kidnappings the military began. Discomfort and protests, limited by the fear that the military generated, began only much later, as it became apparent that anybody could become a victim. In Turkey, much of the population either accepted or supported the persecution of Armenians (Staub, 1989a). In Cambodia, once the Khmer Rouge won the civil war and the killings and the use of people in slave labor began, most people were part of either the perpetrator or the victim group.

Other Nations as Bystanders

Fear contributed to the passivity of internal bystanders, in Germany and elsewhere. External bystanders, other nations and organizations outside Germany, had little to fear, especially at the start of Jewish persecution, when Germany was weak. Still, there was little response (Wyman, 1984). In 1936, after many Nazi atrocities, the whole world went to Berlin to participate in the Olympics, thereby affirming Nazi Germany. American corporations were busy doing business in Germany during most of the 1930s.

Christian dogma was a source of anti-Semitism in the whole Western world. It designated Jews as the killers of Christ and fanned their persecution for many centuries in response to their unwillingness to convert (Girard, 1980; Hilberg, 1961). It was a source of discrimination and mistreatment, which led to murder and further devaluation. In the end, profound religious-cultural devaluation of Jews characterized many Christian nations.

In addition, people outside Germany were also likely to engage in just-world thinking and to further devalue Jews in response to their suffering in Germany. The German propaganda against Jews also reached the outside world. Moscovici's (1973, 1980) research suggests that even seemingly unreasonably extreme statements about attitude objects have influence, if initially not on behavior, then at least on underlying attitudes. As a consequence of these processes, anti-Semitism increased in the Western world in the 1930s, in the United States reaching a peak around 1938 (Wyman, 1968, 1984).

These were some of the reasons for the silence and passivity. Among other reasons for nations to remain passive in face of the mistreatment by a government of its citizens are their unwillingness to interfere in the "domestic affairs" of another country (which could be a precedent for others interfering in their internal affairs) and the economic (trade) and other benefits they can gain from positive relations with the offending nation (Staub, 1999a).

At the time of the genocide of the Armenians, Turkey was fighting in World War I. Nations already fighting against Turkey in the war, perhaps not surprisingly, did speak out against the atrocities. As Turkey's ally, Germany might have been able to exert influence on Turkish policy, but it did not try to do so (Trumpener, 1968). At the time of the disappearances in Argentina, most nations of the world were silent. The Carter administration did speak out against the policy and helped some people in danger, but it took no serious action, such as a boycott, against the Argentine government.

Rwanda presents a recent, disturbing example of international passivity. The civil war began in 1990, with the Rwandan Patriotic Front, a small group of Tutsis who were refugees from prior violence against Tutsis or their descendants, entering the country as a military force. The French immediately began to provide military aid to the government. France continued its aid in subsequent years without protesting the occasional killings of hundreds of Tutsi peasants. Before the genocide began in April 1994, there were warnings of impending violence by human rights organizations. The commander of United Nations peacekeepers received confidential information that a genocide was being planned and asked his superiors permission to destroy arms that were being assembled. He was instructed to do nothing. After the genocide began, most of the UN peacekeepers were withdrawn. The United States and other nations went to extreme lengths to avoid the use of the term *genocide*, while about 700,000 Tutsis were killed over a period of 3 months, between two thirds and three fourths of the total Tutsi population. Apparently the purpose in not using the word *genocide* was to avoid invoking the UN Genocide Convention and thereby the moral obligation to respond (des Forges, 1999; Gourevitch, 1998).

Silence and passivity change bystanders, whether they are individuals or whole nations. They can diminish the subsequent likelihood of protest and punitive action by them. In turn, they encourage perpetrators, who often interpret silence as support for their policies (Staub, 1989a; Taylor, 1983). Complicity by bystanders is likely to encourage perpetrators even more.

THE POWER OF BYSTANDERS

Could bystanders make a difference in halting or preventing mass killing and genocide? Some lines of research and the evidence of real events indicate bystanders' potential to exert influence.

Whether or not one person verbally defines the meaning of a seeming emergency as an emergency greatly affects the response of other bystanders (Bickman, 1972; Staub, 1974). When bystanders remain passive, they substantially reduce the likelihood that other bystanders will respond (Latané & Darley, 1970; Staub, 1978).

Real-life events also show the influence of bystanders, even on perpetrators. In Denmark, the climate of support for Jews apparently influenced some German officials. They delayed deportation orders, which gave the Danish population the time needed to mount and complete a massive rescue effort, taking the approximately 7,000 Danish Jews to neutral Sweden in small boats. In Bulgaria, the actions of varied segments of the population, including demonstrations, stopped the government from handing over the country's Jewish population to the Germans (Fein, 1979). Even within Germany, in spite of the Nazi repression, the population could exert influence. When the euthanasia program became known, some segments of the population protested: the Catholic clergy, some lawyers' groups, the relatives of people killed, and those in danger. As a result, the official program of euthanasia killing was discontinued (Dawidowicz, 1975; Lifton, 1986). There was little response, however, to the mistreatment of Jews. Added to anti-Semitism and other cultural preconditions, the *gradual* increase in mistreatment would have contributed to passivity.

Hitler's attitude also indicates the potential power of bystanders. He and his fellow Nazis were greatly concerned about the reactions of the population to their early anti-Jewish actions, and they were both surprised and emboldened by the lack of adverse reactions (Dawidowicz, 1975; Hilberg, 1961). As I have noted, the population even initiated actions against Jews, which further shaped Nazi views (Staub, 1989a) and stimulated additional official "measures" (Hilberg, 1961).

In the French Huguenot village of Le Chambon, under the leadership of their pastor, André Trocme, the inhabitants saved several thousand refugees, a large percentage of them children (Hallie, 1979). The behavior of the villagers influenced members of the Vichy police. Telephone calls to the presbytery began to inform villagers of impending raids, which enabled them to send the refugees into the neighboring forest. The deeds of the village doctor, who was executed, and his words at his trial influenced a German major, who in turn persuaded a higher officer not to move against the village (Hallie, 1979).

There is also evidence that the practice of torture diminishes in response to negative publicity and reactions by "external bystanders." This was demonstrably the case in South American countries (Stover & Nightingale, 1985). But frequently there is resistance to taking action not only within nations but also in smaller institutions. The practice of putting dissidents into mental hospitals had continued for a long time in the former Soviet Union. A detailed case history showed the resistance of the International Medical Association to condemn this practice (Bloch & Reddaway, 1984). Often organizations, while they may encourage their members to act, do not want to act as institutions, even when their weight and influence are needed. Lack of punitive action or even of condemnation by important bystanders, or support by some, may negate the efforts of others and encourage and affirm perpetrators.

In Iran, after the fundamentalist revolution, the persecution of the Baha'i, a long-persecuted community, has intensified. Over 200 Baha'i were executed in a short period of time. Representations by Baha'i living in other countries to their own governments and to the international community led to UN resolutions, as well as resolutions by individual nations condemning the persecution of the Baha'i in Iran. This led to a cessation of further executions (Bigelow, 1993), although they resumed on a much smaller scale in the 1990s. The international boycott of South Africa apparently also had important influence, which contributed to the abolition of apartheid and the change in government.

By speaking out and taking action, bystanders can elevate values prohibiting violence, which over time perpetrators had come to ignore in their treatment of the victim group. Most groups, but especially ideologically committed ones, have difficulty seeing themselves, having a perspective on their own actions and evolution (Staub, 1989a). They need others as mirrors. Through sanctions bystanders can also make the perpetrators' actions costly to them and induce fear of later punitive action. The earlier bystanders speak out and act, the more likely that they can counteract prior steps along the continuum of destruction or inhibit further evolution (see Staub, 1989a; 1999a). Once commitment to the destruction of a group has developed, and the destruction is in process, nonforceful reactions by bystanders will tend to be ineffective.

THE RANGE OF APPLICABILITY OF THIS CONCEPTION

The conception presented in this chapter can be applied, with modifications, to many forms of mistreatment by groups of members of other groups. It can be used in a tight, even predictive, manner, or as a framework theory that offers understanding. To use it in prediction (and therefore hopefully in prevention), the degree to which the components are present in a specific instance – the level of difficult life conditions and of relevant cultural characteristics, the point at which the group is located on a continuum of destruction, and the activities of bystanders – must be carefully assessed (Staub, 1989a, 1999a). The theory needs to be appropriately modified as it is applied to varied forms of group hostility, in varied contexts. The history of a group, relationships between groups, and the form and nature of any group conflicts must be assessed, and the influences specified here examined in relation to the specific and particular context.

In certain cases difficult life conditions may increase the likelihood of a group turning against others, but they are not central starting points. Even group conflict, where each side wants something from the other, may not be important. The motivation for violence may not originate in the frustration of basic needs described earlier. This is primarily the case when genocide or mass killing develops out of self-interest, as in the destruction of the Ache Indians in Paraguay in the service of the economic development of the forests that were their home. In cases of mass killing or genocide of indigenous peoples (Hitchcock & Twedt, 1997), self-interest is often a central motive. However, difficult life conditions and a history of conflict between groups still make such violence more likely. Intense devaluation of the victim group, which is often present in extreme forms, and other cultural characteristics are central contributors.

In certain cases of group conflict, including what has recently been called *ethnopolitical violence*, "ideologies of antagonism" (Staub, 1989a, 1992a, 1999a) may be a cultural condition that easily gives rise to the motivation for violence. This refers to the outcome of a long history of hostility and mutual violence. Such ideologies are worldviews in which another group is perceived as an implacable enemy, bent on one's destruction. The welfare of one's own group is best served by the other's demise. Economic or other gains by the antagonist group can be experienced as a threat to one's own group and/or group self-concept and can activate hostile motives. While a history of hostility and violence can create a realistic fear of the other, usually the extremely negative view of the other is resistant to changes in reality. The group's identity or self-definition has come to include enmity toward the other. Ideologies of antagonism seemed to have roles in the start or maintenance of violence in the former Yugoslavia, between Israelis and Palestinians, and in Rwanda. They can have an important role even if only a segment of a population holds the ideology.

Difficult life conditions are also not primary initiators of hostility and war that are based on essential conflicts of interest. The beginning of the

Palestinian-Israeli hostility is an example of this, with the two groups claiming the same territory as living space. While the conflict of interests has been real, certainly much more so than in a case like the Falklands War, negotiation resulting in compromise that fulfills the essential needs of both groups (Rouhana & Kelman, 1994) was slowed by psychological elements such as identification by both groups with a particular territory and perceptions or beliefs about the other that, among some part of the membership, probably amounted to ideologies of antagonism.

Using the theory presented here, for example, considering cultural characteristics other than devaluation by itself, which is a defining characteristic of racism, as well as instigating conditions, can help us better understand racism. It can help us understand other types of violence as well, for example, youth violence (Staub, 1996) and the unnecessary use of force by police against citizens (Staub, 1992a, 2002). Police violence involves intense us – them differentiation and the devaluation of citizens by the police, an evolution of increasing violence with changes in norms and standards as part of the group's culture, and passive bystanders (which includes fellow officers and superiors). It is intensified by difficult life conditions (Staub, 1992a, 2002).

Much of the theory is also applicable to terrorism. Terrorism is violence by small groups against noncombatants. It occurs in response to difficult life conditions and/or group conflict which frustrate basic needs, reduce opportunities and hope, create perceptions of injustice, and the experience of having been wronged. At times, great culture change and the inability of people to integrate tradition with new ways of life play a role. The impact of culture change is especially great on people living in societies that are both traditional and repressive.

Small terrorist groups are often less radical at the start. They may begin trying to bring about political and social changes working within the political system (McCauley & Segal, 1989). Over time, they become more radical, due to a combination of the difficulty in bringing about change and dynamics within the group, with members affirming their status and identity by advocating more extreme positions in the direction of already established ideology. The ideology, which is invariably present, becomes more radical, and the devaluation of and hostility toward the ideological enemy more intense. The violence, once it begins, intensifies.

When the theory requires some adjustment appropriate to types of violence and context, many elements of it are still usually present in generating group violence. These minimally include a history of devaluation of the other, the evolution of destructiveness (which has sometimes occurred over a long period preceding a flare-up of current antagonism), and the role of bystanders. Usually, some form of destructive ideology and then ideological justification for violence also exist. A further qualification of the theory in certain instances, such as deep-seated ethnic conflicts, would be that when groups have already progressed far along the continuum of destruction, it is more difficult for bystanders to exert influence.

OTHER VIEWS OF INTERGROUP CONFLICT

We do not have psychological theories of the origins of group violence to compare with this theory. There are, however, varied theories of intergroup relations and conflict. Realistic group conflict theory (LeVine & Campbell, 1972) emphasizes conflicts over scarce, tangible resources. Frustration-aggression-displacement theory (LeVine & Campbell, 1972) identifies frustration within the group as a source of scapegoating and hostility toward other groups. Psychocultural interpretation theory (Volkan, 1988) points to dispositions in groups that lead to threats to identity and fears of survival, which interfere with the resolution of ethnic conflict. Social identity theory (Tajfel, 1982; Turner, 1987) has stressed that individuals' identity is to a substantial degree a social identity, based on membership in a group. Social categorization, the classification of individuals into different categories, leads to stereotyping and discrimination. The desire for a favorable social comparison is an important motive that leads to elevation of one's group by diminishing and discriminating against others. This enhances group self-concept and individual self-esteem.

Aspects of these theories are congenial to the theory presented here, with realistic group conflict theory, which in its basic form assumes that conflict is purely over real, material resources, as well as power, without considering psychological elements, the least congenial. The present theory, which may be called *sociocultural motivation theory*, focuses on a multiplicity of interacting influences, with intense group violence as their outcome. They include cultural dispositions, life conditions, and group conflict. While life conditions and group conflict create frustration and the experience of threat, they do not directly lead to violence. The theory identifies the way groups attempt to satisfy basic needs as the starting point for the evolution of increasing violence.

While the social nature of individual identity is important, except when the role of prior devaluation or an ideology of antagonism is predominant, it is not social comparison but other motives that are regarded as central in leading a group to turn against others. The essential and unique aspects of the present theory include focus on change or evolution in individuals and groups, the potential of bystanders to influence this evolution, and the necessity to consider how a multiplicity of factors interact.

THE PSYCHOLOGY OF HEROIC HELPERS

In the midst of violence and passivity, some people in Germany and Nazi-occupied Europe endangered their lives to save Jews. To do so, helpers of German origin had to distance themselves from their group. Some rescuers were marginal to their community: They had a different religious background, were new to the community, or had a parent of foreign birth (London, 1970; Tec, 1986). This perhaps enabled them to maintain an independent perspective and not join the group's increasing devaluation of Jews. Many rescuers came from families with strong moral values and held strong moral and humanitarian values themselves, with an aversion to Nazism (London, 1970; Oliner & Oliner, 1988). Many were "inclusive" and regarded people in groups other than their own as human beings to whom human considerations apply (Oliner & Oliner, 1988). Interviews with rescuers and the rescued indicate that individual rescuers were characterized by one or more of the three primary motivators that have been proposed for altruistic helping: a value of caring or "prosocial orientation" (Staub 1974, 1978, 1995), with its focus on the welfare of people and a feeling of personal responsibility to help; moral rules or principles, the focus on living up to or fulfilling the principle or rule; and empathy, the vicarious experience of others' suffering (London, 1970; Oliner & Oliner, 1988; Tec, 1986). These were often accompanied by a hatred of Nazism.

Marginality in relation to the perpetrators or to the dominant group does not mean that rescuers were disconnected from people. In the largest study to date, Sam and Pearl Oliner (1988) found that rescuers were deeply connected to their families and/or other people. They described a large proportion (52%) of rescuers as "normocentric," or norm centered, characterized by "a feeling of obligation to a special reference group with whom the actor identified and whose explicit and implicit values he feels obliged to obey." Some normocentric rescuers were guided by internalized group norms, but many followed the guidance of leaders who set a policy of rescue. Some belonged to resistance groups, church groups, or families that influenced them. In Belgium, where the queen and the government-in-exile and church leaders set the tone, most of the nation refused to cooperate with anti-Jewish policies, and the underground actively helped Jews, who as a result were highly active in helping themselves (Fein, 1979). But normocentric influence can lead people in varied directions. In Poland, some priests and resistance groups helped Jews, while other priests encouraged their communities to support the Nazi persecution of Jews, and some resistance groups killed Jews (Tec, 1986).

Many rescuers started out by helping a Jew with whom they had a past relationship. Some were asked by a Jewish friend or acquaintance to help. The personal relationship would have made it more likely that altruistic-moral motives as well as relationship-based motives would become active. Having helped someone they knew, many continued to help.

Even in ordinary times a feeling of competence is usually required for the expression of motivation in action, or even for its arousal (Ajzen, 1988; Bandura, 1989; Staub, 1978, 1980). When action endangers one's life, such "supporting characteristics" (Staub, 1980) become crucial. Faith in their own competence and intuition, fearlessness, and high tolerance for risk are among the characteristics of rescuers derived from interviews both with rescuers and with the people they helped (London, 1970; Oliner & Oliner, 1988; Tec, 1986).

Although this is less supported by a body of evidence, it seems that some rescuers were adventurous and pursued risky, dangerous activities in their earlier lives (London, 1970). Adventurousness might reduce the perceived risk and enhance the feeling of competence to help. According to personal goal theory, it may also partly transform the risk to potential satisfaction, adding a source of motivation.

Heroic helpers are not born. An analysis of two specific cases shows the roots and evolution of heroism. The many-faceted influences at work can be seen in the case of Raoul Wallenberg, who saved the lives of tens of thousands of Hungarian Jews (Marton, 1982). Wallenberg was a member of a poor branch of an influential Swedish family. He had wide-ranging travel and work experience and was trained as an architect. In 1944, he was the partner of a Hungarian Jewish refugee in an import-export business. He had traveled to Hungary several times on business, where he visited his partner's relatives. Earlier, while working in a bank in Haifa, he encountered Jewish refugees arriving from Nazi Germany, which was likely to arouse his empathy. In 1944, he seemed restless and dissatisfied with his career.

On his partner's recommendation, Wallenberg was approached by a representative of the American War Refugee Board and asked to go to Hungary as a Swedish diplomat to attempt to save the lives of Hungarian Jews who were then being deported to and killed at Auschwitz. He agreed to go. There was no predominant motive guiding his life at the time, like a valued career, which according to personal goal theory would have reduced his openness to activators of a conflicting motive. The request probably served to focus responsibility on him (Staub, 1978), his connection to his business partner and his partner's relatives enhancing this feeling of responsibility. Familiarity with Hungary and a wide range of past experience in traveling, studying, and working in many places around the world must have added to his feeling of competence. In Hungary, he repeatedly risked his life, subordinating everything to the cause of saving Jewish lives (Marton, 1982).

Wallenberg's commitment seemingly increased over time, although it appears that once he got involved, his motivation to help was immediately high. Another well-known rescuer, Oscar Schindler (Keneally, 1982), clearly progressed along a "continuum of benevolence." He was a German born in Czechoslovakia. In his youth, he raced motorcycles. As a Protestant, he left his village to marry a Catholic girl from another village. Thus, he was doubly marginal and also adventurous. Both his father and his wife were opposed to Hitler. Still, he joined the Nazi Party and followed the

German troops to Poland, where he took over a confiscated factory and, using Jewish slave labor, proceeded to enrich himself.

However, in contrast to others in a similar situation, Schindler responded to the humanity of his slave laborers. From the start, he talked with them and listened to them. He celebrated birthdays with them. He began to help them in small and large ways. In some rescuers, the motivation to help followed witnessing the murder or brutal treatment of a Jew (Oliner & Oliner, 1988). Schindler had a number of such experiences. His actions resulted in two arrests and brief imprisonments from which he freed himself by invoking real and imaginary connections to important Nazis. Both Schindler and Wallenberg possessed considerable personal power and seemed to enjoy exercising this power to save lives.

To protect his slave laborers from the murderous concentration camp Plaszow, Schindler persuaded the Nazis to allow him to build a camp next to his factory. As the Soviet army advanced, Schindler moved his laborers to his hometown, where he created a fake factory that produced nothing, its only purpose to protect the Jewish laborers. In the end, Schindler lost all the wealth he had accumulated in Poland but saved about 1,200 lives.

Like perpetrators and bystanders, heroic helpers evolve. Some of them develop fanatic commitment to their goal (Staub, 1989a). The usual fanatics subordinate themselves to a movement that serves abstract ideals. They come to disregard the welfare and lives of at least some people as they strive to fulfill these ideals. I regard some of the rescuers as "good fanatics," who completely devoted themselves to the *concrete* aim of saving lives.

Probably in every genocide and mass killing there are heroic helpers, but there is a significant body of scholarship only on rescuers of Jews in Nazi Europe. In Rwanda, as well, there were Hutus who acted to save Tutsis. A very few spoke out publicly against the killings, and some or perhaps all of these were killed (des Forges, 1999). In 1999, I interviewed a few people who were rescued and one rescuer in Rwanda, enough only to gain some impressions (Staub, 2000; Staub & Pearlman, 2001). Rwanda is a highly religious country, and while some high-level church leaders betrayed the Tutsis and became accomplices to genocide (des Forges, 1999; Gourevitch, 1998; Prunier, 1995), it seems from the reports of those who were rescued that some of the rescuers acted out of religious motives, living up to religious ideals. (Research by Oliner & Oliner [1988] suggested that about 15% of rescuers of Jews acted out of religious motives.) Another impression that came out of the interviews was that perhaps because of the horrible nature of the violence in Rwanda, where in addition to the military and paramilitary groups with many very young members, some people killed neighbors and some even betrayed members of their own families who had a Tutsi or mixed ethnic background, some of those who were rescued did not trust the motives or character of their rescuers. They could not quite believe that these motives were truly benevolent rather than based on some kind of self-interest.

The research on rescuers of Jews and other information suggest that over time the range of concern of engaged helpers usually expands. For example, the Mothers of the Plaza del Mayo in Argentina began to march in the plaza to protest the disappearances of their own children. They endured persecution, and some were kidnapped. However, as they continued to march, they developed a strong commitment to universal human rights and freedom (Staub, 1989a), a concern about the persecution and suffering of people in general.

THE HEROISM OF SURVIVORS

The heroism of rescuers has slowly come to be known, acknowledged, and celebrated. The heroism of survivors has remained, however, largely unrecognized. Parents, often in the face of impossible odds that can immobilize people, took courageous and determined actions to save their families. Children themselves often showed initiative, judgment, courage, and maturity that greatly exceeded what we normally imagine children to be capable of.

In information I gathered, primarily from child survivors (who were less than 13 years of age when the Holocaust began), in conversations and questionnaires, they described many amazing acts, of their own and of their parents. Parents found ways to hide children, so that they might live even if the parents were killed. Young children lived with an assumed identity, for example, as a Catholic child in a boarding school. One survivor was a seven-year-old child in a hospital. She has already recovered from scarlet fever but to be safe remained in the hospital. There was a raid on the hospital, so she put on clothes that were hidden under her mattress and walked out of the building, through a group of uniformed men, to the house of a friendly neighbor ten blocks away who brought her the clothes in the first place.

Their actions, which saved their own lives and the lives of others, were in turn likely to shape these survivors' personality. It was probably an important source of the capacity of many of them, in spite of the wounds inflicted by their victimization, to lead highly effective lives.[3]

[3] (Summary of material from E. Staub, Another form of heroism: Survivors saving themselves and its impact on their lives. Unpublished manuscript, University of Massachusetts at Amherst. Draft of chapter to appear in O. Feldman and P. Tetlock, *Personality and politics: Essays in honor of Peter Suedfeld*, in preparation).

THE OBLIGATION OF BYSTANDERS

We cannot expect bystanders to sacrifice their lives for others. But we can expect individuals, groups, and nations to act early along a continuum of destruction, when the danger to themselves is limited, and the potential exists for inhibiting the evolution of increasing destructiveness. This will only happen if people – children, adults, whole societies – develop an awareness of their common humanity with other people, as well as of the psychological processes in themselves that turn them against others. Institutions and modes of functioning can develop that embody a shared humanity and make exclusion from the moral realm more difficult. Healing from past victimization (Staub, 1998), building systems of positive reciprocity, creating crosscutting relations (Deutsch, 1973) between groups, and developing joint projects (Pettigrew, 1997) and superordinate goals can promote the evolution of caring and nonaggressive persons and societies (Staub, 1989a, 1992b, 1999a).

References

Abraham, D. (1987). *The collapse of the Weimar Republic.* New York: Holmes and Meier.

Ajzen, I. (1988). *Attitudes, personality and behavior.* Chicago: Dorsey Press.

Allport, G. (1954). *The nature of prejudice.* Reading MA: Addison-Wesley.

Bandura, A. (1989). Human agency in social cognitive theory. *American Psychologist, 44,* 1175–1184.

Bandura, A., Underwood, B., & Fromson, M. E. (1975). Disinhibition of aggression through diffusion of responsibility and dehumanization of victims. *Journal of Research in Personality, 9,* 253–269.

Bem, D. L. (1972). Self-perception theory. In L. Berkowitz. (Ed.), *Advances in experimental social psychology* (Vol. 6). New York: Academic Press.

Berkowitz, L. (1962). *Aggression: A social psychological analysis.* New York: McGraw-Hill.

Bettelheim, B. (1979). Remarks on the psychological appeal of totalitarianism. In *Surviving and other essays.* New York: Vintage.

Bickman, L. (1972). Social influence and diffusion of responsibility in an emergency. *Journal of Experimental and Social Psychology, 8,* 438–445.

Bigelow, K. R. (1993). A campaign to deter genocide: The Baha'i experience. In H. Fein (Ed.), *Genocide watch.* New Haven, CT: Yale University Press.

Bloch, S., & Reddaway, P. (1977). *Psychiatric terror: How Soviet psychiatry is used to suppress dissent.* New York: Basic Books.

Bloch, S., & Reddaway, P. (1984). *Soviet psychiatric abuse: The shadow over world psychiatry.* London: Victor Gollancz.

Brewer, M. B. (1978). In-group bias in the minimal intergroup situation: A cognitive-motivational analysis. *Psychological Bulletin, 86,* 307–324.

Browning, C. R. (1992). *Ordinary men: Reserve Battalion 101 and the final solution in Poland.* New York: HarperCollins.

Buss, A. H. (1966). The effect of harm on subsequent aggression. *Journal of Experimental Research in Personality, 1*, 249–255.

Card, J. J. (1983). *Lives after Vietnam: The personal impact of military service*. Lexington, MA: Lexington Books.

Chandler, D. P. (1983). *A history of Cambodia*. Boulder, CO: Westview.

Craig, G. A. (1982). *The Germans*. New York: New American Library.

Crawley, E. (1984). *A house divided: Argentina, 1880–1980*. New York: St. Martin's.

Dawidowicz, L. S. (1975). *The war against the Jews: 1933–1945*. New York: Holt, Rinehart and Winston.

DeJong, A. (1978). *The Weimar chronicle: Prelude to Hitler*. New York: New American Library.

DeJong, W. (1979). An examination of self-perception mediation of the foot-in-the-door effect. *Journal of Personality and Social Psychology, 34*, 578–582.

des Forges, A. (1999). *Leave none to tell the story: Genocide in Rwanda*. New York: Human Rights Watch.

Deutsch, M. (1973). *The resolution of conflict: Constructive and destructive processes*. New Haven, CT: Yale University Press.

Devereux, E. D. (1972). Authority and moral development among German and American children: A cross-national pilot experiment. *Journal of Comparative Family Studies, 3*, 99–124.

Dicks, H. V. (1972). *Licensed mass murder: A socio-psychological study of some SS killers*. New York: Basic Books.

Dimont, M. I. (1962). *Jews, God and history*. New York: Signet.

Duster, T. (1971). Conditions for guilt-free massacre. In N. Sanford & C. Comstock (Eds.), *Sanction for evil*. San Francisco: Jossey-Bass.

Egendorf, A., Kadushin, C., Laufer, R. S., Rothbart, G., & Sloan, L. (1981). *Summary findings. Legacies of Vietnam: Comparative adjustment of Vietnam veterans and their peers* (Vol. 1). Washington, DC: U.S. Government Printing Office.

Eisenberg, N. (1986). *Altruistic emotion, cognition and behavior*. Hillsdale, NJ: Erlbaum.

Elms, A. C., & Milgram, S. (1966). Personality characteristics associated with obedience and defiance toward authoritative command. *Journal of Experimental Research in Personality, 2*, 282–289.

Epstein, S. (1980). The self-concept: A review and the proposal of an integrated theory of personality. In E. Staub (Ed.), *Personality: Basic aspects and current research*. Englewood Cliffs, NJ: Prentice-Hall.

Etcheson, C. (1984). *The rise and demise of democratic Kampuchea*. Boulder, CO: Westview.

Fein, H. (1979). *Accounting for genocide: Victims and survivors of the Holocaust*. New York: Free Press.

Fein, H. (1993). Accounting for genocide after 1945: Theories and some findings. *International Journal of Group Rights, 1*, 79–106.

Freedman, J. L., & Fraser, S. C. (1966). Compliance without pressure: The foot-in-the-door technique. *Journal of Personality and Social Psychology, 4*, 195–202.

Friedrich, V. (1989). From psychoanalysis to the "Great treatment": Psychoanalysis under National Socialism. *Political Psychology, 10*, 3–27.

Fromm, E. (1965). *Escape from freedom*. New York: Avon.

Gibson, J. T., & Haritos-Fatouros, M. (1986). The education of a torturer. *Psychology Today, 20*, 50–58.

Girard, P. (1980). Historical foundations of anti-Semitism. In J. Dimsdale (Ed.), *Survivors, victims and perpetrators: Essays on the Nazi Holocaust.* New York: Hemisphere.

Goldhagen, D. J. (1996). *Hitler's willing executioners: Ordinary Germans and the Holocaust.* New York: Knopf.

Goldstein, J. H., Davis, R. W., & Herman, D. (1975). Escalation of aggression: Experimental studies. *Journal of Personality and Social Psychology, 31*, 162–170.

Gourevitch, P. (1998). *We wish to inform you that tomorrow we will be killed with our families.* New York: Farrar, Straus and Giroux.

Greene, F. D. (1895). *The Armenian crisis in Turkey: The massacre of 1894, its antecedents and significance.* New York: Putnam's.

Grusec, J. E., Kuczynski, L., Rushton, J. P., & Simutis, Z. M. (1978). Modeling, direct instruction, and attributions: Effects on altruism. *Developmental Psychology, 14*, 51–57.

Hallie, P. P. (1979). *Lest innocent blood be shed: The story of the village of Le Chambon and how goodness happened there.* New York: Harper and Row.

Harff, B., & Gurr, T. R. (1990). Victims of the state genocides, politicides and group repression since 1945. *International Review of Victimology, 1*, 1–19.

Harff, B., Gurr, T. R., & Unger, A. (1999, November). *Preconditions of genocide and politicide: 1955–1998.* Paper presented at the Conference on Differing Approaches to Assessing Potential Genocide, Politicides and Mass Killings, Vienna, Virginia.

Haritos-Fatouros, M. (1988). The official torturer: A learning model for obedience to the authority of violence. *Journal of Applied Social Psychology, 18*, 1107–1120.

Harris, M. B. (1972). The effects of performing one altruistic act on the likelihood of performing another. *Journal of Social Psychology, 88*, 65–73.

Heider, F. (1958). *The psychology of interpersonal relations.* New York: Wiley.

Herman, J. (1992). *Trauma and recovery.* New York: Basic Books.

Hilberg, R. (1961). *The destruction of the European Jews.* New York: Harper and Row.

Hitchcock, R. K., & Twedt, T. M. (1997). Physical and cultural genocide of various indigenous peoples. In S. Totten, W. S. Parsons, & I. W. Charny (Eds.), *Century of genocide: Eyewitness accounts and critical views.* New York: Garland.

Janoff-Bulman, R. (1985). The aftermath of victimization: Rebuilding shattered assumptions. In C. R. Figley (Ed.), *Trauma and its wake.* New York: Bruner/Mazel.

Janoff-Bulman, R. (1992). *Shattered assumptions.* New York: Free Press.

Keneally, T. (1982). *Schindler's list.* New York: Penguin.

Kren, G. M., & Rappoport, L. (1980). *The Holocaust and the crisis of human behavior.* New York: Holmes and Meier.

Kuper, L. (1981). *Genocide: Its political use in the twentieth century.* New Haven, CT: Yale University Press.

Latané, B., & Darley, J. (1970). *The unresponsive bystander: Why doesn't he help?* New York: Appleton-Crofts.

Lerner, M. (1980). *The belief in a just world: A fundamental delusion.* New York: Plenum.

Lerner, M. J., & Simmons, C. H. (1966). Observer's reaction to the "innocent victim": Compassion or rejection? *Journal of Personality and Social Psychology, 4*, 203–210.
LeVine, R. A., & Campbell, D. (1972). *Ethnocentrism: Theories of conflict, ethnic attitudes and group behavior.* New York: Wiley.
Lewin, K. (1938). *The conceptual representation and measurement of psychological forces.* Durham, NC: Duke University Press.
Lifton, R. J. (1986). *The Nazi doctors: Medical killing and the psychology of genocide.* New York: Basic Books.
London, P. (1970). The rescuers: Motivational hypotheses about Christians who saved Jews from the Nazis. In J. Macaulay & L. Berkowitz (Eds.), *Altruism and helping behavior.* New York: Academic Press.
Luther, M. (1955–1975). *Works: On the Jews and their lies* (Vol. 47). St. Louis, MO: Muhlenberg Press.
Mack, J. (1983). Nationalism and the self. *Psychoanalytic Review, 2*, 47–69.
Marton, K. (1982). *Wallenberg.* New York: Ballantine.
Mayer, M. (1955). *They thought they were free: The Germans, 1933–45.* Chicago: University of Chicago Press.
McCann, L. I., & Pearlman, L. A. (1990). *Psychological trauma and the adult survivor: Theory, therapy, and transformation.* New York: Bruner/Mazel.
McCauley, C. R., & Segal, M. D. (1989). Terrorist individuals and terrorist groups: The normal psychology of extreme behavior. In J. Groebel & J. F. Goldstein, *Terrorism.* Sevilla: Publicaciones de la Universidad de Sevilla.
Merkl, P. H. (1980). *The making of a stormtrooper.* Princeton, NJ: Princeton University Press.
Milgram, S. (1965). Some conditions of obedience and disobedience to authority. *Human Relations, 18*, 57–76.
Milgram, S. (1974). *Obedience to authority: An experimental view.* New York: Harper and Row.
Milgram, S., & Toch, H. (1969). Collective behavior: Crowds and social movements. In G. Lindzey & E. Aronson (Eds.), *The handbook of social psychology* (2nd ed.). Reading, PA: Addison-Wesley.
Miller, A. (1983). *For your own good: Hidden cruelty in child-rearing and the roots of violence.* New York: Farrar, Straus and Giroux.
Moscovici, S. (1973). *Social influence and social change.* London: Academic Press.
Moscovici, S. (1980). Toward a theory of conversion behavior. In L. Berkowitz (Ed.), *Current issues in social psychology.* New York: Academic Press.
Nairn & Simon. (1986, June). Bureaucracy of death. *New Republic*, pp. 13–18.
Nathan, O., & Norden, H. (Eds.). (1960). *Einstein on peace.* New York: Avenel Books.
Nunca Mas. (1986). *The report of the Argentine National Commission on the Disappeared.* New York: Farrar, Straus and Giroux.
Oliner, S. B., & Oliner, P. (1988). *The altruistic personality: Rescuers of Jews in Nazi Europe.* New York: Free Press.
Peters, E. (1985). *Torture.* New York: Basil Blackwell.
Pettigrew, T. F. (1997). Generalized intergroup contact effects on prejudice. *Personality and Social Psychology Bulletin, 23*, 173–185.
Platt, G. M. (1980). Thoughts on a theory of collective action: Language, affect and ideology in revolution. In M. Albin, R. J. Devlin, & G. Heeger (Eds.),

New directions in psychohistory: The Adelphi papers in honor of Erik H. Erikson. Lexington, MA: Lexington Books.
Prunier, G. (1995). *The Rwanda crisis: History of a genocide.* New York: Columbia University Press.
Rouhana, N. N., & Kelman, H. C. (1994). Promoting joint thinking in international conflicts: An Israeli-Palestinian continuing workshop. *Journal of Social Issues, 50,* 157–178.
Rummel, R. J. (1994). *Death by government.* New Brunswick, NJ: Transaction.
Staub, E. (1974). Helping a distressed person: Social, personality and stimulus determinants. In L. Berkowitz (Ed.), *Advances in experimental social psychology* (Vol. 7). New York: Academic Press.
Staub, E. (1975). To rear a prosocial child: Reasoning, learning by doing, and learning by teaching others. In D. DePalma & J. Folley (Eds.), *Moral development: Current theory and research.* Hillsdale, NJ: Erlbaum.
Staub, E. (1978). *Positive social behavior and morality: Social and personal influences* (Vol. 1). New York: Academic Press.
Staub, E. (1979). *Positive social behavior and morality: Socialization and development* (Vol. 2). New York: Academic Press.
Staub, E. (1980). Social and prosocial behavior. In E. Staub (Ed.), *Personality.* Englewood Cliffs, NJ: Prentice Hall.
Staub, E. (1986). A conception of the determinants and development of altruism and aggression: Motives, the self, the environment. In C. Zahn-Waxler, M. Cummings, & R. Ianotti (Eds.), *Altruism and aggression: Social and biological origins.* Cambridge, MA: Cambridge University Press.
Staub, E. (1987). Commentary. In N. Eisenberg & J. Strayer (Eds.), *Empathy and its development.* New York: Cambridge University Press.
Staub, E. (1988). The evolution of caring and nonaggressive persons and societies. In R. Wagner, J. DeRivera, & M. Watkins (Eds.), Positive approaches to peace. *Journal of Social Issues, 44,* 2, 800.
Staub, E. (1989a). *The roots of evil: The origins of genocide and other group violence.* New York: Cambridge University Press.
Staub, E. (1989b). Steps along the continuum of destruction: The evolution of bystanders, German psychoanalysts and lessons for today. *Political Psychology, 10,* 39–53.
Staub, E. (1992a). Understanding and preventing police violence. *Center Review,* 6, 1 and 7.
Staub, E. (1992b). Transforming the bystander: Altruism, caring and social responsibility. In H. Fein (Ed.), *Genocide watch.* New Haven, CT: Yale University Press.
Staub, E. (1993). Motivation, individual and group self-concepts, and morality. In T. Wren & G. Noam (Eds.), *Morality and the self.* Cambridge, MA: MIT Press.
Staub, E. (1995). How people learn to care. In P. G. Schervish, V. A. Hodgkinson, M. Gates, & associates (Eds.), *Care and community in modern society: Passing on the tradition of service to future generations.* San Francisco: Jossey-Bass.
Staub, E. (1996). Cultural-societal roots of violence: The examples of genocidal violence and of contemporary youth violence in the United States. *American Psychologist, 51,* 117–132.

Staub, E. (1998). Breaking the cycle of genocidal violence: Healing and reconciliation. In J. Harvey (Ed.), *Perspectives on loss: A source book*. Washington, DC: Taylor and Francis.

Staub, E. (1999a). The origins and prevention of genocide, mass killing, and other collective violence. *Peace and Conflict: Journal of Peace Psychology, 5*, 303–336.

Staub, E. (1999b). The roots of evil: Social conditions, culture, personality and basic human needs. *Personality and Social Psychology Review, 3*, 179–192.

Staub, E. (2000). Mass murder: Origins, prevention and U.S. involvement. In *Encyclopedia of violence in the United States*. New York: Scribner's.

Staub, E. (2000). Genocide and mass killing: Origins, prevention, healing and reconciliation. *Political Psychology, 21*, 367–382.

Staub, E. (2002). *Understanding and preventing police violence*. In S. Epstein & M. Amir, (Eds.), *Policing, security and democracy*. Huntsville, TX: Office of Criminal Justice Press.

Staub, E., & Pearlman, L. A. (2001). Healing, forgiveness and reconciliation after genocide. In S. J. Helmick, and R. L. Peterson, (Eds), *Forgiveness and reconciliation*. Radnor, PA: Templeton Foundation Press.

Staub, E., & Rosenthal, L. (1994). Mob violence: Social-cultural influences, group processes and participants. In L. Eron & J. Gentry (Eds.), *Reason to hope: A psychosocial perspective on violence and youth*. Washington DC: American Psychological Association.

Steiner, J. M. (1980). The SS yesterday and today: A socio-psychological view. In J. Dimsdale (Ed.), *Survivors, victims and perpetrators: Essays on the Nazi Holocaust*. New York: Hemisphere.

Stover, E., & Nightingale, E. O. (1985). *The breaking of bodies and minds: Torture, psychiatric abuse and the health professions*. New York: Freeman.

Sykes, G. M., & Matza, D. (1957). Techniques of neutralization: A theory of delinquency. *American Sociological Review, 75*, 664–670.

Tajfel, H. (Ed.). (1982). Social identity and intergroup relations. Cambridge: Cambridge University Press.

Tajfel, H., Flamant, C., Billig, M. Y., & Bundy, R. P. (1971). Societal categorization and intergroup behavior. *European Journal of Social Psychology, 1*, 149–177.

Taylor, F. (Ed.). (1983). *The Goebbels diaries, 1939–1941*. New York: Putnam.

Tec, N. (1986). *When light pierced the darkness: Christian rescue of Jews in Nazi-occupied Poland*. New York: Oxford University Press.

Toch, H. (1965). *The social psychology of social movements*. New York: Bobbs-Merrill.

Toynbee, A. J. (1915). *Armenian atrocities: The murder of a nation*. London: Hodder and Stoughton.

Trumpener, U. (1968). *Germany and the Ottoman Empire, 1914–1918*. Princeton, NJ: Princeton University Press.

Turner, J. C. (1987). *Rediscovering the social groups: A self-categorization theory*. New York: Basil Blackwell.

Volkan, V. D. (1988). *The need to have enemies and allies*. Northvale, NJ: Jason Aronson.

Von Maltitz, H. (1973). *The evolution of Hitler's Germany: The ideology, the personality, the moment*. New York: McGraw-Hill.

Wilson, P. J. (1980). Conflict, stress and growth: The effects of war on psychosocial development among Vietnam veterans. In C. R. Figley & S. Leventman (Eds.), *Strangers at home: Vietnam veterans since the war.* New York: Praeger.

Wyman, D. S. (1968). *Paper walls: America and the refugee crisis, 1938–1941.* Amherst: University of Massachusetts Press.

Wyman, D. S. (1984). *The abandonment of Jews: America and the Holocaust, 1941–1945.* New York: Pantheon.

Zimbardo, P. G. (1969). The human choice: Individuation, reason, and order versus deindividuation, impulse, and chaos. In *Nebraska symposium on motivation.* Lincoln: University of Nebraska Press.

23

Steps Along a Continuum of Destruction

Perpetrators and Bystanders

One of the most important roots of persistent or extreme violence is an evolution or change in individuals and groups that results from their own actions. Once perpetrators begin to harm people, the resulting psychological changes make greater harm-doing probable. However, early public reactions can counteract these changes and inhibit further violence.

JUST-WORLD THINKING

One psychological consequence of harm-doing is further devaluation of victims. According to the just-world hypothesis, which has received substantial experimental support, people tend to assume that victims have earned their suffering by their actions or character.[1] Perhaps we need to maintain faith that we ourselves will not become innocent victims of circumstance. However, blaming the victim is not universal; some people turn against the perpetrators. For example, a minority of individuals blame the experimenter instead of devaluing a student receiving electric shocks in an experiment.[2] Prior devaluation should make it more likely that victims are blamed.

People believe in a just world with different degrees of conviction.[3] Those whose belief is strong derogate poor people, underprivileged groups, or minorities. Strong belief in a just world is associated with rigid application of social rules and belief in the importance of convention, as opposed to empathy and concern with human welfare.[4] It is ironic and seemingly paradoxical (although not truly paradoxical, because the belief that the world is just is not identical to regarding justice as an ideal or to the desire to promote justice) that the belief that the world is a just place

Reprinted from E. Staub (1989). *The roots of evil: The origins of genocide and other group violence.* New York: Cambridge University Press, pp. 79–88. Reprinted with the permission of Cambridge University Press.

leads people to accept the suffering of others more easily, even of people they themselves harmed.

People do not devalue victims whose innocence is clearly and definitely established.[5] But how often can that be done? How can Jews or blacks, communists or anticommunists, be cleared of misdeeds, evil intentions, or faults inherent in their nature, particularly in a climate of prejudice? Devaluation is especially likely if the victims' continued suffering is expected.[6] To feel empathy results in empathic distress. To avoid that, people distance themselves from victims. This can be accomplished by devaluation. Under difficult life conditions, concern about the self also diminishes concern about others' suffering.

LEARNING BY DOING AND THE EVOLUTION OF EXTREME DESTRUCTIVENESS

The importance of learning by doing became evident to me through studies in which my associates and I induced children to engage in helpful acts and found that afterward they helped and shared more.[7] Children who taught a younger child, wrote letters to hospitalized children, or made toys for poor hospitalized children became more helpful on later occasions than children who spent the same time in activities that were similar in nature but not helpful to others.[8] Examining past research (much of it conducted to test unrelated hypotheses such as the effects of modeling) I found evidence for the same conclusion.[9] The research offers support for the view of some philosophers that morality is learned through moral action. Learning by doing is a basis for developing values, motives, the self-concept, and behavioral tendencies.

Even if initially there is some external pressure, it often becomes difficult to experience regular participation in an activity as alien. People begin to see their engagement in the activity as part of themselves. The less force is used, the more this happens. People come to see themselves as agents and begin to consider and elaborate on the reasons for their actions. If there are benefits to others, even imagined ones, they begin to find the activity worthwhile and its beneficiaries more deserving. If there is harm to others progressively the victims' well-being and even lives will lose value in their eyes. In other words, people observe their own actions and draw inferences both about those affected by them and about themselves.[10] They attribute to themselves such characteristics as helpfulness or toughness or willingness to harm. Further actions consistent with their changing views of themselves become likely.

Other experiments have explored the "foot in the door" phenomenon.[11] When people are asked for a small favor and comply, they become more likely to agree later to a larger favor than they would if they had been immediately asked for the larger favor. For example, they are more likely to agree to put a large campaign sign on their front lawn if they earlier agreed to put on a small one.

When helping persists for some time, with increasing risk to the helper, the helper's commitment often grows. Rescuers of Jews in Nazi-occupied Europe often responded first to the need of a friend or acquaintance and then went on to help others, sometimes becoming active in underground railroads. Some who intended to hide a family for only a day or two decided to keep hiding them for years. Still other helpers, such as the Swede Raoul Wallenberg and the German Oscar Schindler, became obsessed with their mission to save lives.

The evolution from indifference to total devotion is clear in the case of Oscar Schindler.[12] He followed the German army into Poland, took over a confiscated factory, and enriched himself, using Jewish slave labor. However, he treated his Jewish laborers as human beings, talked to them, listened to them. He started doing them small favors, then greater ones. Later he established a camp next to his factory to protect his workers from the SS, especially the murderous commander of the nearby concentration camp. He repeatedly endangered his life and sacrificed all his possessions, while saving the lives of twelve hundred Jews.

People also change as they harm others. Many experiments use the "teacher-learner paradigm," in which a "teacher" gives a "learner" electric shocks every time the learner makes an error. Even without any instruction to do so, teachers tend to increase the intensity of the shocks over time.[13] When there is instruction to increase the shock level, in the obedience experiments, the increase is gradual, step by step, so that learning by participation makes obedience easier. Both in these experiments and in real life, repeatedly and increasingly harming others makes it difficult to shift course. Unusual events offer decision points; in the obedience studies many who decided to stop did so when the learner-victim began to protest. However, the pressures of authorities and the system and changes that result from past harm-doing often combine with predispositions to override such opportunities.

Learning by doing is also found in research using verbal reinforcements. One person is instructed to speak either approving or disapproving words in response to certain words used by another person.[14] As time passes, the intensity of both rewarding and punishing verbal reinforcements tends to increase. In addition, the learners are devalued by those who punished them.*

* There was no control or neutral condition, so it is uncertain to what extent rewarding in itself led to a positive evaluation and punishing to a negative evaluation. The change in evaluation did not occur when participants only *role-played* rewarding or punishing another (imagined) person. But even under these conditions, the increase in rewards or punishments occurred.

How does harmful behavior become the norm? What internal changes take place in people? Doing harm to a good person or passively witnessing it is inconsistent with a feeling of responsibility for the welfare of others and the belief in a just world. Inconsistency troubles us.[15] We minimize it by reducing our concern for the welfare of those we harm or allow to suffer. We devalue them, justify their suffering by their evil nature or by higher ideals. A changed view of the victims, changed attitude toward that suffering, and changed self-concept result.

Hannah Arendt describes a turning point for Eichmann. When he was first exposed to the bodies of massacred Jews, he reacted with revulsion. But "higher ideals" (that is, powerful motives) such as Nazi ideology and loyalty to the Führer, as well as a desire to advance his career, led him to ignore his distress and continue with his "work." The distress eventually disappeared.[16] Bruno Bettelheim described the inner struggle of a man who was against the Nazis but had to use the obligatory greeting "Heil Hitler." Even such a limited participation can result in substantial psychological reorganization.[17]

The Greek torturers also learned by participation.[18] First they stood guard outside interrogation and torture cells. Then they witnessed torture and provided help in beating up prisoners. They had to perform these duties satisfactorily before they were given a role as torturers.

Ideological movements and totalitarian systems induce members to participate. Members must follow special rituals and rules; they must join in educational or work activities for building the new society. The more they participate, the more difficult it becomes for them to distance themselves from the system's goals and deviate from its norms of conduct, not only overtly but also internally.

Bystanders also learn and change through passive or semiactive participation. Germans who boycotted Jewish stores or abandoned Jewish friends had to find reasons. The danger of resistance was one reason, but it was not enough to account for the wide-ranging participation and for the actions of the system itself that most Germans came to accept and like. The truly passive also, as a result of not taking any contrary action, come to accept the suffering of victims and the behavior of perpetrators.

Another very important phenomenon is self-persuasion, especially among leaders and decision makers. As they create propaganda or devise plans against victims, they reinforce and further develop their own world view. Psychological research shows that when people are asked to persuade others to a certain point of view, they also convince themselves and change their own views.[19]

Leaders or decision makers are also affected by the consequences of their own actions. Violence instigated by propaganda and official acts reinforces the leaders' views and intentions. In Germany random murders of Jews and looting of Jewish shops made Nazi leaders decide that further official acts against Jews were needed. This may happen even when the acts of violence are instigated by the leaders themselves and intended as justification for their policies.

Compartmentalization and Integration

In *1984* George Orwell shows one way complicity evolves. His protagonist, Winston Smith, hates the repressive system of Big Brother, but he occasionally enjoys his work – rewriting history to conform to the current propaganda line. In the middle of Hate Week, the enemy country becomes an ally, and the ally an enemy. All previous history must be rewritten. He and others at the Ministry of Truth work feverishly, day and night, for over a week. "Insofar as he could remember, he was not troubled by the fact that every word he murmured into the speak-write, every stroke of his ink pencil was a deliberate lie. He was as anxious as everyone else in the Department that the forgery should be perfect."[20]

This kind of compartmentalization enables people to focus and act on goals that conflict with important values. When the discrepancy persists, a splitting of the self can occur that enables people to live with it. Usually, further progression along a continuum will lead to moral exclusion and other changes that lead to a personal integration that allows destructive goals and behavior. Occasionally the split may remain and enlarge.

Dedicated or fanatical perpetrators may come to value killing; there is no inconsistency or need for splitting. However, less fully committed perpetrators must be able to compartmentalize. They may concentrate on the immediate task, ignoring ethics and long-term consequences. Many Nazi doctors focused on medical "achievements" in their cruel experiments.[21] Camp commanders focused on efficiency. Bureaucrats prepared regulations and train schedules for transporting victims. Over time, internal changes will increasingly diminish the need to compartmentalize.

Two psychological developments are of great importance: *a reversal of morality, and relinquishing a feeling of responsibility* for the welfare of the victims. To a greater or lesser extent, most human beings learn that they are responsible for the life and welfare of others. A feeling of responsibility for others' welfare is central to people helping and not hurting others.[22] Feelings of responsibility are subverted by excluding certain people from the realm of humanity or defining them as dangers to oneself and one's way of life and values. At the extreme, a complete reversal of morality may occur, so that murder becomes a service to humanity. This is well expressed in a conversation described in testimony at Nuremberg by a Nazi who "worked" at Belzec, one of the extermination camps. When asked: "Wouldn't it be more prudent to burn the bodies instead of burying them? Another generation might take a different view of these things," he responded:

"Gentlemen, if there is ever a generation after us so cowardly, so soft, that it would not understand our work as good and necessary, then, gentlemen, National Socialism will have been for nothing. On the contrary we should bury bronze tablets saying that it was we, we who had the courage to carry out this gigantic task!"[23]

The feeling of responsibility can also be subverted through the assumption of responsibility by leaders. Himmler told the SS that he and the Führer would assume all the responsibility for their actions – and that they were discharging a heroic duty requiring tremendous sacrifice.[24] In Argentina, superior officers signed release forms for each kidnapping, which relieved the direct perpetrators of responsibility.[25] In the obedience studies, the experimenter assumed full responsibility for the consequences of shocking the learner. In a variant of this research, participants who had an observer role and were told that they were responsible for the learner's welfare induced the "teachers" to administer weaker shocks.[26] Research on helping in emergencies (for example, when someone falls and is injured or has a sudden asthma attack) shows that a witness is likely to help if circumstances focus responsibility on him or her (for example, he or she is the only person present or has a special competence) or if other people make the witness responsible by instructions or orders. When circumstances diffuse responsibility, helping is much less probable.[27] Persons with greater ego strength or a greater personal feeling of responsibility for others' welfare are less affected by the presence or passivity of others.[28] The others in this case are strangers. Members of a close-knit group are likely to be more affected by each other.

Specialization and bureaucratization make violence easier, partly by subverting the feeling of responsibility.[29] Peck notes that in conversations with Pentagon officials at the time of the My Lai incident members of each group involved claimed that their role was circumscribed and disclaimed responsibility.[30]

As the destruction process evolves, harming victims can become "normal" behavior. Inhibitions against harming or killing diminish, and extraneous motives can enter: greed, the enjoyment of power, the desire for sex or excitement. This is helped along by the belief that the victims do not matter and deserve to suffer, and even that any form of their suffering furthers the cause the perpetrators serve.

The further the destruction has progressed, the more difficult it is to halt it. Human beings have a tendency to complete what they start. Kurt Lewin described this in terms of a goal gradient: the closer you are to a goal, the stronger the motivation to reach it.[31] Interruption of goal-directed behavior is a source of tension; the closer the goal, the greater the tension.

Cognitive consistency theories also present human beings as motivated to reach closure.[32] The further you have progressed toward a goal, the more difficult it is to give up. Combined with personal and societal changes this explains why Germans, while losing the war, diverted substantial resources for the continued killing of Jews. Continued killing may also have served to give the Nazis a feeling of power and invulnerability as their fortunes declined.[33]

A progression of changes in a culture and individuals is usually required for mass killing or genocide. In certain instances – the Armenian genocide, for example – the progression takes place over decades or even centuries and creates a readiness in the culture. In other cases there is a speedy evolution of ideology, personalities, or social conditions that ready people for mass killing.

"Vicarious" rather than direct participation can also contribute to this evolution. Members of Nazi movements outside Germany identified with German Nazis and vicariously participated in their practices.[34] This prepared them for their role as perpetrators when their country was later occupied by or allied itself to Nazi Germany. However, several such countries had themselves enacted anti-Jewish laws, so that learning by direct participation also occurred.

THE ROLE AND POWER OF BYSTANDERS

Bystanders, people who witness but are not directly affected by the actions of perpetrators, help shape society by their reactions. If group norms evolve to tolerate violence, they can become victims. Bystanders are often unaware of, or deny, the significance of events or the consequences of their behavior. Since these events are part of their lifespace, to remain unaware they employ defenses like rationalization and motivated misperception, or avoid information about the victims' suffering.

Bystanders can exert powerful influence. They can define the meaning of events and move others toward empathy or indifference. They can promote values and norms of caring, or by their passivity or participation in the system they can affirm the perpetrators.[35]

Research on helping in emergencies has shown that, when a number of people are present, responsibility is diffused, and each person is less likely to help.[36] Another consequence is what Bibb Latane and John Darley call pluralistic ignorance.[37] People tend to inhibit expressions of feeling in public. In an emergency, the fact that all bystanders are hiding their feelings may lead them all to believe that there is no need for concern and nothing need be done. Hiding reactions is also common when suffering is inflicted by agents of society on members of a minority.

As I have noted, psychological research shows that a single deviation from group behavior can greatly diminish conformity.[38] In emergencies the likelihood of helping greatly increases when one bystander says the situation is serious or tells others to take action.[39] When a society begins to mistreat some of its members, resistance by bystanders, in words and action, will influence others and inhibit the personal changes that would result from passivity.

Even the behavior of governments can be strongly affected by bystanders – individuals, groups, or other governments. Repeatedly when they faced substantial opposition, the Nazis backed away. They did not persist, for example, when Bulgaria (where the people protested in the streets) refused to hand over its Jewish population or when, within Germany, relatives and some institutions protested the killing of the mentally retarded, mentally ill, and others regarded as genetically inferior.[40] Public protest in the United States greatly affected the war in Vietnam. Amnesty International groups have freed political prisoners all over the world simply by writing letters to governments.

A lack of protest can confirm the perpetrators' faith in what they are doing. Hitler saw the lack of response both in Germany and in the outside world to the persecution of Jews as evidence that the whole world wanted what only he had the courage to do. A refusal to cooperate can raise questions in the minds of perpetrators. According to Helen Fein, resistance in Denmark, Italy, and Bulgaria raised doubts in the minds of some Nazi functionaries in those countries.[41] Perpetrators may question not only whether they can get away with it, but also whether what they are doing is right.

Why then are bystanders so often passive and silent? Sometimes silence results from fear, but that is not the whole explanation. Everywhere people tend to accept a definition of reality provided by "experts," their government, or their culture. Lack of divergent views, just-world thinking, and their own participation or passivity change bystanders' perception of self and reality so as to allow and justify cruelty.

Outsiders may also respond little, although they have less to fear. They too are subject to these processes of change. They too are affected by the propaganda or ideology used to justify mistreatment. Before World War II, for example, anti-Semitism increased in many countries.[42] Hitler's propaganda joined with an existing anti-Semitic base and just-world thinking and enabled people in economic trouble to blame Jews.

Ideological conceptions and romantic notions of what is good can mislead us. Very few people, in retrospect, glorify the violence of the Chinese Cultural Revolution. But at the time, some voices in the United States celebrated this "rejuvenation" of the revolution.

Another reason for outside indifference is that governments usually do not see themselves as moral agents obliged to endanger their interests by interfering in the "internal affairs" of other countries. With rare exceptions they protest only when they see their self-interest endangered (see Chapters 16 and 17).

Notes

1. Lerner, M. J., & Simmons, C. H. (1996). Observer's reaction to the "innocent victim": Compassion or rejection? *Journal of Personality and Social Psychology, 4*, 203–10.
   Lerner, M. (1980). *The belief in a just world: A fundamental delusion*. New York: Plenum Press.
   Smith, R. E., Keating, J. P., Hester, R. K., & Mitchell, H. E. (1976). Role and justice considerations in the attribution of responsibility to a rape victim. *Journal of Research in Personality, 10*, 346–57.
2. Lerner and Simmons, Observer's reaction.
3. Rubin, Z., & Peplau, L. A. (1973). Belief in a just world and reactions to another's lot: A study of participants in the national draft lottery. *Journal of Social Issues, 29*, 73–93.
   Idem. (1975). Who believes in a just world? *Journal of Social Issues, 31*, 65–89.
4. Staub, E. (1978). *Positive social behavior and morality*. Vol. 1, *Social and personal influences*. New York: Academic Press.
5. Ibid.
6. Lerner and Simmons, Observer's reaction.
   Lerner, *Belief in a just world*.
7. Staub, E. (1975). To rear a prosocial child: Reasoning, learning by doing, and learning by teaching others. In D. DePalma & J. Folley (Eds.), *Moral development: Current theory and research*. Hillsdale, N.J.: Lawrence Erlbaum Associates.
   Idem. (1979). *Positive social behavior and morality*. Vol. 2, *Socialization and development*. New York: Academic Press, chap. 6.
8. Staub, To rear a prosocial child.
   Idem. *Positive social behavior*, vol. 2, chap. 6.
9. DeJong, W. (1979). An examination of self-perception mediation of the foot-in-the-door effect. *Journal of Personality and Social Psychology, 34*, 578–82.
   Freedman, J. L., & Fraser, S. C. (1966). Compliance without pressure: The foot-in-the-door technique. *Journal of Personality and Social Psychology, 4*, 195–202.
   Harris, M. B. (1972). The effects of performing one altruistic act on the likelihood of performing another. *Journal of Social Psychology, 88*, 65–73.
   Staub, *Positive social behavior*, vol. 2, chaps. 5 and 6.
10. Bem, D. J. (1972). Self-perception theory. In L. Berkowitz (Ed.), *Advances in experimental social psychology*, vol. 6. New York: Academic Press.
11. Freedman and Fraser, Compliance without pressure.
   DeJong, Examination of self-perception mediation.
12. Keneally, T. (1983). *Schindler's list*. New York: Penguin Books.
13. As an example of this finding see: Buss, A. H. (1966). The effect of harm on subsequent aggression. *Journal of Experimental Research in Personality, 1*, 349–55.
   For a list of relevant references see:
   Goldstein, J. H., Davis, R. W., & Herman, D. (1975). Escalation of aggression: Experimental studies. *Journal of Personality and Social Psychology, 31*, 162–70.

14. Goldstein et al., Escalation.
15. Bem, Self-perception theory.
    Eisenberg, N., & Cialdini, R. B. (1984). The role of consistency pressures in behavior: A developmental perspective. *Academic Psychology Journal, 6*, 115–26.
    Staub, *Positive social behavior*, vol. 2.
16. Arendt, H. (1963). *Eichmann in Jerusalem: A report on the banality of evil*. New York: Viking Press.
17. Bettelheim, B. (1979). Remarks on the psychological appeal of totalitarianism. In *Surviving and other essays*. New York: Vintage Books.
18. Haritos-Fatouros, M. (1979). The official torturer: Learning mechanisms involved in the process. Relevance to democratic and totalitarian regimes today. Unpublished manuscript, University of Thessaloniki, Greece.
    Gibson, J. T., & Haritos-Fatouros, M. (1986). The education of a torturer. *Psychology Today*, *20*, 50–58.
19. For a review see:
    Fishbein, M., & Ajzen, I. (1975). *Belief, attitude, intention and behavior*. Reading, Mass.: Addison-Wesley.
20. Orwell, G. (1949). *1984*. New York: Harcourt & Brace, p. 151.
21. Lifton, R. J. (1986). *The Nazi doctors: Medical killing and the psychology of genocide*. New York: Basic Books.
22. Latané, B., & Darley, J. (1970). *The unresponsive bystander: Why doesn't he help?* New York: Appleton-Crofts.
    Staub, *Positive social behavior*, vol. 1.
    Tilker, H. A. (1970). Socially responsive behavior as a function of observer responsibility and victim feedback. *Journal of Personality and Social Psychology*, *4*, 95–100.
23. Poliakov, L. (1954). *Harvest of hate: The Nazi program for the destruction of the Jews in Europe*. Syracuse, N.Y.: Syracuse University Press, pp. 12–13.
24. Hilberg, R. (1961). *The destruction of the European Jews*. Chicago: Quadrangle Books.
    Dawidowicz, L. S. (1975). *The war against the Jews: 1935–1945*. New York: Holt, Rinehart & Winston.
25. Amnesty International Report. (1980). *Testimony on secret detention camps in Argentina*. London: Amnesty International Publications.
26. Tilker, Socially responsive behavior.
27. Staub, *Positive social behavior*, vol. 1.
    Bickman, L. (1972). Social influence and diffusion of responsibility in an emergency. *Journal of Experimental Social Psychology*, *8*, 438–45.
    Staub, E. (1974). Helping a distressed person: Social, personality, and stimulus determinants. In L. Berkowitz (Ed.), *Advances in experimental social psychology*, vol. 7. New York: Academic Press.
28. Wilson, J. P. (1976). Motivation, modeling and altruism: A person x situation analysis. *Journal of Personality and Social Psychology*, *34*, 1078–86.
    Schwartz, S. H., & Clausen, G. T. (1970). Responsibility norms and helping in an emergency. *Journal of Personality and Social Psychology*, *16*, 299–310.
29. Hilberg, *Destruction*.

30. Peck, M. S. (1982). *People of the lie: The hope of healing human evil.* New York: Simon & Schuster.
31. Lewin, K. (1938). *The conceptual representation and measurement of psychological forces.* Durham, N.C.: Duke University Press.
    Lewin, K. (1948). *Resolving social conflicts.* New York: Harper.
    Hornstein, H. A. (1976). *Cruelty and kindness: A new look at aggression and altruism.* Englewood Cliffs, N.J.: Prentice-Hall.
32. Heider, F. (1958). *The psychology of interpersonal relations.* New York: Wiley.
    Festinger, L. (1957). *A theory of cognitive dissonance.* Evanston, Ill.: Row-Peterson.
33. Becker, E. (1975). *Escape from evil.* New York: Free Press.
34. For example, in Hungary:
    Lacko, M. (1976). *Nyilasok, Nemzetiszocialistak, 1935–1944* (The Arrow Cross, National Socialists). Budapest.
35. Staub, *Positive social behavior*, vol. 1.
36. Latané and Darley, *Unresponsive bystander.*
37. Ibid.
38. Asch, S. E. (1951). Effects of group pressure upon the modification and distortion of judgements. In H. Guetzkow (Ed.), *Groups, leadership, and men.* Pittsburgh: Carnegie Press.
39. Staub, Helping a distressed person.
40. Fein, H. (1979). *Accounting for genocide: National responses and Jewish victimization during the Holocaust.* New York: Free Press.
    Davidowicz, *War against the Jews.*
    Lifton, *Nazi doctors.*
41. Fein, *Accounting for genocide.*
42. Wyman, D. S. (1984). *The abandonment of the Jews: America and the Holocaust, 1941–1945.* New York: Pantheon Books.

24

The SS and the Psychology of Perpetrators

The Interweaving and Merging of Role and Person

The SS (Schutzstaffel) was created as an elite bodyguard for Hitler in the early 1920s and eventually became the organization that had primary responsibility for the Nazi genocide. The following section, taken from the chapter called "The SS and the psychology of perpetrators," shows how people evolved with their roles. The personalities of the SS men and the roles they fulfilled intersected, merged, and became deeply interwoven.

Given the initial self-selection, the progressive identification with the institution, the evolution of the SS into a system devoted to mass murder in the context of changes in the larger system of Germany, and learning through participation, the psychological condition of many SS members came to fit the role they were to fulfill. They became well adapted to their functions, following the rules and operating procedures and treating their victims as contaminated material to be disposed of.

The "ideal" SS man was not personally brutal and did not enjoy the suffering of victims. He could even treat individual Jews well while serving the machinery of their murder. This level of development is demonstrated by a fictional character, O'Brien, in George Orwell's *1984*. O'Brien, the torturer of Winston Smith, inflicts indescribable pain and terror, but does so in a kindly manner, as if it is a necessary task against his inclination. Dr. Wilhelm Pfonnerstiel, professor of hygiene at the University of Marburg and SS lieutenant colonel, reporting after the war on a wartime visit to the concentration camp at Belzec, said: "I wanted to know in particular if the process of exterminating human beings was accompanied by any act of cruelty. I found it especially cruel that death did not set in until 18 minutes

Reprinted from E. Staub. (1989). *The roots of evil: The origins of genocide and other group violence.* New York: Cambridge University Press, pp. 137–141. Reprinted with the permission of Cambridge University Press.

had passed."[1] He was also concerned about the welfare of the SS men administering the extermination.

Not all SS members became "perfect." Even in a total organization like the SS, some traveled unique paths. Despite self-selection some had initially greater capacity for empathy for Jews, whereas others had deep-seated hostility or found pleasure in harming people. As a result, what they learned from experience differed. Some SS may have brutalized victims to maintain a dehumanized view of them and their own commitment to murder. Although worse for the victims, this may represent a shakier commitment, a lesser capacity to accept murder as a normal operating procedure. Others were provoked by the victims' helplessness and their lack of response to beatings and humiliations. People who need to experience power over others require a response or they will escalate violence.[2]

In his book *Schindler's List*, Thomas Keneally describes the behavior of Amos Goeth, the commandant of the labor camp (later concentration camp) at Plaszow.*[3] He would come out onto the balcony of his villa in the morning with a rifle and binoculars and scan the campground. When he saw a prisoner doing something that displeased him – pushing a cart too slowly, standing rather than moving, or committing some other unfathomable crime – he would shoot the prisoner. The life of any Jew in contact with him was in constant danger. He beat his Jewish maid mercilessly if he found the slightest speck of dirt or if his soup was not the right temperature. According to the reports of survivors Goeth believed, at least in his sentimental moods, that this Jewish maid, Helen Hirsch, and others who worked for him were "loving servants." This is also attested by the tone of a note asking her to send clothes and reading material when the SS arrested him for black marketeering. This man, who was even more cruel and sadistic than his SS role required, apparently had no capacity to see his behavior from the perspective of others.

Research has shown that one type of incestuous father is an authoritarian tyrant who regards his wife and children as chattel. In addition to incest, he physically abuses members of his family.[4] Amos Goeth may have been this kind of person, run amok in a system that has run amok. He was unable to appreciate that his prisoners, these "objects" in his possession, had feelings and needs of their own that did not fit his needs and preferences – a not uncommon human blindness but in this case extreme in degree.

While understanding the perpetrators as individuals is important, an essential truth is that they acted in a system that allowed and encouraged behavior like Goeth's. Jan Karski, a representative of the Polish Civil Directorate, witnessed even more random violence when he infiltrated the

* This book is a fictionalized accout of actual events, based on evidence from many sources, including interviews with former camp inmates and material at Yad Vashem, the Holocaust memorial and museum in Jerusalem.

Warsaw ghetto in October 1942 to gain firsthand knowledge of the conditions he was to report to Allied and Jewish spokesmen in London and the United States. He found everywhere "hunger, misery, the atrocious stench of decomposing bodies, the pitiful moans of dying children, the desperate cries and gasps of a people struggling for life against impossible odds."[5] Once a companion seized his arms and rushed him into a building, to a window:

"Now you'll see something. The hunt. You would never believe it if you did not see it yourself."

I looked through the opening. In the middle of the street two boys, dressed in the uniform of the Hitlerjugend, were standing. They wore no caps and their blond hair shone in the sun. With their round, rosy-cheeked faces and their blue eyes they were like images of health and life. They chattered, laughed, pushed each other in spasms of merriment. At that moment, the younger one pulled a gun out of his hip pocket and then I first realized what I was witnessing. His eyes roamed about, seeking something. A target. He was looking for a target with the casual, gay absorption of a boy at a carnival.

I followed his glance. For the first time I noticed that all the pavements about them were absolutely deserted. Nowhere within the scope of those blue eyes, in no place from which those cheerful, healthy faces could be seen was there a single human being. The gaze of the boy with the gun came to rest on a spot out of my line of vision. He raised his arm and took careful aim. The shot rang out, followed by the noise of breaking glass and then the terrible cry of a man in agony.[6]

In the reciprocal evolution of system and persons, some SS and other Nazis (the Hitlerjugend in Karski's report) came to enjoy their limitless power over other humans. The freedom to completely control others' lives and bodies might give some people a dizzying sense of power or perhaps the experience of both abandonment and strength as in an intense sexual experience. Their background and experience also prepares some people for sadistic pleasure, which develops out of a history of connection between one's own pleasure and others' pain.

One's own advantage or satisfaction can be regularly associated with others' disadvantage or suffering: a bully might forcefully take away toys from other children; rivalry may lead to good feelings when a sibling suffers. Past hurts or feeling diminished can lead people to feel elevated relative to others who suffer. Satisfactions gained from power and from others' suffering can fuse. SS members had many experiences that taught sadism. Coming to enjoy their victims' suffering also had a special function: it could erase doubt and make "work" satisfying. The SS could also feel satisfaction from successfully combating "evil."

Keneally offers a glimpse of another individual path.

Poldek Pfefferberg was told about the list by an SS NCO named Hans Schreiber. Schreiber, a young man in his mid-twenties, had as evil a name as any other SS man in Plaszow, but Pfefferberg had become something of a mild favorite of his in that way that was common to relations – throughout the system – between individual prisoners and SS personnel. It had begun one day when Pfefferberg, as a group leader in his barracks, had had responsibility for window cleaning. Schreiber inspected the glass and found a smudge, and began browbeating Poldek in the style that was often a prelude to execution. Pfefferberg lost his temper and told Schreiber that both of them knew the windows were perfectly polished and if Schreiber wanted a reason to shoot him, he ought to do so without any more delay. The outburst had, in a contradictory way, amused Schreiber, who afterward occasionally used to stop Pfefferberg and ask him how he and his wife were, and sometimes even gave Poldek an apple for Mila. In the summer of 1944, Poldek had appealed to him desperately to extricate Mila from a trainload of women being sent from Plaszow to the evil camp at Stutthof on the Baltic. Mila was already in the lines boarding the cattle cars when Schreiber came waving a piece of paper and calling her name. Another time, a Sunday, he turned up drunk at Pfefferberg's barracks and, in front of Poldek and a few other prisoners, began to weep for what he called "the dreadful things" he had done in Plaszow. He intended, he said, to expiate them on the Eastern Front. In the end, he would.[7]

It seems that when Pfefferberg refused to react as a helpless victim, but reacted with an intensity and humanness not fitting the victim role, Schreiber slipped out of the role of executioner. Pfefferberg's anger awoke in Schreiber a human response. That, and his subsequent kindness to Pfefferberg, nurtured in him a consideration for others. One reason for the effectiveness of Oskar Schindler, who saved 1200 Jews, and Raoul Wallenberg, who saved tens of thousands, was that they reacted contrary to the expectations of the SS and Hungarian Nazis.[8] In facing Nazis accustomed to fear and trembling, they acted with self-assurance and authority, sometimes even demanding help in helping Jews.

As the SS became a large, complex, partly bureaucratic elite, more men became members who were not self-selected or selected by authorities for their ability to fulfill task requirements. At one point the whole German equestrian society was incorporated into the SS. Most of these new members became socialized into the SS system. Some late joiners, however, made an incorrect self-selection; they were unaware of some of the requirements of membership or did not anticipate their own reactions to them. These reactions, based perhaps on "inclusive" moral values, inhibited their evolution and resulted in a gap between the role and the person. There were probably few such members in the SS, owing not only to initial self-selection and socialization into the system, but also to dismissal and quitting. Those who did not fit the requirements of SS training, such as extreme obedience and physical courage, were screened out.[9] Those whose values and world view did not fit them for membership could drop out.

A few SS men were relatively humane, at least at times.[10] Prisoners reported that on occasion their lives were saved by SS guards. We can imagine that even very small, casual acts of humanity would have great impact on prisoners searching for humanity in an overwhelmingly cruel, inhumane system.

Only in a very few reported instances was the motivation of a kind SS member clearly to save a Jew. Keneally tells the story of an SS guard who accompanied two children and their fathers from Schindler's camp to Auschwitz and then accompanied three hundred women from Auschwitz back to Schindler's camp, acting in a humane, friendly, helpful manner all the way, at one point even crying in response to their sorrow.[11] All this happened, however, near the end of the war, when the footsteps of the western Allies on one side and the Russians on the other could almost be heard. We do not know to what extent the behavior of this man (and others) was the result of a changed perspective due to changed circumstance that led him to think about his own culpability and to fear retribution.

Notes

1. Kren and Rappoport, *Holocaust*, p. 61.
2. Perry, D. G., & Perry, L. C. (1974). Denial of suffering in the victim as a stimulus to violence in aggressive boys. *Child Development*, 45, 55–62.
3. Keneally, T. (1983). *Schindler's list*. New York: Penguin Books.
4. Gelinas, D. J. (1985). Unexpected resources in treating incest families. In M. A. Karpel (Ed.), *Family resources: The hidden partner in family therapy*. New York: Guilford Press.
5. Karski, J. (1944). *Story of a secret state*. Boston: Houghton Miffin, p. 330.
6. Ibid., pp. 331–2.
7. Keneally, *Schindler's list*, p. 292.
8. Marton, K. (1982). *Wallenberg*. New York: Ballantine Books.
9. Kren and Rappoport, *Holocaust*.
10. Keneally, *Schindler's list*.
11. Ibid.

25

The Origins of Genocide

Rwanda

INSTIGATORS

Intensely difficult economic and political conditions preceded the genocide in 1994 in Rwanda. Hutus, who constituted about 85% of a population of eight million people, with Tutsis making up about 14%, killed somewhere between 600,000 and 800,000 Tutsis. About 50,000 Hutus were also killed, either because they were politically moderate or because they came from the southern part of the country and were mistrusted by the current Hutu leadership from the Northwest (for historical information, see des Forges, 1999; Gourevitch, 1998; Kressel, 1996; Prunier, 1995; Smith, 1998).

In an already densely populated country, there was great population growth. In the late 1980s the price of coffee, the primary export of Rwanda, had substantially declined, as did the price of tin, the major mineral produced in Rwanda. In a highly authoritarian political system, where the elite grew rich while the population suffered, there were demands for greater rights by various groups. The economic problems and political pressures created divisions among the Hutu elite, who were vying for positions of advantage.

The invasion by the Tutsi Rwandan Patriotic Front (RPF) in 1990, consisting of refugees or children of refugees who fled after previous massacres, intensified political turmoil. Although this invasion was stopped, the RPF went on the offensive again in 1992 and then a year later after massacres of Tutsi peasants. Thus, in addition to difficult life conditions created by economic problems, there was both intense conflict between the dominant group and subordinate groups and a civil war. A peace agreement was signed in 1993 that was to create a multiparty system, with power-sharing

Reprinted from E. Staub (1999). The origins and prevention of genocide, mass killing and other collective violence. *Journal of Peace Psychology, 5*, 303–337. Included here are parts of pp. 310–336. Reprinted with permission of Lawrence Erlbaum Associates.

by several groups. The RPF, which propagated national unify, would have controlled 5 out of 21 ministries.

EVOLUTION

About 50,000 Tutsis were killed in 1959, even before the country gained independence from Belgian rule in 1962, with more violence in the early 1960s and in the 1970s. There was only limited violence after that until the 1990s, with the Hutus firmly in control. There was substantial discrimination, with Tutsis excluded from or marginalized in the administration of the country. In the early 1990s, there were small-scale massacres. A simple but powerful ideology of "Hutu power" developed and was propagated by the elite, which included advocacy of the destruction of Tutsis (des Forges, 1999; Gourevitch, 1998; Prunier, 1995). Earlier mass killings, followed by discrimination and periodic violence against a group, represent an evolution that, especially when combined with an ideology of antagonism, make a seemingly sudden flare-up of intense violence possible. In this context, the invasion of the RPF and the resulting mutual violence also enhanced the potential for more intense violence.

THE ROLE OF ELITES

An extensive media campaign, especially involving radio, was used against Tutsis; the propaganda called them cockroaches and incited fear and hatred. Although the RPF did commit some atrocities (killing of noncombatant civilians) after the genocide began (des Forges, 1999), there were earlier, false reports of atrocities by them. People were told that the Tutsis were going to return to reclaim all their property. Paramilitary groups were created and prepared to engage in genocide. The Hutu president was assassinated, apparently by the Hutu leadership, possibly in part as a result of a power struggle and in part to subvert the multiparty system and power-sharing with Tutsis that he had agreed to. The genocide began immediately after this.

The genocide was organized and systematic, its aim the elimination of the Tutsi population. Des Forges (1999) presents evidence that an extremist Hutu leadership strategically used the image of the Tutsi as an absolute menace, together with threats to and violence against dissidents. What the accounts do not sufficiently stress is that even when such images are strategically used, they tend to be based on psychological realities, such as intense devaluation, antagonism, and fear. Although the genocide was primarily perpetrated by the army and paramilitary groups, the tactics used by the leadership, combined with the historical division between Tutsis and Hutus and the tendency to obey authorities, succeeded in involving a significant although probably relatively small portion of the population as perpetrators. However, some Hutus tried to protect Tutsis. Most of the few who did so publicly were killed. As the genocide began, Hutus were killed for political reasons. Later, some were killed for their property (des Forges, 1999). As violence evolves, such expansion of it is quite common (Staub, 1989).

THE ROLE OF BYSTANDERS

In response to the first invasion by the RPF, the French sent troops to support the government. They made no response to "small-scale" massacres of Tutsis that followed, such as the killings of about 2,000 Tutsi peasants in 1993. As passionately described by Gourevitch (1998), the international community made no response to reports of the impending violence against the Tutsi, which came from varied sources, including Human Rights Watch. The United Nations (UN) took no action on the information about plans for a genocide that the head of the UN peacekeeping troops, General Dallaire, received from a highly placed Rwandan. As the genocide began, some Belgian peacekeepers were killed. Partly under Belgian influence, the UN removed its peacekeepers. Not to invoke the genocide convention, which would have created strong pressure to take action, the world, including and in part led by the U.S. government, avoided the use of the term *genocide* (see des Forges, 1999).

CULTURAL PREDISPOSITIONS

The division between Tutsis, who were cattle-herding warriors conquering ethnically diverse farming peoples in the fifteenth century, and Hutus, who were farmers, over time became primarily a division of economic status and political power. The Tutsis ruled, in a complex relationship with the Hutus, until early in the twentieth century. The Belgian colonizers created structural changes in the relation between Hutu and Tutsi that greatly enhanced Tutsi dominance and Hutu exploitation, intensifying Hutu hostility toward Tutsis. Soon after the Hutu revolution in 1959, when many Tutsis were killed, Rwanda gained independence, leaving the Hutu majority to rule the country.

The Hutu government had total control over the population. Everyone was registered. People had to carry ethnic identity cards and were not allowed to move without registering. Tutsis had no access to the public domain. Observers have reported that child-rearing was authoritarian (Smith, 1998), the culture was characterized by strong respect for and obedience to authority, and society was organized in a highly hierarchical fashion. There also had to be some woundedness among the Hutu, due to their past experiences as a subordinate, badly treated group. Even though the Tutsis suffered discrimination, their past history, culture, and better education enabled them to have good jobs in the small but important private sector. This situation – a devalued, disliked group doing relatively well – intensifies hostility, as many instances show, including the Jews in Germany and the Armenians in Turkey (Staub, 1989).

GENOCIDE AND AFTER THE GENOCIDE

It was in this cultural and societal context that intensely difficult life conditions developed, consisting of economic problems, social injustice, political unrest and demands by the population, divisions within the Hutu leadership, and the invasion by a Tutsi army. It was in this context that intense anti-Tutsi feelings were propagated by the leadership and an effective machinery for the destruction of the Tutsi was developed that centered around the use of paramilitary groups and parts of the army. The motivations discussed in previous sections, the anti-Tutsi ideology and propaganda, fear of the Tutsi, violence against Hutus who did not cooperate, and obedience to leaders, led segments of the population to participate in the killings. The killings were finally brought to an end by the victory of the RPF.

The renewed passivity of bystanders following the genocide has contributed to renewed violence. Huge numbers of Hutus left the country after the victory of the RPF and were settled in refugee camps outside the border. Among them were the perpetrators of the genocide. They were not separated from the rest of the refugees. After a while they renewed their violence against the Tutsis, at first with incursions into the country from the camps. Later some of them returned with the rest of the refugees and continued the killings from inside the country. Others continued the violence from the neighboring Congo (Gourevitch, 1998), contributing to a war in that country.

References

Cairns, E., & Darby, J. (1998). The conflict in Northern Ireland. *American Psychologist, 53*, 754–760.

Carnegie Commission on the Prevention of Deadly Conflict. (1997). *Preventing deadly conflict: Final report*. New York: Carnegie Corporation of New York.

Charny, I. (1991). Genocide intervention and prevention. *Social Education*, 124–127.

Comas-Diaz, L., Lynes, M. B., & Alarcon, R. D. (1998). Ethnic conflict and the psychology of liberation in Guatemala, Peru, and Puerto Rico. *American Psychologist, 53*, 778–792.

des Forges. A. (1999). *Leave none to tell the story: Genocide in Rwanda*. New York: Human Rights Watch.

Fein, H. (1979). *Accounting for genocide: Victims and survivors of the Holocaust*. New York: Free Press.

Fein, H. (1990). Genocide: A sociological perspective [Special issue]. *Current Sociology, 38*, 1–126.

Fein, H. (1994). *The prevention of genocide*. New York: City University of New York.

Gourevitch, P. (1998). *We wish to inform you that tomorrow we will be killed with our families*. New York: Farrar, Straus & Giroux.

Kelman, H. C. (1973). Violence without moral restraint: Reflections on the dehumanization of victims and victimizers. *Journal of Social Issues, 29*, 4, 25–61.

Kelman, H. C., & Hamilton, V. C. (1989). *Crimes of obedience*. New Haven: Yale University Press.

Kressel, N. J. (1996). *Mass hate: The global rise of genocide and terror*. New York: Plenum.

Kuper, L. (1981). *Genocide. Its political use in the twentieth century*. New Haven, CT: Yale University Press.

Prunier. G. (1995). *The Rwanda crisis: History of a genocide*. New York: Columbia University Press.

Rouhana, N. N., & Bar-Tal, D. (1998). Psychological dynamics of intractable ethnonational conflicts: The Israeli–Palestinian case. *American Psychologist, 53*, 761–770.

Smith, N. S. (1998). The psychological roots of genocide. *American Psychologist, 53*, 743–753.

Staub, E. (1989). *The roots of evil: The origins of genocide and other group violence*. New York: Cambridge University Press.

Staub, E. (1996a). Cultural–societal roots of violence: The examples of genocidal violence and of contemporary youth violence in the United States. *American Psychologist, 51*, 117–132.

Staub, E. (1996b). Preventing genocide: Activating bystanders, helping victims and the creation of caring. *Peace and Conflict: Journal of Peace Psychology, 2*, 189–201.

Suedfeld, P. (Ed.). (1990). *Psychology and torture*. Washington, DC: Hemisphere.

26

Bystanders as Evil

The Example of Rwanda

The passivity and/or complicity of "bystander nations" was especially horrifying in the case of Rwanda. It is important to examine it as a case study of what should not happen. In addition to considering perpetrators of great and "unjustified" violence as evil, should passivity that allows great harm to others ever be considered evil?

The circumstances bystanders face in a situation such as Rwanda are different from those of witnesses who see in front of them a person who is in great distress and needs help (des Forges, 1999). Even then, circumstances are usually ambiguous: There is pluralistic ignorance, diffusion of responsibility, and the diffidence of many people to step forward (Latané & Darley, 1970; Staub, 1974). However, circumstances preceding collective violence are often more ambiguous. Perpetrators usually claim self-defense or other good reasons for what they do. When there is mob violence against a victim group, which often is instigated by authorities, participants and the authorities usually claim that it was the spontaneous response of the population to threat, danger, and violent actions by others.

In this spirit, perhaps, France sent troops to help the Rwandan government in 1990, when a small rebel group that called itself the Rwandan Patriotic Front (RPF) entered the country from Uganda. This group consisted primarily of Tutsi refugees who had lived in Uganda since they escaped earlier waves of violence against Tutsis, beginning in 1959. The French help temporarily stopped the RPF, but its activities intensified again after massacres of Tutsi peasants by Hutus, who make up about 85% of the population in Rwanda. France did not complain to the government about these massacres and continued to help militarily (Gourevitch, 1998; Prunier, 1995). In 1993, the government and the RPF agreed, in the Arusha

Reprinted from E. Staub (1999). The roots of evil: Personality, social conditions, culture and basic human needs. *Personality and Social Psychology Review*, 3, 179–192. Included here are pp. 185–187. Reprinted with permissions of Lawrence Erlbaum Associates.

accords, to a multiparty government that would include the RPF. The accord prohibited the acquisition of more arms by the parties, but France continued to send arms to the government.

Bystanders often respond to events on the basis of a history of relationships they have had with the parties involved. They refrain from assessing and making decisions on the basis of actual events, moral principles, and human suffering. They either do not exercise prudence or good judgment, which the ancient Greeks regarded an essential element of morality (Staub, 1978), or they act on the basis of sentiments and what they regard as their interests. France may have acted as it did, in part, because of a friendship between President Mitterrand of France and the president of Rwanda, Habyarimana. France also may have acted as it did because the RPF came from Uganda, which in the colonial era was ruled by England, and France feared that an Anglophile influence would spread into an area of Africa they considered their domain (Gourevitch, 1998; Prunier, 1995).

However, France was not the only culprit. Information about impending violence and later about the ongoing genocide against Tutsis had come to the rest of the world from many quarters. Human Rights Watch issued alarming reports. The commanding general of the United Nations peacekeeping force, Major General Dallaire, received information from a person within the Rwandan president's circle of plans for a genocide against the Tutsis. He was not allowed to take action but was told by his superiors within the United Nations to communicate this information to President Habyarimana, whose circle prepared the plans for genocide (des Forges, 1999).

As the violence began in April 1994, some Belgian peacekeepers were killed. Belgium withdrew its contingent of peacekeepers, and the United Nations followed, withdrawing most of them. As the genocidal proportions of this violence emerged, General Dallaire claimed, and many now believe, that he could have stopped it all with 5,000 troops. However, no one was interested in such action. Within a few months, as many as 800,000 people were killed (some estimate 1 million; see Gourevitch, 1998), most of them Tutsis, but also more than 50,000 Hutus who were seen as politically "moderate" or who were from the South in contrast to the group in power, which came from the Northwest. (For an application of the conception of the origins in genocide to Rwanda, see Chapter 25 in this book.)

The United States was a passive bystander but also acted in ways that made a response by others less likely. The United Nations, other nations, and the United States resisted calling the violence genocide, so that the genocide convention, which requires or at least creates strong pressure for a response, would not be invoked. The United States resisted and slowed down a vote in the Security Council on sending back peacekeepers, even though U.S. troops were not required. The United States refused to provide equipment but insisted on leasing it to the United Nations. The United

States and the United Nations haggled over the amount to be paid for the equipment, while every day many thousands of people were killed (Gourevitch, 1998).

Does it make sense to call the passivity and at times complicity by bystander nations "evil" in the face of information about impending violence, and especially in the face of actual, very large-scale violence? Previous selections suggest both that such passivity (and, of course, even more support or complicity) makes the evolution toward genocide more likely by encouraging and affirming perpetrators, and that bystander nations have great potential influence in inhibiting this evolution. In addition, at times, the need for action is clear and there are low-cost ways to at least attempt to exert influence (see also Staub, 1989, 1996a, 1996b, 1999; 2000).

Passivity and various forms of support for perpetrators by outside nations contribute to extreme harm. Often, there is no provocation to justify even limited violence against the victims, much less genocide – or passivity in the face of it. The passivity and complicity often persist. In its physical properties, the situation is highly dissimilar from allowing a young child to drown while one is watching, but in its meaning, it is similar. Perhaps it is also like passively watching while someone is drowning the child, without even calling out to the person to stop. Although passivity is different from action, in terms of the definition of evil offered previously, the kind of passivity and complicity I discuss here is comparable in its effects to the actions that may be called evil. Even passivity in this case involved action – as tortuous contortions by a spokeswoman for the U.S. State Department in avoiding the use of the term *genocide* in relation to Rwanda indicated, together with other actions to stop the international community from responding. Calling certain kinds of passivity and especially complicity evil might have influence on the behavior of nations, which is important for the prevention of future genocides.

Highly questionable actions on the part of international humanitarian organizations and the United Nations followed the genocide. The RPF defeated the government army and stopped the genocide. Elements of this army, together with paramilitary groups – the *interahamwe* – were the prime perpetrators of the genocide. These "genocidaires," together with huge numbers of Hutus – who either participated in the genocide, were pressured or forced by the genocidaires, or frightened by the propaganda about the Tutsis' murderous intentions – fled into neighboring countries. The 1.5 million to 2 million refugees lived in camps, the largest ones in Zaire, very near the Rwandan border. These camps were run by the former army and the *interahamwe*. They ruled over the refugees, stopped those who were so inclined from returning home, used the aid they received as a source of income, and bought large shipments of arms that were delivered to the camps. After awhile, they began incursions into Rwanda, killing many Tutsis and some Hutus who were regarded as sympathetic to Tutsis, and destroying and stealing property. The humanitarian organizations and international community did nothing to deal with this situation, allowing not only ongoing violence but the buildup of the capacity for continuing the genocide. Although some humanitarian organizations, aware of what was happening, pulled out, others immediately took their place.

Part of the problem seemed to be systemic. Humanitarian organizations have a mandate, which is to provide assistance. They do not ask why people need help or make policy judgments as to who should or should not receive help. Under these circumstances, a split self may develop, as in the hero of George Orwell's *1984* (1949) who opposes the totalitarian system and understands the absurdity of the government declaring the friend of yesterday an enemy and the enemy of yesterday a friend, but nonetheless goes about his job with great enthusiasm, erasing written information about the past and replacing it with a false history that is consistent with current circumstance (Staub, 1989). However, part of the problem also may have been what Gourevitch (1998) described as a well-known syndrome, "clientitis," the tendency by humanitarian organizations to see only, and be taken in by, the perspective of their client.

The reason for the United Nations and the international community to do nothing about the situation in the camps may have been similar to their usual reasons for inaction: a difficult situation, the absence of clear national interest to motivate action, and a disregard of the human costs of passivity. Besides, action was already taken – people in the camps were being helped. Perhaps there is also some truth to more sinister motives seen by Kegame, the vice president of Rwanda (Gourevitch, 1998): Africans, like the Tutsi-led RPF, took events into their own hands, in Rwanda and in Zaire, without guidance and influence by the international community. Moreover, these actions defeated the aims of major international actors, particularly France, who supported the Hutu genocidaires until the very end.

Passivity was certainly not all due to blindness. In the first few months after the genocide, there was discussion within the United Nations of assembling an international force to disarm the "militants" in the camps and separate out from the rest of the refugees the criminal elements and the political forces planning a continuation of the genocide. However, in response to a request for volunteers by the United Nations Secretary-General, no country was willing to provide troops.

References

des Forges, A. (1999). *Leave none to tell the story: Genocide in Rwanda*. New York: Human Rights Watch.

Gourevitch, P. (1998). *We wish to inform you that tomorrow we will be killed with our families*. New York: Farrar, Straus & Giroux.

Greven, P.(1991). *Spare the child: The religious roots of punishment and the impact of physical abuse*. New York: Knopf.

Latané, B., & Darley, J. (1970). *The unresponsive bystander: Why doesn't he help?* New York: Appleton-Century-Crofts.

Lifton, R. J. (1986). *The Nazi doctors: Medical killing and the psychology of genocide*. New York: Basic Books.

Orwell, G. (1949). *Nineteen eighty four*. New York: Harcourt, Brace & World.

Prunier, G. (1995). *The Rwanda crisis: History of a genocide*. New York: Columbia University Press.

Staub, E. (1974). Helping a distressed person: Social, personality and stimulus determinants. In L. Berkowitz (Ed.), *Advances in experimental social psychology* (Vol. 7, pp. 203–342). New York: Academic.

Staub, E. (1978). *Positive social behavior and morality: Social and personal influences* (Vol. 1). New York: Academic.

Staub, E. (1989). *The roots of evil: The origins of genocide and other group violence*. New York: Cambridge University Press.

Staub, E. (1996a). Cultural–societal roots of violence: The examples of genocidal violence and of contemporary youth violence in the United States. *American Psychologist*, *51*, 117–132.

Staub, E. (1996b). Preventing genocide: Activating bystanders, helping victims and the creation of caring. *Peace and Conflict: Journal of Peace Psychology*, *2*, 189–201.

Staub, E. (1999). The origins and prevention of genocide, mass killing and other collective violence. *Peace and Conflict: Journal of Peace Psychology*, *5*(4), 303–337.

Staub, E. (2000). Mass murder: Origins, prevention and U.S. involvement. In *Encyclopedia of violence in the United States*. New York: Scribner's.

27

Individual and Group Identities in Genocide and Mass Killing

IDENTITY AND THE ORIGINS OF MASS KILLING AND GENOCIDE: BRIEF REVIEW

I will review and extend here the exploration of origins by describing how individual and group identities are involved in the paths to genocide or mass killing. To begin, severe economic problems deeply impact people. Unemployment, or the inability to provide for oneself and one's family owing to severe inflation, makes people feel insecure and ineffective. Such conditions call into question people's personal identity and self-worth: Who am I if I have no work and cannot take care of the basic material needs of myself and my family? At the same time that identity is questioned, ties to one's group can also weaken because the problems originate in society and social conditions.

Intense political conflict and disorganization also affect people's experience of their group and perception of the world. Rapid social change, which often occurs at times of economic and political crises, adds to social chaos and disorganization. Since substantial social change requires adjustment, even positive change places demands on people.

The different elements of difficult life conditions, which may occur separately but frequently are present in some combination, frustrate many of the basic needs. In difficult times, focusing on their own needs, people become disconnected from each other. At times when they need it most, people lack connection and support. The social upheaval makes their old worldview inadequate in providing a comprehension of reality: an understanding of

Reprinted from E. Staub (2001). Individual and group identities in genocide and mass killing. In R. D. Ashmore, L. Jussim, and D. Wilder, (Eds.), *Social identity, intergroup conflict, and conflict reduction*. New York: Oxford University Press, pp. 159–184. Included here are pp. 163–170.

how people, society, and the world operate, and of their own role or place in the scheme of things.

As a result, when a society experiences persistent, intense life problems, its members desperately need a renewed basis for identity, security, a sense of effectiveness, connection to other people, and comprehension of reality. They turn for identity and the fulfillment of other basic needs to a new group, or to leaders who strengthen the group through scapegoating outsiders or offer it new identity, meaning, and hope through ideologies that promise a better life and offer the fulfillment of basic needs.

IDENTITY, SCAPEGOATING, AND IDEOLOGY

Three types of "identities" are discussed in this chapter: first, *personal identities*, or the ways in which individuals answer the question, Who am I?; second, *social identities*, or the extent to which individual identity is rooted in, or connected to, the group; third, *group self-concepts*, or the socially shared way members perceive and experience their group. Relevant to all of them is a group's culture and the social and political institutions that both express and shape that culture. The nature of individual identity is shaped by culture; in turn, the identities that characterize individuals maintain the culture. Social identity theory has focused on how people categorize themselves (and others) as members of groups, how they identify themselves with certain groups, and the tendency they have to enhance themselves by comparing their group favorably with other groups (Tajfel, 1982; Turner, 1987; Myers, 1999). It emphasizes the psychological experience of rootedness in and connection to the group.

But social identities also have content, as defined by the culture. "We" are intelligent and hardworking, or easygoing and ready to enjoy life, or brave and ready to fight for our rights or for maintaining important values. The content of social identity is what I refer to as group self-concept. While social identity theory stresses the tendency to favorably evaluate one's group, group self-concept can be positive or negative (superior or weak and vulnerable). As in the case of individual identity, consciously held views and evaluations of the group can exist side by side with feelings about and valuations of the group that may not be consciously held, such as a sense of vulnerability or weakness.

Individual identity is, in part, a social identity rooted in groups to which one belongs ranging from family to nation (Tajfel, 1978; 1982; Turner, 1987; Bar-Tal & Staub, 1997). It is not surprising, therefore, that in difficult times people try to strengthen their identity through personal identification with some group. A good social identity – an identity based in a group that is seen in a positive light, for example, as effective and powerful – can also be a good source of security, feelings of effectiveness and control, and connection. The values and worldview of the group also provide a comprehension of reality.

Scapegoating some other group can strengthen both individual and group identity and also help fulfill other needs. If another group is viewed as responsible for life problems, then neither I nor my group are to blame. Scapegoating at such times is usually a social process in that it is done together with like-minded others. This not only builds identity but strengthens security and connection.

Ideologies are almost always a part of the genocidal process. I see ideologies as visions of social arrangements that tell people how to live life. They are blueprints for the organization of societies and relations among individuals. The ideologies created or adopted in difficult times offer the satisfaction of basic needs. They promise people a better life. Sometimes their stated purpose is to improve life for all human beings – what I have called "better world ideologies." Communism has been such an ideology. Nationalistic ideologies promise better life to people in a particular group by enhancing the group's wealth, power, or purity (Staub, 1989b).

Often, ideologies have both better life and nationalistic components. This was true of the Nazi ideology. The Khmer Rouge ideology was ostensibly a better world ideology, focusing on total social equality. But it was group based, looking to the group's history as a simple agricultural society for ways to create this social equality. Without explicit elaboration it also included a strongly nationalistic agenda. This expressed itself in the especially intense violence against the Vietnamese in Cambodia, in hostility to Vietnam, an ancient enemy, and in genocidal violence against other minorities in Cambodia.

Legitimizing ideologies (Levin, Sidanius, Rabinowitz, & Frederico, 1998; Staub, 1989b, 1999) offer justifications for the power and privilege of dominant groups. Violent reactions by powerful groups to demands by subordinate groups for rights and privilege have been one of the most frequent sources of mass killing since World War II (Fein, 1993). In my view, this response of dominant groups is not simply to a threat to their power and privilege. They also respond to a threat to their identity and worldview (Staub, 1989b). They have come to see themselves as rightfully occupying positions of power and influence, owing to their background, history, diligence, intelligence, bravery, or other aspects of their presumed nature. The world is arranged the "right way" with them in power.

People usually hold or turn to and adopt ideologies as part of a group or a movement. At times some people create or put together ideas that form the ideology, as did Hitler (1925) or the leaders of the Khmer Rouge in Cambodia (Staub, 1989b). However, it is when shared among a group of people that an ideology comes to life. The ideology defines the group and gives the group and its individual members a positive social identity.

It also provides a basis for connection. Participating in the movement can make people feel effective and in control. The goals of the movement become the motivating force for members. The ideology and the movement that arise from it often become central sources of people's identity and comprehension of reality.

While human beings need positive visions in difficult times, the ideologies that emerge usually identify another group as an enemy. This group is seen either as the cause of problems, or as standing in the way of the ideology's fulfillment, or both. They, therefore, become the objects of hostility. Harmful actions begin to be directed at them.

THE ROLE OF INDIVIDUAL IDENTITIES IN GENOCIDE

Certain individual identities that a culture promotes make the genocidal process more likely. Research and theory have identified differences in the type of self-concept or individual identity that is shaped by individualist and collectivist cultures (Triandis, 1994). Differences in women's and men's identities in Western societies, including the United States, have also been noted (Sampson, 1988). It has been proposed, for example, that male identity is more autonomous, more like the identity shaped by individualistic cultures, while female identity is more relational, like identities shaped by collectivist cultures.

Considering conditions that give rise to genocide, both relational/collectivist and autonomous/individualist identities may have vulnerabilities. Difficult life conditions may especially frustrate autonomous persons. They have learned to stand on their own, but now they are unable to effectively fend for themselves or their families. American soldiers who became prisoners of war in the Korean War had more difficulty in resisting brainwashing than, for example, Turkish soldiers, seemingly because the former were trying to face it alone while the latter supported each other (Kincaid, 1959).

Relational identities may also create difficulties. People with such identities may feel interconnected with other people in a way that makes it especially difficult to speak out against and oppose the direction the group is beginning to take. As their group or society begins to scapegoat, identify an enemy, discriminate, or take other harmful actions against another group, they are more likely to remain silent and go along. This makes more probable the evolution of increasing discrimination and violence.

I have suggested that relational/collectivist identities may be differentiated into *embedded* and *connected* (Staub, 1993). The embedded identity, which I just described, is characterized by a strong connection to other people that also embodies dependence on the group and an inability to separate from it. In contrast, people who have developed connection to others as inherent to their identities, but who also have learned to stand on their own, to be separate, have connected selves or identities.

The nature of personal identity has implications for people's relationship to their group. People with connected selves may be less likely to give themselves up to the group in difficult times. They may be less likely to relinquish their own identity and give themselves over to a social or group identity than people with embedded selves. Seemingly paradoxically, because they can use others for support more effectively, those with connected self-concepts may be even less likely to do this than people with autonomous/individualist identities. As a result, people with connected selves may be less likely than those with either embedded or autonomous identities to remain passive as the evolution of harm-doing begins. They may be more likely to speak out and oppose actions contrary to their own values, or to the values they believe the group ascribes to. This is extremely difficult to do but is essential in halting the evolution of increasing violence.

I am suggesting that identity-related differences in individuals' relationship to the group have implications for group violence. Related to this, I have proposed that some individuals are "constructively" patriotic while others are "blindly" patriotic (Staub, 1997). In research exploring this we find that constructive patriots express love for their group, but also a willingness to question and criticize the policies and practices of the group that are contrary to caring values and concern for human welfare, or contrary to what they see as important group values (Schatz & Staub, 1997; Schatz, Staub, & Lavine, 1999). Although this has not been assessed in the research, I expect that constructive patriots would have connected identities. In contrast, blind patriots, who I expect to have either individualist or embedded self-concepts, love their group but are unwilling to criticize it or to question its policies or practices. Different identity types and associated relationships to the group have clear implications for supporting or opposing destructive views and group practices.

Other classifications of individual identities that are relevant to genocide are possible. Some people may have secure identities (Staub, 1993). Presumably their basic need for security has been fulfilled in the course of their lives, especially early lives. Perhaps they also have had experiences with taking effective action to protect themselves. As a result they feel reasonably secure in the world. They would be less affected by instigating conditions, such as difficult life conditions, and less moved to the psychological and social processes that were described as a consequence of such conditions. Others, perhaps due to the frustration of the need for security early in life, including victimization or other traumas, may develop insecure identities, making it more likely that these psychological processes leading to genocide unfold in response to instigating conditions.

AUTHORITY ORIENTATION AND IDENTITY

Observation and research indicate that in many cases of genocide or mass killing the society has been characterized by strong respect for authority (Gourevitch, 1998; Kressel, 1996; Smith, 1998; Staub, 1989b, 1999). "Authority orientation" in the culture is a term I prefer to "authoritarian personality" because it focuses purely on respect for authority and hierarchy, without implications of repression of sexual feelings and other characteristics that have been described as aspects of the authoritarian personality.

Authority orientation affects the nature of identity in a number of ways. Individuals who have embedded selves are connected to others through networks of dependent relationships. People in an authority-oriented culture also seem deeply embedded in the group, but this is based on their orientation to authority. The experiences they have as this orientation is developed in them, normally from early childhood on, diminish the evolution of a strong independent self.

In the face of difficult life conditions or group conflict, people who have relied on leaders for guidance and protection will find it more difficult to bear the threat, anxiety, and frustration of basic needs. When policies and practices are instituted in a group that harm others, they will be less willing to speak out and to oppose the authorities and the rest of the group. Strong respect for authority also makes obedience to immoral orders by authorities more likely.

THE NATURE OF GROUP SELF-CONCEPT

Weakness, Superiority, and a Positive Self-Concept

The nature of group self-concept (by which I mean the way members consensually see and experience their group) is also important. How do members of a group, people who identify with a group, see their group? What is their conception and experience of the group? And how do differences in group self-concept predispose toward mass killing or genocide? I have hypothesized (Staub, 1989b) that *both* a sense of weakness and vulnerability, *and* feelings and beliefs of superiority, may make it more likely that groups will turn to and engage in systematic violence against others. When a group feels weak and vulnerable, life problems in the society or conflict with other groups will intensify vulnerability and the need to defend oneself. Elevating the group, scapegoating another group, creating "positive visions" that identify enemies, and self-defense through aggression become more likely.

A sense of superiority, when frustrated, may also become a powerful source of psychological processes and actions that contribute to genocide. Feeling superior makes individuals and groups vulnerable to disconfirmation of their superiority and, as a result, likely to experience narcissistic wounds (Baumeister, 1997). However, a self-concept of superiority is different from a high self-esteem. Feelings of superiority may be the result of a history of success by a society in many realms combined with the usual ethnocentrism of groups that leads to interpretation of this success as evidence of the group's superiority. But more often, a belief in one's superiority is exaggerated and may represent a compensatory identity. In the lives of most individuals and groups there are enough small and large experiences of ineffectiveness, failure, and loss that, under normal conditions, a more moderate sense of self would develop.

A positive identity in individuals is likely to arise from experiences of nurturance and affirmation and from success in overcoming obstacles. Comparable experiences on the group level can give rise to positive group self-concepts. The absence of these may lead to low self-concept. Their absence, or negative experiences, overlaid with experiences of success but without incorporating the difficult, painful experiences into one's identity, can lead to a feeling of superiority, which is what I regard as a compensatory identity. In children a defensive self-esteem or defensive egotism, which was found to be different from high self-esteem, was associated with more bullying of others. Defensive self-esteem was ascribed to children who described themselves and were described by others as having positive self-esteem, but were also described by others as "always wants to be the center of attention; thinks too much of himself or herself; can't take criticism" (Salmivalli, Kaukiainen, Kaistaniemi, & Lagerspetz, 1999, p. 1271).

Germany may be a good example of having a superior group self-concept. The group self-concept of Germans early in this century was extremely positive, of a kind that may be described as a superior compensatory identity. This was due to recent military successes, economic strength, a history of cultural achievement, effective civic institutions, and an internal climate that propagated self-satisfaction with German culture and society beyond what is "normal" ethnocentrism (Staub, 1989b).

These positive experiences might account for what seems was an early twentieth-century German sense of superiority. But Germans also had a history of problems and suffering. Many Germans died in wars in previous centuries. During the Thirty Years' War (1618–1648), a third of Germany's population died (Craig, 1982). After struggles among many smaller units, Germany became a single country only late in the nineteenth century. History leaves its mark, and perhaps underlying the outward sense of group superiority there was also a deep-seated national vulnerability. Germany was then frustrated by a series of events beginning with the loss of World War I. These included a revolution that overthrew the monarchy, hyperinflation, economic depression, political chaos, and actions by other countries that Germans felt were humiliating to them (e.g., the French occupying the Ruhr district to ensure the receipt of compensation Germany was forced to pay after World War I). Whether it was defensive egoism, or normal ethnocentrism, or even a "genuine" sense of superiority, the nature of their group identity was likely important in Germans' reactions to the intense life problems following World War I.

A decade ago I wrote: "in groups and in individuals very high self-evaluation often masks self-doubt. Persistent life difficulties may contradict high self-evaluation and bring self-doubt to the surface. Even when there is no underlying self-doubt, a very high self-evaluation may be associated with limited concern for others. Among individuals, a *moderately* positive self-concept is most strongly associated with sensitivity and responsiveness to other people" (from Staub, 1989b, p. 55; see also Jarymowitz, 1977; Reese, 1961). This still seems a reasonable conclusion. Both individuals and groups have to value themselves in order to value other people, but not value themselves so strongly that others do not matter, or so highly and unrealistically that setbacks are experienced as devastating blows to collective and personal self-worth.

References

Bar-Tal, D., & Staub, E. (1997). Introduction: The nature and forms of patriotism. In D. Bar-Tal & E. Staub (Eds.), *Patriotism in the lives of individuals and groups*. Chicago: Nelson-Hall.

Baumeister, R. F. (1997). *Evil: Inside human violence and cruelty*. New York: W. H. Freeman.

Craig, G. A. (1982). *The Germans*. New York: New American Library.

des Forges, A. (1999). *Leave none to tell the story: Genocide in Rwanda*. New York: Human Rights Watch.

Fein, H. (1993). Accounting for genocide after 1945: Theories and some findings. *International Journal of Group Rights*, *1*, 79–106.

Gourevitch, P. (1998). *We wish to inform you that tomorrow we will be killed with our families*. New York: Farrar, Straus & Giroux.

Hitler, A. (1925). *Mein Kampf*. Translated by Ralph Manheim. Boston, MA: Houghton Mifflin Company.

Jarymowitz, M. (1977). Modification of self-worth and increment of prosocial sensitivity. *Polish Psychological Bulletin*, *8*, 45–53.

Kincaid, E. (1959). *In every war but one*. New York: Norton.

Kressel, N. J. (1996). *Mass hate: The global rise of genocide and terror*. New York: Plenum Press.

Levin, S., Sidanius, J., Rabinowitz, J. L., & Frederico, C. (1998). Ethnic identity, legitimizing ideologies and social status: A matter of ideological asymmetry. *Political Psychology*, *19*, 373–404.

Myers, D. (1999). *Social psychology*. New York: McGraw-Hill.

Reese, H. (1961). Relationships between self-acceptance and sociometric choices. *Journal of Abnormal and Social Psychology*, *62*.

Salmivalli, C., Kaukiainen, A., Kaistaniemi, L., & Lagerspetz, K. M. J. (1999). Self-evaluated self-esteem, peer-evaluated self-esteem, and defensive egotism as predictors of adolescents' participation in bullying situations. *Personality and Social Psychology Bulletin, 25,* 1268–1278.

Sampson, E. E. (1988). The debate on individualism. *American Psychologist, 47,* 15–22.

Schatz, R., & Staub, E. (1997). Manifestations of blind and constructive patriotism. In D. Bar-Tal & E. Staub (Eds.), *Patriotism in the lives of individuals and groups.* Chicago: Nelson-Hall.

Schatz, R., Staub, E. & Lavine, H. (1999). On the varieties of national attachment: Blind versus constructive patriotism. *Political Psychology, 20,* 151–175.

Smith, N. S. (1998). The psychocultural roots of genocide. *American Psychologist, 53,* 743–753.

Staub, E. (1989a). Steps along the continuum of destruction: The evolution of bystanders, German psychoanalysts and lessons for today. *Political Psychology, 10,* 39–53.

Staub, E. (1989b). *The roots of evil: The origins of genocide and other group violence.* New York: Cambridge University Press.

Staub, E. (1993). Individual and group selves, motivation and morality. In T. Wren & G. Noam (Eds.), *Morality and the self* (pp. 337–359). Cambridge: MIT Press.

Staub, E. (1997). Blind versus constructive patriotism: Moving from embeddedness in the group to critical loyalty and action. In E. Staub & D. Bar-Tal (Eds.), *Patriotism.* Chicago: Nelson-Hall.

Staub, E. (1999). The origins and prevention of genocide, mass killing, and other collective violence. *Peace and Conflict: Journal of Peace Psychology, 5* (4), 303–336.

Tajfel, H. (1978). Social categorization, social identity and social comparison. In H. Tajfel (Ed.), *Differentiation between social groups* (pp. 61–76). London: Academic Press.

Tajfel, H. (1982). Social psychology of intergroup relations. *Annual Review of Psychology, 33,* 1–39.

Triandis, H. C. (1994). *Culture and social behavior.* New York: McGraw-Hill.

Turner, J. C. (1987). *Rediscovering the social groups: A self-categorization theory.* New York: Basil Blackwell.

28

Mass Murder

U.S. Involvement as Perpetrator, Passive Bystander, Helper

This chapter examines the involvement of the United States in mass murder: as perpetrator, as indirect actor involved in creating conditions contributing to mass murder, as well as a bystander that supported perpetrators, remained passive, or actively attempted to halt mass murder.

THE UNITED STATES AS PERPETRATOR: MASS KILLING OF NATIVE AMERICANS

Native Americans, profoundly different in appearance and ways of life from the whites arriving from Europe, were seen as primitive, uncivilized, with no culture. Over time, they came to be also seen as violent and dangerous. Devaluation, fear and self-interest, wanting the land on which Native Americans lived, all affected policies toward them. There was an evolution of increasing harm-doing that led to mass murder.

At first, Native Americans were to be civilized, presumably to lessen their difference from other Americans and to enable them to function in America. Trade, religious missions and conversion, white schooling for the children were all to serve these purposes (Sheehan, 1973). These "civilizing" acts were seen as altruistic. Native Americans were changing in response, but not to a sufficient degree. They continued to live tribal lives and occupy huge areas of land. The policy was changed to relocate Native Americans to the West. This would both remove them from the vicinity of other Americans and provide land. Many tribes resisted relocation, which was to be enforced by the U.S. Army. There were many battles, especially after 1829, when Andrew Jackson became president. Some tribes fought until few remained alive. The policies and practices toward

Reprinted from E. Staub (2000). Mass murder: Origins, prevention, and U.S. involvement. *Violence in America: An Encyclopedia, Vol.* 2. New York: Charles Scribner's Sons, pp. 1, 6–17, 23–25. 1999 Gale Group. Reprinted by permission of The Gale Group.

Native Americans became increasingly harsh. While there seemed to be no overall plan, and probably no conscious intention of extermination, these practices constituted mass murder. These practices were made possible by a view of Native Americans as profoundly inferior. They were implicitly supported by the ideology of manifest destiny, which affirmed the right of Americans to expand westward. They were supported by the participation of many Americans who accepted free land or bought land taken from Native Americans at a low cost. They were supported by the passivity of the rest of the population (Pronovost, 1998).

The policy of relocation and the increasing violence against Native Americans was also justified by their violence. This was probably primarily the result of the tremendous upheavals in their lives and the violence against them after the arrival of Europeans in America. Members of certain tribes, like the Apache, came to be seen as intent to destroy whites. The army was ordered to kill every member of that tribe, a genocidal policy (Tebbel, 1966).

LYNCHINGS OF AFRICAN AMERICANS

Between 1865 and 1955 more than 5,000 black people were killed by lynch mobs in the U.S. The killings were perpetrated mostly in the South. In combination, this represents a form of mass murder. Lynchings took place in the context of deep-seated devaluation and hostility. Black people, when they were originally brought to the Americas, were devalued because they were different in appearance, language, ways of life, culture. In addition, violently taking them from their homes, making them into and keeping them as slaves, had to be justified. They had to be seen as less human, especially in a country that was founded on the basic principles of the dignity, rights, and equality of human beings. The laws and social customs after emancipation, like desegregation, continually reinforced the devaluation. In the climate of devaluation and persecution that existed, and especially once lynching became an established practice, the motivation for it could easily arise. Self-interested motivation could also enter: some lynchings were initiated by a white person starting a rumor about a provocative or criminal act by a black business competitor. Given the underlying social and psychological base, sometimes lynchings occurred relatively spontaneously. At other times they were planned, especially by the Ku Klux Klan.

An implicit blueprint or normative pattern is indicated by newspaper accounts of lynchings in the South around the turn of the century. A Negro was accused of a crime, like the murder of a white person or the rape of a white woman. The community responded with outrage. A mob formed, usually of men and boys (who were thereby socialized into mob conduct and lynching). The mob captured the accused, or overran a jail where he (occasionally she) was held. The victim was carried to a place of execution and frequently underwent horrendous torture. Women and children were often present as spectators. The victim was then hanged or burned. Not infrequently, the "real" perpetrator was later found and lynched (Ginzburg, 1988).

MASS KILLING AT MY LAI

In war, usually "enemy images" are created that express fear, hostility, and anger. They make it easier for soldiers to fight and kill and for the population to accept the hardship of war and provide support for it. There is usually also an ideology, whether nationalism, or in the case of Vietnam, anticommunism and the defense of liberty. The immediate danger to their lives and the hostility and anger generated when their friends are killed create additional hostility in soldiers. In Vietnam, the belief that civilians aided and abetted the enemy contributed to feelings of distrust and hate of Vietnamese people in general.

"Charlie" Company had experienced many of the stresses and dangers that surrounded the war in Vietnam: heat, discomfort, unpredictable danger from mortar rounds in the night, booby traps, mines. For a period of a month before they entered the village of My Lai, they were unable to engage the enemy while suffering casualties from mines and booby traps. They were described as being in an anticipatory mood on the eve of the operation, looking forward to finally doing what they were there for.

However, they found not a single combatant in the village of My Lai, only unarmed women, children, and old men. Using a variety of methods, the company killed around five to six hundred of these unarmed villagers. The largest number of people were killed in the hamlet My Lai 4, where the first platoon of the company, commanded by Lieutenant William L. Calley, killed villagers in groups of twenty to forty with rifles, machine guns, and grenades (Peck, 1983).

In war, the engagement by soldiers in violence and the orientation toward the enemy that is partly created, partly develops, makes the evolution of increased violence probable. Without strong restraint imposed by authorities, brutality in fighting and violence against civilians become likely. In Vietnam the policy of body counts, of judging success by how many enemies were killed, probably contributed to this evolution.

Other atrocities, such as rape and murder of civilians, were also committed by American soldiers in Vietnam. In one postwar study of Vietnam veterans, 20% of the men acknowledged having witnessed atrocities; in another study 9% admitted having personally committed atrocities (Herman, 1992). The military and civilian authorities were passive bystanders to atrocities. Bystanders include individuals and groups who are in a position to know about harmful, violent behavior, but do not take in or avoid relevant information. The authorities ignored information they had or was available, allowing atrocities to happen. The media in the United States did not report rumors of atrocities. There was nothing done to counteract the forces that make such behavior probable.

DRESDEN AND HIROSHIMA

The carpet-bombing of the German city of Dresden during World War II, by Allied forces, killed much of the population of that city. Enemies are usually intensely devalued, and more so as a war goes on, with intense "enemy images" created. But there were also special sources of hostility toward Germany. Germany initiated the war, it engaged in tremendous atrocities, it was working on the development of an atom bomb. Its victory would have been a great threat to America. All this made not only the Nazi rulers of Germany, but to some extent all Germans, seen as evil. It was hoped that the bombing of Dresden would bring Germany to its knees.

With Japan also, there were special sources of hostility, such as the surprise Japanese attack on Pearl Harbor, Japanese atrocities in China and other places, Kamikaze pilots and the determination of Japan and its soldiers. The belief that without demonstrating the devastating power of the United States Japan would fight to the last resort was the motivation and/or justification to use the atom bomb in Hiroshima and Nagasaki. Perhaps the use of the bomb was also intended to communicate a message to the rest of the world, especially the Soviet Union, about American power. Perhaps there was also a strong desire to see how the bomb operated. The atom bomb was used in a context of heavy bombing of Japanese cities, particularly Tokyo, that had already created many civilian deaths.

Both the bombing of Dresden and the use of the atom bomb in Japan seem an outcome of the evolution of increasing violence. A system of destruction existed, the "other" was seen as evil and intent on destroying the United States. The distinction between soldiers and civilians broke down.

HATE CRIMES IN THE UNITED STATES

While most hate crimes in the United States are actions against individuals, some, like the bombing of the Federal Building in Oklahoma, are directed at large numbers of people. Hate groups in the United States have a long history, with the Ku Klux Klan a prominent example. They reemerged in the last decades probably in part as a result of tremendous societal changes. Even positive changes such as increased civil rights for everyone and greater rights for women demand difficult adjustment by individuals. But these changes will not seem positive to people who are intensely prejudiced or need to feel superior to women or minorities. While the characteristics of hate groups in the United States around the turn of the century vary, they have some common elements. One of these is intense devaluation of African Americans and Jews. Another is a tendency to see the government as part of a conspiracy against the American people. A third is having many young members, who tend to have experienced substantial neglect or abuse in their lives (Ezekiel, 1995). The group provides them with connection to other people, a sense of identity and a worldview.

THE UNITED STATES AS ACTOR IN THE INTERNATIONAL REALM

Contributing to Conditions Leading to Mass Murder

The United States has contributed to conditions leading to the genocide in Cambodia. It involved Cambodia in the Vietnam War by pursuing Vietnamese troops into Cambodia. It destabilized the country by supporting the overthrow of the Cambodian ruler, Norodom Sihanouk. It extensively bombed heavily populated areas because they were in the hands of the communists, the Khmer Rouge. This turned the peasants against the government, which they incorrectly believed asked for the bombing, radicalized them, and made it easier for the radical Pol Pot group to gain their support. It accidentally helped the Pol Pot group as other Khmer Rouge factions competing with them for power were decimated by heavy U.S. bombing in the course of a major communist offensive in 1973 (Etcheson, 1984). The United States has also contributed to conditions for mass killing in Central and South American countries, particularly in Guatemala. In Guatemala in 1954 the democratically elected president was overthrown in an invasion by the United States. He was seen as a leftist. The action to overthrow him was probably motivated by a combination of anticommunist ideology and the policy of containing communism, and by the desire to protect U.S. economic interests in Guatemala. The same motivations subsequently led to the support of violent regimes in other South American countries.

Decades of military rule followed in Guatemala. In the context of fighting guerrillas (that is, subordinate groups rising up against the dominant group), many civilians were killed, especially from the native Indian population. Villages and their inhabitants were destroyed, individuals disappeared (were abducted and killed) (Comas-Diaz et al., 1998). The United States all along supported these governments. Some members of the military that participated in killings were at times on the CIA payroll.

The School of the Americas trained South American military personnel in counterinsurgency techniques. Some of them later participated in severe human rights violations: the disappearances in Argentina and abducting, torturing, and killing people in other South American countries. In 1964 Defense Secretary McNamara told the U.S. Congress: "The primary objective in Latin America is to aid, whenever necessary, the continual growth of the military and paramilitary forces, so that together with the police and other security forces, they may provide the necessary internal security" (Nunca Mas, 1986, p. 444). However, the United States continued to provide support while these forces, including those members of it that were trained in the United States, engaged in gross human rights violations, including torture and the murder of people who were peacefully working for political change or tried to improve the lives of poor people.

The United States as Passive Bystander

Contributing to conditions that lead to mass killing and being passive bystanders to violence are not always clearly separable. This is demonstrated by the United States increasing its aid to El Salvador in 1984, even though about 40,000 people were killed there between 1979 and 1983, a large percentage of them extrajudicial executions by security forces. A few years later, however, there was intense international pressure on the government of El Salvador, including pressure by the United States. It became known that a group of Jesuit priests and nuns who had been killed were killed by government forces. Seemingly the combination of this pressure, and a successful offensive by the guerillas, finally led the government to engage in serious negotiations. Effective UN participation in the negotiations helped lead to the resolution of the long civil war.

In another instance, in 1936 the nations of the world, including the United States, affirmed Nazi Germany by holding the Olympics in Berlin. U.S. corporations were busy doing business in Germany during the 1930s, in the course of increasing persecution of Jews and other forms of aggression by Germany. During the 1930s and early '40s the United States accepted only 10% of the Jewish refugees the already existing immigration quotas allowed into the country (Wyman, 1984). Most of the people denied entry into the United States and elsewhere later died in extermination and labor camps.

In the 1980s, after Iraq attacked Iran, and continuing after Iraq was using chemical weapons against its Kurdish citizens, the United States and other countries were providing military equipment and economic aid to Iraq. The United States saw Iraq as a counterweight to a fundamentalist, hostile Iran. Since violence evolves when bystanders support perpetrators, it is not surprising that Iraq engaged in further violence, invading Kuwait.

The United States and the international community were also passive bystanders to the genocide in Rwanda. There were warnings of impending violence and even of plans for genocide, for example, from Human Rights Watch and from the commander of the UN peacekeeping force in Rwanda. These warnings were ignored. Once the genocide started, the use of the term "genocide" was avoided so that the UN genocide convention, which requires a response, would not be activated. The size of the UN force was greatly reduced. Attempts to build it up again were especially slowed by

U.S. resistance, perhaps a result of careful checking of all elements of the situation by the government and the Pentagon in order to avoid intensifying the negative attitude of Congress toward the UN.

The United States as Active Bystander

The international boycott of South Africa, in which the United States had a significant role, had a seemingly important role in overthrowing the system of apartheid there. After years of hesitation the limited bombing by NATO, led by the United States, stopped the fighting in Bosnia. The subsequent efforts by the international community, again led by the United States, have greatly increased the chance of peace in Bosnia.

In other parts of the world as well, the United States has been a constructive actor. In Israel its participation as active bystander, as promoter of and partner in working for peace at various times, probably substantially reduced the degree of violence by both parties. In Northern Ireland the United States was one of the parties that helped to move Protestants and Catholics to negotiation, which led to an agreement that offers hope for ending the centuries-old feud and violence.

THE INTERNAL IMPACT OF U.S. ACTIONS IN THE WORLD

As I noted in passing, starting in the 1960s the United States has experienced very great social changes, of many kinds, creating social upheaval. While the United States economy greatly improved during the 1980s, before that there was a decline in U.S. economic strength. There was political turmoil represented in the civil rights movement and inner-city riots, the anti-Vietnam War movement, and the results of the assassination of leaders. There were other important movements, like feminism. Families have changed greatly. Accompanying all this was a kind of social malaise in the country, a self-doubt, a confusion about the identity of America and its people. A part of the reason for this social malaise was probably also the psychological and social impact of U.S. behavior in the world. Citizens of the United States have had a conception of the United States as a moral country. Many people came to see the Vietnam War, the intense destruction the United States has perpetrated on a faraway people, as disconfirming this conception. Being involved elsewhere in the world in the creation of murderous systems, or supporting such systems, or remaining passive in the face of violence against innocent people have raised doubts in the minds of many citizens of the United States about their country as one that uses its power to promote goodness to enhance human welfare.

The confused morality of U.S. actions in the international realm has probably contributed to the unwillingness of the American people to accept loss resulting from humanitarian action and the fear of politicians to risk

American lives in any good cause. As a result, the United States would invade Panama to capture Noriega, a drug-dealing tyrant formerly on the CIA payroll, but fear to take risks for humanitarian causes.

Remaining passive bystanders in the face of others' suffering can create callousness. It is nearly impossible to see great suffering, to do nothing, and to continue to feel caring and empathy. To protect themselves from guilt and empathic suffering, individuals and groups that remain passive need to distance themselves from victims. As a result, their passivity may reduce the likelihood of later action by them.

References

Comas-Diaz, L., Lykes, M. B., & Alarcon, R. D. (1998). Ethnic conflict and the psychology of liberation in Guatemala, Peru, and Puerto Rico. *American Psychologist, 53*, 778–792.

Etcheson, C. (1984). *The rise and demise of democratic Kampuchea*. Boulder, CO: Westview Press.

Ezekiel, R. S. (1995). *The racist mind: Portraits of American neo-Nazis and Klansmen*. New York: Penguin Books.

Ginzburg, R. (1988). *100 years of lynchings*. Baltimore: Black Classic Press.

Herman, J. (1992). *Trauma and recovery*. New York: Basic Books.

Nunca Mas (1986). *The report of the Argentine national commission on the disappeared*. New York: Farrar, Straus & Giroux.

Peck, M. S. (1983). *People of the lie. The hope of healing human evil*. New York: Simon and Schuster.

Pronovost, J. (1998). The mistreatment of Native American people. Unpublished paper. University of Massachusetts at Amherst.

Sheehan, B. (1973). *Seeds of extinction*. Chapel Hill: University of North Carolina Press.

Tebbel, J. (1966). *The compact history of the Indian wars*. New York: Hawthorne Books Inc.

Wyman, D. S. (1984). *The abandonment of Jews: America and the Holocaust, 1941–1945*. New York: Pantheon Books.

29

When Instigation Does Not Result in Mass Murder

Ethnic, religious, political, or national groups can coexist, as they do in Switzerland and in the United States. In Tanzania, in contrast to the rest of Africa, ethnic groups have lived together harmoniously. This is in part because there are a number of groups, and none has been dominant. Also, the different groups live in the periphery of the country with relatively limited contact. In addition, until recently, government policy has actively prohibited ethnic association and organization (Young, 1998).

Inattention to past violence between groups and to the resulting wounds may be a serious problem, as in the case of the former Yugoslavia, where Marshal Tito maintained such a policy. Prohibiting ethnic association creates some danger when the policy is lifted and other circumstances change; the earlier prohibition intensifies the focus on ethnicity. In Tanzania, there has recently been such an increased focus. Probably the best policy is to create structures that protect each group's rights and interests, foster connections, promote shared goals, and provide education about each other.

The conception I advanced offers explanation for why instigating conditions at times do not lead to group violence. Less intense instigating conditions, weaker cultural predisposing characteristics, more positive behavior of leaders, and less use of scapegoating and destructive ideologies – partly perhaps because of the nature of cultural characteristics – all may have a role. Active bystanders seem especially important.

So are preventive efforts, whether naturally occurring or intentionally created, like the existence and creation of positive contact between groups as ways to overcome past antagonism, as well as societal healing. Given

Reprinted from E. Staub (2001). Ethnopolitical and other group violence: origins and prevention. In D. Chirot and M. Seligman (Eds.), *Ethnopolitical Warfare: Causes, Consequences and Possible Solutions*. Washington, DC: American Psychological Association, From Ch. 18, pp. 289–304. Included here are pp. 298–301.

such efforts there can be a positive evolution, which prepares groups for creating agreements and developing structures for the resolution of conflict. Both with regard to causation and the avoidance or prevention of group violence, this is a probabilistic conception: The presence and intensity of certain conditions affects the likelihood of evolution either toward violence or positive relations. Important research is to be done in carefully evaluating the degree of presence of all these conditions both in cases of mass murder and their absence. Here I will briefly look at a few instances.

When instigating conditions exist and/or an evolution toward mass killing has already started, the role of bystanders appears highly significant in halting it. In South Africa, the international boycott had great importance. Preceding this, South Africans, who are very sports minded, were made constantly aware by the exclusion of South African athletes from international events that the world disapproved of apartheid. As the boycotts proceeded, the business community, unwilling to be ruined, supported the abolition of apartheid (Pogrund, 1991). The business community had been deeply engaged with the West and was therefore probably not only materially but also psychologically affected by the boycotts.

The actions of one particular bystander were also significant. The husband of a friend of Winnie Mandela, a White South African lawyer, took it upon himself to influence his friend, the justice minister Jacobus Coetsee, to see Nelson Mandela in a different light and initiate contact with him (Sparks, 1994). The character of Mandela, as it later showed itself to the world, and as it appeared to Coetsee on their first meeting, was also important. It is likely to have led to greater trust by members of the government in engaging with him and the movement he represented.

The role of positive leadership was also important, particularly the leadership of F. W. De Klerk, who started his presidency by legalizing Black liberation organizations and their sympathizers, which had been outlawed for 30 years. But such leadership in part depends on public attitudes and moods, as are affected by the behavior of bystanders and by the existence of like-minded others, like Coetsee.

In Bosnia, the limited military intervention by NATO stopped the fighting and killing. Continued involvement by NATO and the United States in peace negotiations and in peacekeeping efforts led to a peace agreement, giving Bosnia a chance to halt a continuing cycle of violence. There are ongoing efforts by outside groups to create positive connections among members of the different ethnic and religious groups, bringing them together for dialogue, problem solving, and other joint efforts. There are many efforts as well to help people heal from the effects of the violence and destruction. Mostly these efforts are directed at individuals: More group approaches to healing are required (Staub, 2000).

In Northern Ireland there have been centuries of violence between Protestants and Catholics. In 1921 the primarily Catholic Republic of

Ireland was established. After that, many Catholics in the remaining Northern Ireland, which continued to be part of the United Kingdom, wanted to join the Republic, and many Protestants wanted continuing union with Great Britain.

The most recent cycle of violence began in the mid-1960s. Although the bombings, the destruction of buildings, and the killing of people was highly destructive to the morale of the society, "only" 3,000 people were killed and about 30,000 injured. A strong British military presence helped prevent escalation. So did a strong police presence, with a substantial increase in the number of police and with military personnel the police could call on (Cairns & Darby, 1998). Military, police, and other authorities also managed to control the inflow of arms. Restraint by the British military helped to not inflame the situation.

The nature of leadership, which in part emanated from London, was also very important. Inequalities have been reduced, with Catholics gaining improved housing and employment. Many efforts have existed at the community level and in schools to create contact between groups. All this prepared the ground for negotiations and the ensuing agreement in 1998.

Bystanders, third parties, had a very important role in this as well. The British Prime Minister, Tony Blair, was deeply engaged. Former U.S. Senator George Mitchell mediated talks between the parties, and President Bill Clinton provided support and encouragement. It was important as well that most of the parties, including those that had participated in the fighting, participated in the talks. They had a voice, they could represent their constituencies and then work with them on behalf of the agreement. It is instructive that the violence that followed on the agreement was primarily initiated by marginal groups not included in the negotiations (personal communication from the Director of Initiative on Conflict Resolution and Ethnicity, Mari Fitzduff, August 1998).

Although Jews and Arabs fought several wars, the violence between Jews and Palestinians in Israel and the West Bank remained limited in scale. The continuous involvement of the United States, its engagement, may have had an important role in this. Initially Israel and subsequently both Israel and Palestinians needed the United States for support and mediation. The watchful eyes of others is crucial in limiting group violence. Nations as bystanders, like the United States and Norway in the Oslo accords, have also been crucial in bringing the parties together for peace negotiations.

In addition, Israel is a democratic country with a plurality of values and points of view. Many voices have urged peace and accommodation with Palestinians. Many groups have worked to create contact and educate the groups about each other (Rouhana & Bar-Tal, 1998). For example, in the Israeli village of Neve Shalom Jews, Israeli Muslim Arabs, and Christian Arabs live together. This village brought many young people together for contact and shared education about the other. For many years outside parties have also brought Jews and Palestinians together, in dialogue groups, conflict resolution workshops, and the like. The best known, at least among psychologists, have been the problem-solving workshops of Herbert Kelman and his associates (Kelman, 1990; Rouhana & Kelman, 1994). Graduates of these groups have later been involved in the peace negotiations as advisers and even participants.

In the American South, at the time of the civil rights movement, bystanders were very important in limiting violence. The physical presence of the National Guard and military was important in inhibiting violence, but so was their symbolic role as representatives of the U.S. government and its people. Contrast this with the history of the approximately 5,000 lynchings in the South in the second part of the last century and the first part of this one (U.S. Bureau of Census, 1960), with local people frequently watching and encouraging the lynchers, who would remain unpunished (Ginzburg, 1988).

Preceding the civil rights movement, contact with Black people within the military and around the military bases in the South began to diminish devaluation and hostility by many White people. The Supreme Court decision on desegregation and other national legislation began to change the national climate. Just as violence evolves step by step, so does the possibility of constructive, positive relations between groups.

TOWARD THE TWENTY-FIRST CENTURY

The pace of technological, cultural, and social change in the world is tremendous, deeply affecting people and frustrating basic needs. Without significant preventive and ameliorative efforts, people are likely to continue to turn to ethnic or other "identity" groups and to ideologies for identity, connection, and a hopeful vision of life. In addition, in the age of television and other telecommunication, people become aware of their poverty and relative deprivation, as well as the possibility of better lives. An expanding vision of individual and group rights strengthens their perception of injustice and their belief in their right to better lives. Because they are likely to see this in group terms, they are likely to demand greater rights and privileges for their group, threatening the interests and identity of dominant groups and their worldview or legitimizing ideology. The potential for group conflict leading to violence will, therefore, be great. Preventive efforts are essential for the creation of a more peaceful century than the one we have left behind.

References

Cairns, E., & Darby, J. (1998). The conflict in Northern Ireland. *American Psychologist, 53*, 754–760.

Ginzburg, R. (1988). *100 years of lynching*. Baltimore, MD: Black Classic Press.
Kelman, H. C. (1990). Applying a human needs perspective to the practice of conflict resolution: The Israeli–Palestinian Case. In J. Burton (Ed.), *Conflict: Human needs theory*. New York: St. Martin's Press.
Pogrund, B. (1991). *The transformation in South Africa.* (Lecture). University of Massachusetts, Department of Journalism.
Rouhana, N. N., & Bar-Tal, D. (1998). Psychological dynamics of intractable ethno-national conflicts: The Israeli–Palestinian case. *American Psychologist, 53*, 761–770.
Rouhana, N. N., & Kelman, H. C. (1994). Promoting joint thinking in international conflicts: An Israeli–Palestinian continuing workshop. *Journal of Social Issues, 50*, 157–178.
Sparks, A. (1994, April). Letter from South Africa: The secret revolution. *The New Yorker*, pp. 56–89.
Staub, E. (2000). Genocide and mass killing: Origins, prevention, healing, and reconciliation. *Political Psychology, 21(2)*, 367–383.
U.S. Bureau of Census. (1960). *Historical statistics of the United States: Colonial times to 1957*. Washington, DC: U.S. Government Printing Office.
Young, C. (1998, June–July). *How has Tanzania maintained ethnic peace in a troubled region?* Presentation at the conference on Ethno-Political Warfare: Causes and Solutions, Derry/Londonderry, Northern Ireland.

30

Persian Gulf Conflict Was Reflection of Stormy Undercurrents in U.S. Psyche

The United States and its allies have successfully prosecuted a war against Iraq. Although amazingly few allied lives were lost, there was great destruction to Iraq and many Iraqi deaths. It seems important to explore what led the U.S. to turn speedily to war, rather than pursue alternatives. I will focus on how cultural and psychological factors shaped the reactions, motivations, and behavior of the leadership and people of the United States. We are usually unaware of these influences, even though they have great power, and even shape political and economic motives.

Many nations supported Iraq after it attacked Iran and continued to support it in spite of the use of chemical weapons, the mass killing of Kurds in Iraq, and other atrocities. Following the Iraqi invasions of Kuwait there was long overdue response: stationing enough troops in Saudi Arabia to avert an attack and international sanctions. According to many observers the sanctions had a good chance of success in forcing Iraq, with its one-product economy, to withdraw from Kuwait. Real talks with Iraq may have provided Saddam Hussein the cover he needed to withdraw. Success in accomplishing this without war would have set an example for future behavior by the community of nations and discouraged future aggression.

Instead, the U.S. leadership put massive additional forces into Saudi Arabia and promoted a UN resolution that both authorized the use of force to expel Iraq from Kuwait and set a deadline for Iraq to leave. The president offered talks that, as he repeatedly said on television, were only an offer to deliver the "ultimatum" in person. Many experts on Arab culture have said that face-saving was essential for Hussein, but as the talks were defined participation in them would probably have meant loss of face for him.

Reprinted from E. Staub (1991). Persian Gulf conflict was reflection of stormy undercurrents in U.S. psyche. *Psychology International*. Published by the Office of International Relations of the American Psychological Association, Washington, DC, pp. 1, 8–9.

My recent book, *The Roots of Evil: The Origins of Genocide and Other Group Violence*, analyzes the background conditions that lead a group to turn against another or, as in this instance, make turning to aggression and war easier and more likely. These include persistent cultural characteristics and time-bound societal conditions – which I call difficult life conditions – that can give rise to intense psychological needs in group members that sometimes find outlet in group violence.

One important characteristic is a group's or society's self-concept, the shared view group members hold of their society. Strength, power, and superiority in relation to others have been noted as part of the group self-concept of the United States. This self-image has been frustrated by great social change and attendant social upheaval, and the relative loss of economic power and prestige by the U.S. over the past 20 years. Recently there have been intense problems with drugs, crime, homelessness, education, the savings and loan and banking crises, and the beginnings of a recession. All this can result in a need – in both a people and its leaders – to defend societal and individual self-image. One way for Americans to overcome feelings of powerlessness and helplessness was to focus on superior military power in fighting against an enemy. They could join together in a shared identity as citizens of America as their country began successfully to fight "evil."

Severe social problems can also make a people's worldview ineffective in the essential task of comprehending reality. People often turn to or create an ideology that provides the image of a better life – a nationalist or universalist "better world" ideology that offers hope and a new guide to living and understanding life. These ideologies also always identify enemies that stand in the way of their fulfillment – Nazi ideology is a classic example. Although its role in the psychology of the American people is not yet clear, Bush's New World Order, in which nations will not aggress against other nations, is a version of such an ideology. Peoples and nations are often destroyed to fulfill such higher ideals, which can genuinely motivate leaders and a people, or be used to gain support, or both.

Another important cultural characteristic is a history of aggression that becomes a normal operating procedure and makes further aggression acceptable. The United States has used force frequently since World War II – and this "habit" seems to have become stronger in recent years as this country invaded Grenada and Panama, sent fighter-bombers into Libya, and created and supported the Contra and UNITA surrogate armies. My research has shown that aggressors learn by doing, and that unless their aggression is checked both individuals and groups become more aggressive over time. Just as Iraq's aggression against Iran and its own Kurdish people made renewed aggression more likely, so the history of the use of force by the U.S. made a military solution easier in Iraq.

Another influence is the tendency of most groups to differentiate strongly between "us" and "them" and devalue at least certain out-groups. When a group nears or engages in violence, its devaluation of an enemy or victim usually becomes intense. While there are no explicit "enemy" images of Iraqis, the president and other leaders and the media used extremely devaluative statements for Iraq and the Iraqis. Saddam Hussein was demonized, turning from a U.S. ally whose atrocities against his neighbors and countrymen had long been ignored into the outstanding threat to humanity and the world in our consciousness.

From the onset of the war the emphasis in the U.S. has been on supporting "our boys" and focusing on their potential loss of life and suffering. As in the invasion of Panama, there was little attention paid to the loss of "their" lives from the intense bombing. Euphemisms were used, like "collateral damage" for the killing of civilians. There were accounts of the destruction of tanks, but no mention of the people in them. There was an almost complete absence of information about and images of Iraqi injuries and death in the media due to a combination of military censorship and perhaps self-censorship by the media. As a result, empathy and the awareness of shared humanity with the Iraqi people were less likely to be aroused. Group violence often builds step by step, with each small action making the next one seem acceptable. President Bush shaped events in ways that built commitment to a war that seemed increasingly inevitable: placing an increasingly large force in Saudi Arabia, getting the UN resolutions passed, and making it seem that he was willing to talk while Hussein was not.

As in other instances of group violence, the step-by-step nature of this process brought about changes in people that made new steps acceptable. It is highly probable that through these actions the president and our leadership also shaped their own inclination to go to war.

As the war started there was an immediate shift of attitude in the U.S., in support of it. Tom Brokaw reported about a week into the war that an NBC-*Wall Street Journal* poll found 90% of the population supporting its continuation until it was brought to a satisfactory end. There was a rise in the sale of flags and other patriotic items. This upsurge of support may have come from a feeling of purpose and power and shared identity as Americans that at least temporarily replaced the confusions of our contemporary national life, and perhaps from an upsurge of enmity against Iraq, now our opponent in a war.

In addition, what we know about "bystanders" to violence indicates that it is very difficult to oppose one's group, or even to distance oneself internally from it. This is especially so when there is strong national unity on an issue that binds people together. Even those who do not speak out feel uncomfortable and subject to external and internal pressures to join the majority.

Many commentators have noted that the president has had difficulty articulating the nation's reasons for going to war with Iraq. Oil was certainly one factor; others were stopping Iraq from becoming a dominant power in the region and diminishing its capacity for destroying its neighbors. But "national interests" are defined in the framework of cultural and psychological factors that also shape a nation's modes of fulfilling its goals.

By military standards the allied victory in Kuwait and Iraq was easy. But violence is unlikely to shape the future in a positive way, to lead nations to include the value of human rights and nonaggression in their definitions of national interest. The feeling of strength, power, and unity the war affirmed for so many Americans and the increasing acceptance that this was simply fought for moral reasons can make the future use of force by the United States even more likely.

31

Mob Violence

Cultural–Societal Sources, Instigators, Group Processes, and Participants

Ervin Staub and Lori H. Rosenthal

INTRODUCTION

Definitions

Before examining mob violence, a number of terms need to be defined and differentiated: crowd, mob, riot, mob violence, group violence, and crowd behavior. According to a dictionary of psychology (Chaplin, 1985), a *crowd* is a collection of people who share a common interest and whose emotions may be easily aroused; a *mob* is a crowd acting under strong emotional conditions that often lead to violence or illegal acts. The primary distinction between a crowd and a mob is the level of shared emotion, as well as some forms of (destructive) expressions of emotion. A riot is an instance of *mob violence*, with the destruction of property or looting, or violence against people. A *riot* has been described as an unplanned or unorganized expression of anger or rage, without a focused goal (Levin & Mehlinger, 1975). However, riots can and often do serve shared motives of the participants.

Milgram and Toch (1969) suggested that mob violence is primarily expressive or serves a need for immediate gratification, whereas social movements are organized efforts to change social conditions (which may be the background activators of mob violence). However, we contend that crowd behavior and mob violence can also be vehicles of social movements.

We use the term *group violence* to refer to organized violence by the state or by a dominant group in society against subgroups that are defined as enemies. Examples of group violence include genocide, mass killing, and

Reprinted from E. Staub and L. Rosenthal (1994). Mob violence: Cultural–societal sources, instigators, group processes, and participants. In L. Eron and J. Gentry (Eds.), *Reason to hope: A psychosocial perspective on violence and youth*. Washington, DC: American Psychological Association, pp. 281–313. Included here are pp. 281–282, 284–291, and 293–305.

the systematic use of torture (Staub, 1989). *Crowd behavior*, in the form of marches, demonstrations, and mob violence, can also be part of group violence (e.g., the Kristallnacht in Nazi Germany).

There is little discussion in the literature of the minimum number of people that constitutes a crowd or mob. LeBon (1895) wrote that at certain moments half a dozen men might constitute a psychological crowd. One of the defining criteria for Spilerman (1970) in studying racial disorders was the involvement of 30 or more individuals. In contrast, Morgan and Clark (1973) defined a crowd as "the activities of four or more people acting in concert" (p. 612), although the disorders they actually studied involved 50 or more people.

The level of prior organization of violent groups varies. Truly spontaneous mob action and highly organized group violence represent end points of a continuum. Our consideration of mob violence includes the behavior of groups that have an informal organization, but not of groups, like the SS in Nazi Germany, that have carried out institutional mandates.

A distinction between two types of mob and group violence, which will be called *conserving* and *reforming* types, may be useful. The conserving type is a response by a group to threats of identity or status, whether real or experienced, and whether the group's status is high or low. The reforming type is an attempt, usually by a less powerful group, to change the social order.

Organization and Leadership

Destructive actions by mobs can vary from spontaneous emergence to various degrees of leadership and preexisting organization. For example, in the United States around the turn of the century, lynchings frequently occurred relatively spontaneously, but also occurred as the result of the planned activity of a Ku Klux Klan group with an organized leadership. In contrast, Milgram and Toch (1969) note the relative absence of planning and leadership in the civil rights riots in the 1960s.

Violence at soccer games initiated by groups of young English soccer fans (Buford, 1992) has been neither truly spontaneous nor highly organized. The fans share an understanding, a mindset or preparedness for violence. Over time an informal blueprint has developed that guides the actions of the participants, who are united as fans of the same team, with a shared history. New fans are socialized into the ways of the group. An informal leadership also exists. Disruptive and violent confrontation between police and spectators at the Australian Grand Prix motorcycle races also showed an "institutionalization" of the conflict or normative elements (Cuneen & Lynch, 1988).

A similar implicit blueprint or normative pattern is suggested by newspaper accounts of lynchings in the South that occurred around the turn of the century (Ginzburg, 1988; Peretti & Singletary, 1981) (see description in Chapter 27). An implicit blueprint or normative pattern of behavior also appears to exist for inner-city riots, with their focus on looting and destruction of property. There has been a long tradition of riots in the United States; between the 1830s and 1850s in just four cities (Baltimore, Philadelphia, New York, and Boston), 35 major riots took place (Perry & Pugh, 1978). In recent times, television images have spread scripts for rioting. (In addition, radio and TV reporting in the 1960s and helicopter surveillance of the 1992 L.A. riot pointed out areas that had no police protection, encouraging people to join rioting in those areas.)

INSTIGATING EVENTS, BACKGROUND CONDITIONS, AND PARTICIPANT CHARACTERISTICS

Early Theories

LeBon (1895) wrote that collective outbursts arise in particular historical periods, conditioned by important cultural factors. At the same time he believed that unruly or violent crowds, like those in revolutionary movements, are made up of criminals, social misfits, and other marginal people. This potential inconsistency (if there are understandable social reasons why would only the socially marginal act?) led to approaches emphasizing either social–environmental conditions or the personal frustration and social marginality of participants as explanations of mob violence, the latter sometimes referred to as the riff-raff theory.

Convergence theories (see Milgram & Toch, 1969; Sears & McConahay, 1973) propose that people with similar characteristics join to form crowds and violent mobs. Perpetrators of group violence tend to share certain characteristics, like an "authority orientation," and ideology (Staub, 1989). People who become "soccer hooligans" or participants in a race riot or revolutionary mob violence are also likely to share certain characteristics.

However, convergence theories tend to be theories of social marginality. They suggest that members of unruly or violent crowds are violence-prone, antisocial, criminal persons. But the combination of characteristics that lead individuals to join a crowd and remain part of it when it becomes a violent mob is likely to depend on a combination of specific factors, like the nature of instigating conditions and the population and location involved (e.g., a minority group, neighborhood, or prison).

Contagion theories emphasize immediate environmental conditions that act on individuals who happen to be nearby when some precipitating event occurs (Sears & McConahay, 1973). Contagion, "the spread of affect or behavior from one crowd participant to another" (Milgram & Toch, 1969, p. 550), is an important process that helps in understanding how a collection of individuals join in a shared purpose, but does not explain what instigates the affect and creates the sensitivity of people to it. A few people whose interests and inclinations are at odds with the rest of a crowd are unlikely to be the source of contagion. Neither convergence nor contagion theories emphasize the important role of social conditions, cultural characteristics, and their interaction with instigating events as origins of mob violence.

Instigating Events

Observation and evidence suggest that, frequently, specific events are the starting points for violent collective disturbances. Only 10% of urban riots that occurred between 1964 and 1968 did not have an apparent precipitating incident (Downes, 1968). A high percentage of contemporary civil disorders in the United States, including the Watts riot, were precipitated by the killing, arrest, assault on, or search of African American men and women by the police (Feagin & Hahn, 1973). Innocent verdicts against police officers who were believed to be guilty have been starting points for riots, notably in the Rodney King case. The killing of Martin Luther King also precipitated many riots (Downes, 1968). The lynching of African Americans often followed criminal acts or rumors of such acts against a White person (Ginzburg, 1988).

Downes (1968) made an important distinction among three types of hostile racial "outbursts": early pogroms in which Whites attacked African Americans who offered little resistance; race riots in Northern cities in 1915, 1935, and 1943 in which Whites and African Americans engaged in collective violence against each other; and riots in the 1960s with mostly African American participants, whose actions were directed primarily against local merchants and police "whom they consider responsible for a great deal of racial injustice" (Downes, 1968, p. 505).

Lieberson and Silverman (1965), who examined race riots in the United States between 1913 and 1963, noted that there were only four instances in which they did not have an identifiable precipitating event. The precipitating events of these riots, some of which were started by Whites, tended to be violations of important mores involving violence or interracial relations.

There was a relatively substantial percentage of "spontaneous" outbursts of hostility by African Americans against Whites in 1967, without identifiable precipitating events (Downes, 1968). According to Morgan and Clark (1973) this was the year when "the perceive value of racial disorders as social protest" (p. 613) was greatest in the African American communities. However, the many earlier riots in the 1960s may have made rioting a relatively normative behavior. Moreover, this was a period of general social disorder in the United States, with societal changes arising out of the civil rights movement, feminism, and the escalation of the Vietnam War and antiwar protest. Conditions of social disorganization contribute to the motivation for civic disturbances, like riots, and weaken inhibitions.

Authorities taking away a privilege can be a specific instigator, as in the case of some prison riots (Colvin, 1982). The starting point for the Berkeley Free Speech movement, which included the occupation of university buildings by students, was the university administration's decision to prohibit political activities by students, like the distribution of leaflets and solicitation of funds, on a piece of land where such activity had customarily taken place (Lipset & Wolin, 1965). Especially when a predisposition exists, frustrating events can instigate mob violence. For violence-prone soccer fans, their team's loss or taunts and other provocation by opposing fans can be precipitating events for rioting (Buford, 1992).

Moreover, specific instigation is often a process rather than an event. The investigation of precipitating incidents in the 1960s of 24 riots in 20 cities and 3 universities showed that a series of incidents preceded each. These occurred over a period of weeks or months, both expressing and creating tension in the community. These incidents, or rumors based on them, involved either police action (40%), African American protest (22%), or White racist acts (17%) (U.S. Riot Commission, 1968).

The incidents were interpreted in light of community grievances. One of them, frequently, has been police brutality. Although the extent of police violence is not clear, there is evidence of strong devaluation and fear of African American people among the White officers of the 1960s and a tendency to favor the use of excessive force (Stark, 1972). In one study, 15 previously safe drivers who put Black Panther stickers on their rear bumper received 33 tickets for traffic violations in 17 days (Heussenstamm, 1971).

Frequently, reciprocal changes in the behavior of involved parties are the precursors of mob violence. Rumors and mounting tension affected the behavior of corrections officers in Attica preceding the prison riot (Perry & Pugh, 1978). Similarly, rumors and mounting tension in a community are likely to affect police behavior. Inappropriate control attempts and undue force by the police in turn create hostility in the community.

The same types of events only occasionally, not inevitably, instigate mob violence. At least part of the explanation of why they do so at specific times lies in background conditions (which are discussed in the next section). Frequently, in the context of these conditions, the instigator is not the event, but rumors that greatly transform it. Social conditions that give rise to feelings of injustice, anger, or hostility give certain events their instigating power or lead to the creation of rumors.

Social and Cultural Background Conditions

Societal Climate. There are periods of time that have a dominant societal climate, and maybe even more than one, that influences both the occurrence and the interpretation of instigating events. For example, in the Berkeley Free Speech movement the students reacted to the university administration taking away their rights to political activity in a climate formed by the civil rights movement. In addition, potential leadership existed through the experience of some students in the civil rights movement (Milgram & Toch, 1969).

The urban riots in the 1960s occurred in a societal climate created by the desegregation decisions of the Supreme Court and the civil rights movement. There was an increased awareness of discrimination and injustice, and increased expectation by African Americans of improvement in their social and economic conditions. There was also a less punitive climate for intense expressions of African American frustration.

The disappearance of lynching also had to do with a changing societal climate. Such acts became unacceptable, and violators could expect forceful negative reactions. Changes in societal climate in part express changes in and in part help to transform, over time, culture and societal institutions, such as segregation.

Riots are more frequent during wars (Perry & Pugh, 1978), probably in part because of greater acceptance of violence. Usually, however, a number of background conditions coexist: substantial social changes in wartime create social upheaval, which is another background condition for mob violence.

Relative Deprivation, Injustice, and Hope. While the data are not uniform, overall, the perception of relative deprivation and the experience of injustice seem to be important conditions for mob violence. The role of these factors in the urban riots of the 1960s is suggested by the findings that riot participants were better informed politically than nonparticipants and either had experiences with or strong feelings about discrimination and police violence (McPhail, 1971). Moreover, the urban African American community interpreted the riots as protests against racial discrimination (Caplan & Paige, 1968; Sears & Tomlinson, 1978).

As mentioned earlier, prison riots frequently occur after previously granted privileges are withdrawn. The 1980 New Mexico prison riots occurred after employment opportunities and recreational programs that had been introduced were sharply curtailed (Colvin, 1982; Useem, 1985). According to the Official Report of the New York State Special Commission (New York State Special Commission, 1972), very bad conditions preceded the Attica prison riot. Inmates were deprived of phone calls and letters. There were complex rules of which inmates were not informed and which were enforced arbitrarily, with some inmates but not with others. Many rules were petty, used to harass and abuse inmates. There were unclear and unfair parole practices. There was also strong racism with abusive treatment, as White correction officers from rural areas interacted with inner-city African American and U.S. Latino inmates. All this occurred when the social climate of the 1960s, including the riots, increased awareness of injustice and strengthened the identity of African Americans, including inmates (New York State Special Commission 1972; Perry & Pugh, 1978; Wicker, 1975). One can also argue that social disorganization characterized Attica preceding the riot (see discussion in next section).

Societal changes sometimes create awareness of injustice without changes in the actual conditions of people. But frequently crowd disturbances and mob violence occur after improved social and economic conditions, as profoundly repressed or downtrodden people seldom are able to rise to action. The French Revolution, characterized by mob actions like the storming of the Bastille, followed improved social conditions (Milgram & Toch, 1969). Rioting in prisons has increased in spite of general improvement in prison conditions (Deroches, 1983) or perhaps because of them.

Based mainly on his analysis of the Russian and French revolutions, Davis (1969) proposed a J-curve of rising expectations to explain this. In this view, groups riot and revolutions begin under improved social conditions because expectations outpace the actual improvement in conditions. The New Urban Black theory (Caplan, 1970; Sears & McConahay, 1973), for example, suggests that certain individuals (e.g., young, from the North or West, with at least some high school education) were brought up to expect social and political equality. But in spite of progress, they continued to experience discrimination. A precipitating incident sparks their frustration and leads to a riot.

In addition to rising expectations, there may be another dynamic at work as well. For motives even to arise, and for their expression in action, it is necessary for people to have at least minimal confidence in their ability to fulfill their expectations (Staub, 1980). Under extreme conditions of poverty or repression, people may be preoccupied with survival, afraid of the dangers inherent in public protest or crowd behavior, and lack confidence that their actions can lead to desired outcomes. The easing of conditions may allow anger and the desire for change rooted in social conditions to arise and to be expressed in action.

The inability to exert influence by peaceful means is another background condition for mob violence. Based on an analysis of "racial controversies" involving New York City's African American and Puerto Rican populations, Monti (1979) suggests that violence followed unsuccessful efforts by minority groups to get government and nonminority individuals to act on their grievances. The lack of existing avenues for exerting influence and the experience of empowerment through group action are important elements in mob violence.

Societal Change and Social Disorganization. In many instances, substantial changes in society (in technology, jobs, mores, etc.) or in a particular group's life (e.g., in a prison) precede mob violence. Great social changes often create the experience of chaos and disorganization. They threaten security as well as personal and group identity, make the world and one's future place in it difficult to understand, and loosen community ties and connections among people (Staub, 1989).

Downes (1968), in an analysis of 238 "hostile outbursts" between 1964 and 1968, found that those that reached a high intensity were more likely to occur in larger cities with a larger percentage of non-White population and large influx of non-Whites since 1950. Spilerman (1970) also found that non-White population size was important in the likelihood of community disorders. A certain size of the non-White population appears required to create enough strength and power for crowd actions. Moreover, the influx of a non-White population was likely to change social conditions and affect both minority groups and the White majority.

Frequently, increases in the African American population were not accompanied by similar increases in African American representation in city governments and civic institutions (Perry & Pugh, 1978). Thus, the avenues for dealing with the needs and grievances of the African American population remained restricted as their numbers increased.

The behavior of violent English soccer fans, many of whom had good jobs, according to Buford (1992), may be due to the experience of social disorganization. Tremendous social changes have taken place in many countries in the past few decades, including England, frustrating needs for group identity, connection, and power. Most of these can be satisfied, at least to a degree, by belonging to a group that engages in the shared devaluation of outsiders, like foreigners or fans of other teams, and shared violence against them.

Cultural and Subcultural Characteristics

A preexisting negative orientation toward members of another group is almost always a contributing element in mob violence, making it more likely that other background conditions and instigating events provoke mob violence. This negative orientation can take the form of deep-seated devaluation of and hostility toward certain groups in society, as in the case of lynchings of African Americans. Frustration and hostility can be displaced into a target "preselected" by the history of devaluation; basic needs for identity, comprehension, and connection can be served as members of a group turn together against a scapegoated group. Another form of negative orientation is mutual antagonism between two groups. Relations between police and minority groups in many U.S. cities have been one example of this.

Both in violent confrontations between police and spectators at Australian Grand Prix motorcycle races (Cuneen & Lynch, 1988) and disruptive group behavior at motorcycle races in the United States (Shellow & Roemer, 1966), cultural differences between a working-class, motorcycle subculture on the one hand and community and police on the other hand appear to play a role. Overreactions by the police in exercising control and the opportunity for motorcyclists to act out anti-authority feelings appear to contribute to the riots.

In the United States, great social changes, and in earlier times economic problems, have reactivated hostility and violence against devalued minorities, as noted elsewhere in this chapter. In East European countries the collapse of communism has created economic problems, loss of security, and tremendous social change. In East Germany a historically authoritarian culture (Staub, 1989) and a nearly unbroken history of authoritarian rule have made it difficult for people to face the uncertainties of a democratic, capitalistic system. This has combined with a German history of devaluation of non-Germans and led to mob violence against "foreign" residents in Germany. In Yugoslavia, in addition to great social change, deep-seated mutual devaluation by ethnic groups has played a role in both mob violence and organized military actions.

A history of hostility can create an "ideology of antagonism" (Staub, 1989, 1992a), a view of the other as an enemy who is a threat to the self. When such an ideology of antagonism exists, even without threatening action, simply a gain by the other group can lead to negative social comparison (Tajfel & Turner, 1979) that diminishes and threatens the self. The first attacks by Azerbaijanis on Armenians in the dissolving Soviet Union were apparently the result of rumors that the Armenians were getting better housing. This happened, however, in the overall context of profound social change, as the Soviet Union was collapsing.

A history of violence in society, and specifically mob violence, makes such violence more normal and acceptable (Staub, 1989). The United States does have a history of frequent violence of many kinds, including rioting, labor violence, and vigilante actions (Levin & Mehlinger, 1975; Perry & Pugh, 1978). As noted earlier, cultural and subcultural norms that develop for these kinds of activities frequently appear to guide mob violence.

Characteristics of Mob Participants

Participant characteristics vary. Contrary to LeBon and other early theorists, at least when riots or mob actions are in part motivated by reforming tendencies, participants in them usually have not been marginal individuals.

There has been substantial research on the participants in urban riots in the United States in the 1960s, using a variety of data: interviews of riot area residents, interviews with eyewitnesses, arrest records, and a study of arrestees in Detroit. Rioters tended to be lifelong residents of their cities. The typical rioter was an African American unmarried male between 15 and 24 years of age (61.3% of self-reported rioters, 52.5% of arrestees; for ages 15 to 35, 86.3% and 80.8% are the comparable percentages). Rioters were substantially better informed about social and political issues, somewhat better educated, and more involved in civil rights efforts than uninvolved residents in the same areas. The two groups were equal in income and education, but the rioters were more often unemployed. Riot participants expressed strong racial pride, were hostile to Whites – as well as middle-class African Americans – and felt that they were barred from better jobs, which they deserved, because of discrimination (Caplan & Paige, 1968; Sears & McConahay, 1969; U.S. Riot Commission, 1968, especially pp. 128–129). As in the urban riots, in a riot on an inpatient treatment ward no difference was found between rioters and non-rioters in socioeconomic status, number of prior arrests and incarcerations, or age (Marohn, Dalle-Molle, Offer, & Ostrov, 1973).

The U.S. Riot Commission report (1968) indicated that early property damage in the 1960s riots was targeted against symbols of the White establishment, whereas later destruction was associated with profitable looting. Youth with lower socioeconomic status, according to Mason and Murtagh (1985), got involved in this second phase. However, the looting in the inner-city riots appeared to be an expression of community beliefs that because of past persecution and discrimination the people had a right to the goods they were taking. Friends and family groups participated together (Perry & Pugh, 1978). Similarly, in revolutionary France, criminals frequently joined crowds, changing their focus from revolutionary ideals to destruction and thievery (Craik, 1837).

The McCone Commission (McCone, 1966) depicted the Watts rioters as consisting of fringe members of the community, criminals, and the chronically unemployed, who were expressing their personal frustration without community support. Sears and Tomlinson (1978) found, in contrast, that members of the African American community saw the Watts riot as a meaningful protest against injustice and repression by the White society. They saw rioters as people like themselves and were more sympathetic to them than to those who tried to stop them. Rioters were, in fact, connected to their communities, as measured by church attendance and other indexes (Sears & McConahay, 1973).

There were riots and mob actions, however, in which participants compare unfavorably with nonrioters. In the Detroit riots of 1943, 97 African Americans and 8 Whites were imprisoned for their participation. A much larger percentage of African American participants were from the Southern states than people in a nonrioting control group. The rioters were older and less educated, and 74% were unskilled workers with records of prior conflicts with law enforcement agencies (Akers & Fox, 1944).

Many disturbances during the period that includes 1943 were started by Whites, with African Americans defending themselves (Downes, 1968), rather than acting out of discontent with social conditions. In addition, rioting in 1943 may have been a greater deviation from social norms, involving more risk of extreme consequences. Therefore, people who participated were less established in their communities and perhaps more desperate, with less to lose.

In a prison riot (Moss, Hosford, Anderson, & Petracca, 1977), African American inmates involved in the riot had more prior arrests, more prior prison commitments, were younger at the age of first arrest, and had lower grade achievement tests and more deviant scores on the MMPI than those inmates in a control group. In a riot at an inpatient treatment center for delinquent adolescents (Marohn et al., 1973), riot participants engaged in more delinquent behavior and showed less impulse control in the days preceding the riot than those who did not participate. The instigators were well liked by the staff and were not dealt with firmly when they began to act up, supporting the literature that indicates that the use of too much power by control agencies like the police tends to provoke riots, while laxness and undercontrol also makes rioting more likely (Shellow & Roemer, 1966).

In a study of Italian soccer fans, those who participated in serious disturbances were generally young, unemployed, poorly educated, and fanatical in their commitment to their team. Researchers reported that aggressive mob action depended on group norms and on the group's acceptance of violence (Zani & Kirchler, 1991). In contrast, Buford (1992) believed that many of the highly fanatical English soccer fans had decent jobs. Social and family disorganization and the more normative nature of soccer violence in England may have brought a wider range of people to it.

Research on Indiana University basketball fans found that after their team's loss, strongly committed fans experienced more negative moods and lower self-esteem, and predicted that they would perform worse on a task (Hirt, Zillman, Erickson, & Kennedy, 1992). English soccer fans, and perhaps Italians as well, for whom being a fan is a way of life and a form of group membership, may be intensely affected by their team's loss. Through violence and the experience of power over others, they may regain positive group and individual identities.

The Role of Leaders, Bystanders, and Control Agencies

These are topics about which relatively little firm knowledge exists. In political movements, it is clear that leaders at times incite followers to mob action. However, mob violence or riots that are not tied to political movements seem frequently leaderless, or the process of their instigation by individuals has not been identified. Buford (1992) described an informal leadership among violent soccer fans, the group looking up to certain individuals who at times emerge to initiate and guide violence. He described one case in which such a person guided the group with the help of very young teenage "lieutenants."

We also know relatively little about the role of bystanders, witnesses who do not participate. The potential of bystanders to influence the behavior of other people, by their passivity or action (Latané & Darley, 1970), or by what they say (Staub, 1974), is great. There is also real life evidence that bystanders can influence the behavior of perpetrators of organized group violence (Hallie, 1979; Staub, 1989).

We know that in the urban riots of the 1960s, some members of the community tried to stop violence by rioters (U.S. Riot Commission, 1968), but they had little success (Waskow, 1966). As in the case of organized group violence (Staub, 1989), the earlier bystanders act in the evolution of mob formation the greater their potential influence. Their impact is likely to be greatest during the buildup period, before intense feelings and a shared purpose arise and turn into destructive action.

The role of control agencies, like the police and other authorities, is important. Police behavior has often been a specific instigator of urban riots. However, we do not know how often police behavior was overly forceful and how often it was perceived that way because of the operation of background instigators, longstanding grievances, or repeated incidents before the instigating event. Individuals who interpret, for others, particular police actions as violence, or who create rumors, may have significant influence.

Both overly forceful and provocative behavior by police and relinquishing control and influence appear to have a role in initiating and maintaining mob violence. Police behavior is often shaped by lack of understanding, devaluation, and fear of particular groups of people. With careful planning to shape police perception and action, riots of certain kinds can be avoided, as they were during motorcycle races in Maryland in 1965 (Shellow & Roemer, 1966). When riots begin, a fast police response has been found to limit the extent of violence (Downes, 1968).

The unresponsiveness of societal institutions and agencies to the problems and grievances of groups of people, and their feelings of powerlessness to exert influence through legitimate channels, are important sources of rioting. Depending on circumstances, the power to exert a relatively specific influence, like inhibiting police violence or getting a response to prisoner grievances, or political influence to bring about social change, should make mob violence less likely.

But the kinds of changes people seek are not always in the power of governments to provide. In Eastern European countries there have been demonstrations and riots when collapsing communist governments reduced subsidies for basic staples, like bread or milk. In Germany following the loss of World War I, intensely difficult life conditions created both unorganized and organized mob actions. These conditions were the result of longstanding cultural, economic, and historical processes, which involved other nations as well.

Democratic and responsive political institutions, relative economic equality among subgroups of a society, and the absence or weakness of cultural characteristics that promote intergroup conflict (devaluation, authority orientation, etc.) are among the conditions that can be expected to minimize the chances of mob violence in difficult times.

SOCIAL AND PSYCHOLOGICAL PROCESSES THAT GENERATE MOB VIOLENCE

Instigating events, background conditions, and the characteristics of the actors involved, especially when combined with the behavior of control agencies and bystanders, may go a long way to explain the occurrence of mob violence. But such an account would be incomplete without an understanding of the social and psychological processes that occur during and after a group is formed. These include shared definitions; contagion and modeling; deindividuation; group polarization, group mind, and the loss of self; and evolution toward increasing violence. These processes can lead to crowd formation and can change a crowd into a violent mob.

Shared Definitions. People "milling around" and spreading information are part of the definitional process in the formation of a mob. As Festinger (1950) suggested, especially when there is situational ambiguity, people turn to information from other people to define the meaning of events. Research on rumor indicates, however, that information is greatly transformed in the course of transmission (Perry & Pugh, 1978). For example, Lieberson and Silverman (1965) wrote

> The Harlem riot during World War II started when a Negro woman was arrested by a white policeman for disorderly conduct. A Negro soldier, on leave, tried to stop him and the ensuing fight ended with both men in the hospital, the policeman with a battered head and the soldier with a pistol wound in the shoulder. Of greatest interest here is the account of the incident that spread through the Negro community: a Negro soldier was said to have been shot in the back and killed by a white policeman in the presence of the Negro's mother. (p. 889)

Contagion and Modeling

Starting with LeBon, those concerned with crowds have stressed the speed by which feelings and actions spread. Contagion can contribute to crowd formation, to a shared definition of events, and to the formation of a shared purpose.

Observations indicate that affect can spread fast both among animals and people (Staub, 1987). How affect spreads is unclear. Psychoanalysts view the spread of affect as an inborn, unconscious process that is observable in infants. Empathy can certainly be an automatic response to and at least a partial matching of another's emotion.

It may also be the case that given shared inclinations and specific instigators, people freely express and even exaggerate their emotions in a crowd. This is in contrast to their usual tendency to hide their emotions in public (Latané & Darley, 1970).

There is likely to be a sensitivity to other people that underlies contagion, perhaps because of identification with others who are seen as members of one's group, shared dissatisfactions, concerns, and values, or shared antagonism toward a potential victim group. Without that, affect in some people can arouse the opposite affect in others. Although in interviews after riots people sometimes express shock at their own actions (Freedman, Carlsmith, & Sears, 1974), it is unclear whether people who participate in mob violence ever act contrary to their inclinations.

The role of modeling has been noted in contagion. Circular reaction has been proposed as a mechanism: one person responding to another's affect and that person's reaction feeding back to the first one (Allport, 1924). Affect and actions spread not only within a group, but, as a result of information in the media and images on TV, to other people as well.

Contagion has been used to describe the spread of affect and action among an already assembled group of people, as well as beyond a group to people in other locations. Although riots can spread like contagion in classical epidemics (Burbeck, Raine, & Stark, 1978), there are both contagion and noncontagion periods (Midlarsky & Suda, 1978), and civil disturbances have spread more contagion-like in some Latin American countries than in others (Govea & West, 1981). The reasons for these differences require further exploration.

Deindividuation

LeBon suggested the rôle of anonymity in crowd behavior. Festinger, Pepitone, and Newcomb (1952) proposed the related concept of deindividuation, further developed and elaborated by others (Diener, 1980; Zimbardo, 1969). In deindividuation, self-awareness and personal identity are lost and replaced with identification with the goals and actions of the group. Over time, the concept has taken on the meaning as well of the loss of the operation of personal moral standards.

Research findings suggest that anything that makes people less identifiable increases deindividuation, as suggested by behavioral outcomes. Wearing hoods and not being called by name led female subjects to give twice as many shocks to others (Zimbardo, 1969). Lack of identifiability also increased the use of obscene language in group discussion (Singer, Brush, & Lublin, 1965). The use of masks by warriors was related to greater aggression (Watson, 1973).

Anonymity and the psychological condition of deindividuation are likely to lead to a diffusion of responsibility for the welfare of others, and a reduction in fear of blame and punitive consequences. This is suggested by decreased helping in emergencies as the number of bystanders increases (Latané & Darley, 1970). When people are alone, social norms focus responsibility on them for helping a distressed person (Staub, 1978); in groups responsibility is diffused.

As the number of people in a group increases, deindividuation may also increase. For example, when a person contemplates jumping off a building, the larger the number of observers, the more likely they are to encourage jumping (Mann, 1981). Mullen (1983, 1986) proposed, on the basis of an analysis of 60 newspaper accounts, that as the ratio of members of crowds, specifically of lynch mobs, to the number of potential victims increases, lynchers become less self-attentive and their level of atrocity increases.

But being in a group does not by itself increase aggression. Individuals alone with a victim are sometimes more aggressive than a group of people (Diener & Wallbom, 1976). Being with others can decrease anonymity. In actuality, people often join crowds with friends and know at least some other people present (Reicher & Potter, 1985). Perhaps anonymity is not a necessary condition for the loss of a separate identity and loss of the operation of customary moral standards when a group becomes cohesive and emotions rise. And members of a mob are usually anonymous to outsiders.

Reicher and Potter (1985) suggest that the focus on anonymity, deindividuation, and contagion show a continued adherence by social psychologists to early and conservative notions about the mindlessness of groups and the social marginality of participants. They argue, and the review and analysis in this chapter supports their argument, that mob violence frequently arises out of social conditions that give rise to a collective perception by members of a group of themselves and their social world. The members of a crowd act in terms of common social identification.

At the same time, mob violence is extreme behavior that is often at odds with the prior behavior of participants. These social–psychological processes appear to be involved in their facilitation. With repetition, as particular mob actions become normative, these processes are less likely to be required in order for violence to occur.

Group Polarization, Group Mind, and the Loss of Self

LeBon has stressed that in a crowd a group mind takes over, which he believed was irrational. Marx (1848), in contrast, believed that crowds are purposeful and serve an important role in creating social change. The earlier discussion suggests that the behavior of mobs is guided by understandable motives. But a group is more than a collection of separate individuals.

Research in social psychology has shown that members of a group arrive at positions that are more extreme than the average position of those who make up the group (Moscovici & Zavalloni, 1969; Myers & Bishop, 1970; Stoner, 1962). Such "group polarization" happens even in the course of orderly discussions of issues. In crowds, mutual influence is likely to be greater because of contagion, deindividuation, and conformity pressures that increase as a group identity develops.

There can be a loss of individual self and a giving of oneself over to the group, which may be experienced as a falling away of the limitations inherent in the self and of the boundaries restricting connections to other people. The resulting sense of abandon and feelings of connection and oneness can be intensely satisfying, whether they happen in mobs, or in self-development groups that are fashionable in the United States. Mob action can also create or enhance feelings of excitement and power.

Buford (1992) gives a sense of this groupness as he describes how English soccer fans in Italy respond to a policeman firing a gun into the air. They begin with the destruction of property; then they turn against the police:

> I had never seen trouble escalate so quickly. The firing of the handgun now seemed ludicrous; it had served only to inflame. The crowd that was now running back down the street was a different crowd from the one that had fled in panic from the tear gas. It had become different the moment it started destroying property – the familiar border. It was liberated now, and dangerous, and had evolved to that giddy point where it was perfectly happy to run amok with a comprehensive sense of abandon and an uninhibited disregard for the law. It was running hard, the people in it angry and wild. They were screaming something, I couldn't make it out – it was some kind of aggressive howl – but its object was clear enough: It was the police. (Buford, 1992, p. 292)

Buford (1992) also described the experience of English soccer fans in the course of violent action as a form of peak exerience, seemingly addictive in nature.

Evolution Toward Increasing Violence

Psychological and behavioral evolution takes place in groups and in individual members of groups. People change as a result of their own actions. Children who are led to help others become more helpful (Staub, 1975, 1979). "Teachers" who shock "learners" tend to increase the level of shock they use over time (Buss, 1966; Goldstein, Rosnow, Raday, Silverman, & Gaskell, 1975). In the course of organized group violence, whole groups enter into a process of change along a "continuum of destruction" that may end in extreme violence, like mass killing or genocide (Staub, 1989). Such evolution can take place even in the course of a single incidence of mob violence and even more so over repeated instances (e.g., of lynching, soccer violence, or mob action that is part of a social movement). Even vicarious participation, through TV or other media, can be a source of such change (Staub, 1989).

Buford (1992) described what he regarded as "threshold acts" that may be performed by a single person but that move violence from one level to another. Redl (1943) wrote about initiatory acts among violent youths. Threshold acts may exert influence through modeling, disinhibition, and contagion, and may be one means by which change or evolution in a group is furthered. Turner and Killian's (1972) emergent norm theory proposes the emergence of group norms as an explanation of crowd behavior. Group norms are an outcome of an evolution.

Buford (1992) describes a pattern of behavior in which a group of fans surrounds and kicks a person lying on the ground. This action had become part of the script for the group's behavior. Once a group develops such violent scripts and norms, it is extremely difficult for individuals to deviate from them.

As in the case of organized group violence (Staub, 1989), the psychological changes in individuals may include increased devaluation of victims and changes in the self that make violence more acceptable. People may turn to beliefs and "ideals" that justify destructive actions as just or moral. Individual standards are lost as people give themselves over to the group and adopt group standards. As a shared perspective and identification with the group evolve or enlarge, deviation by individuals becomes less likely. The social controls that people normally exert on each other to inhibit violence now serve violence.

THE PARTICIPATION OF YOUTH IN MOB VIOLENCE

Although adequate information about the percentage of participants by age is not available, both in urban riots (Sears & McConahay, 1973; U.S. Riot Commission, 1968) and in groups of violent soccer fans (Buford, 1992), male adolescents and young adults seem to be the most frequent participants. As discussed earlier, participants, especially in postwar African American urban riots, have not usually been criminals or delinquents: 56% of juveniles between the ages of 10 and 19 who were arrested or referred to the L.A. probation department during the Watts riot had one or no previous contact with the police, 48% attended church regularly, and 53% were doing average or better in school (Sears & McConahay, 1973).

The motives of young participants may include frustration, hostility, the desire to create social change, and personal gain. But part of the reason for their greater participation may be that the motives fulfilled through participation in a crowd or mob activity are especially satisfying for young, developing persons.

Developmental Issues

In cultures where young people are led to distance themselves from their families, they need to create their own, separate identity. This attracts them to groups, including cults and gangs. But even semi-organized groups like violent soccer fans or a crowd that becomes a mob can provide them with connection, belonging, and self-definition. The positive social identity they gain from group membership (Tajfel & Turner, 1979) depends partly on the group's perceived status and rank, which in certain subcultures will depend on toughness and violence (Gaskell & Smith, 1986). As needs increase under difficult life conditions, the satisfaction gained from connection to a group would also increase.

As they seek self-definition and identity, young people may be more open to the lure of "higher ideals," both legitimate ones like fighting injustice and illegitimate ones proclaimed by leaders and advocated by destructive ideologies. Because they seek separateness from their families, but still need guidance and support, the potential influence of leaders on young people is greater.

In addition, to the extent that young people are less socialized, have fewer internalized societal norms and prohibitions, and have developed less impulse control, they are likely to be more vulnerable to contagion and deindividuation. They may change more easily, adopt emerging group norms, and lose their identity in a group.

Other factors intrinsic to youth may be attraction to the excitement of mob action and less fear of legal consequences or harm to themselves. This may be partly due to feelings of invulnerability; it is due to their courage as well as their malleability that armies and revolutionary groups induct them or work to attract them, or that youth are attracted to them (Etcheson, 1984; Staub, 1989). For example, the Khmer Rouge soldiers were extremely young (Etcheson, 1984) and the Greek torturers were young people inducted into the military police (Haritos-Fatouros, 1988). Young people may also feel they have less to lose, because they have few possessions and limited obligations and commitments.

There are other factors contributing to young people's participation that are not intrinsically tied to age, but are more likely to be present among young people, especially young Black males in the United States at this time. These are unemployment and limited opportunity.

Individual and Family Characteristics

There has been very little research on the personal characteristics and family experiences of youthful participants in crowd action and mob violence. Particularly when mob violence does not arise as a relatively direct protest against social conditions and is not the result of intense devaluation and hate shared by a society or subculture, it is important to investigate these characteristics and experiences. Even if participants have no criminal record, they may possess personal characteristics that create an inclination for aggressive behavior, such as a negative view of human beings, weak or undeveloped moral values (Staub, 1971, 1989), lack of aggression anxiety (Baron, 1977) or a perception of aggression as acceptable and normal (Huesmann & Eron, 1984), and low self-esteem. Experiences in the home, like rejection or hostility (Bandura & Walters, 1959; Dodge, 1993; Huesmann, Eron, Lefkowitz, & Walder, 1984; Staub, 1993), can contribute to the development of such predisposing characteristics. To the extent that this occurs, interpersonal aggressiveness and participation in some types of mob violence would be related.

Youth Groups as Mobs

Violence committed by loosely knit groups of adolescents appears to be an emerging form of youth violence in the United States. The information about these groups is, as yet, extremely limited and speculative.

The word "wilding" was made familiar by the group of adolescents who, after they attacked several victims in Central Park in New York, severely beat and raped a female jogger.[1] Only one of the youths involved had prior police contact. Other instances of violence by small groups of youth have also been recently reported (Gibbs, 1989).

Scheidlinger (1992) suggests the emergence of "loosely structured 'packs' (small crowds) of teenagers who engage in senseless violence" (p. 1). He suggests that these groups have shifting membership and lack affectionate ties and a sense of shared identity among members. He contrasts them with the organized gangs of the 1960s, which were characterized by group loyalty, cohesion, and stable leadership. Whereas gangs in the 1960s usually fought with each other, violence by packs is more random, with little empathy for the victims. In Scheidlinger's view, moblike processes such as deindividuation, contagion, and "group psychological intoxication" (Redl, 1943) characterize these groups. Scheidlinger's (1992) hypotheses about the existence and nature of such groups come from limited observations and discussions with adolescent participants in group counseling.

Crimes by teenagers have often been committed in small groups. For example, one extensive study found that 43% of rapes in Philadelphia were committed by pairs or groups of youth mainly between 15 and 19 years

[1] However, according to information that has come to light since (a confession by a man in prison), these young men were not the rapists.

old. Among the Kikuyu, which Sanday (1981) identifies as a rape-prone society, it is normative for boys to roam the countryside looking for women to rape as an initiation into sexual behavior.

Research is needed to determine how common "packs" are, the characteristics of participants in them, the social and psychological processes by which they operate, and the similarities and differences between them and violent groups of teenagers in the past. Deindividuation and contagion probably always characterized groups of teenagers engaged in violence. However, in stable groups norms develop that guide behavior, which may make violence less random, if not less extreme.

Many authors, including Scheidlinger (1984), have noted the crucial role of the peer group in social and moral maturation. He suggests that when deviant behavior among adolescents becomes frequent, causes are likely to reside in social patterns of families and communities.

Tremendous societal changes have taken place in the United States in the past 25 years. The civil rights movement, feminism, changes in sexual mores, divorce, increase in single-parent families, and drug use are among the examples and consequences of social change (Staub, 1989, 1992b, 1996). The impact on families and children has been profound. The children who are most severely affected, a kind of "new youth" who experienced lack of affection as well as disorganization and lack of structure in their early lives, may find it difficult to establish and to function within structures in their peer groups. Experiences of neglect and of abuse would intensify the problem, limiting affective ties to others, trust, and caring.

In the absence of persistent affective ties and stable sources of identity, even temporary connections, such as packs, can be of substantial emotional value. The violence by such groups may be intensified by the excitement that results from the experience of connection to some and power over others. The absence of affective ties and mistrust of people would limit empathy and concern about the welfare of others. In their homes, through films and TV, and in their peer group such teenagers may even have learned to value violence and see it as a source of manhood (Toch, 1969).

The Impact of Mob Violence on Young People

As suggested in the discussion of evolution in groups, mob violence will shape participants and may particularly shape the younger ones. The nature of actions (destruction of property, looting, physically harming others, killing people), their frequency, and the combination of motives they serve – political, ideological, psychological need-fulfillment, excitement, or material gain – should all influence how participants change. Among the likely effects are a changed perception (devaluation) of victim groups and human beings in general, an increase in the acceptability of aggression, changes in self-perception and feelings of empowerment, and in many cases stronger group ties, especially if the mob has an identifiable composition (Staub, 1989, 1990, 1993). Laboratory research on the psychological and behavioral effects of engaging in aggressive behavior, alone and with others, is greatly needed.

The effect of violence on nonparticipating young people depends on many factors. There is substantial evidence that a wide range of conditions traumatize children and create posttraumatic stress (McCann & Pearlman, 1990). For example, following a fatal schoolyard sniping incident, being physically closer to the shooting and knowing the deceased child both contributed to a greater posttraumatic syndrome. This included intrusive imagery, emotional constriction and avoidance, loss of interest in significant activities, fears of recurrence, anxiety, sleep difficulties, and difficulties in paying attention in school (Pynoos et al., 1987).

Children and youth who are part of a victim group, especially in the case of recurrent violence, like lynchings in the United States or pogroms against Jews in Eastern Europe, can be expected to show not only intense posttraumatic stress, but fear of and hostility toward the perpetrators and, based on just world thinking (Lerner, 1980; Staub, 1989), in-group devaluation (Tajfel, 1982a, 1982b). Those who are not members of a victim group are also likely to show posttraumatic stress, probably based on physical proximity, age and discriminatory ability, empathy, degree of identification with the victims, and general security and anxiety level.

Other research, for example, with Cambodian children who were relocated to the United States following concentration camp experiences (Kinzie, Sack, Angell, Manson, & Rath, 1986; Sack, Angell, Kinzie, & Rath, 1986), suggests that the characteristics of children's families and family relationships will moderate both the short-term and long-term impact of witnessing violence. Close in-group ties lessen the extent to which devaluation and discrimination by out-groups become in-group devaluation (Tajfel, 1982b).

SUMMARY AND CONCLUSIONS

When it comes to mob violence, difficult life conditions can affect a whole society, or a specific group of people. These conditions can involve economic problems or decline, political upheaval, or great social changes that create the experience of disorganization and chaos with loss of guiding values and sense of community. Relative deprivation, the perception of unfair treatment and injustice, and powerlessness in improving one's fate or affecting change also function as instigators of mob violence. The easing of repression, discrimination or economic problems can also give rise to mob violence by decreasing fear, empowering people, and increasing hopes for change that may remain essentially unfulfilled. In addition, the changes involved in creating such improvements can themselves contribute to social disorganization. Under these conditions, devaluation of or antagonism between groups can create a persistent cultural potential for mob violence.

Evidence suggests that specific instigating events are often the starting points for mob violence. The assassination of political leaders, police brutality, and withdrawal of privileges are among the kinds of precipitants often found. Frequently, the interpretation of the event rather than simply the event's occurrence seems to be the potent precipitant.

Particular group processes are also implicated in mob violence. Rumors about an event, contagion, modeling, deindividuation, group polarization, group mind, loss of self, and evolution toward increasing violence are among the processes that may change a crowd into a violent mob. Leaders and bystanders can also function to provoke or inhibit violence.

An individual's reasons and motivations for participation in mob violence can include frustration, hostility, exploding anger, and the desire to hurt; the desire for institutional and social change motivated partly by self-interest and partly by response to perceived injustice; feelings of connection to and unity with others; a sense of identity the person gains; feelings of control, power, and even intense excitement and peak experience that arise from group processes; or the desire for personal gain.

When a mob turns against a particular victim group, as in the case of lynching, perhaps the most prejudiced will participate. But given shared prejudice, or a shared cultural devaluation of and hostility toward the group to which potential victims belong, it may be other characteristics that lead participants to join. The people who joined the SS shared the general German and Nazi anti-Semitism, but only a percentage (mostly in leading positions) were extremely anti-Semitic (Merkl, 1980).

Under some conditions, demographic characteristics like employment status, race, class, and other group memberships may be powerful selectors. Under other conditions, the types of needs that arise in response to difficult circumstances, and the extent to which individuals possess these needs (for positive identity, connection to others, a comprehension of reality), may determine participation. Clearly, self-selection for participation in mob violence needs to be further explored.

To gain a better understanding of mob violence, fine-grained analyses are needed that identify background conditions, the groups that are most affected, relevant aspects of culture and current societal norms and climate, and not only demographic but personality characteristics of participants.

References

Akers, E. R., & Fox, V. (1944). The Detroit rioters and looters committed to prison. *J. Crim. Law Criminol.*, 35, 105–110.

Allport, F. H. (1924). *Social psychology*, Boston: Houghton Mifflin.

Bandura, A., & Walters, R. H. (1959). *Adolescent aggression*. New York: Ronald Press.

Baron, R. A. (1977). *Human aggression*. New York: Plenum.

Buford, B. (1992). *Among the thugs: The experience, and the seduction, of crowd violence*. New York: Norton.
Burbeck, S. L., Raine, W. J., & Stark, M. J. (1978). The dynamics of riot growth: An epidemiological approach. *Journal of Mathematical Sociology, 6*,1–22.
Buss, A. (1966). Instrumentality of aggression, feedback, and frustration as determinants of physical aggression. *Journal of Personality and Social Psychology, 3*, 153–162.
Caplan, N. S. (1970). The new ghetto man: A review of recent empirical studies. *Journal of Social Issues, 26*, 59–73.
Caplan, N. S., & Paige, J. M. (1968). A study of ghetto rioters. *Scientific American, 219*, 15–21.
Chaplin, J. P. (1985) *Dictionary of psychology* (2nd ed.). New York: Doubleday.
Colvin, M. (1982). The 1980 New Mexico prison riot. *Social Problems, 29*, 119–153.
Craik, G. L. (1837). *Sketches of popular tumults*. London: Knight.
Cuneen, C., & Lynch, R. (1988). The social meanings of conflict in riots at the Australian Grand Prix motorcycle races. *Leisure Studies, 7*, 1–19.
Davis, J. L. (1969). The J-curve of rising and declining satisfactions as a cause of some great revolutions and a contained rebellion. In H. D. Graham & T. R. Gurr (Eds.), *Violence in America*. New York: Bantam Books.
Deroches, F. J. (1983). Anomie: Two theories of prison riots. *Canadian Journal of Criminology, 25*, 173–190.
Diener, E. (1980). Deindividuation: The absence of self-awareness and self-regulation in group members. In P. P. Paulus (Ed.), *Psychology of group influence*. Hillsdale, NJ: Erlbaum.
Diener, R., & Wallbom, M. (1976). Effects of self-awareness on anti-normative behavior. *Journal of Research in Personality, 10*, 107–111.
Dodge, K. A. (1993). Social cognitive mechanisms in the development of conduct disorder and depression. *Annual Review of Psychology, 44*, 559–584.
Downes, B. T. (1968). Social and political characteristics of riot cities: A comparative study. *Social Science Quarterly, 49*, 504–520.
Etcheson, C. (1984). *The rise and demise of democratic Kampuchea*. Colorado: Westview Press.
Feagin, J. F., & Hahn, M. (1973). *Ghetto revolts*. New York: Macmillan.
Festinger, L. (1950). Informal social communication. *Psychological Review, 57*, 271–292.
Festinger, L., Pepitone, A., & Newcomb, T. (1952). Some consequences of deindividuation in a group. *Journal of Abnormal and Social Psychology, 47*, 382–389.
Freedman, J. L., Carlsmith, J. M., & Sears, D. O. (1974). *Social psychology* (2nd ed.). Englewood Cliffs, NJ: Prentice-Hall.
Gaskell, G., & Smith, P. (1986). Group membership and social attitudes of youth: An investigation of some implications of social identity theory. *Social Behaviour, 1*, 67–77.
Gibbs, N. C. (1989, May 8). Wilding in the night. *Time*, pp. 20–21.
Ginzburg, R. (1988). *100 years of lynchings*. Baltimore, MD: Black Classic Press.
Goldstein, J. H., Rosnow, R. L., Raday, T., Silverman, I., & Gaskell, D. (1975). Punitiveness in response to films varying in content: A cross-national field study of aggression. *European Journal of Social Psychology, 5*, 149–165.

Govea, R. M., & West, G. T. (1981). Riot contagion in Latin America. *Journal of Conflict Resolution, 25*, 319–358.
Hallie, P. P. (1979). *Lest innocent blood be shed. The story of the village of Le Chambon, and how goodness happened there.* New York: Harper & Row.
Haritos-Fatouros, M. (1988). The official torturer: A learning model for obedience to the authority of violence. *Journal of Applied Social Psychology, 18*, 1107–1120.
Heussenstamm, F. K. (1971). Bumper stickers and the cops. *Trans-action, 8*, 32–33.
Hirt, E. R., Zillman, D., Erickson, G. A., & Kennedy, C. (1992). Costs and benefits of allegiance: Changes in fans' and self-ascribed competencies after team victory versus defeat. *Journal of Personality and Social Psychology, 63*, 724–734.
Huesmann, L. R., & Eron, L. D. (1984). Cognitive processes and the persistence of aggressive behavior. *Aggressive Behavior, 10*, 243–251.
Huesmann, L. R., Eron, L. D., Lefkowitz, M. M., & Walder, L. O. (1984). Stability of aggression over time and generations. *Developmental Psychology, 20*, 1120–1134.
Kinzie, J. D., Sack, W. H., Angell, R. H., Manson, S., & Rath, B. (1986). The psychiatric effects of massive trauma on Cambodian children: I. The children. *Journal of the American Academy of Child Psychiatry, 25*, 370–376.
Latané, B., & Darley, J. M. (1970). *The unresponsive bystander: Why doesn't he help?* New York: Appleton-Century-Crofts.
LeBon, G. (1895). *The crowd.* London: Unwin.
Lerner, M. J. (1980). *The belief in a just world: A fundamental delusion.* New York: Plenum.
Levin, M. A., & Mehlinger, H. D. (1975). *Violence and society.* Boston: Houghton Miffin.
Lieberson, S., & Silverman, A. R. (1965). The precipitants and underlying conditions of race riots. *The American Journal of Sociology, 62*, 14–20.
Lipset, S. M., & Wolin, S. S. (1965). *The Berkeley student revolt.* New York: Anchor Books.
Mann, L. (1981). The baiting crowd in episodes of threatened suicide. *Journal of Personality and Social Psychology, 41*, 703–709.
Marohn, R. C., Dalle-Molle, D. Offer, D., & Ostrov, E. (1973). A hospital riot: Its determinants and implications for treatment. *American Journal of Psychiatry, 130*, 631–636.
Marx, K. (1888). *Manifesto of the communist party.* Chicago: Charles H. Kerr. (Original work published 1848.)
Mason, D. T., & Murtagh, J. A. (1985). Who riots? An empirical examination of the "new urban Black" versus the social marginality hypotheses. *Political Behavior, 7*, 352–373.
McCann, L., & Pearlman, L. A. (1990). *Psychological trauma and the adult survivor.* New York: Brunner/Mazel.
McCone, J. A. (Ed.) (1996). Violence in the city: An end or a beginning? Los Angeles: Governor's Commission on the Los Angeles Riots.
McPhail, C. (1971). Civil disorder participators: A critical examination of recent research. *American Sociological Review, 36*, 1058–1073.
Merkl, P. H. (1980). *The making of a storm trooper.* Princeton, NJ: Princeton University Press.
Midlarsky, E. & Suda, W. (1978). Some antecedents of altruism in children: Theoretical and empirical perspectives. *Psychological Reports, 13*, 187–208.

Milgram, S., & Toch, H. (1969). Collective behavior: Crowds and social movements. In G. Lindzey & E. Aronson (Eds.), *The handbook of social psychology* (2nd ed., Vol. IV). Reading, MA: Addison-Wesley.

Monti, D. J. (1979). Patterns of conflict preceding the 1964 riots: Harlem and Bedford-Stuyvesant. *Journal of Conflict Resolution, 23*, 41–69.

Morgan, W. R., & Clark, T. N. (1973). The causes of racial disorders: A grievance-level explanation. *American Sociological Review, 38*, 611–624.

Moscovici, S., & Zavalloni, M. (1969). The group as a polarizer of attitudes. *Journal of Personality and Social Psychology, 12*, 124–135.

Moss, C. S., Hosford, R. E., Anderson, W. R., & Petracca, M. (1977). Personality variables of Blacks participating in a prison riot. *Journal of Consulting and Clinical Psychology, 45*, 505–512.

Mullen, B. (1983). Operationalizing the effect of the group on the individual: A self-attention perspective. *Journal of Experimental Social Psychology, 19*, 295–322.

Mullen, B. (1986). Atrocity as a function of lynch mob composition: A self-attention perspective. *Personality and Social Psychology Bulletin, 12*, 187–197.

Myers, D. G., & Bishop, G. D. (1970). Discussion effects on racial attitudes. *Science, 169*, 778–789.

New York State Special Commission on Attica. (1972). *Official report*. New York: Praeger.

Oliner, S. B., & Oliner, P. (1988). *The altruistic personality: Rescuers of Jews in Nazi Europe*. New York: Free Press.

Peretti, P. O., & Singletary, D. (1981). A theoretical–historical approach to black lynching. *Social Behavior and Personality, 9*, 227–230.

Perry, J. B. & Pugh, M. D. (1978). *Collective behavior: Response to social stress*. New York: West.

Pynoos, R. S., Frederick, C., Nader, K., Arroup, W., Steinberg, A., Eth, S., Nunez, F., & Fairbanks, L. (1987). Life threat and posttraumatic stress in school-age children. *Archives of General Psychiatry, 44*, 1057–1063.

Redl, R. (1943). Group psychological elements in discipline problems. *American Journal of Orthopsychiatry, 13*, 77–81.

Reicher, S., & Potter, J. (1985). Psychological theory on intergroup perspective: A comparative analysis of "Scientific" and "lay" accounts of crowd events. *Human Relations, 38*, 167–189.

Sack, W. H., Angell, R. H., Kinzie, J. D., & Rath, B. (1986). The psychiatric effects of massive trauma on Cambodian children: II. The family, the home and the school. *Journal of the American Academy of Child Psychiatry, 25*.

Sanday, P. R. (1981). The sociocultural context of rape: A cross-cultural study. *Journal of Social Issues, 37*, 5–27.

Scheidlinger, S. (1984). The adolescent peer group revisited. Turbulence or adaptation? *Small Group Behavior, 15*(3), 387–397.

Scheidlinger, S. (1992). *On adolescent violence: Some preliminary group process observations*. Unpublished manuscript, Albert Einstein College of Medicine, Bronx, NY.

Sears, D. O., & McConahay, J. B. (1969). Participation in the Los Angeles riot. *Social Problems, 17*, 3–20.

Sears, D. O., & McConahay, J. B. (1973). *The politics of violence: The new urban blacks and the Watts riot*. Boston: Houghton Mifflin.

Sears, D. O., & Tomlinson, T. M. (1978). Riot ideology in Los Angeles: A study of Negro attitudes. *Social Science Quarterly, 49*, 485–503.

Shellow, R., & Roemer, D. V. (1966). The riot that didn't happen. *Social Problems, 14*, 221–233.

Singer, J. E., Brush, C. A., & Lublin, S. C. (1965). Some aspects of deindividuation: Identification and conformity. *Journal of Experimental Social Psychology, 1*, 356–378.

Spilerman, S. (1970). The causes of racial disturbances: A comparison of alternative explanations. *American Sociological Review, 20*, 408–414.

Stark, R. (1972). *Police riots, collective violence and law enforcement*. Belmont, CA: Wadsworth.

Staub, E. (1971). The learning and unlearning of aggression: The role of anxiety, empathy, effcacy and prosocial values. In J. Singer (Ed.), *The control of aggression, violence: Cognitive and physiological factors* (pp. 93–125). San Diego, CA: Academic Press.

Staub, E. (1974). Helping a distressed person: Social, personality and stimulus determinants. In L. Berkowitz (Ed.), *Advances in experimental social psychology* (Vol. 7, pp. 293–344). San Diego, CA: Academic Press.

Staub, E. (1975). To rear a prosocial child: Reasoning, learning by doing and learning by teaching others. In D. DePalma & J. Folley (Eds.), *Moral development: Current theory and research*. Hillsdale, NJ: Erlbaum.

Staub, E. (1978). *Positive social behavior and morality: 1. Personal and social influences*. San Diego, CA: Academic Press.

Staub, E. (1979). *Positive social behavior and morality: 2. Socialization and development*. San Diego, CA: Academic Press.

Staub, E. (1980). Social and prosocial behavior: Personal and situational influences and their interactions. In E. Staub (Ed.), *Personality: Basic aspects and current research* (pp. 236–295). Englewood Cliffs, NJ: Prentice-Hall.

Staub, E. (1987). The meanings, clarification and functions of empathy: A commentary. In N. Eisenberg & J. Strayer (Eds.), *Empathy and its development*. Cambridge: Cambridge University Press.

Staub, E. (1989). *The roots of evil: The origins of genocide and other group violence*. Cambridge: Cambridge University Press.

Staub, E. (1990). The psychology and culture of torture and torturers. In P. Suedfeld (Ed.), *Psychology and torture* (pp. 49–77). New York: Hemisphere.

Staub, E. (1992a). *Bystandership with focus on the use of force*. Manual for proposed course, developed for the Commission of Peace Officers' Standards and Training, Department of Justice, State of California. Amherst: University of Massachusetts.

Staub, E. (1992b). The origins of caring, helping and nonaggression: Parental socialization, the family system, schools, and cultural influence. In S. Oliner, P. Oliner, L. Baron, L. Blum, D. L. Krebs, & M. Z. Smolenska (Eds.), *Embracing the other: Philosophical, psychological, and historical perspectives on altruism* (pp. 390–413). New York: New York University Press.

Staub, E. (1993 August). *Societal–cultural, familial and psychological origins of youth violence*. Paper presented at the 101st Annual Convention of the American Psychological Association, Toronto, Canada.

Staub, E. (1996). The cultural–societal roots of violence: The examples of genocidal violence and of contemporary youth violence in the United States. *American Psychologist, 51* 117–132.

Stoner, J. A. F. (1962). *A comparison of individual and group decisions involving risk.* Unpublished master's thesis, Massachusetts Institute of Technology, Cambridge.

Tajfel, H. (1982a). *Human groups and social categories.* Cambridge: Cambridge University Press.

Tajfel, H. (1982b). Social psychology of intergroup relations. *Annual Review of Psychology, 33,* 1–39.

Tajfel, H., & Turner, J. C. (1979). An integrative theory of intergroup conflict. In W. G. Austin & S. Worchel (Eds.), *The social psychology of intergroup relations.* Pacific Grove, CA: Brooks-Cole.

Toch, H. (1969). *Violent men.* Chicago, IL: Aldine.

Turner, R., & Killian, L. M. (Eds.). (1972). *Collective behavior* (2nd ed.). Englewood Cliffs, NJ: Prentice-Hall.

U.S. Riot Commission. (1968). *Report.* New York: Bantam Books.

Useem, B. (1985). Disorganization and the New Mexico prison riot of 1980. *American Sociological Review, 50,* 677–688.

Waskow, A. I. (1966). *From race-riot to sit-in: 1919 and the 1960's.* New York: Doubleday.

Watson, R. I., Jr. (1973). Investigation into deindividuation using a cross-cultural survey technique. *Journal of Personality and Social Psychology, 5,* 4–15.

Wicker, T. (1975). *A time to die.* New York: Quadrangle/The New York Times Book Co.

Zani, B., & Kirchler, E. (1991). When violence overshadows the spirit of sporting competition: Italian football fans and their clubs. *Journal of Community and Applied Social Psychology, 1,* 5–21.

Zimbardo, P. G. (1969). The human choice: Individuation, reason and order versus deindividuated impulse and chaos. In W. I. Arnold & D. Levine (Eds.), *Nebraska symposium on motivation.* Lincoln: University of Nebraska Press.

32

Understanding and Preventing Police Violence

INTRODUCTION

A selected number of issues critical to "police violence" will be the focus of this article.

- What leads to the use of "unnecessary force" against what groups of people, and
- What can we do to eliminate the use of "unnecessary force"?

There are advantages to starting in the "middle" as one seeks to understand and prevent police violence. Once the use of unnecessary force starts within a system, an evolution begins. Groups and individuals learn by doing. When they help others they are likely to learn from that and become more helpful. When they harm others and use force against others, they are likely to change as individuals and as groups. And it becomes easier for them to use force later on. This is a problem inherent in the work of police officers and others working in the broad field of security because their work sometimes *requires* the use of force. So that is already the starting point for the possibility of the development of the use of more force.

When individuals use force, especially excessive force, they have to justify it somehow. One way to justify it is to *devalue* your victim, even more than you may have devalued that person before. It then becomes easier to harm him or her even more. Another facet of the same process, which may seem to be paradoxical at first glance, is imputing great strength

Reprinted from E. Staub (2001). Understanding and preventing police violence. In S. Einstein & M. Amir, *Policing, security and democracy: Special aspects of democratic policing*. Huntsville, TX: The Office of International Criminal Justice Inc., pp. 221–229. Reprinted with permission. The postscript to this chapter is reprinted from E. Staub (1992). Understanding and preventing police violence, *Center Review, 6*, 1–7. A publication of the Center for Psychology and Social Change: An affiliate of the Harvard Medical School, Cambridge, MA. Reprinted with permmission from the Center for Psychology and Social Change.

and power to the "identified victim" by demonizing him or her, so as to justify what you plan to do by the supposed need to protect yourself.

We tend to believe and feel that the world is a just place. This is a pretty strong feeling or belief. And, if the world is just, those who suffer must deserve their suffering, either because of their character or because of their actions. Ironically, using this *"just world"* thinking, we then think that our own victims also deserve their suffering, and so we devalue them. Left on our own, once unnecessary use of force begins, it is likely to evolve, with a continuing progression of steps. In order to stop it or inhibit it, there has to be something in others' behavior or in the system that says this is inappropriate, this is not going to work.

"Bystanders" in a policing and/or security context are officers who themselves don't engage in "unnecessary force" or don't use any violence, at least initially, but who are witnesses to these events. The power of bystanders is very great, and they don't even have to do anything extraordinary to use this power. By speaking out at the time each of us can make a tremendous impact. By simply saying, *"stop that," "that's not right," "that's not appropriate,"* you and I can have a tremendous impact. What one person says – not even what one person does – powerfully influences the behavior of other people. A bystander does not even have to say to another person what not to do, or what to do. It is enough to share the meaning of a situation in a certain way. In a study that I conducted when a person in another room heard a crash and someone in pain, what another person said greatly affected the first person's actions. When the second person said, for example, *that sounds bad, maybe we should do something* the first person was much more likely to initiate helpful action.

The trouble is that it can be extremely difficult for any police officer to speak out. Police officers are part of a group that has developed strong bonds – a shared identity. In this shared identity, *who you are* depends upon your membership in the group. Just by speaking up at a certain time you may be separating yourself from colleagues. You put yourself aside, and in some sense, you endanger yourself. So it becomes difficult for officers not only to speak up, but even to think in opposition. Because if you think that this is wrong, that this is bad, you may have to take action in order to live up to your own thoughts. Therefore, it is easier not to think. We need to overcome this difficulty on the part of police officers to speak up.

Not only does the behavior of perpetrators of the use of "unnecessary force" change as they harm others, bystanders also change when they remain silent. You have to deal with the events you see and with the fact that you don't speak up or act. One way to do this is to join in devaluing the people who are victims of unnecessary force; to say to yourself *they* deserved it. It is okay. Over time there will be a shift in the whole system. The norms of the system change and allow such behavior. Obviously it is essential to counteract this process.

Higher-ups in the police system and police organization have an essential role in this. *Accountability* at every level is essential. It is not enough that police higher-ups set the necessary standards. They must make clear statements against the use of unnecessary force and help police officers define the meaning of such behavior in ways that make it unacceptable. The important task is for everyone – from the top to the bottom – to work on creating and maintaining a system in which this kind of behavior becomes deviant, and worth speaking out against.

Once unnecessary violence starts to happen, as a group of officers begins to act in an unnecessarily forceful way in a community, there are consequences. One of the basic principles of human behavior is that of *reciprocity*. If you help people there is a tendency for them to feel kindly toward you. If you harm people, there is a tendency for them to feel angry and to want to retaliate. Once you begin to use unnecessary force in a community, you generate a lot of anger, a lot of hostility, increasing degrees of hostility, and various forms of retaliation. Retaliation can be as simple as the community withholding support for the work of police officers. When a police officer is in trouble and members of the community could do something to help, nobody is there. This is an expression of hostility. Or there can be active forms of hostility. And of course, as the community becomes more hostile, the officers become more hostile, and a vicious cycle is in place.

One problem with this vicious cycle is that usually neither side sees its own role in it. If you are an officer and if your community acts in hostile, negative, and antagonistic way toward you, all you see is their behavior. You don't see how your own actions or the actions of your colleagues may have contributed to this. Therefore, rather than looking at yourself and seeing what you need to change, the tendency is to respond with anger to the community, and to increase the use of force.

All too often this is what happens once the use of "unnecessary force" begins. Sometimes it is a very difficult judgment to decide whether force is needed and, if so, how much. But frequently, it is not a matter of difficult judgment: force is clearly not necessary, or very limited force is sufficient.

Let us consider:

- Why would officers use force when it is not necessary?
- How does use of force originate?

As previously noted, the work of police officers, by its nature, *sometimes* requires the *appropriate use of force*. That can, under certain conditions, be a starting point toward inappropriate use of force. Another source often is that certain groups, such as police groups, face difficult or dangerous tasks in which group members are very strongly dependent upon each other. As a result of this a special bond is likely to form. Since connection within the group is very important, special ways are used to increase a feeling of community. This can and does include drawing a sharp differentiation between *"us,"* the members of this group, and others. This phenomenon is not specific to police officers; it can and does include groups that engage in difficult, dangerous work. Sometimes this is legitimate work, such as policing. At other times it may be illegitimate, criminal "work" such as the work of torturers, which at times a society can make "acceptable." In all such instances there is a tendency to create and to maintain a strong bond, and a strong differentiation between *us* and *them*. A "we versus them" separation is a general human tendency, which can become intensified in such groups. This differentiation can lead some groups of police officers to see all citizens, or all members of a particular subgroup of society, as *"them,"* as potential lawbreakers. *"We"* represent the law. *"They"* are potential or even probable lawbreakers.

This situation is influenced by the fact that there is a lot of devaluation of, or prejudice against, certain groups in our society. Minority groups are already defined by society as a *"them,"* and the people who become police officers pick this up. As they grow up, it is part of their – our – culture. Imagine, for example, a young kid growing up in that part of the community in Boston that responded with intense anger and violence at the time the Boston schools were integrated through bussing. If a person grows up in that climate, as he enters police work, he will carry this culturally learned devaluation.

In addition, officers in particular cities or neighborhoods of cities may have more frequent, dangerous and threatening interactions with members of certain groups. Danger, threat and attack on oneself tend to give rise to aggression. If you experience more of this in relation to members of some group, you may further devalue that group as a whole. The point about prejudice and devaluation of groups is that you don't select some individuals and say that these people are dangerous and criminal. Rather you devalue the whole group. Such devaluation often has several elements.

- One is simply that these people are "worse than the rest of us," "they are stupid," or "lazy," etc.
- Another element is seeing and experiencing these people – them – as dangerous, and as dangerous to oneself.
- There is a third element in the tendency to devalue certain groups, and that is that by devaluing others you can elevate yourself. You can feel better about yourself, better about who you are, feel stronger, more important in relation to certain other people, and in general, by devaluing others.

These processes are all too common in day-to-day living and adapting.

What else can contribute to the beginning of the use of excessive force? Another thing that might contribute is difficult conditions of life in society. Life conditions can be difficult economically, politically, or because there is a lot of social change. I would suggest to you that in this society there have been moderately difficult life conditions for the last 25 years. It started perhaps with the assassination of leaders such as President Kennedy, and Martin Luther King, in the USA. These difficult conditions were also created by potentially positive events such as the civil rights movement and feminism, which while having very positive elements, nonetheless, create great changes. It becomes unclear to people how the world operates and how "things" should be and how life should be lived. This is very disconcerting, even threatening. It is reasonable to posit that, partly for these reasons, there has been an increase in violence in our society. These conditions are disorganizing and at certain points in time, when the changes are great, they represent a kind of chaos for individuals as well as for systems.

Great changes in family structure, many single parents, drugs and drug use and misuse, and the sexual revolution are but a few of the additional events and processes that represent tremendous social changes. These dynamic, complex phenomena affect us both as individuals and as members of a society in which life is less ordered or comprehensible. In our own personal lives, we are affected by the way in which we live with our mates or how we relate to people. "Maleness" and the meaning of "maleness," for example, have become different. An aspect of this is that males are also blamed for many things that go on that people have identified, "tagged" as being problematic. Some of this "tagging" is justified. But whether it is justified or not, it is very difficult to bear. All these things have a tremendous impact on people. And people can't separate their lives cleanly. "This is my life out in the world." "This is my life as a police officer." These events can and do affect people, their level of frustration, and their response under stressful conditions.

Self-selection is a further element as a source of violence. One can talk about the selection of people for policemen and what criteria are used. You-me-whoever are selected for jobs and tasks. But there is also the complex process of self-selection. There are some people who want to become police officers or work as part of security services. Not everybody is equally inclined to join the police force. Most likely it is not the same person who yearns to be a librarian and who yearns to be a police officer. Entering the police force you know that you are or will be exposing yourself to danger, that you have to be willing to use force as part of your work. There are characteristics associated with "self-selection." Sometimes these characteristics come in positive forms and sometimes not. A positive form might be a person wanting to be a police officer who feels strong and has a sense of personal power, a person who can influence things. A negative form might be a person who values strength and power but doesn't feel strong and powerful; who feels weak and relatively powerless. Such a person may hope that through police work he or she may gain a sense of strength and power together perhaps with respect and status.

In "hot pursuit," police officers may become excited and therefore more likely to use force. I have heard of discussions, however, that suggest an additional critical element. When somebody has to be pursued that person challenges the pursuer. Some officers may feel that this shows a kind of disrespect. A police officer wants to enforce the law and this person defies him or her. The result can be a sense of being personally challenged. Responding to this challenge with punishment, by the use of force, reaffirms for some officers a feeling of authority, a feeling of strength. Power over the body of another human being is one of the ultimate forms of power. That you can do what you will with another's body can give some people such a feeling of power.

What can we do to reduce the use of unnecessary force? It is essential to set standards, to set rules of conduct, to create accountability. However difficult that must be, this accountability must be both internal and external, that is, relative to the police force as a unit and also relative to the community. There has to be *both* kinds of accountability. Police chiefs, deputy chiefs, supervisors, and so on, can exert tremendous influence by speaking up and explaining where they stand. After all, police officers want to be part of the system. That system, the community which they are part of, is important for them. The clearer the standards of acceptable behavior, the more likely it is that police officers will respond to these limits and "norms." Impunity also creates problems. It is important that deviation from significant norms are to have consequences.

Positive, active *"bystandership"* is also very important. Police officers are likely to often remain passive because of the kind of bond they have with their fellow officers. They may feel that trying to redirect or influence a fellow officer who is emotionally aroused, or threatening or actually harming a civilian, they will be seen as unsupportive or even hostile. However, entering into such a situation, taking over from an emotionally aroused fellow officer, and directing him or her away from or stopping the use of unnecessary force is positive teamwork. It helps the civilian, it helps the fellow officer who may get into serious trouble, and it helps to bring about good police work. Police officers can create the kind of system that they want to be both part of and proud of through such actions. Training in "bystandership" can be very important for "democratic policing."

Another extremely important, if not critical, process to create and maintain can be called *cross-cutting relations* between the police forces and the communities and neighborhoods that they serve. Everybody now talks about "community policing" and what that involves. It involves, in its most basic sense, contact with members of the community. But "community policing" needs to go further than that. *Cross-cutting relations* means deep, ongoing, sensitive, equitable, engagement by members of different groups with each other. Viable and effective democratic community policing demands such contacts between police officers and members of the community that they serve. Deep involvement! Respectful involvement! We know that just being neighbors doesn't reduce prejudice and the devaluation of people. Psychologists have done research starting in the 1940s and 1950s which documented that, for example, when Blacks and Whites simply live near each other prejudice does not diminish. In fact, it can even increase. What is necessary, critical, is that there be a real connection, real involvement. This can be in play or in work.

What do I mean? I mean things such as community projects that people can plan and do together. In Amherst, Massachusetts, a few years back, somebody initiated the building of a playground for one of the local schools. It was done by volunteers. The material was donated by local businesses. All segments of the community came, including students from the university, people from the community, and police officers. People talked about this experience glowingly afterwards. Some people came for a four-hour stint, which was the required amount of time to participate, and then remained for the whole, long weekend. They came back because it was so satisfying to work together.

This sort of thing has positive effects. It can, for example, overcome *devaluation*. You see and experience the other person as a human being. It develops feelings of connection. Many types of joint projects can be created, in the course of which members of the police force and the community can develop shared goals that override some of their conflicts. Then they work for these shared goals. And people learn by doing. This happens in the realm of violence and also happens in the realm of positive relations. When we act to help another, we come to value that other person more. We come to feel connection(s) to that "other." We come to value that "other" PERSON as a person, and not simply hold some image of that person as the member of some group. This is not just changing and developing the attitudes of police officers toward the community, it is also changing and developing the attitudes of community members toward the police.

Another element that is extremely important is education in "cultural awareness." When we consider and talk about "cross-cutting relations," the education that people get is through their direct, immediate experience. Children can learn to be caring about other people or aggressive toward others as a function of the kind of experience that they have with others, with adults and peers – how much benevolence or malevolence and how much they themselves engage in. Experiential learning is at the core of this. Preaching to people does not educate them. What is necessary is facilitating opportunities for meaningful, prosocial relationships and experiences with others as PEOPLE.

But education in the realm of *cultural awareness* is also very important. What forms does it need to take? One form is academic. People need to understand the culture of the other group. One good way to do this is to come to understand the particular characteristics of the other, and how their ways of operating in the world have developed. What functions do these characteristics serve for this group? How did they adopt these kinds of behavior and ways of being? Frequently groups (and individuals) have become who they are as they responded to the circumstances of life they faced. This kind of learning is especially important when we start off by looking down at the "other," saying, "*How can they be that way*?" There are good reasons for why each group is the way that it is . . . although the reasons may not be obvious.

There is another important element in this and that is education in *interpersonal styles*. Even in "cross-cutting relations," when the opportunities exist to work together, we have to understand all kinds of "little things" about members of the "other group." Some people, for example, don't smile at the time that we expect them to smile. There may be all kinds of behaviors, rituals, and life styles that are different from one's expectations. And when this is so there is a tendency, if we are not informed either by experience or education, to think that something is wrong with "them." The point is that "they" are different. Some people have written about teachers who, when they encounter, for example, Mexican-American children, become very annoyed. As they talk with these children, especially when there is a discipline problem, and explain what they want or what they think, these children look down instead of looking at them. The teacher may think that these kids are being impertinent, that they challenge them and challenge their authority. But, actually, in Mexican cultures, children are taught to act that way with people in authority, by looking down when these people talk to them. They are supposed to show respect that way. It is such a simple thing and yet a serious misinterpretation can result, creating inappropriate, unnecessary anger and hostility. And this example may be switched to a police officer stopping a minority youth on the street, or a probation officer speaking to a young minority-group probationer.

Another important consideration is to develop the appropriate and necessary physical and verbal skills in peace officers in order to more effectively respond to the demands of all kinds of situations. Research shows that aggressive children are less capable of expressing themselves and are, therefore, less capable of shaping situations in such a way that they get what they want, except by force. So already being aggressive, rather than communicating in words, is characteristic of aggressive children. It is very important for police officers to learn to express themselves and to express clearly what they want as police officers: to explain, reason, give clear commands, not to be distressed by verbally challenging behavior, but have a verbal way to respond to them.

Verbal as well as physical skills are important sources of confidence. The more you feel good about your competence and your ability to handle situations, the less you need to use violence. When one has realistically based confidence in oneself and knows and senses that one can do whatever one needs to do, when somebody challenges you, you don't need to respond to that challenge with force.

It is also crucial to learn to listen. To begin to listen and to take in what people say. Here again the characteristics of some police officers, the nature of the system, and how the system has shaped them, the police organization to which they belong and identify with, are important. For example, given the standards and values of a police unit, officers may feel that listening to somebody and taking them seriously may be demeaning. They think, "*I need to look tough*." They may feel that they even endanger themselves by listening.

One may create situations that are self-fulfilling prophecies. For example, one can say, and believe, "*I cannot talk to these people. I have to act tough, to act forcefully*." Then the "others" would respond tough and forceful, and a vicious cycle begins; a progressive escalation. And you may say to yourself, "*Oh well, I knew that you couldn't talk to these people*." Another important consideration is training that involves perspectives, ways of looking at things, how to interpret things. For example, it is crucial to help police officers move away from a tendency to interpret the behavior of others as being an affront, from interpreting it as being personal. In a way, when someone tries to get away from a police cruiser, when they have to be pursued, they are doing "their thing." And I, the mandated upholder of "law and order" don't want *them* to do "their thing." But that's what *they* are doing! To perceive this in such a manner rather than becoming enraged that *they* dare to do this can be very valuable to a police officer. A mindset that makes such experiences less personal must be part of the ongoing training of police officers.

It is valuable to use role playing in such training. Role playing is a very effective tool. It even re-creates a lot of the gut reactions. I have worked with people who have a terrible time expressing anger. I remember one particular person. The only time that he was able to express anger was in the form of knocking someone on the head and knocking him out. Having expressed anger in this way, the person said to himself, "*of course I cannot express anger because of how I react*." And this particular person, when we did role playing, in the beginning, could not express anger even in role playing, because it was so arousing for him. Role playing has many important uses in learning new forms of behavior and reworking emotional reactions.

Another important but different aspect of training is to create a change in self-awareness. This includes an increase in the knowledge about, and an awareness of how a group operates; how we ourselves adapt and operate. When people – each one of us – become aware that devaluing or looking down on certain people may not have to do with *who* "they" are but may have more to do with who we are, as well as who we aren't, a tremendous and necessary shift in our own consciousness occurs. This inevitably has great significance. An increase in self-awareness can and does lead us to reevaluate others.

Finally, there has to be some special training for certain officers. Certain officers, for reasons already noted, such as interpreting the behavior of the "other" as an affront to themselves, tend to frequently respond with anger. Anger can be automatic in response to certain circumstances over which the person has little control. Something happens that causes a short-circuit: anger and a violent response. This has to be broken down. Control can be learned. People who operate this way, including police officers, can learn to shift from an automatic response sequence, to once again consciously think about the *meaning of events* to which they respond. New viable ways of seeing and perceiving, new interpretations of events must be introduced, new ways of officers "talking to themselves." This relearning can be crucial. While only a small number of police officers may manifest this problem to an extreme degree, others may have it to a smaller degree. Police officers letting themselves go in this way may frequently be part of the reality of policing in states that are going through a transition from totalitarian or authoritarian political systems and in which the "old guard" police and security officers remain on the job because there simply aren't sufficient appropriate new recruits to meet the "law and order" and social control needs of the country-in-transition. Effective training of new officers in such situations is of crucial importance. A final factor to consider are the kinds of selection methods used for police recruits, special task assignments, as well as a variety of special service security agents. Many of the (mis) behaviors noted in this chapter are not abnormal. They are the outcome of human tendencies and psychological processes given certain contextual-situational backgrounds.

It is incumbent upon us – all of us – to create and to use appropriate methods to discover and document the use of "police violence" and address its sources; condemnation alone will not work. Accountability, the nature of the culture in a particular police system, positive "bystandership" and the other elements that were noted must be considered.

In summary, we, the constituents within a democracy, need to understand, and members of the police force and police officers need to understand:

- the powerful, complex tendencies that exist in groups that can and do lead to unnecessary use of force – both against the innocent as well as the guilty – and
- the kinds of training that ought to be instituted to reduce the use of "unnecessary force," if "democratic policing" is to be an integral part of our democratic society, processes, and values.

Selected Reading

Staub, E. (1989). *The roots of evil: The origins of genocide and other group violence.* New York: Cambridge University Press.

POSTSCRIPT: ACTIVE BYSTANDERSHIP IN PREVENTING THE USE OF UNNECESSARY FORCE BY POLICE

The preceding chapter is a revised version of a talk I gave in September 1991 at a seminar on reducing the use of unnecessary force by police, organized in the wake of the Rodney King incident by the Commission on Police Officers Standard and Training (POST), an agency of California's Department of Justice. When the Los Angeles police tried to stop Rodney King and he did not stop, a chase followed, after which he was beaten by a number of officers, while lying on the ground, with other officers standing in a circle around them and watching the beating. The event became famous because unknown to the police someone videotaped the scene and the video was shown on television. Later, the police officers were tried, and when they were acquitted, a major riot erupted in Los Angeles.

I was asked by POST to give the opening talk at the seminar, in which there were about 200 participants – police chiefs, police instructors, representatives of police rank and file and of community organizations. After that I was asked to develop a program to reduce the use of unnecessary force by police that can be introduced into the police academies.

POST was especially interested in my focus on the role of "bystanders," in this instance fellow officers whose intervention can inhibit or stop the use of unnecessary force. I developed a proposal for a course on "Bystandership," or active intervention. I presented this proposal in Sacramento in July 1992 in a two-day workshop to 20 participants, ranging from chiefs to field officers from around California. Their tasks were to evaluate the proposal, and then advise POST on how to use the approach.

The Sources of Police Violence

The basis for this proposal was my analysis of the origins of police violence described in this chapter. My analysis of police violence originated in my understanding of the many kinds of group violence described in my book, *The Roots of Evil: The Origins of Genocide and Other Group Violence*.

Groups and individuals change as a result of their own actions; they learn by doing. When they harm others, or use force against others, it becomes easier for them to use force again. People justify harming others partly by devaluing their victims, and they perceive themselves as increasingly willing to use force for what they regard as good reasons. This is a problem inherent in police work in that the work sometimes *requires* the use of force, which can be a starting point for the use of unnecessary force and the evolution of police violence.

Once the unnecessary use of force begins, it will expand, unless the response of "bystanders" – people who witness it or know about it – indicates that such actions are inappropriate and unacceptable. These people can be fellow officers, superiors, or community groups and agencies. Both experimental and real-life evidence show that by what they say and do people can influence each other, and bystanders can influence perpetrators' actions. Like other uniformed groups engaged in dangerous work, police officers develop strong bonds and an identity deeply rooted in the group. These bonds make it difficult for them to oppose one another's actions and thereby endanger their relationship to fellow officers – even to oppose them in thought, since that can create internal conflict. But when *bystanders* remain silent they affirm the perpetrators, and they themselves change, for example, by joining perpetrators in devaluing victims. Over time there can be a shift in the whole system that will make violence acceptable.

Superior officers can speak out strongly against the use of unnecessary force and create accountability by investigating allegations and punishing perpetrators. When they remain passive bystanders they allow the development of a violent system; this, apparently, was the case in Los Angeles.

The strong bond within police units can create a differentiation between "us" (the police) and "them" (which potentially includes all outsiders, who come to be seen as potential lawbreakers). And officers will tend to devalue most and become most violent against groups devalued by society.

Police violence generates anger and the desire to retaliate. Members of a community may withhold support from police officers or engage in hostile actions. A vicious cycle can result, with mutual anger and increasing police violence.

Space allows only a listing of other contributors to police violence: lack of verbal and physical skills to effectively deal with interactions with citizens; lack of cultural awareness that would enable officers to understand and effectively communicate with various groups of citizens; the characteristics of some individuals who join the police, such as valuing strength and power without feeling strong and powerful, and an associated tendency to interpret the behavior of citizens (for instance, Rodney King not stopping his car) as a personal challenge; and, finally, the way some people, including police officers, deal with the impacts of difficult life conditions, such as the tremendous social changes and social disorganization in the United States.

An Avenue for Reducing Police Violence

What are the central elements of training in bystandership? First an effort must be made to create a change in perspective – from seeing intervention as action against fellow officers to seeing it as effective teamwork, serving the shared goals of police work, protecting the rights of citizens, and keeping fellow officers out of trouble. Second, the issue of disloyalty can be avoided and the effectiveness of intervention increased by training officers to notice when interactions between fellow officers and citizens develop in ways that make the use of unnecessary force probable, and to intervene to shape situations so that unnecessary force is not used. Training is also required for ways to intervene when unnecessary force is used.

Watching and discussing film clips that depict such situations, along with role playing and rehearsing interventions, are among the central aspects of the training. Officers can play the roles of *acting* officers, *bystanding* (or intervening) officers, as well as citizen-victims. Playing the victim role could help officers understand the perspective – the feelings, thoughts, and actions – of a citizen. Following an intervention officers should discuss what happened, partly to resolve any negative feelings.

Ideally, an aspect of positive bystandership would be for officers to speak out when their superior officers remain passive in the face of police violence. The hierarchical culture, however, makes this extremely difficult. It is essential, therefore, to expose top administrative officers to these ideas so that they understand their own role in allowing a violent culture to develop and their responsibility to act to support and reward active intervention by officers in the field.

The group assembled in Sacramento strongly supported the idea of police training in bystandership, or active intervention, at all levels – starting with chiefs – not only in relation to the use of force but also in other domains, such as interpersonal conflict or racism within the police. They also supported the central ideas for methods of training to promote active bystandership. They did not support all suggestions: for example, they thought that creating joint projects for police and community, which I proposed as an avenue for cross-cutting relations or deep engagement, should not be part of this training; they did not support the idea that officers role-play victims; and they were uncertain about the best name for the program.

The special consultant's report to POST said the following:

> Based on feedback from the committee, personally listening to portions of Dr. Staub's presentation, reviewing his materials, and consulting with POST staff, the following recommendations are made:
>
> "Bystandership" should be replaced with the term "intervention" or other similar terminology.
>
> Training relative to intervention should be incorporated with other POST courses already developed.
>
> The subject of intervention should be taught to all levels of police officers (Basic Course through Executive Development).
>
> Some of the members from the Bystandership Committee should be reconvened to assist with the integration of intervention into other POST courses.
>
> The police organization must be supportive of officers who employ intervention tactics.

PART V

THE AFTERMATH OF MASS VIOLENCE

Trauma, Healing, Prevention, and Reconciliation

33

Preventing Group Violence

There was hope after World War II that the horrors of the Holocaust, Nazi Germany's crusade against Jews, and the killing of millions of other people would bring such violence to an end forever. Instead, collective or group violence has become commonplace in the second part of the twentieth century. Cambodia, China, Indonesia, Tibet, East Timor, Argentina, El Salvador, Chile, Guatemala, Colombia, Bosnia, and Rwanda are only some of the better-known places where such violence has been perpetrated. Its forms have also been numerous, including genocide, mass killing, abductions or disappearances of large numbers of individuals, and widespread torture (Suedfeld, 1990).

Without effective prevention, the frequency of such violence is likely to rise further in the twenty-first century. Poverty, the experience of injustice, and social and psychological disorganization that prevents the meeting of basic human needs in a rapidly changing world tend to lead people to turn to ethnic, religious, national, or other "identity" groups to strengthen individual identity and to gain support and security. This, combined with ideologies that groups adopt in difficult times, whether Nazism, communism, nationalism, racial supremacy, or something else, frequently leads to antagonism and violence against other groups.

Understanding the influences that lead to collective violence is necessary for prediction; both understanding and prediction are essential for prevention. For effective prevention, it is highly important to further our understanding of commonalities in both causes and methods of prevention as well as to respect the particulars of each potentially violence-producing situation.

Reprinted from E. Staub (1999). The origins and prevention of genocide, mass killing, and other collective violence. *Peace and Conflict: Journal of Peace Psychology, 5*, 303–336. Included here are pp. 304, 314–320.

HALTING VIOLENCE

When reactions or interventions by bystanders or outsiders are early, perpetrators' commitment to violence against a victim group is often still limited. The motivation for mass killing or genocide may not yet have evolved; inhibitions against violence may not yet have disappeared. A plan of action or a system to execute it may not yet exist. Persistent efforts by external bystanders, nations, and the international community are likely to be effective even without the use of military force.

From Early Warning to Early Action

Recent attention has focussed on early warning. It is important to have a valid conceptual base for identifying, collecting, and analyzing relevant information. The conception of the origins of collective violence described in earlier chapters offers a system for identifying relevant information both for halting violence and for prevention (the presence of difficult life conditions and group conflict; scapegoating; ideologies; cultural characteristics like devaluation, authority orientation, and so on; change in the degree of discrimination or other forms of harm inflicted on a group, which is especially important in indicating the need to halt violence; and the passivity of bystanders). Other systems, overlapping with this one, have also been proposed (Bond & Vogele, 1995; Charny, 1991; Harff & Gurr, 1990; Kuper, 1984).

The European Community has proposed the establishment of a center for early warning, but practical efforts to implement it have not followed (Rupesinghe, 1996). Because important motivational and mediating processes are psychological in nature, many kinds of psychologists, including political, social, and peace psychologists, should be involved in the specification of the type of information needed, the development of assessment tools, and research in evaluating the validity of information.

An even more important issue is the use of information. The UN, nongovernmental organizations (NGOs), and the embassies of various nations already provide a great deal of early information. But in Rwanda and elsewhere, information has not led to action. Actions to halt and prevent group violence will become more likely if standards are developed for *when* action is required, *what* actions are required depending on circumstances, and *who* is to take action, and if institutions responsible for activating responses are created or strengthened.

Without effective institutions whose job is to activate response, early warning is unlikely to lead to action, especially early action. The institutions of the UN, which have been so ineffective in Rwanda and elsewhere, need to be strengthened. Appropriate institutions within regional organizations, such as the Organization of African States, must also be created. However, because the UN and regional organizations rely on and require for action the help of member nations, and because nations sometimes may need to take the lead, it would be extremely important to establish corresponding institutions within national governments. These institutions would be responsible for processing information about actual and potential violence against groups (relevant to either halting or preventing violence) and play the required role, in cooperation with international organizations, in activating responses.

From Passivity to Humanitarian Intervention

Many kinds of bystanders have potential influence, including individuals, community groups, NGOs, nations, and international organizations (Rupesinghe, 1996). But as discrimination, persecution, and violence evolve beyond a certain point, the influence and power of states and the community of nations is required to halt further violence.

Why do they usually remain passive? At least in theory, the principle of nonintervention in each other's internal affairs guides states' relations. There was seemingly permanent warfare in Europe until the treaty of Westphalia, in 1648, with its central principles of the sovereignty of states and nonintervention. The principle of nonintervention became part of the UN charter, which states in article 2(7) that "nothing contained in the present Charter shall authorize the United Nations to intervene in matters which are essentially within the domestic jurisdiction of any state."

Perhaps governments believe that by not intervening they uphold an orderly international system. However, in practice states do intervene, but usually for self-serving reasons. The United States has engaged in or supported a number of self-serving and ideologically guided military interventions: in Guatemala in 1954, helping to overthrow a democratically elected president; in Nicaragua; in Panama; and elsewhere.

Another reason for passivity is that states like to have complete jurisdiction over their citizens. They avoid interference in others' affairs, so that others won't interfere in their affairs. This has been shown by the unwillingness of states to include political groups under the genocide convention and by continuing attacks by some states on principles of human rights. Abiding by a principle of humanitarian intervention may also require states to go against an ally or business partner identified as a perpetrator nation, as well as to assume some of the burdens of intervention.

States have traditionally acted to further what they view as their national interest, usually defined in terms of power, wealth, or influence. They have not seen themselves as moral agents with responsibility for the welfare of people outside their borders. This seems not only immoral but shortsighted, because violence usually expands, and nations that have turned against their own citizens ultimately have often turned against other nations as well, as did Germany, Iraq, Argentina in the Falklands war, and others.

Nations that have close ties to a perpetrator nation are especially likely to remain passive or provide continuing support. Unfortunately, such close ties usually generate loyalty not to the citizens of a country, certainly not to a minority within the country, but to its government. Because these countries have maximum potential influence (Fein, 1994), they have a special responsibility to act.

Nations have also withheld support that the UN needs to deal with human rights issues. They are especially reluctant to provide material support or force. In Rwanda, only one nation out of 60 responded to the Secretary General's plea for more troops, and 2 out of 50 for his plea for police officers (Ramsbotham, 1995).

In spite of all this, concern about human rights and the physical safety and basic rights of individuals and groups has been greatly expanding. These concerns are expressed in various international conventions and institutions within the UN. But for nations to act, the international climate must change further. Citizens must exert influence on their governments.

Psychologists can contribute by elucidating some of the psychological sources of passivity. They can publicize already-existing knowledge and gather new information about diffusion of responsibility (Latané & Darley, 1970; Myers, 1996); about the differentiation between "us and them," which makes violence against "them" easier and action on behalf of "them" less likely; about both perpetrators and bystanders excluding victims from the moral and human realm and blaming victims (Lerner, 1980; Opotow, 1990; Staub, 1990); and about other processes that lead either to passivity or action by bystanders (Myers, 1996; Oliner & Oliner, 1988; Staub, 1993). However, we need to know much more about how to activate bystanders, and especially groups, including nations. Psychologists can also use already-existing knowledge to help citizens influence their governments, so that they act in behalf of people outside their own borders.

In summary, it is important to develop criteria that differentiate between self-serving, "imperial" interventions and humanitarian interventions; to establish both the principle of intervention *for the protection of human rights* and appropriate forms of intervention; to develop institutions whose job is to activate early responses; and to create an international climate that leads to action.

Forms of Intervention

All or nearly all violence-generating situations, no matter how important their objective elements, have important psychological dimensions. Psychologists must participate both in devising and executing methods of intervention. If time allows it, intervention may best start with high-level private communication. This may include condemnation of the policies and practices that harm the victim group, specification of actions that the international community will take if they continue, and offers of help with mediation and conflict resolution. Positive inducements, material aid, support, and efforts to help fulfill a group's basic needs are important. Doing all this in private enables the leaders of the perpetrator group to change course without losing face, without appearing weak in front of their followers. Such psychological considerations in shaping bystander actions are of profound importance. However, if victimization continues, public condemnation and then action by the international community must follow.

Nations and the community of nations, by what they say and do, can reaffirm and possibly to some degree reinstate in the eyes of perpetrators the humanity of the victims. They can raise concern among perpetrators about their image in the eyes of the world and create fear of the consequences of their actions to themselves. They can also help fulfill some of the goals that motivate violence, both material and psychological, in other ways. The media, if it can penetrate into the perpetrator country, given the censorship that usually accompanies such situations, can communicate the perspective of the outside world and thereby move some internal bystanders to action.

If all this is ineffective, nations can intensify their response by withholding aid, by sanctions and boycotts. The earlier such actions and the more uniformly nations abide by them, the more effective they are likely to be. Further study is required of how to use sanctions and boycotts so that they will effectively bring about psychological change in the attitudes and motives of perpetrators and internal bystanders.

An international boycott had an important role in bringing apartheid to an end in South Africa, partly because the business community in South Africa was unwilling to suffer the damage it inflicted. But its effectiveness may have been enhanced by preceding actions such as decades of exclusion of South African athletes from international competition (Pogrund, 1991). In an extremely sports-minded country, this has continuously communicated to South Africans the world's disapproval of apartheid.

Sanctions have been less effective in some other instances. The reasons for this may include that they start late, or without private warnings and dialogue, or both; that not all nations adhere to them; that powerful rulers are unwilling to publicly give in; and that sanctions at times aim not only to stop violence but to topple the leadership (e.g., Iraq and Cuba).

However, harm-doing might have been much greater in some instances, like Bosnia, without boycotts and other actions that showed concern and vigilance by the world. At times boycotts have limited effects in changing policies but harm the population of a country, as in Cuba and Iraq. Targeting sanctions so that they penalize those most responsible for the crisis (e.g. freezing leaders' personal assets; Carnegie Commission on Preventing Deadly Conflict, 1997) may enhance the effectiveness of sanctions and reduce the suffering of the general population.

At times a military response is essential to stop violence. Limited military action in Bosnia, for example, was effective in bringing the violence to an end. A UN force of some kind has long been advocated (Fein, 1994; Institute for Genocide Studies, 1999), perhaps consisting of volunteers, but it has not been created. But the earlier other measures are used and the more extensive they are, the less will be the need for military action.

To be effective, actions by bystanders require wisdom and sensitivity. The definition of a situation very much matters: How bystanders see it and what sense they make of it shapes their actions. For example, seeing Iraq as an important counterweight to Iran, rather than as an aggressor that is violent both internally and against outsiders, created United States support for Iraq. In Somalia, seeing General Adid as a warlord who was the primary source of the violence, rather than as a leader of one of several factions and a representative of a significant group of people, led the United States to focus on him and attempt to capture him (Farer, 1996). This resulted in retaliation, the killing of American soldiers. Because of the legacy of the Vietnam War, the American people and American leaders became frightened about another quagmire. Sensitivity and wisdom are required in all preventive efforts by outsiders, especially knowledge about and openness to the requirements of a specific culture (Wessels & Montiero, 2001).

Special Envoys and Advisory Teams

As part of an early response, special envoys (see Carnegie Commission on the Prevention of Deadly Conflict, 1997), working with advisory teams, can be useful in efforts either to halt or prevent group violence.

On the one hand, they can carry private and public messages from the international community. On the other hand, in their interactions with leaders, special envoys can to some degree address the psychological forces that drive leaders, as well as followers. It is frequently assumed that leaders act purely out of opportunistic motives, to gain and hold power, or to develop influence over their supporters. This view is so deeply ingrained that it was offered as an explanation of Hitler's anti-Semitic policies, even after World War II, and even by a wise psychologist like Gordon Allport (Allport, 1954).

But leaders are also members of their group and the product of its culture, including its devaluation of and enmity toward certain others. They are also affected by conditions of life in their society. As they propagate scapegoating and destructive ideologies and initiate harmful actions against the designated victim, they are fulfilling their own and their groups' needs, but in destructive ways. They create (usually false) understanding of causes, offer hopeful (but ultimately destructive) visions, make people feel effective, create connections and strengthen identity in the group.

Frequently, perpetrators also carry a feeling of prior victimization. The Serbs were ruled by Turkey for five centuries, until late in the nineteenth century. Hundreds of thousands of Serbs were killed by Croats during World War II, with Muslims allied to Croats (Staub, 1996). When Croatia declared independence, the Serbs attacked Croatia, and after the Croat counterattack, about 200,000 Serbs were ousted, or ethnically cleansed, from Croatia.

In Rwanda, not only were the Hutus long subordinated to the Tutsis, but they witnessed Tutsi massacres of Hutus in Burundi (and after the genocide, Tutsi killings of Hutu refugees in Zaire). Leaders in part act out of their group's woundedness, as well as their own corresponding woundedness, as in the case of Serb leaders (e.g., Mladic, the military commander in Bosnia, whose parents were killed by Croats during World War II).

In their interaction with leaders, the aim of diplomats and professionals who work with them should be to move beyond formal diplomatic engagement. In an effort to help the group move to constructive modes of need fulfillment, they should try to help leaders generate inclusive visions that bring members of different groups together in the service of shared goals. To the extent possible, they should act as agents of healing and reconciliation.

Even though they carry the message that violation of the rights of others is unacceptable to the international community, they can show genuine appreciation of and empathy for the past suffering of the group and its leaders. Special envoys may be the only party situated to engage in such constructive efforts with leaders of a group that has begun an evolution toward group violence. Psychologists have important roles to play, in developing a knowledge base, providing training, and participating as members of such teams.

Let us examine post-genocide events in Rwanda and the conduct of the international community. With the return of Hutu refugees to Rwanda from neighboring countries in 1996, many former members of the militias and the military who were the prime perpetrators of the genocide also returned. At least some of them resumed killing Tutsis, mainly in the northwest region of the country that has long been the center of Hutu extremism. The government forces have apparently killed Hutu civilians in retaliation (Drumtra, 1998). In such a situation, over time, a "siege mentality" (Rouhana & Bar-Tal, 1998) can develop. A government that seems to have been genuinely interested in creating a just and peaceful society, and has punished its own soldiers for unjustified violence (Drumtra, 1998), might increasingly engage in what it sees as defensive violence.

Although Rwanda has received some humanitarian aid, the international community has taken no discernible action to help stop the continued Hutu violence against Tutsis. However, by the middle of 1999, the government of Rwanda succeeded in bringing such violence to a halt. Still, a combination of high-level, visible condemnation by the international community, third parties (perhaps high-level special envoys) working with both sides, and the introduction of international peacekeepers can be important actions by the international community in such situations.

References

Allport, G. W. (1954). *The nature of prejudice*. Reading, MA: Addison-Wesley.

Bond, D., & Vogele, W. (1995). *Profiles of international "hotspots."* Unpublished manuscript, Harvard University, Cambridge, MA.

Carnegie Commission on the Prevention of Deadly Conflict. (1997). *Preventing deadly conflict: Final report*. New York: Carnegie Corporation of New York.

Charny, I. (1991). Genocide intervention and prevention. *Social Education*, 124–127.

Drumtra, J. (1998). *Life after death: Suspicion and reintegration in post-genocide Rwanda*. Washington, DC: U.S. Committee for Refugees, Immigration and Refugee Services of America.

Farer, J. (1996). Intervention in unnatural humanitarian emergencies: Lessons of the first phase. *Human Rights Quarterly, 18*, 1–22.

Fein, H. (1994). *The prevention of genocide*. New York: City University of New York.

Harff, B., & Gurr, T. R. (1990). Victims of the state genocides, politicides and group repression since 1945. *International Review of Victimology, 1*, 1–19.

Institute for Genocide Studies. (1999). *Ever again? Evaluating the United Nations Genocide Convention on its 50th anniversary*. New York: University of New York.

Kuper, L. (1984). *International action against genocide*.

Latané, B., & Darley, J. (1970). *The unresponsive bystander: Why doesn't he help?* New York: Appleton-Crofts.

Lerner, M. (1980). *The belief in a just world: A fundamental delusion*. New York: Plenum.

Myers, D. (1996). *Social psychology*. New York: McGraw-Hill.

New York Times Conference on the Internet. (1996). *Bosnia: Uncertain path to peace*. Forum on Healing and Reconciliation.

Oliner, S. B., & Oliner, P. (1988). *The altruistic personality: Rescuers of Jews in Nazi Europe*. New York: Free Press.

Opotow, S. (Ed.) (1990). Moral exclusion and injustice. *Journal of Social Issues*, *46*(1).

Pogrund, B. (1991). *The transformation in South Africa*. Lecture, University of Massachusetts of Amherst.

Ramsbotham, D. (1995). The changing nature of intervention: The role of UN peacekeeping. *Research Institute for the Study of Conflict and Terrorism, 282*, 1–28.

Rouhana, N. N., & Bar-Tal, D. (1998). Psychological dynamics of intractable ethnonational conflicts: The Israeli–Palestinian case. *American Psychologist, 53*, 761–770.

Rupesinghe, K. (1996). *From civil war to civil peace: Multi-Track solutions to armed conflict*. Unpublished manuscript, International Alert.

Staub, E. (1990). The psychology and culture of torture and torturres. In P. Suedfeld (Ed.), *Psychology and torture* (pp. 49–77). Washington, DC: Hemisphere.
Staub, E. (1993). The psychology of bystanders, perpetrators and heroic helpers. *International Journal of Intercultural Relations*, *17*, 315–341.
Staub, E. (1996). Preventing genocide: Activating bystanders, helping victims and the creation of caring. *Peace and Conflict: Journal of Peace Psychology*, *2*, 189–201.
Suedfeld, P. (Ed.). (1990). *Psychology and torture*. Washington, DC: Hemisphere.
Wessels, M., & Montiero, C. (2001). Psychological intervention and post-conflict reconstruction in Angola: Interweaving Western and traditional approaches. In D. Christie, R. V. Wagner, & D. Winter (Eds.), *Peace, conflict and violence: Peace psychology for the 21st century*. Englewood Cliffs, NJ: Prentice-Hall.

34

Kosovo

The Need for Flexible Bystander Response

The many failures of response by the international community were followed by a very delayed but effective response in Bosnia. Once serious bombing of the Serb military began, it speedily led to a halting of violence, followed by the Dayton peace negotiations. Even in Kosovo, the response was delayed: Warnings about potential violence in Kosovo had started to come in the late 1980s. The bombing began after negotiations and after significant ethnic cleansing had taken place (Adelman, 1999). But, at least, there was a bystander response before large-scale violence.

A likely reason for this was awareness of, attention to, and a commitment that has developed in Bosnia to stopping Serb aggression, an evolution in a positive direction. The same leaders were on the scene. The failure of a response in Rwanda, and the apology by President Clinton to the Rwandan people that acknowledged responsibility, may have added at least to his motivation to act. This evolution has not led, however, to the creation of international institutions that might be helpful in other crises. The specificity of concern and commitment does not offer the hope of more active bystandership by the community of nations.

Given that bombing stopped Serb aggression in Bosnia, it was understandable that the same method was tried in Kosovo. But this was a different situation, given the symbolic meaning of Kosovo for Serbs, their view of it as essential to their identity. It was evident within a few days that instead of stopping violence, the NATO bombing was creating great suffering, especially for Albanians who were being expelled and killed by Serbs, and increasingly for Serbian civilians as well.

Reprinted from E. Staub (1999). The origins and prevention of genocide, mass killing, and other collective violence. *Peace and Conflict: Journal of Peace Psychology, 5*, 303–336. Included here are pp. 328–329.

Flexibility, the capacity to change course, is essential when the means intended to stop violence create rather than relieve suffering and destruction. Effective change in strategy requires understanding of history, culture, and the needs of both members of a society and its leaders. Given their history, the needs of the Serbs for a feeling of security and for identity as a people must have been intense. The Serbs, victimized in the past and having constructed an image of themselves as a victimized people, once again could see themselves as victims. Perhaps much of the violence in the former Yugoslavia would have been prevented if the world had responded to the Serbs when communism collapsed and Yugoslavia began to collapse, with awareness of the need to contain their readiness for violence, but also with awareness of their woundedness and need for security and identity.

There has been a quality to Serb behavior that may be regarded as suicidal, and suicide is usually born out of some form of desperation. With the whole world watching, with the most powerful alliance perhaps in the history of the world threatening and later attacking, they have engaged in terrible violence, both in Bosnia and in Kosovo. Explaining this as Milosovic's way of maintaining power seems insufficient. Beliefs about a hostile world and about the need for self-defense are likely to be involved.

After a period of bombing that showed the seriousness of the world community as represented by NATO, a shift in NATO policy would have been useful. Showing respect for the Serbs, in spite of their actions, for their history and their victimization, might have made a difference. President Clinton, Kofi Annan, and other important leaders could have offered to meet with Milosovic, perhaps in a neighboring country, involving the Russians as the Serbs' only supporters. Giving Milosovic and the Serbs such respect and recognition, combined with an uncompromising demand that Serb aggression stops, might have created new possibilities. Such an approach might have saved lives and reduced human suffering.

Whatever will be the immediate resolution, the complex problems of Kosovo will have to be addressed. Serb feelings about Kosovo, the longstanding hostility between Serbs and Albanians, the effects of this most recent violence, the insistence of the Kosovo Liberation Army on independence make a "solution" for Kosovo hard to come by. In complex situations like this, it is essential to protect people, to create conditions that make them secure. It is also essential to create processes that over time can lead to a resolution. These processes include mediation and conflict resolution, healing and reconciliation, economic and other support, and committed third parties who participate.

Reference

Adelmann, H. (1999) "Early warning and ethnic conflict management: Rwanda and Kosovo." Unpublished manuscript, York University, Toronto.

35

The Effects of Violence On Groups and Their Members

Groups of people who have been victims of intense persecution, violence, mass killings, and genocide are deeply affected. This is true, of course, of individual survivors of mass killings or genocides, who were in camps or in territories where the violence occurred and who were personally targeted as victims. But it is also true of members of the victim group who were not in direct danger. They are also deeply affected by the persecution and the attempt to eliminate all or part of their group.

For most people, individual identity is deeply rooted in their group identity (Bar-Tal & Staub, 1997; Staub, 1997a), especially in the case of racial, ethnic, and even religious groups, with membership in the group often not experienced as a matter of choice. The deaths of many others belonging to the group, the knowledge that, except for circumstances (often accidental ones like geography), one would have been killed, and the effects of the genocide on the whole group have deep impact on individuals, ranging from survivor guilt, to devaluation of oneself and one's group, to insecurity and the perception of the world as hostile.

Past victimization affects people's assumptions about the world (Janoff-Bulman, 1992). It deeply frustrates basic human needs like the need for security, for a positive identity, for a sense of effectiveness and control, for positive connections to others, and for a usable, meaningful comprehension of reality, including one's own place and role in the world (Staub, 1989, 1996). It creates schemas or beliefs about what the world is like and what other people are like that make the constructive fulfillment of these needs more difficult. These include a negative view of human beings, of the world,

Reprinted from E. Staub (1998). Breaking the cycle of genocidal violence: Healing and reconciliation. In J. Harvey (Ed)., *Perspectives on Loss*. Washington DC: Taylor and Francis, pp. 231–238. Included here are pp. 231–232. Copyright 1998. Reproduced by permission of Taylor and Francis, Inc., http://www.routledge-ny.com.

and of one's ability to protect oneself and fulfill important goals in life (Staub, 1989).

For these reasons members of a victim group have diminished capacity for leading satisfying, happy lives. In addition, a group that was the victim of violence has an increased potential for violence. The victims' intense insecurity in the world diminishes their capacity to consider others' perspective or needs, especially at a time of threat to the self. The capacity of groups of people to see their own role in hostile relations with other groups is limited even under the best circumstances and will be diminished by past victimization. People in the group may come to believe that violence is necessary to protect themselves and will respond with violence to conflict, threat, or hostility.

Victimization can also be part of a history that creates an "ideology of antagonism" (Staub, 1989, 1997b). This concept refers to a view of the other group as the enemy, bent on damaging or destroying one's own group, and a view or conception of one's group as an enemy of the other. Such ideologies are usually the result of a history of mutual hostility and violence. But in line with the limited perspective taken by groups of people already noted, even when harm-doing has been mutual and a victimized group has also victimized the other, groups and their individual members tend to focus on their own pain. They rarely take in the pain of the other or consider their own responsibility for it.

References

Bar-Tal, D., & Staub, E. (1997). Introduction: The nature and forms of patriotism. In D. Bar-Tal and E. Staub (Eds.), *Patriotism in the lives of individuals and groups.* Chicago: Nelson-Hall.

Janoff-Bulman, R. (1992). *Shattered assumptions.* New York: The Free Press.

Staub, E. (1989). *The roots of evil: The origins of genocide and other group violence.* New York: Cambridge University Press.

Staub, E. (1996). Cultural-societal roots of violence: The examples of genocidal violence and of contemporary youth violence in the United States. *American Psychologist, 51,* 117–132.

Staub, E. (1997a). Blind versus constructive patriotism: Moving from embeddedness in the group to critical loyalty and action. In D. Bar-Tal and E. Staub (Eds.), *Patriotism in the lives of individuals and groups.* Chicago: Nelson-Hall.

Staub, E. (1997b). *Halting and preventing collective violence: The role of bystanders.* Background paper for participants in Beyond Lamentation: A Symposium on the Prevention of Genocide, Stockholm, June 13–16.

36

Healing, Reconciliation, and Forgiving after Genocide and Other Collective Violence

Ervin Staub and Laurie Anne Pearlman

This chapter will explore the impact of collective violence on victims and, to some degree, on perpetrators as well. It will consider the role of healing, forgiveness, and reconciliation in building a better future in societies in which such violence had taken place. As a primary example, the chapter will focus on Rwanda, where the authors have been conducting a project on healing, forgiveness, and reconciliation.

Healing, reconciliation, and forgiveness are deeply interrelated. Healing and reconciliation help break cycles of violence and enhance the capacity of traumatized people for psychological well-being. Forgiving is essential for reconciliation to take place and both arise from and contribute to healing.

OVERVIEW: THE NEED TO HEAL, FORGIVE, AND RECONCILE

Victimization of one group by another that leads to great suffering by a group has intense and long-lasting impact. Members of the victim group feel diminished, vulnerable. They see the world as a dangerous place.[1] They tend to see other people, especially outside groups and their members, as hostile. Their capacity to live life well, to be happy, is diminished. When the group is in conflict with another group, when it is threatened, its members are less able to see the other's point of view, to consider the other's needs. The group is more likely to strike out, in the belief that it is defending itself. However, it may actually become a perpetrator of violence against others.[2] Alternatively, depending on the group's culture and circumstances, the group's capacity to stand up for its interests and rights may be impaired.

Reprinted from E. Staub & L. A. Pearlman (2001). Healing, reconciliation, and forgiving after genocide and other collective violence. In S. J. Helmick and R. L. Petersen, (Eds.), *Forgiveness and reconciliation: Religion, public policy and conflict transformation*. Radnor, PA: Templeton Foundation Press, from Ch. 11, pp. 205–217.

Healing is essential both to improve the quality of life of the group's members and to make it less likely that the group becomes a perpetrator of violence. Because of the numbers of people involved, and because the injury happened to the group as a whole, it is important for healing to take place at the group level, in the community of others. A community for healing may consist of a small number of people from the group, the whole group, or both members of the group and people from outside the group. Traumatized people require at least a rudimentary feeling of security for healing to begin. When there is continued threat from the other, depending on circumstances, healing may be difficult or even impossible.

When one group has victimized another, or when there has been mutual victimization by two groups, if the groups continue to live near each other, reconciliation is essential both to stop a potentially continuing cycle of violence and to facilitate healing. As reconciliation begins, it increases security and makes healing more possible. As healing progresses, reconciliation becomes more possible. This is a cycle in which progress in one realm fosters progress in the other.

Reconciliation is more than the coexistence of formerly hostile groups living near each other. It is more even than formerly hostile groups interacting and working together, although working together for shared goals is one important avenue to overcoming hostility and negative views of the other and moving toward reconciliation.[3] Reconciliation means coming to accept one another and developing mutual trust. This requires forgiving. Reconciliation requires that victims and perpetrators come to accept the past and not see it so much as defining the future as simply a continuation of the past, that they come to see the humanity of one another, accept each other, and see the possibility of a constructive relationship.

Forgiving is difficult. The very idea of it can be offensive after horrible events like the Holocaust, the genocide in Rwanda, or the genocidal violence in Tibet. Even to people outside the victim group, the idea that survivors should forgive following genocide is an affront, an anathema. It is inconceivable to them and incomprehensible how victims or anyone else would or should forgive the perpetrators. It is even difficult for many survivors to consider forgiving those members of the perpetrator group who have not personally participated in violence, either because they belong to the perpetrator group or because they were passive bystanders. Nonetheless forgiving is necessary and desirable. It paves the way for reconciliation and furthers healing, thereby making a better future possible. And when groups live together without reconciliation following group violence, as in Bosnia and Rwanda, feelings of insecurity and the danger of violence are ever present. In addition, research with individuals has shown that in some situations forgiving benefits those who were harmed. It improves the psychological well-being of victims. It lifts the burden of anger and the desire for revenge. Conversely, people who do not forgive their transgressors have more psychological difficulties. When people forgive, a psychological and spiritual burden may be lifted from them.[4]

Healing, reconciliation, and forgiving are hindered by certain conditions and facilitated by others. As we have noted, survivors are likely to feel greatly diminished as persons and as members of their group, both in general and specifically in relation to the perpetrator group. Genuine forgiveness in this state may not be possible. "Forgiving" perpetrators in this state may be more psychological and spiritual capitulation to a powerful other than real forgiveness. The perpetrator group, even if it has no more genuine power, will represent great power in the psychological experience of the survivors. Continued threat, whether real or mainly in the mind of the survivors, adds to the difficulty of healing, forgiving, and reconciliation. It is for these reasons that both some degree of real security and the beginnings of healing are important starting points.

For reconciliation to occur, perpetrators also must heal. Often there has been mutual violence between groups, so that both are victims and both are perpetrators. Even when the distinction between perpetrator and victim is clear, a group sometimes becomes the perpetrator of violence because it had previously been victimized or suffered greatly for other reasons. Even when this is not the case, perpetrators are wounded because of their violent, often horrible actions. Perpetrators must heal from the wounds they have inflicted on themselves, as they harmed others.[5] Healing can open perpetrators to face their deeds, to engage with their victims, and to enter into a process that leads to reconciliation. Members of the perpetrator group who have themselves not engaged in violence also need to heal from the impact of their own group's actions.

The common tendency for perpetrators is to continue to justify their past actions, as they tend to do while they are perpetrating them, by devaluing and dehumanizing the victims. They make their former victims into a dangerous enemy bent on their own destruction, an enemy of higher values and ideals, the enemy of a vision of a better life.[6] Perpetrators can thus protect themselves from facing what they have done by blaming their victims. In this and other ways they surround themselves with a protective shell. As they begin to face their deeds, perpetrators can also begin to forgive themselves.[7] Paradoxically they may also have to "forgive" the survivors, who are a living testament to their own or their group's terrible actions.

Survivors of genocide endure extreme harm and tremendous losses, including the murder of loved ones and others in the group in which survivors' identity is rooted, and the attempt to eliminate their entire culture and community. For these survivors, healing, forgiving, and reconciliation seem to present an even greater psychological-spiritual demand than for survivors of other forms of victimization. Most people identify with their group, and their own identity is based to an important extent on their membership in their group.[8] Thus even people who have themselves not been harmed, or were not even present, are likely to be greatly affected. And those who suffered direct personal losses are likely to be even more affected.

GENOCIDE IN RWANDA

We will consider the case of Rwanda, where we are conducting a project on healing, forgiveness, and reconciliation. Much of what we write below seems relevant to other instances of genocide and mass killing, while some is specific to or takes special forms in Rwanda. As we will note, the material is partly from scholarly sources, partly from interviews with individuals and personal stories people told in the course of a two-week workshop that we conducted in Rwanda in September 1999.[9]

A Brief History

Rwanda was under the colonial rule of Belgium in the first part of the twentieth century. The Tutsis, who are the minority (in 1994 they were about 14% of the population of 8 million people, with Hutus about 85%), were dominant until 1959. At that point, about 50,000 of them were killed in a Hutu revolution. When the country become independent in 1962, the Hutus took power. There were large-scale massacres of Tutsis in the 1960s and '70s. Discrimination and occasional, smaller-scale killings of Tutsis continued into the 1990s.[10]

In 1990 a Tutsi group, the Rwanda Patriotic Front (RPF), invaded the country. They were stopped, with help from the French military, but fighting renewed later, partly in response to massacres of Tutsi peasants. Groups of Hutus within the country also demanded more political freedom and rights and created political parties. In 1993 the Arusha peace accord was signed. It was to lead to the creation of a government including the RPF as well as other political elements. However, while he signed the accords, President Habyarimana also brought intense anti-Tutsi elements into his government.

In April 1994 the president's plane was shot down, probably by extremist Hutus. The genocide began immediately. Altogether perhaps as many as 800,000 people were killed within three months. About 50,000 of these were Hutus. They were regarded as enemies because they were politically moderate, or they came from a certain region of the country, or for other reasons. Violence usually evolves and intensifies – as did the violence against Tutsis over several decades – and in the end some Hutus were also killed by individual perpetrators for personal reasons.[11] The genocide was brought to a stop by the victory of the RPF over the government forces.

The genocide in Rwanda was unusual and especially gruesome in certain respects. First, a very large number of people were killed in a very short time. Second, a great deal of the killing was person-to-person, rather than impersonal. While guns and even grenades were used, machetes, which require close contact between perpetrator and victim, were often used. Third, while the military and paramilitary groups, the latter often made up of very young people, perpetrated much of the killing, substantial killing was also perpetrated by a segment of the population. People were killed by neighbors, and even relatives – a Tutsi married into a Hutu family, or children and adults in a family who were of mixed ethnic background.[12]

Survivors' Experiences in Rwanda: The Difficulty in Forgiving

The Tutsis we talked to in Rwanda had very varied experiences during the genocide, but all had relatives killed and were themselves in great danger. The following stories come from interviews of survivors, especially people who were helped by Hutus, from experiences people described in a workshop we conducted (see below), and from extensive conversations with individuals.

The parents and four of six siblings of one Tutsi man were killed. He himself was lying on the ground with other men who were to be killed, but for reasons he does not know he was let go.

A pregnant woman saw her husband taken away and was told soon after that he had been killed. Men came for her repeatedly, but one of her former household workers, a Hutu man, sent another Hutu man to her house to protect her. This latter man repeatedly endangered his own life to stop the killers from taking her away, facing off the men who came for her.

A young woman described how her neighbors came into her house and killed her father and brothers, but then protected her, her mother, and sister from other killers. They even buried the men they killed.

One man described how his sister, a Tutsi, was given to the killers by her Hutu husband and his family. The man and his wife and children were hidden by a series of people, for a time in the house of a bishop. When remaining there became dangerous, the bishop transported them in the trunk of his car to another place, going twice through a roadblock to do this as he transported different members of the family. In contrast, other highlevel church officials in various churches betrayed their Tutsi parishioners.[13] The church was intertwined with the government and the ruling circle, and when the genocide began many high-level church officials became its tools.

Another Tutsi woman's Hutu husband was involved in having her mother killed. Then the husband died. Her brother would not help her children, because they were children of the man who was responsible for the killing of his mother.

In addition to carrying the past within them, most Tutsis have constant reminders of the genocide and of what has happened to them. One woman whose husband and children were killed adopted a child who survived by staying for a long time in a pile of corpses. This child has great difficulty exercising self-control. He behaves like a very young child and wants to be taken care of like an infant. Another woman whose family was killed has no home and no money to pay tuition so her children cannot go to school (there is no publicly funded education in Rwanda, as is true in many African countries).

While the Tutsis who lived in Rwanda had very painful experiences, others returned from exile. Some, like the mother of a taxi driver with whom we became acquainted in Kigali, returned just before the genocide, when the situation had eased and the plan was to include varied parties, including Tutsis, in the government. She and other such returnees were killed.

But even those who returned after the genocide stopped have had very difficult and painful experiences. They or their parents left Rwanda after earlier massacres. They returned to a devastated country. With memories of the violence their parents experienced, with a life spent as refugees and exiles in other countries, they also find it extremely difficult to forgive and reconcile. However, many of them realize that the only hope for creating a functioning society lies in reconciliation. They dominate the current government and the policy of this government is "unity and reconciliation."

When we ask about forgiveness, we have to ask, forgive whom? What of different kinds of perpetrators: the planners, those who killed, others who in some ways assisted in or benefited from the killings? What of members of the perpetrator group who have not perpetrated violence but are implicated by membership in the group and many of them by their passivity? What of the outside world, which often remains passive in the face of increasing violence against a victim group?[14] The disregard of information about impending violence and then of the actual genocide was especially shocking in the case of Rwanda.[15] What about the members of the perpetrator group who actually helped Tutsis? Does their behavior in some way offer an entry point toward forgiving the others?

Even under circumstances that promote forgiveness, it is likely to take place at a different pace and to different degrees in relation to different groups of people. A first reasonable goal may be for members of a victim group to move toward, and for others to facilitate, forgiving in relation to those who have not themselves planned or directly perpetrated violence.

The injuries in Rwanda are very great, and even people who were saved by others suspect those who saved them. The woman mentioned above who was saved by the Hutu stranger who came to her house and persisted in protecting her appeared to have difficulty accepting what he did as coming from benevolent motives. She fluctuated between seeing his action as arising from goodness and suspecting him of some unidentified self-interest. This is not surprising, considering that in the course of the genocide some Hutu men "saved" Tutsi women by taking them to their house and keeping them in sexual slavery.[16] When the man who saved her came to see her for the first time since the genocide, just before our interview in September 1999, she wondered what he might want and talked about being protected from him, if necessary, by the authorities.

A family – a husband, wife, and their grown children – saved another person. The husband decided to help her and was in charge, directing the others. She was hidden in a pit the family dug in a cow pasture; they handed food to her through a small hole. After a while she was moved to another such pit, with the children in the family not knowing where she was, so that they would not accidentally give her away or put themselves in danger.

Afterwards the man who helped this woman was arrested, accused of complicity in the killing of some children. In an interview with one of the man's sons, he told us that the family was hiding these children in another hole, but the children climbed out, came to the house, were seen by the killers, and taken away. His father is wrongly accused. But paraphrasing what the woman said whom the family saved: "He saved my life, and even if I knew something I would not testify against him, but some people helped one person and killed others." While interviewing the woman who was saved by the Hutu man that her worker had sent to her house, the interviewer (ES) said that two people, not one, saved her. But she said (again, in a paraphrase): "The worker was there when my husband was killed. And later he refused to tell me where my husband's body was."

An "Intervention" to Help with Healing, Reconciliation, and Forgiveness

Theory, research, and practical experience in working with traumatized individuals suggest that prolonged avoidance of memories of painful, traumatic experiences limits healing. Engaging with such experiences under safe conditions, when others support people, is important for healing to occur. In these and in other ways reconnecting with people helps to overcome the fear and distrust that victimization and other traumatic experiences create. Other people acknowledging the pain and suffering that a particular person and a victimized group has suffered, showing empathy and caring, both people in one's own group and those in the outside world, can be important for healing after collective violence.[17]

In our project in Rwanda we conducted a two-week seminar to promote healing, forgiveness, and reconciliation.[18] The participants in this training were Rwandese staff members of organizations from around the country that work with groups in the community. Some of the organizations try to help people heal, others try to help them reconcile, and most of them work with some form of community building, such as helping people work together in agriculture.

The training had experiential and psychoeducational elements. The experiential component included people repeatedly writing or drawing something to represent an experience they had during the genocide.[19] It soon became apparent that given Rwandese culture, with its focus on oral rather than written language, it was better for some people to simply think about their experience. This was followed by people telling each other, in small groups, what they wrote, drew, or thought about. People told about intense and painful experiences. They received strong support from other members of the group.

Before this process began, we discussed the importance of empathic responding to others' experiences. We demonstrated both lack of response and overresponse, like taking over by offering advice or immediately begining to tell one's own story. Many of the participants responded to painful stories by simply crying with the person who told the story.

We worked with a mixed group, both Hutus and Tutsis. Given the realities in Rwanda – the genocide by Hutus against Tutsis with the Tutsis now in power – it may not be surprising that the Hutus, who participated well in the workshop in general, did not tell their "stories" of experiences during the genocide. Still, we believe that hearing the painful stories of Tutsis – stories told mostly with a focus on what happened to the victims, hardly mentioning perpetrators – could promote empathy in Hutus and contribute to reconciliation.

The psychoeducational part of the training included brief lectures and discussion of various topics. One of them was about the origins of genocide, the influences leading to it. We will discuss this in the next section. Another was about the impact of trauma on individuals and communities. We expect that understanding the continuing impact of their experiences on them will help transform these experiences. A third topic was avenues toward healing: what is required for and what facilitates healing. A fourth topic was basic human needs, providing a framework for understanding psychological trauma and healing.[20]

The aim of the workshop was to provide tools that may be useful for participants in their work with community groups. An additional component of the workshop was to help participants from different organizations integrate the material from the workshop with the way they usually work with organizations. Local collaborators are continuing to help participants apply material from the workshop to their work with community groups.

CONTRIBUTORS TO HEALING, RECONCILIATION, AND FORGIVENESS AFTER COLLECTIVE VIOLENCE: THE CREATION OF PEACEFUL SOCIETIES

The following discussion applies to varied "transitional societies" that are trying to rebuild after collective violence such as genocide, mass killing, or intense civil war. However, as an example, we will focus again on Rwanda.

Empowerment: Helping People Find Their Voice

The unity and reconciliation commission in Rwanda has begun in a wise manner. It gathers groups of people and asks them what they need in order to reconcile. One potential benefit of this is that people engage with the idea of reconciliation. Another is that they can help identify what they need for reconciliation to take place. A third is that by expressing their views and then, ideally, actively engaging with each other and with the process, they are creators and actors. This is valuable since healing, forgiveness, and reconciliation can only be facilitated but not created or imposed by others.

Truth

The truth provides a base for healing, forgiving, and reconciliation. The use of truth commissions after collective violence has become a common practice, from Argentina to other South American countries, to South Africa and elsewhere.[21]

Describing what has happened acknowledges the pain and suffering of the victims. When violence has been one-sided rather than mutual, truth-telling validates the victims' innocence. It thereby helps mitigate one psychological effect of victimization, the survivors' tendency to feel that something must be wrong with them. Proclaiming the truth also tells victims that the world does not regard such behavior as acceptable, which contributes to feelings of safety and begins to restore the group's connection to the world community.

In addition, individuals and groups who harm others and then are accused of wrongdoing easily feel that they are the victims. Convincingly documenting their violent actions makes it more difficult for perpetrators to claim or feel this. It makes it more difficult for them to continue to blame the victims.

The truth is often complicated. Often harm-doing is mutual. Even when one group is clearly the perpetrator of genocide, as in Rwanda, there has often been some form of mutual victimization in the course of prior history. Acknowledging this may help perpetrators heal and open themselves to their victims.

Perpetrators acknowledging the truth can be of great value. As one woman in Rwanda said, spontaneously introducing the idea of forgiveness: "How can I forgive them, if they don't tell me the truth, if they don't acknowledge what they did?"

Testimonies, Memorials, Group Ceremonies

When whole groups have been affected, large numbers of people must be involved in healing. Testimonials as to what has happened, memorials and ceremonies in which people grieve together can help people reexperience and acknowledge the pain and losses of traumatic events in a supportive context. Survivors and members of the perpetrator group joining together can facilitate mutual healing and reconciliation. The presence of outsiders can also be helpful; the process of bearing witness expresses acknowledgment, empathy, and support.

However, such events can be destructive as well as constructive. Rather than healing, they can maintain woundedness and build identity through enmity and nationalism.[22] This seemed to have happened with the Serb focus on their defeat by Turkey in the fourteenth century. The ceremonies created ought to offer visions of inclusive connections and a positive future.

Justice

Justice as Punishment. Even victims of simple unfair treatment often express their need for justice. People deeply resent impunity. People in Rwanda repeatedly expressed their desire that the perpetrators be punished. What kind of punishment is needed and what other avenues are open to creating the experience of justice that facilitates healing, forgiveness, and reconciliation and the creation of a peaceful society?

Individual responsibility is important. This involves identifying, to the extent possible, higher- and lower-level decision makers, more and less important direct perpetrators, and people who were more and less important facilitators. When many people are involved, healing requires that punishment be limited in scope, with a focus on those especially responsible. This helps to avoid creating new wounds.

The involvement of the community in the process of punishment can be both healing and empowering. In Rwanda the government is re-creating the Gacaca to deal at least with lower-level perpetrators. Traditionally, when someone did harm to another in the community, the elders gathered to hear what happened and to decide about punishment. The punishment functioned as restitution, allowing the perpetrator to come back into the community. In its current form people will be elected to the Gacaca.

At the same time, international tribunals punishing important perpetrators can reduce feelings of resentment by members of the perpetrator group. They are more likely to see justice as impartial. Unfortunately, recent international tribunals, both the one dealing with Bosnia, and especially the one dealing with Rwanda, have been poorly funded, slow, and ineffective.

Justice as Improvement in Economic Well-Being. Collective violence, in addition to everything else, usually leaves survivors impoverished. Some of those whose relatives were killed in South Africa or who were themselves victimized feel unjustly treated because changes in the government and the truth and reconciliation process have not substantially improved their economic condition.[23] At a meeting of women from Kigali with the unity and reconciliation commission in Rwanda, some women said that to experience justice they need their economic situation to improve.

Fair and just government policies are important. But to create economic justice is extremely difficult, especially in a poor society like Rwanda. If much is taken away from the Hutus, they will feel that this is revenge against them. Extensive public discussion of the conditions of the country and of what might represent justice under the circumstances might be helpful. Economic help by the international community that immediately improves people's lives and promotes long-term development can be of great value.

Restorative Justice. Restorative justice, or justice based on restitution, is an ancient concept. It stands in contrast to retributive justice, whose goal is to punish the perpetrator. In the past two decades, people have been attempting to apply restorative justice systematically in cases of victimization in an effort to provide reparations, restore community, resolve conflict, restore both perpetrators and victims into the moral and social realms (in the eyes of the larger community and one another), and provide accountability for the actions of perpetrators.[24] Restorative justice implies trying to show through actions that the perpetrators are sorry, understand the pain they have caused, and want to make amends. In Rwanda and other countries affected by genocide or collective violence, restorative justice would require the victims and the larger community to agree on reparations that the perpetrators would make to the community. In contrast to retributive justice, where reparations mean punitive sanctions, causing pain to the perpetrator, in a restorative justice model reparation means acting to benefit those whom one has harmed. The goals would be for the community to have a sense that justice has been served, that the offenders and their offenses have been denounced and held accountable, that a sense of peace has been restored. The community is healing and a process of establishing safety and trust has begun. Such a process requires the active involvement of the perpetrators, who are participants in rather than victims of the process, and could contribute to healing, forgiving, and reconciliation.

Understanding the Origins of Genocide or Collective Violence

The information we provided in our workshop in Rwanda about the origins of genocide and mass killing, exemplifying principles by reference to various cases, including the genocide in Rwanda, and the discussions that followed, had a powerful impact on participants.[25] Learning that others had similar fates and coming to understand how certain influences contribute to genocide seemed to help participants feel they were not outside history and human experience, that as terrible as it was what happened in their society is a human process. It seemed to reconnect them with humanity. One woman said, "If this happened to other people, then it doesn't mean that God abandoned the people of Rwanda."

It seemed that perpetrators were also humanized to some extent in the eyes of victims. Perhaps members of the perpetrator group were humanized in their own eyes. Perpetrators acted in response to societal, cultural, and psychological forces. Most of the influences that usually lead to genocide were present in Rwanda:[26] economic and political chaos in society and a civil war; a history of intense devaluation of and discrimination against a group; intense propaganda by leaders intensifying hostility; strong obedience to authority; a history of violence against a group (in Rwanda the Tutsis) that prepared the possibility of new and greater violence; and passivity by many bystanders (within and outside of society) and support for and hence complicity by some nations with the perpetrators. Understanding does not reduce the responsibility of perpetrators, who can choose to act differently, but may make forgiveness more possible and certainly facilitates healing. Finally, participants in our workshop seemed to feel that understanding the forces that lead to genocide might allow action to be taken to prevent genocide. One woman said, "If people created this, then people can solve it."

Exposing leaders to information about the origins of genocide may be valuable. It may promote healing and help them use the understanding they have gained for breaking the cycle of past violence. Leaders may not be open to such information, since they usually develop their own visions of the past and future. But knowledge gained from the study of collective violence around the world is likely to be useful to them in addressing cultural elements and societal processes that contribute to violence. The task is daunting. Since culture is deeply rooted, existing forms of it often feel comfortable and preferred, and are resistant to change. Moreover, certain elements of culture, which can contribute to genocidal violence, serve leaders well. One of these is obedience to authority, which seemed to have significantly contributed to genocide in Rwanda, as people responded to the propaganda and the orders of leaders to kill. Working to change such cultural elements requires self-sacrifice and commitment by leaders.

Perpetrators Asking for Forgiveness

Although some research suggests that forgiving does not necessarily require anything from the perpetrator, other research on forgiveness has shown that harm-doers acknowledging their responsibility for causing harm, apologizing for their actions, and asking for forgiveness contribute to victims forgiving perpetrators.[27] The latter finding is highly consistent with comments people made in Rwanda.

The explicit focus of our work in Rwanda was on healing and reconciliation. Our background research, including interviews with informants, indicated that people were not ready to talk about forgiveness. But by the time we conducted our workshop in September 1999 we found that this was not the case. Participants spontaneously talked about forgiveness. They expressed their need, in order to be able to forgive, for perpetrators to acknowledge what they had done, apologize, and ask for forgiveness.

This may have reflected in part the influence of the government, which is encouraging perpetrators who are in prison to confess and ask for forgiveness. By doing so, perpetrators can reduce their punishment. At the same time such behavior may facilitate healing, forgiveness, and reconciliation by victims. But instead of genuine remorse, perpetrators can pretend regret, without genuine change in their attitudes toward their deeds or their former victims. Such empty apologies can inflame the rage of victims, as has indeed happened for many witnesses to the truth and reconciliation process in South Africa. Healing by perpetrators may make their request for forgiveness more genuine.

Acknowledgment of Harm Suffered by Perpetrators

Knowledge by victims of harm that perpetrators have suffered and harm inflicted on the perpetrator group by the victims' own group can contribute to reconciliation. Past victimization often contributes to perpetrators' actions. Acknowledgment of the harm perpetrators have suffered may weaken the protective shell of victim-blaming and further the process leading to reconciliation.

Under Belgian rule the Tutsi dominance over Hutus was enhanced. Hutus became more subordinate, their rights, opportunities, and well-being further diminished. In most genocides and mass killings members of the perpetrator group oppose their group's actions or try to save individual members of the victim group. In Rwanda a few Hutus publicly opposed the genocide and were killed. Others were killed because they were politically moderate, probably in part because it was assumed that they would not support the genocide.[28] Some Hutus endangered themselves to help individual Tutsis. Spreading the information about these facts would be constructive. Along the way, Tutsis' skepticism about those who helped others would have to be addressed.

Hutu civilians were also killed, after the genocide began, as the Rwanda Patriotic Front fought against the government army.[29] Such tragic, reciprocal killings almost always occur when a group perpetrates great atrocities on the other. These killings, too, must be acknowledged if healing and reconciliation are to succeed.

After the genocide was stopped, perhaps as many as two million Hutus escaped from Rwanda, including many of the perpetrators. Soon they began incursions into Rwanda, killing more Tutsis. In 1996 the government allowed Hutus to return. The returnees included many genocidaires, who resumed killing Tutsis in the northwestern part of the country. In the course of trying to stop them, again Hutu civilians were killed.[30]

Before the return of the refugees from Zaire (which by that time had become the Democratic Republic of the Congo), in the course of the civil war there, the rebel army was supported by the Rwandese military in its fight against the Mobutu government. An unknown but possibly large number of Hutu refugees were killed. Finally, in neighboring Burundi, which has been ruled since its independence by a Tutsi minority, there have been periodic massacres of Hutus.

It seems even more difficult for a government than for ordinary members of a group to admit to "wrongdoing" by the group, to violations of human rights by its army and people. This is especially the case when the "wrongs" committed seem minor to the group relative to the wrongs inflicted on the group. However, this is an essential part of the truth. It is essential for mutual healing, forgiveness, and reconciliation.

WORKING TOGETHER FOR SHARED GOALS

One important way for people to overcome hostility and negative views of each other is deep engagement, in the course of which they can experience each other's similarity and humanness. Working together for shared goals, which are superordinate to people's and their groups' separate and at times conflicting goals, can promote this deep engagement. The relationships that individuals develop to each other in the course of this can extend to the group as a whole. Interpersonal contact between offenders and offended after transgressions may facilitate forgiving.[31]

Governments, organizations at different levels of society, and community groups can all promote such deep engagement. These can involve creating shared ceremonies and memorials, as discussed above, or building new institutions of the society. It can involve joint projects in any realm, from agriculture to business enterprise, to building new houses, to attending to children's needs. Indeed, children's needs and the desire for a better world for the next generation seems to be one likely universal meeting point for opposing groups.

Those who provide aid, like the United States Agency for International Development (USAID), are in a natural position to promote such engagement by members of hostile groups. They can offer incentives to them to join in development projects. As benevolent third parties they can help shape these projects to promote both success in development work and in the human relations required for the continued peaceful development of society.

Attention to Children

Children are deeply affected by violence in society, especially genocide and war.[32] They are directly affected, by losing parents and other relatives and suffering as well as witnessing violence. They are indirectly affected as the actions and emotions of parents and other relatives, people around them who have been deeply traumatized, impact them. We now know from work with Holocaust survivors, Vietnam veterans, and survivors of severe and early childhood abuse that trauma is transmitted through the generations.

To help children heal as well as overcome the devaluation, fear, and hostility of the other implanted in them in the course of their socialization is of profound importance for breaking cycles of violence. Many avenues must be used, but their experience in school (of deep engagement with children who are members of the other group) and school programs provide a natural opportunity.[33] Watching traumatized parents commit themselves to healing and reconciliation may also be a powerful change agent for children.

Finding Meaning: Working to Prevent Renewed Violence

People who have been greatly victimized need to find meaning in what seems senseless: their suffering. An aspect of healing is to make meaning of one's experience.[34] One way to find meaning after a genocide is to devote oneself to creating a world in which people will not inflict violence on each other. People who have greatly suffered, when they have healed to some extent, often devote themselves to helping other people. This is "altruism born of suffering," in contrast to the usual development of altruism through positive, growthful experiences.[35]

Participants in our workshop were eager to discuss what they might do to make renewed violence, a new genocide, less likely. Working together with others to accomplish this, for example, to help people heal, to overcome antagonism and help members of the two groups work together, to enhance varied aspects of justice, to reduce unquestioning obedience to authority helps to fulfill basic needs that were deeply frustrated by the genocide. Such work contributes to a feeling of efficacy, to a positive identity, to positive connections to other people, to an understanding of the world or a worldview that is hopeful and constructive. All this enhances a sense of security. Making a contribution, serving others and the community, also helps fulfill a need for transcendence, an important aspect of spirituality.[36]

Government Policies: The Behavior of Leaders

The behavior and direction given by authorities are very important in every society – but especially in one with strong respect for authority. In Rwanda the previous leaders led the group to genocide. The current leaders can be contributors to the creation of lasting peace. It would be valuable for leaders themselves to undergo some of the processes that promote healing and open people to reconciliation. In Bosnia wounded leaders, like General Mladic whose parents were killed by Croats during World War II as part of the mass killing of hundred of thousands of Serbs, led Serbia to great violence.

As refugees or children of refugees, as members of a group that has suffered so much harm and violence, the current Tutsi leaders of Rwanda must be wounded. Depending on their personal experience and level of healing, the creation of the unity and reconciliation process may be primarily a wise, thoughtful strategy, and it may also be based on genuine desire. The more it is a combination of the two, the more likely it is to survive the difficulties and vicissitudes of the long road to a healed society.

Notes

1. L. I. McCann & L. A. Pearlman, *Psychological trauma and the adult survivor: Theory, therapy, and transformation* (New York: Brunner/Mazel, 1990); and L. A. Pearlman & K. W. Saakvitne, *Trauma and the therapist: Countertransference and vicarious traumatization in psychotherapy with incest survivors* (New York: W. W. Norton, 1995); J. L. Krupnick & M. J. Horowitz, "Stress Response Syndromes: Recurrent Themes," *Archives of General Psychiatry 38* (1981): 428–35.
2. See Chapter 35, this volume.
3. G. W. Allport, *The nature of prejudice* (Reading, Mass.: Addison-Wesley, 1954); T. F. Pettigrew, "Generalized Intergroup Contact Effects on Prejudice," *Personality and Social Psychology Bulletin* 23, no. 2 (1997): 173–85; and E. Staub, "The Origins and Prevention of Genocide, Mass Killing, and Other Collective Violence," in *Peace and Conflict: Journal of Peace Psychology* 5 (1999); and E. Staub, *A brighter future; Raising caring and nonviolent children* (in preparation).
4. R. H. Al-Mabuk, R. D. Enright, & P. A. Cardis, "Forgiveness Education with Parentally Love-Deprived Late Adolescents," *Journal of Moral Education* 24

(1995): 427–44; S. R. Freedman & R. D. Enright, "Forgiveness as an Intervention Goal with Incest Survivors," *Journal of Consulting and Clinical Psychology 64* (1996): 983–92; M. J. Subkoviak, R. D. Enright, C. Wu, E. A. Gassin, S. Freedman, L. M. Olson, & I. Sarinopoulos, "Measuring Interpersonal Forgiveness in Late Adolescence and Middle Adulthood," *Journal of Adolescence 18* (1995): 641–55; M. E. McCullough & E. L. Worthington, "Promoting Forgiveness: A Comparison of Two Brief Psychoeducational Group Interventions with a 'Waiting List' Control," *Counseling and Values 40* (1995): 55–69; D. F. Greenwald & D. W. Harder, "Sustaining Fantasies and Psychopathology in a Normal Sample," *Journal of Clinical Psychology 50*, no. 5 (1994): 707–10; M. L. Zelin, S. B. Bernstein, C. Heijn, R. M. Jampel, P. G. Myerson, G. Adler, D. H. Buie Jr., & A. M. Rizzuto, "The Sustaining Fantasy Questionnaire: Measurement of Sustaining Functions of Fantasies in Psychiatric Inpatients," *Journal of Personality Assessment* 47 (1983): 427–39; J. M. Templeton, *Worldwide laws of life: 200 eternal spiritual principles* (Philadelphia: Templeton Foundation Press, 1997).

5. E. Staub & L. A. Pearlman, "Healing, Forgiveness, and Reconciliation in Rwanda," grant proposal to the John Templeton Foundation, 1998; and Staub, "Origins and Prevention of Genocide, Mass Killing, and Other Collective Violence."
6. Staub, "Origins and Prevention of Genocide, Mass Killing, and Other Collective Violence."
7. Templeton, *Worldwide laws of life.*
8. H. Tajfel, "Social Categorization, Social Identity, and Social Comparison," in *Differentiation between social groups*, ed. H. Tajfel (London: Academic Press, 1978), 61–76; J. C. Turner, *Rediscovering the social groups: A self-categorization theory* (New York: Basil Blackwell, 1987); and D. Bar-Tal & E. Staub, "Introduction: The Nature of Patriotism," in *Patriotism in the lives of individuals and groups*, ed. D. Bar-Tal & E. Staub (Chicago: Nelson-Hall Publishers, 1997).
9. Staub & Pearlman, "Healing, Forgiveness, and Reconciliation in Rwanda"; E. Staub, *The roots of evil: The origins of genocide and other group violence* (New York: Cambridge University Press, 1989); E. Staub, L. A. Pearlman, and A. Hagengimana, "Manual for Facilitators of Healing Through Understanding and Connection Project," Project on Healing, Forgiveness and Reconciliation in Rwanda, supported by the John Templeton Foundation, manuscript in English and Kinyarwanda, Trauma Research, Education, and Training Institute, Inc., South Windsor, Conn., 1999.
10. G. Prunier, *The Rwanda crisis: History of a genocide* (New York: Columbia University Press, 1995); A. des Forges, *Leave None to Tell the Story: Genocide in Rwanda* (New York: Human Rights Watch, 1999); and N. S. Smith, "The Psychocultural Roots of Genocide," *American Psychologist 53* (1998): 743–53.
11. Staub, *Roots of evil*; Staub, "Origins and Prevention of Genocide, Mass Killing, and Other Collective Violence."
12. Prunier, *The Rwanda Crisis*; des Forges, *Leave none to tell the story*; and Smith, "Psychocultural Roots of Genocide," 743–53.
13. des Forges, *Leave none to tell the story.*
14. Staub, *Roots of evil.*

15. Gourevitch, 1998; and Staub, "Origins and Prevention of Genocide, Mass Killing, and Other Collective Violence."
16. C. Bonnet, "Le Viol des Femmes Survivantes du Genocide du Rwanda," in *Rwanda: Un genocide du XX, siècle,* ed. R. Verdier, E. Decaux, & J. Chretien (Paris: Editions L'Harmattan, 1995); United Nations, *Report of the special rapporteur on violence against women, its causes and consequences addendum: Report on the mission to Rwanda on the issues of violence against women in situations of armed conflict,* UN document number E/CN. 4/1998/54/ADD.I.
17. E. Foa & B. Rothbaum, *Treating the trauma of rape: Cognitive behavioral-therapy of PTSD* (New York: Guilford, 1997); J. Herman, *Trauma and recovery* (New York: Basic Books, 1992); McCann & Pearlman, *Psychological trauma and the adult survivor;* L. A. Pearlman, "Healing and Forgiving in Trauma Victims," paper in the symposium, Healing, Forgiving, and Reconciliation in Individuals and Groups, International Society of Political Psychology, Montreal, Quebec, 1998; E. Staub, "Breaking the Cycle of Genocidal Violence: Healing and Reconciliation," in *Perspectives on loss: A source book,* ed. J. Harvey (Washington, D.C.: Taylor & Francis, 1998).
18. E. Staub, "Genocide and Mass Killing: Origins, Prevention, Healing, and Reconciliation," *Political Psychology, 21,* no. 2 (2000): 367–82; Staub & Pearlman, "Healing, Forgiveness, and Reconciliation in Rwanda"; Staub, Pearlman, & Hagengimana, "Manual for Facilitators of Healing Through Understanding and Connection Project."
19. Pennebaker, 1990.
20. Staub, *Roots of evil;* McCann and Pearlman, *Psychological trauma and the adult survivor;* K. W. Saakvitne, S. J. Gamble, L. A. Pearlman, & B. T. Lev, *Risking connection: A training curriculum for working with survivors of childhood abuse* (Lutherville, Md.: Sidran Press, 2000); Pearlman & Saakvitne, *Trauma and the therapist.*
21. Nunca Mas, *The report of the Argentine national commission on the disappeared* (New York: Farrar, Straus, Giroux, 1986).
22. See Staub, "The origins and prevention of genocide..." and Chapter 35, this volume.
23. B. Hamber, "The Burdens of Truth," *American Imago 55,* no. 1 (1998): 9–28.
24. G. Brazemore & M. Umbreit, "Rethinking the Sanctioning Function in Juvenile Court: Retributive or Restorative Responses to Youth Crime," *Crime and Delinquency 41,* no. 3 (1995): 296–316.
25. Staub, *Roots of evil;* Staub, Pearlman, & Hagengimana, "Manual for Facilitators of Healing Through Understanding and Connection Project."
26. Staub, *Roots of evil;* Staub, "Origins and Prevention of Genocide, Mass Killing, and Other Collective Violence."
27. Freedman & Enright, "Forgiveness as an Intervention Goal with Incest Survivors," 983–92; R. J. Bies & T. M. Tripp, "Beyond Distrust: Getting Even and the Need for Revenge," in *Trust in organizations: Frontiers of theory and research,* ed. R. M. Kramer & T. R. Tyler (Thousand Oaks, Calif.: Sage, 1996), 246–60; and M. N. O'Malley & J. Greenberg, "Sex Differences in Restoring Justice: The Down Payment Effect," *Journal of Research in Personality 17* (1983): 174–85; M. H. Gonzales, D. J. Manning, & J. A. Haugen, "Explaining Our Sins: Factors

Influencing Offender Accounts and Anticipated Victim Responses," *Journal of Personality and Social Psychology* 62 (1992): 958–71.

28. des Forges, *Leave none to tell the story;* Prunier, *The Rwanda crisis.*
29. des Forges, *Leave none to tell the story.*
30. J. Drumtra, *Life after death: Suspicion and reintegration in post-genocide Rwanda* (Washington, D.C.: U.S. Commission for Refugees, Immigration and Refugee Services of America, 1998).
31. Pettigrew, "Generalized Intergroup Contact Effects on Prejudice," 173–85; L. A. Gerber, "Experiences of Forgiveness in Physicians Whose Medical Treatment Was Not Successful," *Psychological Reports 61* (1987): 236; and "Transformation in Self-Understanding in Surgeons Whose Treatment Efforts Were Not Successful," *American Journal of Psychotherapy 44*, no. 1 (1990): 75–84.
32. *Peace and Conflict*, Special Issue: "The Graca Machel/UN Study on the Effects of War on Children," *Peace and Conflict: Journal of Peace Psychology 4*, no. 4 (1998).
33. N. Eisenberg, *The caring child* (Cambridge: Harvard University Press, 1992); E. Staub, "Altruism and Aggression in Children and Youth: Origins and Cures," in *The psychology of adversity*, ed. R. Feldman (Amherst: University of Massachusetts Press, 1996); Staub, "Genocide and Mass Killing," 367–82.
34. Herman, *Trauma and recovery*; Pearlman and Saakvitne, *Trauma and the therapist.*
35. Pearlman & Saakvitne, *Trauma and the therapist*; Valent 1998; Staub, "Basic Human Needs and Their Role in Altruism and Aggression"; Eisenberg, *The caring child*; Staub, "Altrusim and Aggression in Children and Youth."
36. Staub, *Roots of evil*; Staub, "Basic Human Needs and Their Role in Altruism and Aggression"; Staub, "Genocide and Mass Killing," 367–82.

37

Healing, Forgiveness, and Reconciliation in Rwanda

Project Summary and Outcome, with Addendum on Other Projects

Ervin Staub and Laurie Anne Pearlman

In this project, we provided training in a seminar/workshop to 30 people in Rwanda. They were mainly staff of NGOs that worked with groups of people in the community. These staff were working with religious and secular groups in the areas of healing and community building. To the extent we could determine, 21 of them were Tutsi and 9 Hutu (information about ethnicity is difficult to establish in Rwanda at this time). Our purpose was to prepare participants to use the training, or elements of it, in their own work with groups in the community. A primary purpose of the training was to promote psychological healing from the traumatic effects of the genocide as well as skills in promoting healing in others (in Tutsi survivors, in Tutsis who returned from other countries after the genocide, and Hutus who were affected by the violent actions of their own group and other aspects of the situation in Rwanda). The training also aimed to promote reconciliation, and in turn initiate a process of forgiveness, or more broadly, a more positive orientation toward members of the other group.

The training had psycho-educational and experiential components. The former consisted of lectures and discussion. One topic was the origins of genocide and mass killing. Brief lectures, based on the work of Ervin Staub (as described in his book, *The Roots of Evil: The Origins of Genocide and Other Group Violence*, and other publications) as well as other scholars, were followed by extensive discussion in which participants applied what they learned to understanding the genocide in Rwanda.

Exploring the origins of genocide seemed to have powerful effects on the participants. Survivors seemed to feel reincluded in the human realm,

Reprinted from E. Staub and L. A. Pearlman (2001). Healing, forgiveness, and reconciliation in Rwanda: Project summary and outcome. *Final Report to the John Templeton Foundation.*

This project was supported by the Templeton Foundation. Further information on the project can be found at the website www.heal-reconcile-rwanda.org.

as they came to see the horrors they had experienced as the result of understandable human processes and realized the extent to which such tremendous violence has also taken place in other countries. They appeared more open to perpetrators whose actions, however horrible, seemed at least somewhat comprehensible, rather than simply evil. They expressed the desire to prevent future violence using the understanding they gained. Another important lecture topic was the role of basic human needs and their frustration in both originating genocide and in the aftermath of genocide. A further topic was the psychological effects of trauma, and specifically of genocide, on survivors and on all members of the victim group, as well as on members of the perpetrator group. This portion of the training was based in part on previous work by Laurie Pearlman (including her book, *Psychological Trauma and the Adult Survivor*), as well as that of other trauma experts. This topic was intended to help foster understanding and acceptance by participants of how they and others had been affected by the events surrounding the genocide.

There was also a lecture and discussion of avenues to healing from trauma. An important avenue is engagement with traumatic experiences, talking about them under safe conditions. As part of the training we worked on how to respond to other people's stories empathically. A final component was a lecture on traumatic grief, based in part on research done by research teams in the United States on this topic and in part by interviews conducted after the genocide by our Rwandese collaborator, Dr. Athanase Hagengimana. Again, the purpose was to provide a normalizing framework for participants' experiences.

The discussion of these topics was likely to have experiential meaning, to engage and create change not only in thought and knowledge, but also feelings. In addition, participants talked in small groups about their experiences during the genocide, empathically supporting each other. They told powerful stories, which many of them said they had never told anyone before. We thought that the beneficial effect of these experiences with regard to forgiveness and reconciliation would be enhanced by the presence of members of both groups. While Hutus in the group did not talk much about their experiences during the genocide, their presence and empathic response were likely to further a positive orientation by Tutsis toward Hutus, and perhaps even healing by Tutsi survivors. While there was not enough time to do this extensively, we made some effort to help participants integrate the approach we used with the type of training they and their organization traditionally did with groups in the community.

To evaluate the effects of training, we examined three groups. In one set of (*integrated*) groups, participants in our training integrated our approach with their own and used this integrated approach with groups in the community. In another set of (*traditional*) groups, facilitators from the same or similar organizations as the integrated groups, but who did not participate in our training, used their usual or traditional approach with groups in the community. In both cases, these groups were newly created and met for a period of three weeks, twice a week. There was also a *control* group, which did not receive any training, but completed the same questionnaires at the beginning and end of the program.

To allow us to evaluate the effects of treatments, questionnaires were administered to all participants as the groups began, before any training or interaction, immediately after the training, and two months later. Those in the control group were administered questionnaires at about the same times. There was a questionnaire to assess *traumatic experiences*. A second questionnaire assessed the *effects of trauma*. This had several parts. It assessed posttraumatic stress disorder, other trauma symptoms, traumatic grief, and beliefs about self and others. Because this last part was less reliable, it was not included in most of the analyses. These questionnaires were in part taken from previous measures, and in part created by us and our collaborator, a Rwandese psychiatrist, with sensitivity to the expression of trauma in Rwandese culture.

Based on the research literature, other existing measures and our discussions with Rwandese "cultural consultants," we also developed a questionnaire to assess forgiveness, or more broadly, orientation to the other group. We used a part of this measure in our final analyses that was derived from factor analyses and was theoretically meaningful. A high score on this measure means that a person saw violence as having had complex origins, expressed a willingness to work with members of the other group for a better future, and was open to forgiveness – under certain conditions (see below). A fourth questionnaire asked about demographic information – including ethnic group membership, which is highly sensitive information at this time in Rwanda.

FINDINGS

Our participants reported a very large number of traumatic experiences. The main analyses focused on the Tutsi participants, since the number of Hutu participants was too small for meaningful, separate analyses. However, analyses with the whole group showed similar results.

Tutsi participants in the integrated group started out with greater trauma and less positive other orientation/forgiveness than participants in the other two groups. We could not establish the reason for this initial difference. Over time, the level of trauma in the integrated group decreased – on the delayed post-test, two months after the end of the treatment, it was significantly less than at the beginning. Controlling for initial differences, we found that their level of trauma was less on the delayed post-test than the trauma in the other two groups, whose participants started out with less trauma.

However, not only did participants in the integrated group get better, but those in the other two groups got worse. Since there seemed no other reason for this (for example, no evidence of deteriorating conditions in the country during this period), the most likely reason is that the administration of the questionnaire reactivated trauma. In the control group, there was nothing to counteract this reactivation. In the traditional group, the experiences of participants did not succeed in counteracting this. In the integrated group, participants' experiences were apparently sufficiently healing to reduce the original level of trauma and protect people from reactivation.

Analysis of the other orientation measure showed findings similar to those with trauma. At the start Tutsi participants in the integrated group were more negative about members of the other group (including less "conditional forgiveness," as we called it, since a readiness for forgiveness was conditional on acknowledgement of harmful action and apology by the perpetrator group) than participants in the other two groups. However, on the delayed measure they showed significantly more positive other orientation than at the time of the first administration, and when we controlled for initial difference, they also showed significantly more positive orientation than Tutsi participants in the other two conditions. In summary, the procedures we used in training facilitators increased their effectiveness with members of the community in reducing the level of trauma and promoting more positive orientation by Tutsis toward Hutus.

Additional Work in Rwanda on Healing, Reconciliation, Prevention, and Rebuilding Society

I, my coworker Dr. Laurie Anne Pearlman, and other associates have continued the work we have described in this and the previous chapter. We conducted seminars/workshops with high-level leaders of the country (government ministers, the heads and members of national commissions, the President and Vice President of the Supreme Court, members of parliament, and leaders of political parties and others); with community leaders; with journalists; with trauma specialists, and other groups. In all of this work we used some or all of the principles and approaches we have described, but we further developed them for the best use by particular groups.

With national leaders, for example, we discussed the influences that lead to genocide and the traumatic impact of genocide on people and avenues to healing. We then discussed the implications of such information both on what policies leaders need to develop, and what methods of implementing policies are required, in order to prevent new violence and develop constructive relations between groups and a peaceful society. We have worked with journalists on how they can use such information to present news in a way that helps to overcome rather than intensify hostility. More specifically, we discussed how they can present the *gacaca* – a communal justice system in which 250,000 people elected from the population serve in judging the large majority of about 115,000 prisoners accused of perpetrating the genocide – in a way that helps people understand how someone has become a perpetrator, and helps limit retraumatization by survivors who hear testimonies about terrible acts.

For descriptions of some of this work and for references to published material please go to *www.heal-reconcile-rwanda.org* or start at www.umass.edu/peacepsychology and look for links.

38

Further Avenues to Prevention

DIALOGUE, CONFLICT RESOLUTION, PROBLEM SOLVING, AND OTHER JOINT PROJECTS

Dialogue groups, engagement in problem solving by antagonistic groups, conflict resolution, and joint projects serve a number of positive goals. They can help overcome devaluation and foster healing and reconciliation. They can also resolve political issues and point to solutions for practical problems.

Creating contact is one of their significant contributions. Deep engagement by members of groups with each other, ideally under conditions of equality and other supporting conditions, can help overcome negative stereotypes and hostility (Allport, 1954; Cook, 1970; Deutsch, 1973; Pettigrew, 1997; Staub, 1989). The creation of joint goals and shared efforts in their behalf are extremely valuable (Deutsch, 1973; Sherif, Harvey, White, Hood, & Sherif, 1961; Staub, 1989).

In dialogue groups, members describe the pain and suffering of their group. They are led to express empathy and to assume responsibility for their group's role in causing the other's suffering (Fisher, 1997; Volkan, 1988). In problem-solving workshops (for example, Kelman, 1990; Rouhana & Kelman, 1994), which are one version of conflict resolution approaches (Fisher, 1997, 2000), members address real-life issues, practical as well as political, that have to be resolved for the groups to live in peace. Some of the processes that take place in dialogue groups must occur, and can occur, relatively naturally in the course of problem solving. Both parties are aware of their own difficulties, but their awareness expands. Like themselves, members of the other group endanger themselves as they act to promote peace, given the fear of and enmity in each group toward the other.

Reprinted from E. Staub (1999). The origins and prevention of genocide, mass killing, and other collective violence. *Peace and Conflict: Journal of Peace Psychology, 5*, 325–328.

Practitioners of these approaches have emphasized the importance of the frustration of basic needs in originating conflict and of the fulfillment of the basic needs of protagonists in resolving it (Burton, 1990; Fisher, 1997; Kelman, 1990; Rothman, 1992). Kelman has suggested that the failure to fulfill needs for identity, security, recognition, participation, dignity, and justice, or threat to such needs, significantly contributes to the origins, escalation, and perpetuation of conflict between groups. He noted that the Israelis became more open to talking with the Palestine Liberation Organization (PLO) when they perceived it as less intent on destroying them, and members of the PLO became more willing to talk when their identity was affirmed by the international community. Christie (1997) has suggested that the fulfillment of the needs for security, identity, material well-being, and self-determination is central to peace-building.

Dialogue groups and problem-solving workshops must be small to work well. Membership is at times confidential, to protect participants from hostility in their communities. At other times, members are officials who are sent by leaders (Fisher, 1997). To bring about change in group relations, these groups must include influential individuals. As practical circumstances make this feasible, the processes that take place ought to be extended to the larger community through public events, literature, and the media.

Dialogue groups and problem-solving workshops provide significant contact. But members of antagonistic groups can also create other joint projects: rebuilding ruined houses, cleaning up neighborhoods, participating in business projects, and so on. In Macedonia, journalists from different ethnic groups joined in teams. Together they interviewed ordinary people belonging to the different groups and wrote articles about their lives, which were published in the papers of each ethnic group (Manoff, 1996).

When there is antagonism and hostility between groups, the creation of shared goals and joint efforts often requires the committed effort of active bystanders, of third parties who are willing to foster and guide engagement between hostile parties. Given the psychological components of all these efforts, clinical, social, political, and other kinds of psychologists, and professionals in specialities like conflict resolution, have a potentially important role in envisioning, initiating, and executing them. NGOs, the UN, individual nations, and single individuals have all initiated such efforts, but a much more organized approach is required to make them the powerful tools in prevention they can be.

REBUILDING COMMUNITIES

The approaches required to heal and rebuild communities, both to improve individual lives and to avoid continued violence, are extremely multifaceted. In addition to generalizable needs, there are specific local needs. In addition to knowledge brought by psychologists and other

Western specialists, local culture, custom, and knowledge must be drawn on. Communities can only be rebuilt by their members (Wessels & Montiero, 2001).

For example, Angola is a country that has been greatly impoverished and its communities severely impacted by decades of violence between a government initially supported by the Soviet Union and rebels supported by the United States. Many adolescents were forced or enticed into joining the two armies. These adolescents may have killed people even in their own villages. They need to heal as individuals and, to recreate normal community life, they must be reintegrated into their communities.

This requires traditional ceremonies, with the engagement of the whole community. This process can be helpful to all members of a community devastated by war, disorder, and poverty. Psychological education that helps adults understand and thereby respond more effectively to the impact of traumatic experiences on young people can facilitate this process. Such youth also need schooling and jobs, which is not available to most of them. Outside help with economic development and with rebuilding of institutions is often essential (Wessels & Montiero, 2001).

CULTURE CHANGE AND DEMOCRATIZATION

It is difficult for external bystanders to further culture change in a society. People feel a right to their culture and resist interference. Help in rebuilding local communities offers one avenue to culture change. Helping countries with democratization is another relatively accessible way to this. At times of great societal upheavals, as in Eastern Europe after the collapse of the Soviet Union, there has been danger that nationalistic and other extreme ideologies and violent movements would emerge. Some bystanders tried to help develop institutions that maintain a "civil society" (Sampson, 1996). Outsiders have participated in developing school programs that promote good citizenship, a well-functioning media, and other institutions. When this is appropriate and accepted, outsiders can also help create inclusive visions and practices. As democracy develops, takes hold, and acquires roots, culture is likely to become more pluralistic and less authority oriented.

THE ROLE OF THE MEDIA

The importance of the media in combating human rights violations has long been recognized (see Manoff, 1996). The media can play a crucial role in preventing group violence. It can report human rights violations and present groups in ways that diminish rather than enhance antagonism. It can identify issues between parties and articulate their positions in nonconfrontational ways. It can call attention to the psychological needs that underlie conflict. It can point to the passivity of bystanders, or their collaboration with perpetrators, and it can mobilize bystanders. Inattention by the media can allow violence against groups to unfold with little public knowledge.

How the media presents victims and perpetrators greatly affects public attitudes. By devaluing victims and giving the benefit of the doubt to perpetrators, the media can generate passivity. Consider that in 1938, after years of increasing persecution of Jews in Nazi Germany, there were intensely anti-Semitic radio programs in the United States (e.g., that of Father Coughlin; Wyman, 1968, 1984). The media can join people as they follow an inclination to devalue victims, which may arise from a belief that the world is a just place and people who suffer must have deserved it (Lerner, 1980), as well as from other psychological processes. Such reporting by the media can lead people to distance themselves from victims. Alternatively, accurate reporting by the media can generate empathy with the victims' plight, caring, and action.

Providing members of the media with relevant training is essential. The training should promote psychological knowledge about origins and effects of violence. It should also promote self-awareness. Membership in one's culture affects attitudes and the perception of events. It can lead to favoring certain groups based on past relations with them and to favoring their ideology. It can lead to self-censorship due to dominant cultural perspectives (Staub, 1989). For example, when Franco ruled Spain, the editors of *Time Magazine* rejected a report on Spanish communists because it made them "look too good" (Gans, 1980). Lack of familiarity with faraway lands (e.g., not knowing who Tutsi and Hutu are) is probably another important reason for ignoring the evolution toward intense violence.

A crucial way for bystanders to promote human rights is by fighting censorship, intimidation, and control of the media by authorities. Even sanctions seem justified to protect freedom of the media. To counteract censorship, at times outside news broadcasts on radio and television in the country's language may be appropriate.

But media freedom is a complex issue, and international standards for media responsibility are needed. The anti-Semitic radio broadcasts of Father Coughlin during the 1930s in the United States were highly popular, and they continued until it was discovered that he had used verbatim translations of speeches by Goebbels, the Nazi propaganda minister (Wyman, 1968). Sometimes hate and nationalism are propagated by government-controlled media, sometimes by elites who have control over the media, and sometimes by individuals. And sometimes journalists who write the truth are killed (Committee to Protect Journalists, 1997).

References

Allport, G. W. (1954). *The nature of prejudice*. Reading, MA: Addison-Wesley.
Burton, J. W. (1990). *Conflict: Human needs theory*. New York: St. Martin's Press.

Christie, D. J. (1997). Reducing direct and structural violence: The human needs theory: *Peace and Conflict: Journal of Peace Psychology, 3*, 315–332.

Committee to Protect Journalists. (1997). *Effects on the press in 1996: A world-wide survey of the committee to protect journalists*. New York: Author.

Cook, S. W. (1970). Motives in conceptual analysis of attitude-related behavior. In W. J. Arnold & D. Levine (Eds.). *Nebraska symposium on motivation*. Lincoln: University of Nebraska Press.

Deutsch, M. (1973). *The resolution of conflict: Constructive and destructive processes*. New Haven, CT: Yale University Press.

Fisher, R. J. (1997). *Interactive conflict resolution*. Syracuse, NY: Syracuse University Press.

Fisher, R. J. (2000). Social psychological processes in interactive conflict analysis and reconciliation. In Ho-Won, Jeong (Ed.), *From conflict resolution to peace building*. Dartmouth Publishing.

Gans, H. (1980). *Deciding what's news*. New York: Vintage.

Kelman, H. C. (1990). Applying a human needs perspective to the practice of conflict resolution: The Israeli–Palestinian Case. In J. Burton (Ed.), *Conflict: Human needs theory*. New York: St. Martin's Press.

Lerner, M. (1980). *The belief in a just world: A fundamental delusion*. New York: Plenum.

Manoff, R. (1996). *The mass media and social violence: Is there a role for the media in preventing and moderating ethnic, national, and religious conflict?* Unpublished manuscript, New York University.

Pettigrew, T. F. (1997). Generalized intergroup contact effects on prejudice. *Personality and Social Psychology Bulletin, 23*, 173–185.

Rothman, J. (1992). *From confrontation to cooperation: Resolving ethnic and regional conflict*. Newbury Park, CA: Sage.

Rouhana, N. N., & Kelman, H. C. (1994). Promoting joint thinking in international conflicts: An Israeli–Palestinian continuing workshop. *Journal of Social Issues, 20*, 157–178.

Sampson, S. (1996). The social life of projects. Importing civil society to Albania. In C. Hann & E. Dunn (Eds.), *Civil society: Challenging western models*. London: Routledge & Kegan Paul.

Sherif, M., Harvey, D. J., White, B. J., Hood, W. K., & Sherif, C. W. (1961). *Intergroup conflict and cooperation: The robber's cave experiment*. Norman: University of Oklahoma Book Exchange.

Staub, E. (1989). *The roots of evil: The origins of genocide and other group violence*. New York: Cambridge University Press.

Volkan, V. D. (1988). *The need to have enemies and allies*. Northvale, NY: Jason Aronson.

Wessels, M., & Montiero, C. (2001). Psychological intervention and post-conflict reconstruction in Angola: Interweaving Western and traditional approaches. In D. Christie, R. V. Wagner, & D. Winter (Eds.), *Peace, conflict and violence: Peace psychology for the 21st century*. Englewood Cliffs, NJ: Prentice-Hall.

Wyman, D. S. (1968). *Paper walls: America and the refugee crisis, 1938–1941*. Amherst: University of Massachusetts Press.

Wyman, D. S. (1984). *The abandonment of Jews: America and the Holocaust*, 1941–1945. New York: Pantheon.

39

Commentary

Human Destructiveness and the Refugee Experience

I was in the midst of writing *The Roots of Evil: The Psychological and Cultural Origins of Genocide* and had finished an analysis of the "autogenocide" in Cambodia, when I was invited to attend a meeting of the seminar on Southeast Asia in which students wrote essays about their life experiences. I heard one student describe in personal terms the horrors in Cambodia that I knew so well from my research. But the tragedy of students from other Southeast Asian countries was also manifest in this meeting: young people, children and adolescents, fearing for their lives or in the hope of greater security and human dignity left their countries, alone or with their families.

Being a refugee is a tragically common human experience. Unfortunately, repression and violence that lead people to escape from their own country and seek refuge elsewhere have always existed. It is all too frequent in our century. Huge numbers of people were displaced and became stateless in Europe during the first part of the century. Millions of people became refugees in the wake of the Second World War. But this saga seems never ending, and the flow of those seeking refuge continues.

CREATING REFUGEES: THE ORIGINS OF REPRESSION, TORTURE, MASS KILLINGS

A group of young Cambodian students in Paris, all members of the French Communist party, comrades in Communist study groups, became political associates and, ultimately, associates in designing a vision of a society that they attempted to fulfill by genocide. Their road from Paris in the 1950s to

Reprinted from E. Staub (1989). Commentary: Human destructiveness and the refugee experience. In L. Nguyen & J. Halpem (Eds.), *The far east comes near*. Amherst: University of Massachusetts Press, pp. 198–205.

winning a civil war in 1975 and gaining power both over their enemies in the civil war and among the Cambodian Communists was a long one.

Once they came to power they killed many officers in the army and government officials, many professionals and intellectuals – doctors, teachers, lawyers. These people were enemies and judged incapable of building and living in the society that Pol Pot, the prime minister, and his associates designed – a society based on the land, on the peasantry, totally self-sufficient, with complete equality among members.

They evacuated the cities and drove people into the countryside, forcing them to build villages from scratch, without expertise and without help. They made these people spend long, long days building irrigation systems or working the fields. Although there was an extreme shortage of food, they prohibited the gathering of food from the forests, a traditional mode of survival at times of scarcity in Cambodia. They established many stringent rules of conduct and killed people for even slight infractions, at times after one or two warnings, at times without warning. Practices varied somewhat in different areas of the country and during different periods of the four-year rule of the Khmer Rouge, as the Cambodian Communists called themselves. With less than total consistency, they broke up families. Through direct murder and starvation they killed one to two million people. They imposed profound suffering on all.

They created many refugees. The impact on refugees varies depending on the nature of the repressive system in their country of origin and the individual experience of the victims. There are commonalities, however, in any experience of repression, threat, and danger, in escape, and in entry into a new society.

Human beings have certain basic needs. They need a feeling of security, a freedom from danger and threat of attack. They need some feeling of control over their immediate fate and their future lives. They need to believe that they can protect themselves and fulfill their essential goals. Important for both security and a feeling of control is at least a moderate trust in the world. People also need a sense of connection to other people, some feeling of community. Under the conditions that lead people to escape from their homes and start life in a different country usually none of these needs are fulfilled.

The conditions that create refugees may lead to the experience of total helplessness in face of the brutal power of the system. Depending on the extent that they are singled out as a limited subgroup of society, members of victimized groups may develop a growing self-doubt and self-devaluation: Am I persecuted because something is wrong with me? This happened to many Jews who were persecuted by the Nazis and others; it happened to Armenians as they were persecuted (and about a million of them killed) in Turkey; it happens to mistreated minorities in many countries. It happened to Cambodians, especially city people and the educated who were driven from their homes. And those who were not killed were degraded, mistreated, enslaved, forced to witness others' degradation and murder. Their experience must lead many refugees to a view of the world as hostile, dangerous, unpredictable.

The experience of refugees will profoundly affect both their worldview and their self-concept. Their feelings of helplessness may be counteracted as refugees initiate their escape and entry into a new country. After all, in highly significant ways, they are taking charge, they are exercising control over their lives. This may strengthen their belief in their capacity to create a new life for themselves. In addition, as people move to a new country, the sharp break makes it possible for them to discriminate between the old and the new, to be aware of the greater benevolence of their new environment, of freedom and possibilities.

Still, at deep levels, basic effects remain. Those who experienced extreme cruelty and great suffering may be left with deep wounds: doubts about their self-worth, about the goodness and trustworthiness of human beings. In most refugees, a feeling of vulnerability and a sensitivity to danger may be easily reawakened. Former refugees describe their anxiety upon encountering policemen, agents of repression in their former lives, or upon crossing borders, which reminds them of past insecurity and homelessness. Hostility directed at them may have greater impact, may threaten them at deeper levels. I have experienced these and other revivals of a dormant but still existing self.

THE ROLE AND OBLIGATIONS OF BYSTANDERS

What is the obligation of other human beings toward refugees and toward the destructiveness that creates refugees? A basic obligation of those who offer refuge is true acceptance and hospitality. Refugees, human beings much like ourselves, have experienced pain, suffering, and the collapse of their former existence, and they have a deep need to create a new existence. We must reach out to refugees as we hope others would reach out to us. As a nation we must open our doors to those who are persecuted and in danger, whether from El Salvador or Cuba, regardless of the political ideology of the system that they are escaping from. All nations have practical limitations, in resources and space, but within those limitations, which are less restrictive for a large and wealthy country like the United States, we must open our doors to innocent victims.

But there is also another profound obligation. You and I and our nation as a bystander must not ignore the suffering that countries around the world inflict on their own citizens. We must not deny that it is happening, or close our eyes to it and ignore it, as the United States and Britain and many other countries did during the Holocaust and at other times. As the genocide in Cambodia began, the world was very slow to respond. Moreover, all too often ideology or "national interest" shapes the response to perpetrators and inhibits help for victims. When partly in response to self-destructive provocations Vietnam invaded Cambodia and put an end to the murderous Khmer Rouge rule, our government and China joined as strange bedfellows in recognizing the ousted Pol Pot regime as the legitimate representative of Cambodia in the United Nations.

Individuals, groups, nations of the world, and the community of nations have an obligation to exert the maximum influence in their power, which is great in the case of the United States, to stop governments from mistreating their citizens. All countries and, considering our traditional values and potential influence, especially the United States should follow a consistent policy of expressing views and shaping relations with foes and friends to support human rights, foster respect for the life, welfare, and safety from persecution of individuals, and foster individual rights and freedom.

When a government does mistreat its citizens we – individuals, human-rights groups, governments – must call the attention of perpetrators to basic rights and moral values and show that we consider their disregard to be of the greatest significance. We must do all that we can to make perpetrators aware of the costs of their atrocities to themselves, through diplomacy, boycotts, ostracism in the international community, and in other ways. We must make perpetrators aware that they won't escape punishment for their actions.

Through our positive acts, taking in refugees and reaching out to them, and through our attempts to inhibit human destructiveness, we can genuinely contribute to a "better world."

40

A Vision of Holocaust Education in Holocaust Centers and Schools

SOME GENERAL GOALS

Holocaust education has become widespread in schools and education centers. It has the potential to benefit many people:

To see the evil (destructiveness) human beings are capable of; understand its sources, where it comes from; see the potential for it in each of us; see the human potential and their own potential for goodness.

To develop the capacity to see what around us (in the characteristics of culture, society, people's actions) may promote human destructiveness and what is required by us to promote goodness rather than evil in ourselves and society.

To become aware of their potential as bystanders and perpetrators, as well as helpers, and of how they actually act in the world.

To help Jews – survivors, descendants, members of the group targeted in the Holocaust – as well as members of other groups that suffered violence against them, and people in general, become aware of their suffering and pain, which is part of the life of many people, adults and children. Holocaust education can also help with healing, and with opening up to other people's suffering and need.

To become aware of the difference they can make in the world, the choices they can make in their own lives.

Many people within and outside the Jewish community may become interested in and open to education about the Holocaust if it is made relevant to their own lives. What happened in the Holocaust, its origins and human consequences, has profound relevance to many aspects of contemporary life. Holocaust education at its best will draw lessons from the Holocaust that inform and improve both Jewish life and human life in general, both today and in the future. An approach that does that may conflict with an approach to Holocaust education that focuses on the uniqueness of the Holocaust. But the latter approach diminishes what teaching about the Holocaust can offer the world: the potential of Holocaust education to improve the world.

The following is applicable, although at times in somewhat different ways, both to Holocaust education in the schools, and in Holocaust Education Centers that serve both children and adults. In both settings, Holocaust education should involve people emotionally and experientially, not just convey information and knowledge. In referring to "people," I mean both young people and adults.

SPECIFIC AIMS AND APPROACHES

A starting point for Holocaust education is information about what happened, the actual events of the Holocaust. These include conditions in Germany at the time, the increasing persecution of Jews, how Jews were collected, and the different ways they were killed, the death camps, the broad range of people involved, the passivity of Germans who were not perpetrators, and the passivity of the rest of the world. With some audiences, this has to start from scratch.

How could the Holocaust happen? How could Germans perpetrate such horrible violence? Understanding the roots of the Holocaust is important. What was the role of individuals, of the culture, of the nature of society? This understanding can then be applied to our lives today to make violence less likely and to promote its opposite: caring about the welfare of other human beings and acting in their behalf.

My attempt to understand the origins of the Holocaust and other violence against ethnic, religious or political groups is described in my book, *The Roots of Evil: The Origins of Genocide and Other Group Violence.* It discusses difficult conditions of life in a society and people's responding to it by scapegoating and creating destructive ideologies, the evolution of increasing discrimination and violence against a group, and the passivity of bystanders.

The predispositions for such violence include a history of devaluation of a group of people and discrimination against them, too much respect for and obedience to authorities, a monolithic rather than pluralistic society, unhealed wounds from past violence, lack of courage to speak out against discrimination and violence against people, and some other elements of culture and society. Sometimes these elements take idiosyncratic and specialized forms in different societies. In Germany ideas about "racial hygiene," involving the medical profession, added to the devaluation of Jews. The division between the rulers and the intellectuals in the cities and the peasants in the countryside was a basis of devaluation in Cambodia.

The understanding of the origins of the Holocaust can thus be expanded to other violence against groups and their members. Education about what happened in the Holocaust and its causes can be followed by information about other intense violence against groups, in Turkey, Cambodia, Bosnia, and Rwanda, and about hate crimes and youth violence in America.

Learning about the history and causes of the Holocaust can show people the human potential for evil, and our individual potential to participate in evil or remain passive in the face of evil. It can also show the importance of awareness of social forces and of self-awareness, and one's responsibility in making choices, speaking out and taking action. It can develop in people both the capacity to notice forces in the world (or in their own environment) that may promote violence and destruction and the willingness and ability to oppose them.

Holocaust education should show the long-term consequences of the Holocaust, the impact on human beings and communities. Not only did millions die, but survivors, and all Jews, have been profoundly affected. It should show the emotional wounds of survivors, how these wounds are handed down through the generations. It should also be inclusive by showing the wounds inflicted by genocide or mass killing on other groups of people – Armenians, Rwandans, and so on. It is sometimes difficult to go beyond the intense suffering brought by the Holocaust to the pain of others, but ultimately, when we open ourselves to others' pain, it is healing. Holocaust education may also show the significance of the world reaching out to survivors and helping them heal, and the further wounds inflicted by the world ignoring the suffering of victimized peoples. This happened to the Armenians, as much of the world joined Turkey in denying that the genocide against the Armenians had occurred.

It is also worthwhile, for many reasons, to teach about the role of "victims." Often victims are blamed and devalued. Why Jews did not resist more is a question some people have asked. Showing the psychological effects of being surrounded by force, the helplessness people feel when they are abandoned by friends, neighbors, business associates and even spouses, as it happened to Jews in Germany and other European countries, can help explain the "passivity" of victims. This approach to Holocaust education can also help people who have been victimized as individuals, or members of some other group, by understanding their own experiences of victimization.

Understanding survival also has great value. While mostly not overtly resisting, Jews who survived were often highly active and courageous in saving their children, relatives, other people, and themselves. Both parents and children have often acted decisively in the face of an overwhelming threat to their lives. Survival was often the result of a combination of courageous, determined action, help by other people, and luck.

Teaching about rescuers and resistance can show the possibilities of caring in the midst of evil. However, it is important to provide a proper balance in Holocaust education, to show the possibilities of goodness as well as human destructiveness and the suffering it creates.

Stories of rescue are inspiring. But it is also important to help people understand what led rescuers to act when so many were passive or joined the perpetrators. Many rescuers learned to draw less sharp lines between "us" and "them," which indicates that we need to raise children so that they will be "inclusively" caring. Other aspects of rescuers' childhoods are highly consistent with what we know from contemporary research about raising caring and helpful children: it requires affection, constructive guidance, positive discipline, helpful models, and so on. Rescuers often developed increasing commitment to helping once they began: like evil, so goodness evolves, and both perpetrators and heroic helpers create themselves. Education about rescuers can provide a framework for further exploration of passive bystanders versus active helpers. It can also provide a framework for education about ways to raise caring, nonviolent children. The role of both parents and teachers is important in this.

Holocaust education should help people heal. Holocaust education should engage members of the Jewish community in activities that promote healing. It should draw in others to join the Jewish community in these healing events. Memorials and ceremonies, poems, art, music, plays, writing about personal, family, and group experiences, and feelings related to them, can all contribute to healing.

By exposing people to the tremendous suffering created by the Holocaust, by supporting them in feeling empathy for its victims and survivors, and by enabling them to experience their own pain and feel empathy for themselves, Holocaust education can be instrumental in helping both Jews and non-Jews heal. This is important because unhealed psychological wounds can be an important source of violence: by parents against children, by groups against other groups. They also, of course, diminish well-being, the quality of life.

Many children and adults carry tremendous pain due to different kinds of victimization or losses in their lives. I believe that this pain can separate people from others, stopping them from engagement with the world and caring about others' welfare. But pain and loss can also give rise to caring about and helping other people. Many survivors of the Holocaust, for example, are in the "helping professions" and have worked for positive social change. For this to happen people must understand that others have also suffered greatly and to experience connection to and support from at least some other people. Grieving for others can contribute to healing. Healing in connection to others can promote caring about other people and altruism.

I am suggesting that getting members of groups who have experienced discrimination and violence and those who have been individually victimized involved with Holocaust education can reduce violence in the world.

Perhaps this may seem paradoxical, but I believe that exposure to information about the tragic, painful events of the Holocaust, and to ceremonies and memorials, can be healing for non-Jews, especially those who have themselves been victimized. This healing effect can be enhanced when combined with other experiences, like writing about the impact of exposure to these events, and writing about one's own experiences of pain and victimization. Guiding people in this process requires sensitivity and some prior knowledge and experience.

It may be worthwhile for Holocaust education to address the extremely difficult and sensitive question of forgiveness: is it possible to forgive those who did these horrible things, or their children, or Germans and their European collaborators? What is required for it, and how can forgiveness take place?

On the one hand, for many people, the idea of forgiveness in the context of the Holocaust is anathema. On the other hand, the activities of One by One, an organization that brings together children of survivors and children of perpetrators of the Holocaust, seem to have great appeal to both non-Jews and Jews. And forgiveness has some important uses, one of which is to help those who have been victimized heal.

Forgiveness is also important for reconciliation. Reconciliation with Germans is not a significant life issue for Jews. But in other instances of violence by groups against other groups, as in Bosnia, Rwanda, or between Israelis and Palestinians, people who live intertwined with each other, it is a highly significant issue. So may it be for people in the United States living in the inner cities who belong to different groups. Reconciliation requires that victims forgive, if not the perpetrators, at least members of the group that perpetrated violence. It also requires perpetrators, or members of the group in general, to assume responsibility for the group's actions. Both are outcomes: they happen as a result of "processes" within and between groups. Moreover, since at times both parties may be either victims or perpetrators, each party must both forgive and assume responsibility. Education about all this can be an important part of Holocaust education.

Holocaust education should move people to take action in the world. Combating devaluation of groups of people and discrimination against them; acting to stop violence in one's community in part by building community; acting to influence one's government to work on preventing genocide in the world; helping to create "caring schools" that develop caring in children are a few of the possible avenues for relevant action.

Creating community is of special importance. Frequently, this requires reaching out across boundaries that divide groups, by race, religion and so on, which contribute to hostility and violence. Successful reaching out, by finding shared goals and creating joint projects, can teach young people that "us" and "them" does not have to be an operative principle in life. Creating caring schools is also of special importance. Such schools don't teach caring, but the way they operate provides children with experiences that promote caring.

The more that members of the community, Jews and non-Jews, young and old, can be involved in creating programs for Holocaust education, the greater the learning that might follow. They can create stories, poems, art, plays, and gather relevant material. They can be involved in many ways.

41

Out of Hiding

It was with reluctance that I went to New York last year for the first conference of people who, as children, survived the Holocaust in hiding. These were the children of miracles. They survived when the overwhelming majority of European Jews were killed by Nazi Germany, at times aided by collaborationist governments that handed over their Jewish populations for extermination. Their survival was a manifestation of the human capacity for goodness even in the darkest of times.

Perhaps my reluctance to attend this conference stemmed from an unwillingness to revisit the dark times of my own wartime experience. All my professional life I have studied, as a psychologist, what leads individuals and groups to be caring and helpful, or to turn against and harm others. Until recently, however, I paid little attention to the origins in my own childhood of this lifelong concern with the roots of cruelty and kindness, and of my desire to do what little I can to help create a more caring world.

I was a young Jewish child in Hungary at the time of the Holocaust. When the Nazis began to deport Jews from Budapest, a wonderful Christian woman hid me and my sister with a Christian family. She returned us to our mother after a while, when we received "letters of protection," and we survived in a "protected house" until Soviet troops liberated the city.

While more than 450,000 Hungarian Jews were sent to their deaths in Auschwitz, thousands of Jewish women, children, and old men survived in similar protected houses in Budapest, tenuously shielded by letters of protection (although raiding Hungarian Nazis, the "Arrow Cross," often refused to respect these documents).

Reprinted from E. Staub (1992 Winter). Out of hiding: Children who survived the Holocaust share their memories. Amherst: *Massachusetts Magazine*, *3*, 22–24. Copyright 1992. Reprinted with permission from *Massachusetts Magazine*.

The Swedish diplomat Raoul Wallenberg created the first protected houses, and a couple of other embassies in Budapest followed his example. Wallenberg designed an official-looking letter of protection that guaranteed the bearers Swedish citizenship after the war. He was constantly persuading, cajoling, and threatening Hungarian officials to respect these documents. By this and other means he saved 10,000–30,000 lives; some sources put the number as high as 100,000.

My family's wartime experience was extremely unusual: while letters of protection saved my life and the lives of my mother and sister, my father also survived. He escaped during a stopover in Budapest as his brigade from a forced labor camp was being transported to Germany. He was the sole survivor of this group, and I was the only one among my Jewish friends whose father survived the horrors of the Holocaust.

I wrote briefly about this personal history in the preface to my 1989 book *The Roots of Evil: The Origins of Genocide and Other Group Violence*. But that did not mean I was ready to pay attention to my experience. When an Australian psychiatrist friend (who also survived the Holocaust as a child in Budapest) wrote me that he was coming to attend the Hidden Child Conference in New York, I invited him for a visit, but in spite of his strong urging, I had no intention of going to the conference myself. My friend's quiet persistence overcame my resistance and I decided to go – for one day.

At the conference, the 1,600 people in attendance filled a huge room, with the press present in large numbers. Most of the speakers were survivors of the Holocaust, many of them hidden children who have devoted their lives to working with other survivors.

One important theme the speakers sounded was the long neglect of child survivors, especially of hidden children who had not been in the Nazi extermination and labor camps. If parents survived, they were often silent about what had happened, some even lying to their children, which created walls between parent and child. Some parents may have wanted to protect children from the pain of the past, unaware that knowing, remembering, and "processing" the experience of trauma is part of healing.

Children were hidden or hid themselves in many places: in cellars and attics, in barns, in buildings with secret compartments or concealed rooms, wandering in the forest, as members of Christian families, or in cloisters. Some families successfully passed themselves off as Christian. My Australian friend's family did this for a while – until two men in trench coats arrested his parents one day, leaving the five-year-old boy alone on the street.

Silence was often a key to survival during the Holocaust. One friend remembers hiding in a small room with a number of other children and adults while the Arrow Cross searched the house. The parents placed their hands over the children's mouths to keep them quiet. Later, after the war, some hidden children remained psychologically in hiding, prisoners of their own silence, unable to explore their early trauma.

Maintaining silence was probably also a result of shame that some survivors felt. There is a common human tendency to believe that the world is a just place and therefore to assume that people who are victimized must deserve their fate. This is one of the reasons that bystanders devalued and failed to help victims of the Holocaust. Victims are often victimized again when this "just world" thinking leads them to devalue themselves.

Some hidden children remained in hiding with Christians for a long time, or were even converted to Christianity, or were scared to be Jewish after the war, and suffered from resulting confusions of identity. Many continued to feel this confusion as they emigrated to other countries, feeling like strangers everywhere.

Outside the large conference room in New York, people milled around between sessions. Some of them filled bulletin boards with notices, pictures, articles about lost relatives – still hoping and searching after all these years.

The real work of the conference took place in small groups – separate workshops for hidden children, for spouses, for the children of hidden children. As I sat in one small workshop after another, striking similarities emerged in the way participants talked about themselves. They described feelings of not belonging, of looking in from the outside, of keeping themselves at arm's length from other people. They talked about the difficulty of claiming things for oneself – for example, time to talk about oneself. They responded with recognition as one person after another talked about his or her seriousness, lack of spontaneity, difficulty in just playing. Difficulty in exposing oneself to scrutiny or judgment, and struggle to overcome a "film" which separates oneself from others were also common experiences.

Not surprisingly, many people in the workshops talked about how important it was to have a sense of control over the events in their lives. Some said that they felt they had to justify their existence by achieving. As one of the speakers said: "We were strong. Steadfastly fixed on goals to be achieved, we were restless achievers." Their Holocaust experiences also led many of the hidden children to care deeply about human suffering and devote themselves to helping others.

Psychologists now know that early trauma, even if much less severe than the traumas of the Holocaust, has a long-lasting impact on people. The wonders of human life include the dual capacity to go on and live life effectively and intensely, and still be deeply affected by early trauma.

From early on, a strong sense of community was evident at the conference. The shared suffering, shared fate, made for intense connection in the small workshops. This was a place where people felt understood, without having to explain themselves.

Some people told me weeks after the conference that confronting the past had awakened old memories and brought forth feelings of anxiety, helplessness, or loss. Yet they continued to explore the past after the conference was over. Many others reported breaking their silence at the conference in a way they had never done before, or experiencing empathy with themselves as well as trust and deep connection to others, all important aspects of healing.

Despite my original intentions, I stayed through the second day of the conference. I left moved and, yes, uplifted by the experience, and by the caring and love that got me there.

42

Review of *Legacy of Silence: Encounters with Children of the Third Reich*

Book Review

Legacy of Silence: Encounters with Children of the Third Reich. By Dan Bar-On. Cambridge: Harvard University Press, 1989.

In the last two decades increasing attention has focused on how human beings deal with and make sense of their victimization and trauma. After long neglect of their experience and fate, attention has focused on how survivors of the horrors of the Holocaust have been affected by and deal with their experiences, and on how children of the survivors have been affected by growing up with their deeply traumatized parents. In this book Dan Bar-On examines how the children of the perpetrators of the Holocaust, the children of Nazis involved in the extermination policy or process, deal with the circumstances their lives handed them.

He made contact with 58 children of perpetrators and interviewed all but nine who refused to see him. There is an introductory and a concluding chapter, and 13 chapters that present individual interviews. The author asks questions and provides brief statements – of his emotional reactions, thoughts, or interpretations – at a few points along the way and at the end of each interview. But he is primarily an unobtrusive although important presence. He provides a frame for the interviewees' stories.

The interviews show the immense struggle of the children of perpetrators to comprehend what happened, to create a tolerable relationship to their dead or still alive perpetrator father, and to build their own identity in the shadow of this heritage. At least as significant about this book is the view it provides of life in Nazi Germany from the vantage point of youth in perpetrator families, ranging in age from very young children to

Reprinted from E. Staub (1995). Legacy of Silence: Encounters with Children of the Third Reich. *Political Psychology, 16*, 3, 651–655. Reprinted by permission of Blackwell Publishers Ltd.

young adults, and the views it provides of the Holocaust, and of postwar Germany and its relationship to its past.

The author offers limited conceptualization, which seems acceptable given the complex, many-faceted, and deeply experiential nature of the interview material. But as a result, to make the reader of this review familiar with the book, I must provide glimpses of the material in the interviews, highlighting some major themes along the way.

One of the children of perpetrators, whose father was a doctor in Auschwitz but was acquitted after the war because he tried to help Jews in the camp, supposedly does not learn about his father's activities until he is 20 years old, when he sees his father's picture on television. But at 18 he surprises his educated parents, who value intellectual life, by signing up as a chef's apprentice. He works as a chef, never talks to his father about what he did or did not do, and sees human nature as the same now and thinks that many would like to do to the Turks what was done to the Jews. The author believes that this person "knew," without really knowing.

Another son, whose father committed suicide (as did the fathers of several other interviewees) when he was a baby, has become a professor of history but avoids studying the Hitler era. Although he claims that he views his father as a historical figure, without emotional connection to him or his role, and he considers what happened as a mass or group phenomenon, he does not have children for fear that somehow the genes responsible for his father's behavior would be transmitted. He also wonders whether he is normal, because he does not suffer enough from his heritage. The son's adaptation was clearly influenced in this case by the active role of his mother. She was married to his father only briefly, did not feel loyal to him, and openly talked about what happened. The nature of the family, usually silent and unsupportive, has an active role in the adaptation of the children of perpetrators.

This son has an ongoing struggle between distancing himself from and indirectly defending his father, for example, by suggesting that people were taken in by slogans, pushed in a certain direction, "... a direction they weren't in agreement with...." (p. 65) and then lost control and were driven from the outside. A theme present in many interviews is the struggle between facing the truth and experiencing pain versus the desire to explain and justify.

The theme is present for a number of daughters who have been very close to their perpetrator fathers. One daughter, deeply engaged with her father, who committed suicide after the war, on the one hand struggles with the past and on the other distances herself from it to the point of denial. She has had great difficulty in engaging with Jews in any way. The focus of her struggle seems to be to maintain her love for her father, while facing the fact that he was one of Hitler's close associates, and creating an independent identity for herself. While she has a successful academic life, like several of the interviewees she is unmarried, which she attributes to the past.

One daughter, an illegitimate child, who strongly rejects the father, struggles with her mother, who continues to idealize the father. Perhaps liberated by her rejection of her father, she asks significant questions about the process by which Germany arrived at such horrors and about postwar Germany's refusal to engage with its past.

Another mode of adaptation is reflected by a nephew of Heydrich, head of the Gestapo. During the war the nephew felt like a crown prince because of his association with his famous uncle. But after the war there were "nineteen years during which he did little but deal with his family's past...." He now performs cabaret songs from the 20s and 30s, some of them by Jews mourning the fate of Jews.

As I have noted, the book provides a lens into the nature and practices of Nazi Germany, including its racial-biological views and the intention to improve the human race by allowing only the "pure and noble" to reproduce, computations about the costs of maintaining the "burdensome individuals" who were to be killed in the euthanasia program, and institutions that sucked in people, like children who yearned to join the Hitler Youth.

In an understated but powerful way the book also brings the reader close to the tragedy of the Holocaust. The author, walking in a Jewish cemetery in a small town, sees a memorial stone telling the date the Jews were rounded up, how many were gassed, and where. A letter from the only reluctant Nazi in the book to his son describes his horror as he sees the Jews of a small Polish village killed.

Through the interviews the book also provides a picture of postwar Germany's relationship to the Holocaust, which mostly lies somewhere between ignoring it and repressing it. The schools did not teach about it, and when one of the children of the perpetrators attempted to do so, parents protested. There was a legacy of silence not only in the perpetrator families, but in the society as a whole. People did not talk about the Holocaust and nobody acknowledged any role in it. As one interviewee said: "I also discovered that these ordinary people, these normal people don't have any biography for the years between '33 and '45.... they became innocent as lambs."

The history of the people interviewed was extremely varied; they cannot be understood simply as members of a category, the children of perpetrators. One of the interviewees, who was older during the war, carried his own guilt. His father, a religious man, who joined the Nazi party, when sent to Poland was deeply disturbed by the suffering of the Jews. He made friends with and tried to help some. When he saw all the Jews in the village killed he became deeply disturbed, unable to function. He suffered greatly not only during the war, when he could not talk about this, but also afterwards.

The son, who was indoctrinated by the Hitler Youth in which he was made a leader, was disturbed and confused by his father's feelings and unable to empathize with him. As Bar-On notes, "his story shows once again that even if knowledge of the extermination process was available early on, the proregime belief system made it seem, in one interviewee's word, like 'pure BBC propaganda'" (p. 327). Later, this interviewee is deeply stricken by his father's suffering, by his past distance from his father and inability to feel with him, by the extent the Hitler Jugend succeeded in indoctrinating him, and by his hard-hearted actions during that period. He says "just imagine what if this generation, which has been psychologically trained and geared up for it, what if this generation had been let loose on mankind. Then what occurred with the Jews, why it would pale in comparison..." (p. 213).

Age differences, whether the perpetrator continued to live, the sex of the child, the relationship to the perpetrator, usually the father, the degree of the involvement with the system (three of the perpetrators were very high-ranking Nazis), and the nature of the family as a system seem to be among the influences on the mode of the child's later adjustment. But given the many variations and the relatively small number of cases described in the book, there is insufficient information for drawing conclusions about the role of these factors.

The author, in the last chapter, offers a summary of some of the apparent themes: for example, silence about the extermination program even among the families of high-ranking Nazis who had to know about it; the loneliness of people who began as children of heroes and became overnight children of criminals; a "double wall" phenomenon, both parents and children erecting walls around their feelings about the atrocities that the parents were involved in; the distortions and gaps in the parents' stories and the failure in learning the truth through them when sons or daughters attempted to penetrate their parents' silence; the difficulties these offspring had in establishing stable relationships and families of their own; the inability of parents to help them; the unmentionable issue of the children of perpetrators in a society that "prefers a more convenient history, more comforting illusions" (p. 329). As in the case of Holocaust survivors at first, at least one therapist advises one of the children of perpetrators to forget about the past and move on.

This is a rich book, and its understated, experience-based glimpses of the Holocaust, Nazi Germany, and postwar Germany make it deeply affecting. In my own work I attempted to answer the questions that his book repeatedly asks: How could the Holocaust happen? How did this come about? In doing this work, I spent a great deal of time reading, thinking, and writing about the Holocaust. While I believe that I have developed a plausible, meaningful understanding of how the Holocaust and genocides in general happen (Staub, 1989), as I was reading this book I dreamt about human beings being killed one by one and woke up with a deep sense of incomprehension.

While the interviews touch on it in many ways, the book does not adequately address the impact on children of living with their perpetrator parents after the war. An analogous situation has been true of child survivors of the Holocaust: recently their experience during the Holocaust has become a focus of attention, but not the impact of growing up with deeply traumatized parents. In the case of perpetrators, not only were the parents affected by the loss of war, greatly damaged status, and danger to themselves, but the perpetrators must have been a particular kind of person, if not because they selected themselves or were selected for their roles, then because of the personal change that must have taken place in them while they fulfilled their roles (see Staub, 1989).

Human beings need to come to terms with life, and when they face extraordinary circumstances, they have to engage in extraordinary psychological maneuvers to do so. I have proposed (Staub, 1989) that human beings have certain basic needs, and a normal life requires that these needs be satisfied at least to a moderate degree. In the case of the children of perpetrators these needs – for security, for comprehension of reality, for a positive identity, for a sense of effectiveness and control, for positive connection to people – have been frustrated and challenged by their circumstances. The book shows, I believe, their struggle to fulfill these needs using the personal, familial, and societal tools at their disposal.

Reference

Staub, E. (1989). *The roots of evil: The origins of genocide and other group violence.* New York: Cambridge University Press.

43

What Can We Learn from This Tragedy? A Reaction Days after September 11, 2001

Can the recent tragedy on our own shores teach us empathy for all people?

Who does not agree that the perpetrators of the horrible acts of last Tuesday must be stopped and punished? But more is necessary to combat terrorism. Feelings of injustice, disregard, deprivation, and humiliation are significant roots of terrorism. When people with deep grievances are unable to get any kind of redress, a breeding ground for terrorism exists. Such people will not necessarily turn to terrorism. They may turn against each other or even against their families. Or they may simply suffer.

But the possibility of taking action in their own behalf or the behalf of their family or group will be very appealing. And violent actions are often framed by "leaders," whatever the leaders' motives, as expressions of higher ideals, such as the welfare of their people, serving justice, or the will of God. People in pain and others who identify with them can replace helplessness with a sense of meaning and purpose by striking out against those they see as their enemies, or the enemies of these higher ideals.

I believe the United States is a special target for terrorism for several reasons. One is that many people see some of our actions as a nation and some of the actions of U.S. corporations as contributor to their own and others' suffering. Another is that we are a source of and a symbol of great changes in the contemporary world. As the foremost and most successful practitioners of capitalism, and as a source of many contemporary cultural trends that contribute to change, overturn tradition, and thereby create confusion about how to live life, both people whose lives are difficult and those whose lives have been deeply affected by circumstance and change see us, or can be led to see us, as responsible.

Versions of this commentary were published in the *Springfield Union-News*, Springfield, MA, on September 30, 2001, and in the Winter 2001 *Newsletter of the Society for the Study of Peace, Conflict and Violence: Peace Psychology Division of the American Psychological Association*.

To stop terrorism, our great and powerful country must become more concerned with the fate of people everywhere. Tragedy can bring people together and create caring and empathy. In New York and across the country people have been reaching out to each other in moving and striking ways. We can create more satisfying lives for ourselves by holding on to such generosity and concern about our fellow Americans in more normal times. In a similar spirit, our pain ought to lead us to open our hearts to people's suffering everywhere.

A coalition of many nations is needed to exert many forms of influence and stop nations from "hosting" or sponsoring terrorists. But such a coalition should also act to help people in refugee camps, or living in great poverty, at times due to systems that limit their rights and opportunities. Help by economic aid, but at least as importantly by providing expertise and training, by promoting true democracy, by doing whatever caring nations can do. Such a coalition would be impossible to maintain, and a spirit of empathy would die, if we indiscriminately bombed and killed many innocent people in response to the violence we have suffered.

If we truly expand our empathy, we will stop being passive bystanders to the many kinds of suffering in the world. We will not again be passive in the face of the extraordinary suffering of people who are victims of mass killing and genocide. When during the Holocaust the Allies, flying near Auschwitz to bomb factories, were asked to bomb the railroads leading there, or the gas chambers where huge numbers of people were killed every day, those responsible decided that no plane could be spared for this. When hundreds of thousands of people were being killed in Rwanda, with pictures of a river filled with bodies, the world did nothing. The U.S. even slowed down the return of some peacekeepers that was contemplated.

If we as a nation become more caring about the lives and suffering of people everywhere, our lives will be enriched. Just as it is enriched today when we act, or just see our fellow Americans act in behalf of others.

PART VI

CREATING CARING, MORALLY INCLUSIVE, PEACEFUL SOCIETIES

44

Changing Cultures and Society

For wide-ranging change in personalities to occur, changes in culture and social institutions are required, and vice versa. Change can be initiated at any point. However, it is essential, when change begins in the personalities and values of groups of individuals, that this be followed by or codified in change in the culture: that is, changes in the functioning of institutions or the creation of new institutions. Such cultural change is required for individual change to be supported and for it to spread to a substantial degree. It is the actions of collectivities, of groups, and of nations that create antagonism or build positive connection and cooperation.

CREATING SYSTEMS OF POSITIVE RECIPROCITY

Frequently, those concerned with peace focus on already existing antagonisms and hostility. For example, relations between the United States and the U.S.S.R. have been characterized by a cycle of negative reciprocity and retaliation for harmful actions, imagined or real (Deutsch, 1983: Osgood, 1962; White, 1984). Proposals for change often focus on halting or reversing the cycle, for example, by unilateral positive acts designed to encourage reciprocation by the other party (Osgood, 1962; White, 1984). The focus of such proposals has usually been arms control and disarmament, with the hope that reciprocal actions can lead to a diminished nuclear threat.

However, research on reciprocity indicates that reactions to another's behavior greatly depend on the intentions attributed to the other (Schopler, 1970; Staub, 1978). If seemingly positive acts are believed to result from selfish intentions (for instance, the desire to gain benefits by inducing

Reprinted from E. Staub (1988). The evolution of caring and nonaggressive persons and societies. In R. Wagner, J. De Rivera, and M. Watkins (Eds.), Psychology and the promotion of peace. *Journal of Social Issues*, 44(2), 81–100. Included here are pp. 93–100. Reprinted by permission of Blackwell Publishers Ltd.

reciprocity), they will frequently not be reciprocated. When devaluative stereotypes and ideologies of antagonism exist – when nations are already in a system of negative reciprocity – they are frequently too untrusting of each other either to initiate or to respond to acts that they believe might weaken their security.

For a negative system of reciprocity to change, for trust to evolve, the parties may often need to begin by initiating positive acts in very simple, risk-free ways. They can move from diplomatic contact to cultural and academic exchanges, to cooperation in activities that do not require substantial trust, to more significant and potentially self-sacrificial acts. At times, however, highly significant positive initiatives do find an immediate response, as in the case of Anwar Sadat's offer to go to Jerusalem. The danger to Sadat was probably seen as evidence of his positive intentions. The more convincing is the demonstration of positive intent, the more likely is a positive response (Schopler, 1970).

Creating positive reciprocity is also important when no antagonism or hostility exists. It is an important aspect of positive inter-group and international relations, and in turn it contributes to cultural-societal change – to positive conceptions of the other, to a changed view of one's group in relation to others, and to the creation of institutions that serve cooperation.

CROSS-CUTTING RELATIONS

Positive reciprocity between groups can take place with relatively little direct contact among members, or it can provide opportunity for contact. Lack of contact helps create and maintain us – them differentiation and judgments of differentness in values, beliefs, and ways of life. *Cross-cutting relations,* a term proposed by Morton Deutsch (1973), are essential to develop an appreciation of alikeness as human beings and a feeling of connectedness. Deutsch used the term to refer to the integration and joining of societal subgroups in work, in education, or in recreation. Cultural and educational exchanges and joint projects provide opportunities for cross-cutting relations between nations. For positive feelings and connection to result, it is essential to educate members of both groups about each other's work habits, customs, interpersonal styles, and the like. Otherwise cultural differences may irritate and provoke.

Significant joint projects can serve the self-interest of each party and provide vehicles for cross-cutting relations. Such projects can serve shared, superordinate goals (Sherif, 1966; Worchel, 1979) that are more important than the separate and potentially conflicting interests of each party. Joint cultural, scientific, and technical endeavors can include such diverse projects as filmmaking, AIDS research, and international manufacturing projects, and they can lead to extensive and politically significant projects like joint space exploration. Progressively, an international economic (and scientific and cultural) order may evolve in which all countries have a stake. Maintaining this economic order then would become another superordinate goal.

Scientists, academics, artists, and businessmen can all make important contributions to such developments. For example, many scientific organizations and groups work for disarmament and peace. They spend a great deal of energy on educating the public about nuclear issues, lobbying for arms control, and developing relations with like-minded scientists in other countries. They could expand their contributions by designing, lobbying for, and executing joint projects. The psychological and practical interconnectedness of a wide range of individuals and of nations offers the promise of a peaceful world, and the institutions that evolve for designing and administering such projects become new social realities.

STEPS ALONG THE CONTINUUM OF BENEVOLENCE

Not only children but also adults become more helpful as a result of their own prior helping (De Jong, 1979; Freedman & Fraser, 1966; Harris, 1972: Staub, 1978). Acting to benefit others can result in personal changes that lead to more significant helping. It can promote a more positive evaluation of the welfare of people who have benefited from one's actions and of people in general, and a perception of oneself as a caring person willing to extend effort and make sacrifices for others' sake. It can lead to increased concern for and commitment to others' welfare (Eisenberg & Cialdini, 1984; Grusec, 1981; Staub, 1975, 1979, 1986).

Hostility and antagonism between groups that result in genocide or war frequently represent the end point of a progression, an evolution. Whole groups, not only individuals, learn and change as a result of their own actions. Hostile or harmful actions by a group often represent *steps along a continuum of destruction* that prepare them for more violent acts (Staub, 1989). Similarly, caring and benevolence can evolve, and a group's own positive actions can be steps that prepare them for greater benevolence.

We need to greatly expand the opportunities for both children and adults to act in others' behalf. My experience with a variety of relevant research studies indicates that children would willingly do a great deal in others' behalf, given the opportunity, the chance to choose activities that fit their inclinations, and some guidance by socializers. Adults' participation in helping others is also essential, if they are to guide children to such activities, and if the values of caring and connection are to evolve in a group. There is substantial involvement by Americans in volunteer activities, and the range of voluntary community service in America is great, from providing transportation for old people to contributing to United Way (Harmon, 1982). In England, volunteering to donate blood has become widely practiced, contributing to a spirit of community (Titmus, 1971). Those concerned with peace need to focus their attention on this basic means of fostering personal and cultural change, generating ideas and creating opportunities for needed service to others at home and abroad. Acting to satisfy human needs and producing real benefits to others can be highly satisfying. Thus, such programs, once started, can inspire many people to participate in them.

Part of this effort must be to create opportunities for help across group and national lines. The Peace Corps is a model of service to people in other countries. Mutual Peace Corps programs among nations, so that each party provides service to the other, would be especially valuable. Advanced technical or academic knowledge should not be a prerequisite for this. At the least, everybody can teach others about their own customs and ways of life. Such mutual Peace Corps programs would include all the essential components of change that I have discussed: individuals acting to benefit others, cross-cutting relations among peoples, and a system of positive reciprocity among nations.

Important public figures can help create both inspiration and practical possibilities for such activities, as in John F. Kennedy's call, which led many people to join the Peace Corps. National leaders can exert great influence in creating positive attitudes, as Richard Nixon did by his visit to China and Sadat did by his visit to Jerusalem. If such temporary positive attitudes are translated into positive actions and supporting institutions, lasting change will result. Peace workers' success in educating the public and influencing politicians to initiate such actions and programs will be more likely if their focus is on basic ways of relating to people in other nations rather than on domains of conflict and competition. Positive acts that focus on human connection and basic human welfare may be relatively uncontroversial, thus preparing the way for further progress along the continuum of benevolence.

ROLES FOR WRITERS, ARTISTS, AND THE MEDIA

Books, films, and other cultural products sometimes have substantial impacts on the attitudes, beliefs, and actions of whole societies. *Dr. Strangelove* and *The Day After* are examples of films that mobilized the public spirit, and the BBC television report on starvation in Ethiopia resulted in a worldwide effort to help. Those devoted to creating a peaceful world must work to recruit artists, writers, and the media to this effort. Educational efforts about us – them differentiation, enemy images, ideologies of antagonism, and the sources of violence and war, should particularly be directed toward those who shape the public awareness. Members of the peace movement need to make continuous efforts to establish personal contact with those who work in the public domain in order to make them aware of their potential contribution in diminishing cultural-societal predispositions to violence and enhancing positive orientations toward outside groups.

CONCLUSION

To create a world characterized by the values and practices of caring and cooperation among groups, and to reduce the predisposition for inter-group conflict and group violence, committed groups of individuals must work for long-term change. Tendencies toward hostility and violence cannot be directly changed. They will change as socialization practices promote in children a positive orientation to other human beings, and as positive acts and cross-cutting relations among groups result in changed values, changed self-concepts, changed attitudes toward other groups, and changes in culture and social institutions.

References

DeJong, W. (1979). An examination of self-perception mediation of the foot-in-the-door effect. *Journal of Personality and Social Psychology, 37,* 2221–2239.

Deutsch, M. (1973). *The resolution of conflict: Constructive and destructive processes.* New Haven, CT: Yale University Press.

Deutsch, M. (1983). The prevention of World War III: A psychological perspective. *Political Psychology, 4,* 3–31.

Eisenberg, N., & Cialdini. R. B. (1984). The role of consistency pressures in behavior: A developmental perspective. *Academic Psychology Bulletin, 6,* 115–126.

Freedman, J. L., & Fraser, S. C. (1966). Compliance without pressure: The foot-in-the-door technique. *Journal of Personality and Social Psychology, 4,* 195–202.

Grusec, J. (1981). Socialization processes and the development of altruism. In J. P. Rushton & R. M. Sorrentino (Eds.), *Altruism and helping behavior* (pp. 65–91). Hillsdale, NJ: Erlbaum.

Harmon, J. D. (Ed.). (1982).*Volunteerism in the eighties*. Washington, DC: University Press of America.

Harris, M. B. (1972). The effect of performing one altruistic act on the likelihood of performing another. *Journal of Social Psychology, 88,* 65–73.

Osgood, C. E. (1962). *An alternative to war or surrender*. Urbana: University of Illinois Press.

Schopler, J. (1970). An attribution analysis of some determinants of reciprocating a benefit. In J. Macaulay & L. Berkowitz (Eds.), *Altruism and helping behavior* (pp. 231–241). New York: Academic Press.

Sherif, M. (1966). *In common predicament: Social psychology of intergroup conflict and cooperation.* Boston: Houghton Miffin.

Staub, E. (1975). To rear a prosocial child: Reasoning, learning by doing, and learning by teaching others. In D. DePalma & J. Folley (Eds.), *Moral development: Current theory and research* (pp. 113–136). Hillsdale, NJ: Erlbaum.

Staub, E. (1978). *Positive social behavior and morality: Social and personal influences* (Vol. 1). New York: Academic Press.

Staub, E. (1979). *Positive social behavior and morality: Socialilization and development* (Vol. 2). New York: Academic Press.
Staub, E. (1981). Promoting positive behavior in schools, in other educational settings, and in the home. In J. P. Rushton & R. M. Sorrentino (Eds.), *Altruism and helping behavior* (pp. 109–134). Hillsdale, NJ: Erlbaum.
Staub, E. (1986). A conception of the determinants and development of altruism and aggression: Motives, the self, the environment. In C. Zahn-Waxler, E. M. Cummings, & R. Ianotti (Eds.), *Altruism and aggression: Social and biological origins* (pp. 135–164). New York: Cambridge University Press.
Staub, E. (1989). *The roots of evil: The origins of genocide and other group violence.* New York: Cambridge University Press.
Titmus, R. (1971). *The gift relationship: From human blood to social policy.* New York: Pantheon Books.
White, R. K. (1984). *Fearful warriors: A psychological profile of U.S. – Soviet relations.* New York: Free Press.
Worchel, S. (1979). Cooperation and the reduction of intergroup conflict: Some determining factors. In W. G. Austin & S. Worchel (Eds.), *The social psychology of intergroup relations.* Monterey, CA: Brooks/Cole.

45

Transforming the Bystanders

Altruism, Caring, and Social Responsibility

THE PASSIVITY OF BYSTANDERS

People often remain passive both in the face of the mistreatment of groups of people, such as discrimination, torture, mass killing, and genocide, and in the face of events in their society that harm or endanger everyone, such as the destruction of the environment or the nuclear arms race. Socially responsible action is both similar to and different from helping and altruism directed at individuals. To the extent it derives from a feeling of responsibility, its focus is the social good, which includes one's own good but extends to one's group, other groups, and possibly all of humanity. Some of our knowledge of bystander passivity comes from researchs on emergency helping[1] and some from analyses of the psychology of perpetrators, bystanders, and heroic helpers in genocides and mass killings.[2]

Type I Bystanders: Passivity in the Face of Mistreatment and Violence

There are two categories of Type I bystanders. Those who witness the mistreatment of members of a group of their own society but remain passive are internal bystanders. They may accept demands by the perpetrators that they participate in the persecution, even gradually joining the group. Their silence and their semiactive role often encourage the perpetrators. For example, in Nazi Germany most Germans participated to a greater or lesser degree in the system the Nazis established. They boycotted stores, owned by Jews, broke off relations with Jewish friends, and so on. Some even initiated anti-Jewish actions before the government ordered them to – businesses fired Jewish employees or refused to give them paid vacations.[3]

Reprinted from E. Staub (1992). Transforming the bystanders: Altruism, caring, and social responsibility. In H. Fein (Ed.), *Genocide watch*. New Haven, CT: Yale University Press, from Ch. 10, 162–181. Included here are pp. 168–170, 172–181.

Other nations and outside groups who remain passive are external bystanders. By maintaining friendly relations with an offending nation, they also encourage the perpetrators. Coming to understand the psychology of bystanders, internal and external, can help us arrive at ways to increase caring and social responsibility.

Internal bystanders may legitimately fear an often brutal system, but that is an insufficient explanation for their passivity. In Germany people protested against the euthanasia program and brought it (though not all the killings) to an end,[4] but they did not protest the persecution of Jews. Outsiders may remain silent even when they have nothing to fear – as did the nations of the world and the corporations that conducted business with Germany between 1933 and 1939. Like internal bystanders, they come to support the persecutors through important symbolic gestures. The Olympics were held in Germany in 1936, for example, and Jewish runners were withdrawn from a U.S. relay team though Germany did not request it. And the United States sold oil to Germany in the mid-thirties, which helped its air war against Republican Spain.

Type II Bystanders: Passivity in the Face of Societal Issues

One reason for passivity among Type II bystanders is that the goals and values that predominate in a society may be contrary to caring and social responsibility. Acquisitiveness, a focus on self-interest, and an individualism that conflicts with and diminishes feelings of connection and community make moral values and social responsibility less important in the hierarchy of individual and group goals.

Another reason is that people tend to respond to the immediate. Earning a living, caring for children, and fulfilling everyday responsibilities are urgent tasks that detract from the impulse to take action toward fulfilling long-term group goals. The need to perform one's daily tasks is powerful enough to dominate even those people who have strong motives that promote caring and social responsibility. Moreover, it is one thing to have other-oriented goals and values and feel personal responsibility for the welfare of other individuals and another thing to feel responsible for broad human issues like the fate of minorities or the poor, the environment, or nuclear disarmament. Concern for broader issues, in most people, seems less developed, which makes internal activation of social goals and values unlikely. And to the extent that issues are abstract and remote, external activation is also less likely.

Diffusion of responsibility and pluralistic ignorance are other inhibitors of socially responsible feelings and action.[5] Some people may feel that it is the government's responsibility to act; others, that everyone in the group or all of humanity share the responsibility, thus diminishing individual responsibility and absolving the individual from the need to act. When there is limited public discussion of an issue, a condition of pluralistic ignorance exists. If no one seems concerned, the issue seems unimportant and action unnecessary. In addition, the authorities often define opposition to official policies (which may be creating or at least not addressing the problems) as unpatriotic and disloyal.

Finally, given the magnitude of societal problems, the individual's feeling of powerlessness inhibits action. Even if motives are strong, they will not be expressed in action unless the individual has some faith in the possibility of their fulfillment. How can one person stop discrimination and persecution of minorities or the devastation of the environment? In the real world, people acting alone have little influence in such large matters.

Given inaction, individuals shift awareness away from these issues to lessen their feelings of danger, personal responsibility, and guilt. The result is often called *denial*, although it does not fit the traditional psychoanalytic meaning of the term. Thoughts about such matters are avoided, but the issues are probably not repressed or denied in the psychoanalytic sense. Another term, *psychic numbing*, has been used to explain the relatively passive acceptance by people of the nuclear arms race in spite of the dangers it poses, but that term, too, does not seem to fit the phenomenon well. Psychic numbing is a diminished emotional responsiveness that results from severe trauma, such as the experience of nuclear attack in Hiroshima or other intense bombing, the experience of survivors of Nazi concentration camps, or the experience of combat.[6] It is unlikely to result from daily life in a Western post-industrial society, however threatening the possibility of nuclear war.

Perhaps similar and more straightforward explanations are the following. First, there is a kind of gating or screening of phenomena, given the overload of events in the modern world impinging on us. This is similar to Stanley Milgram's description of what happens to inhabitants of large cities.[7] Second, there is inattention to and avoidance of events and information that have a negative emotional impact on us, especially if we do not believe we have the capacity to deal with them, to control them. Nonetheless, desensitization and inattention to social issues are not of such a nature that people cannot be mobilized for action.

MOBILIZING BYSTANDERS

It is useful to know first what one hopes to accomplish by mobilizing bystanders. Ultimately, I would hope for a world in which human relationships are characterized by caring and connection, in the relations both of individuals and of groups. Human rights would be respected, which means not only safety from physical harm but also fulfillment of basic needs for food and shelter and thus at least minimal social justice. In the world I seek, individuals' psychological needs would not be met at the expense of others, and genuine conflicts would not be resolved through aggression. Connection and caring for others would be valued more than wealth and power. This would require at least a minimal feeling of security, which the group must provide; otherwise security will be sought by means of acquiring wealth and power.[8] A view of shared interests would contribute to socially responsible action.

For such a world to come about, children and adults in the long run must develop certain personal characteristics, such as a prosocial value orientation and empathy. As I noted earlier, socialization in the home and schools and certain experiences with other people shape these characteristics. Members of groups, whether nations or subgroups of societies, must develop an appreciation of one another's humanity. They need to initiate positive acts and respond to other's positive acts, which promotes reciprocity. Systems of positive reciprocity can be expanded by joint enterprises serving shared goals that are superordinate to individual and potentially conflicting goals. The realms for shared goals can include the environment, nuclear arms, economic cooperation, and other such matters. To further, evolve and maintain positive connections with and views of others, people need to develop cross-cutting relations; members of different groups must be integrated in their living, working, and playing together.[9]

The Value of Self-Awareness and Information

Self-awareness can minimize the impact of the psychological processes that inhibit caring, helping, and socially responsible actions and that promote moral exclusion. Disseminating information and education can be extremely useful to create self-awareness. Building awareness both of human tendencies for us-them differentiation and for devaluing those who suffer and of how the words and actions of other bystanders may inhibit us from responding to individual suffering and societal problems can reduce the power of such inhibitory forces. My belief in this is fortified by my impression of greater sensitivity in students exposed to such information and by research showing that information about inhibiting conditions increases later helping behavior in emergencies.[10]

Education needs to go beyond the simple dissemination of information, however. It should include training and experience that help people observe and catch themselves devaluing sufferers or thinking that victims have brought on their suffering by their own actions or character and thus deserve to suffer. It needs to raise awareness in people of the influence of their own needs on their thinking and actions.

Providing information has additional value. Frequently people avoid becoming involved with others' needs, or with societal and world issues, as they busily pursue their own private lives. But if they become aware of the intensity and urgency of the needs of other people or of problems in their society and the world, they are more likely to take action. The outpouring of aid to starving Ethiopians in the mid-1980s was stimulated by a television program about them.

Information about the lives, circumstances, feelings, habits, and customs of people who are persecuted or of those with persistent need (such as the homeless) can increase individuals' attention and concern. Education and information that stresses the shared humanity of different groups of people, their shared needs and aspirations, can promote their inclusion in one's moral realm. It can also lead to a consideration of the balance of one's own and others' needs and awareness of one's advantage, which can activate caring. Information that expands knowledge about the environment, nuclear arms, the economic interdependence of the world, and problematic government policies will expand cognitive networks and the impact of these issues on thought, feelings, and action.

Abstractions do not suffice to humanize persons and groups, and to bring to life general societal and global issues. As Tversky and Kahneman have suggested, people need "availability heuristics," images or memories by which they can make hypothetical possibilities real.[11] Facts alone do not provide these heuristics. Distant issues must be brought near both by enlarging knowledge about them through the creation of availability heuristics – that is, by making real the suffering of people or the potential impact of conditions like environmental pollution on individual lives – and by showing their relevance for the self and for important personal goals.

To help individuals overcome the feeling of personal helplessness, information should be disseminated about the tremendous potential power of bystanders. There is much evidence showing that people can greatly influence the behavior of others. This has been demonstrated in both experimental research[12] and real-life events.[13] For example, in Nazi Europe the behavior of a sympathetic population[14] and that of a group of helpers-rescuers[15] repeatedly influenced not only other bystanders but also perpetrators. The nineteenth-century abolitionists are another example of the impact strong commitment can have. Research findings have also shown that a minority, by clearly and strongly expressing its attitudes and beliefs, can greatly influence majority views.[16]

But even when individuals become aware of the potential of bystanders to exert influence, they can still feel personally helpless and ineffective if they do not know avenues for effective action. They need to learn how they, if they act, can contribute to ultimate goals and to become aware of meaningful intermediate goals – in other words, how to measure and appreciate progress. Other factors that encourage continued involvement in efforts that usually bring only slow results include support by like-minded others, strong values, and as a result of engaging in action, the development of a principled commitment to action itself.

In fact, antinuclear activists, in contrast to nonactivists, tend to believe more in their political power. As they act they become more knowledgeable about what can be done. In addition, once they are involved, they come to depend less on actual results, but continue to act because they see action as necessary and right. With their actions congruent with their values, with their whole motivational system probably more integrated,[17] these activists acquire an increased sense of inner integrity.[18]

For effective action, it is important to approach and engage in dialogue with members of the media, writers, politicians, and others who can reach the public. But the potential influence of every person must be made clear: in speaking to others and influencing others' knowledge and ways of thinking; in initiating behavior that benefits others, changes the self, and brings about reciprocal actions that build connections; in initiating cross-cutting relations; and so on.

The Self and Its Relationship to Others

An individual's embeddedness in a group can reduce the person's likelihood of responding to the group's harming those in subgroups as well as to official policies that are potentially destructive. There has been recent recognition that the valuing of autonomous selves that characterizes Western thinking is not universal, but that various groups value and promote different forms of the development of identity and the self-concept. Some promote a self-definition that is more relational: other people are part of the self-concept, or connection to others is inherent in the self, or the boundaries of the self are fluid. Some authors in the past decade have suggested that women in our society have more relational selves.[19] Gilligan has also suggested that women's morality is based on care and responsibility, whereas men's is based on rules and logic.[20] Whether these differences are tied to gender or not, the possibility they suggest of different types of connections between self and others is important. In some Asian societies individual selves are less delineated, less autonomous, more inherently relational.[21]

Family and couples therapists stress that for people to function well in modern families good differentiation must exist between themselves and both people in their families of origin and their current mates. But those with autonomous, self-contained identities may have more difficulty in developing values that lead them to respond to the needs of other persons or to act to promote the social good.

On the other hand, people who have undifferentiated selves and are *embedded* in a group cannot arrive at an independent definition of reality or take action against a destructive course the group might be pursuing. The capacity to be separate is required for "group-awareness" – self-awareness extended to one's group – and for critical consciousness, the capacity to hold views different from those dominant in the group. It is also required for "critical loyalty," the ability to oppose group policies and practices that one sees as destructive or as carrying a destructive potential. Japanese culture has traditionally promoted connection between the individual and the group – and kamikaze pilots may have been one result.

We need to create a third category to make sense of the findings and theoretical ideas, that of the *embedded self*. As I define it, the relational or *connected* self is less self-contained and more connected to others than an autonomous self, but the person is differentiated and flexible and can separate the self from others and from the group. An embedded self is less differentiated than a connected self and its identity more defined by group membership, whether the group is the family or a nation.[22] The authoritarian child rearing and schools that characterized Germany before World War II made it difficult to develop either autonomous or connected selves and tended to give rise to embedded selves.[23] We must strive to create cultures and institutions that promote the evolution of connected selves.

To mobilize people it is necessary to show the relationship of issues, causes, and events to their selves, desires, values, and ideals. But when we appeal to ideals, we must keep in mind the destruction that has been wrought in the name of higher ideals. The improvement of the world must not become an abstraction; it must be grounded in the welfare of individual human beings. In that framework the future of children, the shared humanity of all people, the satisfactions of connections and of helping others in need, the ideals of peace and justice, can appeal to many.

It has been claimed that opposing the policies of the government and the attitude of the majority is unpatriotic. But the true benefits of such opposition to the group, how opposition serves important values, should be recognized. The mistreatment of groups of people within one's society, the mistreatment of people in other countries, the destruction of the environment, and the nuclear arms race seem diverse issues. What connects them is the valuing of persons and groups, the valuing of human welfare, and the great potential of bystanders to make a difference.

Notes

1. B. Latané & J. Darley, The *unresponsive bystander: Why doesn't he help*? (New York: Appleton-Century-Crofts, 1970); Staub, *Positive social behavior*, vol. 1.
2. Staub, *The roots of evil*.
3. R. Hilberg, *The destruction of the European Jews* (New York: Harper and Row, 1961).
4. Robert J. Lifton, *The Nazi doctors: Medical killing and the psychology of genocide* (New York: Basic Books, 1986).
5. Latané and Darley, *The unresponsive bystander*.
6. Robert J. Lifton, *The broken connection: On death and the continuity of life* (New York: Touchstone Books, 1979).

7. Stanley Milgram, "The Experience of Living in Cities," *Science 167* (1970): 1461–1468.
8. Staub, *The roots of evil.*
9. Ibid.
10. A. Beaman, et al. "Increasing Helping Rates through Information Dissemination: Teaching Pays," *Personality and Social Psychology Bulletin* 4 (1978): 406–411.
11. A. Tversky & D. Kahneman, "Judgment under Uncertainty: Heuristics and Biases," *Science 185* (1974): 1124–1131.
12. L. Bickman, "Social Influence and Diffusion of Responsibility in an Emergency," *Journal of Experimental and Social Psychology 8* (1972): 438–445; Staub, "Helping a Distressed Person."
13. Staub, *The roots of evil.*
14. Fein, *Accounting for genocide* (New York: Free Press, 1979).
15. P. P. Hallie, *Lest innocent blood be shed: The story of the village of Le Chambon, and how goodness happened there* (New York: Harper and Row, 1979); Staub, *The roots of evil.*
16. S. Moscovici, "Toward a Theory of Conversion Behavior," in *Current issues in social psychology*, ed. L. Berkowitz (New York: Academic Press, 1980).
17. Staub, *The roots of evil.*
18. M. G. Locatelli & R. R. Holt, "Antinuclear Activism, Psychic Numbing, and Mental Health," *International Journal of Mental Health* (special issue, "Mental Health Implications of Life in the Nuclear Age," ed. M. Schwebel) *15* (1986): 143–162.
19. J. Surrey, *Self-in-relation: A theory of women's development* (Wellesley, Mass.: Stone Center, Wellesley College, 1985).
20. C. Gilligan, *In a different voice: Psychological theory and women's development* (Cambridge: Harvard University Press, 1982).
21. J. R. Weiss, F. M. Rothbaum, & T. C. Blackburn, "Standing Out and Standing In: The Psychology of Control in America and Japan," *American Psychologist* 39 (1984): 955–969.
22. Ervin Staub, "Individual and Group Selves, Motivation and Morality," in *Morality and the self*, ed. W. Edelstein & T. Wren (Cambridge: MIT Press, 1993); see also Chapter 27, in this book.
23. A. Miller, *For your own good: Hidden cruelty in child-rearing and the roots of violence* (New York: Farrar, Straus & Giroux, 1983); Staub, *The roots of evil.*

46

Blind versus Constructive Patriotism

Moving from Embeddedness in the Group to Critical Loyalty and Action

We constantly see in the world what may be called blind patriotism: an intense alignment by people with their nation or group and uncritical acceptance of and support for its policies and practices, with an absence of moral consideration of their consequences or disregard of their impact on the welfare of human beings who are outside the group or are members of its subgroups. There is celebration of any apparent gain by the group regardless of the means by which it is achieved, a tendency to act in the spirit of the dictum "my country right or wrong." Blind patriotism often has destructive consequences not only for other groups, but ultimately for one's own group as well. What are its origins, and might there be desirable, ideal, or "constructive" forms of patriotism?

When a government or a dominant group in society embarks on a destructive course of action that may ultimately lead to mass killing, genocide, or war, reactions by the population have the potential to inhibit the evolution of greater destructiveness (Staub, 1989). But usually the "bystanders," members of the population who are not directly involved as either perpetrators or victims, remain passive. In part, this is due to blind patriotism, which leads to loyalty to the group regardless of the nature of its conduct, or at least creates an embeddedness in the group that makes it difficult to oppose its direction.

In dictionary definitions love and devotion to one's country are central aspects of patriotism (for example, *Webster's*, 1967). For Bar-Tal (1993) "... in its fundamental form patriotism refers to attachment of group members to their group and the country in which they reside," and "the basic element of patriotism is the desire to belong to a group which is positively evaluated" (p. 48).

Reprinted from E. Staub (1997). Blind versus constructive patriotism: Moving from embeddedness in the group to critical loyalty and action. In D. Bar-Tal and E. Staub (Eds.), *Patriotism in the lives of individuals and groups*. Chicago: Nelson-Hall Publishers, from Ch. 10, 213–228.

On the one hand, people can be led by their attachment and desire to belong, to positively value and uncritically support any action of their group (blind patriotism). On the other hand, their attachment to the group can lead people to stand up against the policies and actions of the group that they see as betrayal of the group's basic values, or basic human values, or as contrary to the group's interests in the long run (constructive patriotism). By doing so they go beyond defending the identity of the group. They participate in the incessant task of *constructing* a positive identity for the group.

Since policies, practices, institutions, and cultures are always imperfect, and require change as social conditions and circumstances in the world change, and since national policies and practices are conducted by governments made up of individuals who have varying worldviews, individual personalities, and responses to events, the capacity and willingness by citizens to engage in corrective actions is essential. However, individuals can also be blindly patriotic by unquestioning adherence to a political movement or party that claims to serve the group or the nation by advocating policies and practices that ignore the welfare and rights of others. In the name of patriotism such groups can oppose a government that attempts to carry out humane and reasonable policies. The Nazis in their opposition to the Weimar Republic provide one of many possible examples. Thus blind versus constructive patriotism as types of attachments and beliefs can be tied to entities like nations or governments, leaders, or political movements.

Constructive patriotism requires balancing attachment to and consideration for the well-being of one's own group with an inclusive orientation to human beings, with respect for the rights and welfare of all people. In its everyday practice it requires gathering information, questioning, and evaluation, and the willingness to take corrective action even if that goes contrary to current government policy or powerful political forces. Its last stage, corrective action, often requires courage, since governments and traditionally patriotic groups usually do what they can to define "true" patriotism as loyalty to themselves and their ideas that allows no questioning and criticism, that is, as blind patriotism.

Both the benefits and destructive potentials of patriotism have been noted in the past, and distinctions have been drawn between "good" and "bad" kinds of patriotism. Their conceptualizations have varied greatly, including military versus civic patriotism (Curti, 1946) and pseudopatriotism versus genuine patriotism (Adorno et al., 1950). These and related distinctions have not been greatly elaborated or extensively explored. In this chapter the concepts of blind and constructive patriotism, their nature, and their origins are developed in detail. The next chapter includes empirical evidence collected to support the distinction between these two forms of patriotism and to explore their nature.

THE ROOTS OF BLIND PATRIOTISM

Blind patriotism requires uncritical loyalty to an entity like the nation or state, and to a conception, vision, or ideology and related practices that purport to serve that entity. It also requires the absence or the willingness to disregard moral values that demand consideration for the welfare of human beings not included in the entity or group that is the object of one's patriotic attachment. What are the social experiences in the course of the development of a child and the attendant psychological processes that serve blind patriotism?

Us–Them Differentiation

Children have a biologically based tendency to create differentiations among people. Strong attachment to caretakers and fear of strangers begin to manifest themselves about the same time, around six months of age. But both positive attachment, secure rather than anxious or ambivalent, and experience with varied strangers seem to decrease stranger anxiety (Shaffer, 1988).

However, through experiential learning, as they are guided to interact with members of their own group but not with others, through exposure to the devaluation of certain others that is part of most cultures, and through modeling the words and actions of others, children usually come to distance themselves from and regard those outside the group as different, alien, and less good. Piaget and Weil (1951) have shown that Swiss children developed clear stereotypes of other nations, usually devaluative, by nine to ten years of age. The strong differentiation that children learn between "us" and "them," and the tendency to devalue "them" and/or elevate "us" relative to them (Brewer, 1978; Staub, 1989; Tajfel et al., 1971), is one source of blind patriotism. They enable children and the adults they become to exclude people outside their group from the moral realm (Opotow, 1990; Staub, 1990) and to disregard their rights and well-being, especially when they see them as in conflict with the interests of their own group.

The Rootedness of Personal Identity in the Group

A second source of blind patriotism is the nature of personal identity. We are social beings and define ourselves in terms of our relationship to others; in particular, our identity is rooted in the groups to which we belong. Patriotism is one outcome of this. An important answer to the question "Who am I?" is the answer, "I am a member of this group." Both children's physical and psychological embeddedness in their own group, and the way the group is emphasized in most groups, make group membership a central aspect of people's self-definition. Tajfel (1978) stressed the importance of social identity, which is the part of the self-concept that derives from membership in the social group and the value and emotional significance attached to that membership. In addition to the rootedness of their personal identity in the group, or a social identity, people also acquire a group self-concept, a conception of the group that is normally shared with other members.

The rootedness of the self in the social group is probably unavoidable and in certain forms highly beneficial. Once upon a time the group in which the self was rooted may have been the tribe, or even an extended family. But as several authors have suggested, in the modern age it tends to be the nation (Berlin, 1979; Mack, 1983). However, since attachment to and rootedness in groups other than country or society can also serve identity building and maintaining functions, patriotism may be a usual, not the one and only essential group source of identity.

Individuals vary in the *extent* to which and the *manner* in which their personal identity is rooted in and derives from their group identity. That is, blind and constructive patriotism can be stable personal characteristics. Groups can socialize children in ways that promote or lessen the rootedness of individual identity in group identity and shape its form of expression as constructive or blind patriotism.

However, since rootedness in the group has important functions not only for the individual but also for maintaining the group, (Schatz, 1993), groups usually regard it as essential to get the loyalty of citizens. An important element of socialization in most societies is the development of this loyalty to the group. This happens in many ways, including the teaching of geography, the group's (idealized) history, and the provision of examples of heroic patriotism, with the result that in people's psychological interior the group will have a dominant place.

While blind and constructive patriotism are stable characteristics of persons and their predominance will vary across groups, social conditions can also increase or decrease their presence in a group. Frequently, when the need for a positive personal identity is unfulfilled, people will turn to and seek satisfaction from a positive group identity, from being members of a valued group. This tends to happen, for example, when people face difficult conditions of life in their society with which, as individuals, they cannot cope effectively. These difficult conditions include economic problems, political conflict and disorganization, and great, rapid social change (Staub, 1989).

To gain a positive identity from their group, people tend in difficult times to elevate it, often by devaluing or through group violence diminishing others. In doing so they come to idealize their own group more which makes their allegiance to it more rigid and promotes blind patriotism (Staub, 1989). Whether difficult life conditions or other conditions (e.g., external threat to the group) move people to more intense and more unquestioning allegiance to the group in its existing form (e.g., the government or current leaders), or whether they turn to alternative symbols, authorities, and political movements, or even abandon the group (e.g., emigrate), depends also on cultural and contextual influences.

For example, in Germany, elements of the historical and cultural background, including the history of monarchy, the hierarchical organization of society, and the strong respect of authority, created a great deal of hostility to the Weimar Republic. Many Germans did not see it as a true representative of Germany and Germanness. As a result, in response to intensely difficult life conditions, they found alternative objects for identification and expressions of their patriotism, like communism on the one hand, or Nazism and other right-wing movements on the other (Staub, 1989).

Dimensions of the Self: Security, Types of Connectedness

Personal identity, that is, the self, has many dimensions. Some are relevant to patriotism and help determine its form, whether blind or constructive. Individuals may grow up feeling secure in the world, or insecure and defensive. While varied elements of personality are likely to influence the nature of a person's patriotism (aspects of personal identity, values, political beliefs), a secure identity is likely to diminish blind patriotism, since it makes standing apart, on one's own, more possible. An intense connection to a group or political movement can be motivated by the need to compensate for an insecure self and enhance feelings of personal security.

Other relevant dimensions of personal identity or self are the degree and *nature* of its connectedness to other people and/or the group. The latter variation may be conceptualized as ranging from disconnection, to autonomy, to connection, to embeddedness (Staub, 1993).

Disconnected people may be seen as people who have developed an identity that is walled off, separate, and resists entering into connection with others. Autonomous people have developed individuated selves, with a capacity to stand on their own. While they can also learn to develop connection to others, and experience caring for others, connection and caring are not inherent aspects of their developing and developed selves (Staub, 1993).

Recent advances in self theory have struggled with the strong emphasis on the autonomous self in Western societies, particularly the United States. It has been noted that in many societies people develop selves that are more connected or tied to others (Sampson, 1988, described this as ensembled individualism). Feminist psychologists have proposed that women, rather than developing autonomous selves, develop selves-in-relation (Surrey, 1985) in the course of their normal development. Thus both the possibility and existence of developing selves that are inherently tied to or connected to others have been proposed.

But there is a danger for group function of selves tied to others. Deep connection can make it difficult to stand apart from the group and resist or oppose its other members, or the direction set by leaders, whether the group is the nation, a political party or movement, a church, or any other group. But standing apart, questioning, opposing, and resisting may be required at times to halt a destructive evolution in the group and is an aspect of constructive patriotism. I have differentiated, therefore, between *connected* and *embedded* selves, as two ways that the self can be tied to others (Staub, 1993).

Connected individuals develop in connection, and connection (and caring) become integral to their identity. This is similar to the concept offered by the Stone Center of selves-in-relation (Surrey, 1985). But in my conception individuals with connected selves also develop a sense of individuality and the capacity to separate themselves from other people and the group. In contrast, embedded individuals have not become separated and individuated. Theirs is a self dependent on other people and the group, and embedded in the group; a self that is incomplete on its own, and must be sustained through unbroken connection (Staub, 1993). While positive connection to others is a basic human need (Staub, 1996), and all people require connection over time to maintain their psychological integrity, individuals with connected selves can endure disconnection and standing in opposition to others when this is required to fulfill their important values, while embedded individuals cannot.

Culture and socialization promote different types of selves. For example, the United States has been regarded as a country that promotes autonomous selves, Japan as a country that promotes deep ties (Weiss, Rothbaum, & Blackburn, 1984) of a kind that may be described as embeddedness. Japanese socialization does foster the capacity to stand on one's own in dealing with members of other groups. This capacity seems to be based on a confidence that accompanies a feeling of oneness with one's group, which in turn makes it difficult to take a critical stance in relation to it.

Social psychologists have written about individuals who adopt a group identity and do not differentiate between personal identity and group identity, in ways that overlap with the concept of embeddedness (see, for example, Tajfel, 1993). Jarymowitz (1991) found that persons who show less differentiation between self and we schemas are more likely to categorize people in terms of their group membership. She believes that the personal identity of such people is not well developed and their social identity is dominant.

Autonomous selves can also pose a problem for group function. Stress, frustration, threat to the self, or attack on the self can all result from individual circumstance or from difficult conditions of life shared by members of a society, such as economic problems, political conflict, or great social change. These tend to give rise to basic needs: the need for security, for a positive self-concept, for a comprehension of changing realities, for connection to others, and for hope (Staub, 1989). Instead of turning toward each other in mutual support, and working together to fulfill these basic, important needs, people who face difficult life conditions tend to become preoccupied with their own needs and compete for limited resources. An autonomous self makes turning toward others and fulfilling basic needs by joining others less likely. For example, during the Korean war Turkish prisoners of war were intensely supportive of each other, and fared better psychologically than American prisoners who offered each other little support (Kincaid, 1959).

Since the need for connection and mutual support is great in difficult times, and since turning toward others to receive or provide support and connection is more difficult for autonomous than connected (or embedded) persons, autonomous individuals may overcome their disconnection and isolation by joining together to fight "enemies." Scapegoating, ideologies that create enemies, and confrontation with other groups are all in part means of joining together, thereby fulfilling basic needs. They can generate blind patriotism and nationalism, or commitment to universalistic movements like communism, depending on the guiding ideology and its "ideals."

For individuals with embedded selves it is difficult to stand on their own. This will especially be the case when life conditions are difficult, which leads them, even more than other people, to look for guidance by leaders, rather than resist destructive leaders or group processes (Fromm, 1965; Staub, 1989). Their embeddedness would also make it especially difficult for them to deviate from the group, and therefore even to notice, much less speak out against, a destructive course of action.

THE INTERACTION OF SHARED CULTURE AND DIFFICULT LIFE CONDITIONS

Regardless of the type of self a group promotes, when it comes to the needs and interests of the group, and when the group faces stress, threat, or attack, it will demand submission of the individual to the group. It will demand that people function as if they were embedded in the group, that they follow its guidance.

The meaning of events at a particular time is defined, and goals are set, by individuals in positions of power and influence. Leaders control the apparatus of the state, and through it try to define the meaning of events in a unified way. They set goals and determine a course of action to fulfill them on the basis of this definition of reality. At certain times, such as in response to external threat and danger, the level of social control by leaders will increase and the availability of alternative information decrease.

In these cases individuals will strongly experience their "group" as the actor.

The tendency to support the group, or at least submit to it, is also strengthened by a shared culture. In spite of class and educational differences, leaders and group members are shaped and guided by the same basic culture. Culture, in its essence, is a shared perspective on events, shared worldviews and meanings, values, and rules. To the extent leaders' views and actions are formed by the culture they share with the people, their definition of events and identification of goals and actions will find resonance among the people.

One aspect of shared culture is a shared group self-concept. In certain groups the culture may evolve a view of the group as special and superior – and therefore as possessing special rights – that goes beyond "normal" ethnocentrism (Staub, 1989). The group self-concept of the United States includes, in my view, such a belief in the nation's superiority (Staub, 1991). This has contributed to the easy acceptance by citizens of state actions like the invasion of Grenada and Panama, or turning to war against Iraq (without sufficient diplomatic effort to attempt to bring about Iraq's withdrawal from Kuwait).

While all cultures tend to promote respect for authority and obedience to leaders, substantial variations exist. The more the culture promotes these, the more naturally will people accept their leaders' guidance, regardless of its direction. Such "authority orientation" creates a form of embeddedness. When life conditions in a society are very difficult, which usually creates social chaos and disorganization, people in an authority-oriented society will have an especially difficult time standing on their own in facing life problems. They will yearn for and seek guidance. Germany is a classic example of a country that promoted strong respect for and obedience to authority (Craig, 1982; Girard, 1980), cultural characteristics creating a predisposition for group violence (Staub, 1989).

Members of a society share the experience of conditions and events that affect the whole group. The similarity in their psychological reactions is enlarged by the shared culture, which mediates – diminishes or enhances the significance, and shapes the meaning of – the events and conditions. The United States, for example, has experienced moderately difficult conditions of life for several decades. Even positive social movements like feminism, the civil rights movement, and the anti–Vietnam War movement greatly affect relations between people and create social disorganization. There have also been changes in sexual mores, family structure and family life, drugs and violence on TV and in everyday life, and a relative loss by the United States of economic power and influence in the world. The impact of these conditions was enhanced by the societal self-concept of being superior, which was frustrated and challenged by life problems. The upsurge of patriotism after the war against Iraq began was partly the result of this combination of difficult life conditions and societal self-concept. The war reaffirmed for many citizens the strength, power, and superiority of the United States (Staub, 1991; Chapter 30, this volume).

Difficult life conditions give rise to intense needs, including the need to protect a positive view of one's identity. By focusing on the goodness, strength, or power of their group, people can strengthen and protect their own diminished and threatened identity. Thus, in difficult times, the group becomes more important. Similarly, when the group is threatened or is under attack, an intense feeling of "usness," of community and shared identity, strengthen feelings of security and individual identity.

Individuals tend to align themselves with their group, and the group tends to demand their loyalty, especially in times of difficulty, stress, or danger. As a result, even internal deviation from the group becomes extremely difficult. A perspective on events that is at odds with the group is dangerous, since it may eventually bring the person into outward conflict with the group. In contrast, merging with the group, giving oneself over to the group, has great psychological payoff. People can shed a powerless, ineffective, frustrated, and hence burdensome self. They can find connection, feel empowered, and even experience transcendence as they shift from self-focus to unity with a greater whole.

Given heterogeneity and pluralism in a society, as in the United States, subgroups of society tend to have varying and often conflicting values. This can have some very positive consequences: through contact and learning to work out differences in the public domain, intense devaluation of each other can diminish, which makes genocidal violence less likely (Staub, 1989). However, the differences among groups also diminish a sense of oneness. Responding to difficult life conditions by finding a shared external enemy, like Panama or Iraq, and rising above variations in ethnic, racial, or religious identifications and the attendant conflicts in values and goals, the resulting experience of unity can be especially satisfying.[1]

THE ORIGINS OF CONSTRUCTIVE PATRIOTISM

Ideally, individuals would develop a capacity for both critical consciousness and critical loyalty toward their group. Critical consciousness means the capacity to independently evaluate information, rather than simply adopt "group" (authority) perspectives on events. This requires at least minimal information about the true nature of events (which points to the

[1] Patriotism in the United States is especially strong, and the need to feel a sense of unity that overrides the country's pluralism may be one explanation for it. Another has been proposed by Janowitz (1985): that individualism in the United States and the attendant lack of community create feelings of aloneness and isolation, which in turn give rise to strong patriotism to ameliorate them.

role and importance of the media). It also requires knowledge of how information tends to be biased in one's group or influenced by its culture and political process.

Critical loyalty means commitment to the group's ultimate welfare and to universal human ideals and values, rather than to a policy or course of action adopted by the group at any particular time. It also means the willingness and capacity to deviate from – not support, but resist and attempt to change – the current direction of one's group, whether the group is the nation, state, or a political movement that itself is in opposition to existing governmental policies and actions. Critical loyalty requires that a person not be embedded in the group, and that he or she has bases for judgment that provide the grounds for an independent stance. These may be personal values or basic values of the group that stand in conflict with current practice.

There can be many criteria for judging a nation: how well it takes care of its citizens, in terms of security, material well-being, the opportunity for self-expression, and so on; to what extent there is justice and fairness in the treatment of different subgroups of society, whether these differences are ethnic, religious, or class-based; its relationship to other nations, whether friendly and cooperative or aggressive and seeking dominance; and so on. Many of these criteria involve the application of moral values, in terms of human welfare, justice, and inclusiveness, or the extent to which the rights and welfare of all citizens, as well as of human beings outside the nation's boundaries, are considered and respected.

Is one country's consideration of the well-being of individuals outside its borders a reasonable criterion for patriotism? Why should it not be? Is my love of a person not affected by his or her caring for versus cruelty toward people? Harming others can be justified, as in the case of necessary self-defense. But the acceptance of unnecessary violence toward others or indifference to others' fate are relevant criteria in evaluating and responding to the actions of one's nation.

How might critical consciousness and critical loyalty evolve? The core requirements for their existence include: a connected but not embedded self; self-awareness, knowledge of one's group, and knowledge of group processes that have a destructive potential; and the development of autonomous values. Socialization and experience at home and in schools can encourage critical consciousness and independence of judgment. Membership in varied groups can diminish embeddedness. The more people in a society practice critical consciousness and critical loyalty, the more they can support each other in the practice of constructive patriotism.

Might culture and social institutions evolve so that a society comes to value people speaking out in opposition to the current course of the group, and accepts, attends to, and even celebrates those who speak out and act in ways that offer society a mirror in which to see itself? A core question, both conceptual and practical, is that of the right balance between and synthesis of connection and community, on the one hand, and an independent perspective that enables people to act on universalistic human and moral values, on the other hand.

The Evolution of Caring and a Connected Self

I have proposed that people can develop connected selves. Inherent in such selves are connection and caring, as well as a firm identity with a capacity for independence, and thereby for critical consciousness and critical loyalty.

For such a self to develop, children require love and affection, which leads them to see and experience other people in a positive light. In an affectionate relationship, they can experience empathy from and with others. Children also require guidance that includes reasoning, so that rules become understandable, rooted in values, rather than arbitrary. They require the use of induction, or people pointing out to them the consequences of their behavior on other people – both harmful and helpful (Hoffman, 1970, 1975). This makes others important, enlarges awareness of others' inner experience and humanity, and leads to awareness by children of their responsibility toward others and capacity to diminish or improve others' welfare. The development of connected selves also requires guidance that leads children to reach out to others, to show caring and help, so that they learn by doing or participation (Staub, 1975, 1979, 1986). All this develops a positive orientation to and connection to others, caring about others' welfare, and helpful behavior (Staub, 1978).

For constructive patriotism this caring orientation needs to develop beyond the child's immediate environment, toward people belonging to varied subgroups of a nation, and toward society in general. The danger of traditional patriotism is that the loyalty and love for the group can become an abstraction. This is a danger in any "higher" ideal, be that freedom, communism, or patriotism. Commitment to higher ideals and to a group can be a form of transcendence of the self, an experience of unity with something higher, beyond the self, that is deeply satisfying. Unfortunately, commitment to and the pursuit of abstract ideals often leads to a disregard of persons, whether by communists, Nazis, or members of religious groups of many varieties. Blind patriotism can lead even to the destruction of members of one's own group so as to fulfill the abstract love for the group.

Constructive patriotism, on the other hand, requires love of the group with an awareness of the concrete existence and well-being of the *individuals* who are members of the group. It also requires, especially in our global age, that caring and concern extend to humanity in general. Constructive patriotism must, therefore, embody the higher ideal or value of human welfare, with respect and consideration for the needs and welfare of specific human beings.

The development of a connected self requires an environment that allows individuality, including differentness. Children must be allowed and even encouraged to speak out and express themselves, and when necessary assert themselves. Self-expression and self-assertion need not break connection. When performed without physically harming or psychologically diminishing others, they can even build connection and help develop the identity of a group, like a classroom or a peer group. Children's participation in defining and creating community, for example, in deciding about community standards of behavior like classroom rules, helps build both aspects of a connected self – other orientation and connection, and the sense of one's own identity.

Self-Awareness and Knowledge about Groups

To become active bystanders who oppose a destructive course of action by their group, it is important for people to gain awareness of the psychological tendencies and reactions in themselves that contribute to turning against and victimizing others, or to passively accepting others' suffering. Differentiating between us and them, devaluing people regarded as "them," just-world thinking or the belief that people get what they deserve and those who suffer must deserve it due to their actions or character (Lerner, 1980), and the exclusion of people from the moral universe (Opotow, 1990; Staub, 1989, 1990) are among these psychological tendencies and reactions. Through instruction in school and in the home, television programs, literature, and in other ways, children and adults can acquire knowledge that, over time, can lead to an awareness of these processes in themselves and others around them.

Knowledge of characteristics and processes in groups that contribute to repression or group violence, and learning to notice these in one's own group, are important for constructive patriotism. To provide this knowledge or type of self-awareness requires a new approach to teaching children and informing citizens. It requires teaching history that, rather than idealizing the past, identifies destructive actions and processes in the group's past, and explores the cultural and psychological reasons for them. The schools, the media, writers and artists, and all citizens can play an important part in this.

The Role of Values

Critical consciousness requires one's own vantage point to evaluate events. Critical loyalty requires a basis for separating oneself from current group practice. Personal values, and/or adherence to values to which the group is committed (by its constitution or basic social organization) but does not currently follow, can provide these.

The world that we now live in, the global interconnection that is increasingly evident – in the shared dangers of nuclear and environmental destruction, diseases like AIDS that respect no national borders, and the interrelatedness of the world economy – more than ever requires values that can be grounds for both constructive patriotism and positive connections between groups. Thus, the values that provide the grounds for critical conciousness and loyalty ought not be simply those that inhibit violence and destruction. They must be positive values that promote caring and connection among human beings, including connection across group lines – racial, religious, ethnic, and national.

Values of connection, caring, and responsibility for others' welfare need to be inclusive, that is, apply to all human beings regardless of their group membership. When blind patriotism leads to disregard for others' needs, it requires devaluation of other groups, which can be so extreme that these groups and their members are excluded from the moral realm (Opotow, 1990; Staub, 1990). Inclusive values of caring, which humanize others (Oliner & Oliner, 1988; Staub, 1989), are essential to provide the grounds for constructive patriotism.

Certain practices develop caring across group lines. They include positive reciprocity, "cross-cutting" relations (Deutsch, 1973) among members of different groups, that is, deep involvement with each other in joint projects, whether work or play, and the development of shared goals that are super-ordinate to separate and conflicting goals. All this involves an evolution, where beginning actions change people and lead to further actions (Staub, 1988, 1989, 1992).

But constructive patriotism is not only resistance to destructive group practice. It is also a commitment to one's group – not in its opposition to other groups, but as part of the human family. This commitment entails social responsibility, the feeling of responsibility for the group and its welfare, which motivates constructive action on behalf of the group and in its relationship to other groups.

CONSTRUCTIVE PATRIOTISM AND THE INTERCONNECTEDNESS OF NATIONS

Is patriotism, even its constructive form, still a viable psychological phenomenon in our global age? Or is it outmoded in any form? Is love for and a desire to belong to a group outmoded in an age that has begun to stress both human interconnectedness and the connection of human beings to the earth and the universe? In my view human beings have not yet evolved psychologically in ways that would make deep ties to concrete and accessible groups unnecessary. This need for concrete ties can probably be best satisfied in smaller groups, but for many people their nation remains a major avenue for fulfillment. These ties are still needed by most people as a ground of their identity. Moreover, while the creation of smaller communities may reduce the role and importance of patriotism for individuals, constructive patriotism, as noted above, is one motivation leading individuals to work for the improvement of their society and to maintain its accountability to moral standards.

An important question for constructive patriotism is the balance of the relationship between one's own nation and other nations, and commitment to one's nation versus humanity. "Should one" buy American products and promote trade practices that benefit one's nation? Perhaps so, when the alternative is to buy the products of nations that are technologically highly developed, like Japan or Germany, but not when the alternative is to buy the products of poor nations.

In general, the relationship between and balance of group interest and universal human interrelatedness requires attention and exploration. Human limitations must also be considered. It is easier for human beings to devote themselves to improving education in their community, while it requires a broader vision, social responsibility, or other comparable sources of motivation to work for improving education in one's country. It is even more removed from the self and a more abstract goal to work on improving education in the whole world, and requires vision, inclusive values, competencies, and institutions to connect the self to such a goal. The relative obligations to personal welfare, others' welfare, group welfare, human welfare, and the welfare of the natural environment, as well as their psychological bases, remain important questions for exploration and discussion.

References

Adorno, T. W., Frenkel-Brunswik, E., Levinson, D. J., & Sanford, R. N. (1950). *The authoritarian personality.* New York: Norton.

Bar-Tal, D., (1993). Patriotism as fundamental beliefs of group members. *Politics and the Individual* 3:45–63.

Berlin, I. (1979). Nationalism: Past neglect and present power. *Partisan Review* 45:350.

Brewer, M. B. (1978). In-group bias in the minimal intergroup situation: A cognitive-motivational analysis. *Psychological Bulletin* 86:307–24.

Craig, G. A. (1982). *The Germans.* New York: The New American Library.

Curti, M. (1946). *The roots of American loyalty.* New York: Columbia University Press.

Deutsch, M. (1973). *The resolution of conflict: Constructive and destructive processes.* New Haven, CT: Yale University Press.

Fromm, E. (1965). *Escape from freedom.* New York: Avon Books.

Girard, P. (1980). Historical foundations of anti-semitism. In J. Dimsdale (Ed.), *Survivors, victims and perpetrators: Essays on the Nazi Holocaust.* New York: Hemisphere Publishing Company.

Hoffman, M. L. (1970). Conscience, personality, and socialization technique. *Human Development* 13:90–126.

(1975). Altruistic behavior and the parent–child relationship. *Journal of Personality and Social Psychology* 31:937–43.

Janowitz, M. (1985). *The reconstruction of patriotism: Education for civic consciousness.* Chicago: University of Chicago Press.

Jarymowitz, M. (1991). The self/we schemate and social categorization effects. Paper presented at the conference on Changing Stereotypes, Université René Descartes, Paris, September 3–6.

Kinkaid, E. (1959). *In every war but one.* New York: Norton.

Lerner, M. (1980). *The belief in a just world: A fundamental delusion.* New York: Plenum Press.

Mack, J. (1983). Nationalism and the self. *The Psychology Review* 2:47–69.

Oliner, S. B., & Oliner, P. (1988). *The altruistic personality: Rescuers of Jews in Nazi Europe.* New York: Free Press.

Opotow, S. (Ed.). (1990). Moral exclusion and injustice. *Journal of Social Issues 46,* No. 1.

Piaget, J., & Weil, A. (1951). The development in children of the idea of the homeland and of relations with other countries. *International Social Science Bulletin* 3:570.

Sampson, E. E. (1988). The debate on individualism. *American Psychologist* 47:15–22.

Schatz, R. T. (1993). Patriotism and intergroup conflict, *Peace Psychology Bulletin* 2(3).

Shaffer, D. R. (1988). *Social and personality development.* Monterey, CA: Brooks-Cole.

Staub, E. (1975). To rear a prosocial child: Reasoning, learning by doing, and learning by teaching others. In D. DePalma & J. Folley (Eds.), *Moral development: Current theory and research.* Hillsdale, NJ: Erlbaum.

(1978). *Positive social behavior and morality: Personal and social influences* (Vol. 1). New York: Academic Press.

(1979). *Positive social behavior and morality: Socialization and development* (Vol. 2). New York: Academic Press.

(1986). A conception of the determinants and development of altruism and aggression: Motives, the self, the environment. In C. Zahn-Waxler (Ed.), *Altruism and aggression: Social and biological origins.* Cambridge, MA: Cambridge University Press.

(1988). The evolution of caring and nonaggressive persons and societies. In R. Wagner, J. DeRivera, & M. Watkins (Eds.), Positive approaches to peace. *Journal of Social Issues* 44:81–100.

(1989). *The roots of evil: The origins of genocide and other group violence.* New York: Cambridge University Press.

(1990). Moral exclusion, personal goal theory and extreme destructiveness. In S. Opawa (Ed.), Moral exclusion and injustice. *Journal of Social Issues* 46:47–65.

(1991, Spring). Persian Gulf conflict was reflection of stormy undercurrents in U.S. psyche. *Psychology International* 1–9. Washington, DC: American Psychological Association.

(1992). Transforming the bystander: The origins of caring and social responsibility. In H. Fein (Ed.), *Genocide watch.* New Haven, CT: Yale University Press.

(1993). Individual and group selves, motivation and morality. In W. Edelman & T. Wren (Eds.), *Morality and the self.* Cambridge, MA: MIT Press.

(1996). The cultural-societal roots of violence: The examples of genocidal violence and of contemporary youth violence in the United States. *American Psychologist* 51:117–33.

Surrey, J. (1985). *Self-in-relation: A theory of women's development*. Wellesley, MA: The Stone Center, Wellesley College.

Tajfel, H. (1978). Social categorization, social identity and social comparison. In H. Tajfel (Ed.), *Differentiation between social groups* (pp. 61–76). London: Academic Press.

(Ed.) (1993). *The social dimension*. Cambridge: Cambridge University Press.

Tajfel, H., Flamant, C., Billig, M. Y., & Bundy, R. P. (1971). Social categorization and intergroup behavior. *European Journal of Social Psychology* 1, 149–77.

Webster's Third New International Dictionary. (1967). Springfield, MA: G. & C. Merriam.

Weiss, J. R., Rothbaum, F. M., & Blackburn, T. C. (1984). Standing out and standing in: The psychology of control in America and Japan. *American Psychologist* 39:955–69.

47

Manifestations of Blind and Constructive Patriotism

Summary of Findings

Based on Work with Robert Schatz

I have proposed the existence of two types of patriotism: blind and constructive. Blind patriotism is an attachment to country that is characterized by unquestioning acceptance of its policies and practices and unquestioning allegiance. It is expressed in agreement with questions like "I would support my country right or wrong"; "People should not constantly try to change the way things are in America"; and "It is un-American to criticize this country." Constructive patriotism combines attachment, love of country, with the capacity and willingness to question, criticize, and work for change. It is expressed in agreement with questions like "My love of country demands that I speak out against popular but potentially destructive policies"; "People should work hard to move this country in a positive direction"; and "If you love America, you should notice its problems and work to correct them." Constructive patriots say, in essence, because I love my country I have to question problematic policies and practices. This study considers the manifestations of these two kinds of patriotism in attitudes and behaviors toward one's own country and toward other countries.

The participants were undergraduate students at the University of Massachusetts at Amherst. They completed a questionnaire that intended to assess types of patriotism. The results showed that constructive patriotism was positively related to scores on a measure of prosocial value orientation, understood here to assess positive valuation of human beings and a feeling of personal and social responsibility for others' welfare. This measure also included items assessing the belief that the responsibility for

This study is described in detail in R. Schatz & E. Staub (1997). Manifestations of blind and constructive patriotism: Personality correlates and individual-group relations. In E. Staub & D. Bar-Tal (Eds.), *Patriotism in the lives of individuals and groups*. Chicago: Nelson-Hall Publishers. It is also described in R. T. Schatz, E. Staub, & H. Levine, On the varieties of national attachment: Blind versus constructive patriotism. *Political Psychology*, *20*, 151–175.

others' welfare extends to all human beings. Blind patriotism, on the other hand, was negatively related to prosocial value orientation. Constructive patriotism was positively related while blind patriotism was negatively related to feelings of empathy. Constructive patriotism was negatively related to "just-world thinking," the belief that the world is just and people get what they deserve, while blind patriotism was positively related to it. These findings support the assumption that the willingness of constructive patriots to question and oppose policies and practices destructive to people would be based on values and beliefs that affirm human welfare.

The two types of patriots differed in what they consider important in social practices, and how they see the United States. The survey asked subjects to rate how positively or negatively they saw a variety of attributes, as well as the degree to which these characterized the United States in their view. Respondents categorized as blind patriots rated attributes associated with "power/strength" and "capitalism/materialism" as more desirable, while constructive patriots rated attributes associated with "equality/fairness" as more desirable. Blind patriots believed that equality and fairness were more characteristic of the United States than did constructive patriots, whereas constructive patriots were more likely than blind patriots to see the United States as characterized by power and capitalism. For blind patriots the ratings of desirability of attributes and the extent they saw desirable attributes characterize the country were more closely associated than for constructive patriots. This may indicate the greater embeddedness of blind patriots in their group/country.

Although both types of patriots expressed similar levels of positive feelings toward the United States, constructive patriots were significantly more likely to express negative feelings as well. Differences were also found between groups in behaviors that expressed their "relationship with the United States." Symbolic allegiance was more important for blind patriots, who rated symbolic behaviors, such as flying the American flag and saying the Pledge of Allegiance, as the most expressive of their relationship to the United States. This suggests a somewhat abstract relationship by blind patriots to their country. In contrast, constructive patriots reported that they gather more political information and engage in more political activism than blind patriots. They reported these concrete activities as more expressive of their relationship with the United States than performing symbolic behaviors.

Because constructive patriots express greater desire for change and are more willing to criticize the government, it is not surprising that they engage in more political activity. Because blind patriots are more likely to view the United States in a completely positive light, they might feel little need to be politically active and might even condemn people who are. However, blind patriots might also become politically active if conditions threaten their positive vision of the country.

Blind patriots rated themselves as more conservative than did constructive patriots and were more supportive of a conservative political agenda, including a strong military, and the strengthening and expansion of capitalist practices. We would anticipate that the conservative orientation of blind patriots would lead them to oppose multiculturalism and advocate for a common identity as Americans. Blind patriotism was linked to measures related to "cultural purity," to seeing American culture as under threat by the adoption of foreign cultural practices in the United States and by the adoption of U.S. practices in other countries. The latter was expressed, for example, in the view that the Japanese adopting baseball as a national sport may diminish baseball as an American national pastime.

The study also examined participants' attitudes toward other countries. We found that blind patriotism was strongly related to "militaristic nationalism," while constructive patriotism was unrelated to it. Further, blind patriotism was negatively related to concern for global welfare and mutual assistance among nations. Constructive patriotism, in contrast, was positively related to internationalism. As expected, blind patriotism was positively related to a measure of the perception of national vulnerability. No significant relationship was found between constructive patriotism and vulnerability.

This study supports the view that blind and constructive patriotism can be empirically distinguished. They represent very different ways of being patriotic. Patriotism, whatever its form, demands loyalty to one's country. Ultimately, for a peaceful world, the critical question is: Can a person strongly identify himself or herself with all of humanity and still be a patriot? Our findings suggest that caring, humanistic values, and emotional connections to other human beings, as expressed in empathic feelings, can be related to a type of patriotism that we have called constructive. In future work, the possibilities for joint, integrated, patriotic, and universalistic identities ought to be further explored.

48

The Ideal University in the Real World

INTRODUCTION

What might the ideal university be like? Not the ideal university in a nonexistent ideal world, but in the real world of today, in the U.S. How might the University of Massachusetts strive to become an ideal university?

We must consider and specify core values that the university ought to transmit to students and core values that the university ought to embody in the way it functions. We must also consider how these values are to be fulfilled, how they are to be implemented. I will first specify and discuss *core values*, and then methods or means of their implementation.

Rarely do institutions (or individuals) specify and consciously examine the values they strive to fulfill. To do so has substantial benefits. It is difficult to move toward desired ends, to fulfill one's purpose without knowing that purpose. For example, if a university hopes to transmit certain values to students, clearly specifying what they are is essential to develop optimal ways to transmit them.

Decision making is difficult enough when values and goals are explicit. When decision making is based on *implicit* values, as it often is, the force

Reprinted from E. Staub (1987). The ideal university in the real world. *Occasional Papers III*, The Institute for Advanced Study in the Humanities. University of Massachusetts, Amherst.

This statement draws on prior work of my own (Staub, 1979, 1982, 1989), on a brief presentation (by Richard O'Brien), on brief written statements on the ideal university (by Roland Chilton, Rachel Clifton, Seymour Epstein, Lou Fisher, Haim Gunner, Joel Halpern, George Levinger, Jay Savereid, Michael Wolff) and on discussions among these and other members (Jules Chametzky, Miriam Levin, Mason Lowance, Linda Slakey, Meyer Weinberg) of a yearlong Faculty Forum on "Current events and values in American life" that took place under the auspices of the Institute for the Advanced Study in the Humanities, University of Massachusetts, Amherst, from January through December 1986. The members of the forum listed above participated in discussions involving the ideal university. This statement also draws on discussion about values in other realms in which other members of the forum participated (Irving Howards, Paul Hollander, Patricia Hunt, Gerald Platt, Gerald Weinstein).

of circumstance and conflicting interests (especially when they join with conflicting although less essential values) make it much easier to disregard or submerge essential values. Doing so repeatedly, in specific instances, can lead over time to a drift away from these values.

An additional reason to attempt to specify core values of an ideal or optimally functioning university is lack of agreement about such values within the university community. As values remain implicit, at times potential conflicts are avoided, but at the cost of possibly great loss in effectiveness in fulfilling important values, in fulfilling the true functions and purposes of the university. At other times conflicts arise but without a clear awareness of their source in value differences. Attempting to specify core values can lead to a process of discussion, exploration, and self-education within the university community.

CORE VALUES IN THE IDEAL UNIVERSITY

The university is a place to discover and transmit knowledge. At the same time, the university cannot be a place of the mind alone. It must do what it can to educate, both through direct instruction and by their experience in the university, multifaceted human beings who are prepared to live in the world and contribute to the world – to their community, to their nation, to human beings in general. We must concern ourselves with a university transmitting knowledge and skills, a university contributing to students living their lives as full human beings who can use their many potentials well, and the university contributing to students' "positive orientation" to other human beings.

There are a fair number of core values. Some may be called "process" values, which ought to guide all behavior within the university (see basic values below). Others help define and specify the central functions of the university (education and the creation of new knowledge). Still others relate to the creation of community and the nature of community life within the university and to the relations of the university and the larger society of which it is a part.

BASIC VALUES AND PRINCIPLES

"Absolute" Values and Rules

Moral philosophers have long attempted to specify moral principles, basic, essential principles or rules of conduct. We can specify values and principles that we regard as especially relevant to university life, or principles that have universal validity which the university wants to stress as well. These include: *truth, honesty, openness, justice and respect for the rights of others, free and democratic societal processes, and service to and the willingness to make sacrifices in others' behalf.*

These values have universal applicability. Many of them have special meaning in a university community. Honesty in research, in reporting research results, and in teaching are essential. The search for truth, the discovery and creation of new knowledge, is a basic task of the university. An open mind, the appreciation of different perspectives on reality, different ways of framing experience, different basic assumptions or theories, is essential in the search for truth. It is also essential in contributing to *tolerance* of and respect for human beings in general as well as among members of the university community who at times hold highly varied views, beliefs and ideals. Thus, while the university ought to strive to live by, and transmit certain core values, it should also have great tolerance for people with differing values.

It is important to limit a list of such values to those most significant. Only then are we likely to use these core values as a guide to conduct. As we examine such values our aim should be to pare them down, to limit their number.

The Underlying Essential Value: Human Welfare

Such values or principles of conduct are *not* absolutes. They are to serve human welfare. This is important because every principle can be reified or distorted. Truth can become a dogmatic, official, dehumanizing truth, as in Nazi Germany, including the universities of Nazi Germany. The other basic values can also be subverted by the way they are interpreted and institutionalized. Service to the community may become killing "enemies" in unjust or unnecessary wars, or help in suppressing people who deviate from an official political line or from group consensus.

Taken in combination, the principles listed above are less likely to be misused. The primary protection from misuse is, however, to remain aware of the basic, underlying, ultimate purpose that these principles serve. As we use these principles, as we attempt to transmit them, as we create institutional structures around them, we must always be aware that they are intended to guide behavior, human relationships and community life so as to protect and enhance human welfare. We must always test the ways these principles are used by the criterion of whether they serve human welfare, or whether instead, in their direct and immediate effects (in contrast to claims that they fulfill abstract ideals), they diminish human beings.

EDUCATION AND THE CREATION OF KNOWLEDGE

Multifaceted Education, the Love of Learning, Preparation for Life

One central function of the university is education. In the course of their experience at the university, students should come to value learning, or to value it more. They should acquire a love of learning. The university should maximize the opportunities for students to experience the satisfactions inherent in discovering new ideas, new facts, and their interrelations, in the creation of ideas and the experience of discovery, in entering new realms of knowledge. Beyond providing substantive knowledge, this love of learning and of intellectual creativity is a profoundly important enduring contribution that the university can make to its students.

Substantively, their education should provide students with a wide range of knowledge; it should generate wide-ranging interests and awareness by students and appreciation by them of their many different potentials. As examples of range and of preparation for the rest of the students' lives, the university education should provide refinement of aesthetic appreciation, learning about music but also learning to enjoy music, and so on.

Their education should inform students about different cultures and ways of life, about different perspectives on reality, and help them gain awareness of their shared humanity with other human beings. General skills in thinking and information processing can develop in the context of such multifaceted learning. Both a *critical consciousness and commitment to learning and to the search for truth* ought to be fostered in students. They are both important and provide a necessary balance for each other. A multifaceted education will help evolve skills and capacities, it can result in a lifelong commitment to learning, and it is likely to lead to fuller and more satisfying lives.

Focused Education, Specific Skills and Information, Preparation for a Career

In our complex world specific skills and in-depth knowledge in specific domains are essential in preparing students for the pursuit of a career, and in fulfilling the needs of society. To provide such education must be a basic goal of the contemporary university, both in its service to its students and to the society in which the university exists.

Here a difficult and vexing problem arises: how to fulfill the values and goals of both multifaceted and focused education. The changing cycles and shifting philosophies in undergraduate curricula in American universities since World War II partly reflect the search for a proper balance, the emphasis on one after a while replaced by an emphasis on the other. If the university is to make a contribution to the quality of lives and to an enlightened, harmonious and well functioning society, multifaceted education must receive at least as much emphasis as focused education. The concern with balance must be especially great in the education of students whose focused work is in areas of knowledge, for example, mathematics or engineering, which are inherently less multifaceted, in comparison, for example, to focused work in the humanities. It is a potential source of conflict that faculty in such areas may not highly value multifaceted education.

Self-Awareness as an Outcome of Education

Enhancing self-awareness (accompanied by enhanced awareness of others) is a potentially highly significant goal of education. The significance of self-awareness in human life is great. The capacity to see oneself, the knowledge of certain psychological tendencies of and processes in human beings, and an awareness of these tendencies and processes in oneself can profoundly affect the mode of relating to each other by individuals and members of groups.

People may strongly hold certain values, but without this kind of awareness it is often difficult to live by them. There is a profound tendency among human beings to create us–them differentiation (a tendency that starts soon after birth with the infant's affectionate tie to caretakers and fear of strangers) and to devalue "them," those who are members of the out-group. There is a profound tendency to maintain a belief in justice, and to see innocent victims as somehow having deserved their suffering. When their self-interest motivates people to deviate from their moral values, it is a common tendency to create justifications. The knowledge of and the capacity to see the operation of these and other psychological processes in oneself (e.g. the capacity to "catch oneself") can have profound effects.

Educating students in ways that enhance their self-awareness is far from a commonly held value. The importance of self-awareness is not widely recognized and even if it is, the university as the institution to promote self-awareness is not necessarily accepted. "Academic" knowledge offered by the social sciences, through the study of literature and drama and in other ways, is an important component of such education. The university should also include other components to foster self-awareness.

It has been an oft expressed hope that a good liberal education would diminish the inclination for violence and cruelty, that it would "civilize" its recipients. Although no carefully controlled study is available, historical evidence suggests that this is a false hope. It points to highly educated perpetrators of the Holocaust, planners of the genocide in Cambodia, and originators of and participants in other cruelties. A multifaceted education that succeeds in fostering self-awareness has a better chance to diminish aggression of many types and to foster positive relations between individuals and groups.

Individual Responsibility

University education and life in the university as a community ought to foster a sense of personal responsibility in students, both for themselves, in their own lives, and in relation to the various groups that they are part of and human beings in general. It ought to help students develop a strong identity, with an awareness of responsibility for decisions and actions.

An aspect of responsibility to self and to others is the awareness of the need to balance self-interest and the interest of others. Each person possesses, and the university fosters, personal motives, such as the motive for achievement. Under what circumstances should self-interest, personal motives, predominate over the needs and interest of others, and when should the latter supersede the former? A university should help students explore such basic issues, in light of core values.

Research, Scholarship, the Creation of New Knowledge

Together with its educational function, this is the central function of the university and another core value. In its most basic form, this is a generally accepted value, as is the value of education.

However, in this realm also, issues and questions abound, such as the value of basic versus applied research and whether it is acceptable to conduct research that produces knowledge that has destructive uses. Another issue is the evaluation of creative scholarship. Is a large quantity of research and scholarly writing the best index of creativity? Is public interest in a particular domain of research or scholarship a good index? In some realms, another question is the relative value of research on highly specific issues versus that on larger questions: for example, research that dissects psychological or societal functioning into small components versus research that explores greater wholes. An exploration of such questions, which involves a specification of values, should guide efforts at implementation.

THE UNIVERSITY AS A COMMUNITY: THE VALUE OF COMMUNITY AND COMMUNITY LIFE AS A MEANS OF EDUCATION

A basic concern of many people – educators, social scientists, social thinkers, and people in public life – is the relative lack of community in American life. Perhaps in part this expresses the relatively low value placed on community, especially in comparison to the strongly held value of individualism, whether it is an economic individualism (material pursuits) or expressive individualism (the pursuit of self fulfillment) (Bellah et al. 1985).

The university is a place where a strong, meaningful community can be created. It is a place where students and other members can learn to value community. It is an ideal setting for students to learn about the relationship of the community and the individual, the rights and obligations of each, and to participate in creating a "good" community. As any fair-sized community, the university community is inevitably a complex system. It has many subgroups and subsystems; students, faculty, administration, different branches of the administration, varied kinds of maintenance staff, police. Most of these can be further subdivided. Even if we agree on core values, such agreement would have to evolve over time through varied forms of community building, will never be complete, and will always be in flux as new members enter the community and as the community is affected by the values and conditions that exist in the larger society. Even with relatively good agreement, the needs, goals, and interests of subsystems and subgroups will vary, partly due to their different functions, which also result in different perspectives, and at times give rise to conflict.

It is important to recognize these differences, to specify them, and to attempt to resolve them, guided by the core values of the university. Students may want rules and privileges that administrators are unwilling to grant. Hostility may develop among subsystems. Crises may arise, for example when students, protesting some university action, or the way the university participates in the larger world (e.g. investment in companies that do business in South Africa, or allowing CIA recruiters on campus), disrupt normal processes. In the relations of subgroups in the system or between individuals there may be examples of racism, sexism, or in general deviation from the basic values of the community.

Conflicts, crises, offer tremendous opportunities for education and for community building. How does the community respond to conflict, to provocation, to the breaking of rules, to interference with the usual business of the community? Are conflicts and crises resolved by discussion of facts and values, by mutual persuasion, by negotiation and arbitration, that is, in the context of minimal force and no physical force, or are they resolved by the dictates of authority and the use of force? How much effort is put into dealing with conflict in ways that are consistent with the core values?

The range of conduct that is accepted, even if at times reluctantly, ought to be broad and when possible conduct that exceeds such limits ought to be dealt with in ways that have educational value. In most contemporary communities in America some actions of individuals will be totally unacceptable and require punishment and possible exclusion. Where does a community draw the limit, and how is such unacceptable conduct dealt with? While at times inevitable, only in the most extreme instances should the university give up its autonomy in governing itself, for example, by calling in the police. When such outside agents enter, since the university has no control over them, their actions may be entirely at odds with the core values of the community.

While our tolerance within the community for self expression and the expression of values should be great, a "good community" must insist on mutual tolerance. Diminishing and harming others and violence, whether for personal reasons or due to group membership, should activate established institutions and processes to educate, to demand reparation, and if necessary to punish. In the progressively more ideal community such actions will bring forth strong community-wide reactions. The more behavior conflicts with or negates core values in general and the *basic* values and principles that I discussed earlier, the less tolerance it should receive.

The building of community is a constant, continuing task of exploration, self-definition and implementation. The faculty and the administration both have important roles in shaping community and creating its educational function (see the section below on implementation). Participation in community building and learning to be responsible members of a community can themselves be major components of university education. Students are relatively inexperienced, and university life represents a tremendous increase in independence for most of them and the first significant opportunity to exert influence as part of a community.

On the one hand, in an ideal community, members will learn to respect each other and each other's rights regardless of race, sex, religion, physical handicap, or other differences. On the other hand, the community ought to allow and even encourage members in expressing their differences with the group, especially differences in basic values, or their feelings of being unjustly treated, even by strong protest, unpleasant as such protest might be. Without members at times forcefully (but nonviolently) expressing their views, especially if they have no other way to make themselves heard, the community may gradually evolve practices and create structures that are contrary to core values, with a resultant change in values. (In varied publications, I have developed the concepts of learning by participation and steps along the continuum – of destruction or benevolence, depending on the direction of steps – and reviewed substantial evidence in their support. A progression of such steps results in changes in persons and in the group as a whole.) The value of *critical loyalty*, the commitment to create the best possible society in serving human welfare, even if it requires questioning, criticism, and protest (or skeptical loyalty), and the value of respect for the community, must both be transmitted to students. The resolution of such at times conflicting values is a source of personal and moral growth.

Human beings need to feel connected to others. They also need to feel significant in relation to other human beings and their group. A community can fulfill these and other needs. This, in turn, will have significant consequences. For example, individuals who identify with a group they value (the university community), who feel connected to other members of the group, who feel significant, are unlikely to be violent.

THE RELATIONSHIP OF THE UNIVERSITY TO THE LARGER COMMUNITY

This relationship is simply a fact of life: values enter in shaping and guiding it. The university, in its basic functions, serves society: in both multifaceted and focused education part of the knowledge it transmits must be knowledge essential for life in that society. At least some of the knowledge it generates is directly in the service of society. One question we might ask is about the proper balance between seeking and aiming to transmit "universal" truths, versus knowledge specifically relevant to and needed by the existing society. In finding this balance and in other ways, the university and the larger society of which it is a part will, at times, be in conflict.

Society expects loyalty and at least moderate adherence to its values by the university. In addition, the university is impacted by the forces active in society, by its guiding values and their modes of implementation, and by its mores: by poverty, rape and other kinds of violence, by the drug culture, sexism, racism, and anti-Semitism, as well as by lessening discrimination, affirmative action, and the like. Certain conditions in society place specific demands on the university. The disruption of family life requires that the university act in loco parentis (for example by helping students deal with emotional needs) at a time when the role of parents itself is in flux.

A specification of the core values by which the university wishes to live and that the university wishes to transmit to students makes it possible to consciously shape the relationship of the university to the larger world, according to the core values, within practical limits. It also makes it possible to attempt to prepare students for the larger world in ways that inoculate them against certain influences, preempt destructive influences in their lives once they leave the university, and help maintain their values. They can learn to value justice within the university setting, and aware of injustice in the world be prepared not to accept injustice in the outside world as an acceptable way of life. They may come to value critical loyalty in the university setting and live by this value in communities they later enter and in their role as citizens of their nation.

As we consider the university as a community that lives by certain values, the question arises whether the university as an institution, as a whole, should ever take a stand in relation to the outside world: a political stand, or a stand on social policy, on major societal issues. The flow of the argument up to this point, the logic inherent in it, suggests that in some cases this becomes an obligation.

While the university might endanger itself, might generate antagonism in outside powers or the public, so do individuals or other institutions if they act contrary to the interests or preferences of powerful others. The consequences to a university that is more dependent on the rest of society, such as a publicly funded university, can be greater. Nonetheless, in extreme instances, for example, if a powerful movement such as Nazism gains strength, if one's own country engages in actions in the world that are profoundly contrary to the core values of the university and of the larger society as well, it is essential that important institutions stand in opposition. We frequently enough cite the examples of important institutions remaining silent, in many countries, as it happened during the Holocaust in Germany, or at the time of the disappearances in Argentina, and even during the McCarthy era or early during the Vietnam War in the U.S. This stands as a warning to us. To be effective, to live by their values, and ultimately even to limit danger to themselves, institutions, including universities, ought to express themselves before extreme and uncontrollable conditions evolve.

It is not just financial dependence, but many other ties, that stop individuals and universities from taking a stand. Basically, it is difficult to stand in opposition and risk the condemnation of one's group: critical loyalty is difficult both for individuals and institutions. This is doubly relevant, in that, ultimately, institutions don't take stands: their governing bodies or leaders do.

Part of the obligation of the university, in extreme circumstances, is not simply to take a stand, to oppose, whether in words or actions. It is also to educate, to remind society of basic values that they might be betraying or that a particular group threatens. Unfortunately, it is highly unusual for universities (apart from groups of students) to act in these ways.

Why should a university know better than the rest of society? All segments of society have an obligation to participate in steering society on a humane as well as effective course. The university is in a better position than most groups to engage in the public exploration of wide-ranging ideas and issues. Its relative independence as a community makes it easier to evolve an independent perspective rather than accept the currently dominant views, the societal definition of reality. The university (and its individual members) will be more likely to assume the stance of critical loyalty toward society if as a community it succeeds in developing a strong sense of identity, and a culture of commitment within the community, based on core values.

There are many ways to take a stand, and some may have practical and symbolic significance with little danger to the university. A university takes a strong stand against racism, for example, if it admits members of a persecuted group. However, very mild "stands" may ultimately coopt an institution. While survival as an institution is an essential value, and the ability to fulfill the functions of teaching and scholarship extremely important, so are the core values of the ideal university.

MEANS AND METHODS OF CREATING THE IDEAL UNIVERSITY

The fulfillment of core values, the creation of the ideal university, is inevitably an ongoing process. It is a way of life. This realization must not mean that we delay, that we postpone, that we don't act. The effort to fulfill these core values should have high priority. Part of it may best be institutionalized, perhaps in the form of a permanent committee of administration, faculty, staff, and students who are charged with reviewing university processes and suggesting ways to implement core values. Existing conditions can be examined in the light of core values. Ongoing change efforts might focus on realms where the discrepancy from the ideal is especially great.

There are "realities of life" facing those who administer a university and all those who work on shaping it, which require pragmatism. However, in working to fulfill core values, this must be a principled pragmatism that retains a vision of and commitment to creating the ideal university.

In the following, I will briefly discuss selected aspects of and issues in implementation. I will focus on principles of implementation in contrast to actual practices. Principles and methods of implementation themselves embody values. We must strive to make these presumably subordinate values consistent with core values.

The Role of the Faculty

The role of the faculty in implementing core values is central. First, to fulfill the goals of multifaceted education, faculty members must be both inspiring and multifaceted themselves. Narrow specialization may enhance the capacity to create knowledge in certain fields. However, to the extent it limits the breadth of knowledge and the evolution of "personhood" it may make it impossible for faculty members to provide multifaceted education and to be effective role models for a "multifaceted person." The problem is complex, however, and possibly both intrinsic and systemic. Do a single-minded commitment to creative work, and the capacity for high-level research and scholarship, which presumably result in worthwhile contributions to knowledge, inevitably lead to narrow specialization, at least in fields that are inherently specialized? Or can this be avoided? This is the intrinsic side. The systemic aspects are, first, that the reward system both within the university and in the larger society strongly supports single-minded focus within frequently highly specialized areas and, second, that the faculty faces multiple and often conflicting demands.

To encourage greater breadth in the faculty, more wholeness as scholars, persons, and teachers, the university might offer incentives for faculty to participate in interdisciplinary seminars and in interdisciplinary teaching. Participation in the life of the university community is another route to greater depth.

Independently of this, the faculty's participation in the community is essential if there is to be a real university community. Faculty members ought to be involved in undergraduate life, as teachers, role models, advisors in residential settings, and for extracurricular activities. They can serve the community by conflict resolution and crisis management both in formal committees created for such purpose and informally. They can help parties to discuss, to negotiate, to engage in the processes of peaceful conflict resolution. They can both help manage conflict and educate in the process. As they enter the flow of life, they will themselves be educated: through their participation, they learn and change.

The *multiple demands* on the faculty include not only both multifaceted and focused teaching, creative research and scholarship, participation in community life and in the life of students, but various types of administrative service within the community and frequently service to the institutions of society beyond the university. How can the faculty fulfill all these demands? There are no easy solutions. Excellent support systems – secretarial help, teaching and research assistants – may lighten the load. Part of the problem is thus financial. It may also help to limit faculty administrative roles to areas where the faculty can make special contributions. However, since a good part of the problem is systemic, to the extent certain roles are neglected, such as participation in undergraduate life, admonishing the faculty will not be enough. It requires a specification of the relative importance of different roles and functions in the light of core values, careful thought about how to create an optimal balance of functions, and system changes that induce and lead the faculty to create such balance in their activities. A less than fully satisfying but probably inevitable solution is that different faculty members fulfill a different combination of functions.

The Role of the University Administration

Like the faculty, the administration must also enter the life of the community. Members of the administration must also be full members of the community. They must participate in community discussions of values, of community issues, in an exchange of ideas. In general, the more there are "cross-cutting" relations (Deutsch, 1973; Staub, 1989) among subgroups within a system, members of subgroups both working and playing together, the less there is mutual devaluation. Conflict becomes easier to resolve. The understanding of the other's needs will be greater. We must design ways for the different segments of the university population to both work and play together.

The administration must work to open channels for the different subgroups within the university to express themselves, and to exert influence. That is, we must work toward increasingly democratic processes. The opportunity to express their views and to exert influence might well diminish disruptive modes of self-expression by student groups.

A university administration also has multiple demands. It must be responsive to the university community, if there is to be a well functioning university, if the core values of the community are to be fulfilled, and if there is to be education through community building and community life. It must also be responsive to outside forces. It must attend to power, money, and political context, as well as to the service that the university is to provide to society.

The primary service ought to be, however, the kind of educated and responsible citizens the university provides society, and the new knowledge it generates. As I noted earlier, however, the university must respond to specific needs of society. As just one example, the university must train teachers needed by society. The quality of its teacher training affects society, and in part determines the knowledge and personality of students who enter the university.

The core values of a university and the values and expectations of society with regard to the university are likely to differ, especially in the case of public universities. Legislators may value focused education and applied research, which provide specific tangible benefits, with less interest in multifaceted education and basic research. Part of the continuing task of the university is to communicate its core values and to persuade society of their worth.

At times, administrators must feel caught between internal and external forces. Consulting different subgroups within the university and cooperating with them in the evolution or setting of policy may reduce conflict within the university and enhance the sense of community. The university community developing a clear identity based on core values would provide guidance both in administering the university within and shaping its relationship to the outside world. It would not resolve conflicts between these "two worlds," but would provide a better blueprint to follow in working for their resolution.

UNDERGRADUATE LIFE IN THE UNIVERSITY

Residential life. Living in relatively small communities within the larger community, such as a residential college system or other group living that is limited in size and scale, creates opportunities for connection, for intimacy, and for intellectual interchange. It is a source of identity. To serve the purposes of the larger community such residential units should not be exclusive or discriminatory. It is an open question whether and what kind of instruction ought to take place within these smaller entities.

Extracurricular activities. Persons evolve, interests evolve, and much learning takes place through participation in varied activities. There is some research showing that in smaller high schools that provide students with opportunities for active (rather than audience) participation, students develop into more involved, responsible persons (Gump & Friesen, 1964). Student art exhibits, theater groups, music groups, political groups and activities, student government can be significant aspects of multifaceted education. An ideal university is characterized by a student culture with wide-ranging activities of this sort.

TEACHING: QUALITY AND MODES

Teaching styles and quality. To provide the type of education that I discussed in the section on values requires motivation, skill, and multifaceted faculty members. I touched on the issues of motivation and personal evolution in the discussion of faculty role.

The development of teaching skills is also important. Providing faculty with nonevaluative feedback can become a basic operating procedure of the university. Videotaping lectures as well as seminars and expert guidance in viewing the tapes can go a long way toward improved teaching. Although such services are available, their common use requires "cultural" change.

"Deep learning." In addition to the usual courses, it is essential to deepen knowledge and promote self-awareness by providing courses that draw on or *generate* life experience. These courses can also connect experience with concepts, with substantive knowledge. Some courses might focus on students coming to know each other's life experiences. As students share experiences, at times similar at other times highly divergent, as they enter each other's worlds, and as they are guided in this exploration by concepts, their knowledge of human beings and their awareness of themselves, of others, and of their shared humanity with others will evolve. For example, Southeast Asian refugee students and students from New England might learn more in these realms by sharing their experiences in a seminar setting than in any other way. In other courses students may explore moral dilemmas, entering them and attempting to solve them. As they wrestle with basic conflicts between the dictates of different values in such "as if" experiences, whatever knowledge they gain from relevant courses on ethics or values will deepen and become personal. While some such courses already exist, this form of teaching and learning should be encouraged.

Education as part of community life. Public lectures, teach-ins, ongoing community discussions are important tools of education. The Kaleidoscope project at the University of Massachusetts has developed a format to discuss significant, value laden and conflictful issues in a "civil" manner. Many opportunities and avenues must be created for such community explorations.

There are many specific problems and issues that a university community faces: alcoholism, drug abuse, emotional problems, and so on. The administration of a university should draw on the resources of the community, not only faculty but students, in dealing with these. Students can educate each other about drug and alcohol problems, provide each other co-counseling as support. As people teach, they learn. Problems might resolve themselves as due to wide-ranging student participation the student culture changes.

SUMMARY STATEMENT

There are a substantial number of core values, which define and elaborate on the functions of the university. The goal of creating an ideal university is itself a core value. To create an ideal university we must engage in discussion and debate, in the exchange of ideas, in order to forge increasing agreement about core values and about priorities among them. To varying but not equal degrees, we can work on fulfilling all core values at the same time. It is also essential to set enduring priorities (which remain responsive to the realities of the real world) so that efforts to create the ideal university will not be nullified by constantly shifting policies.

In various senses (e.g. the focus on excellence, attention to human relations and civility issues, community efforts such as Mass Transformation, etc.) this university has already embarked on a process of creating the ideal university. This must be an ongoing process, the process itself valuable. At the bottom of the core values is the motivation to enhance human welfare. In shaping the vision of the ideal university, we must be guided by the question: What kind of world would such a university help to create?

References

Bellah, P. N., Madsen, R., Sullivan, W. M., Swindler, A., & Lipton, S. M. (1985). *Habits of the heart. Individualism and commitment in American life*. New York: Harper & Row.

Deutsch, M. (1973). *The resolution of conflict: Constructive and destructive processes*. New Haven, CT: Yale University Press.

Gump. P. V., & Friesen, W. V. (1964). Participation in nonclass settings. In R. G. Barker & P. V. Gump (Eds.), *Big school, small school: High school size and student behavior*. Stanford, CA: Stanford University Press.

Staub, E. (February 1982). Proposal for including human relations in the general education curriculum. From the working group on human relations. The appended documents for the Report of the Faculty Senate and the Committee on General Education. University of Massachusetts, Amherst.

Staub, E. (1986) A conception of the determinants and development of altruism and aggression: Motives, the self, the environment. In C. Zahn-Waxler (Ed.), *Altruism and aggression: Social and biological origins*. Cambridge: MA: Cambridge University Press.

Staub, E. (1979). *Positive social behavior and morality, Vol. 2: Socialization and development*. New York: Academic Press.

Staub, E. (1989). *The roots of evil: The origins of genocide and other group violence*. Cambridge: Cambridge University Press.

49

Conclusion

Creating Caring Societies

CONCLUSIONS: BUILDING BLOCKS OF GOODNESS IN INDIVIDUALS AND SOCIETIES

In concluding the book, I will add some thoughts about what is required for individuals and groups, including nations, to not act violently, but instead to care about and promote others' welfare. What are the cultural, social, and psychological requirements for a peaceful world that nourishes the human spirit and helps individuals develop their personal and human potentials? Along the way I will comment further on influences leading to violence and make some reference to the evolution of terrorism.

BASIC HUMAN NEEDS

This book has identified many influences that lead to helping or harm-doing. A basic needs perspective can help us to go beyond those influences, to give a sense of wholeness and coherence to our understanding of the roots of evil and goodness, and to point to ways that we can generate goodness.

To briefly summarize, human beings have fundamental, shared needs. These include a need for security, for a positive identity, for a sense of effectiveness, for both positive connection to other people and autonomy, for a comprehension of reality. Another need, which emerges most strongly when the needs I have described are reasonably satisfied, is the need for transcendence. This is an aspect of spirituality – the need to go beyond one's own material concerns and beyond the self. When these needs are fulfilled, people are well on their way to harmonious,

This chapter was written as the conclusion for this book. It is partly based on the author's Presidential Address to the International Society for Political Psychology, and a slightly revised version of it was also published in that Society's journal, *Political Psychology* (2003, vol. 24, 1–21) as the author's presidential address.

caring relationships with others, as well as continued growth in their lives.

Certain conditions in children's lives, such as warmth and affection from adults and peers, and effective guidance, especially when this guidance is not punitive, have been found to contribute to caring for and helping others. Important forms of guidance include reasoning, such as the explanation of the reasons for rules and pointing out to children the consequences of their behavior for other people, and the example of other people. The experiences that these practices provide are likely to fulfill basic needs. In contrast, neglect, hostility, harsh treatment or abuse by parents and peers, lack of structure and guidance contribute to aggression. Such experiences frustrate basic needs. Similarly, social conditions that frustrate basic needs, like economic deterioration, great and rapid societal changes and social disorganization, and intense conflict and the threat of or actual attack by other groups, are instigators of violence by groups.

Poverty has many negative effects, including an adverse effect on the way parents treat and guide their children. But economic *deterioration* can have especially strong effects. In addition to frustrating the basic needs I described, it usually enhances the already existing discrepancy between more and less privileged groups. It activates or intensifies the experience of injustice. Social injustice, or comparisons between self and other, or one's group and other groups, that lead to a belief that one is unfairly treated, gives rise to anger and resentment and potentially to violence. Justice is a powerful human motive. Possibly, it is another basic need. But it may be, instead, that injustice frustrates many of the basic needs I have described, especially the need for a positive identity, as a person is treated with less respect and feels less worthy, and the need for effectiveness and control, since injustice means that one's actions can't bring about the outcomes one deserves.

However, people have different, and potentially divergent and competing definitions of justice, the two primary ones equity and equality, and even different views of what constitutes equity or equality. As a result, a person or a group may experience injustice, which motivates them to create justice, while others, especially people in conflict with them, may not recognize or acknowledge the existence of injustice.

It is likely that children whose basic needs have been constructively fulfilled also develop resilience. Their needs may be less deeply frustrated by difficult personal or social conditions. They may be less likely to respond with violence to personal frustration. They may be less attracted to destructive ideological visions and less likely to join potentially destructive movements as avenues to fulfill needs frustrated by social conditions.

Obviously, the fulfillment of basic needs is not just an individual matter. Even apart from societal crises constituted by difficult life conditions or group conflict, in everyday life the nature of culture, relations between groups, the institutions of society, the existence and nature of local communities provide the frame in which families and individuals live. They greatly affect the extent to which basic needs are fulfilled under normal, everyday conditions. They shape how children are treated, determine to a greater or lesser extent who is poor and who is rich, affirm or diminish people as individuals and members of groups, shape connections among people. It would make great sense to evaluate the "goodness" of societies in terms of the ease or difficulty of fulfilling basic needs, and to identify desirable social changes in terms of their probable contribution to the fulfillment of basic human needs. I will give here a few examples of what in the life of a society might fulfill or frustrate basic needs.

Differentiating "them" from "us" and devaluing them is central to violence against them, while a positive view of the other is central to helping "them." Even without any violence, devaluation and discrimination, for example, media images that devalue a group – whether a minority, women, or any other group – will frustrate a number of needs of members of the devalued group. An obvious one is the need for positive identity. Certain kinds of negative images have the potential to incite harmful action, thereby also frustrating the need for security. Extreme negative images, and especially discrimination and physical threat that may accompany them, obviously affect connections between groups, but can also affect connections within a devalued group. Devaluation, threat, and frustration can break down the ability of members of a group to connect to and support each other.[1] Affirming the humanity of members of a devalued group – in the media, in literature, through laws and societal practices, in everyday relations – will help fulfill their basic needs. Humanizing the other is likely to have many significant benefits.

The fulfillment of basic needs of whole groups, and whole nations, is affected by their relationship to other groups. Being accepted and respected by other nations, being engaged with and connected to others can help fulfill the basic needs of group members, and of leaders. Isolation contributes to violence within families, to child and spouse abuse. Connection to other nations makes genocide by groups less likely.[2]

The existence of many and varied community organizations, whether religious or secular, helps fulfill the basic need for connection. The more there are, and the more varied in nature and accessible, the less dependent people will be on any one of them, and the less likely that they will passively remain part of an organization that becomes destructive.

When conditions in a society lead many young women without life partners, especially teenagers, to have children, this will frustrate a number of basic needs, most likely of the mothers, but even more of the children. Young, single mothers, especially if they are poor, are more likely to abuse their children. They would also be more likely to neglect them, to not provide them with the warmth and guidance they need. The presence of supportive adults in their lives, for example, a grandmother, greatly improves their parenting.[3]

Certain practices in families are important in fulfilling basic needs. Eating family dinners together and reading to young children can foster connection. However, fostering connection while also allowing and even fostering autonomy is important. Especially in an individualist culture, as children get older, it becomes important for them to be able to make decisions for themselves, to have time for themselves.

While all children need both connection and autonomy, the ideal balance will depend on the nature of the larger culture, how individualist or collectivist it is. The individualist cultures of the United States and Europe, especially Western Europe, focus on autonomy, individuals making decisions for themselves, acting to fulfill individual goals. The need for connection, although shaped so that it perhaps becomes less central, is still a basic need, but more difficult to fulfill. In the collectivist cultures of much of the rest of the world the focus is on membership in the group, people acting to fulfill goals that serve not their own purposes, or at least not only theirs, but also their family or whole group. Rules to live by are more restrictive.[4] The need for autonomy may become less important, but still necessary to fulfill, though more difficult.

RAISING INCLUSIVELY CARING, MORALLY COURAGEOUS CHILDREN

Even among people who have learned to care about others' welfare, caring can be limited to those in their own group. To create a nonviolent, caring world, to create goodness, extending the boundaries of "us" is essential. Inclusive caring, the extension of caring to the "other," ideally to all human beings, develops through words and images that humanize all people, through the example of models who show caring for people regardless of their group membership, and through one's own experience of connection to varied people.

Moral courage is also important for a nonviolent, caring world, the courage even in the face of opposition and potential disapproval and ostracism, to express important values in words and actions. A positive sense of self and confidence in one's judgment are sources of strength to act according to one's values. Support from like-minded others can greatly contribute, as in the case of the abolitionists in the United States, who even when acting alone, facing hostile groups while advocating the abolition of slavery, were supported by their feelings of connection to other abolitionists. People may also find support from internalized, imagined others – like parents who exemplify moral values, or a belief in what God requires them to do. Affirmation when a child or teenager speaks out against cruelty or injustice, or simply expresses beliefs or points of view that are contrary to those of others, can help develop moral courage.

Because morally courageous people, as active bystanders, can make a crucial difference at important moments, in many settings, it is essential that we learn more about the origins of moral courage and create conditions that help it develop. Not being embedded in the group, which makes an independent perspective possible, may be an important precondition for moral courage. (A fair percentage of rescuers of Jews during the Holocaust were in some way marginal to their communities.[5]) Constructive, in contrast to blind, patriotism gives people a separate enough perspective to question problematic policies and practices of their group. People who are both morally committed and courageous can help overcome the inertia of social systems, activate other bystanders, and work on creating societies and an international community that promote harmony and caring in human relations.

TYPES OF VIOLENCE: INTERPERSONAL, GROUP (GENOCIDE, MASS KILLING TERROR), AND WAR

There are different cultures of violence, different conditions that lead to different types of violence. I have presented earlier some reasons for the very high level of interpersonal violence in the United States. They include neglect and harsh treatment of children; culture changes that affect parents' confidence in providing guidance to their children as well as the frequency of divorce and its attendant effects on some children; lack of community and of support for parents and other caretakers of children, including welfare and other social policies that make life stressful for poor people and difficult to adequately attend to children; the availability of weapons; art and media that have come to idolize violence. Creating the opposite conditions would reduce individual violence.

The highly individualistic, competitive beliefs or worldview that characterize American culture also contribute. Given the belief that everybody has the opportunity to pursue success, individuals who have not succeeded are likely to be greatly frustrated. Young people who feel hopeless, which can be due to difficult social conditions, often become members of violent movements, such as Nazi storm troopers in Germany or paramilitary groups that killed many people in the genocide in Rwanda. In the United States, in addition to individual violence, these conditions and experiences by individuals also contribute to the generation of groups with extreme ideologies that identify either minorities or the state or both as their enemies.

Out of this hate crimes and terrorist violence arise. Many young members of extreme right-wing groups in the United States had harsh, painful childhood experiences that are likely to diminish hope in the future and the capacity to build a good life.[6]

There seems to be, in contrast, little chance of genocide or mass killing within the United States. While devaluation, prejudice, and racism do exist, they have greatly declined, certainly since World War II. Laws and social practices have evolved to protect the rights of individuals regardless of group membership, even if not equally – there are great disparities in how the justice system treats whites and minorities and racial profiling has become notorious – to a substantial enough degree that the evolution of harm-doing or violence toward a subgroup of society has become highly unlikely.

But the United States has engaged numerous times since World War II in violence against other countries. It has overthrown democratically elected governments, using the Marines as in Guatemala or supporting internal factions as in Chile. It has militarily attacked Panama, Libya, Iraq, Afghanistan and other countries. One likely source of these actions is the "group self-concept" of the United States.[7]

Groups are ethnocentric, seeing their values and beliefs as superior to those of others.[8] As citizens of a great power the people and the leaders of the United States seem to have developed a perhaps even stronger than usual belief in their country's specialness and superiority. As part of this the United States has developed ideologies and principles, such as the Monroe Doctrine, that affirm its right to interfere in the affairs of others. Two world wars and the cold war, in which the United States was both the savior and victor and saw itself that way, have strengthened and extended this view to other areas of the world. The United States also has the power to back up its group self-concept and beliefs about its role in the world. In addition to its own views of itself, not infrequently the world turns to the United States and expects it to take action. (All this, combined with the effects of 9/11, may have led to the recent "Bush Doctrine.")

While at times the use of force is necessary and can be constructive, like protecting groups that are harmed, a group inclined to aggression tends to use it to serve its goals, or turn to it when it should use other, peaceful means to serve constructive goals. Both have been the case with the United States. The problematic nature of the group beliefs and psychology that at times have led to destructive violence by the United States has also expressed itself in an unwillingness to participate in international conventions – whether they have to do with the rights of the child, the abolition of land mines, the establishment of an International Criminal Court to try perpetrators of genocide and other great human rights violations, or other matters. Self-examination and the resulting self-awareness can be a starting point for changes in culture, including group beliefs that lead to violence against outside groups, by nations that intend to be and claim to be constructive members of the international community.

HALTING THE EVOLUTION OF VIOLENCE BY SOCIAL MOVEMENTS

Frequently, groups that engage in ethnic/political violence, as well as terrorist groups, start with grievances, often some form of injustice, and political action to bring about change. People who are dissatisfied or want to justify their actions may claim injustice, even where there is none. But the grievances can be real, deeply felt, an authentic source of motivation, and the changes groups advocate can have deep legitimacy.

For example, in Argentina in the 1960s and early 1970s a number of groups wanted to bring about social changes, to enhance the rights, opportunities, and material well-being of less privileged groups. Some of them, like the Montoneros, later turned to terrorism, with counterterrorism and great violence by a military government not only against them, but also against people who held liberal political views or tried to improve the conditions of poor people.[9] Mob violence is also often initiated by grievances and attempts to redress them that receive no response. In the United States it is often demands for better treatment by the police of people living in certain neighborhoods, usually members of minority groups.[10]

The more authorities and societies respond in positive and effective ways to grievances by groups and to the political and social movements that arise from them, the less likely that they will turn violent. However, in a country that practices repression, the easing but not lifting of repression increases hopes and expectations. This may lead to further demands and revolutionary movements. An effective response to grievances, whether they have to do with concerns by people in a particular neighborhood or with the concerns of large groups, has to be multifaceted, involving constructive actions, continued engagement, and the building of relationships among parties.

Unfortunately, dominant, powerful groups don't easily yield power and privilege, and they may come to consider even limited demands as encroaching on their power and privilege. This can be true even in a democracy, especially when the prevalent ideology holds that since everyone has an equal opportunity the advantages of privileged groups have been earned and are therefore deserved. Thus justice as equity can be used to proclaim the grievances of the less privileged as unjustified. But the engagement of different parties is crucial for nonviolent social change. Just being heard can be of great importance to people who feel aggrieved and are trying to bring about change. It can lead to a continuation of a nonviolent process.

Facilitating the evolution of democracy can be a contribution to peaceful change processes. But issues I raise here also apply to democracies. Since democracy is rarely complete, often not genuinely participatory, and in a capitalist country it is individualist and competitive, many individuals and groups can feel left out, experience injustice, and may feel unheard, their basic needs frustrated. Creating a social and political system that is responsive to the needs, conditions, and grievances of individuals and groups, a society that is just and benevolent, will reduce violence and create harmony. In a democracy every person can contribute to this.

IDEOLOGY, COMMUNITY, AND TERRORISM

Movements that end in mass violence or come to practice terrorism attract adherents for several reasons. One is the existence and experience of genuine grievances. Another is that certain people seek the connection, identity, and leadership offered to them by a group. They may have frustrated needs and resulting problems with identity and seek ways to relinquish a burdensome self. They may have difficulty finding purpose and direction in their lives. Difficult conditions of life can intensify these needs. Or they can give rise to them in people who under normal conditions are able to manage their lives. Some persons may harbor resentment and hostility that draws them to movements that are destructive from the start, in that a significant element of their ideology is enmity toward some group.

However, some groups that become violent may provide at the start a positive vision, ideals, and hope. Such visions may appeal not only to people moved by personal, individual concerns, or enmity toward particular groups, but also to people who are genuinely concerned about human suffering and want to improve lives – their own, their families', but also those of people in their community or larger society, perhaps the lives of all human beings. Caring, idealistic, morally committed persons do, of course, get involved in social movements.

Over time some groups become more radical, their ideology more extreme, the means by which they attempt to achieve their ideals more violent. Violence can become the end itself rather than the means. This is partly because social change is so difficult to bring about, partly because of the dynamics of such groups. Along the way most members will undergo varying degrees of personal transformation. While especially early on members do leave such groups, as time progresses the dynamics of the group, such as intense connection among members, increasingly shared vision, separation from the rest of the world so that there is no moderating influence, and strong disapproval and the possibility of revenge against those who abandon the group, may keep members in the group. Members expressing radical views, to be heard and to gain influence within the group, and the group engaging in violent actions all contribute to change or transformation in individuals and the group. Research on terrorist groups, like the Baader-Meinhof gang in Germany, the Red Brigade in Italy, and many others, offers a picture consistent with all this.[11]

It also may apply to the terrorists of September 11, 2001. Thomas Friedman wrote in one of his *New York Times* columns that the men who perpetrated that attack came from highly traditional Islamic societies. All of them moved to Europe. There they experienced intense culture clash between the views they held and the extreme openness of the societies they encountered. Traditional societies that are also repressive, where custom, law, and authorities combine to limit exposure to new ideas and ways of life, make it especially difficult for people to deal with culture change. In the contemporary age, in spite of tradition and repression, changes in the world often seep in. But restrictive tradition and change are difficult to integrate, making it difficult for people to generate a usable, meaningful comprehension of reality.

Friedman writes that these young men were also greatly affected by the lack of respect for Muslims in Europe. Their disorientation and exclusion led to great influence over them of the teachings of radical mosques and prayer groups that they joined, and led them to go to Afghanistan, where they received training in Osama Bin Laden's camps.[12]

Here again, a basic needs perspective is helpful. Community is crucial in fulfilling needs for connection and identity. David Buss, an evolutionary psychologist, suggests that we humans have evolved over time in close-knit groups and need the connection they offer for well-being and happiness. However, in the modern age, people living in big cities and nuclear families lack community.[13] They may turn to or create communities, such as gangs or ideological movements, that generate destruction. Societies ought to be creative in building communities that help people constructively fulfill basic needs. Institutions of learning and other communities ought to help young people integrate the old and the new. Communities should enable youth on the margin to constructively participate in social processes. For example, Arnold Goldstein, a pioneer in youth violence reduction, has developed a strategy for creating "prosocial gangs." Rather than trying to break up a gang, he would guide it to positive action. He would help them create legitimate enterprises: rather than sell drugs, own laundromats.[14]

Healing from Past Wounds and Altruism Born of Suffering

Healing from past wounds diminishes evil and creates goodness. Not only members of victimized groups, but also many children and adults in the course of "normal" existence have painful, wounding experiences, what I call "life injuries":[15] exclusion by peers, conflict with and at times the resulting loss of friends, divorce, the death of loved ones, and others. These can be a source of vulnerability, mistrust of other people, unhappiness in life, as well as hostility and violence. Healing requires that people engage with their painful experiences, have their suffering and pain acknowledged, receive empathy, and experience loving connections.

Such corrective experiences can lead to what I have called "altruism born of suffering." Many people who have been neglected, physically or sexually abused, survived persecution, torture or genocide against their group, rather than becoming hostile or vengeful against the world devote themselves in significant ways to helping others. Many child survivors of the Holocaust have jobs in which they help people.[16] Even partial healing, which healing from deep psychological wounds usually is, seems to lead some people to become caring and helpful. Many want to do what they can so that other people won't suffer as they have.

A very significant source of healing and probably of altruism born of suffering is the experience of loving connection and support. Loving connections have been found to be important in the development of resilience in children, the ability to function well in spite of difficulties, obstacles, and painful experiences early in life. Loving connections before trauma or life injuries, which fulfill basic needs, help people endure them better. After trauma or life injury they help people heal from them. They offer those who have suffered an image of possibilities in life different from what their painful experiences have shown.

One of my students, a very bright, very attractive young woman, had a terrible year in eighth grade. There was a boys' clique that dictated the rules by which the girls were to behave. In addition to sexual teasing, they would touch the girls – their breasts, their buttocks. They engaged in many degrading actions, which most of the girls endured. They even acted as if they welcomed them. Because she did not go along with this, she was viciously teased and ostracized, not only by the boys but by the girls as well. The teachers witnessed all this but did nothing, even making comments to her like "boys will be boys." She suffered all this without yielding, but suffered greatly.

In her home life, however, she received a great deal of love and affection before this, and much love and support while this was happening. She also saw her parents as moral, spiritual people, instilling in her both an understanding of others (she came to interpret the behavior of the boy who was the main gang leader as a child of busy socialites who paid little attention to him), as well as independence. She believes that it was the combination of her background and her suffering that year that led her to engage in many and varied activities to help others: volunteering with mentally and physically disabled children, spending time in a town in a poor area of the country helping to rebuild it after it was devastated by a disaster, serving as a peer mentor, as a tutor, and as a counselor for emotionally disturbed girls, volunteering at many charities and organizations, being the kind of person to whom others turn for consolation, and more.

Positive temperamental characteristics have also been found to contribute to resilience in children. This may be, at least in part, because an "easy," appealing temperament generates interest and may lead to loving connections. However, adults should be capable of choice, and should reach out to children needing loving connections even if they are shy, withdrawn, moody, intense, or impulsive, that is, even if they don't have an easy temperament.

As with moral courage, our knowledge of the roots and nature of altruism born of suffering is quite limited. I have already presented the hypotheses that healing from past wounds and loving connections are among these roots. Having had active bystanders intervene in one's behalf at times of victimization or suffering, a form of love, may also play a role. Positive actions by a person in his or her own behalf, whether as a child or an adult, and the actions of important people like parents in saving their families from harm inflicted on them, may also contribute. Many of the child survivors of the Holocaust were helped by bystanders, by their parents, and, young as they were, by their own actions.

Effective self-protection under extreme conditions powerfully affirms one's efficacy and control. Learning that persecution and violence can be evaded and thus defeated may also show people the potential for goodness in the world. However, victimized people who evade persecution and violence primarily by the use of personal violence may learn something different. Children who are treated by parents or other people with great harshness and who learn to use violence in their defense may believe that only violence will give them security, a feeling of control, a positive identity. This may start them on the road to a life of violence.[17]

When individuals or groups of individuals are completely focused on their injuries and pain, or preoccupied with the dangers the world poses for them, it is understandable that they may hardly notice others' suffering. But when such people heal, when their pain eases, as they become less self-focused and feel reasonably safe, and as they see the possibilities of human goodness, it makes sense that their past suffering could and would enable them to understand and to respond to others' need. What is true of individuals is probably also true of groups. While past suffering makes violence by them more likely, healing combined with certain conditions may enhance their empathy, caring, and helping. This may have been the case with Huguenots in the village of Le Chambon, whose inhabitants saved thousands of Jews during the Holocaust.[18] Having known great religious persecution, they may have understood more and empathized more with others who were persecuted.

I expressed the hope in this book that empathy and altruism born of suffering will characterize the United States in the wake of the attacks of September 11. Like all countries, the United States has had painful experiences in the course of its history – to name a few, the Civil War, the

Depression, slavery and its aftermath, the Vietnam War, inner-city riots. But the attack of September 11, 2001, was a highly unusual, unique experience.

People in the country pulling together, the successful war against Afghanistan, and the demonstration of strength and power by the United States have rebuilt a reasonable sense of security and have had healing effects. These expressions of strength, however, also seemed to have reestablished the feeling of rightness and superiority that I have noted before, interfering with the recognition of similarities in our pain and the pain of weak, helpless victims elsewhere. This is indicated, for example, by the quiet acceptance by the U.S. government, apparently in exchange for support of the war against terrorism, of varied countries around the world engaging in violence and human rights violations against members of opposition groups, calling them terrorists. An important subject for exploration is what might move groups who have suffered to altruism born of suffering. What social processes, in addition to healing from past wounds, might be required, and how might they be generated? And what might help groups to "see themselves," to have a perspective on themselves?

RECONCILIATION AND A SHARED COLLECTIVE HISTORY

To prevent new violence and promote positive relations between formerly hostile groups, or individuals, requires not only healing, but also reconciliation. Healing can create greater openness to other people and may be an essential precondition for, and contributor to, reconciliation. When there are perpetrators and victims, perpetrators must also heal. Often perpetrators of great violence have been wounded before, which was one of the influences leading to their violence. But even if that is not the case, they have almost certainly been wounded by their own violent acts. At the very least, they would have closed themselves to their victims. Over time the decline in their capacity for empathy, guilt, and other moral feeling would be likely to extend to more and more people.

Reconciliation also requires some sense of justice. Only one source of this is the punishment of wrongdoers. Acknowledgment by perpetrators of the harm they have done, especially if they are accompanied by expressions of regret and apology, and social arrangements that make future harm-doing less likely (and which in the process acknowledge that unacceptable suffering was imposed on victims) contribute to a sense of justice and to reconciliation. So does compensation that improves the lives of survivors of violence,[19] who may have been greatly impoverished in the course of the violence against them, or as a result of the psychological aftereffects of the violence on them.

Another important element of reconciliation, between both individuals and groups, is a vision of the past that is acceptable to all parties, a shared collective history. Usually the parties' view of what has happened is profoundly contradictory. Groups blame each other for the conflict and violence and see their own actions as justifiable self-defense. In an interview I conducted in a prison in Rwanda with "Agnes," the justice minister of the country at the time of the genocide, she said the reason for the genocide was "the past slavery of the Hutus." Perpetrators also minimize the harm they have inflicted and see the other as exaggerating his or her suffering,[20] a research finding with individuals that almost certainly applies to groups as well.

An important tool for the creation of a shared history is the understanding of the roots of violence and harm-doing, the kind of understanding that has been offered in this book. Using its elements and applying them to the groups' history, it is possible to see how persecution and violence have come about. Such an exploration of the genocide in Rwanda can show the traditionally greater power and privilege of Tutsis over Hutus. The Belgian colonialists had the Tutsis administer the country for them, further enhancing their power and privilege and leading to the abuse of this power. The Hutu experience of repression and injustice led to anger and the desire for revenge. In a Hutu uprising in 1959 over fifty thousand Tutsis were killed.

Such an exploration can also point to the mutual devaluation, antagonism, and fear that would have existed at this point. This explains why, under the Hutu rule that followed as the country became independent, there was discrimination as well as violence against Tutsis, including periodic mass killings. It was in reference to this history that Agnes claimed that the genocide was the outcome of the enslavement of Hutus by Tutsis, several decades before.

A thorough examination of what has generated violence in the course of two groups' history with each other, in a way that creates understanding and even empathy, can contribute to acceptance of both what the other has done and what one's own group has done. It can lead to acknowledging and taking responsibility for the actions of one's own group, without the usual justifications. It can lead to a shared collective memory. It can lead to teaching children a history that does not sustain the antagonism. It makes peaceful engagement with the other possible.

Even if the issue is not reconciliation between two parties living together, an exploration of problematic aspects of a country's past has great value. A truthful engagement with the past that is also empathic with mistakes made creates self-awareness that can lead to more constructive actions in the future. Such aspects of the past in the United States may include the Vietnam War, slavery and the long history of repression of black people that followed, overthrowing democratic governments, and supporting dictatorships. In European countries it may include the behavior of European countries in the colonial era and complicity with Nazi Germany in the extermination of the Jews and in other matters. The healing may be from wounds inflicted by one's own country's conduct and reconciliation is with one's own country.

EDUCATION THAT PROMOTES CARING AND PEACE

As the preceding discussion indicates, education to prevent violence and promote caring is important. In our work in Rwanda we found that learning about the roots of genocide had very great impact on people. They seemed to feel humanized by learning about the genocides that have happened to others, and by coming to see the roots of their terrible experience as understandable. Learning about forces that influenced perpetrators and passive bystanders was an aspect of a broader set of experiences, including learning about trauma that results from victimization and about paths to healing, and people in small groups talking about their painful experiences during the genocide.

An experimental evaluation found that when people who were so trained conducted relatively brief training with groups in the community, two months after the training the participants in the community groups had fewer trauma symptoms and developed a more positive attitude toward members of the other group. This change occurred both over time and in comparison to groups led by people we did not train, who used the methods they have traditionally used, and control groups.[21]

Education in these realms has to be more than instruction. To the extent it consists of information, it has to engage people's experience. At the very least, it has to combine information and discussion and bring about not just knowledge but *experiential understanding*. By this I mean a joining and integration of facts and ideas with life experiences, thus creating a deep, "organismic" understanding that reaches beyond thought to feelings.

Such experiential education and healing from past wounds are relevant in many contexts. They are needed by young people in inner cities of the United States who are exposed to and traumatized by having friends and relatives killed, witnessing shootings and seeing dead bodies, and feeling unsafe walking the streets. They are needed by children and adults who have been physically or sexually abused, and by women, and men, who have been victims of physical abuse by a spouse or partner.

CULTURE, PERSONALITY, AND SELF-AWARENESS

Devaluation in contrast to positive evaluation of others; very strong respect for and the tendency to obey authority versus reasonable respect and the willingness to raise questions about, challenge, and oppose potentially destructive policies and actions; inequality and the experience of injustice versus a reasonable distribution of power and privilege; monolithic political organization and values versus pluralism and democracy; unhealed wounds versus processes of healing and reconciliation all contribute, respectively, to violence or peaceful, harmonious relations between groups and among individuals in a society. The creation of cultures and political arrangements that promote the positive sides of these cultural characteristics is important.

Beyond avenues already discussed in this book, self-awareness and awareness of the culture and practices of one's group are of great importance. Individuals (and groups) who are unaware of the impact of their behavior on others will react very differently from those who see how their actions have contributed to others' actions. Without such awareness, if the other's action is negative, an intensifying cycle of hostile interactions may follow. Many conflicts, for example, the Israeli and Palestinian conflict, are sustained by the unwillingness or inability of each party to consider the reactions that its own actions create.

Aggressive boys who tend to initiate aggression toward their peers and are unpredictable in their behavior are unpopular among their peers, but are unaware of this. They become more aggressive over time and many of them later engage in criminal violence. In contrast, nonaggressive boys who are unpopular know it. It is presumably this awareness and the adjustment it makes possible that contributes to their greater acceptance by peers over time.[22] Going a step deeper and becoming aware of the origins of one's own or one's group's actions in thoughts, feelings, values, beliefs, and motives also has great value. It makes choice and self-control possible.

Awareness of the larger world is also important. Terrorism, usually defined as violence by small groups against noncombatants, and state terrorism, violence by the state against its nonviolent citizens, should be completely unacceptable. It should be distinguished from people fighting against a violent, repressive system.

But the roots of such violence are essential to understand, and in the United States there has been a relative absence of public exploration after the attacks of September 11 both of the roots of terrorism in general and of how U.S. actions and the nature of the country might have contributed to hostility toward the United States The sources of hostility to the United States in the Arab world might include sanctions against Iraq, which made sense at the start, since sanctions have at times been effective in influencing governments, but were continued after it became evident that they were not accomplishing their aims but were creating much suffering in the population. They might include support for repressive systems; the United States as a creator of much contemporary culture that seeps into traditional societies that are also repressive and have difficulty handling culture change[23] (which then leads to scapegoating the United States); seeing the United States as the supporter of Israel in the Israeli-Palestinian conflict. While the following may not be of special concern to Arab terrorists or would-be Arab terrorists, they might also include the unwillingness to be good citizens of the international community as shown by U.S. refusal to participate in many international agreements; and possibly U.S. economic policies being seen as a cause of others' poverty. Engaging in critical self-examination makes changes in action possible.

Self-preoccupation interferes with happiness.[24] Complexity in thinking about the self, at least a type of it in which people use many dimensions in describing the self but without necessarily integrating these dimensions, while it buffers to some degree reactions to stress, does not contribute to positive mood and well-being.[25] But constructive self-examination and self-awareness must, seemingly by definition, make meaningful choice possible. They can motivate and help create positive change in oneself and one's group. It is important to help children develop a capacity to reflect on their experiences and gain self-awareness. It is important for societies as well to practice self-examination, without censorship, and even in a democracy to overcome the self-censorship[26] that is imposed by culture, prevailing values, and the prevailing views of the group that may have become difficult to question.

GOODNESS AND OPTIMAL HUMAN FUNCTIONING

Many of the experiences that contribute to a person becoming caring, helpful, and an active bystander in response to harm-doing also contribute to optimal human functioning. By this I mean our continued growth as persons, the unfolding and evolution of our positive human and personal potentials. I mean the capacity both to live a full and satisfying internal/emotional life, a fulfilling and constructive life of relationships, and a creative and purposeful work life. It is likely that some of the internal and relational aspects of optimal functioning are similar in most people, including self-awareness, empathy, respect for other people, and a feeling of effectiveness in the world. These qualities include what Abraham Maslow and Carl Rogers have identified as qualities of a self-actualized person and Daniel Goleman has described as emotional intelligence.[27]

Optimal human functioning is an outgrowth of the fulfillment of basic needs. While, as I have noted, we can expect uniformity in some processes that characterize persons whose basic needs have been primarily fulfilled, as well as in processes involved in fulfilling basic needs – for example, affirming a child and what she or he does – there will be differences in content, for example, what activities the child is engaged in and for what the child is being affirmed. Thus, the realms in which a person develops efficacy, the nature of the person's identity, the elements of his or her worldview will vary. People who are highly skilled, and whose identity is invested, in the study or practice of literature, in carpentry, or in social interaction may all be optimally functioning individuals. In different cultures, aspects of optimal functioning will look different. It is likely, however, that optimal human functioning will express itself, whatever the profession, activity, or culture, in some degree of creativity, at least in creativity in living.

Goodness is likely to be one expression of optimal functioning. A group of caring, morally committed people who have been studied, including university presidents and successful business people who have used their skills to promote others' welfare, as well as people working full-time to feed, clothe, or in other ways benefit poor people or promote positive social change, reported deep satisfaction from helping others. The considerable time they spent on such activities was not a sacrifice for them. Their personal goals embodied helping others: acting in others' behalf brought a fulfillment of their own personal goals as well.[28] Their deep caring and moral commitment was the outcome of a personal evolution. As adults, they shaped themselves through choices they made and the actions and experiences these choices led to. In the end, their caring about others was a wholly integrated part of themselves.

ACTIVE BYSTANDERSHIP REVISITED

A crucial theme of this book is the role of bystanders: that passivity by witnesses greatly contributes to the evolution of evil, and that creating goodness requires active bystandership by individuals, organizations, communities, and nations. Speaking out can stop those who do harm from doing more harm, whether it is a child in a school, an adult in a workplace, or a group that is beginning to develop a destructive ideology. A caring peer or teacher can be a turning point in a child's life, remembered forever. "Third parties" are often essential for the peaceful resolution of conflict. Active bystanders can help create caring schools. Working together, people can promote the cultural/societal characteristics that in turn create and maintain harmony, goodness, and peace.

Although individuals can have great influence, to create social change it is necessary for people to work together. To be active bystanders requires caring values, a feeling of responsibility, as well as a feeling of efficacy, the belief that one can bring about positive ends. Active bystandership is also facilitated by mutual support, people working together for a shared cause. We have seen in this book that often people support each other as they work together for destructive ends. Fortunately, people can support and inspire each other working for beneficial ends as well.

Active bystandership entails risk. The risks are usually lower when bystanders act early in a sequence of events, and when they act skillfully. Whether attempting to stop children, adults, or groups from harming others, words and actions can exert positive influence, or they can confront. Often the former is more beneficial and sufficient; at times the latter is necessary. Active bystandership also has many potential rewards, like immediate benefits to someone's welfare, awareness of long-term benefits, and the satisfaction inherent in living up to one's values. Its rewards include the benefits of pursuing one's enlightened self-interest, the gains for one's self, one's children, and grandchildren in living in a more harmonious, caring society and world that one's actions help to create. A great reward, in the end, is knowing that one has been leading a worthwhile life. Erik Erikson[29] describes as a last stage of psychosocial development integration versus despair. In looking back on our lives, integration and contentment may come from not having focused only on ourselves, from having lived as true members of the human community.

Notes

1. Tajfel, H. (1982). Social psychology of intergroup relations. *Annual Review of Psychology, 33*, 1–39.
2. Harff, B., Gurr, T. R., & Unger, A. (1999). Preconditions of genocide and politicide: 1955–1998. Paper presented of the Conference on Differing Approaches to Assessing Potential Genocide, Politicides and Mass Killings. Sheraton Premier Hotel, Vienna, Virginia, November 18.
3. For a review, see Staub, E., *A brighter future: raising caring and nonviolent children.* New York: Oxford University Press (in preparation).
4. Triandis, H. (1989). The self and social behavior in differing cultural contexts. *Psychological Review*, Vol. 96, No. 3, pp. 506–520; Matsumoto, D., Kitayama, S., & Markus, H. (1994). Culture and self: How cultures influence the way we view ourselves. Chapter 2 in D. Matsumoto, *People: Psychology from a cultural perspective*. Brooks/Cole.
5. Tec, N. (1986). *When light pierced the darkness: Christian rescue of Jews in Nazi-occupied Poland*. New York: Oxford University Press.
6. Ezekiel, R. S. (1995). *The racist mind*. New York: Penguin Books.
7. Staub, E. (1989). *The roots of evil: The origins of genocide and other group violence.* New York: Cambridge University Press.
8. Sumner, W. G. (1906). *Folkways* New York: Ginn.
9. Staub, E. *The roots of evil*.
10. Staub, E., Rosenthal, L. (1994). Mob violence: Societal-cultural sources, group processes and participants. In L. Eron and J. Gentry (Eds.), *Reason to hope: A psychosocial perspective on violence and youth*. Washington, DC: American Psychological Association.
11. McCauley, C. R., & Segal, M. D. (1989). Terrorist individuals and terrorist groups: The normal psychology of extreme behavior. In J. Groebel, & J. F. Goldstein, *Terrorism*. Sevilla: Publicaciones de la Universidad de Sevilla.
12. Friedman, T. L. (2002). The two domes of Belgium. *The New York Times*, January 27, p. 13.
13. Buss, D. M. (2000). The evolution of happiness. *American Psychologist. 55*, 15–24.
14. Goldstein, A. P., Glick, B., & Gibbs, J. C. (1998). *Aggression replacement training: A comprehensive intervention for aggressive youth.* Champaign, IL: Research Press.
15. Staub, E. *A brighter future: Raising caring and nonviolent children*. New York: Oxford University Press (in preparation).

16. Valent, P. (1998). Child survivors: A review. In J. Kestenberg & C. Kahn (Eds.), *Children surviving persecution: An international study of trauma and healing*. New York: Praeger.
17. Rhodes, R. (1999). *Why they kill*. New York: Knopf.
18. Hallie, P. P. (1979). *Lest innocent blood be shed. The story of the village of Le Chambon. and how goodness happened there*. New York: Harper and Row.
19. Gibson, J. L. (in press). Truth, justice and reconciliation: Judging the fairness of amnesty in South Africa. *American Journal of Political Science*.
20. Baumeister, R. F. (1997). *Evil: Inside human violence and cruelty*. New York: Freeman and Co.
21. Staub, E., Pearlman, A. L., Hagengimana, A., & Gubin, A. Healing, forgiving and reconciliation: An intervention and its experimental evaluation in Rwanda. Unpublished manuscript, Department of Psychology, University of Massachusetts at Amherst. See also www.heal-reconcile-rwanda.org
22. Zakriski, A., Jacobs, M., & Coie, J. (1997). Coping with childhood peer rejection. In S. A. Wolchik & I. N. Sandler (Eds.), *Handbook of children's coping: Linking theory and intervention*. New York: Plenum Press.
23. Staub, E. (in press). Notes on terrorism: Origins and prevention. *Peace and Conflict: Journal of Peace Psychology*.
24. Lubomirsky, S. (2001). Why are some people happier than others? The role of cognitive and motivational processes in well-being. *American Psychologist, 56*, 239–250.
25. Rafaeli-Mor, E., & Steinberg, J. (2002). Self-complexity and well-being: A review and research synthesis. *Personality and Social Psychology Review, 6*, 31–58.
26. See discussion of self-censorship in Staub, E., *The roots of evil*.
27. Maslow, A. H. (1987). *Motivation and personality* (3rd ed.). New York: Harper and Row (original work published in 1954); Rogers, C. R. (1961). *On becoming a person*. Boston: Hougton Mifflin. Goleman, D. (1995). *Emotional intelligence*. New York: Bantam Books.
28. Colby, A., & Damon, W. (1992). *Some do care*. New York: The Free Press.
29. Erikson, E. H. (1959). Identity and the life cycle. Selected papers. *Psychological Issues*. 1 (Monograph 1). New York: International Universities Press.

Appendix

What Are Your Values and Goals?

In recent years there has been much debate about which values and goals guide our lives. To help us get a sense of what Americans value today, we'd like to know what is most important to you. How essential are independence and self-reliance? Where do human relationships, human needs and helping others fit in?

By filling out and mailing in this questionnaire, you can contribute to an understanding of our society, to a true picture of who we are as a people. The questionnaire will also help you learn about yourself – about how you see people and the world and what is important to you.

PART I: HUMAN RELATIONS

People have different views of – and orientations to – others. Consider each statement below and indicate the extent to which you agree or disagree with it. There are five possible ratings: Strongly Disagree (1), Disagree (2), Neutral (3), Agree (4), and Strongly Agree (5). *Rate each statement by circling the number that best describes your opinion of how you see yourself.*

People usually get what they deserve, good or bad.

Strongly agree **Strongly disagree**

1 2 3 4 5 (1:6)

Reprinted from E. Staub (1989, May). What are your values and goals? *Psychology Today*, 46–49. Reprinted with permission from *Psychology Today*, Copyright © 1989 Sussex Publishers, Inc. Part I is the measure of prosocial value orientation (or caring) that was used in several studies described in this book.

This questionnaire was developed in part on the basis of past questionnaires by S. Schwartz; L. Berkowitz and K. Lutterman; R. Christie; M. Rokeach; J. P. Rushton; A. Mehrabian and N. Epstein; and E. Staub with H. Feinberg, S. Grodman, W. Levinson, and S. Rosenblum.

We all have the right to concern ourselves with our own goals first and foremost, rather than with the problems of other people.

Strongly agree **Strongly disagree**

1 2 3 4 5 (7)

I feel a moral duty to help people who suffer.

1 2 3 4 5 (8)

As long as they keep within the law, business people should do as they like.

1 2 3 4 5 (9)

To bring relief to needy people requires, first and foremost, changes in social and economic policies.

1 2 3 4 5 (10)

I usually make decisions without being influenced by other people's feelings.

1 2 3 4 5 (11)

I get angry when I see someone mistreated.

1 2 3 4 5 (12)

I would feel obligated to do a favor for a person who needs it, even if she/he has not shown gratitude for past favors.

1 2 3 4 5 (13)

Some people are completely trustworthy.

1 2 3 4 5 (14)

I often become more irritated than sympathetic when I see someone crying.

1 2 3 4 5 (15)

Individuals can do little to alleviate suffering in the world.

1 2 3 4 5 (16)

Only the government can solve social problems like poverty and homelessness.

1 2 3 4 5 (17)

People from different religious and ethnic groups are different in basic ways.

1 2 3 4 5 (18)

Most people have a vicious streak that will come out, given a chance.

1 2 3 4 5 (19)

Generally speaking, people won't work hard unless forced to.

1 2 3 4 5 (20)

Bonds to people are more important to me than independence or personal freedom.

1 2 3 4 5 (21)

There is more need and suffering in the United States now than in past decades.

1 2 3 4 5 (22)

It makes me sad to see a lonely stranger in a group.

1 2 3 4 5 (23)

I value sensitivity to people and try to understand others' feelings and situations.

1 2 3 4 5 (24)

I need more companionship and emotional support in my life.

Strongly agree **Strongly disagree**

1 2 3 4 5 (25)

Most people are basically good.

1 2 3 4 5 (26)

There is no excuse for lying.

1 2 3 4 5 (27)

Most people who are poor are either unmotivated or have limited innate capacity or both.

1 2 3 4 5 (28)

You can't blame a person who is completely involved in important work for being insensitive to those around him or her.

1 2 3 4 5 (29)

All of us should give some of our time for the good of our town or country.

1 2 3 4 5 (30)

I don't want to pay more taxes to expand social welfare programs.

1 2 3 4 5 (31)

If a friend of mine wanted to injure an enemy of his/hers. I would consider it my duty to stop him/her.

1 2 3 4 5 (32)

When I act in a caring way, it is only to get approval and/or to avoid disapproval.

1 2 3 4 5 (33)

I am concerned about the welfare of human beings everywhere in the world.

1 2 3 4 5 (34)

Most people who get ahead in this world are honest, good people.

1 2 3 4 5 (35)

People should always help themselves rather than expect help from others.

1 2 3 4 5 (36)

The best way to handle people is to tell them what they want to hear.

1 2 3 4 5 (37)

Most people with serious problems brought their problems on themselves.

1 2 3 4 5 (38)

I feel sympathy for people who suffer.

1 2 3 4 5 (39)

God expects us to help others.

1 2 3 4 5 (40)

All people share basic needs and desires.

1 2 3 4 5 (41)

It is in my power to do things that improve the welfare of others.

1 2 3 4 5 (42)

The biggest difference between most criminals and others is, criminals get caught.

Strongly agree **Strongly disagree**

1 2 3 4 5 (43)

Individuals should be ready to inhibit their own pleasures if they inconvenience others.

1 2 3 4 5 (44)

To the extent that I follow moral standards it is only to avoid trouble.

1 2 3 4 5 (45)

It is not enough to rely on the authorities; every person should act to dissuade others from criminal acts.

1 2 3 4 5 (46)

If we all volunteer time and effort, social problems like poverty and homelessness can be overcome.

1 2 3 4 5 (47)

People frequently intrude into others' private affairs when they try to help them.

1 2 3 4 5 (48)

I feel a responsibility to contribute to the welfare of people who suffer.

1 2 3 4 5 (49)

People who suffer are often innocent victims of circumstance.

1 2 3 4 5 (50)

PART II: YOUR GOALS AND VALUES

People live by different values and pursue different goals. Which are the most important for you in guiding your life? In the following columns, *check the **six** goals or values that are the **most important** to you. Then check the **six least important** to you.*

	Most Important	**Least Important**
Improving society	☐	☐ 51
Pleasure/fun	☐	☐ 52
Wealth	☐	☐ 53
Enjoyment of beauty	☐	☐ 54
Creating justice	☐	☐ 55
Financial security	☐	☐ 56
Friendship	☐	☐ 57
Success in a career	☐	☐ 58
Privacy	☐	☐ 59
World at peace	☐	☐ 60
Recognition and respect	☐	☐ 61
Helping others	☐	☐ 62
Emotional support and security	☐	☐ 63

	Most Important	Least Important
Community	☐	☐ 64
Use of my intellect	☐	☐ 65
Cooperation	☐	☐ 66
Power	☐	☐ 67
Connection to others	☐	☐ 68
Independence	☐	☐ 69
Generosity	☐	☐ 70
Equality	☐	☐ 71
Responsibility for others	☐	☐ 72
Personal growth	☐	☐ 73
Approval from others	☐	☐ 74
Adventure	☐	☐ 75
Moral goodness	☐	☐ 76
Competence and control	☐	☐ 77

PART III: PERSONAL BACKGROUND

Please fill in (or check off) one answer to each question.

Age: ______ (78–79)

Sex: Female ☐ 80-1 Male ☐ -2

Your highest level of education completed: ______________________ (81)

Was your family of origin:

Working class/blue collar ☐ 82-1
Lower middle class ☐ -2
Middle class ☐ -3
Upper middle class ☐ -4
Upper class ☐ -5

Do you consider yourself to be:

Working class/blue collar ☐ 83-1
Lower middle class ☐ -2
Middle class ☐ -3
Upper middle class ☐ -4
Upper class ☐ -5

Your racial and ethnic background: __________ (84–85)

Are you currently:

Employed full-time ☐ 86-1
Employed part-time ☐ -2
Full-time student ☐ -3
Homemaker ☐ -4
Unemployed ☐ -5
Retired ☐ -6

Occupation (be as specific as possible): __________ (87–88)

What is your level of satisfaction with your work life?

Very low ☐ 89-1
Low ☐ -2
Medium ☐ -3
High ☐ -4
Very high ☐ -5

How financially secure do you feel?

Very secure ☐ 90-1
Fairly secure ☐ -2
Neither secure nor insecure ☐ -3
Fairly insecure ☐ -4
Very insecure ☐ -5

Marital status:

Single ☐ 91-1
Married ☐ -2
Divorced or separated ☐ -3
Widowed ☐ -4

Do you have children?

No ☐
Yes ______ (92)
(number)

Number of siblings in your family of origin (including yourself): ________ (93)

PART IV: HOW YOU HELP

A. We know little about how much and in what ways Americans help each other. Please look at each type of helping listed below and indicate by checking one box under the FREQUENCY column, whether you have ever helped in that way and how frequently. (For now, please ignore the columns called FEELINGS and TIME.)

	FREQUENCY					*FEELINGS*	*TIME*
	Never	**Once**	**A Few Times**	**Quite Often**	**Very Often**		
1. I have given directions to a stranger.	☐ 94-1	☐ -2	☐ -3	☐ -4	☐ -5	______ (6–7)	______ (30)
2. I have given money to a charity.	☐ 95-1	☐ -2	☐ -3	☐ -4	☐ -5	______ (8–9)	______ (2)
3. I have done volunteer work for a charity.	☐ 96-1	☐ -2	☐ -3	☐ -4	☐ -5	______ (10–11)	______ (4)
4. I have donated blood.	☐ 97-1	☐ -2	☐ -3	☐ -4	☐ -5	______ (12–13)	______ (6)
5. I have delayed an elevator for a stranger.	☐ 98-1	☐ -2	☐ -3	☐ -4	☐ -5	______ (14–15)	______ (8)
6. I have picked up a hitchhiker.	☐ 99-1	☐ -2	☐ -3	☐ -4	☐ -5	______ (16–17)	______ (40)
7. I have offered my seat on a bus or train to a stranger.	☐ 100-1	☐ -2	☐ -3	☐ -4	☐ -5	______ (18–19)	______ (2)
8. I have helped a friend move.	☐ 11:1-1	☐ -2	☐ -3	☐ -4	☐ -5	______ (20–21)	______ (4)

	FREQUENCY					*FEELINGS*	*TIME*
	Never	**Once**	**A Few Times**	**Quite Often**	**Very Often**		
9. I have helped a stranger in an emergency (sudden illness, accident).	☐ 2-1	☐ -2	☐ -3	☐ -4	☐ -5	______ ______ (22–23)	______ (6)
10. I have served food in a soup kitchen.	☐ 3-1	☐ -2	☐ -3	☐ -4	☐ -5	______ ______ (24–25)	______ (8)
11. I have tried to console someone who was upset.	☐ 4-1	☐ -2	☐ -3	☐ -4	☐ -5	______ ______ (26–27)	______ (50)
12. I have spent time working for causes (like peace, social justice, or the environment).	☐ 5-1	☐ -2	☐ -3	☐ -4	☐ -5	______ ______ (28–29)	______ (2)

B. Sometimes we feel good about helping, sometimes not – perhaps because circumstances pushed us into it. Look again at the list above. For each type of help that you have performed, think of the ***last occasion*** when you helped in that way. In the FEELINGS column, write ***two*** of the following terms that best describe how you felt ***afterward***: good, bad, joyful, let down, high, low, powerful, incompetent, valuable, worthless, a good person, stupid, needed, taken advantage of, neutral.

C. Then, in the TIME column, give, when possible, the approximate ***time*** when this happened (e.g., last week, last month, 5 months ago, 1 year ago, 3 years ago, etc.).

D. Other ways you help: Name up to ***three*** additional types of helping that you have engaged in. For each way you've helped, indicate its frequency. Then write down your feelings after the last occasion (again using the adjectives listed above) and its approximate time.

	FREQUENCY					*FEELINGS*	*TIME*
	Never	**Once**	**A Few Times**	**Quite Often**	**Very Often**		
1. ______ ______	☐ 54-1	☐ -2	☐ -3	☐ -4	☐ -5	______ ______ (57–58)	______ (63)
2. ______ ______	☐ 55-1	☐ -2	☐ -3	☐ -4	☐ -5	______ ______ (59–60)	______ (5)
3. ______ ______	☐ 56-1	☐ -2	☐ -3	☐ -4	☐ -5	______ ______ (61–62)	______ (7)

E. If you work as a volunteer or unpaid staff, list the organizations you work for and your role in them: ______________________________
______________________________ (69–70)

F. Is there a type of unpaid service you'd like to do if you could find an organization that did it? ______________________________ (71–72)

G. On average, how many hours a month do you spend:
Working as a volunteer for a charity:
______________________________hours (73–74)
Helping people in other ways:
______________________________hours (75–76)

H. In comparison to past years, is the time and effort you now spend to help people *(Check one)*:

Much less	☐ 77-1	More	☐ -4
Less	☐ -2	Much more	☐ -5
About the same	☐ -3		

I. Compared to other people, do you feel you help *(Check one)*:

Much less	☐ 78-1	More	☐ -4
Less	☐ -2	Much more	☐ -5
About the same	☐ -3		

PART V. BELIEFS & FEELINGS

Please fill in (or check off) one answer to each question.

Your political orientation:

Check one (79)		*Check one* (80)	
Democrat	☐ -1	Conservative	☐ -1
Republican	☐ -2	Moderate	☐ -2
Independent	☐ -3	Liberal	☐ -3
Other _____	☐ -4	Other _____	☐ -4

How strong is your religious or spiritual faith?

None	☐ 81-1	Strong	☐ -4
Little	☐ -2	Very strong	☐ -5
Moderate	☐ -3		

Your participation in formal religion is:

None	☐ 82-1	High	☐ -4
Low	☐ -2	Very high	☐ -5
Medium	☐ -3		

Your religious affiliation: ______________________________ (83)

Your level of satisfaction with your life is:

Very high	☐ 84-1	Low	☐ -4
High	☐ -2	Very Low	☐ -5
Medium	☐ -3		

How would you describe your health?

Very poor	☐ 85-1	Good	☐ -4
Poor	☐ -2	Very Good	☐ -5
Medium	☐ -3		

How many times did you see a doctor last year?

0–1	☐ 86-1	11–15	☐ -4
2–5	☐ -2	16 or more	☐ -5
6–10	☐ -3		

How well do you like yourself?

Not at all	☐ 87-1	A fair amount	☐ -4
A little	☐ -2	Very much	☐ -5
Moderately	☐ -3		

OPTIONAL: We would welcome a note or brief letter from you about why you help people – or why you don't help. Do you think that charitable activities do any good? You might tell us briefly about any dramatic experience you have had with helping or being helped – or not being helped when you needed it.

Index

The index uses two different methods of citing authors referred to in the book. When author names are mentioned in the text, the corresponding index entries consist of page numbers alone. When there are endnotes in the text instead of author-name citations, the index entries include the page number and the note number, followed in parentheses by the page number on which the numbered citation to the author's note appears.